Orlando Bump, U.S. Declaration of Independence

Notes of Constitutional Decisions

being a digest of the judicial interpretations of the Constitution of the United States, as contained in the various federal and state reports

Orlando Bump, U.S. Declaration of Independence

Notes of Constitutional Decisions
being a digest of the judicial interpretations of the Constitution of the United States, as contained in the various federal and state reports

ISBN/EAN: 9783337192563

Printed in Europe, USA, Canada, Australia, Japan

Cover: Foto ©Suzi / pixelio.de

More available books at **www.hansebooks.com**

NOTES

OF

CONSTITUTIONAL DECISIONS:

BEING A DIGEST OF

THE JUDICIAL INTERPRETATIONS

OF THE

CONSTITUTION OF THE UNITED STATES,

AS CONTAINED IN THE VARIOUS

FEDERAL AND STATE REPORTS.

Arranged under each Clause of the Constitution.

TOGETHER WITH AN APPENDIX,

CONTAINING THE DECLARATION OF INDEPENDENCE
AND ARTICLES OF CONFEDERATION.

By ORLANDO F. BUMP.

NEW YORK:
BAKER, VOORHIS & CO., PUBLISHERS,
66 NASSAU STREET.
1878.

BAKER & GODWIN, PRINTERS,
25 Park Row, New York.

PREFACE.

THIS work consists of the Constitution of the United States, with notes under each clause and section, referring to all the cases in which it has ever been construed or applied, whether the cases arose in the Federal or State courts. Where the cases, upon a particular subject, have been numerous, the notes have been arranged under appropriate subdivisions. The practitioner is thus enabled to tell, at a glance, whether there is any decision upon the particular point which he is considering. The importance of the field covered by the work can be readily seen by even a hasty glance at its contents. In American jurisprudence there is no field that is more prolific of important questions than that of constitutional law, and of these the most important are those that pertain to the Federal Constitution. The importance of the subjects that are committed to the control of the National Government, the nice discrimination between the powers of the State governments and the National Government, and the restrictions that have been placed upon the powers of both for the protection of private rights, have given rise to an immense amount of litigation, and the establishment of principles that are all-pervading in their consequences. The results are embodied in this volume. They constitute the permanent, fundamental and supreme law of the country. This law has been settled by litigation extending over a period of more than eighty years, and may be regarded as nearly unchangeable. No pains have been spared to make the work exhaustive. It is possible that some cases may have been overlooked, but, if this is so, it is not because there has been any lack of diligence in hunting for them, but because there is great difficulty in making a work like this complete.

ORLANDO F. BUMP.

BALTIMORE, January 1st, 1878.

TABLE OF CASES.

Abbott v. Bayley, 287, 290.
Abercrombie v. Baxter, 152.
Ableman v. Booth, 263, 267, 278, 298, 311, 334, 335, 336, 359.
Achison v. Huddleson, 127.
Adams v. Day, 285.
Adams v. Logan, 153.
Adams v. Palmer, 143.
Adams v. Smith, 226.
Adams v. Storey, 5, 72, 155, 158, 316.
Adams v. Way, 336.
Addison v. Saulnier, 236.
Agnew v. Platt, 162.
Agricultural Branch Railroad Co. v. Winchester, 203.
Aguirre v. Maxwell, 106.
A. & G. Railroad Co. v. Allen, 178, 179.
A. & G. Railroad Co. v. State, 193.
Ah Fong, Ex parte, 50, 378.
Ah Fook, Ex parte, 376.
Ahl v. Gleim, 90.
Ala. & Fla. Railroad Co. v. Kenney, 180.
Albany Railroad Co. v. Brownell, 191.
Albee v. May, 115, 123, 139.
Aldrich v. Kenney, 3, 285.
Aldridge v. Tuscumbia Railroad Co., 115.
Alexander v. Gibson, 72, 155.
Alexander v. Kilpatrick, 225.
Alexander v. Railroad Co., 107, 237, 239.
Alexander Stephens, Ex parte, 18, 68, 262, 268.
Alicia, The, 277.
Allen v. Buchanan, 163.
Allen v. Colby, 89, 344.
Allen v. McKeen, 127, 165, 168, 187, 188, 193.
Allen v. Sarah, 287, 294, 350.
Allen v. Shield, 225.
Alley v. Denson, 153.

Allis v. State Bank, 215.
Almy v. People, 235.
Am. Ins. Co. v. Canter, 87, 249, 262, 269, 300, 303.
Amy v. Smith, 127, 229, 291.
Amy Warwick, The, 86.
Anderson v. Baker, 114, 119, 363.
Anderson v. Comm., 194.
Anderson v. Dunn, 11, 19.
Anderson v. Wheeler, 159.
Andrews v. Russell, 115, 123, 148.
Andrews v. State, 343.
Angelo De Giacomo, 103.
Ankrim, In re, 14.
Ann Ryan, The, 48, 238, 294.
Anon., 10, 193, 194, 211.
Anthony v. Halderman, 380.
Antoni v. Wright, 131, 134, 147, 172.
Appold, In re, 71.
Archy, Ex parte, 288.
Armington v. Barnet, 179, 180.
Armistead v. State, 251.
Armstrong v. Commissioners, 153.
Armstrong v. Jackson, 139.
Armstrong v. Lecompte, 154.
Armstrong v. Treasurer, 179.
Aspinwall v. Commissioners, 205, 207.
Astrom v. Hammond, 128, 339.
Att. Gen. v. Bank of Charlotte, 174.
Att. Gen. v. Bay State Mining Co., 291.
Att. Gen. v. Clergy Society, 187.
Att. Gen. v. Railroad Companies, 171, 190, 193.
Att. Gen. v. Stevens, 52.
Atwater v. Townsend, 156, 158.
Atwater v. Woodbridge, 123, 174.
Augsbury v. Crossman, 77.
Augusta v. Earle, 364.
Augusta v. Sweeny, 144.
Augusta Bank v. Augusta, 218.
Auld v. Butcher, 229.
Aurora Turnpike Co. v. Holthouse, 168, 186, 219.

TABLE OF CASES.

Austin v. Boston, 326.
Austin v. Sandel, 369.
Austin v. State, 292.
Avery v. Fox, 352, 356.
Aycock v. Martin, 152, 227.

Babcock v. Middleton, 137.
Babcock v. Weston, 158.
Backus v. Lebanon, 180.
Bacon v. Howard, 286.
Bagnell v. Broderick, 301.
Bailey v. Gentry, 112, 120, 128, 221, 227, 336.
Bailey v. Hollister, 194.
Bailey v. Maguire, 174.
Bailey v. Milner, 111, 333.
Bailey v. Railroad Co., 53, 167, 337.
Bailey v. Trustees, 191.
Bains v. The James Catherine, 360.
Baker v. Herndon, 149.
Baker v. Wheaton, 155.
Baker v. Wise, 40, 56, 108, 240, 289, 293, 294, 342.
Baldwin v. Bank, 159.
Baldwin v. Comm., 134.
Baldwin v. Hale, 157, 158, 159.
Baldwin v. Newark, 218.
Ballantine v. Haight, 72, 156, 158.
Ballard v. Ridgeley, 214.
Ballard v. Webster, 159.
Balt. & Ohio Railroad Co. v. Van Ness, 356.
Balt. & S. Railroad Co. v. Nesbit, 123, 168, 225.
Bancher v. Fisk, 158, 159.
Banet v. Alton & Sangamon Railroad Co., 196, 198, 199, 200.
Bangor Railroad Co. v. Smith, 189, 190.
Bank v. Bank of Cape Fear, 112, 128, 148, 163.
Bank v. Clarke, 110, 111.
Bank v. Commissioners, 323, 324.
Bank v. Daniel, 364.
Bank v. Deming, 132, 172.
Bank v. Domigan, 219.
Bank v. Dudley, 358.
Bank v. Earle, 291.
Bank v. Edwards, 132, 172.
Bank v. Halstead, 100, 336.
Bank v. Hamilton, 180, 181, 185.
Bank v. Hart, 218.
Bank v. Longworth, 213.
Bank v. McVeigh, 148, 195.
Bank v. New Albany, 132, 172, 207.

Bank v. Northumberland, 261.
Bank v. Okely, 361.
Bank v. Osborn, 268.
Bank v. Planters' Bank, 366.
Bank v. Spilman, 110.
Bank v. Squires, 159, 160.
Bank v. Supervisors, 324.
Bank v. Wister, 366.
Bank of Cape Fear v. Edwards, 175.
Bank of Columbia v. Att. Gen., 186.
Bank of Commerce v. New York, 316.
Bank of Md. v. Ruff, 169.
Bank of Penn. v. Comm., 172.
Bank of U. S. v. Northumberland Bank, 261, 268.
Bank of U. S. v. Roberts, 261, 267, 268, 273.
Bank of Washington v. State, 133.
Bank Tax Case, 325.
Banks v. Mayor, 324, 325.
Banta v. McNeil, 42.
Baptiste v. State, 50, 291.
Barber v. Andover, 180.
Barber v. Minturn, 155.
Barber v. Rogers, 76.
Barbour v. Barbour, 143.
Barden v. Supervisors, 24.
Barings v. Dabney, 147, 150.
Barker v. Jackson, 229, 360.
Barker v. People, 341, 346, 361.
Barker v. Pittsburgh, 143.
Barkley v. Glover, 228.
Barlow v. Gregory, 150.
Barnaby v. State, 57.
Barnes v. Barnes, 227.
Barnes v. State, 38.
Barnet v. Barnet, 141.
Barnett v. Barbour, 231.
Barney v. Chittenden, 62.
Barque Chusan, The, 29.
Barrell v. Benjamin, 293.
Barrett, Ex parte, 335.
Barron v. Mayor, 341, 342, 346.
Barry v. Iseman, 123, 125.
Barry v. Mercein, 277.
Barry, Ex parte, 276.
Barton v. Morris, 141.
Bass v. Fontleroy, 206, 207.
Bass v. Mayor, 142, 144.
Battle v. Corporation, 240, 292.
Baugher v. Nelson, 115, 149, 211, 337.
Bay v. Gage, 123.
B. C. & M. Railroad v. State, 181, 183.
Beach v. Walker, 141.

TABLE OF CASES.

Beal v. Burchstead, 156.
Beal v. Nason, 229.
Beall v. State, 48, 234, 235.
Beatty v. U. S., 261.
Beavens, Ex parte, 67, 68, 97.
Beck v. Parker, 76.
Beckerford, In re, 71.
Bedford Railroad Co. v. Bowser, 202.
Beekman v. Railroad, 140.
Beer v. Hooper, 161.
Beers v. Haughton, 217, 336.
Beers v. Rhea, 156, 158.
Beers v. State, 133.
Beirne v. Brown, 216.
Bela Judd, In re, 74.
Belfast, The, 269, 271, 272.
Bell v. Perkins, 141.
Bell v. Roberts, 141, 229.
Bellona Company's Case, 180.
Benedict v. Vanderbilt, 239.
Benford v. Gibson, 143.
Benjamin T. Greenough, Ex parte, 296.
Bennett v. Boggs, 34, 57, 58, 271, 287, 294, 338.
Benson v. New York, 163, 181, 205.
Bergen, In re, 375, 377.
Berrett v. Oliver, 137.
Berry v. Bellows, 333.
Berry v. Haines, 125, 230.
Berry v. Ransdall, 229, 230.
Bertemeyer v. Iowa, 375.
Berthelemy v. Johnson, 143.
Berthelon v. Betts, 77.
Berthold v. Fox, 224.
Berthold v. Holman, 224.
Berwick, John D., Ex parte, 335.
Bethune v. Dougherty, 141, 211.
Betts v. Bagley, 72, 157.
Bibb v. Commissioners, 331.
Biddle v. Comm., 46, 47, 233, 234, 321.
Bigelow v. Pritchard, 215.
Billings v. Hall, 126.
Billis v. State, 109, 110.
Billmeyer v. Evans, 227.
Binghamton Bridge v. Chenango Bridge, 163, 166, 167.
Bish v. Johnson, 200.
Bishop v. Loewen, 73.
Bissell v. Briggs, 283, 285.
Black v. Del. & Rar. Canal Co., 202, 203.
Black v. Lusk, 80, 87.
Blackford v. Peltier, 229.
Blackman v. Gordon, 115.
Blackman v. Green, 162.

Blair v. Mil. & P. Railroad Co. 183.
Blair v. Pathkiller, 62, 306.
Blair v. Ridgley, 114, 119, 308.
Blair v. Williams, 120, 121, 122, 123, 228.
Blanchard v. Haynes, 84.
Blanchard v. Russell, 72, 122, 130, 155, 158, 159, 317.
Blanchard v. Sprague, 83.
Blanchard v. The Martha Washington, 30.
Blanchard's Factory v. Warner, 84.
Blann v. State, 121, 149.
Bleakley v. Williams, 135, 152, 206.
Bleakney v. Farmers' Bank, 148, 186.
Bloodgood v. Railroad Co., 140.
Bloomer v. McQuewen, 350.
Bloomer v. Stolley, 20, 83, 84.
B. & M. Railroad Co. v. White, 204.
Board v. Bearse, 90.
Board v. Fowler, 136.
Board v. Pleasants, 48, 233.
Board v. Scearce, 184.
Boardman v. De Forrest, 155.
Bode v. State, 232.
Bodley v. Gaither, 139.
Bollman, Ex parte, 277, 280, 281.
Bolton v. Johns, 216.
Bonaparte v. Camden & Amboy Railroad Co., 138, 140, 346, 359.
Booe v. Junction Railroad Co., 203.
Booth v. Booth, 141.
Booth v. Woodbury, 89, 90.
Boring v. Williams, 358.
Boston v. Cummins, 141.
Boston & L. Railroad Co. v. Salem & L. Railroad Co., 171, 180, 364.
Boston Water Power Co. v. Railroad, 180.
Bowdoinham v. Richmond. 205.
Bowen v. Johnson, 284, 286.
Bowerbank v. Morris, 258.
Bowlin v. Comm., 370.
Boyce v. Tabb, 154, 369.
Boyd v. Ellis, 346.
Boyer v. Dively, 66.
Boykin v. Shaffer, 35, 38.
Boyle v. Turner, 158.
Boyle v. Zacharie, 158.
Braddie v. Brownfield, 224.
Bradford v. Cary, 204.
Bradford v. Farrand, 158.
Bradwell v. State, 287, 289, 375.
Brainard v. Williams, 261.
Brainerd v. Colchester, 175.

TABLE OF CASES.

Branch v. Baker, 155.
Brandon v. Gaines, 210.
Branin v. Conn. & P. Railroad Co., 185.
Brashear v. Williams, 65, 66.
Braynard v. Marshall, 159.
Breed v. Cunningham, 150.
Breitenbach v. Bush, 228.
Breitenbach v. Turner, 25.
Brengle v. McClellan, 284, 285.
Brest v. Smith, 156.
Brewer v. Kidd, 335.
Brewer v. Otoe Co., 135.
Brewster v. Hough, 172.
Bridge Co. v. Hoboken Land Co., 134, 170.
Bridgeport v. Hubbell, 115, 205.
Bridgeport v. Railroad Co., 148.
Brien v. Clay, 216, 338.
Brig Wilson v. U. S., 27, 28, 29.
Brigham v. Henderson, 161.
Brighton Bank v. Merick, 159.
Bright Star, The, 33, 56.
Brinsfield v. Carter, 133.
Brinton v. Seevers, 141.
Briscoe v. Anketell, 229, 230.
Briscoe v. Bank, 5, 17, 108, 109, 110, 112.
Bristoe v. Evans, 139.
Bristol v. New Chester, 205.
Brittle v. People, 299.
Britton v. Butler, 88.
Broadway, In re, 151.
Bronson v. Kinzie, 121, 123, 209, 211, 221, 223, 225.
Bronson v. Newberry, 217.
Brooklyn Central Railroad Co. v. Brooklyn City Railroad Co., 140.
Brooklyn Park v. Armstrong, 137.
Brown v. Bridge, 161.
Brown v. Collins, 159.
Brown v. Dillahunty, 217.
Brown v. Duchesne, 83.
Brown v. Fairmount Co., 201.
Brown v. Hummel, 165.
Brown v. Penobscot Bank, 184.
Brown v. Read, 333.
Brown v. State, 5, 7, 19, 26, 32, 46, 232, 233, 234, 236, 312, 322, 337.
Brown v. Storm, 123.
Brown v. U. S., 88.
Brown v. Ward, 227.
Bruce v. Schuyler, 221.
Brumagin v. Tillinghast, 235.
Bruns v. Crawford, 123.
Bryan v. Cattell, 144.

Bryan v. Moore, 152.
Bryan v. State, 342.
Bryson v. Campbell, 143.
Buchanan v. Smith, 332.
Buck v. Vasser, 332.
Buckner v. Finley, 364.
Buckwalter v. U. S., 273.
Buffalo & N. Y. City Railroad Co. v. Dudley, 194, 202, 203, 204.
Buie v. Parker, 88.
Bulkley v. N. Y. & N. H. Railroad Co., 192.
Buller v. Palmer, 229.
Bulow v. Charleston, 326.
Bumgardner v. Circuit Court, 227.
Bunker v. Green, 23.
Bunn v. Gorgas, 227.
Burbanks v. Williams, 339.
Burford, Ex parte, 277, 344.
Burke v. Tregre, 251.
Burlock v. Taylor, 293.
Burns v. State, 375.
Burrall v. Rice, 159.
Burt v. Merchants' Ins. Co., 356.
Burt v. Williams, 227.
Burton's Appeal, 138.
Burton v. Emerson, 221.
Bush v. Lester, 72.
Bush v. Peru Bridge Co., 170.
Bush v. Shipman, 112, 205.
Butler v. Chariton, 206.
Butler v. Hopper, 101, 298.
Butler v. Pennsylvania, 126, 144, 337.
Butler v. State, 35.
Butler v. Toledo, 115.
Butler v. Walker, 194.
Butz v. City, 125.
Byrd v. Badger, 158.
Byrne v. State, 109, 111.
Byrne v. Stewart, 115.

Cabell v. Cabell, 143.
Cæsar Griffin, Ex parte, 4, 341, 379.
Calder v. Bull, 114, 115, 117, 120, 225, 337, 338, 364.
Calder v. Kurby, 144.
Calhoun v. Calhoun, 125, 154, 308, 369.
California Pacific Railroad Co., 70.
Call v. Hagger, 229.
Callicott, Theophilus C., In re, 253.
Camden & Amboy Railroad Co. v. Briggs, 38, 183.
Camden & Amboy Railroad Co. v. Commissioners, 132, 172, 175, 178.

Camden & Amboy Railroad Co. v. Hillegas, 175.
Cameron v. Wurtz, 284.
Camp v. Smith, 302.
Campbell v. Claudius, 158.
Campbell v. Morris, 287, 290, 293.
Campbell v. State, 357.
Campbell v. T. & N. O. Railroad Co., 152.
Campbell v. U. S., 81.
Canal Co. v. Railroad Co., 127, 129, 132, 163, 241.
Canfield v. Hunter, 227.
Cannon v. New Orleans, 237, 238.
Caperton v. Martin, 115.
Capron v. Johnson, 159.
Carl Wehlitz, Ex parte, 68.
Carlton, Ex parte, 335.
Carpenter v. Northfield Bank, 25.
C. & A. Railroad Co. v. People, 184.
Carey v. Conrad, 161.
Carey v. Giles, 187.
Cargill v. Power, 224.
Carpenter v. Comm., 115.
Carpenter v. The Emma Johnson, 271.
Carroll v. Boyd, 333.
Carroll v. Perry, 302.
Carroll v. Rossiter, 223.
Carroll v. Safford, 302.
Carson v. Carson, 118, 143.
Carson R. L. Co. v. Patterson, 45.
Carter v. Bennett, 284.
Carter, Perkins, Ex parte, 115, 298, 304, 320, 321.
Cary v. Curtis, 261.
Cassard et al. v. Kroner, 78.
Cassell v. Backrack, 232.
Catlin v. Munger, 219, 221.
Central Bank v. Empire Stone Dressing Co., 148.
Central Bank v. Little, 110.
Central Bank v. Pratt, 97.
Central Bridge v. Lowell, 180, 207.
Central R. & B. Co. v. State, 188.
Central Railroad Co. v. Ward, 330, 331.
C. & F. Railroad Co. v. Hecht, 185.
Chadwick v. Moore, 228.
Chamberlain v. Perkins, 77.
Champaign Bank v. Smith, 146.
Champion v. Memphis & Charleston Railroad Co., 198.
Chancely v. Bailey, 275, 328, 330.
Chandler v. Siddle, 75.
Chapman v. Miller, 27, 37, 41, 294, 295.
Chappell v. Williamson, 330.
Charles A. Dana, Ex parte, 279.
Charles E. Hopson, Ex parte, 335.
Charles River Bridge v. Warren Bridge, 123, 166, 170, 337, 338.
Charleston v. Rogers, 7, 39, 57, 318.
Chase v. Flagg, 159.
Chemung Canal Bank v. Lowery, 295.
Cherokee Nation v. Georgia, 64.
Cherokee Nation v. State, 3, 59, 27, 276.
Cherokee Tobacco, The, 60, 314.
Cherry v. Jones, 369.
Ches. & O. Canal Co. v. Key, 354, 356.
Chesapeake Bank v. First Nat. Bank, 98.
Chesnut v. Shane, 141.
Chicago v. Lunt, 324.
Chicago, B. & Q. Railroad Co. v. Haggerty, 183.
Chicago, B. & Q. Railroad Co. v. Iowa, 39, 172, 184.
Chicago v. Sheldon, 125.
Childress v. Emory, 359.
Chilvers v. People, 55.
Chirac v. Chirac, 67, 255.
Chisholm v. Coleman, 332.
Chisholm v. Georgia, 275.
Chitty v. Glenn, 231.
Choteau v. Molony, 306.
Choteau v. Richardson, 158, 161.
Christmas v. Russell, 285.
Church v. Chambers, 40.
Churchman v. Martin, 118.
Chusan, The, 37, 269, 272.
Chy Lung v. Freeman, 29, 49.
Cisco v. Roberts, 30.
Citizens' Bank v. Degnoodt, 215.
City v. Ahrens, 39, 235.
City v. Boatman's Ins. & Trust Co., 172.
City v. Boffinger, 39.
City v. Churchill, 318, 321, 323, 326, 327.
City v. Cov. & Cin. Bridge Co., 197.
City v. Erie Canal Co. 169.
City v. Han. & St. Jo. Railroad Co., 176.
City v. Ill. Cent. Railroad Co., 145.
City v. Lamson, 125.
City v. McCoy, 39.
City v. Menard, 58.
City v. Metropolitan Bank, 193.

TABLE OF CASES.

City Nat'l Bank v. Mahan, 109.
City v. Railroad Co., 142.
City of Richmond v. R. & D. Railroad Co, 175.
City of Roxbury v. Railroad Co., 190, 191.
City v. Russell, 205.
City v. Society, 178.
City v. Stevenson, 24.
City v. The Nautilus, 239.
Claflin v. Houseman, 273.
Clark v. Clark, 143.
Clark v. Dick, 113, 264, 346.
Clark v. Hatch, 158.
Clark v. Martin, 228.
Clark v. Mitchell, 352.
Clark v. Monongahela Navigation Co., 196, 200, 201.
Clark v. Sickel, 105.
Clark v. Smith, 305, 308.
Clark v. Ticknor, 152.
Clark v. U. S., 360.
Clarke v. Ray, 77.
Clay v. Smith, 162.
Clay v. State, 93.
Clemens v. Conrad, 23.
Clement L. Vallandigham, Ex parte, 275, 277.
Clinton Bridge, The, 26, 27, 33, 50, 313.
Coates v. New York, 140.
Cochran v. Darcy, 225.
Cochran v. Van Surlay, 123.
Cockrum v. State, 343.
Coffin v. Rich, 155, 169.
Coffin v. State, 144.
Coffman v. Bank, 209, 212, 227.
Coffman v. Keightly, 90.
Cohens v. Virginia, 4, 5, 6, 92, 268, 274, 275, 277, 278, 316, 328, 329, 365, 366.
Colby v. Dennis, 225.
Coles v. Madison, 115, 207.
Collector v. Day, 23, 334.
Collet v. Collet, 67.
Collins v. Chicago, 326.
Collins v. Rodolph, 158, 162.
Collins v. Sherman, 166, 170.
Collins v. Society, 42.
Colt's Estate, 284.
Colt v. Eves, 358.
Columbus Ins. Co. v. Curtenius, 52, 53.
Columbus Ins. Co. v. Peoria Bridge Co., 51, 52, 53.
Comer v. Folsom, 90, 142.
Comm. v. Alger, 41.

Comm. v. Aves, 298.
Comm. v. Bacon, 144.
Comm. v. Bean, 116.
Comm. v. Bedford Bridge, 52.
Comm. v. Bird, 135.
Comm. v. Bonsall, 192.
Comm. v. Breed, 52.
Comm. v. Clapp, 235, 338.
Comm. v. Clary, 94.
Comm. v. Cullen, 187.
Comm. v. Dennison, 276, 296, 297, 363.
Comm. v. Eastern Railroad Co., 193.
Comm. v. Essex Co., 191, 194.
Comm. v. Farmers' Bank, 164, 186.
Comm. v. Fayette Co. Railroad Co., 188, 192, 193.
Comm. v. Feely, 273.
Comm. v. Fitzgerald, 298.
Comm. v. Fox, 335.
Comm. v. Gardner, 117.
Comm. v. Green, 283, 285.
Comm. v. Griffin, 26, 40, 289.
Comm. v. Griffith, 298, 344.
Comm. v. Hall, 297.
Comm. v. Hitchings, 341.
Comm. v. Intoxicating Liquors, 185.
Comm. v. Irish, 90.
Comm. v. Kimball, 125, 235, 363, 364.
Comm. v. Lewis, 96, 98, 103, 321.
Comm. v. Merrill, 348.
Comm. v. Milton, 287, 289, 291, 294.
Comm. v. Morrison, 21, 95, 98, 316, 321, 322, 324, 326, 329.
Comm. v. Murray, 89.
Comm. v. Ober, 48, 235.
Comm. v. O'Hara, 73.
Comm. v. Phillips, 116.
Comm. v. Pomeroy, 342.
Comm. v. Schaffer, 274.
Comm. v. Towles, 69, 287.
Comm. v. Tracy, 295, 297.
Comm. v. Young, 93, 94.
Commercial Bank v. Chambers, 211.
Commercial Bank v. State, 130, 164, 168, 186, 209, 210.
Commissioner v. Jarvis, 187.
Commissioners v. Brandt, 49.
Commissioners v. Cuba, 41.
Commissioners v. Holyoke W. P. Co., 192.
Commissioners v. Lucas, 208.
Commissioners v. Pidge, 52, 54.
Conant v. Van Schaick, 155.
Concord Railway v. Greely, 346.

TABLE OF CASES. xi

Confiscation Cases, 282.
Conkey v. Hart, 211, 222.
Conner v. Elliott, 288, 295.
Conner, John O., In re, 95.
Conner v. New York, 143.
Continental Ins. Co. v. Kasey, 264.
Converse v. Bradley, 161.
Converse v. Burrows, 224.
Conway v. Taylor, 55.
Cook v. Moffat, 156, 158.
Cook v. Oliver, 330, 333.
Cook v. Rogers, 76.
Cook v. Smith, 146.
Cook v. State, 176.
Cooke v. Cooke, 332.
Cooley v. Philadelphia, 5, 18, 27, 28, 30, 33, 36, 37, 41, 42, 108, 234, 238, 317, 318.
Coosa River Steamboat Co. v. Barclay, 215.
Corbin v. Marsh, 353, 355.
Corfield v. Coryell, 31, 34, 57, 58, 271, 287, 294.
Coriell v. Ham, 218.
Cornelius v. Glen, 139.
Cornell v. Hichens, 214.
Corner v. Miller, 73.
Cornet v. Winton, 308.
Corning v. Greene, 133.
Corporation v. Overton, 55.
Cory v. Carter, 370, 378.
Cov. & L. Railroad Co. v. Kenton, 207.
Cowles v. Brittain, 47, 233.
Cowser v. State, 333.
Cox v. Berry, 230.
Cox v. State, 54, 126.
Coxe v. Martin, 228.
Coxe v. McClenachan, 13.
Craig v. Dimock, 23.
Craig v. Kline, 38.
Craig v. State, 109, 111.
Craighead v. Bank, 110, 221.
Crandall, In re, 236.
Crandall v. State, 43, 326, 337.
Cranson v. Smith, 85.
Crapo v. Kelly, 161.
Crawford v. Bank, 219.
C. R. & B. Co. v. State, 193.
Crease v. Babcock, 188, 189.
Crenshaw v. Slate River Co., 139, 151.
Crescent G. C. Co. v. New Orleans G. Co., 206.
Crittenden v. White, 85.
Cronise v. Cronise, 143.

Crosby v. Hanover, 180.
Cross v. Harrison, 250.
Crow v. Coons, 160.
Crow v. State, 47.
Cubreth, Ex parte, 297.
Culbreath v. Hunter, 227.
Cully v. Balt. & O. Railroad Co., 375.
Cummings v. Maxwell, 229.
Cummings v. Savannah, 47, 233.
Cummings v. State, 113, 115, 119.
Curiac v. Albadie, 80, 87.
Curran v. State, 109, 110, 124, 164, 169, 195, 209, 211.
Currie v. Mutual Assurance Society, 204.
Curtis v. Gibbs, 3, 283.
Curtis v. Leavitt, 148.
Curtis v. Morehouse, 170.
Curtis v. Whitney, 129, 146.
Curry v. Davis, 154.
Curry v. Landers, 213.
Cushing v. The James Gray, 41.
Cusic v. Douglas, 226.
Cutter v. Folsom, 70.
Cutts v. Hardee, 214.
Cynosure, The, 40.

Dabb's Case, 335.
Dale v. Governor, 133.
Dailey v. Burke, 213.
Damman v. Commissioners, 134.
Dana, Chas. A., Ex parte, 279.
Daniel Ball, The, 29, 31, 32, 33, 35, 36.
Daniel Deckert, In re, 72.
Danley v. State Bank, 215.
Darrington v. Branch Bank, 109, 110.
Darlington v. U. S., 356.
Dart v. Houston, 206.
Dartmouth College v. Woodward, 4, 126, 143, 163, 165, 166, 337.
Dash v. Van Kleeck, 115, 127.
Daughdrell v. Life Ins. Co., 132, 172.
Dausin v. Champlin, 336.
Davenport v. Davenport, 207.
David Howes, In re, 14.
Davidson v. Smith, 161.
Davis, Jefferson, Ex parte, 379.
Davis v. Ballard, 115, 123, 209, 224.
Davis v. Bronson, 123.
Davis v. Central Railroad Co., 219.
Davis v. Dashiel, 47, 233, 236.

Davis v. Gray, 139, 365.
Davis v. Peirse, 119, 216, 228, 289, 290, 293.
Davis v. State Bank, 142.
Davis v. The Seneca, 269, 270.
Davison v. Champlin, 262, 273.
Dawson v. Shaver, 336, 358.
Dawson v. State, 118.
Day v. Bardwell, 71, 77.
De Cordova v. Galveston, 229.
Decuir v. Benson, 50, 376.
Degant v. Michael, 318.
Deichman's Appeal, 151.
Delafield v. State, 272, 273, 274.
De la Howe v. Harper, 225.
Del. Railroad Co. v. State, 146.
Del. Railroad Co. v. Tharp, 198, 199.
Del. Railroad Co. v. Thorp, 188.
Del. Railroad Tax, 45, 172, 173, 178.
Delmas v. Ins. Co., 154, 333.
Delorme v. Ferk, 24.
De Lovis v. Birt, 269, 270.
Demerritt v. Exchange Bank, 159.
Den v. Jersey Co., 36.
Dentzel v. Waldie, 141.
Denver v. Hobart, 144.
Depew v. Trustees, 35, 299.
Derby Turnpike Co. v. Parks, 128, 137, 163, 164.
D'Wolf v. Rabaud, 359.
Dickey v. Turnpike Co., 82, 95, 356.
Dickinson v. Dickinson, 117, 118.
Dikeman v. Dikeman, 146.
Dingman v. People, 132, 185.
Dinsmore v. Bradley, 158.
District Attorney, Case of, 257.
Dittmars v. Myers, 333.
Dobbins v. Commissioners, 323.
Dodge v. Coffin, 285.
Dodge v. Woolsey, 125, 132, 173, 278, 311, 317, 319, 364.
Dole v. Irish, 65.
Doll v. Evans, 260.
Donnell v. State, 298, 318.
Donnelly v. Corbett, 158, 159, 161, 162, 217.
Dooley v. Smith, 80, 87.
Dorman v. State, 38.
Dormire v. Cogley, 227.
Doty v. Strong, 12, 13.
Dougherty v. Fogle, 216.
Doughty v. Sheriff, 225.
Douglass v. Stephens, 291, 294.
Dover v. Portsmouth Bridge, 51, 52, 53, 54, 241.
Downham v. Alexandria, 48, 292.

Doyle v. Continental Ins. Co., 264.
Dranguet v Rost, 154.
Dred Scott v. Sandford, 6, 66, 67, 68, 287, 288, 290, 291, 299, 300, 303, 304, 305, 342.
Drehman v. Stifle, 113, 123, 153.
Dresser v. Brooks, 70.
Druecker v. Salomon, 281, 282.
Dryden v. Comm., 30.
Ducat v. Chicago, 291.
Duer v. Small, 292.
Duke v. Navigation Co., 299.
Dulany v. Tilghman, 141.
Duncan v. Darst, 336.
Dundas v. Bowler, 124, 148, 261.
Dunham v. Lamphere, 36, 58, 294.
Dunlap v. Rogers, 161.
Dunn, Ex parte, 102.
Durand v. Hollins, 255.
Durfee v. Railroad Co., 202, 203, 204.
Durousseau v. U. S., 277.
Duvall v. Fearson, 285.
Dwight v. Simon, 74.
Dyer v. Tuscaloosa Bridge Co., 139.
Dyke v. McVey, 301.
Dynes v. Hoover, 90.

Eakin v. Raub, 336, 337.
Eames, Lucius, In re, 73.
Earle v. Johnson, 227.
Easterly v. Goodwin, 159, 161.
Easton v. N. Y. & L. B. Railroad Co., 52.
Easton Bank v. Comm., 172.
Eaton v. Sweetser, 159.
Ebersole v. Adams, 76.
Edelward's Appeal, 23.
Edmondson v. Ferguson, 129, 228.
Edward Klein, In re, 69, 70, 73.
Edwards v. Dixon, 153.
Edwards v. Elliott, 358.
Edwards v. Jagers, 124.
Edwards v. McCaddon, 230.
Edwards v. Panama, 30, 37, 303.
Edwin Heyward, Ex parte, 298.
Eells v. People, 298, 317, 320.
Ehrenzeller v. Canal Co., 187.
Einer v. Beste, 157.
Eldridge v. Cowell, 41.
Electoral Count, 243, 244, 368.
Eli Horton, In re, 74.
Elkinson v. Deliesseline, 40.
Elliott v. Elliott, 118.
Elliott v. Van Voorst, 336.
Ellis v. State, 379.

TABLE OF CASES. xiii

Elmore v. Grymes, 359.
Elwell v. Tucker, 153.
Ely v. M. & B. Manuf. Co., 360.
Ely v. Peck, 262, 273.
Emanuel Roberts, Ex parte, 335.
Emory v. Greenough, 158.
Empire City Bank, In re, 194.
Enfield Bridge Co. v. Connecticut River Co., 163, 164, 166, 180.
Enfield Bridge Co. v. Railroad Co., 163, 170, 179.
English v. New Haven Co., 191.
English v. State, 343.
English v. Supervisors, 136.
Erie Co. v. State, 44.
Erie & N. E. Railroad Co. v. Casey, 189.
Erie Railroad Co. v. Comm., 173.
Ervine's Appeal, 350, 352.
Eu-che-lah v. Welsh, 301.
Evans v. Eaton, 20.
Evans v. Jordan, 83, 120.
Evans v. Montgomery, 216.
Evans v. Richmond, 331.
Evans v. Robinson, 120.
Evans v. Weiss, 120.
Evansville, H. & N. Railroad Co. v. Comm., 173, 178.
Everhart v. Phila. & W. C. Railroad Co., 197.
Exchange Bank v. Hines, 132, 172, 173, 218.

Fagan, Ex parte, 102.
Fain v. Headerick, 333.
Fales v. Wadsworth, 214.
Fall v. Suter, 170.
Fanney v. Montgomery, 298.
Fanning v. Gregoire, 55.
Farmers' Bank v. Comm., 173.
Farmers' Bank v. Gunnell, 150.
Farmers' Bank v. Smith, 72, 155, 316, 317, 319.
Farmers' National Bank v. Dearing, 98, 316.
Farnsworth v. Vance, 120, 228.
Farwell v. Rockland, 144.
Felch v. Bugbee, 159.
Fell v. State, 144.
Fellows v. Blacksmith, 315.
Fellows v. Denniston, 314, 315.
Fellows v. Lee, 306.
Ferguson v. Landram, 89, 90.
Ferguson v. Miners' & Manuf. Bank, 188.

Ferrand, Ex parte, 335.
Ferrira v. Keevit, 158.
Ferris v. Coover, 278.
Fessenden v. Willey, 159, 160.
Field, Anson, Ex parte, 101, 344.
Fielden v. Lahens, 152.
Fife v. State, 343.
Fifield v. Close, 23.
Fire Department v. Helfevistein, 291.
Fire Department v. Noble, 291.
Fire Department v. Wright, 291.
F. & M. Ins. Co. v. Hurrah, 291.
Fireman's Association v. Loansbury, 291.
First Nat. Bank v. Douglas, 325.
First Nat. Bank v. Lamb, 98, 99.
Fisher v. Cockerill, 115, 139.
Fisher v. Lacky, 217.
Fisher v. Wheeler, 156, 158.
Fisk v. Montgomery, 74.
Fisk v. Union Pacific Railroad Co., 264.
Fiske v. Foster, 158.
Fitch v. Livingston, 39, 58, 317, 320.
Fitch v. Railroad Co, 170.
Fitchburg Railroad Co. v. Grand Junction Railroad Co., 191.
Fitzpatrick v. Hearne, 154.
Flannagan v. Philadelphia, 53.
Fleming v. Page, 87, 88, 249.
Fletcher v. Peck, 128, 137, 138, 139, 305, 308, 337.
Fletcher v. R. & B. Railroad Co., 139.
Flint & F. P. Co. v. Woodhull, 189.
Florentine v. Barton, 151.
Florida v. Georgia, 241, 276.
Floyd v. Recorder, 298.
Fogg v. Williams, 138.
Folsom v. U. S., 107.
Forcheimer v. Holly, 23, 154, 333.
Ford v. Clinton, 23.
Ford v. Hale, 216.
Ford v. State, 379.
Forsyth v. Marbury, 115, 120, 226, 229.
Fort Plain Bridge Co. v. Smith, 170, 188.
Foster v. Chamberlain, 30.
Foster v. Commissioners, 62.
Foster v. Davenport, 33, 41.
Foster v. Essex Bank, 186.
Foster v. Jackson, 358.
Foster v. Neilson, 313.

Foster v. Port Wardens, 41.
Fowler v. Halbert, 139.
Fowler v. Lindsey, 275.
Fox v. State, 79, 81, 319, 341.
Fox v. Woods, 333.
Francis Hatch, The, 243.
Frank Knowles, Ex parte, 6, 67, 68, 262, 263.
Franklin Bank v. State, 173.
Frazer v. Seibern, 326.
Free v. Haworth, 219.
Freeborn v. Pettibone, 223.
Freeborn v. Smith, 262.
Freedman v. Sigel, 24.
Freedman v. Robinson, 317.
Freeman v. How, 336.
Freleigh v. State, 144.
French v. O'Brien, 77.
French v. Tomlin, 154, 333.
Frey v. Kirk, 156, 158, 160.
Fry v. L. & B. S. Railroad Co. 200, 201.
Fuller v. Spear, 58.
Fults v. Fox, 143.
Furman v. Nichol, 147.

Gaines v. Buford, 138, 139.
Gaines v. Fuentes, 264, 266.
Gaines v. Rives, 112.
Galena & C. Railroad Co. v. Loomis, 181, 183.
Galena Railroad Co. v. Appleby, 183.
Gantly v. Ewing, 221.
Gardner v. Collector, 14, 15.
Gardner v. Jeter, 216.
Gardner v. Lee's Bank, 162.
Gardner v. State, 132, 172.
Garland, Ex parte, 103, 252, 253.
Garlington v. Priest, 227.
Garr v. Bright, 365.
Garrett v. Beaumont, 229.
Garrett v. Cheshire, 225.
Garrison v. Mayor, 151.
Gatzweiller v. People, 205, 207.
Gault's Appeal, 126, 146.
Gautden v. Stoddard, 369.
Geery's Appeal, 78.
Gelston v. Hoyt, 260.
Genesee Chief v. Fitzhugh, 269, 270, 271.
Geo. B. Keeler, In re 243.
George Doll, Ex parte, 260.
Geo. H Corliss, In re, 243.
George Kirk, In re, 318.
George Peters, Ex parte, 63.
Geo. T. Duerson, In re, 72.

Geo. W. Dillard, In re, 72.
George v. Concord, 20, 25, 79, 80, 87, 362.
George v. Gamble, 308.
German Liederkranz v. Schieman, 23.
Gibbons v. Ogden, 17, 18, 19, 20, 26, 27, 28, 29, 32, 34, 37, 39, 41, 57, 95, 284, 312, 318, 321.
Gibson v. Choteau, 301.
Gilbert v. Commissioners, 144.
Gile v. Hallock, 301.
Gilman v. Contra Costa, 135.
Gilman v. Cutts, 230.
Gilman v. Lockwood, 158.
Gilman v. Philadelphia, 32, 34, 36, 50, 51, 52.
Gilman v. Sheboygan, 231.
Gilmer v. Lime Point, 312, 356.
Gelpcke v. Dubuque, 125.
Gist, Ex parte, 256, 259, 260, 263, 274.
Gittings v. Crawford, 277.
Gittner v. Gorham, 298.
Glenn v. Glass Co., 161, 162.
Glenn v. Hodges, 298.
Glenn v. Humphreys, 162, 336.
Glover v. Powell, 35, 54, 151.
Godfrey v. Beardsley, 306.
Goenen v. Schroeder, 153, 223.
Goggins v. Turnipseed, 152.
Golden v. Prince, 72, 129, 155.
Gold Hunter, The, 270.
Goldsmith v. Brown, 136.
Goodall v. Tuttle, 71.
Goodell v. Jackson, 65.
Goodman v. McGehee, 333.
Gordon v. Appeal Tax Court, 174, 177.
Gordon v. Baltimore, 172.
Gordon v. Canal Co. 216.
Gordon v. Kerr, 313.
Gordon v. U. S., 277.
Gorman v. Pacific Railroad, 181, 183.
Goshen v. Stonington, 142.
Gotcheus v. Matheson, 103.
Governor v. Gridley, 204, 229.
Governor v. Madrazo, 366.
Gowen v. Penobscot Railroad Co., 169.
Gozzler v. Georgetown, 140.
Graham v. State, 219.
Graham v. Stucken, 277.
Grammar School v. Burt, 138.
Grand Gulf & P. B. R. Co. v. Buck, 178.
Grand Gulf Railroad Co. v. State, 217.

Graniteville Manuf. Co. v. Roper, 147.
Grannahan v. Railroad Co., 185.
Grant v. U. S., 354.
Grantly v. Ewing, 223.
Grapeshot, The, 250, 251, 261.
Gratiot v. U. S., 257.
Graves v. State, 298, 318.
Gray v. Coffin, 169.
Gray v. Monongahela Navigation Co., 196, 197, 201.
Gray v. Munroe, 217, 350.
Grayson v. Lilly, 227.
Great Barrington v. Berkshire, 151.
Greely v. Townsend, 263.
Green v. Biddle, 127, 128, 130, 139, 209, 241, 336, 358.
Green v. Sarmiento, 283, 284.
Green v. Savannah, 359.
Green v. Shumway, 114, 119.
Green v. Sizer, 111, 333.
Green v. State, 39, 236.
Greenfield v. Dorris, 130, 222.
Greenleaf v. Township, 206.
Greenville & Col. Railroad Co. v. Coleman, 198.
Gregg v. Hilsen, 77.
Gregory v. Shelby College, 144.
Griffin v. Kentucky Ins. Co., 188.
Griffin v. McKenzie, 229.
Griffin v. Wilcox, 101, 246, 247, 248, 351.
Griffing v. Gibb, 41, 53, 58.
Griffith v. Bank, 110.
Griffith v. Shipp, 216.
Griffith v. Thomas, 227.
Grim v. Weisenberg School District, 142.
Grimball v. Ross, 128, 229, 336, 337.
Grimes v. Bryne, 209, 225.
Grimes v. Doe, 149.
Griner, In re, 89.
Griswold v. Hepburn, 21, 25, 79.
Griswold v. Pratt, 73.
Grogan v. San Francisco, 137, 208.
Grosvenor v. Chesley, 213.
Groton v. Hurlburt, 35, 52.
Grover & Baker S. M. Co. v. Butler, 85.
Grover v. Coon, 224.
Grover v. Slaughter, 26, 40.
Grubbs v. Harris, 215.
Guild v. Rogers, 209, 222.
Guillote v. New Orleans, 357.
Gunn v. Barry, 124, 226.
Gut v. State, 116.

Gutierrez, Ex parte, 118.
Guy v. Hermance, 58.

Hackley v. Geraghty, 239.
Hadfield v. New York, 221.
Haggin v. Squires, 285.
Hague v. Powers, 1, 20, 25, 79, 80, 87.
Haight v. Grist, 23.
Halderman v. Beckwith, 37, 39, 57, 58.
Hale v. Huston, 333.
Hale v. Ross, 158.
Hale v. Sharp, 333.
Hale v. Wilder, 306.
Hall v. Boardman, 157, 160.
Hall v. Carey, 187.
Hall v. Hall, 332.
Hall v. Keese, 369.
Hall v. State, 144.
Hall v. Winchell, 157.
Halley v. Hoeffner, 369.
Hamilton Avenue, In re, 170.
Hamilton v. Dillin, 88.
Hamilton v. Keith, 171.
Hamilton v. Pleasants, 333.
Hamilton Company v. Massachusetts, 325.
Hammett v. Anderson, 155, 156.
Hamrick v. House, 153.
Hanauer v. Woodruff, 333.
Hancock v. Ritchie, 216.
Haney v. Marshall, 293.
Haney v. Sharp, 273.
Hanford v. Barbour, 231.
Hanford v. Obrecht, 23.
Han. & St. Jos. Railroad Co. v. Chacklett, 178.
Han. & St. Jos. Railroad Co. v. Marion, 142.
Hardeman v. Downer, 225, 226, 309.
Hardy v. Waltham, 173, 179.
Harlan v. People, 81.
Harlan v. Sigler, 216, 217.
Harlan v. State, 330, 333.
Harness v. Green, 284.
Harris v. Shaw, 153.
Harrison v. Mayor, 233, 235.
Harrison v. Young, 170.
Hart v. Cornwall, 179.
Hart v. State, 118.
Hartford v. Hartford Bridge Co., 205.
Hartford Bridge Co. v. East Hartford, 166, 189.

Hartford Bridge Co. v. Union Ferry Co., 166, 337.
Hartford Fire Ins. Co. v. Doyle, 264.
Hartford & New Haven Railroad Co. v. Crosswell, 195, 196, 199, 200.
Hartung v. People, 116, 117.
Hasbrouck v. Shipman, 228.
Hastings v. Fowler, 70.
Hatch v. Burroughs, 154, 330.
Havemeymer v. Iowa County, 125.
Hawkins et al., In re, 76.
Hawkins v. Filkins, 124, 329, 330.
Hawkins v. Learned, 76.
Hawkins v. Miss. & Tenn. Railroad Co., 201.
Hawley v. Hunt, 159, 161.
Hawthorne v. Calef. 155.
Hayburn's Case, 260, 265.
Haynes v. State, 144.
Hays v. Pacific Mail Steamboat Co., 46.
Hazen v. Union Bank, 124, 165.
Head v. Starke, 332.
Head v. University, 151.
Hedgman v. Board, 373.
Hedgman v. State, 380.
Helfenstein v. Cave, 225.
Helm v. First Nat'l Bank, 85.
Hempstead v. Reed, 157.
Henderson v. Mayor, 33, 37, 49, 321.
Henderson v. Railroad Co., 201.
Henkel, In re, 226.
Hennen, Ex parte, 257, 258.
Henry Brenneman. In re, 71.
Henry E. Hayne, Ex parte, 243.
Henry v. Lowell, 99, 298, 318.
Hepburn v. Curts, 220.
Hepburn v. Griswold, 80, 87, 355.
Herbert v. Easton, 214, 232.
Herman v. Phalen, 318.
Herrick v. Randolph, 175.
Herring v. Selding, 156.
Hess v. Johnson, 113.
Hess v. Warts, 148.
Hester v. Memphis & Charleston Railroad Co., 199.
Hewitt, Ex parte, 225.
Hewitt v. N. Y. & O. M. Railroad Co., 193.
Heyward v. Judd, 210, 223, 224.
Hickland v. State, 291.
Hickman v. Jones, 333.
Hickox v. Tallman, 214.

Hicks v. Brown, 158.
Hicks v. Euhartonah, 59, 61.
Hicks v. Hotchkiss, 5, 160.
Hill v. Boyland, 332, 339.
Hill v. Kessler, 226.
Hill v. Low, 298.
Hill v. Smith, 211.
Hill v. State, 342.
Hill, J. J., Ex parte, 335.
Hinckle v. Riffert, 220.
Hinckley v. C. N. & St. P. Railroad Co., 193.
Hinkley v. Marean, 156, 158.
Hinson v. Lott, 47, 48, 232, 333, 234.
Hintrager v. Bates, 80, 87.
Hiriart v. Ballou, 359.
Hitchcock v. Aicken, 3.
Hoag v. Hunt, 157.
Hodgson v. Millward, 264, 268.
Hoffman v. State, 348.
Hogg v. Canal Co., 127.
Holcomb v. Tracy, 229.
Holden v. Joy, 65, 301.
Holland v. Dickerson, 224.
Holland v. Pack, 66.
Hollida v. Hunt, 85.
Hollingsworth v. Virginia, 365.
Hollister v. Union Co., 138, 346.
Holloway v. Sherman, 223.
Holly Springs S. & J. Co. v. Marshall, 174, 327.
Holman v. Bank, 123.
Holmes v. Holmes, 143.
Holmes v Jennison, 2, 241, 254, 255, 317.
Holmes v. Lansing, 209, 217.
Holt v. State, 118.
Holyoke v. Lyman, 192.
Home Ins. Co. v. Augusta, 145.
Home of the Friendless v. Rouse, 163, 172, 173.
Homer v. Brown, 336.
Homestead Cases, 124, 225, 309, 318, 330.
Hood v. Maxwell, 330.
Hopkins v. Jones, 215, 223.
Hoppins v. Jenckes, 13.
Horn v. Lockhart, 332, 333.
Horne v. Green, 324, 326.
Horton, Eli, In re, 74.
Hospital v. Philadelphia, 174.
Houghton v. Maynard, 159.
Houston v. Deloach, 332.
Houston v. Jefferson College, 153, 187, 192.

TABLE OF CASES. xvii

Houston v. Moore, 5, 7. 90, 91, 92, 262, 272, 273, 317, 320, 336, 337, 338.
Howard v. Bugbee, 223.
Howard v. Insurance Co., 185.
Howe v. Carpenter, 23.
Howell v. State, 46, 322, 233.
Howes, David, In re, 14.
Howze v. Howze, 225.
Hoyt v. Benner, 23.
Hubbard v. Callahan, 152.
Hubbard v. Northern Railroad Co., 261.
Hubbard v. Supervisors, 325.
Huber v. Reily, 273, 350, 351, 364.
Hubert v. Horter, 76.
Hudspeth v. Davis, 227.
Hughes, Wm. H., Ex parte, 251, 296.
Hughes v. Davis, 285.
Hughes v. Cannon, 141.
Hughes v. Stinson, 333.
Humphrey v. Pegues, 132, 172, 174.
Humphreys v. U. S., 260.
Hunsaker v. Borden, 135.
Hunt v. Gregg, 221.
Hunt v. Palao, 100.
Hunt v. State, 62.
Hunter v. Cobb, 22, 23.
Hunter v. Martin, 278.
Huntington v. Bishop, 358.
Huntington v. Central Pac. Railroad Co., 327.
Huntington v. Texas, 331.
Huntress, The, 269, 270, 360.
Huntsman v. Randolph, 133.
Huntzinger v. Brock, 229.
Husted, Ex parte, 335.
Hutchinson v. Thompson, 52.
Hyatt v. Esmond, 190.
Hyatt v. McMahon, 188, 190.
Hyatt v. Whipple, 190.
Hyde v. Planters' Bank, 217.
Hyde v. State, 144.
Hyer v. Wave, 41.
Hylton v. U. S., 104, 105, 337.

Ill. Cent. Railroad Co. v. County, 132, 172.
Ill. Cent. Railroad Co. v. U. S., 302.
Illinois College v. Cooper, 195.
Ill Railroad Co. v. Beers, 197.
Ill. Railroad Co. v. Zimmer, 196, 197, 200.
Ill. & Mich. Canal Co. v. Railroad Co., 133, 170.

Impeachment of Wm. W. Belknap, 259.
Independent Insurance Co., In re, 75.
Indian Canon Road v. Robinson, 170.
Indianapolis Railroad Co. v. Kercheval, 183.
Ingersoll v. Skinner, 235.
Inglehart v. Wolfin, 224.
Ingraham v. Dooley, 214.
Inman Steamship Co. v. Tinker, 237, 239.
Ins. Co. v. Comstock, 358.
Ins. Co. v. New Orleans, 373.
International Assurance Society v. Commissioners, 324.
Iowa City v. Foster, 144.
Iron City Bank v. Pittsburgh, 188, 191, 193.
Irvin v. Turnpike Co., 196, 199, 200.
Irvine v. Armstead, 331.
Irvine v. Marshall, 301.
Irvine, In re, 70, 71.
Isley v. Merriam, 160.
Iverson v. Shorter, 223, 230.

Jack v. Martin, 5, 298, 316, 318.
Jackson v. Butler, 119, 216, 293.
Jackson v. Goodell, 65.
Jackson v. Lamphire, 141, 229.
Jackson v. Porter, 305, 306.
Jackson v. Rose, 262, 272, 273.
Jackson v. The Magnolia, 271.
Jackson v. Winn, 140.
Jackson v. Wood, 65, 341, 346, 357.
Jacob Spangler, Ex parte, 335.
Jacobs v. Smallwood, 152, 210, 227.
Jacoway v. Denton, 88, 124, 125, 154.
Jacques v. Marchand, 155.
James Egan, Ex parte, 248.
James P. Martin, Ex parte, 45, 236.
James River Co. v. Thompson, 180.
James Romaine, Ex parte, 295.
James v. Comm., 342, 361.
James v. Stull, 222.
Jane v. Comm., 346.
January v. January, 228.
Jefferson Bank v. Skelly, 132, 173.
Jefferson Davis, Ex parte, 379.
Jemison v. Planters' Bank, 217.
Jeremiah Ferguson, Ex parte, 335.
John Baxter, Ex parte, 103.
John L. Clark, Ex parte, 296.
John Merryman, Ex parte, 101, 258.

B

TABLE OF CASES.

John R. Platt, In the matter of, 344, 351.
John T. Phillips, 349.
John White, Ex parte, 297.
John W. A. Smith, In re, 72.
John W. Smith, In re, 72.
John Ziegenfuss, In re, 73.
Johnson v. Bentley, 211.
Johnson v. Bond, 229.
Johnson v. Comm., 132, 172.
Johnson v. Drummond, 237, 240.
Johnson v. Duncan, 101, 122, 209, 210, 211, 212, 227.
Johnson v. Gordon, 264, 278.
Johnson v. Higgins, 210, 228.
Johnson v. Johnson, 66.
Johnson v. Jones, 248, 352.
Johnson v. McIntosh, 305, 306, 307.
Johnson v. Monell, 264.
Johnson v. Thompkins, 298.
Johnson v. Winslow, 210.
Johnston v. Riley, 297.
Joice v. Scales, 284, 286.
Jolly v. Draw Bridge Co., 52, 53, 57.
Jones' Appeal, 143.
Jones v. Brandon, 225.
Jones v. Crittenden, 130, 131, 210, 227, 237.
Jones v. Eisler, 63.
Jones v. G. & C. Railroad Co., 183.
Jones v. Harker, 80, 87.
Jones v. Horsey, 162.
Jones v. Keep, 23.
Jones v. Laney, 65.
Jones v. McMahon, 227.
Jones v. People, 238.
Jones v. Seward, 247.
Jones v. Van Zandt, 298.
Jones v. Walker, 255, 312, 313, 314.
Jordan v. Cobb, 232.
Jordan v. Dayton, 85.
Jordan v. Dobson, 83, 84.
Jordan v. Hall, 75.
Jordan, In re, 71, 72.
Joseph De Cabrera, Ex parte, 261.
Joseph Smith, 297.
Joslyn v. Pacific Mail Steamship Co., 203.
Jourdan v. Barrett, 301, 302.
Journeay v. Gardner, 162.
Journeay v. Gibson, 141.
Joy v. Jackson & Mich. Plank Road, 197.
Joy v. Thompson, 220.
Juan, Leon, Ex parte, 273.

Judd, Bela, In re, 74.
Judd v. Ives, 74.
Judson v. State, 172, 173.
Julia v. McKinney, 288.
Justices v. Murray, 358, 361.

Kansas Indians, The, 60, 62, 63.
Karrahoo v. Adams, 66.
Kauffman v. Oliver, 298.
Kean et al, In re, 72.
Kearney, Ex parte, 277.
Kearney v. Taylor, 142.
Keeler, Geo. B., In re,
Keene v. Mould, 70, 71.
Keller v. State, 235.
Kellogg v. Union Co., 43, 54.
Kelly v. Crapo, 161.
Kelly v. Drury, 159.
Kelly v. McCarthy, 142, 143.
Kemp, Nicholas, In re, 103.
Kendall v. Badger, 158.
Kendall v. U. S., 242, 243, 261.
Kennett v. Chambers, 260.
Kenowsha, Rockford & Rock Island Railroad Co. v. Marsh, 198, 202.
Keokuk v. Packet Co., 239.
Keough v. McNitt, 119, 228.
Keppel v. Petersburg Railroad Co., 331.
Kerr, In re, 72, 180.
Kierski v. Matthews, 80, 87.
Kimball v. Taylor, 251.
Kimberly v. Ely, 156.
Kimbro v. Bank, 216.
Kincaid v. Francis, 290, 293.
King v. Dedham Bank, 123.
King v. Stevenson, 159.
King v. W. & W. Railroad Co., 213.
Kingsley v. Cousins, 218.
Kinney v. Sherman, 216.
Kirtland v. Molton, 214.
Kittredge v. Warren, 71.
Klaus v City, 215.
Klein, Edw., In re, 69.
Kleinschmidt v. Dunphy, 359, 360, 361.
Kneedler v. Lane, 19, 87, 89, 90, 91, 101, 338, 362.
Knight v. Dorr, 216.
Knowles, Frank, Ex parte, 67, 68.
Knox v. Lee, 331.
K. N. P. Co. v. Keokuk, 238, 239.
Kohl v. U. S., 356.
Kansas Pacific Railroad Co. v. Mower, 183.

TABLE OF CASES.   xix

K. & P. Railroad Co. v. Palmer, 201.
Krebs v. State Bank, 215.
Kulp v. Ricketts, 264, 268.
Kumler v. Traber, 179.
Kunkle v. Franklin, 142.
Kunzler v. Kohaus, 2, 69, 70.
Kyle v. Jenkins, 114, 119.
Kynoch v. Ives, 269, 270.

Lain v. Shepardson, 147.
Lake View v. Rose Hill Cem. Co., 182, 185.
Lalor v. Wattles, 70.
Lampton v. Bank, 110.
Landon v. Litchfield, 123, 175, 178, 179.
Lang v. Randall, 69.
Lange, Ex parte, 349.
Lanman v. Lebanon Valley Railroad Co., 200.
Lans v. Randall, 69.
Lansing v. County, 221.
Lansing v. Smith, 138.
Lapsley v. Brashears, 121, 129, 131, 209, 210, 228, 337, 364.
Larrabee v. Talbott, 74, 161.
Latham v. Clarke, 232.
Latham v. Smith, 23.
Latham v. U. S., 80.
Lathrop v. Brown, 216.
Latimer v. Poteet, 305.
Lavender v. Goswell, 74, 79.
Lawrence, In re. 133, 143.
Lawrence v. Miller, 220.
Lawson v. Miller, 333.
Layton v. New Orleans, 205.
Leach v. Smith, 154.
League v. De Young, 153, 225, 318.
Leak v. Commissioners, 151, 232.
Leathers v. Shipbuilders' Bank, 215, 219.
Le Bur, Ex parte, 335.
Lee Co. v. Rogers, 125.
Lee v. Davis, 152.
Lee, Oliver & Co.'s Bank, Ex parte, 124, 189, 194.
Lee v. Tillotson, 358.
Legal Tender Cases, 6, 20, 80, 81, 87, 96, 100, 337, 355.
Leitensdorfer v. Webb, 249, 250, 262.
Lemmon v. People, 29, 36, 38, 288, 289, 290.
Leonard, The, 270.
Leonard v. The Volunteer, 270.
Le Roy v. East S. C. Railway, 173.

Lessley v. Phipps, 225.
Levering v. Washington, 150.
Levi v. Thompson. 302.
Levison v. Krohne, 227.
Levison v. Norris, 227.
Lewis v. Brackenridge, 222.
Lewis v. Broadwell, 229.
Lewis v. Elmendorf, 13.
Lewis v. Harbin, 229.
Lewis v. Lewis, 227.
Lewis v. McElwain, 211.
Lewis v. Randall. 23.
Lexington v. Aull, 175.
License Cases, 37, 47, 232, 233, 234, 235, 320.
License Tax Cases, 22, 23.
Lick v. Faulkner, 80, 87.
Lincoln v. Smith, 38, 342.
Lincoln Bank v. Richardson, 186.
Lindsey v. Burbridge, 228.
Linn v. State Bank, 110, 111.
Lin Sing v. Washburn, 27, 28, 30, 50, 319.
Linthicum v. Fenly, 76.
List v. Wheeling, 136, 150.
Little v. Barreme, 246.
Little v. Gould, 83.
Liverpool Ins. Co. v. Massachusetts, 45.
Livingston v. Hollenbrock, 146.
Livingston v. Jefferson, 263.
Livingston v. Mayor, 341, 346, 358.
Livingston v. Moore, 140, 213, 215, 341, 358.
Livingston v. Van Ingen, 32, 83, 85.
L. & N. Railroad Co. v. Davidson, 207.
Lobdell v. Fowler, 333.
Lobdell v. Hall, 63.
Lobrano v. Nelligan, 155.
Locke v. Dane, 115, 141, 142.
Locke v. New Orleans, 115.
Lockett v. Usry, 210.
Lockhart v. Yeizer, 229.
Lockington's Case, 335.
Logwood v. Planters' Bank, 124.
Lonas v. State, 375.
Long, Ex parte, 298.
Longfellow v. Patrick, 209.
Longis v. Creditors, 74.
Lord v. Chadwick, 115.
Lord v. G. N. & P. Steamship Co., 33.
Lord v. Litchfield, 175.
Lord v. Thomas, 136.
Loring v. State, 146.

Lothrop v. Stedman, 190.
Lott v. Cox, 240.
Lott v. Mobile Trade Co., 240.
Lott v. Morgan, 239.
Loud v. Pierce, 70, 71.
Loughborough v. Blake, 8, 21, 92, 104, 105.
Louisa Simpson, The, 243.
Louisville C. & L. Railroad Co. v. Comm., 173.
Louisville Railroad Co. v. Letson, 366.
Louisville Turnpike Co. v. Lounsbury, 186.
Louisville v. University, 149, 165, 205.
Low v. Austin, 232, 233.
Low v. Commissioners, 41, 279, 357, 360.
Lowry v. Francis, 128.
Lowry v. McGhee, 112.
Lowry v. Weaver, 62.
Lucas v. Sawyer, 143.
Lucius Eames, In re, 73.
Lunt v. Hunter, 58.
Luther v. Borden, 308, 309.
Lyman v. B. & W. Railroad Co., 183.
Lynch v. Hoffman, 114, 119.
Lytle v. Whicher, 369.

Macaulay v. Kellogg, 367.
Mackey v. Coxe, 66.
Madison & Ind. Railr'd Co. v. Whiteneck, 183.
Maenhut v. New Orleans, 136.
Magee v. Young, 143.
Mager v. Grima, 235.
Magill v. Parsons, 98, 268.
Magruder v. Marshall, 230.
Maguire v. Card, 270.
Maguire v. Maguire, 143.
Malony v. Fortune, 223.
Maltbie v. Hotchkiss, 76, 78.
Maltby v. Cooper, 229.
Maltby v. Reading & Col. Railroad Co., 145, 146.
Manly v. Raleigh, 205.
Manning v. State, 116.
Marbury v. Madison, 3, 4, 242, 243, 257, 275, 311, 336.
Margaret, The, 360.
Marietta & Cin. Railroad Co. v. Elliott, 187, 199, 200.
Marietta v. Fearing, 204.
Mark Strouse, Ex parte, 344, 349.
Markoe v. Hartranft, 327.

Marks v. Donaldson, 208.
Marsh v. Burroughs, 124, 148, 154, 309.
Marsh v. Putnam, 156.
Marshall v. Donovan, 378.
Marshall v. Grimes, 55.
Martha Ann, The, 58.
Martha Washington, The, 30.
Martin, Ex parte, 263, 274, 298, 359.
Martin, James P., Ex parte, 45.
Martin v. Berry, 73, 74, 77.
Martin v. Hewitt, 331, 333.
Martin v. Horton, 333.
Martin v. Hunter, 1, 2, 5, 19, 262, 264, 265, 266, 272, 273, 277, 278, 279, 316, 329, 339, 362.
Martin v. Mott, 90.
Martin v. Penn. & Geo. Railroad Co., 201.
Martin v. Snowden, 22, 23, 104, 351.
Martin v. Somerville Co., 222.
Martin v. State, 116.
Martin v. Waddell, 36.
Martinetti v. Maguire, 83.
Mary Washington, The, 270.
Mason v. Boom Company, 263.
Mason v. Haile, 217.
Mason v. Nash, 72.
Mass. Gen'l Hospital v. State Mutual Life Assurance Co., 192.
Master v. Pratts, 42, 239.
Matheny v. Golden, 132, 173, 179.
Mather v. Bush, 155.
Mather v. Chapman, 141.
Mathews v. Rucker, 232.
Mathing v. Golden, 125.
Matthews v. Ray, 67.
Matthews v. Zane, 14.
Matthewson v. Weller, 225.
Maxey v. Wise, 141.
Mayer v. Hillman, 76.
Maynard v. Newman, 21, 25, 79, 80.
Maynes v. Moore, 215.
Mayor v. Balt. & Ohio Railroad Co., 174, 175, 178.
Mayor v. Cooper, 261, 264, 267.
Mayor v. Miln, 49, 318, 320, 321.
Mayor v. N. & W. Railroad Co., 190, 193.
Mayor v. Pitts. & C. Railroad Co., 189.
Mayor v. Proprietors, 178.
Mayor v. Second Ave. Railroad Co., 149.
Mayor v. State, 111, 205.

TABLE OF CASES. xxi

Maysville Turnpike Co. v. How. 167.
McCall v. McDowell, 19, 101, 102.
McCardle, Ex parte, 277.
McCarty v. Gibson, 161, 162.
McCaulay v. Kellogg, 367.
McCauley v. Brooks, 129, 153.
McClung v. Silliman, 336.
McClure v. Owen, 125.
McClurg v. Kingsland, 84.
McComb v. Board, 135.
McConnell v. Wilcox, 93, 300.
McCormick v. Alexander, 213.
McCormick v. Humphrey, 264.
McCormick v. Pickering, 70, 71.
McCormick v. Rusch, 228.
McCoy v. Washington, 111. 140.
McCracken v. Hayward, 121, 122, 129, 130, 211, 221.
McCracken v. Poole, 111.
McCracken v. Todd, 62.
McCray v. Junction Railroad Co., 196, 200.
McCready v. State, 58, 294.
McCready v. Wilcox, 102.
McCreary v. State, 218.
McCulloch v. State, 5, 7, 17, 18, 95, 97, 98, 99, 100, 312, 316, 318, 321, 322, 323, 325, 326, 329, 362.
McElmoyle v. Cohen, 283, 284, 286.
McElwain v. Mudd, 154, 369.
McFarland v. Butler, 119, 216, 293.
McFarland v. McKnight, 56.
McFarland v. State Bank, 109, 110.
McGar v. Nixon, 333.
McGavish v. State, 174.
McGee v. Mathis, 128, 145.
McIntire v. Wood, 261.
McIntyre v. Ingraham, 169, 217.
McKeen v. Northampton, 151.
McKeithen v. Terry, 226.
McKenny v. Compton, 229.
McKim v. Voorhies, 336.
McKim v. Willis, 160.
M'Kinney v. Carroll, 139, 230, 231.
McLaren v. Pennington, 188.
McLeod v. Burroughs, 166.
McLeod v. Sav. A. & G. Railroad Co., 170.
McMechen v. Mayor, 149.
McMillan v. McNeill, 158.
McMillan v. Sprague, 208, 219.
McMillen v. Anderson, 376, 377.
McMillen v. Boyles, 142.
McNealy v. Gregory, 113, 124, 154.

McRee v. Railroad Co , 170.
McReynolds v. Smallhouse, 43.
McRoberts v. Washburne, 139.
Mead v. Dayton, 161.
Meade v. U. S., 354.
Meador, Ex parte, 344, 349, 350.
Meadow Dam Co. v. Gray, 202, 204.
Mechanics' Bank v. Bridges, 325.
Mechanics' Bank v. Debolt, 132, 173.
Mechanics' Bank v. Thomas, 132, 173.
Mechanics' Bank v. Union Bank, 250, 261.
Medbury v. Hopkins, 156.
Meekins, Kelly & Co. v. Creditors, 74.
Melcher v. Boston, 323.
Menges v. Wertman, 141.
Mercer's Case, 217.
Merchants' Ins. Co., In re, 75.
Merryman, John, Ex parte, 101, 258.
Metcalf v. St. Louis, 39.
Metropolitan Bank v. Van Dyck, 3, 4, 5, 18, 19, 20, 25, 79, 80, 87, 90, 96, 98, 99, 100, 103, 337, 355.
Metropolitan Board v. Barrie, 38, 144.
Metropolitan Railroad Co. v. Highland Railway, 190.
Metzger, In re, 313.
Michigan Bank v. Hastings, 163.
Michigan Central Railroad Co. v. Slack, 24, 355.
Micou v. Tallassee Bridge Co , 170.
Middlesex Turnpike Corporation v. Locke, 199.
Middlesex Turnpike Corporation v. Swan, 198, 199, 201.
Middlesex Turnpike Corporation v. Walker, 201.
Milan & R. Plank Road Co. v. Husted, 132, 172, 173.
Miles v. King, 141.
Millar v. State, 63.
Miller v. Comm., 229.
Miller v. Gould, 333.
Miller v. Little, 301.
Miller v. McQuerry. 298, 359.
Miller v. Moore, 216.
Miller v. New York, 51.
Miller v. Railroad Co., 191, 194.
Miller v. State, 189, 192.
Miller v. U. S., 86, 87, 355, 357, 360.
Milligan, Ex parte, 6, 247, 248, 279, 357.

Milligan v. Hovey, 100.
Mills v. Duryea, 284.
Mills v. St. Clair, 55, 166.
Mills v. Williams, 205.
Milne v. Huber, 210, 211.
Milner v. Pensacola, 206.
Milwaukee v. Milwaukee, 208.
Miners' Bank v. U. S, 165. 189.
Minor v. Happersett, 309, 373. 375.
Minot v. P. W. & B. Railroad Co., 45, 173, 174.
Mintzer v. Montgomery, 326.
Miss. C. Railroad Co. v. State, 331.
Miss. River Telegraph Co. v. First National Bank, 262.
Mitchell v. Burlington, 125.
Mitchell v. Cothrans, 216.
Mitchell v. Lenox, 284.
Mitchell v. Manuf. Co., 71.
Mitchell v. Rome Railroad Co., 198.
Mitchell v. Steelman, 26, 28, 30, 95, 319.
Mitchell v. United States, 305, 307.
Mobile Railroad Co. v. State, 133, 189, 195, 338.
Mobile School Com. v. Putnam, 206.
Moffat v. Soley, 261.
Mohawk Bridge Co. v. Railroad Co., 170.
Monongahela Navigation Co. v. Coone, 151, 187, 188, 189.
Monroe Savings Bank v. Rochester, 325.
Montello, The, 35, 36.
Montgomery v. Elston, 324, 326.
Montgomery v. Galbraith, 217.
Montgomery v. Kasson, 137.
Montpelier Academy v. George, 163, 165.
Montpelier v. East Montpelier, 207.
Moor v. Veazie, 31, 32, 33, 34, 57, 59.
Moore v. Fowler, 123.
Moore v. Illinois Central Railroad Co., 124, 172.
Moore v. Martin, 224.
Moore v. Mayor, 143.
Moore v. People, 317, 319.
Moore v. State, 185.
Morford v. Unger, 205.
Morgan v. Dudley, 68.
Morgan v. King, 57.
Morgan v. Louisiana, 179.
Morgan v. McGhee, 66.
Morgan v. Neville, 293.
Morgan v. Parham, 46.

Morrill v. State, 47.
Morris v. People, 207.
M. O. & R. R. Railroad Co. v. Gaster, 201.
Morse v. Goold, 209, 210, 225.
Morse v. Hovey, 69, 70.
Morse v. Ins. Co., 264.
Morse v. Rice, 217, 218.
Morton v. Granada Academy, 208.
Morton v. Rutherford, 149.
Morton v. Skinner, 296.
Moses Du Puy, In re, 253.
Moses v. Kearney, 153.
Moses Taylor, The, 266, 272.
Mott v. Penn. Railroad Co., 132, 172.
Motts v. Bennett, 360.
Mount Pleasant v. Clutch, 292.
Mowrey v. Ind & Cin. Railroad Co., 200.
Mudge v. Commissioners, 169.
Mulligan v. Corbins, 138.
Mumford v. Wardwell, 58.
Mumma v. Potomac Co., 187, 188.
Mundy v. Monroe, 211, 223.
Municipality v. Commercial Bank, 177.
Municipality v. Pease, 48, 238.
Municipality v. State Bank, 132, 172.
Municipality v. Wheeler, 115.
Munn v. People, 376.
Munn v. Illinois, 39, 106, 376, 377, 378.
Murch v. Tomeer, 63, 66.
Murdock v. Memphis, 277.
Murphy, Wm., In re, 103.
Murphy & Glover Cases, 113, 119.
Murphy v. Northern Trans. Co., 28.
Murphy v. People, 279, 341, 346, 357.
Murray v. Hoboken Co., 97, 260, 266, 344, 350, 351.
Murray v. McCarty, 287.
Murray v. Patrie, 264.
Murray v. Wooden, 59.
M. W. & M Plank Road Co. v. Reynolds, 193.
Myrick v. Battle, 126, 152.

Naff v. Crawford, 333.
Nat. Bank v. Comm., 322, 325, 327.
Nat. Bank v. Mayor, 326.
Nathan v. Louisiana, 45. 323.
Neaderhouser v. State, 34.
Neass v. Mercer, 215.
Ned, The, 87.

Neil v. State, 127.
Neilson v. Garza, 236.
Nellie Smith, Ex parte, 378.
Nelson v. Allen, 139.
Nelson v. People, 317, 320.
Nelson v. V. & C. Railroad Co., 181, 182, 183.
Nesbit v. Greaves, 76.
Nevitt v. Bank, 130, 187.
New Albany & Salem Railroad Co. v. McNamara, 218.
New Albany & Salem Railroad Co. v. Tilton, 181, 183.
Newark City Bank v. The Assessor, 324.
Newcastle Railroad Co. v. Peru & Ind. Railroad Co., 180.
New Haven v. City Bank, 177.
New Haven v. Sheffield, 175.
New Jersey Co. v. Merchants' Bank, 270.
New Orleans v. Cordeviolle, 115.
New Orleans v. Holmes, 222.
New Orleans v. Turpin, 145.
New Orleans C. & N. Co. v. New Orleans, 231.
New Orleans J. & G. N. Railroad Co. v. Harris, 195, 200.
New Orleans Railroad Co. v. Harris, 195.
New York Indians, 62.
New York v. Dibble, 61.
New York v. Staples, 49.
Newcomb v. Smith, 350, 352, 353, 354, 355.
Newell Smith, Ex parte, 357.
Newkirk v. Chaperon, 210.
Newland v. Marsh, 229.
Newmarket Bank v. Butler, 158, 159.
Newport v. Taylor, 36, 55.
Newton v. Commissioners, 153.
Newton v. Tibbatts, 217.
Nicholas Kemp, In re, 101, 103, 247, 248, 259, 346.
Nichols v. Bertram, 171.
Nichols v. N H. & N. Co., 178.
Nichols v. Som. & Ken. Railroad Co., 167, 183.
Nock v. U. S., 260.
Noel v. Ewing, 142, 143.
Nones v. Edsall, 12, 13.
Norris v. Abingdon Academy, 163.
Norris v. Androscoggin Railroad Co., 183.
Norris v. Boston, 40, 49, 125, 318, 321.

Norris v. Doniphan, 280, 352, 353.
Norris v. Newton, 298.
North Cape, The, 240.
Northeast Railroad Co., Ex parte, 184.
Northern Railroad v. Concord Railroad, 180.
Northern Railroad Co. v. Miller, 202, 203, 204.
Northwestern U. P. Co. v. St. Paul, 239.
North. Mo. Railroad Co. v. Maguire, 146, 173, 342.
North River Co. v. Hoffman, 32.
North Yarmouth v. Skillings, 205.
Norton v. Cook, 158, 159, 162.
Norton v. Pettibone, 141.
Norwalk Co. v. Husted, 132, 172, 173.
Nugent, John, Ex parte, 11, 12.
Nunn v. State, 343.
N. W. Fertilizing Co. v. Hyde Park, 181, 184
N. W. Union Packet Co. v. St. Louis, 239.
N. Y. Life Insurance Co. v. Best, 264.

Oatman v. Bond, 211.
Ochiltree v. Railroad Co., 155.
O'Donnell v. Bailey, 175.
Officer v. Young, 186.
Ogden v. Lee, 306, 307.
Ogden v. Saunders, 5, 120, 121, 122, 123, 124, 125, 155, 156, 158, 284.
Ohio & M. Railroad Co. v. McClelland, 181, 183.
Ohio Trust Co. v. Debolt, 125, 132, 166, 170, 172, 364.
Olcott v. Supervisors, 125.
Oldens v. Hallet, 72, 155, 284.
Oliver Lee & Co.'s Bank, Ex parte, 124, 189, 194.
Oliver v. McClure, 210, 224.
Oliver v. Memphis & L. Railroad Co., 172.
Oliver v. Washington Mills, 292.
O. & L. Railroad Co. v. Veazie, 201, 204.
Olmstead's Case, 335, 365.
Olney v. Angell, 286.
Opinion of Justices, 92, 298, 323, 324.
Ordinary v. Central Railroad Co., 177.
Oriental Bank v. Freeze, 210, 217, 218.

Orono, The. 242.
Osborn v. Bank, 266, 267, 326, 365, 366.
Osborn v. James, 229.
Osborn v. Nicholson, 154, 369.
Osborn v. U. S., 253.
Osborne v. Humphrey, 123, 174, 178, 179.
Osborne v. Mobile, 45.
Oswego Bridge Co. v. Fish, 170.
Owen v. Branch Bank, 109, 110.
Owens v. Bowie, 161.
Owings v. Speed, 1.

Pace v. Burgess, 106.
Pacific Life Ins. Co. v Soule, 22, 105.
Pacific Railroad Co. v. Cass, 176.
Pacific Railroad Co. v. Hughes, 197, 198, 199, 204.
Pacific Railroad Co. v. Maguire, 176.
Pacific Railroad Co. v. Renshaw, 202, 204.
Padelford v. Savannah, 47.
Painter v. Ives, 61.
Palfrey v. Boston, 324.
Palmer v. Commissioners, 52.
Palmer v. Goodwin, 158.
Parent v. Walmsley, 66.
Paris v. Farmers' Bank, 175.
Parker v. Metropolitan Railroad Co., 193.
Parker v. Milldam Co., 54.
Parker v. Redfield, 175, 179.
Parker v. Shannonhouse, 220.
Parkham v. Justices, 350.
Parkinson v. Scoville, 159.
Parks v. Coffey, 333.
Parsons v. Armor, 361.
Parsons v. Ballard, 337.
Parsons v. Bedford, 358.
Paschal v. Whitsett, 211.
Passaic Bridges, The, 34, 52, 53.
Passenger Cases, 2, 21, 22, 27, 28, 29, 37, 46, 48, 49, 101, 107, 236, 316, 321.
Paterson v. Society, 205.
Patin v. Prejean, 220.
Patrie v. Murray, 279, 358.
Patterson v. Comm., 85.
Patterson v. Philbrook, 141, 142.
Paul v. Virginia, 28, 29, 288, 289, 291.
Paup v. Drew, 147.
Pawlett v. Clark, 128.
Payaud v. State, 109, 111.
Payne v. Baldwin, 164, 169, 337.

P. & C. Railroad Co. v. S. W. P. Railroad Co., 182.
Pearce v. Patton, 141, 229.
Peck v. Chicago, 39.
Peete v. Morgan, 39, 240.
Pelton v. Platner, 285.
Pendleton v. State, 40, 291.
Penn. Railroad Co. v. Comm., 235, 239.
Penn. Railroad Co. v. N. Y. Railroad Co., 52.
Penn. Railroad Co. v. Riblet, 183.
Penn. & Ohio Canal Co. v. Webb, 196, 199.
Penn. Tel. Co. v. W. U. Tel. Co., 28, 44.
Penn v. Tollison, 330, 333.
Pennsylvania v. Quicksilver Co., 274, 275.
Penniman v. Meigs, 160.
Pennsylvania College Cases, 189, 192, 195.
Pennywit v. Eaton, 250.
Penobscot Indians v. Veazie, 306.
Penrose v. Erie Canal Co., 217, 226.
Penrose v. Reed, 211.
Pensacola Tel. Co. v. W. U. Tel. Co., 83.
People v. Assessors, 325, 326.
People v. Auditor, 132, 134, 143, 172.
People v. Babcock, 55.
People v. Barton, 327.
People v. Bond, 130, 136.
People v. Bradley, 326.
People v. Brady, 296, 378.
People v. Brooks, 27, 46, 318.
People v. Burrows, 144.
People v. C. & A. Railroad Co., 373.
People v. Carpenter, 217.
People v. Coleman, 47, 233, 235, 292, 323.
People v. Commissioners, 46, 174, 208, 323, 324, 325, 327, 338.
People v. Curtis, 255.
People v. Dawell, 4, 283.
People v. Devlin, 144.
People v. Downer, 29, 49, 236.
People v. Fishkill Plank Road Co., 206.
People v. Fiske, 335.
People v. Gardiner, 324.
People v. Gerke, 254, 255.
People v. Godfrey, 93.
People v. Goodwin, 348.
People v. Hawley, 153.
People v. Hills, 190, 192.

People v. Imlay, 291, 292.
People v. Jenkins, 39.
People v. Lent, 93, 94.
People v. Lippincott, 144.
People v. Manhattan Co., 164.
People v. Marshall, 187.
People v. Mayor, 139.
People v. Merrill, 290, 357.
People v. Mitchell, 207, 215.
People v. Moring, 233, 235, 236.
People v. Morris, 204, 205.
People v. Mortimer, 116.
People v. Naglee, 50, 301, 302, 312, 316, 321, 364.
People v. Plank Road, 168, 181.
People v. Platt, 139, 140.
People v. Power, 207.
People v. Quant, 38.
People v. Quigg, 359, 376.
People v. Railroad Co., 32, 37, 51, 52.
People v. Raymond, 27, 28, 37, 40, 44.
People v. Roe, 39.
People v. Roper, 126, 133, 134, 135.
People v. Schenck, 298.
People v. Sheriff, 319.
People v. Sperry, 42.
People v Supervisors, 136.
People v. Tax Commissioners, 47, 107, 235.
People v. Thurber, 45, 291.
People v. Tillinghast, 136.
People v. Toynbee, 38.
People v. Washington, 67, 312, 369, 370.
People v. White, 81.
People v. Woods, 136.
People v. Wright, 298.
Peoria & Rock Island Railroad Co. v. Preston, 198.
Pepin v. Lachenmeyer, 333.
Pepoon v. Jenkins, 336.
Perdicaris v. Charleston Gas-Light Co., 331.
Perdue v. Ellis, 38, 235.
Pereles v. Watertown, 229, 230.
Perkins, Carter, Ex parte, 115, 298, 304, 320, 321.
Perkins v. Rogers, 86.
Perkins v. Watertown, 205
Permoli v. Municipality, 364.
Perrin v. Oliver, 188, 193.
Perry v. Comm., 116.
Perry v. Langley, 73.
Perry Manuf. Co. v. Brown, 161.

Perry v. Torrence, 46, 240.
Pervear v. Comm., 326, 342.
Peters v. Railroad Co., 180, 185.
Peter Voorhees, Ex parte, 296, 297, 298.
Phalen v. Comm., 144, 230.
Phelen's Case, 335.
Phelps v. Racey, 40.
Phila. W. & B. Railroad Co. v. Bowers, 163, 168, 172, 181, 182.
Phila. W. & B. Railroad Co. v. State, 178.
Phila. & W. Railroad Co. v. State, 131, 172.
Philbrick v. Philbrick, 215.
Phillips v. Bloomington, 55.
Phillips v. Mayor, 144.
Phœbe v. Jay, 149.
Phœnix Ins. Co v. Comm., 291.
Pick v. C. & N. W. Railroad Co., 193, 195.
Pierce v. Carskadon, 114, 119.
Pierce v. Mill, 218.
Pierce v. Somersworth, 180.
Pierce v. State, 255, 320.
Pingry v. Washburn, 187.
Piqua Bank v. Knoup, 278.
Piscataqua Bridge Co. v. N. H. Bridge Co., 179.
Pitcher v. U. S., 354.
Pitkin v. Thompson, 157.
Pittsburgh, F. W. & C. Railroad Co. v. Comm., 146.
Pittsburgh v. Nat'l Bank, 326.
Pitts. & S. Railroad Co. v. Gazzam, 199.
Plank Road Co. v. Arndt, 199.
Planters' Bank v. Sharp, 129, 130, 166, 217, 337.
Platenius v. State, 133.
Platt v. Archer, 75.
Pleasants v. Rohrer, 230.
Plumbly v. Comm., 118.
Plymouth v. Jackson, 165.
Poe v. Duck, 156, 159, 161.
Pol v. Hardie, 225.
Police Jury v. Shreveport, 205, 208.
Pollard, Ex parte, 209, 210, 211, 213, 227.
Pollard v. Hagan, 34, 36, 58, 299, 300.
Ponder v. Graham, 143.
Pool, William, Ex parte, 30.
Pool v. Young, 130, 211, 228.
P. & O. Railroad Co. v. Elting, 197, 198, 199, 201.

TABLE OF CASES.

Portland v. Bangor, 376.
Portland Bank v. Apthorp, 173.
Portland Railroad Co. v. Railway Co., 183.
Port Wardens v. The Charles Morgan, 42, 239.
Port Wardens v. The Martha J. Ward, 36, 42, 239.
Post v. Riley, 155.
Pott v. Supervisors, 134.
Potter v. Kerr, 158, 161.
Potter v. Sturdivant, 154, 219.
Potts v. New Jersey Arms and Ordnance Co., 222.
Potts v. Water Power Co., 220.
Poughkeepsie & S. P. Plank Road v. Griffin, 203.
Powell v. Boon, 251, 309, 332, 379.
Powell v. Sammons, 171.
Powell v. Young, 333.
Powers v. Dougherty Co., 115, 123, 346.
Pratt v. Brown, 151, 303.
Pratt v. Chase, 158.
Pratt v. Jones, 209.
Presbyterian Church v. New York, 140.
Prescott v. State, 346.
Prigeon v. Smith, 232.
Prigg v. Comm., 2, 5, 99, 263, 274, 298, 316, 318, 321.
Prize Cases, The, 86, 87, 242, 246, 247.
Proctor v. Moore, 158.
Proprietors v. Haskell, 190.
Proprietors v. Laboree, 229.
Providence Bank v. Billings, 166, 172, 173, 363.
Provident Ins. v. Massachusetts, 325.
P. S. & P. Railroad Co. v. B. & M. Railroad Co., 184.
Pugh v. Bussell, 72, 155, 158.
Pullan v. Kinsinger, 351.

Quackenbush v. Daks, 225.

Rader v. S. R. District, 219, 221.
Raguet v. Wade, 47, 233, 235, 321.
Railroad Commissioners v. P. & O. C. Railroad Co., 184.
Railroad Co. v. Davis, 346.
Railroad Co. v. Fuller, 38.
Railroad Co. v. Heath, 358.
Railroad Co. v. Johnson, 80, 87.
Railroad Co. v. Leach, 201.
Railroad Co. v. Maryland, 44.
Railroad Co. v. Peniston, 4, 322, 323, 327.
Railroad Co. v. Richmond, 230.
Railway Co. v. Pierce, 264.
Railway Comp'y v. Whitton, 264.
Raleigh & G. Railroad Co. v. Reid, 174.
Ralston v. Lothian, 215.
Rand v. Comm., 118, 232.
Randolph, Ex parte, 337.
Randolph v. Baldwin, 333.
Randolph v. Good, 114, 119.
Randolph v. Middleton, 152.
Ranger v. New Orleans, 136.
Rank, In re, 75.
Rar. & Del. Railroad Co. v. Del. & Rar. Canal Co., 40, 44, 339.
Rathbone v. Bradford, 210, 213, 215.
Raverty v. Fridge, 141.
Rawley v. Hooker, 221.
Ray v. Donnell, 298.
Ray v. Thompson, 331, 333.
Raymond v. Merchant, 159.
R. & B. Railroad Co. v. Thrall, 201.
Read v. Frankfort Bank, 194, 210, 219.
Reapers' Bank v. Willard, 185.
Reardon v. Searcy, 226.
Reavis v. Blackshear, 232.
Reciprocity Bank, In re, 189, 194.
Rector v. Philadelphia, 175.
Redd v. St. Francis Co., 292.
Reddell v. Bryan, 93.
Red River Bridge Co. v. Clarksville, 180.
Reed v. Fullum, 217.
Reed v. Rice, 344.
Reed v. Taylor, 73, 78.
Reed v. Vaughan, 70.
Regents v. Williams, 126, 127, 128, 163, 165, 166, 168, 187, 337.
Reichart v. Felps, 351.
Reiman & Friedlander, In re, 69, 70, 71.
Renner v. Bennett, 93, 94.
Rexford v. Knight, 229, 230.
Reynolds, In re, 73, 75.
Reynolds v. Bank, 25, 80, 87.
Reynolds v. Baldwin, 205.
Reynolds v. Geary, 289.
Reynolds v. Hall, 153.
Reynolds v. State, 116.

TABLE OF CASES.   xxvii

Reynolds v. Taylor, 332.
Rhode Island v. Massachusetts, 275, 276.
Rice v. Rock Island & Alton Railroad Co., 198.
Richard Oliver, In re, 102.
Richards, Ex parte, 298.
Richardson, In re, 14, 15.
Richardson v. Brown, 165.
Richardson v. Monson, 151.
Richland v. Lawrence, 205.
Richmond Railroad Co. v. Louisa Railroad Co., 166, 180.
Riddle v. Hill, 333.
Riddlesbarger v. McDaniel, 25.
Riggs v. Martin, 211.
Riston v. Content, 159.
Rivers v. Moss, 333.
Roach v. Gunter, 154.
Robert Barnard, Ex parte, 356.
Robert D. Bogart, In re, 90, 347.
Robert v. Coco, 225.
Roberts v. Skolfield, 270.
Roberts v. Yates, 40.
Robertson v. Shores, 333.
Robeson v. Brown, 213.
Robinson, Ex parte, 85, 257, 335.
Robinson v. Flanders, 297, 318.
Robinson v. Gardiner, 192.
Robinson v. Howe, 127, 146.
Robinson v. Magee, 120, 121, 122, 130, 212, 229.
Robinson v. Peyton, 286.
Roby v. Boswell, 123.
Roby v. City, 215.
Roche v. Washington, 66.
Rochereau v. Delacroix, 141.
Rockwell v. Hubbell, 225.
Rodemacher v. Mil. & St. P. Railroad Co., 183.
Rodes v. Patillo, 333.
Rodgers v. Bass, 333.
Rodrigues v. Bienvenu, 369.
Rogers v. Railroad Co., 52.
Rohrbacker v. Jackson, 38.
Roosevelt v. Cebra, 155.
Root v. McGrew, 226.
Ropes v. Clinch, 313.
Rose v. Buckland, 301.
Rose v. Estudillo, 135.
Rose v. Himely, 260.
Rosier v. Hale, 221.
Ross County Bank v. Lewis, 132, 173.
Ross v. Jenkins, 114, 119.
Ross v. Riley, 117, 118.

Roundtree v. Baker, 369.
Rowan v. Holcomb, 70.
Rowan v. State, 376.
Rowe v. Granite Bridge, 35.
Rowe v. Page, 73, 77.
Rubideaux v. Vallie, 63.
Rudd v. Schlatter, 231.
Rump v. Comm., 68.
Rundle v. Del. & R. Canal Co., 151.
Russell v. Cheatham, 71.
Russell v. Lowth, 301.
Russell v. Randolph, 225.
Ruth, In re, 71.
Rutland v. Copes, 124, 213.
Rutledge v. Fogg, 250, 251.

Sackett v. Andross, 69, 70.
Sadlier v. Fallon, 336.
Sage v. Dillard, 190, 192.
Sala v. New Orleans, 206.
Salem Turnpike Co. v. Lyme, 170.
Salt Co. v. East Saginaw, 134.
Sampeyreac v. U. S., 352.
Samples v. Bank, 229.
Sampson v. Sampson, 229.
Sanders v. Hillsborough Ins. Co., 185.
Sanders v. Norton, 139.
Sandusky Bank v. Wilbor, 132, 172, 173, 174.
Sanford v. Nichols, 345.
Santo v. State, 235.
Sarah Jane, The, 269, 270.
Sarah Kennedy, In re, 125, 225, 226, 309.
Satterlee v. Matthewson, 123, 148, 363.
Savannah v. State, 37, 41.
Savings Bank v. Allen, 149.
Savings Bank v. Bates, 149.
Savings Institution v. Mankin, 186, 209.
Savoye v. Marsh, 159, 160.
Sayles v. Davis, 24.
Scearcy v. Stubbs, 187.
Schenectady & Saratoga Plank Road v. Thatcher, 202, 204.
Scholey v. Rew, 105.
Scobey v. Gibson, 224.
Scott v. Billgerry, 250, 251, 360, 361.
Scott v. Bogart, 160.
Scott v. Jones, 278.
Scott v. Mather, 139.
Scott v. Willson, 39.
Scott v. The Young America, 269.
Scribner v. Fisher, 159.

TABLE OF CASES.

Scully v. Kirkpatrick, 76.
Seabury v. Field, 58, 300, 301.
Seale v. Mitchell, 223.
Searight v. Stokes, 82.
Sears v. Commissioners, 48, 236, 292.
Selsby v. Redlon, 141.
Sequestration Cases, 227, 330, 331.
Sere v. Pilot, 303.
Seton v. Hanahan, 285.
Seymour v. Hartford, 175.
Seymour v. State, 292.
Shaffer v. Bolander, 221.
Shaw v. Brown, 291.
Shaw v. Lindsay, 333.
Shaw v. McCandless, 30.
Shaw v. Robbins, 156.
Shearon v. Henderson, 333.
Shears v. Solhinger, 73, 75.
Sheehan v. Good Samaritan Hospital, 178.
Sheffield v. Parsons, 237, 239.
Sheldon v. Sill, 261.
Shelor v. Mason, 225.
Shelton v. Johnson, 284.
Shelton v. Wade, 158.
She-mid-go-me-sia v. State, 62.
Shepard v. Taylor, 232.
Sheppard v. People, 117.
Sheppardson's Appeal, 77.
Sherfy v. Argenbright, 333.
Sheriff v. Lowndes, 165.
Sherlock v. Alling, 37, 38.
Sherman v. Bingham, 71.
Sherman v. Smith, 188, 194.
Sherrill v. Hopkins, 159.
Shields v. State, 193.
Shields v. Thomas, 360.
Shipman, In re, 72.
Shipper v. Pennsylvania Railroad Co., 293.
Shollenberger v. Brinton, 18, 19, 20, 25, 79, 80, 87.
Shorter v. Cobb, 88, 154, 309.
Shorter v. Smith, 170, 180.
Shortridge v. Macon, 281, 331.
Shryock v. Bashore, 75, 77, 78.
Shute v. Davis, 261.
Silliman v. Hudson River Bridge Co., 51, 52.
Silliman v. Troy & W. Troy Bridge Co., 52.
Silver Lake Bank v. Harding, 285.
Silverman, In re, 69, 70.
Simeon Bushnell, Ex parte, 298, 334.
Simmons, Ex parte, 298.
Simmons v. Hanover, 142, 210.

Simmons v. State, 145.
Simpson v. Savings Bank, 77, 219.
Sims' Case, 298.
Sinnot v. Davenport, 41, 57, 312, 320.
Sizemore v. State, 81, 82.
Skeen v. Monkeimer, 248.
Slaughter v. Comm., 291, 294.
Slaughter v. Culpepper, 213, 214.
Slaughter House Case, 374.
Slaughter House Cases, 371, 373, 374.
Sloan v. Mo. Pacific Railroad Co., 172, 182.
Small v. Hodgen, 230.
Smedberry v. Bentley, 105.
Smith, Ex parte, 274.
Smith v. Allyn, 261.
Smith v. Appleton, 136.
Smith v. Brown, 157, 159.
Smith v. Bryan, 215.
Smith v. Cleveland, 122, 147.
Smith v. Gardner, 159.
Smith v. Healy, 156.
Smith v. Levinus, 58.
Smith v. Marston, 49.
Smith v. Mead, 156.
Smith v. Merchant, 146.
Smith v. Moody, 287, 291, 292, 370.
Smith v. Morrison, 229, 230.
Smith v. Morse, 209, 226.
Smith v. Nelson, 333, 379.
Smith v. New Orleans, 111.
Smith v. Owen, 113.
Smith v. Packard, 229.
Smith v. Parsons, 155.
Smith v. People, 47, 235.
Smith v. Short, 23.
Smith v. Smith, 158.
Smith v. State, 32, 36, 56, 58, 270, 271, 344.
Smith v. Tucker, 230.
Smoot v. Lafferty, 221.
Sneider v. Heidelberger, 225.
Snyder v. Bank of Ill., 339.
Society v. Coite, 325.
Society v. New Haven, 314.
Society v. Wheeler, 115, 229.
Sommers v. Johnson, 217.
Sommerville v. Marks, 38.
Soule v. Chase, 159, 161.
South Carolina v. Georgia, 36.
Southern Express Co. v. Hood, 45, 236.
Southern Express Co. v. Mayor, 46.
South Western Railroad Co. v. Paulk, 184.

Southworth v. City, 149.
Soutter v. Madison, 221.
Sparks v. Clapper, 148.
Sparrow v. Evansville & Crawfordsville Railroad Co., 123, 200.
Spaulding v. Andover, 208.
Spear v. Peabody, 156, 160.
Speer v. Comm., 48.
Speer v. Directors, 90.
Spencer v. Board, 375.
Spinney, Ex parte, 295, 374, 376.
Spooner v. McConnell, 127, 329.
Sporer v. Eifler, 23.
Sprague v. Ill. Railroad Co., 196, 199, 200.
Springer v. Foster, 158.
Sprott v. Reid, 213.
Sprott v. U. S., 332.
Staats v. Hudson River Railroad Co., 192.
Stacy v. Abbott, 262.
Stafford v. Lick, 141.
Stanley v. Stanley, 169.
Stanmire v. Taylor, 128.
Stanwood v. Green, 344.
Starkweather v. Hawes, 223.
Starr v. Hamilton, 143.
Starr v. Pease, 143.
Starr v. Robinson, 222.
State v. Accommodation Bank, 200.
State v. Adams, 167, 207.
State v. Antonio, 81.
State v. Arlin, 117.
State v. Atkins, 277.
State v. Auditor, 109, 132, 173.
State v. Bank, 132, 172, 176, 218, 226.
State v. Barker, 134, 135.
State v. Barnett, 342.
State v. Barringer, 210.
State v. Batchelder, 302.
State v. Beackins, 112.
State v. Bell, 119.
State v. Bentley, 177.
State v. Bermudez, 229.
State v. Berry, 132, 172.
State v. Betts, 173.
State v. Blundell, 176.
State v. Bond, 115, 118.
State v. Bosworth, 171.
State v. Branin, 177.
State v. Brown, 81, 82.
State v. Browning, 47.
State v. Buchanan, 274.
State v. Buzzard, 343.
State v. Calvin, 110.

State v. Cardozo, 111.
State v. Carew, 227.
State v. Chandler, 343.
State v. Charleston, 46, 106, 107, 232, 233, 239, 240.
State v. Claiborne, 290.
State v. Collector, 176, 326.
State v. Commercial Bank, 132, 173.
State v. Commissioners, 173, 176, 188, 189, 190.
State v. Constitution, 37, 49.
State v. Cooper, 50, 291.
State v. County Court, 132, 172.
State v. County Treasurer, 174.
State v. Cumb. & Penn. Railroad Co., 43, 44.
State v. De La Foret, 276.
State v. Del., L. & W. Railroad Co., 27, 40, 44, 179, 235.
State v. Demarest, 89.
State v. Dews, 133, 143.
State v. Dimish, 335.
State v. Donehey, 235.
State v. Doyle, 264.
State v. Dulle, 172.
State v. Fellows, 145.
State v. Flavell, 176
State v. Foreman, 60, 61, 63.
State v. Fosdick, 48.
State Freight Tax, 27, 28, 37, 43, 44.
State v. Fry, 143.
State v. Garesche, 113, 119, 145.
State v. Gatzweiller, 113, 151.
State v. Garton, 24.
State v. Gazlay, 145.
State v. Georgia Railroad & B. Co, 172, 176.
State v. Gibson, 375.
State v. Glen, 139.
State v. Gray, 133.
State v. Gulich, 335.
State v. Haight, 176, 324, 325, 326.
State v. Han. & St. Jo. Railroad Co., 174, 178.
State v. Hancock, 176.
State v. Hart, 325, 326.
State v. Hawthorn, 144.
State v. Heighland, 113, 119.
State v. Heyward, 165, 168.
State v. Hoge, 109.
State v. Holmes, 144.
State v. Hoppess, 298.
State v. Hudson, 54, 55, 139.
State v. Hunt, 329.
State v. Jackson, 90, 346.

State v. Johnson, 118.
State v. Jones, 133, 153, 229.
State v. Jumel, 343.
State v. Keeran, 119.
State v. Keith, 118.
State v. Kennedy, 47.
State v. Kent, 117.
State v. Keyes, 346, 358.
State v. Kline, 115, 207.
State v. Lathrop, 291.
State v. Leester, 179.
State v. Love, 173.
State v. Manning, 116.
State v. Mansfield, 176.
State v. Matthews, 167, 170, 181.
State v. Mayor, 192.
State v. McBride, 262, 273.
State v. McCann, 374. 378.
State v. McDonald, 117.
State v. McGinty, 228.
State v. Medbury, 288, 289, 294.
State v. Millain, 342.
State v. Miller, 192.
State v. Minton, 172.
State v. Moor, 348.
State v. Moore, 235, 319.
State v. Navigation Co., 303.
State v. Neal, 114, 119.
State v. Newark, 176, 177.
State v. New Haven & N. Railroad Co., 150, 189.
State v. Newsom, 343.
State v. North, 47, 232, 233, 234.
State v. Northern Central Railroad Co., 177, 189.
State v. N. & W. Railroad Co., 175.
State v. Noyes, 171, 182.
State v. Pagan, 49.
State v. Parker, 173.
State v. Paul, 119, 125, 126, 342.
State v. Peckham, 233, 235.
State v. Perry Co., 153, 338.
State v. Person, 188.
State v. Petway, 173, 177.
State v. Phalen, 144.
State v. Pinckney, 34, 47, 233, 234, 236.
State v. Plime, 335.
State v. Powers, 176, 177.
State v. P. W. & B. Railroad Co., 43.
State v. Railroad Co., 168, 205, 207.
State v. Randall, 82, 272, 274.
State v. Robinson, 47.
State v. Ross, 62.
State v. Ryan, 116.
State v. Salomons, 117.
State v. Schumpert, 346.
State v. Sears, 116, 330.
State v. Shapleigh, 46, 232.
State v. Shricker, 342.
State v. Sluby, 232.
State v. Smedes, 144.
State v Smith, 343.
State v. Sneed, 118.
State v. Southern Pacific Railroad Co., 181, 185.
State v. Springfield, 208.
State v. Squires, 115.
State v. Stanton, 276.
State v. Sterling, 144.
State v. Stone, 193.
State v. Sullivan, 116.
State v. Ta-cha-na-tah, 63.
State v. Tassels, 63.
State v. Tombecbee Bank, 168, 169.
State v. Trustees, 277.
State v. Tutt, 274.
State v. Waples, 145.
State v. Wells, 273.
State v. Wheeler, 235.
State v. Wheeling Bridge Co., 51, 52, 106, 107, 127, 242, 275, 351.
State v. Whittemore, 68.
State v. Wilson, 128, 145.
State v. Winona & St. Paul Railroad Co., 179.
State v. Woodruff, 176.
State v. Woodson, 119.
State v. Wright, 81.
State v. Yard, 189.
State Bank v. Charleston, 175.
State Bank v. Knoop, 132, 163, 164, 165, 172, 173, 174, 364.
State Bank v. Madison, 208.
State Bank v. People, 132, 172.
State Bank v. Wilborn, 70.
State Home Society v. Mayor, 178.
State Tax on Foreign Held Bonds, 146.
State Tax on Railway Gross Receipts, 45, 46, 233.
State Tonnage Tax Cases, 237, 240.
Steamboat Co. v. Livingston, 1, 19, 26, 27, 32, 37, 56, 57.
Steamship Co. v. Joliffe, 42.
Steamship Co. v. Port Wardens, 48, 237, 239.
Stearns v. Gittings, 229.
Stearns v. U. S., 262, 273, 312.
Steerman v. State, 56.
Steele v. Thacher, 270.
Steelman v. Mattix, 75, 76.

TABLE OF CASES. xxxi

Steen v. Finley, 152.
Stephen v. Smith, 188.
Stephens, Alexander, Ex parte, 68.
Stephens v. Powell, 188.
Stephens v. St. Louis Nat'l Bank, 229.
Stephenson v. Osborne, 225.
Stepp v. Stahl, 77.
Sterrett v. Houston, 238.
Stetler's Case, 253.
Stetson v. Bangor, 326.
Stevens v. Andrews, 227.
Stevens v. Brown, 38.
Stevens v. Norris, 161.
Stevens v. R. & B. R. Co., 196.
Stewart v. Blaine, 11.
Stewart v. Harry, 37.
Stewart v. Kahn, 88.
St. Louis B. & S. Association v. Lightner, 325.
St. Louis v. Ferry Co , 46.
St. Louis I. M. & S. R. Co. v. Loftin, 174, 177.
St. Luke's Hospital v. Barclay, 277.
Stocking v. Hunt, 222.
Stockwell v. Silloway, 76.
Stoddard v. Harrington, 156, 161.
Stoddart v. Smith, 115, 215, 338.
Stokes v. New York, 39. 57.
Stokes v. Rodman, 115, 148, 210.
Stokes v. Searight, 127.
Stone v. Bassett, 223, 224.
Stone v. Bennett, 229.
Stone v. Tibbetts, 157.
Story v. Furman, 220.
Story v. Jersey City Plank Road Co., 202.
Stow v. Parks, 79.
St. Paul & Pac. Railroad Co. v. Parcher, 179.
St. Paul & Pac. Railroad Co. v. St. Paul, 177.
Strader v. Graham, 299. 364.
Streubel v. Mil. & M. Railroad Co., 134.
Strode v. Comm., 325.
Strong v. Daniel, 227, 230.
Strong v. State, 337.
Strong v. Waterman, 63, 65, 306.
Stuart v. Laird, 262.
Sturges v. Crowninshield, 4, 69, 72, 73, 120, 121, 127, 131, 155, 317, 363.
Sturges v. Spofford, 30.
Succession of John M. Nelson, 141.

Succession of Woodward, 369.
Sullivan v. Brewster. 216.
Sullivan v. Hieskill, 76.
Supervisors v. Miss. & W. Railroad Co. 200.
Susquehanna Canal Co. v. Comm., 146.
Susquehanna Canal Co. v. Wright, 151.
Sutherland v. DeLeon, 115.
Suydam v. Moore, 183, 188.
Suydam v. Receivers, 115, 186.
Swan v. Williams, 352, 354, 356.
Swann v. Buck, 136. 144.
Swasey v. N. C. Railroad Co., 365.
Swickard v. Bailey, 230.
Swift v. Fletcher, 217, 218.
Syracuse Bank v. Davis, 188.

Tabor v. Harwood, 158.
Taggart v. McGinn, 222.
Tarbles' Case, 335.
Tarleton v. Southern Bank, 214.
Tarpley v. Hamer. 218.
Tarver v. Tankersley, 333.
Tate v. Stooltzfoos, 141.
Tatum v. Wright, 291.
Tax Cases, 177.
Taylor v. Barron. 285.
Taylor v. Drew, 61.
Taylor v. Flint, 213.
Taylor v. Morton, 313, 314.
Taylor v. Railroad Co., 353, 354.
Taylor v. Stearns, 126. 151, 209.
Taylor v. Thompson, 89.
Taylor v. Turley, 333.
Teal v. Felton, 272.
Tebbetts v. Pickering, 158.
Telford v. Barney, 62.
Terre Haute & Alton Railroad Co. v. Earp, 197, 198.
Terrett v. Taylor, 128, 137, 138.
Territory v. Coleman, 319.
Territory v. Pyle, 144.
Texas v. Hardenberg, 331.
Texas v. White, 91, 250, 308, 309, 327, 328, 329, 330, 331.
Thames Bank v. Lovell, 37, 43. 239.
Thayer v. Hedges, 19, 20, 21, 25, 79, 80, 87.
Thayer v. Seavey, 127, 218.
Theophilus C. Callicott, In re, 253.
Thomas F. Goodhue, In re. 298.
Thomas Kaine, Ex parte. 101.
Thomas Swan, The, 54, 57.

TABLE OF CASES.

Thomas v. Taylor, 232, 330, 331, 339.
Thompson v. Alger, 70.
Thompson v. Bohannon, 333.
Thompson v. Buckley, 228.
Thompson v. The Catherina, 269.
Thompson v. Guion, 199.
Thompson v. Holton, 145.
Thompson v. Mankin, 330, 333.
Thompson v. Pacific Railroad Co., 97, 327.
Thompson v. N. Y. & Harlem Railroad Co., 170.
Thompson v. State, 333.
Thomson v. Lee County, 125.
Thorington v. Smith, 232.
Thornbury v. Harris, 333.
Thorne v. San Francisco, 223.
Thornhill et al. v. Bank of Louisiana, 74, 75.
Thornton's Case, 298, 318.
Thornton v. Hooper, 123, 133.
Thornton v. McGrath, 142.
Thorp v. B. & O. Railroad Co., 164, 180, 181, 182, 183.
Thurber v. Townsend, 142, 143.
Tillotson v. Millard, 226.
Tilton v. Swift, 142.
Timms v. Grace, 333.
Tobias Watkins, Ex parte, 361.
Tobin v. Trump, 77.
Tobin v. Vicksburg, 237.
Tod v. Fairfield, 264.
Todd v. Neal, 224.
Toledo Bank v. Bond, 132, 172, 173.
Tolen v. Tolen, 143.
Tomlinson v. Branch Bank, 132, 172, 178.
Tomlinson v. Jessup, 193.
Totten v. U. S., 246.
Towle v. Forney, 123.
Towne v. Pace, 148.
Towne v. Smith, 159.
Townsend v. Griffin, 143.
Townsend v. Townsend, 112, 130, 131, 209, 210, 227.
Township v. Talcott, 125.
Tracy v. State, 47, 233.
Trask v. Maguire, 179.
Tredway v. S. C. & St. P. R. Co., 378.
Trigg v. Drew, 147.
Trombley v. Humphrey, 356.
Tropic Wind, The, 86, 247.
Troy & Rutland Railroad Co. v. Kerr, 190, 194, 196, 203.
Trustees v. Aberdeen, 205.
Trustees v. Bailey, 132, 136.
Trustees v. Beers, 137.
Trustees v. Bradbury, 165, 337.
Trustees of Public Schools, In re, 209.
Trustees v. Rider, 120, 124, 126, 127, 128, 133.
Trustees v. State, 165.
Trustees v. Tatman, 205.
Trustees v. Winston, 187, 206.
Tuckahoe Canal Co. v. Railroad, 166, 180.
Tucker v. Ferguson, 175.
Tucker v. Harris, 141.
Tucker v. Potter, 23.
Tuolumne Redemption Co. v. Sedgwick, 218, 224.
Turner v. Bank, 261.
Turner v. Missionary Union, 303, 315.
Turner v. State, 4, 117.
Turner v. Watkins, 224.
Turnpike Co. v. Phillips, 199, 200.
Turnpike Co. v. Railroad Co., 166, 171, 180.
Turnpike Co. v. State, 169, 170.
Turpen v. Commissioners, 144.
Twitchell v. Comm., 342, 357.
T. W. & W. Railroad Co. v. City, 182, 183.
Tyler v. Defrees, 87.
Tyson v. Va. & T. Railroad Co., 203.

Underwood v. Lilly, 142.
Union Bank v. Hill, 23, 24.
Union Bank v. State, 124, 163, 178.
Union Improvement Co. v. Comm., 192.
Union Locks & Canals v. Towne, 195, 199, 200, 202.
Union Pacific Railroad Co. v. Lincoln County, 327.
Union Passenger Railway Co. v. Philadelphia, 178.
Union Railroad Co. v. East Tennessee Railroad Co., 190, 241.
Union Tow Boat Co. v. Bordelon, 45.
University v. Maultsby, 165.
Upton v. Hubbard, 157.
Urton v. Hunter, 157.
U. S. v. ———, 81.
U. S. v. Ames, 94.
U. S. v. Anthony, 375.

TABLE OF CASES. xxxiii

U. S. v. Arredondo, 313.
U. S. v. Avery, 257.
U. S. v. Bailey, 17, 27, 60, 61, 96.
U. S. v. Bainbridge, 89.
U. S. v. 130 Barrels, 361.
U. S. v. Bedford Bridge, 37, 52, 261, 269, 320.
U. S. v. Bevans, 270, 271.
U. S. v. Block, 346.
U. S. v. Bright, 336, 360, 365.
U. S. v. Brooks, 301.
U. S. v. Burr, 3, 280, 281.
U. S. v. Cathcart, 330.
U. S. v. Cha-to-kah-na-he-sha, 60.
U. S. v. Cheneweth, 282.
U. S. v. Cisna, 59, 60, 61, 63.
U. S. v. Cole, 86.
U. S. v. Collins, 349.
U. S. v. Conner, 349.
U. S. v. Conway, 221.
U. S. v. Cook, 307.
U. S. v. Coolidge, 262.
U. S. v. Coombs, 270, 271.
U. S. v. Cooper, 12.
U. S. v. Cornell, 93, 94.
U. S. v. Crawford, 86.
U. S. v. Cruikshank, 99, 100, 329, 342, 343, 357, 371, 374, 375, 376, 377, 378, 379, 380.
U. S. v. Davis, 94.
U. S. v. Dawson, 280, 357.
U. S. v. Dewitt, 57.
U. S. v. Distillery, 103, 344, 349, 359, 360.
U. S. v. Drennen, 263.
U. S. v. Ebert, 347.
U. S. v. Eliason, 246.
U. S. v. Elm, 373.
U. S. v. Ferreira, 256, 260, 265, 313.
U. S. v. Fisher, 95, 97.
U. S. v. Fitzgerald, 300.
U. S. v. Foster, 307.
U. S. v. Fourteen Packages, 360.
U. S. v. Fries, 281, 282.
U. S. v. Furlong, 86.
U. S. v. 43 Gallons, 59, 60, 254.
U. S. v. Gilbert, 280, 349.
U. S. v. Given, 381.
U. S. v. Gould, 29.
U. S. v. Gratiot, 300, 301, 303.
U. S. v. Great Falls Manuf. Co., 139.
U. S. v. Greathouse, 280, 281, 282.
U. S. v. Greiner, 281, 282.
U. S. v. Hall, 103, 374.
U. S. v. Hamilton, 277.
U. S. v. Hanway, 282.

U. S. v. Harding, 349.
U. S. v. Haskell, 348.
U. S. v. Haun, 29.
U. S. v. Hodges, 281, 282.
U. S. v. Holliday, 59, 60, 61.
U. S. v. Home Ins. Co., 232.
U. S. v. Hoxie, 280, 282.
U. S. v. Hudson, 262.
U. S. v. Hughes, 103.
U. S. v. Irma, 360.
U. S. v. James, 13.
U. S. v. Joe, 262.
U. S. v. Keehler, 331.
U. S. v. Keen, 349.
U. S. v. Klein, 253.
U. S. v. Lariviere, 62, 255.
U. S. v. Lathrop, 262, 272, 273.
U. S. v. La Vengence, 360.
U. S. v. Louisville Canal Co., 355.
U. S. v. Macomb, 349.
U. S. v. Marigold, 31, 81, 95, 99.
U. S. v. Maurice, 256, 258, 316, 363.
U. S. v. Maxon, 357.
U. S. v. Maxwell, 346.
U. S. v. Mil. & St. P. Railroad Co., 51.
U. S. v. Minn. & N. W. Railroad Co., 351.
U. S. v. Mitchell, 280, 282.
U. S. v. More, 92, 265, 277.
U. S. v. Morrison, 330.
U. S. v. Norris, 348.
U. S. v. Ortega, 276.
U. S. v. 129 Packages, 261.
U. S. v. Parker, 349.
U. S. v. Percheman, 313.
U. S. v. Perez, 348.
U. S. v. Peters, 336, 365, 366.
U. S. v. Petersburgh Judges, 380.
U. S. v. Pryor, 282.
U. S. v. Ragsdale, 61, 65, 66.
U. S. v. Railroad Bridge Co., 32, 51, 52, 82, 94, 261, 300, 302, 303.
U. S. v. Railroad Co., 24.
U. S. v. Rathbone, 359, 361.
U. S. v. Ravara, 262, 277.
U. S. v. Reese, 380.
U. S. v. Rhodes, 67, 312, 370.
U. S. v. Riley, 22, 348.
U. S. v. Ritchie, 23.
U. S. v. Rogers, 60.
U. S. v. Russell, 353.
U. S. v. Sacramento, 357.
U. S. v. Shanks, 65.
U. S. v. Shawmux, 59.
U. S. v. Sheppard, 346.

TABLE OF CASES.

U. S. v. Shoemaker, 349.
U. S. v. Singer, 22.
U. S. v. Smith, 86, 242.
U. S. v. Ta-wau-ga-ca, 261.
U. S. v. Taylor, 350.
U. S. v. The Betsey, 360.
U. S. v. The James Morrison, 54.
U. S. v. The Queen, 360.
U. S. v. The Seneca, 57.
U. S. v. The William, 30, 54, 107.
U. S. v. Tierney, 93, 94.
U. S. v. Todd, 260.
U. S. v. Townmaker, 349.
U. S. v. Travers, 94.
U. S. v. Villato, 67.
U. S. v. Waller, 346.
U. S. v. Ward, 61, 63.
U. S. v. Watson, 348.
U. S. v. Webster, 246.
U. S. v. Williams, 14, 349.
U. S. v. Williamson, 298.
U. S. v. Wilson, 253, 336.
U. S. v. Wonson, 358.
U. S. v. Worrall, 99, 262.
U. S. v. Wright, 257.
U. S. v. Yellow Sun, 61.
U. S. Express Co. v. Haines, 23.

Van Allen v. The Assessors, 325, 326, 327.
Vance v. Burtis, 331.
Van Hook v. Whitlock, 156.
Vanhorne v. Dorrance, 120, 133, 150, 306.
Van Husan v. Kanouse, 25, 79, 80, 112, 362.
Vannini v. Paine, 86.
Van Nostrand v. Carr, 73, 74.
Van Raugh v. Van Arsdaln, 158.
Van Rensselaer v. Ball, 221.
Van Rensselaer v. Hays, 222.
Van Rensselaer v. Snyder, 209, 222.
Vanuxem v. Hazlehursts, 72, 156, 158, 284.
Van Valkenburg v. Brown, 373, 375, 381.
Vanzandt v. Waddell, 215.
Varick v. Briggs, 141.
Vaux v. Nesbit, 68.
Veazie v. Moor, 26, 31, 32, 34, 56.
Veazie Bank v. Fenno, 21, 22, 24, 25, 105.
Vedder v. Alkenbrack, 225.
Verges v. Giboney, 25.
Vermont C. Railroad Co. v. Burlington, 176.

Vernon v. Henson, 228.
Vinsant v. Knox, 333.
Virginia v. West Virginia, 241, 276.
Visitors v. State, 167.
Volunteer, The, 270.
Von Baumbach v. Bade, 209, 213, 223.
Von Glan v. Varenne, 157, 158.
Vonhein v. Elkus, 76.
Von Hoffman v. Quincy, 122, 209, 212, 221.

Wade v. Richmond, 206.
Wadsworth v. Buffalo H. Association, 306, 307, 308.
Wainwright v. Bridges, 369.
Waite v. Dowley, 327.
Walcott v. People, 45.
Waldo v. Williams, 221, 223.
Waldron v. Railroad Co., 183.
Walker v. Dunham, 144.
Walker v. Peele, 144.
Walker v. Sauvinet, 358, 375.
Walker v. Tipton, 150, 339.
Walker v. Whitehead, 122, 130, 212, 216.
Wall v. Williamson, 65, 66.
Wallace v. State, 332.
Walsh v. Farrand, 155.
Walston v. Comm., 115, 116.
Walter A. Wood Mowing Machine Co. v. Caldwell, 85.
Walter v. Bacon, 141, 142, 217.
Walton v. Bryenth, 23.
Ward v. Flood, 370, 378.
Ward v. Maryland, 289, 292.
Ward v. Morris, 287.
Wardlaw v. Buzzard, 230.
Ware v. Hyer, 270.
Ware v. Hylton, 314.
Waring v. Clarke, 270, 360.
Waring v. Mayor, 236.
Warner v. Uncle Sam, 311.
Warren Manuf. Co. v. Ætna Ins. Co., 14, 284, 291, 292.
Warren v. Mayor, 138.
Warren v. Paul, 23.
Wartman v. Philadelphia, 150.
Washburn v. Franklin, 149.
Washington Bridge Co. v. State, 163, 168.
Washington University v. Rouse, 173, 175.
Water Commissioners, In re, 52.
Watson v. Bourne, 158, 160.
Watson v. Mercer, 123, 141.
Wayman v. Southard, 100, 336.

Weaver v. Fegley, 81, 317, 319.
Weaver v. Lapsley, 225.
Webb v. Moore, 215, 223.
Weber v. Harbor Commissioners, 58.
Webster v. Reid, 62, 313, 339, 361.
Webster v. Rose, 227.
Webster v. Seymour, 94, 335.
Weimer v. Bunbury, 344, 346.
Weister v. Hade, 115.
Welch v. Wadsworth, 148.
Wells, Wm., Ex parte, 252.
Welman's Case, 14.
Welton v. State, 27, 28, 37, 47.
Wendell, In re, 155.
Wendover v. Lexington, 144.
West v. Creditors, 74.
Western Saving Fund v. Philadelphia, 122, 136, 137, 149, 211.
Weston v. Charleston, 146, 322, 323.
West End Co. v. Atlanta Co., 170.
West River Bridge Co. v. Dix, 129, 180.
West. Union Tel. Co. v. Atlantic & Pac. Tel. Co. 28, 37.
West. Union Tel. Co. v. Mayer, 49.
West. Union Tel. Co. v. Richmond, 48.
West. Wis. Railroad Co. v. Supervisors, 193, 194.
Wetherbee v. Johnson, 279, 358.
Wethersfield v. Humphrey, 35.
Whallon v. Bancroft, 361.
Wharf Case, 239.
Wheat v. State, 211, 215.
Wheaton v. Peters, 5, 83.
Wheeler v. Me-shin-go-me-sia, 306.
Wheelock v. Leonard, 156, 157.
Whelan v. U. S., 360.
Whitaker v. Haley, 81.
White v. Cannon, 330, 333.
White v. Comm., 274.
White v. Hart, 88, 125, 154, 309, 330, 369.
White v. McKee, 339.
White v. Railroad Co., 188, 194.
White v. Syr. & Utica Railroad Co., 202, 203.
White v. Wayne, 115, 120.
White v. White, 142, 143.
White v. Wilkins, 220.
White v. Winn, 161.
White River Turnpike Co. v. Railroad Co., 180.
White's Bank v. Smith, 30.
Whitney v. Madison, 324, 325.
Whitney v. Whiting, 158, 159, 160, 161.

Wiggins v. U. S., 354.
Wilard v. Presbury, 92.
Wilckins v. Willett, 11.
Wilcox v. Davis, 228.
Wilcox v. Jackson, 303.
Wilder v. Lumpkin, 224.
Wiley v. Parmer, 292.
Willard v. Longstreet, 231.
Willard v. People, 288, 321.
William B. Hobbs, Ex parte, 375.
William Blount, 259.
William Fetter, In re, 295, 298.
William H. Hughes, Ex parte, 251, 296.
William J. Jordan, Ex parte, 335.
William Jarvis, The, 40.
William Law, Ex parte, 103.
William L. Tate, In re, 379.
William Murphy, In re, 103.
William Pool, Ex parte, 263, 274, 335.
William Wells, Ex parte, 252, 253.
Williams v. Guignard, 157.
Williams v. Haines, 214.
Williams v. Norris, 351.
Williams v. Waldo, 213.
Williams v. Wickerman, 354.
Williams v. Wilkes, 336.
Williamson v. Suydam, 151.
Willis A. Jordan, In re, 72.
Wilmington Railroad Co. v. Reid, 132, 172, 176, 177.
Wilmington & Weldon Railroad Co. v. King, 154.
Wilson v. Bozeman, 333.
Wilson v. Buckman, 90.
Wilson v. Hardesty, 123, 149.
Wilson v. K. C. St. Jo. & C. B. Railroad Co., 38.
Wilson v. Kenna, 23.
Wilson v. Marsh Co., 54.
Wilson v. Mason, 242.
Wilson v. Matthews, 155, 157.
Wilson v. Robertson, 284.
Wilson v. Sharks, 225.
Wilson v. Wall, 268, 307.
Winchester v. Corinna, 90.
Winona & St. Peter Railroad Co. v. Blake, 172, 184.
Winona & St. Peter Railroad Co. v. Waldron, 183.
Winston v. McCormick, 230.
Winter v. Jones, 130, 132, 138, 336.
Winter v. Muscogee Railroad Co., 199.
Winterniz, In re, 77, 78.
Wise v. Rogers, 133.

Withers v. Buckley, 34, 35, 38, 58, 299, 342, 346.
Witherspoon v. Duncan, 302.
Witt v. Follett, 157.
Witter v. M. P. & R. Railroad Co., 198, 199.
Womack v. Dearman, 336.
Wood v. Child, 229.
Wood v. Fitzgerald, 380, 381.
Wood v. Kennedy, 148.
Wood v. New York, 215.
Wood v. Wood, 122, 131, 210.
Woodbridge v. Allen, 158.
Woodbridge v. Wright, 158, 162.
Woodfin v. Hooper, 217.
Woodfin v. Slader, 214.
Woodfork v. Union Bank, 196, 199.
Woodhull v. Wagner, 158.
Woodman v. Kilbourn Manuf. Co., 54, 299.
Woodruff v. Parham, 47, 233.
Woodruff v. Scruggs, 148.
Woodruff v. State, 120, 126, 128, 152.
Woodruff v. Tilly, 154.
Woodruff v. Trapnall, 110, 112, 128, 147.
Woods v. Buie, 210, 213.
Woodson v. Fleck, 332.
Woodson v. Randolph, 23.
Woodworth v. Rogers, 360.
Woolen v. Banker, 85.
Wooley v. Butler, 12.

Worcester v. Georgia, 314, 315.
Worcester v. State, 59, 61, 62, 63, 65.
Works v. Junction Railroad, 52.
Worsley v. Municipality, 48, 238.
Worthington v. Jerome, 161.
Worthington v. Sebastian, 151.
Worthy v. Barrett, 379.
Wray v. Reily, 158.
Wright v. Deacon, 298.
Wright v. Marsh, 62.
Wright v. Overall, 333.
Wright v. Sill, 173.
Wright v. Stiltz, 325.
Wylie, In re, 71.
Wyman v. Mitchell, 157, 161.
Wynehamer v. People, 38.
Wynne, In re, 14.
Wynne v. Wright, 47, 232, 233, 234.

Yarmouth v. Yarmouth, 165.
Yeaton v. Bank, 190.
Yeazel v. Alexander, 38.
Yerger, Ex parte, 275.
Young v. Beardsley, 154.
Young v. Harrison, 163.
Young v. McKenzie, 140, 350.
Young v. Oregon, 136.
Young v. State Bank, 225.
Youngs v. Hall, 135.

Zabriskie v. Hackensack & N. Y. Railroad Co., 202, 203.

NOTES
OF
CONSTITUTIONAL DECISIONS.

THE
CONSTITUTION OF THE UNITED STATES.

WE, the People of the United States, in order to form a more perfect union, establish justice, insure domestic tranquility, provide for the common defense, promote the general welfare, and secure the blessings of liberty to ourselves and our posterity, do ordain and establish this Constitution for the United States of America.

General Principles.

The Constitution did not commence to operate until the first Wednesday in March, A. D. 1789. Owings *v.* Speed, 5 Wheat. 420.

The Constitution should be so construed as best to promote the great objects for which it was made. This end will be best accomplished by avoiding either extreme of the rules of construction, and keeping steadily in view the purposes for which it was instituted. Steamboat Co. *v.* Livingston, 3 Cow. 713; S. C. 1 Hopk. 150; Hague *v.* Powers, 39 Barb. 427.

The Constitution, like every other grant, is to have a reasonable construction according to the import of its terms, and where a power is expressly given in general terms, it is not to be restrained to particular cases, unless that construction grows out of the context expressly or by necessary implication. The words are to be taken in their natural and obvious sense, and not in a sense unreasonably restricted or enlarged. Martin *v.* Hunter, 1 Wheat. 304.

It is manifest that the Constitution has proceeded upon a theory of its own, and given or withheld powers according to the judgment of the American people by whom it was adopted. The courts can only construe its powers, and can not inquire into the policy or principles which induced the grant of them. Martin *v.* Hunter, 1 Wheat. 304.

The Constitution unavoidably deals in general language. It did not suit the purposes of the people in framing this great charter of their liberties to provide for minute specifications of its powers, or to declare the means by which those powers should be carried into execution. It was foreseen that this would be a perilous and difficult, if not an impracticable task. The instrument was not intended to provide merely for the exigencies of a few years, but was to endure through a long lapse of ages, the events of which were locked up in the inscrutable purposes of Providence. It could not be foreseen what new changes and modifications of power might be indispensable to effectuate the general objects of the charter, and restrictions and specifications which at present might seem salutary might in the end prove the overthrow of the system itself. Hence the powers are expressed in general terms, leaving to the legislature from time to time to adopt its own means to effectuate legitimate objects, and to mould and model the exercise of its powers as its own wisdom and the public interests should require. Martin *v.* Hunter, 1 Wheat. 304.

· No uniform rule of interpretation can be applied to the Constitution, which may not allow, even if it does not positively demand, many modifications in its actual application to particular clauses. Perhaps the safest rule of interpretation will be found to be to look to the nature and objects of the particular powers, duties and rights with all the lights and aids of contemporary history, and to give to the words of each just such operation and force, consistent with their legitimate meaning, as may fairly secure and attain the ends proposed. Prigg *v.* Comm. 16 Pet. 539.

No court of justice can be authorized so to construe any clause of the Constitution as to defeat its obvious ends, when another construction, equally accordant with the words and sense thereof, will enforce and protect them. Prigg *v.* Comm. 16 Pet. 539.

The Constitution and the powers confided by it to the general government to be exercised for the benefit of all the States, ought not to be nullified or evaded by astute verbal criticism without regard to the grand aim and object of the instrument and the principles on which it is based. Passenger Cases, 7 How. 283; s. c. 45 Mass. 282.

In expounding the Constitution, every word must have its due force and appropriate meaning; for it is evident from the whole instrument that no word was unnecessarily used or needlessly added. Every word appears to have been weighed with the utmost deliberation, and its force and effect to have been fully understood. No word in the instrument therefore can be rejected as superfluous or unmeaning. Holmes *v.* Jennison, 14 Pet. 540.

The framers of the Constitution spoke through a permanent law to a great nation from the vocabulary of that nation. When they use a term defined in that vocabulary they must be understood accordingly. Kunzler *v.* Kohaus, 5 Hill, 317.

The same words have not necessarily the same meaning attached to them when found in different parts of the same instrument; their meaning is controlled by the context. In common language the same word has various meanings, and the peculiar sense in which it is used in any sentence is to be determined by the context. Cherokee Nation *v.* State, 5 Pet. 1.

Where the words admit of different intendments, that must be selected which is most consonant to the object in view. Aldrich *v.* Kinney, 4 Conn. 380.

Care should be taken to reconcile words apparently discordant, and in such a manner as to give, if possible, meaning to every word. Curtis *v.* Gibbs, 2 N. J. 399.

Adherence must not be had to the letter, in opposition to the reason and spirit of the enactment; and hence to effectuate the object intended it is even proper to deviate from the usual sense of the words. Aldrich *v.* Kinney, 4 Conn. 380.

Every interpretation which leads to an absurdity ought to be avoided, and that is properly denominated absurd which is morally impossible or so contrary to reason that it can not be attributed to a man in his right senses. Aldrich *v.* Kinney, 4 Conn. 380.

Where the object of an instrument admits of no doubt, the expressions should not be rejected as inadequate or incompetent. If they will bear the sense which they were intended to convey without too much constraining their meaning, they should be interpreted accordingly. Hitchcock *v.* Aicken, 1 Caines, 460.

So far as the meaning of any terms is completely ascertained, those by whom they are employed must be considered as employing them in that ascertained meaning, unless the contrary is proved by the context. U. S. *v.* Burr, 2 Burr's Trial, 401.

Affirmative words are often in their operation negative of other objects than those affirmed. Marbury *v.* Madison, 1 Cranch, 137.

A constitution is an instrument of government made and adopted by the people for practical purposes connected with the commerce, business and wants of human life. For this reason, every word should be expounded in its plain, obvious and common sense. Metropolitan Bank *v.* Van Dyck, 27 N. Y. 400.

The various provisions of the Constitution should receive such a construction as will most effectually subserve the great purposes of its formation, and best promote the general welfare of the grantors of the powers contained in it. Metropolitan Bank *v.* Van Dyck, 27 N. Y. 400.

A written constitution, framed by men chosen for the work by reason of their peculiar fitness, and adopted by the people upon mature deliberation, implies a degree of carefulness of expression proportioned to the importance of the transaction, and the words employed are to be presumed to have been used with the greatest possible discrimination. Metropolitan Bank *v.* Van Dyck, 27 N. Y. 400.

The Federal Constitution is not to be construed technically. It was meant to subserve great and beneficial ends, and any narrow and technical construction that makes it defeat those ends and work mischief is obviously a perversion of its real meaning. People *v.* Dawell, 25 Mich. 247.

The Constitution must receive a practical construction. Its limitations and its implied prohibitions must not be extended so far as to destroy the necessary powers of the States, or prevent their efficient exercise. Railroad Co. *v.* Peniston, 18 Wall. 5.

The Constitution should be so construed as to give effect to its different clauses, so far as it is possible to reconcile them, and not let their seeming repugnancy destroy one another. Cohens *v.* Virginia, 6 Wheat. 264; Marbury *v.* Madison, 1 Cranch, 137.

Although the spirit of the Constitution is to be respected not less than its letter, yet the spirit is to be collected chiefly from its words. It would be dangerous in the extreme to infer from extrinsic circumstances that a case for which the words of an instrument expressly provide shall be exempted from its operation. Where words conflict with each other; where the different clauses of an instrument bear upon each other, and would be inconsistent unless the natural and common import of words be varied, construction becomes necessary, and a departure from the obvious meaning of words justifiable. But if in any case the plain meaning of a provision, not contradicted by any other provision in the same instrument, is to be disregarded because the court believes the framers of that instrument could not intend what they say, it must be one in which the absurdity and injustice of applying the provision to the case would be so monstrous that all mankind would without hesitation unite in rejecting the application. Sturges *v.* Crowninshield, 4 Wheat. 122.

Great attention is properly paid to the argument from inconvenience. This argument can not prevail over plain words or clear reason. But on the other hand, a construction which must necessarily occasion great public and private mischief must never be preferred to a construction which will occasion neither, or neither in so great degree, unless the terms of the instrument absolutely require such preference. Ex parte Cæsar Griffin, Chase, 364; S. C. 25 Tex. Supp. 623.

A case which is within the words of the rule, must be within it operation likewise, unless there be something in the literal construction so obviously absurd or mischievous, or repugnant to the general spirit of the instrument as to justify those who expound the Constitution in making it an exception. Dartmouth College *v.* Woodward, 4 Wheat. 518.

The exception of a particular thing from general words, proves that in the opinion of the lawgiver the thing excepted would be within the general clause had the exception not been made. Brown *v.* State, 12 Wheat. 419.

Affirmative words are often, in their operation, negative of other objects than those affirmed, and where a negative or exclusive sense must be given to them, or they have no operation at all, they must receive that negative or exclusive sense. But where they have full operation without it, where it would destroy some of the most important objects for which the power was created, affirmative words ought not to be construed negatively. Cohens *v.* Virginia, 6 Wheat. 264.

A transposition of words or sentences can never be admitted in those cases where consistent meaning can be given to the whole clause as its authors thought proper to arrange it, and where the only doubt is whether the construction which the transposition countenances, or that which results from the reading which the legislature has thought proper to adopt, is most likely to fulfill the supposed intention of the legislature. Ogden *v.* Saunders, 12 Wheat. 213.

The derangement of words and even sentences of a law, may sometimes be tolerated, in order to arrive at the apparent meaning of the legislators to be gathered from other parts or from the entire scope of the law; but this is a hazardous rule to adopt in the construction of an instrument so maturely considered as the Constitution was by the enlightened statesmen who framed it, and so severely criticised by its opponents in the different State conventions which finally adopted it. Ogden *v.* Saunders, 12 Wheat. 213.

There is no mode by which the meaning affixed to any word or sentence by a deliberative body can be so well ascertained as by comparing it with the words and sentences with which it stands connected. Wheaton *v.* Peters, 8 Pet. 591.

Where a construction has been long carried into practice, though unsanctioned by judicial authority, it is worthy of great consideration because it can not be overturned without great inconvenience. Houston *v.* Moore, 5 Wheat. 1; s. c. 3 S. & R. 169; Hicks *v.* Hotchkiss, 7 Johns. Ch. 297; Adams *v.* Storey, 1 Paine, 79; M'Culloch *v.* State, 4 Wheat. 316; Martin *v.* Hunter, 1 Wheat. 304; Briscoe *v.* Bank, 11 Pet. 257; s. c. 7 J. J. Marsh. 349; Cooley *v.* Philadelphia, 12 How. 299; Metropolitan Bank *v.* Van Dyck, 27 N. Y. 400.

Where the commencement of the practice was almost coeval with the Constitution, there is great reason to suppose that it was in conformity to the sentiments of those by whom the true intent of the Constitution was best known. Houston *v.* Moore, 5 Wheat. 1; s. c. 3 S. & R. 169; Ogden *v.* Saunders, 12 Wheat. 213; Martin *v.* Hunter, 1 Wheat. 304;. Prigg *v.* Comm. 16 Pet. 539; Jack *v.* Martin, 12 Wend. 311; s. c. 14 Wend. 509.

Great weight has always been attached, and rightly attached, to contemporaneous exposition. Cohens *v.* Virginia, 6 Wheat. 264.

The opinion of the Federalist has always been considered as of great authority. It is a complete commentary on the Constitution, and is appealed to by all parties on the questions to which that instrument has given birth. Its intrinsic merit entitles it to this high rank, and the part two of its authors performed in framing the Constitution, put it very much in their power to explain the views with which it was framed. Cohens *v.* Virginia, 6 Wheat. 264.

The views of particular members or the course of proceedings in the convention, can not control the fair meaning and general scope of the Constitution as it was finally framed and now stands. It is a finished document, complete in itself, and to be interpreted in the light of history and of the circumstances of the period in which it was framed. Legal Tender Cases, 12 Wall. 457.

The words "people of the United States" and citizens, are synonymous terms, and mean the same thing. They both describe the political body who form the sovereignty, hold the power and conduct the government through their representatives. They are what are called "the sovereign people," and every citizen is one of this people, and a constituent member of this sovereignty. Dred Scott *v.* Sandford, 19 How. 393.

By metaphysical refinement, it might be correctly said that there is no such thing as a citizen of the United States. But constant usage, arising from convenience, and perhaps necessity, and dating from the formation of the Union, has given substantial existence to the idea which the term conveys. A citizen of any one of the States of Union, is held to be and called a citizen of the United States, although technically and abstractly there is no such thing. To conceive a citizen of the United States who is not a citizen of some one of the States, is totally foreign to the idea, and inconsistent with the proper construction and common understanding of the expression as used in the Constitution. Ex parte Frank Knowles, 5 Cal. 300.

The Constitution is a law for rulers and people equally, in war and in peace, and covers, with the shield of its protection, all classes of men at all times and under all circumstances. No doctrine involving more pernicious consequences was ever invented by the wit of man, than that any of its provisions can be suspended during any of the great exigencies of government. Ex parte Milligan, 4 Wall. 2.

In construing the Constitution, no principle not declared can be admissible which would defeat the legitimate operations of a supreme government. It is of the very essence of supremacy to remove all obstacles to its action within its own sphere, and so to modify every power vested in subordinate governments as to exempt its own operations from their influence. This effect need not be stated in terms. It is so involved in the declaration of supremacy, so necessarily implied in it, that the expression of it could not make it more certain. M'Culloch *v.* State, 4 Wheat. 316

In construing clauses in the Constitution which involve conflicting powers of the government of the Union and the governments of the respective States, it is proper to take a view of the literal meaning of the words to be expounded, of their connection with other words, and of the general objects to be accomplished by the prohibitory clause or by the grant of power. Brown *v.* State, 12 Wheat. 419.

In construing the Constitution, courts of justice should breathe a spirit of harmony and conciliation. The powers of the States and of the United States often approach each other so nearly that the line of division is almost invisible. While the laws of both, then, may be executed without clashing, they should be supported unless they are manifestly in violation of the Constitution. Houston *v.* Moore, 5 Wheat. 1; s. C. 3 S. & R. 169; Charleston *v.* Rogers, 2 McC. 495.

ARTICLE I.

SECTION I.

1. All legislative powers herein granted, shall be vested in a Congress of the United States, which shall consist of a Senate and House of Representatives.

SECTION II.

1. The House of Representatives shall be composed of members chosen every second year by the people of the several States; and the electors in each State shall have the qualifications requisite for electors of the most numerous branch of the State legislature.

2. No person shall be a representative who shall not have attained the age of twenty-five years, and been seven years a citizen of the United States, and who shall not, when elected, be an inhabitant of that State in which he shall be chosen.

3. Representatives and direct taxes (*a*) shall be apportioned among the several States which may be included within this union, according to their respective numbers, which shall be determined by adding to the

whole number of free persons, including those bound to service for a term of years, and excluding Indians not taxed, three-fifths of all other persons. The actual enumeration shall be made within three years after the first meeting of the Congress of the United States, and within every subsequent term of ten years, in such manner as they shall by law direct. The number of representatives shall not exceed one for every thirty thousand, but each State shall have at least one representative; and until such enumeration shall be made, the State of New Hampshire shall be entitled to choose three; Massachusetts, eight; Rhode Island and Providence Plantations, one; Connecticut, five; New York, six; New Jersey, four; Pennsylvania, eight; Delaware, one; Maryland, six; Virginia, ten; North Carolina, five; South Carolina, five; and Georgia, three.

Taxes.

(*a*) The object of this regulation is to furnish a standard by which taxes are to be apportioned, not to exempt from their operation any part of the country. Had the intention been to exempt from taxation those who were not represented in Congress, that intention would have been expressed in direct terms. The power having been expressly granted, the exception would have been expressly made. But a limitation can scarcely be said to be insinuated. The words used do not mean that direct taxes shall be imposed on States only which are represented or shall be apportioned to representatives, but that direct taxation, in its application to States, shall be apportioned to numbers. This clause was obviously not intended to create any exemption from taxation, or to make taxation dependent on representation, but to furnish a standard for the apportionment of each on the States. Loughborough *v.* Blake, 5 Wheat. 317.

If a direct tax be laid at all, it must be laid on every State conformably to the rule provided in the Constitution. Congress has clearly no power to exempt any State from its due share of the burden. But this regulation is expressly confined to the States, and creates no necessity for extending the tax to the District of Columbia or the territories. Loughborough *v.* Blake, 5 Wheat. 317.

4. When vacancies happen in the representation from any State, the executive authority thereof shall issue writs of election to fill such vacancies.

5. The House of Representatives shall choose their speaker and other officers, and shall have the sole power of impeachment.

SECTION III.

1. The Senate of the United States shall be composed of two senators from each State, chosen by the legislature thereof, for six years; and each senator shall have one vote.

2. Immediately after they shall be assembled in consequence of the first election, they shall be divided, as equally as may be, into three classes. The seats of the senators of the first class shall be vacated at the expiration of the second year; of the second class, at the expiration of the fourth year; and of the third class, at the expiration of the sixth year: so that one-third may be chosen every second year; and if vacancies happen, by resignation or otherwise, during the recess of the legislature of any State, the executive thereof may make temporary appointments until the next meeting of the legislature, which shall then fill such vacancies.

3. No person shall be a senator who shall not have attained to the age of thirty years, and been nine years a citizen of the United States, and who shall not, when elected, be an inhabitant of that State for which he shall be chosen.

4. The Vice President of the United States shall be president of the Senate, but shall have no vote unless they be equally divided.

5. The Senate shall choose their other officers, and also a president *pro tempore*, in the absence of the Vice President, or when he shall exercise the office of President of the United States.

6. The Senate shall have the sole power to try all impeachments. When sitting for that purpose, they shall be on oath or affirmation. When the President of the United States is tried, the chief justice shall preside; and no person shall be convicted without the concurrence of two-thirds of the members present.

7. Judgment, in cases of impeachment, shall not extend further than to removal from office, and disqualification to hold and enjoy any office of honor, trust, or profit under the United States; but the party convicted shall nevertheless be liable and subject to indictment, trial, judgment, and punishment, according to law.

SECTION IV.

1. The times, places, and manner of holding elections for senators and representatives, shall be prescribed in each State by the legislature thereof; but the Congress may, at any time, by law, make or alter such regulations, except as to the places of choosing senators.

2. The Congress shall assemble at least once in every year, and such meeting shall be on the first Monday in December, unless they shall by law appoint a different day.

SECTION V.

1. Each house shall be the judge of the elections, returns, and qualifications of its own members; and a majority of each shall constitute a quorum to do business; but a smaller number may adjourn from day to day, and may be authorized to compel the attendance of absent members, in such manner and under such penalties as each house may provide.

Whether a senator has been regularly elected is a question exclusively for the Senate of the United States. Anon. 12 Fla. 686.

2. Each house may determine the rules of its proceedings, punish its members for disorderly behavior, and, with the concurrence of two-thirds, expel a member.

Contempts.

The exercise of the powers given over their own members is of such a delicate nature, that a constitutional provision became necessary to assert or communicate it. Constituted as that body is of the delegates of confederated States, some such provision was necessary to guard against their mutual jealousy, since every proceeding against a representative would indirectly affect the honor and interest of the State which sent him. But the express grant does not imply that the Senate or House of Representatives can not punish for contempt. Anderson *v*. Dunn, 6 Wheat. 204; Ex parte John Nugent, 1 Am. L. J. 107.

The House of Representatives has the power to punish an individual for contempt of its dignity and authority and a breach of its privileges. Anderson *v*. Dunn, 6 Wheat. 204.

The Senate has the power to punish contempts of its authority. Ex parte John Nugent, 1 Am. L. J. 107.

The power to punish for contempt does not belong to any other than a legislative or judicial body. Anderson *v*. Dunn, 6 Wheat. 204.

The Senate has the same power to punish contempts in secret as in open session. Ex parte John Nugent, 1 Am. L. J. 107.

The House of Representatives has the power to subpœna witnesses to testify before it, or before one of its committees, and to compel their attendance from any portion of the territorial limits of the United States. It is a necessary incident to the sovereign power of making laws. Wilckins *v*. Willett, 4 Abb. App. 596; s. c. 10 Abb. Pr. 164.

The power to punish for disobedience and contempt is a necessary incident to the power to require and compel attendance. Wilckins *v*. Willett, 4 Abb. App. 596; s. c. 10 Abb. Pr. 164; Stewart *v*. Blaine, 1 McArthur, 453.

A warrant of commitment need not set forth the particular facts which constitute the alleged contempt. Ex parte John Nugent, 1 Am. L. J. 107.

A warrant to commit for contempt may be served anywhere within the boundaries of the United States. Anderson *v*. Dunn, 6 Wheat. 204.

The power to punish for contempt only extends to the power of imprisonment. It may, at first view, and from the history of the practice of legislative bodies, be thought to extend to other inflictions; but every other will be found to be mere commutation for confinement, since commitment alone is the alternative where the individual proves contumacious. And even to the duration of imprisonment a period is imposed by the nature of things, since the existence of the power that imprisons is indispensable to its continuance, and although the legislative power continues perpetual, the legislative body ceases to exist on the moment of its adjournment or periodical dissolution. It follows that imprisonment must terminate with that adjournment. Anderson *v*. Dunn, 6 Wheat. 204.

No court, on a writ of *habeas corpus*, can inquire into the question of contempt, and discharge the prisoner, for the legislative body is the only judge of its own privileges and contempts. Ex parte John Nugent, 1 Am. L. J. 107.

3. Each house shall keep a journal of its proceedings, and from time to time publish the same, excepting such parts as may in their judgment require secrecy; and the yeas and nays of the members of either house, on any question, shall, at the desire of one-fifth of those present, be entered on the journal.

The journal can not be kept secret unless the proceedings themselves are kept secret. Hence each house has a right to hold secret sessions whenever in its judgment the proceedings shall require secrecy. Ex parte John Nugent, 1 Am. L. J. 107.

4. Neither house, during the session of Congress, shall, without the consent of the other, adjourn for more than three days, nor to any other place than that in which the two houses shall be sitting.

SECTION VI.

1. The senators and representatives shall receive a compensation for their services, to be ascertained by law, and paid out of the treasury of the United States. They shall, in all cases, except treason, felony, and breach of the peace, be privileged from arrest during their attendance at the session of their respective houses, and in going to and returning from the same; and for any speech or debate in either house, they shall not be questioned in any other place.

The word "arrest" has a definite meaning, both technical and common, and necessarily implies corporal restraint, and does not apply to a summons which is served by a mere notice of it to the party. Wooley *v.* Butler, 1 B. L. T. 35.

There is no privilege which exempts a member of Congress from the service or the obligation of a subpœna as a witness in a criminal case. U. S. *v.* Cooper, 4 Dall. 341.

A member of Congress can not have a continuance of a pending case as a matter of right, because he is in attendance on Congress. Nones *v.* Edsall, 1 Wall. Jr. 189; contra, Doty *v.* Strong, 1 Pinney, 84.

A member of Congress is privileged from arrest both on judicial and mesne process, and from the service of a summons or other civil process, while in attendance on his public duties. Nones *v.* Edsall, 1 Wall. Jr. 189; Coxe *v.* M'Clenachan, 3 Dall. 478.

This privilege is to be taken strictly, and is to be allowed only while the party is attending Congress, or is actually on his journey going to or returning from the seat of government. Lewis *v.* Elmendorf, 2 Johns. Cas. 222.

The duration of the privilege does not extend to forty days or more before and after each session of Congress, but is limited to a convenient and reasonable time in addition to the actual session of Congress, for each member to go to and return from such session. Hoppin *v.* Jenckes, 8 R. I. 453.

This provision applies to a delegate from a territory as well as to a member from a State, for with the exception of the power to vote, he is a member of the House of Representatives, and entitled to the same constitutional privileges. Doty *v.* Strong, 1 Pinney, 84.

2. No senator or representative shall, during the time for which he was elected, be appointed to any civil office under the authority of the United States, which shall have been created, or the emoluments whereof shall have been increased, during such time; and no person holding any office under the United States shall be a member of either house during his continuance in office.

SECTION VII.

1. All bills for raising revenue shall originate in the House of Representatives; but the Senate may propose or concur with amendments, as on other bills.

A bill for regulating postal rates for postal service is not a bill for raising revenue, and may originate in the Senate. U. S. *v.* James, 13 Blatch. 207.

2. Every bill which shall have passed the House of Representatives and the Senate, shall, before it become a law, be presented to the President of the United States; if he approve, he shall sign it; but if not, he shall return it, with his objections, to that house in which it shall have originated, who shall enter the objections at large on their journal, and proceed to recon-

sider it. If, after such reconsideration, two-thirds of that house shall agree to pass the bill, it shall be sent, together with the objections, to the other house, by which it shall likewise be reconsidered, and if approved by two-thirds of that house, it shall become a law. But in all such cases, the votes of both houses shall be determined by yeas and nays, and the names of the persons voting for and against the bill shall be entered on the journal of each house respectively. If any bill shall not be returned by the president within ten days (Sundays excepted) after it shall have been presented to him, the same shall be a law in like manner as if he had signed it, unless the Congress by their adjournment prevent its return, in which case it shall not be a law.

There are two courses of action by the President in reference to a bill presented to him, each of which results in the bill becoming a law. One of them is by signing the bill within ten days, and the other is by keeping it ten days and refusing to sign it. Gardner *v.* Collector, 6 Wall. 499.

The only duty required of the President, in regard to a bill which he approves, is that he shall sign it; nothing more. The simple signing his name at the appropriate place is the one act which the Constitution requires of him as the evidence of his approval; and upon his performance of this act, the bill becomes a law. Gardner *v.* Collector, 6 Wall. 499.

When the President approves a bill, it is not required that he shall write on the bill the word "approved;" nor that he shall date it. Gardner *v.* Collector, 6 Wall. 499.

When no time is fixed for the commencement of a statute, it takes effect from its date. Matthews *v.* Zane, 7 Wheat. 164; Warren Manuf. Co. *v.* Etna Ins. Co. 2 Paine, 501; In re Ankrim, 3 McLean, 285.

Where the question is as to the effect of a proceeding instituted on the same day on which an act affecting the validity of such proceeding was passed, the precise time at which the act became a law may be inquired into. Fractions of a day or of an hour may be allowed, whenever it will promote substantial justice. In re Richardson, 2 Story, 571; In re Wynne, 4 B. R. 23; S. C. 1 Chase, 227; In re Ankrim, 3 McLean, 285; contra, In re David Howes, 21 Vt. 619; Welman's Case, 20 Vt. 653; U. S. *v.* Williams, 1 Paine, 261.

Every bill which is approved by the President takes effect as a law only by such approval and from the time of such approval. It is the act of approval which makes it a law, and until that act is done it is not a law. The approval can not look backwards, and by relation make that a law at any antecedent period of the same day which was not so before the approval, for the general rule is *lex prospicit, non respicit*. In re Richardson, 2 Story, 571.

In cases of doubt, the time should be construed favorably for the citizens. The legislature have it in their power to prescribe the very moment *in futuro* after the approval when the law shall have effect, and if it does not choose to do so, a court of justice is not called upon to supply the defect. In re Richardson, 2 Story, 571.

A general statute is not to be proved as an issue of fact, but the courts take judicial notice of it. Whenever a question arises as to the existence of a statute, or the time when a statute took effect, or the precise terms of a statute, the court which is called upon to decide it has a right to resort to any source of information which in its nature is capable of conveying to the judicial mind a clear and satisfactory answer to such question, always seeking first for that which in its nature is most appropriate, unless the positive law has enacted a different rule. Gardner *v.* Collector, 6 Wall. 499.

When the president retains the bill, it is his action in retaining it for ten days which makes it a law, and no evidence is required of him by the Constitution to show that he has ever received or considered it. Gardner *v.* Collector, 6 Wall. 499.

If the bill on its return is approved by two-thirds of the members present in each house, that is sufficient, although they do not constitute two-thirds of the whole house. See 19 Law Rep. 196.

3. Every order, resolution, or vote, to which the concurrence of the Senate and House of Representatives may be necessary, except on a question of adjournment, shall be presented to the President of the United States; and before the same shall take effect, shall be approved by him, or being disapproved by him, shall be repassed by two-thirds of the Senate and House of Representatives, according to the rules and limitations prescribed in the case of a bill.

SECTION VIII.

The Congress shall have power—

1. To lay and collect taxes, (*a*) duties, imposts, and excises; to pay the debts, and provide for the common defense and general welfare of the United States; but

all duties, imposts, and excises, shall be uniform throughout the United States:

2. To borrow money (*b*) on the credit of the United States:

3. To regulate commerce (*c*) with foreign nations, and among the several States, and with the Indian tribes:

4. To establish a uniform rule of naturalization, (*d*) and uniform laws on the subject of bankruptcies (*e*) throughout the United States:

5. To coin money, (*f*) regulate the value thereof, and of foreign coin, and fix the standard of weights and measures: (*g*)

6. To provide for the punishment of counterfeiting (*h*) the securities and current coin of the United States:

7. To establish post offices and post roads: (*i*)

8. To promote the progress of science and useful arts, by securing for limited times to authors and inventors the exclusive right to their respective writings and discoveries: (*j*)

9. To constitute tribunals inferior to the Supreme Court:

10. To define and punish piracies (*k*) and felonies committed on the high seas, and offenses against the law of nations:

11. To declare war, (*l*) grant letters of marque and reprisal, and make rules concerning captures on land and water:

12. To raise and support armies; (*m*) but no appropriation of money to that use shall be for a longer term than two years:

13. To provide and maintain a navy:

14. To make rules for the government and regulation of the land and naval forces: (*n*)

15. To provide for calling forth the militia (*o*) to execute the laws of the Union, suppress insurrections, and repel invasions.

16. To provide for organizing, arming, and disciplining the militia, (*p*) and for governing such part of them

as may be employed in the service of the United States, reserving to the States, respectively, the appointment of the officers, and the authority of training the militia according to the discipline prescribed by Congress :

17. To exercise exclusive legislation (q) in all cases whatsoever, over such district, not exceeding ten miles square, as may, by cession of particular States, and the acceptance of Congress, become the seat of the government of the United States ; and to exercise like authority (r) over all places purchased by the consent of the legislature of the State in which the same shall be, for the erection of forts, magazines, arsenals, dock-yards, and other needful buildings ; and,

18. To make all laws which shall be necessary (s) and proper for carrying into execution the foregoing powers, and all other powers vested by this Constitution in the government of the United States, or in any department or officer thereof.

General Principles.

The Federal Government is one of enumerated powers. M'Culloch *v.* State, 4 Wheat. 316.

The Constitution is one of enumeration, and not of definition. Gibbons *v.* Ogden, 9 Wheat. 1; S. C. 17 Johns. 488; 4 Johns. Ch. 150; M'Culloch *v.* State, 4 Wheat. 316.

The Federal Government is one of delegated powers. All powers not delegated to it, or inhibited to the States, are reserved to the States or to the people. Briscoe *v.* Bank, 11 Pet. 257; S. C. 7 J. J. Marsh. 349.

The sovereignty of Congress, though limited to specified objects, is plenary as to those objects. Gibbons *v.* Ogden, 9 Wheat. 1 ; S. C. 17 Johns. 488 ; 4 Johns. Ch. 150.

The Federal Government, though limited in its powers, is supreme in its sphere. M'Culloch *v.* State, 4 Wheat. 316.

The Federal Government can only exercise the powers granted to it. M'Culloch *v.* State, 4 Wheat. 316 ; U. S. *v.* Bailey, 1 McLean, 234.

A Constitution to contain an accurate detail of all the subdivisions of which its great powers will admit, and of all the means by which they may be carried into execution, would partake of the prolixity of a legal code, and could scarcely be embraced by the human mind. It would probably never be understood by the public. Its nature, therefore, requires that only its great outlines should be marked, its important objects designated, and the minor ingredients which compose those objects be deduced from the nature of those objects themselves. M'Culloch *v.* State, 4 Wheat. 316.

The theory of the Constitution is that a few great and leading subjects of control and administration, belonging to and inherent in all sovereign states, and which are of interest to all the States, are singled out and placed within the exclusive jurisdiction of the general government. This government, unlike the confederation of States which acted mainly through the State governments, is constituted with its legislative, judicial and executive departments to act directly upon the people, without the intervention of the State governments, and is organized in such manner as to make, administer and execute all laws necessary or incidental to the full and complete exercise of the sovereign power upon the subject placed within its administration. Ex parte Alexander Stephens, 70 Mass. 559.

The grant does not convey power which might be beneficial to the grantor if retained by himself, or which can inure solely to the benefit of the grantee, but is an investment of power for the general advantage in the hands of agents selected for that purpose, which power can never be exercised by the people themselves, but must be placed in the hands of agents or lie dormant. There is no rule for construing the extent of such powers other than is given by the language of the instrument which confers them, taken in connection with the purposes for which they are conferred. The powers are not to be construed strictly. Gibbons *v.* Ogden, 9 Wheat. 1.

In a general sense, the Federal Government does not possess an omnipotence equal to that of the Parliament of Great Britain. But in respect to all subjects of legislation, which are either expressly or impliedly delegated to it, complete sovereign legislative power is conferred upon Congress, and that body possesses an omnipotence in these things equal to that possessed by the British Parliament or any other supreme legislative body. Metropolitan Bank *v.* Van Dyck, 27 N. Y. 400.

In construing the Constitution and determining the extent of one of its important grants of power to legislate, no distinction can be made between the nature of the power and the nature of the subject on which that power was intended practically to operate, nor can the grant be considered more extensive by affirming of the power what is not true of the subject in question. Cooley *v.* Philadelphia, 12 How. 299.

To understand the nature and extent of the powers conferred by the Constitution, whether substantive or ancillary, it is indispensable to keep in view the objects for which the Constitution was adopted, and for which its powers were granted. When the general purpose of the instrument is ascertained, its language is to be construed, so far as possible, as subservient to that purpose. Shollenberger *v.* Brinton, 52 Penn. 9.

Whenever a particular object is to be effected, the language of the Constitution is always imperative, and can not be disregarded without violating the first principles of public duty. On the other hand, the legislative powers are given in language which implies discretion, as, from the nature of legislative power, such a discretion must ever be exercised. Martin *v.* Hunter, 1 Wheat. 304.

The powers granted to Congress must be construed and applied with reference to the purposes for which the Constitution was made. It is not a mere abstraction to sharpen men's wits upon, but a practical scheme of government, having all necessary power to maintain its existence and authority during peace and war, rebellion or invasion. McCall *v.* McDowell, 1 Deady, 233; S. C. 1 Abb. C. C. 212.

The existence of a power should not be denied because it may be unwisely exercised, nor should it be presumed that abuses will take place. Kneedler *v.* Zane, 45 Penn. 238; S. C. 3 Grant, 465; Metropolitan Bank *v.* Van Dyck, 27 N. Y. 400; Anderson *v.* Dunn, 6 Wheat. 204.

Questions of power do not depend upon the degree to which it may be exercised. If it may be exercised at all, it must be exercised at the will of those in whose hands it is placed. Brown *v.* State, 12 Wheat. 419; Martin *v.* Hunter, 1 Wheat. 304; Metropolitan Bank *v.* Van Dyck, 27 N. Y. 400.

That is a very narrow view which regards any of its specified powers independent of its relation to the others, or to them all aggregated.' Each must be considered as but part of a system, a constituent of a whole. No single power specified is the ultimate end for which the Constitution was adopted. It may be an intermediate end, but it is itself a means for the accomplishment of a single and higher end. Shollenberger *v.* Brinton, 52 Penn. 9.

When Congress have the power to do the same act by virtue of distinct powers, they may exercise which they please, and when they profess to act under one power, there is no necessity to resort to any other. Steamboat Co. *v.* Livingston, 3 Cow. 713; S. C. 1 Hopk. 150; Thayer *v.* Hedges, 23 Ind. 141; Shollenberger *v.* Brinton, 52 Penn. 9.

The exceptions from a power mark its extent, for it would be absurd as well as useless to except from a granted power that which was not granted—that which the words of the grant could not comprehend. Gibbons *v.* Ogden, 9 Wheat. 1; S. C. 17 Johns. 488; 4 Johns. Ch. 150.

Some powers that usually belong to sovereignties were extinguished, but they were not extinguished by implication. When it was intended that governmental powers universally acknowledged as such should cease to exist, they were expressly denied, not only to the States, but to the Federal Government. Shollenberger *v.* Brinton, 52 Penn. 9.

Where a substantive power is granted in a given form, and to an exactly defined extent, or is thus withheld, the grant or prohibition can not be exercised or contravened by a power claimed as incident to some other substantive power. Thayer *v.* Hedges, 22 Ind. 282.

No power, in itself a substantive one, can be exercised or contravened by action under an incidental power. Thayer *v.* Hedges, 22 Ind. 282.

It is not indispensable to the existence of any power claimed for the Federal Government, that it can be found specified in the words of the Constitution, or clearly and directly traceable to some one of the specified powers. Its existence may be deduced fairly from more than one of the substantive powers expressly defined, or from them all combined. It is allowable to group together any number of them, and infer from them all that the power has been conferred. Legal Tender Cases, 12 Wall. 457.

The powers conferred upon Congress must be regarded as related to each other and all means for a common end. Each is but part of a system, a constituent of one whole. No single power is the ultimate end for which the Constitution was adopted. Legal Tender Cases, 12 Wall. 457.

Power over a particular subject may be exercised as auxiliary to an express power, though there is another express power relating to the same subject, less comprehensive. Legal Tender Cases, 12 Wall. 457.

There is no ground for any such distinction as express and implied powers. The terms are used merely for convenience. In fact, the auxiliary powers, those appropriate to the execution of other powers singly described, are as expressly given as any other powers. Legal Tender Cases, 12 Wall. 457.

When investigating the nature and extent of the powers conferred by the Constitution, it is indispensable to keep in view the objects for which those powers were granted. If the general purpose of the instrument is ascertained, the language of its provisions must be construed with reference to that purpose, and so as to subserve it. Legal Tender Cases, 12 Wall. 457.

An act of Congress passed for the direct and primary purpose of annulling a contract or impairing its obligation would be void, but if the primary object of an act is within any of the granted powers it is valid, although it may incidentally impair the obligation of contracts. Hague *v.* Powers, 39 Barb. 427; Metropolitan Bank *v.* Van Dyck, 27 N. Y. 400; George *v.* Concord, 45 N. H. 434; Shollenberger *v.* Brinton, 32 Penn. 9; Evans *v.* Eaton, Pet. C. C. 323; S. C. 3 Wheat. 454; Bloomer *v.* Stolley, 5 McLean, 158; Legal Tender Cases, 12 Wall. 457.

Although Congress can not enable a State to legislate, it may adopt the provisions of a State on any subject. Gibbons *v.* Ogden, 9 Wheat. 1; S. C. 17 Johns. 488; 4 Johns. Ch. 150.

Taxes.

(*a*) The power to lay and collect taxes is expressly given to Congress, in connection with a recital of the objects to which the taxes when collected may be legitimately applied. The recital is not a positive and distinct grant of indefinite power. Comm. *v.* Morrison, 2 A. K. Marsh. 75; Passenger Cases, 7 How. 283; S. C. 45 Mass. 282; Griswold *v.* Hepburn, 2 Duvall, 20; Thayer *v.* Hedges, 22 Ind. 282; vide Maynard *v.* Newman, 1 Nev. 271.

The grant is general without limitation as to place. It consequently extends to all places over which the government extends. If this could be doubted, the doubt is removed by the subsequent words which modify the grant. These words are: "but all duties, imposts and excises shall be uniform throughout the United States." It will not be contended that the modification of the power extends to places to which the power itself does not extend. The power then to lay and collect duties, imports and excises, may be exercised and must be exercised throughout the United States. This term designates the great Republic which is composed of States and Territories. The District of Columbia is not less within the United States than any State. Since then the power to lay and collect taxes, which includes direct taxes, is obviously coextensive with the power to lay and collect duties, imposts and excises, it follows that the power to impose direct taxes also extends throughout the United States. Loughborough *v.* Blake, 5 Wheat. 317.

The power to lay and collect taxes, duties and imposts, gives to Congress a plenary power over all persons and things for taxation, except exports. Such is the received meaning of the word taxes in its most extended sense, and always so when it is not used in contradistinction to terms of taxation having a limited meaning as to the objects to which by usage the terms apply. It is in the Constitution used in both senses; in its extended sense, when it is said that Congress may lay and collect taxes, and in a more confined sense in contradistinction to duties, imposts and excises. Congress may tax persons who come into the United States. Passenger Cases, 7 How. 283; S. C. 45 Mass. 282.

The purpose of the Constitution was to give the power of taxation to Congress in its fullest extent as to everything except exports. This purpose is apparent from the terms in which the taxing power is granted. More comprehensive words could not have been used. Veazie Bank *v.* Fenno, 8 Wall. 533.

The taxing power is given in the most comprehensive terms. The only limitations imposed are, that direct taxes, including the capitation tax, shall be apportioned; that duties, imposts and excises shall be uniform; and that no duties shall be imposed upon articles exported from any State.

With these exceptions, the exercise of the power is in all respects unfettered. Pacific Life Ins. Co. *v.* Soule, 7 Wall. 433.

Congress can not tax exports, and it must impose direct taxes by the rule of apportionment, and indirect taxes by the rule of uniformity. Thus limited and thus only, it reaches every subject, and may be exercised at discretion. But it reaches only existing subjects. License Tax Cases, 5 Wall. 462.

Congress has no power to lay taxes to pay the debts of a State, or to provide by taxation for its general welfare. Congress may tax for the treasury of the Union, and here its power ends. Passenger Cases, 7 How. 283; s. c. 45 Mass. 282.

A tax can not be pronounced unconstitutional, merely because it is oppressive, for Congress is responsible, not to the court, but to the people by whom its members are elected. Veazie Bank *v.* Fenno, 8 Wall. 533.

Duties are things due and recoverable by law. In its widest signification the term is hardly less comprehensive than "taxes." It is applied in its most restricted meaning to customs, and in that sense is nearly the synonym of "imposts." Pacific Life Ins. Co. *v.* Soule, 7 Wall. 433.

Excise is an inland imposition, sometimes upon the consumption of the commodity and sometimes upon the retail sale; sometimes upon the manufacturer and sometimes upon the vendor. Pacific Life Insurance Co. *v.* Soule, 7 Wall. 433.

Impost is a duty on imported goods and merchandise. Pacific Life Ins. Co. *v.* Soule, 7 Wall. 433.

An internal revenue law which is uniform is valid, although its enforcement is suspended by rebellion in some States, and it recognizes such suspension. U. S. *v.* Riley, 5 Blatch. 204.

A tax upon distillers is in the nature of an excise tax, and is uniform in its operation if it is assessed equally upon all manufacturers of spirits, wherever they are. U. S. *v.* Singer, 15 Wall. 112.

Congress may impose a tax on a business which is prohibited by the laws of a State. License Tax Cases, 5 Wall. 462; U. S. *v.* Riley, 5 Blatch. 204.

Congress has the power to raise revenue by a stamp act. Hunter *v.* Cobb, 1 Bush, 239.

Congress has no power to forfeit land absolutely to the United States as a penalty for the non-payment of taxes. Martin *v.* Snowden, 18 Gratt. 100.

Congress has no power to provide that the whole land shall be sold for non-payment of direct taxes in every case, whatever may be the value of the land, and whatever the amount of the tax, for such a course is not necessary and proper to carry the power to tax into execution. Martin *v.* Snowden, 18 Gratt. 100.

Congress can not authorize a trade or business within a State in order to tax it. License Tax Cases, 5 Wall. 462.

The Federal Government is limited in its right to lay and collect taxes to the citizens and their transactions as such, or as acting in the Federal Government officially or otherwise, and cannot lay them on or collect them from individuals on their proceedings when acting, not as citizens transacting business with each other as such, but officially or in the pursuit of rights and duties in and through State official agencies and institutions. Warren *v.* Paul, 22 Ind. 276.

Congress has no power to tax the means and instrumentalities employed by the States for carrying on the operations of their governments, preserving their existence and fulfilling the high and responsible duties assigned to them by the Constitution. Collector *v.* Day, 11 Wall. 113.

Congress can not impose a tax upon the salary of a judicial officer of a State. Collector *v.* Day, 11 Wall. 113.

Congress can not impose an income tax on the compensation allowed by a State to a State's attorney. U. S. *v.* Ritchie, 4 C. L. N. 139.

A stamp tax on writs issued by State courts, is unconstitutional and void. Warren *v.* Paul, 22 Ind. 276; Jones *v.* Keep, 19 Wis. 369; Fifield *v.* Close, 15 Mich. 505; Smith *v.* Short, 40 Ala. 385 ; Union Bank *v.* Hill, 3 Cold. 325 ; Edelward's Appeal, 66 Penn. 89; Tucker *v.* Potter, 35 Conn. 43; Lewis *v.* Randall, 1 Abb. Pr. N. S. 135; S. C. 30 How. Pr. 378; Walton *v.* Bryenth, 24 How. Pr. 357; Ford *v.* Clinton, 25 Iowa, 157; contra, German Liederkranz *v.* Schieman, 25 How. Pr. 388 ; Hoyt *v.* Benner, 22 La. Ann. 353.

Congress has no power to control contracts or impair the legal obligation of contracts made in a State according to her laws, by making them void for want of a stamp. Hunter *v.* Cobb, 1 Bush, 239; Latham *v.* Smith, 45 Ill. 29; Forcheimer *v.* Holly, 14 Fla. 239.

Congress has no power to declare by law what shall or shall not be evidence in a State court.' Latham *v.* Smith, 45 Ill. 29; Forcheimer *v.* Holly, 14 Fla. 239; Clemens *v.* Conrad, 19 Mich. 170; Sporer *v.* Eifler, 1 Heisk. 633; Haight *v.* Grist, 64 N. C. 739; Hunter *v.* Cobb, 1 Bush, 239; Hanford *v.* Obrecht, 49 Ill. 146 ; Craig *v.* Dimock, 47 Ill. 308; Bunker *v.* Green, 48 Ill. 243; U. S. Express Co. *v.* Haines, 48 Ill. 248; Wilson *v.* Kenna, 52 Ill. 43; contra, Woodson *v.* Randolph, 1 Va. Cas. 128; Howe *v.* Carpenter, 53 Barb. 382.

Congress can not tax the salary of a judge of a State court, although his salary is fixed by a body acting under the authority of the Legislature, for the agency which the State may choose to employ for that purpose, can not affect the relation which the two governments bear to each other. Freedman *v.* Sigel, 10 Blatch. 327.

Congress has no power to tax the official bonds given to a State by its officers, for the faithful performance of their duties. State *v.* Garton, 32 Ind. 1; contra, City *v.* Stevenson, 30 Iowa, 526.

There is no distinction between levying a tax upon the exercise of a power reserved to the States, and levying it on all those who seek to enforce their rights or redress their grievances through the instrumentality of the power or upon the means employed to that end. Union Bank *v.* Hill, 3 Cold. 325.

Congress can not impose a tax upon a tax certificate issued by State authority at a tax sale. Barden *v.* Supervisors, 33 Wis. 445.

Congress can not tax the salary of a judge of a State court, although it is paid by a municipal corporation, for the right to tax does not depend upon the mode which the State may choose to raise the revenue applied to the support of the office, or the sources from which it may choose to draw that revenue. Freedman *v.* Sigel, 10 Blatch. 327.

Congress can not require a revenue stamp to be placed upon a tax deed given by a State upon a sale of land for taxes, for it has no power to tax the means or instruments devised by the States for the purpose of collecting their own revenues. Sayles *v.* Davis, 22 Wis. 225; Delorme *v.* Ferk, 24 Wis. 201.

A municipal corporation is a portion of the governmental power of the State, and its revenues are not subject to taxation. U. S. *v.* Railroad Co. 17 Wall. 322.

Congress can not tax the interest due to a municipal corporation, on money advanced by it to a railroad corporation, to aid in building a railroad. U. S. *v.* Railroad Co. 17 Wall. 322.

In order to entitle the revenue of a municipal corporation to exemption from taxation, it must be municipal in its nature. U. S. *v.* Railroad Co. 17 Wall. 322.

Congress may impose a tax upon the notes of State banks issued for circulation. Veazie Bank *v.* Fenno, 8 Wall. 533.

A tax upon the interest due on railroad bonds, which is levied upon all railroads indebted by bond, and in the same amount, and is to be collected in the same manner, is valid although the bonds are held by non-residents. The tax must be uniform throughout the United States, not beyond them. Michigan Central R. R. Co. *v.* Slack, 22 I. R. R. 337.

Borrowing Money.

(*b*) The power to "borrow money," includes or implies the power to issue the requisite securities or evidences of debt for the money borrowed. Hague *v.* Powers, 39 Barb. 427; Metropolitan Bank *v.* Van Dyck, 27 N. Y. 400; Thayer *v.* Hedges, 22 Ind. 282; George *v.* Concord, 45 N. H. 434; Van Husan *v.* Kanouse, 13 Mich. 303.

It is not necessary that these obligations shall be issued only in return for money received, and not for capital or commodities of which money is the representative. As the government requires articles of various descriptions, or the services of men for its exigencies in war and in peace, it may give its own obligations or evidences of indebtedness, and these are valid and properly issued under the power to borrow money. Metropolitan Bank *v.* Van Dyck, 27 N. Y. 400.

It is not essential to the exercise of this power that the contract between the government and the lender or the obligations issued shall provide for the repayment of the money borrowed at any specific future day, or with interest. Metropolitan Bank *v.* Van Dyck, 27 N. Y. 400.

The issue of treasury notes is an exchange of credit for money or property. All political economists recognize the fact that in issuing paper promises to circulate as currency, their makers are in effect borrowing on the credit of these promises whatever of value they receive in exchange for them. Metropolitan Bank *v.* Van Dyck, 27 N. Y. 400.

Borrowing money means neither more nor less than raising supplies on the credit of the government. The issuing and paying out of treasury notes may be a forced loan to the government. Metropolitan Bank *v.* Van Dyck, 27 N. Y. 400.

Congress may constitutionally authorize the emission of bills of credit, make them receivable in payment of debts due to the United States, fit them for use by those who see fit to use them in all the transactions of commerce, provide for their redemption, and make them a currency uniform in value and description, and convenient and useful for circulation. Veazie Bank *v.* Fenno, 8 Wall. 533.

In order to borrow, the government must have credit, and if, in the judgment of Congress, it is either necessary or proper, in order to enhance the credit of the government promises, to make them a legal tender in the payment of private as well as public debts, it has the right to do so. Riddlesbarger *v.* McDaniel, 38 Mo. 138; Hague *v.* Powers, 39 Barb. 427; Metropolitan Bank *v.* Van Dyck, 27 N. Y. 400; Thayer *v.* Hedges, 23 Ind. 141; Breitenbach *v.* Turner, 18 Wis. 140; Reynolds *v.* Bank, 18 Ind. 467; Maynard *v.* Newman, 1 Nev. 271; Carpenter *v.* Northfield Bank, 39 Vt. 46; Shollenberger *v.* Brinton. 52 Penn. 9; Verges *v.* Giboney, 38 Mo. 458; contra, Thayer *v.* Hedges, 22 Ind. 282; Griswold *v.* Hepburn, 2 Duvall, 20.

Congress, by suitable enactments, may restrain the circulation, as money, of any notes not issued by itself. Veazie Bank *v.* Fenno, 8 Wall. 533.

Commerce.

(*c*) The design and object of this power was to establish a perfect equality among the several States, as to commercial rights, and to prevent unjust and invidious distinctions which local jealousies or local and partial interests might be disposed to introduce and maintain. These were the views pressed upon the public attention by the advocates for the adoption of the Constitution, and the decisions have been in accordance therewith. Veazie *v.* Moor, 14 How 568; S. C. 32 Me. 343.

Although the power to regulate is given in the same words in relation to commerce with foreign nations, among the States and with the Indian tribes, yet, as the subject to be regulated is different in each case; and as the relation in which Congress stands to the parties is also different, there is good reason for giving different effect to the same granting words in the several cases. Surely it can not be that Congress may exercise the same powers in regulating commerce among the States as it exercises in regulating commerce with the Indian tribes. If this be admitted, it must also be admitted that the identity of the language in which the power is given to regulate commerce with foreign nations, and among the several States, does not prove that the power itself is as to its extent, and the modes of its legitimate exercise identical in both cases. Comm. *v.* Griffin, 3 B. Mon. 208.

The power is a power to regulate, that is, to prescribe the rule by which commerce is to be governed. This power, like all others vested in Congress, is complete in itself, may be exercised to its utmost extent, and acknowledges no limitations other than are prescribed in the Constitution. The power over commerce with foreign nations and among the several States is vested in Congress as absolutely as it would be in a single government having in its Constitution the same restrictions on the exercise of the power as are found in the Constitution of the United States. Gibbons *v.* Ogden, 9 Wheat. 1; S. C. 17 Johns. 488; 4 Johns. Ch. 150.

Commerce undoubtedly is traffic, but it is something more: it is intercourse. It describes commercial intercourse between nations and parts of nations in all its branches, and is regulated by prescribing rules for carrying on that intercourse. Gibbons *v.* Ogden, 9 Wheat. 1; S. C. 17 Johns. 488; 4 Johns. Ch. 150; Steamboat Co. *v.* Livingston, 3 Cow. 713; S. C. 1 Hopk. 150; Brown *v.* State, 12 Wheat. 419; Groves *v.* Slaughter, 15 Pet. 449; Mitchell *v.* Steelman, 8 Cal. 363.

Navigation is only one of the elements of commerce. It is an element of commerce because it affords the means of transporting passengers and merchandise, the interchange of which is commerce. Any other mode of effecting this is as much an element of commerce as navigation. Clinton Bridge, 1 Wool. 150; S. C. 10 Wall. 454.

The word "commerce" comprehends navigation within its meaning, and a power to regulate navigation is as expressly granted as if that term had been added to the word "commerce." Gibbons v. Ogden, 9 Wheat. 1; S. C. 17 Johns. 488; 4 Johns. Ch. 150; Steamboat Co. v. Livingston, 3 Cow. 713; S. C. 1 Hopk. 150; Brig Wilson v. U. S. 1 Brock. 423; Chapman v. Miller, 2 Spears, 769; Passenger Cases, 7 How. 283; S. C. 45 Mass. 282; Cooley v. Philadelphia, 12 How. 299.

The word commerce refers to trade. U. S. v. Bailey, 1 McLean, 234.

The term "intercourse" includes the transportation of passengers. People v. Raymond, 34 Cal. 492.

Commerce is a unit, its several parts so united and bound together as to be inseparable, and as intercourse is a component part of commerce, the power to regulate commerce includes the power to regulate intercourse. The power comes from the grant, and is co-extensive with the subject to which it relates. Lin Sing v. Washburn, 20 Cal. 534.

Commerce comprehends intercourse for the purposes of trade in any and all its forms, including the transportation, purchase, sale and exchange of commodities between the citizens of the United States and the citizens or subjects of other countries, and between the citizens of the different States. Welton v. State, 91 U. S. 275; S. C. 55 Mo. 288.

The word commerce, as here used, is not limited to the mere buying and selling of merchandise and other commodities, but comprehends the entire commercial intercourse with foreign nations and among the several States. It includes navigation as well as traffic in its ordinary signification, and embraces ships and vessels as the instruments of intercourse and trade, as well as the officers and seamen who control and navigate them. People v. Brooks, 4 Denio, 469.

The words of this clause comprehend every species of commercial intercourse between the United States and foreign nations. No sort of trade can be carried on between this country and any other to which this power does not extend. Commerce, as the word is used in the Constitution, is a unit, every part of which is indicated by the term. Gibbons v. Ogden, 9 Wheat. 1; S. C. 17 Johns. 488; 4 Johns. Ch. 150.

It makes no difference whether the interchange of commodities is by land or by water. In either case the bringing of the goods from the seller to the buyer is commerce. State Freight Tax, 15 Wall. 232; Clinton Bridge, 1 Wool. 150; S. C. 10 Wall. 454.

By the term commerce is meant not traffic only, but every species of commercial intercourse, every communication by land or by water, foreign and domestic, external and internal. State v. Del. L. & W. R. R. Co. 30 N. J. 473; S. C. 31 N. J. 531.

The power to regulate commerce extends to persons as well as things. Lin Sing *v.* Washburn, 20 Cal. 534.

Communication by telegraph is a part of commerce. West. U. Tel. Co. *v.* Atlantic & Pac. Tel. Co. 5 Nev. 102; Penn. Tel. Co. *v.* W. U. Tel. Co. 2 Woods, 643.

The transportation of freight or of the subjects of commerce for the purpose of exchange or sale is a constituent of commerce. State Freight Tax, 15 Wall. 232.

The power to regulate commerce embraces all the instruments by which it may be carried on. Welton *v.* State, 91 U. S. 275; S. C. 55 Mo. 288.

The power includes commerce carried on by corporations as well as commerce carried on by individuals. Paul *v.* Virginia, 8 Wall. 168.

The language of the grant makes no reference to the instrumentalities by which commerce may be carried on. It includes alike commerce by individuals, partnerships, associations and corporations. Paul *v.* Virginia, 8 Wall. 168.

Congress has the power to regulate the vessels as well as the articles they bring. Brig Wilson *v.* U. S. 1 Brock. 423.

The power of Congress to regulate commerce extends to all the immediate agents and vehicles of commerce, and as it extends to these vehicles for some purposes, it must for all. Mitchell *v.* Steelman, 8 Cal. 363.

The power to regulate navigation is the power to prescribe rules in conformity with which navigation must be carried on. It extends to the persons who conduct it as well as to the instruments used. Cooley *v.* Philadelphia, 12 How. 299.

The power extends to the regulation of the navigation of vessels engaged in conveying passengers, whether steam vessels or of any other description, as well as to the navigation of vessels engaged in traffic merely. Murphy *v.* Northern Transportation Co. 15 Ohio St. 553; People *v.* Raymond, 34 Cal. 492; Gibbons *v.* Ogden, 9 Wheat. 1; S. C. 17 Johns. 488; 4 Johns. Ch. 150; Passenger Cases, 7 How. 283; S. C. 45 Mass. 282.

A coasting vessel employed in the transportation of passengers is as much a portion of the American marine as one employed in the transportation of a cargo, and no reason is perceived why such vessel should be withdrawn from the regulating power of that government which has been thought best fitted for the purpose generally. Gibbons *v.* Ogden, 9 Wheat. 1; S. C. 17 Johns. 488; 4 Johns. Ch. 282.

The power authorizes all appropriate legislation for the protection or advancement of either interstate or foreign commerce, and for that purpose such legislation as will insure the convenient and safe navigation of all the navigable waters of the United States, whether that legislation consists in requiring the removal of obstructions to their use, or in subjecting the vessels to inspection and license, in order to insure their proper construction and equipment. The Daniel Ball, 10 Wall. 557; S. C. 1 Brown, 193.

The power to regulate, control or extinguish the liens given by the maritime law for material-men upon foreign vessels does not differ from the power to regulate the shipping of seamen or the navigation of foreign vessels. The Barque Chusan, 2 Story, 455.

The prescribing of rules for the shipping of seamen and the navigation of vessels engaged in the foreign trade, or trade between the States, is a regulation of commerce. The Barque Chusan, 2 Story, 455.

The passage of laws which concern the admission of citizens and subjects of foreign nations to our shores, belongs to Congress, and not to the States. It has the power to regulate commerce with foreign nations. The responsibility for the character of those regulations, and the manner of their execution, belongs solely to the national government. Chy Lung *v.* Freeman, 92 U. S. 275.

The power to regulate commerce includes the power to prohibit the migration or importation of any persons whatever into the States, except so far as this power may be restrained by other clauses of the Constitution. Brig Wilson *v.* U. S. 1 Brock. 423; Gibbons *v.* Ogden, 9 Wheat. 1; s. c. 17 Johns. 488; 4 Johns. Ch. 150; Passenger Cases, 7 How. 283; S. C. 45 Mass. 282; People *v.* Downer, 7 Cal. 169.

Congress has the power to prohibit the importation of slaves into the United States. U. S. *v.* Gould, 8 A. L. Reg. 525; U. S. *v.* Haun, 8 A. L. Reg. 663.

Congress has the power to punish any person who holds or sells a slave imported from a foreign country, although the slave has passed out of the hands of the importer. U. S. *v.* Haun, 8 A. L. Reg. 663; contra, U. S. *v.* Gould, 8 A. L. Reg. 525.

The power to regulate commerce confers no power on Congress to declare the *status* which any person shall sustain while in any State. It ceases in the case of passengers when they arrive in the State. Lemmon *v.* People, 26 Barb. 270; S. C. 20 N. Y. 562; 2 Sandf. 681.

The issuing of a policy of insurance is not a transaction of commerce. Such policies are like other personal contracts between parties, which are completed by their signature and the transfer of the consideration. They are not interstate transactions, though the parties may be domiciled in different States. Paul *v.* Virginia, 8 Wall. 168.

It was never intended that this power should be exercised so as to interfere with private contracts not designed, at the time they were made, to create impediments to commercial intercourse. Railroad Co. *v.* Richmond, 19 Wall. 584.

A law passed to induce immigration for the purpose of settlement is a regulation of commerce, and the Federal Government may pass such a law for immigration, either temporary or permanent, as an essential ingredient of intercourse and traffic. Lin Sing *v.* Washburn, 20 Cal. 534.

Congress may pass laws for the regulation of seamen to be employed in the merchant service, for otherwise commerce could not be carried on. Ex parte Wm. Pool, 2 Va. Cas. 276.

Congress, having created vessels of the United States, has the power to pass a recording act for the security and protection of all persons dealing therein. White's Bank *v.* Smith, 7 Wall. 646; Mitchell *v.* Steelman, 8 Cal. 363; Shaw *v.* McCandless, 36 Miss. 296; Blanchard *v.* The Martha Washington, 1 Cliff. 463; Foster *v.* Chamberlain, 41 Ala. 158.

The regulation of the qualification of pilots, of the modes and times of offering and rendering their services, of the responsibilities which shall rest upon them, of the powers they shall possess, of the compensation which they may demand, and of the penalties by which their rights and duties may be enforced, is a regulation of navigation. Cooley *v.* Philadelphia, 12 How. 299; Dryden *v.* Comm. 16 B. Mon. 598; Cisco *v.* Roberts, 6 Bosw. 494; Edwards *v.* Panama, 1 Oregon, 418.

The passage of an act of Congress relating to pilots does not release a party from a penalty incurred under a State law which is thereby superseded. Sturges *v.* Spofford, 45 N. Y. 446.

The power to regulate commerce is not to be confined to the adoption of measures exclusively beneficial to commerce itself, or tending to its advancement, but in the national system, as in all modern sovereignties, it is also to be considered as an instrument for other purposes of general policy and interest. The mode of its management is a consideration of great delicacy and importance, but the national right or power under the Constitution to adapt regulations of commerce to other purposes than the mere advancement of commerce is unquestionable. The capacity and power of managing and directing it for the advancement of great national purposes is an important ingredient of sovereignty. The degree and extent of the prohibitions can only be adjusted by the discretion of the national government to whom the subject is committed. U. S. *v.* The William, 2 Am. L. J. 255.

Every subject falling within the legitimate sphere of commercial regulation may be partially or wholly excluded when either measure shall be demanded by the safety or by the important interests of the entire nation.

Such exclusion can not be limited to particular classes or descriptions of commercial subjects. It may embrace manufactures, bullion, coin, or any other thing. The power once conceded, it may operate on any and every subject of commerce to which the legislative discretion extends. U. S *v.* Marigold, 9 How. 560.

This power authorizes all appropriate legislation for the protection or advancement of either interstate or foreign commerce, and for that purpose such legislation as will insure the convenient and safe navigation of all the navigable waters of the United States, whether that legislation consists in requiring the removal of obstructions to their use, in prescribing the form and size of the vessels employed upon them, or subjecting the vessels to inspection and license in order to secure their proper construction and equipment. The Daniel Ball, 10 Wall. 557; s. c. 1 Brown, 193.

Commerce with foreign nations and among the several States means nothing more than intercourse with those nations and among those States, for the purposes of trade, be the object of that trade what it may, and this intercourse must include all the means by which it can be carried on, whether by the free navigation of the waters of the several States, or by a passage over land through the States where such passage becomes necessary to the commercial intercourse between the States. It is this intercourse which Congress is invested with the power of regulating, and with which no State has a right to interfere. Corfield *v.* Coryell, 4 Wash. C. C. 371; Moor *v.* Veazie, 31 Me. 360; s. c. 32 Me. 343.

It can not be properly concluded that, because the products of domestic enterprise in agriculture or manufactures, or in the arts, may ultimately become the subjects of foreign commerce, that the control of the means or the encouragement by which the enterprise is fostered and protected, is legitimately within the import of the phrase "foreign commerce," or fairly implied in any investiture of the power to regulate such commerce. A pretension as far reaching as this would extend to contracts between citizen and citizen of the same State, would control the pursuits of the planter, the grazier, the manufacturer, the mechanic, the immense operations of the collieries and the mines, for there is not one of these avocations the results of which may not become the subjects of foreign commerce, and be borne either by turnpikes, canals or railroads from point to point within the several States towards its ultimate destination. Veazie *v.* Moor, 14 How. 568; s. c. 32 Me. 343.

A license to prosecute the coasting trade is a warrant to traverse the waters washing or bounding the coasts of the United States. Such a license conveys no privilege to use, free of tolls or of any condition whatsoever, the canals constructed by a State, or the watercourses partaking of the character of canals exclusively within the interior of a State, and made practicable for navigation by the funds of the State or by privileges she may have conferred for the accomplishment of the same end. Veazie *v.* Moor, 14 How. 568 ; s. c. 32 Me. 343.

The coasting trade means commercial intercourse carried on between different districts in different States, between different districts in the same State, and between different places in the same district on the sea coast or on a navigable river. Steamboat Co. *v.* Livingston, 3 Cow. 713; s. c. 1 Hopk. 150 ; People *v.* Railroad Co. 15 Wend. 113.

An enrollment and license confer no immunity from the operation of the valid laws of a State. If a vessel of the United States, engaged in commerce between two States, is interrupted by a law of a State, the question arises whether the State had the power to make the law, by force of which the voyage was interrupted. This question must be decided in each case upon its own facts. Smith *v.* State, 18 How. 71.

The commerce among the States, which Congress has the power to regulate either directly or incidentally, is that commerce which may be carried on by vessels regularly licensed by the laws of Congress. Steamboat Co. *v.* Livingston, 3 Cow. 713 ; s. c. 1 Hopk. 150.

The commercial power can only be exercised and carried out by legislation. There is no common law in regard to regulations of navigation. In this respect the legislation of Congress is the only remedy known to the Constitution. U. S. *v.* Railroad Bridge Co. 6 McLean, 517.

The word "among" means intermingled with. A thing which is among others is intermingled with them. Commerce among the States can not stop at the external boundary line of each State, but may be introduced into the interior. Commerce among the States must of necessity be commerce with the States. The power of Congress, whatever it may be, must be exercised within the territorial jurisdiction of the several States. Gibbons *v.* Ogden, 9 Wheat. 1 ; s. c. 17 Johns. 488 ; 4 Johns. Ch. 150; Steamboat Co. *v.* Livingston, 3 Cow. 713; s. c. 1 Hopk. 150; Brown *v.* State, 12 Wheat. 419; Moor *v.* Veazie, 31 Me. 360; s. c. 32 Me. 343; Gilman *v.* Philadelphia, 3 Wall. 713; contra, Livingston *v.* Van Ingen, 9 Johns. 507 ; North River Co. *v.* Hoffman, 5 Johns. Ch. 300.

Whenever an article has begun to move as an article of trade from one State to another, commerce in that commodity between the States has commenced. The fact that several different and independent agencies are employed in transporting the commodity, some acting entirely in one State, and some acting through two or more States, does in no respect affect the character of the transaction. To the extent in which each agency acts in that transportation, it is subject to the regulation of Congress. The Daniel Ball, 10 Wall. 557; s. c. 1 Brown, 193.

The lightering or towing of vessels is but a prolongation of the voyage of the vessels assisted to their port of destination, and the vessels so engaged are entitled to the privileges of vessels engaged in the coasting trade, although they are employed only within the limits of the State. Foster *v.* Davenport, 22 How. 244.

Congress has the power to regulate an agency employed in commerce between the States, whether that agency extends through two or more States, or is confined in its action entirely within the limits of a single State. The Daniel Ball, 10 Wall. 557; S. C. 1 Brown, 193; vide The Bright Star, Wool. 266.

The exercise of this power is not limited by bounds of any State. Vessels may be authorized to navigate waters within the bounds of a State, and to pass through a State, if it be practicable to do so, while employed in commerce with foreign nations or among the States. The power was conferred without regard to the jurisdiction of the States. The limits of a State do not constitute any portion of the elements by which the extent of the power is to be ascertained and determined. Moor *v.* Veazie, 32 Me. 343; S. C. 31 Me. 360.

The transportation of a passenger is not complete until he is disembarked, and any law which prescribes the terms on which alone a vessel can discharge her passengers, is a regulation of commerce. Henderson *v.* Mayor, 92 U. S. 259.

The power extends to every part of the voyage, and may regulate those who conduct or assist in conducting navigation in one part of a voyage, as much as in another part or during the whole voyage. Cooley *v.* Philadelphia, 12 How. 299.

Congress has the power to prescribe all needful and proper regulations for the conduct of the traffic over any railroad which has voluntarily become part of a line of interstate communication, or authorize the creation of such roads when the purposes of interstate transportation of persons and property justify or require it. Clinton Bridge, 1 Wool. 150; S. C. 10 Wall. 454.

The power to prescribe the conditions upon which a vessel shall be employed as an instrument of interstate and foreign commerce necessarily carries with it the power to modify the rights of those who use it, whether for the purposes of domestic commerce, or for the purposes of interstate or foreign commerce. Lord *v.* G. N. & P. Steamship Co. 14 Pac. L. R. 297.

The power to regulate commerce does not include the means by which commerce is carried on within a State. Canals, turnpikes, bridges and railroads, are as necessary to the commerce between and through the several States, as rivers, yet Congress has never pretended to regulate them.

The Passaic Bridges, 3 Wall. 782; Veazie v. Moor, 14 How. 568; s. c. 32 Me. 343; Withers v. Buckley, 20 How. 84; s. c. 29 Miss. 21.

In regulating commerce with foreign nations, the power of Congress does not stop at the jurisdictional lines of the several States. It would be a very useless power if it could not pass those lines. The commerce of the United States with foreign nations is that of the whole United States. Every district has a right to participate in it. The deep streams which penetrate the country in every direction, pass through the interior of almost every State in the Union, and furnish the means of exercising the right. If Congress has the power to regulate it, that power must be exercised whenever the subject exists. If it exists within the States, if a foreign voyage may commence or terminate at a port within a State, then the power of Congress may be exercised within a State. Gibbons v. Ogden, 9 Wheat. 1; s. c. 17 Johns. 488; 4 Johns. Ch. 150.

Rivers.

The power comprehends the control to the extent necessary for the purpose of regulating commerce of all navigable waters of the United States, which are accessible from a State other than those in which they they lie. For this purpose they are the public property of the nation, and subject to all the requisite legislation of Congress. Corfield v. Coryell, 4 Wash. C. C. 371; Bennett v. Boggs, Bald. 60; Pollard v. Hagan, 3 How. 212; Gilman v. Philadelphia, 3 Wall. 713.

The exercise of the power is not restricted to waters in which the tide ebbs and flows. There may be commerce and navigation with foreign nations and among the States upon the fresh water lakes and rivers, and to the regulation of such navigation the power will extend. Moor v. Veazie, 31 Me. 360; s. c. 32 Me. 343.

The extent to which the power of Congress to regulate navigation has been conferred, and to which it may be exclusively exercised, is ascertainable by ascertaining the simple fact whether a vessel can be navigated from a port or place within a State, to a port or place within a foreign country or within another State. Moor v. Veazie, 31 Me. 360; s. c. 32 Me. 343.

The power is confined to those streams which are channels of commerce between the States—such as are navigable in fact for vessels of commerce coming out of and returning into the navigable waters of other States by continuous voyages. Neaderhouser v. State, 28 Ind. 257.

Wherever a stream in its course ceases to be a public highway for the commerce between States, at that point its national character terminates, and above that it is within the exclusive jurisdiction of the State. Neaderhouser *v.* State, 28 Ind. 257.

Streams, where they are only navigable for certain kinds of inferior craft, or for certain distances within the State, and where they are not visited by vessels of commerce coming from and going to the navigable waters of other States by continuous voyages, are subject only to the jurisdiction of the State. Neaderhouser *v.* State, 28 Ind. 257.

It is not every ditch in which the tide ebbs and flows through the extensive salt marshes along the coast, and which serve to admit and drain off the salt water from the marshes, that can be considered a navigable stream. Nor is every small creek in which a fishing skiff or gunning canoe can be made to float, deemed navigable, but in order to have this character it must be navigable for some general purpose useful to trade or business. Withers *v.* Buckley, 20 How. 84; S. C. 29 Miss. 21; Boykin *v.* Shaffer, 13 La. Ann. 129; Groten *v.* Hurlburt, 22 Conn. 178; Wethersfield *v.* Humphrey, 20 Conn. 213; Depew *v.* Trustees, 5 Ind. 8; Glover *v.* Powell, 10 N. J. Eq. 211; Neaderhouser *v.* State, 28 Ind. 257; Rowe *v.* Granite Bridge, 38 Mass 344; Butler *v.* State, 6 Ind. 165.

Rivers are navigable waters of the United States, in contradistinction from the navigable waters of the States, when they form in their ordinary condition by themselves or by uniting with other waters, a continued highway, over which commerce is or may be carried on with other States or foreign countries, in the customary modes in which such commerce is conducted by water. The Daniel Ball, 10 Wall. 557; S. C. 1 Brown, 193.

The doctrine of the common law as to the navigability of waters, has no application to this country. Here the ebb and flow of the tide do not constitute any test of the navigability of waters. The Daniel Ball, 10 Wall. 557; S. C. 1 Brown, 193.

The true test of the navigability of a stream does not depend on the mode by which commerce is or may be conducted, nor the difficulties attending navigation. The capability of use by the public for purposes of transportation and commerce, affords the true criterion of the navigability of a river, rather than the extent and manner of that use. If it is capable in its natural state of being used for purposes of commerce, no matter in what mode the commerce may be conducted, it is navigable in fact, and becomes in law a public river or highway. The Montello, 20 Wall. 430.

Those rivers are public navigable rivers in law which are navigable in fact. The Daniel Ball, 10 Wall. 557; S. C. 1 Brown, 193.

Rivers are navigable in fact when they are used, or are susceptible of being used in their ordinary condition as highways for commerce over which trade and travel are or may be conducted in the customary modes of trade and travel on water. The Daniel Ball, 10 Wall. 557; s. c. 1 Brown, 193.

If a river divides into two channels, Congress may erect works to divert the water from one channel into the other for the purpose of improving the navigation. South Carolina *v.* Georgia, 93 U. S. 4.

Congress has the power to control navigable rivers between States to the extent of improving their navigability. South Carolina *v.* Georgia, 93 U. S. 4.

If the natural navigation of a river is such that it affords a channel for useful commerce, the river is navigable in fact, although its navigation may be encompassed with difficulties by reason of natural barriers, such as rapids and sand bars. The Montello, 20 Wall. 430.

Each State, in its capacity as sovereign, owns the navigable waters and the soil under them within its limits. Martin *v.* Waddell, 16 Pet. 367; Pollard *v.* Hagan, 3 How. 212; Den *v.* Jersey Co. 15 How. 426; Smith *v.* State, 18 How. 71.

The territorial limits of a State extend a marine league, or three geographical miles, from the shore. Dunham *v.* Lamphere, 69 Mass. 268.

In ascertaining the line of the shore, the limit does not follow each narrow inlet or arm of the sea, but when the inlet is so narrow that persons and objects can be discerned across it by the naked eye, the line of territorial jurisdiction stretches across from one headland to another of such inlet. Dunham *v.* Lamphere, 69 Mass. 268.

How far Exclusive.

The power to regulate commerce embraces a vast field, containing not only many, but exceedingly various subjects, quite unlike in their nature; some imperatively demanding a single uniform rule operating equally on the commerce of the United States in every port, and some as imperatively demanding that diversity which alone can meet the local necessities of navigation. Either absolutely to affirm or deny that the nature of this power requires exclusive legislation by Congress, is to lose sight of the nature of the subjects of this power, and to assert concerning all of them what is really applicable but to a part. Whatever subjects of this power are in their nature national, or admit only of one uniform system or plan of regulation, may justly be said to be of such a nature as to require exclusive legislation by Congress. Cooley *v.* Philadelphia, 12 How. 299; Newport *v.* Taylor, 16 B. Mon. 699; Port Wardens *v.* The Martha J. Ward, 14 La. Ann. 289; Lemmon *v.* People, 20 N. Y. 562; s. c. 2 Sandf. 681; 26 Barb. 270; Gilman *v.*

Philadelphia, 3 Wall. 713; Stewart *v.* Harry, 3 Bush, 438; State *v.* Pinckney, 10 Rich. 474; License Cases, 5 How. 504; s. c. 13 N. H. 536; Thames Bank *v.* Lovell, 18 Conn. 500; U. S. *v.* Bedford Bridge, 1 W. & M. 401; Savannah *v.* State, 4 Geo. 26; Haldeman *v.* Beckwith, 4 McLean, 286; Gibbons *v.* Ogden, 9 Wheat. 1; s. c. 17 Johns. 488; 4 Johns. Ch. 150; Steamboat Co. *v.* Livingston, 3 Cow. 713; s. c. 1 Hopk. 150; People *v.* Railroad Co. 15 Wend. 113; The Chusan, 2 Story, 455; Chapman *v.* Miller, 2 Spears, 769; Passenger Cases, 7 How. 283; s. c. 45 Mass. 282.

Whenever the subjects over which a power to regulate commerce is asserted are in their nature national, or admit of one uniform system or plan of regulation, they are of such a nature as to require exclusive legislation by Congress. State Freight Tax, 15 Wall. 232.

If the subject is local and not national, the States may legislate concerning it in the absence of any legislation by Congress. Cooley *v.* Philadelphia, 12 How. 299; Edwards *v.* Panama, 1 Oregon, 418.

The transportation of passengers or merchandise through a State, or from one State to another, is of such a nature as to admit of but one regulating power; for if one State can directly tax persons or property passing through it, or tax them indirectly by levying a tax upon their transportation every other may, and thus commercial intercouse between States remote from each other may be destroyed. State Freight Tax, 15 Wall. 232.

The power to regulate the right to land passengers in the United States is national, and belongs exclusively to Congress. Henderson *v.* Mayor, 92 U. S. 259; State *v.* Constitution, 42 Cal. 578.

That portion of commerce with foreign countries and between the States which consists in the transportation and exchange of commodities, is of national importance, and admits and requires uniformity of legislation. The very object of investing this power in the general government was to insure this uniformity against discriminating State legislation. Welton *v.* State, 91 U. S. 275; s. c. 55 Mo. 288.

When Congress makes a law regulating commerce, its authority is paramount and exclusive, and supersedes all State legislation on that subject. People *v.* Raymond, 34 Cal. 492; West. Union Tel. Co. *v.* Atlantic & Pac. Tel. Co. 5 Nev. 102.

State Legislation.

The legislation of a State not directed against commerce or any of its regulations, but relating to the rights, duties, and liabilities of citizens, and only indirectly affecting the operations of commerce, is of obligatory force upon citizens within its territorial jurisdiction, whether on land or water, or engaged in commerce, foreign or interstate, or in any other pursuit. Sherlock *v.* Alling, 93 U. S. 99.

A State law prohibiting the importation from other States of cattle which are calculated to communicate disease to the native cattle is valid. Yeazel *v.* Alexander, 58 Ill. 254; Stevens *v.* Brown, 58 Ill. 289; Somerville *v.* Marks, 58 Ill. 371; Wilson *v.* K. C. St. Jo. & C. B. R. R. Co. 60 Mo. 184.

A State law giving an administrator the right to maintain a suit where the death of the deceased is caused by the wrongful act or omission of another, is valid, although it applies to marine torts committed within the State. Sherlock *v.* Alling, 93 U. S. 99.

A State law prohibiting the floating of logs in a navigable river without their being rafted and joined together, and put under the control and pilotage of men specially placed in charge thereof, is valid. Craig *v.* Kline, 65 Penn. 399.

A State law requiring railroad corporations to fix the rates for the transportation of passengers and freight at a certain time in each year, and make them public and adhere to them, is a police regulation, and not a regulation of commerce. Railroad Co. *v.* Fuller, 17 Wall. 560.

Every State has the right to make improvements in the rivers, watercourses, and highways within its limits. Withers *v.* Buckley, 20 How. 84; S. C. 29 Miss. 21; Boykin *v.* Shaffer, 13 La. Ann. 129.

A State legislature may charter a company to navigate the waters in any State, or even the ocean itself. If the company seek the protection and security of a State charter, they are bound by the restrictions and penalties of that charter. Such restrictions are not regulations of commerce, but limitations on the power of the corporation. Camden & Amboy R. R. Co. *v.* Briggs, 22 N. J. 623.

A State may pass a law prohibiting the sale of any article deemed detrimental to the public good, although it may have been introduced from a foreign country or another State. Lincoln *v.* Smith, 27 Vt. 328; Wynehamer *v.* People, 2 Parker Cr. C. 377; S. C. 20 Barb. 567; 13 N. Y. 378; People *v.* Quant, 2 Parker Cr. C. 410; Perdue *v.* Ellis, 18 Ga. 586; Metropolitan Board *v.* Barrie, 34 N. Y. 657; Dorman *v.* State, 34 Ala. 216; Rohrbacker *v.* Jackson, 51 Miss. 735; contra, People *v.* Toynbee, 20 Barb. 168; S. C. 13 N. Y. 378.

A statute prohibiting the sale of spirituous liquors within certain limits is valid. Dorman *v.* State, 34 Ala. 216; Barnes *v.* State, 49 Ala. 342.

The power of the State to determine the *status* of persons in its territory may be exercised as well in relation to persons *in transitu* as in relation to those remaining in the State. Lemmon *v.* People, 26 Barb. 270; S. C. 20 N. Y. 562; 2 Sandf. 681.

A statute regulating the places in which imported articles may be kept does not interfere with the power of Congress to regulate trade. City *v.* Ahrens, 4 Strobh. 241.

A statute conferring exclusive privilege of navigating the interior navigable rivers of the State is void. Gibbons *v.* Ogden, 9 Wheat. 1; S. C. 17 Johns. 488; 4 Johns. Ch. 150.

The constitutionality of the health laws and quarantine laws of the several States has never been denied. They are considered as flowing from the acknowledged power of a State to provide for the health of its citizens. Gibbons *v.* Ogden, 9 Wheat. 1; S. C. 17 Johns. 488; 4 Johns. Ch. 150; Metcalf *v.* St. Louis, 11 Mo. 102; City *v.* McCoy, 18 Mo. 238; City *v.* Boffinger, 19 Mo. 13; Peete *v.* Morgan, 19 Wall. 581.

The object of inspection laws is to improve the quality of articles produced by the labor of a country, to fit them for exportation, or it may be for domestic use. They act upon the subject before it becomes an article of foreign commerce, or of commerce among the States, and prepare it for that purpose. They form a portion of that immense mass of legislation which embraces everything within the territory of a State not surrendered to the general government, all of which can be most advantageously exercised by the States themselves. Gibbons *v.* Ogden, 9 Wheat. 1; S. C. 17 Johns. 488; 4 Johns. Ch. 150; Charleston *v.* Rogers, 2 McC. 495; Stokes *v.* New York, 14 Wend. 87; Green *v.* State, R. M. Charlt. 368.

Quantity as well as quality is an object of inspection. Charleston *v.* Rogers, 2 McC. 495.

A statute requiring the measurement of coals upon sale thereof is valid. Charleston *v.* Rogers, 2 McC. 495; Stokes *v.* New York, 14 Wend. 87.

An act regulating the floating of timber on navigable rivers is not a regulation of commerce. Scott *v.* Willson, 3 N. H. 321.

A statute regulating the speed of steamboats on a navigable river in passing the wharves of a city is valid. It is a police regulation, and does not conflict with any regulation of commerce by the general government. People *v.* Jenkins, 1 Hill, 469; People *v.* Roe, 1 Hill, 470.

A State law regulating the charges for the storage of grain in warehouses is valid. Munn *v.* Illinois, 94 U. S. 113.

Until Congress acts, a State may regulate the rates to be charged by a railroad corporation for the transportation of freight and passengers, although it is engaged in interstate commerce. Chicago, B. & Q. R. R. Co. *v.* Iowa, 94 U. S. 155; Peck *v.* Chicago & N. W. R. R. Co. 94 U. S. 164.

A State law regulating the navigation of vessels has no operation on commerce carried on between the State and any place out of the State. Haldeman *v.* Beckwith, 4 McLean, 286; contra, Fitch *v.* Livingston, 4 Sandf. 492.

A State law prohibiting any person from having certain game birds in his possession after a certain time, whether killed in the State or brought from another State, is valid, whether the law is regarded as a sanitary measure, or is made for the protection of food. Phelps *v.* Racey, 60 N. Y. 10; S. C. 5 Daly, 235.

A State statute prohibiting colored seamen from coming into the State on board of any vessel, and requiring the master to give bond to transport them out of the State, is void. A State can not thus interfere with navigation, or dictate to the owners of an American vessel the composition of her crew. The Cynosure, 1 Sprague, 88; Elkison *v.* Deliesseline, 2 Wh. Cr. Cas. 56; The William Jarvis, 1 Sprague, 485; contra, Roberts *v.* Gates, 16 Law Rep. 49.

No State is under any legal obligation to give to other States the facilities requisite to interstate commerce. The only obligation of a State in this respect is to allow the citizens of other States to use, equally with her own citizens, such roads or highways as in her discretion she may see fit to construct. A State may, therefore, agree not to permit the construction of a rival railroad for a certain period. Rar. & Del. R. R. Co. *v.* Del. & Rar. Canal Co. 18 N. J. Eq. 546.

A State law regulating commerce can not be made valid because it is contained in the charter of a corporation, for no contract respecting a regulation of commerce can make it constitutional. State *v.* Del. L. & W. R. R. Co. 30 N. J. 473; S. C. 31 N. J. 531.

• A State can not accomplish, by indirect methods, what it is forbidden to do directly. People *v.* Raymond, 34 Cal. 492.

If the real object of an act, as manifested in its provisions, is to direct, regulate or control commerce, although some other purpose may be recited in the preamble or otherwise expressed, the real and not the expressed object must determine the character of the act. Norris *v.* Boston, 45 Mass. 282.

A statute prohibiting the transportation of slaves on a navigable river over which the State has jurisdiction, without the consent of the owner, does not interfere with the rightful power of the Federal Government to regulate commerce, for the act forbidden is in its nature tortious. Church *v.* Chambers, 3 Dana, 274.

A State law prohibiting any vessel from leaving a port in the State without being inspected, for the purpose of protecting the slave property of citizens of the State is valid. Baker *v.* Wise, 16 Gratt. 139.

A statute prohibiting the entrance of negroes within the limits of a State, is not a regulation of commerce. Pendleton *v.* State, 6 Ark. 509; Groves *v.* Slaughter, 15 Pet. 449. Comm. *v.* Griffin, 3 B. Mon. 208.

A State law which requires a vessel engaged in the coasting trade to register the name of the vessel, the names of the owners and their interest therein, before entering the interior waters of the State, is void. Sinnot *v.* Davenport, 22 How. 227; Foster *v.* Davenport, 22 How. 244; contra, Commissioners *v.* Cuba, 28 Ala. 185.

A State law which prohibits any person, other than a port warden, from making a survey of hatches or of damaged goods, is void. Foster *v.* Port Wardens, 92 U. S. 246.

In the absence of regulations by Congress, a State has a right to prescribe at what wharf a vessel may lie, and how long she may remain there, where she may unload and take on particular cargoes, where she may anchor in the harbor, and for what time and what description of light she shall display at night to warn passing vessels of her position, and that she is at anchor and not under sail. Regulations of this kind are necessary and indispensable in every commercial port for the convenience and safety of commerce. They are like to the local usages of navigation in different ports, and every vessel is bound to take notice of them and conform to them. Cushing *v.* The James Gray, 21 How. 184.

A State may establish the line for wharves on a navigable river, and authorize the erection of wharves, if it does not interfere with navigation. Savannah *v.* State, 4 Geo. 26; Comm. *v.* Alger, 61 Mass. 53; Elbridge *v.* Cowell, 4 Cal. 80; Griffing *v.* Gibb, 1 McA. 212.

Whether the erection of wharves will or will not interfere with the navigation of the river, is a question of fact. Savannah *v.* State, 4 Geo. 26.

Pilots.

The mere grant to Congress of the power to regulate commerce, does not deprive the State of the power to regulate pilots. Cooley *v.* Philadelphia, 12 How. 299; Hyer *v.* Wave, 2 Paine, 131.

The acknowledged power of a State to regulate its police, its domestic trade, and to govern its own citizens, may enable it to legislate on the subject of pilots to a considerable extent. Gibbons *v.* Ogden, 9 Wheat. 1; S. C. 17 Johns. 488; 4 Johns. Ch. 150; Chapman *v.* Miller, 2 Spears, 769; Low *v.* Commissioners, R. M. Charlt. 302; Cooley *v.* Philadelphia, 12 How. 299.

A State law requiring the payment of half pilotage fees in case of a refusal to receive a pilot, is valid. There are many cases in which an offer to perform, accompanied by present ability to perform, is deemed by law equivalent to performance. The laws of commercial States and countries have made an offer of pilotage service one of those cases, and a law which does this is not so far removed from the usual and fit scope of laws for the regulation of pilots and pilotage, as to be deemed a covert attempt to legislate upon another subject under the appearance of legislating on the one.

Cooley *v.* Philadelphia, 12 How. 299; Steamship Co. *v.* Joliffe, 2 Wall. 450; Banta *v.* McNeil, 5 Ben. 74.

A State law that imposes a penalty upon any other person than a pilot who pilots or tows a vessel through a dangerous channel, is valid. People *v.* Sperry, 50 Barb. 170.

The fair objects of a law regulating pilots may be secured, and at the same time some classes of vessels be exempted from the charge of half pilotage. The purpose of the law being to cause masters of such vessels as generally need a pilot, to employ one, and to secure to the pilots a fair remuneration for cruising in search of vessels or waiting for employment in port, there is an obvious propriety in having reference to the number, size and nature of employment of vessels frequenting the port. The legislative discretion has been constantly exercised in making discriminations founded on differences both in the character of the trade and the tonnage of vessels engaged therein. Cooley *v.* Philadelphia, 12 How. 299.

The appropriation of the sums received for half pilotage fees, to the use of the society for the relief of distressed and decayed pilots, their widows and children, has no legitimate tendency to impress on the act the character of a revenue law. Whether the sums shall go directly to the use of the individual pilots by whom the service is tendered, or shall form a common fund to be administered by trustees for the benefit of such pilots and their families as may stand in peculiar need of it, is a matter resting in legislative discretion in the proper exercise of which the pilots alone are interested. Cooley *v.* Philadelphia, 12 How. 299.

The States have the power to pass pilotage laws, to license pilots, to regulate their compensation, and to enforce these laws by appropriate penalties. They may discriminate between the different kinds of vessels, according to their size and character, requiring heavier fees, and putting more severe penalties upon some than others. If the fees are not an impost or duty, certainly the penalty is not. It is a substitute for the fees that ought to have been paid. It matters not what the reason for the discrimination is, for it is in the discretion of the Legislature. Collins *v.* Society, 30 Leg. Int. 85.

In the absence of legislation by Congress, the States may establish a board of port wardens and prescribe their duties. Port Wardens *v.* The Martha J. Ward, 14 La. Ann. 289; Port Wardens *v.* The Charles Morgan, 14 La. Ann. 595; Master *v.* Prats, 10 Rob. 459.

State Taxation.

A State has the power to improve navigable rivers within its territory, and impose a toll upon merchandise to compensate for the improvement, although such merchandise passes to and from a port of delivery. It may enact laws for the improvement of navigable rivers within its territories.

Although such enactments may incidentally affect commerce, yet they are not a regulation of commerce, nor are they adopted in virtue of any supposed power to regulate commerce. They are mere municipal regulations. Kellogg *v.* Union Co. 12 Conn. 7 ; Thames Bank *v.* Lovell, 18 Conn. 500; McReynolds *v.* Smallhouse, 8 Bush, 447.

The constitutionality or unconstitutionality of a State tax is to be determined not by the form or agency through which it is to be collected, but by the subject upon which the burden is laid. State Freight Tax, 15 Wall. 232.

A State tax imposed not upon the carrier but upon the freight carried, and because carried, is void so far as it affects commodities transported through the State, or from points without the State to points within it, or from points within the State to points without it. State Freight Tax, 15 Wall. 232; contra, Penn. R. R. Co. *v.* Comm. 3 Grant, 128.

The owner of an artificial highway may exact what he pleases for the use of the way. That right is an attribute of ownership. Tolls and freight are a compensation for services rendered or facilities furnished to a passenger or transporter. A tax is a demand of sovereignty ; a toll is a demand of proprietorship. State Freight Tax, 15 Wall. 232.

A State tax upon the carriage of merchandise from State to State, is in conflict with the Federal Constitution. Merchandise is the subject of of commerce. Transportation is essential to commerce, and every burden laid upon it is *pro tanto* a restriction. No State can, therefore, impose a tax upon freight transported from State to State, or upon the transporter because of such transportation. State Freight Tax, 15 Wall. 232.

A State can not tax persons for passing through it or out of it. Interstate transportation of passengers is beyond the reach of a State Legislature. Crandall *v.* State, 6 Wall. 35 ; S. C. 1 Nev. 294.

A tax upon a railroad corporation for every passenger carried by it is a tax on the passenger, and is void. State *v.* P. W. & B. R R. Co. 4 Houst. 158.

It matters not whether the tax is in terms imposed upon the passenger to be collected by the carrier, or is imposed upon the carrier with power given or recognized and sanctioned to collect it out of the passenger. The difference is one of phraseology merely, not varying in the least degree its effect upon the passenger. State *v.* P. W. & B. R. R. Co. 4 Houst. 158.

A State law which imposes a tax upon coal transported from mines in the State to places beyond the State for sale is void. State *v.* Cumb. & Penn. R. R. Co. 40 Md. 22.

A State law imposing a transit duty on foreign corporations for all goods and passengers carried or transported within the State is invalid. State *v.* Del. L. & W. R. R. Co. 30 N. J. 473; s. c. 31 N. J. 531.

The transportation is as much a part of commerce as the goods themselves. If there can be no commerce between the States without goods, so there can be none without the transportation of the goods. The two must be united to constitute interstate commerce. A tax on transportation is in legal effect a tax on the goods. Whenever the taxation of a commodity would amount to a regulation of commerce, so will the taxation of an inseparable incident or a necessary concomitant of such commodity. Erie Co. *v.* State, 31 N. J. 531; s. c. 30 N. J. 473.

A State law imposing a tax on all passenger contracts for the transportation of passengers beyond the limits of the State is void, although the tax is to be paid nominally by the owner of the vessel. People *v.* Raymond, 34 Cal. 492.

A State act incorporating a railroad corporation may provide a tax for every passenger carried across the State, if the tax is paid by the corporation, and is not to be added to the ordinary rate of fare. Rar. & Del. R. R. Co. *v.* Del. & Rar. Canal Co. 18 N. J. Eq. 546.

A provision in the charter of a railroad corporation that all tonnage carried on the road shall be subject to a certain toll or duty per mile is not a tax on commerce or on the goods, but is simply a mode of taxing the company according to the magnitude of its business. Penn. R. R. Co. *v.* Comm. 3 Grant, 128.

If a State builds a railroad or canal, it may exact any amount whatever of toll or fare or freight, or authorize its citizens, if owners, to do the same. Railroad Company *v.* Maryland, 21 Wall. 456; s. c. 34 Md. 344.

A State, in a charter of a railroad corporation, may reserve a certain portion of the earnings as a bonus for the grant of the franchise. Railroad Company *v.* Maryland, 21 Wall. 456; s. c. 34 Md. 344.

A charter to a corporation is usually treated as a contract, and is not obnoxious to the Constitution, for the Constitution forbids only laws which involve no individual consent as necessary to their existence. Penn. R. R. Co. *v.* Comm. 3 Grant, 128.

It is not material that the tax is levied upon all freight, as well that which is wholly internal as that embarked in interstate trade. An act to tax interstate or foreign commerce is not cured by including in its provisions subjects within the domain of the State. State Freight Tax, 15 Wall. 232; State *v.* Cumb. & Penn. R. R. Co. 40 Md. 22.

A State has the authority to tax the estate, real and personal, of all corporations, including carrying companies, precisely as it may tax similar property when belonging to natural persons, and to the same extent. Such taxation may be laid upon a valuation, or may be an excise, and in exacting an excise from corporations a State is not obliged to impose a fixed sum upon the franchises or the value of them, but may demand a graduated contribution, proportioned either to the value of the privileges granted, or to the extent of their exercise or the results of such exercise. No mode of effecting this, and no forms of expression which have not a meaning beyond this, can be regarded as violating the Constitution. State Tax on Railway Gross Receipts, 15 Wall. 284; Del. Railroad Tax, 18 Wall. 206.

A tax upon the gross receipts of a railroad corporation is valid, for it is a tax upon the corporation measured in amount by the extent of its business, or the degree to which its franchise is exercised. State Tax on Railway Gross Receipts, 15 Wall. 284; Del. Railroad Tax, 18 Wall. 206.

A tax upon the gross receipts of an express company engaged in carrying articles between States, is valid. Southern Express Co. v. Hood, 15 Rich. 66; Walcott v. People, 17 Mich. 68.

A State tax upon a money or exchange broker is valid. No one can claim an exemption from a general tax on his business within the State, on the ground that the products sold may be used in commerce. Nathan v. Louisiana, 8 How. 73.

A State law imposing a tax upon the agents of foreign insurance companies doing business within the State is not a regulation of commerce. People v. Thurber, 13 Ill. 554.

A State law imposing a stamp tax on foreign bills of exchange drawn in the State is valid. Ex parte James P. Martin, 7 Nev. 140.

A State may impose a tax upon the capital of a corporation created by it, although the corporation is created for the purpose of towing vessels and carrying freight and passengers. Union Tow Boat Co. v. Bordelon, 7 La. Ann. 192.

A State may impose a higher tax upon a foreign corporation than it does upon corporations created by its own laws. Liverpool Ins. Co. v. Massachusetts, 10 Wall. 566.

A State tax for the use of each locomotive and car in the State where the railroad is engaged in interstate commerce is void. Minot v. P. W. & B. R. R. Co. 2 Abb. C. C. 323; s. c. 18 Wall. 206; 7 Phila. 555.

A State law imposing a toll upon wood and lumber floating down a river in the course of transportation to another State is void. Carson R. L. Co. v. Patterson, 33 Cal. 334.

A State law requiring every express company or railroad company doing business in the State, and having a business extending beyond the limits of the State, to take out a license is valid, for it is a tax on the business of making contracts within the State for transportation beyond it. Osborne *v.* Mobile, 16 Wall. 479; S. C. 44 Ala. 493; Southern Express Co. *v.* Mayor, 49 Ala. 404.

A State tax upon vessels owned by a citizen of the State, ratably with other property within the State, is valid. Howell *v.* State, 3 Gill, 14; State *v.* Charleston, 4 Rich. 286.

A State may impose a tax on the capital or stock invested by its citizens in steamboats, although they are employed in commerce between the States. Perry *v.* Torrence, 8 Ohio, 521; People *v.* Commissioners, 48 Barb. 157.

A State tax upon the officers and crew of a vessel of the United States is a regulation of commerce, and unconstitutional. People *v.* Brooks, 4 Denio, 469; Passenger Cases, 7 How. 283; S. C. 45 Mass. 282.

A State has no jurisdiction to impose a tax on a vessel temporarily entering its ports for the purposes of commerce, if the home port is in another State. Hays *v.* Pacific Mail Steamship Co. 17 How. 596; St. Louis *v.* Ferry Co. 11 Wall. 423; Morgan *v.* Parham, 16 Wall. 471.

Sale is the object of importation, and is an essential ingredient of that intercourse of which importation constitutes a part. It is as essential an ingredient, as indispensable to the existence of the entire thing, as importation itself. It must be considered as a component part of the power to regulate commerce. Congress has a right not only to authorize importation, but to authorize the importer to sell. Brown *v.* State, 12 Wheat. 419; vide Biddle *v.* Comm. 13 S. & R. 405.

Any penalty inflicted on the importer for selling an imported article in his character of importer is in opposition to the act of Congress which authorizes importation. Any charge on the introduction and incorporation of the articles into and with the mass of property in the country, is hostile to the power given to Congress to regulate commerce, since an essential part of that regulation and principal object of it is to prescribe the regular means for that introduction and incorporation. Brown *v.* State, 12 Wheat. 419; State *v* Shapleigh, 27 Mo. 344.

The line which separates the power of the Federal Government to regulate commerce among the States from the authority of the States to tax persons, property, business, or occupations within their limits, is difficult to define with distinctness. A tax upon imported goods, so soon as the importer has broken the original packages and made the first sale, obstructs importation quite as much as an equal impost upon the unbroken packages before they have gone into the market. State Tax on Railway Gross Receipts, 15 Wall. 284.

The power which insures uniformity of commercial regulation must cover the property which is transported as an article of commerce from hostile or interfering legislation until it has mingled with and become a part of the general property of the country, and subjected, like it, to similar protection, and to no greater burdens. Welton *v.* State, 91 U. S. 275; s. c. 55 Mo. 288.

The commercial power continues until the commodity has ceased to be the subject of discriminating legislation. That power protects it, even after it has entered the State, from any burdens imposed by reason of its foreign origin. Welton *v.* State, 91 U. S. 275; s. c. 55 Mo. 288.

If an importer intends to break the original package and sell the liquor therein contained in violation of the prohibitory law of the State, the package may be forfeited under the State law. State *v.* Blackwell, 65 Me. 556.

No one but the importer himself has the right to sell except as allowed by the laws of the State, and he can sell only in the original packages. State *v.* Robinson, 49 Me. 285.

The products of other States which are brought into a State for sale are not subject to State taxation until a change in the ownership or condition of the merchandise takes place, so that it becomes incorporated with and forms a part of the property of the State. State *v.* Kennedy, 19 La. Ann. 397.

The mere conveyance of property from one State to another will not exempt it from taxation and general regulation by the laws of the latter State. License Cases, 5 How. 504; s. c. 13 N. H. 536; State *v.* Pinckney, 10 Rich. 474.

A State may levy a tax on capital, although it is continuously invested in cotton purchased for exportation. People *v.* Tax Commissioner, 17 N. Y. Supr. 255.

A tax on merchants according to the amount of their capital, without any distinction in regard to the articles in which they deal, is not a tax on imports, nor does it interfere with the power of Congress to regulate commerce. Raguet *v.* Wade, 4 Ohio, 107; License Cases, 5 How. 504; s. c. 13 N. H. 536; Padelford *v.* Savannah, 14 Ga. 438; Smith *v.* People, 1 Parker Cr. Cas. 583.

A State law imposing a tax upon the sale of articles which are not of the growth, product or manufacture of the State, is void. Welton *v.* State, 91 U. S. 275; s. c. 55 Mo. 288; State *v.* North, 27 Mo. 464; State *v.* Kennedy, 19 La. Ann. 397; State *v.* Browning, 62 Mo. 591; Woodruff *v.* Parham, 8 Wall. 123; s. c. 14 Ala. 334; Hinson *v.* Lott, 8 Wall. 148; s. c. 40 Ala. 123; Crow *v.* State, 14 Mo. 237; contra, Davis *v.* Dashiel, Phillips, 114; Morrill *v.* State, 38 Wis. 428; People *v.* Coleman, 4 Cal. 46; Wynne *v.* Wright, 4 Dev. & Bat. 19; Biddle *v.* Comm. 13 S. & R. 405; Cowles *v.* Brittain, 2 Hawks, 204; Cummings *v.* Savannah, R. M. Charlt. 26; Tracy *v.* State, 3 Mo. 3.

A State tax upon telegraph companies, which is graduated to the amount of their business, and does not discriminate in favor of or against any company, is valid. West. U. Tel. Co. *v.* Richmond, 26 Gratt. 1.

A State may impose a tax upon the sale of liquor introduced from another State when a tax to the same extent is imposed upon liquors manufactured in the State. Hinson *v.* Lott, 40 Ala. 123; s. c. 8 Wall. 148.

A tax on business which does not discriminate as to the residence or citizenship of the person engaged in the business, is not a regulation of commerce. Speer *v.* Comm. 23 Gratt. 935.

A State law requiring a license from non-resident traders to vend foreign merchandise is not a regulation of commerce. Sears *v.* Commissioners, 36 Ind. 267.

A State law requiring hawkers and peddlers to take out a license is valid. Comm. *v.* Ober, 66 Mass. 493.

A State tax upon the sale of articles manufactured in the State is valid. Downham *v.* Alexandria, 10 Wall. 173.

A State statute which imposes a penalty upon those who sell articles not of the product of the United States, does not interfere with the power to regulate commerce. Beall *v.* State, 4 Blackf. 107.

A State law imposing a penalty upon those who sell articles brought from another State, and allowing a fee to the inspector for his services, is valid. State *v.* Fosdick, 21 La. Ann. 256; Board *v.* Pleasants, 23 La. Ann. 349.

The States can not constitutionally tax the commerce of the United States for the purpose of paying any expense incident to the execution of their police laws. Passenger Cases, 7 How. 283; s. c. 45 Mass. 282.

A State law requiring a vessel to pay a fee to a port warden, whether he is called on to perform any service or not, is void. Steamship Co. *v.* Port Wardens, 6 Wall. 31.

A State law regulating the rates of wharfage, owing to the intimate and necessary connection of the subject-matter with navigation, may be a regulation of commerce, but is not invalid in the absence of any act of Congress, for the subject is not such as to require it to be considered to be within the exclusive jurisdiction of the national government. The Ann Ryan, 7 Ben. 20; Municipality *v.* Pease, 2 La. Ann. 538.

A municipal ordinance imposing a charge for the use of wharves owned by the city, is valid. Worseley Municipality, 9 Rob. 324; Municipality *v.* Pease, 2 La. Ann. 538.

A State law requiring horses and cattle to be landed at a particular locality, and compelling the owners to pay for the facilities afforded in the wharves erected there is valid. State *v.* Pagan, 22 La. Ann. 545.

A State tax on the gross receipts of a telegraph company is valid, although they accrued from messages which originated or terminated at points outside of the State. Western Union Tel. Co. *v.* Mayer, 6 A. L. T. (N. S.) 500.

Transportation of Persons.

A State statute which requires the master or owner to give a bond for the support of every passenger landed in the United States, but allows a commutation and release from the bond upon the payment of a small sum, is in effect a tax on passengers, and is void. Henderson *v.* Mayor, 92 U. S. 59.

A State statute allowing a commissioner to inspect passengers, and determine who are improper to land, and to prohibit their landing, unless a bond is given, and allowing a commutation for the bond, is void. Chy Lung *v.* Freeman, 92 U. S. 275; contra, Commissioners *v.* Brandt, 26 La. Ann. 29.

A State statute imposing a tax upon passengers coming into the ports of the State, is a regulation of commerce, and therefore unconstitutional and void. Passenger Cases, 7 How. 283; S. C. 45 Mass. 282; People *v.* Downer, 7 Cal. 169; contra, Smith *v.* Marston, 5 Tex. 426.

The right to exclude immigrants is a power to tax them, and the converse of the proposition is also true, that a power to tax is a power to exclude. Passenger Cases, 7 How. 283; S. C. 45 Mass. 282.

A State law which obstructs the entrance into the State of persons who are neither paupers, vagabonds nor criminals, nor in anywise unsound or infirm in body or in mind, is not an exercise of the police power of the State, and is void. State *v.* Constitution, 42 Cal. 578.

It is as competent and as necessary for a State to provide precautionary measures against the moral pestilence of paupers, vagrants, and possibly convicts, as it is to guard against physical pestilence which may arise from unsound and infectious articles imported, or from a ship the crew of which may be laboring under an infectious disease. Mayor *v.* Miln, 11 Pet. 102; S. C. 2 Paine, 429; New York *v.* Staples, 6 Cow. 169.

A statute of a State requiring the captain of every vessel to make a report concerning the passengers brought to a port of the State in the vessel is not a regulation of commerce, but of police. Mayor *v.* Miln, 11 Pet. 102; Norris *v.* Boston, 45 Mass. 282.

The police power of the State may be exercised by precautionary measures against the increase of crime or pauperism, or the spread of infectious diseases from persons coming from other countries. The State may entirely exclude convicts, lepers and persons afflicted with incurable disease, may refuse admission to paupers, idiots and lunatics, and others who from physical causes are likely to become a charge upon the public, until security is afforded that they will not become such a charge, and may isolate the temporarily diseased until the danger of contagion is gone. Ex parte Ah Fong, 3 Saw. 144; s. c. 20 I. R. R. 112.

Where the evil apprehended by the State from the ingress of foreigners is that such foreigners will disregard the laws of the State, and thus be injurious to its peace, the remedy lies in the more vigorous enforcement of the laws, and not in the exclusion of the parties. Ex parte Ah Fong, 3 Saw. 144; s. c. 20 I. R. R. 112.

The extent of the power of the State to exclude a foreigner from its territory is limited by the right in which it has its origin,—the right of self-defense. Whatever outside of the legitimate exercise of this right, affects the intercourse of foreigners with our people, their immigration to this country and residence therein is exclusively with the general government. Ex parte Ah Fong, 3 Saw. 144; s. c. 20 I. R. R. 112.

A State law requiring that negroes coming into the State shall give a bond for their good behaviour, and that they will not become a public charge, is not a regulation of commerce. State *v* Cooper, 5 Blackf. 258; Baptiste *v*. State, 5 Blackf, 283.

A State law which prohibits common carriers from discriminating against passengers on account of race or color, is valid. Decuir *v*. Benson, 27 La. Ann. 1.

Commerce can not be carried on without the agency of persons, and a tax the effect of which is to diminish personal intercourse is necessarily a tax on commerce. A tax on an alien after he has landed as a condition of residence in the State, is void. Lin Sing *v*. Washburn, 20 Cal. 534.

Aliens can not be taxed for the privilege of residing in a State, without reference to their condition or character. They may be taxed as other residents, but they can not be set apart as special subjects of taxation, and compelled to contribute to the revenue of the State in their character of foreigners. Lin Sing *v*. Washburn, 20 Cal. 534.

Every State may tax foreigners within its territorial limits, with the exception of foreign ambassadors, and agents and their retinue. People *v*. Naglee, 1 Cal. 231.

Bridges.

Congress has the power to keep navigable waters open and free from any obstruction to their navigation interposed by the States or otherwise, to remove such obstructions when they exist, and to provide by such sanctions as it may deem proper, against the occurrence of the evil, and for the punishment of offenders. Gilman *v*. Philadelphia, 3 Wall. 713.

The power to regulate commerce includes the power to determine what shall or shall not be deemed in judgment of law an obstruction to navigation. A bridge authorized by an act of Congress will not be deemed an obstruction. Miller *v.* New York, 13 Blatch. 469; State *v.* Wheeling Bridge Co. 18 How. 421.

Congress may legalize a bridge erected across a navigable river flowing between two States. The Clinton Bridge, 10 Wall. 454; S. C. 1 Wool. 150; State *v.* Wheeling Bridge Co. 18 How. 421.

Congress has the power to prescribe the place and manner of constructing bridges across navigable rivers. U. S. *v.* Mil. & St. P. R. R. Co. 5 Biss. 410, 420.

Congress may confer on a chief of a department the right to determine where a bridge which crosses a navigable river, shall be constructed. U. S. *v.* Mil. & St. P. R. R. Co. 5 Biss. 410.

Congress may interpose whenever it shall be deemed necessary by general or special laws. It may regulate all bridges over navigable waters, remove offending bridges, and punish those who shall thereafter erect them. Gilman *v.* Philadelphia, 3 Wall. 713.

Congress can not, by any act subsequent to the erection of a bridge, so legislate as to render its further continuance unlawful, without making proper compensation for the property so taken, if the bridge was erected by State authority in the absence of conflicting legislation by Congress. Dover *v.* Portsmouth Bridge, 17 N. H. 200.

Congress can not, under this clause, construct a bridge over a navigable water. This belongs to the local or State authority within which the work is to be done. U. S. *v.* Railroad Bridge Co. 6 McLean, 517; Dover *v.* Portsmouth Bridge, 17 N. H. 200.

The several States had the power to build bridges before the Constitution was adopted, and have it still, for the power to authorize the building of bridges is not to be found in the Constitution. Gilman *v.* Philadelphia, 3 Wall. 713; Silliman *v.* Hudson River Bridge Co. 4 Blatch. 74, 395; S. C. 2 Wall. 403.

A State having the power to authorize the construction of a bridge, is, as a general thing, exclusively to judge of the time, place and circumstances which call for its exercise. Columbus Ins. Co. *v.* Peoria Bridge Co. 6 McLean, 70.

The power to build bridges over navigable rivers must be considered so far surrendered as may be necessary for a free navigation upon those streams. By a free navigation must not be understood a navigation free from such partial obstacles and impediments as the best interests of society may render necessary. People *v.* Railroad Co. 15 Wend. 113.

A State has the power to build bridges over navigable rivers within its territory, where they shall be necessary for the convenience of its citizens. The right must be so exercised however as not to interfere with the right to regulate and control the navigation of navigable streams. Both governments have rights which they may exercise over and upon navigable waters, and it is the duty of both so to exercise their several portions of the sovereign power that the greatest good may result to the citizens at large. It is the right and duty of the general government to adopt such measures that the commerce and navigation of the country shall not be improperly obstructed; and it is the duty of the State government to afford its citizens all the facilities of intercourse which are consistent with the interest of the community, and which shall not obstruct the powers granted to the general government. A bridge with a draw which shall be opened free of expense for every vessel sailing under a license as a coasting vessel, affords all the accommodations necessary for citizens in the vicinity or for travelers, and does not impede the navigation in any essential degree. Silliman *v.* Troy & W. Troy Bridge Co. 11 Blatch. 274; U. S. *v.* Railroad Bridge Co. 6 McLean, 517; The Passaic Bridges, 3 Wall. 782; People *v.* Railroad Co. 15 Wend. 113; Comm. *v.* Breed, 21 Mass. 460; Commissioners *v.* Pidge, 5 Ind. 13; Comm. *v.* Bedford Bridge, 68 Mass. 339; In re Water Commissioners, 3 Edw. Ch. 290; Att. Gen. *v.* Stevens, Saxt. 369; Hutchinson *v.* Thompson, 9 Ohio, 52; U. S. *v.* Bedford Bridge, 1 W. & M. 401; Groten *v.* Hurlburt, 22 Conn. 178; Palmer *v.* Commissioners, 3 McLean, 226; Works *v.* Junction Railroad, 5 McLean, 425; Penn. R. R. Co. *v.* N. Y. R. R. Co. 18 I. R. R. 142; Rogers *v.* Railroad Co. 35 Me. 319; Silliman *v.* Hudson River Bridge Co. 4 Blatch. 74, 395; S. C. 2 Wall. 403.

A State may, in the absence of legislation by Congress, authorize the erection of a bridge across a navigable river entirely within the limits of the State, although navigation is thereby obstructed. Bridges which are connecting parts of turnpike streets and railroads are means of commercial transportation as well as navigable rivers, and the commerce which passes over a bridge may be much greater than would ever be transported on the water it obstructs. It is for the municipal power to weigh the considerations which belong to the subject, and to decide which shall be preferred, and how far either shall be made subservient to the other. Gilman *v.* Philadelphia, 3 Wall. 713; The Passaic Bridges, 3 Wall. 782; The Albany Bridge Case, 2 Wall. 463; S. C. 4 Blatch. 74, 395; Easton *v.* N. Y. & L. B. R. R. Co. 9 Phila. 475; Dover *v.* Portsmouth Bridge, 17 N. H. 200.

If Congress has regulated navigation upon a navigable river by licensing vessels and establishing ports of entry, no State can pass a law authorizing the erection of a bridge that will interfere with navigation thereon. No State law can hinder or obstruct the free use of a license granted under an act of Congress. State *v.* Wheeling Bridge Co. 13 How. 518; Columbus Ins. Co. *v.* Curtenius, 6 McLean, 209; Columbus Ins. Co. *v.* Peoria Bridge Co. 6 McLean, 70; Jolly *v.* Draw Bridge Co. 6 McLean, 237.

S. C.

BRIDGES.

The mere existence of a port of delivery above a bridge does not render it unlawful if the bridge does not prevent access to the port, and is provided with a draw and an arch for the passage of vessels and boats. Dover *v.* Portsmouth Bridge, 17 N. H. 200.

Congress by conferring the privileges of a port of entry on a town or city, does not thereby prohibit a State from erecting a bridge over a navigable river below the port. The Passaic Bridges, 3 Wall. 782.

Every bridge, except one suspended over a river so as to be above all vessels and water craft, may in one sense be said to be an obstruction, but that delay or risk which is inseparable from the existence which the State has the power to create, does not make it an obstruction in contemplation of law. The necessity is the justification, and for such delay or risk the law will not give a right of action. Columbus Ins. Co. *v.* Peoria Bridge Co. 6 McLean, 70; Jolly *v.* Draw Bridge Co. 6 McLean, 237; Dover *v.* Portsmouth Bridge, 17 N. H. 200.

A partial, local, or slight obstruction which operates only on some specific spot, does not *per se* conflict with the power of Congress to regulate commerce. Any exercise of the right of eminent domain which does not conflict with a regulation of commerce is legitimate. The State must grossly abuse her right by an essential and material obstruction of a communication which it is the duty of the government to keep open. There may be many obstructions which a State may authorize, but if they are not in their nature essential and serious, they must remain so long as the authorities of the State permit them. Griffing *v.* Gibb, 1 McA. 212.

A State may authorize the erection of a close bridge over a navigable creek which is not used as a great public highway. Bailey *v.* Railroad Co. 4 Harring. 389.

Whether a particular bridge is an essential obstruction of navigation is a question of fact, and a State law authorizing its erection is not conclusive on that point. Columbus Ins. Co. *v.* Curtenius, 6 McLean, 209; Columbus Ins. Co. *v.* Peoria Bridge Co. 6 McLean, 70; Jolly *v.* Draw Bridge Co. 6 McLean, 237.

Whether navigation is left free is the test by which to determine whether a bridge is a material obstruction. No precise and absolute rule can be given to determine whether a particular bridge is an obstruction. It must depend upon all the circumstances of each particular case, the character of the river, the trade upon it, and the craft navigating it. Columbus Ins. Co. *v.* Peoria Bridge Co. 6 McLean, 70; Jolly *v.* Draw Bridge Co. 6 McLean, 237.

A State legislature may bridge a navigable river upon such terms and conditions as merely impair and diminish the freedom of navigation without destroying the right altogether. Flannagan *v.* Philadelphia, 42 Penn. 219.

A State may authorize the erection of a bridge over a navigable river flowing between it and another State. Dover *v.* Portsmouth Bridge, 17 N. H. 200.

If a bridge does not obstruct navigation at the time when it is erected, it will not become unlawful by a subsequent accident whereby it is rendered an obstruction. Commissioners *v.* Pidge, 5 Ind. 13.

The provision for the payment of tolls by those who may pass over a bridge built across a navigable river flowing between two States, may perhaps, be regarded as a regulation for them, but is not in such an application a commercial regulation. Dover *v.* Portsmouth Bridge, 17 N. H. 200.

The regulation of the tolls of bridges and turnpike roads, and the fares of railroads and ferries, is in no just sense a regulation of commerce. State *v.* Hudson, 24 N. J. 718; s. c. 23 N. J. 206.

Dams.

If Congress has passed no law to control State legislation over small navigable creeks, into which the tide flows, the respective States may authorize the erection of dams, and otherwise abridge the rights of those who have been accustomed to use them. . Such acts are not repugnant to the power to regulate commerce in its dormant State. Wilson *v.* Marsh Co. 2 Pet. 245; Kellogg *v.* Union Co. 12 Conn. 7; Parker *v.* Mill Dam Co. 20 Me. 353; Glover *v.* Powell, 10 N. J. Eq. 211; Woodman *v.* Kilbourn Manuf. Co. 1 Abb. C. C. 158.

A State may authorize the erection of dams and locks in navigable rivers if navigation is not seriously obstructed thereby. Commissioners *v.* Pidge, 5 Ind. 13; Stoughton *v.* State, 5 Wis. 291.

A State statute imposing a penalty for erecting a dam or other artificial obstruction across any navigable river in the State is not unconstitutional while the power of Congress over the subject lies dormant. Cox *v.* State, 3 Blackf. 193.

A State may improve the navigation of any and all streams within her borders, and authorize the erection in and over them of any works that do not substantially injure them for purposes of navigation. Commissioners *v.* Pidge, 5 Ind. 13.

Ferries.

Congress has no authority to require a license to carry on a ferry over a navigable river at a place altogether within the limits of a State. U. S. *v.* The James Morrison, Newb. 241; U. S. *v.* The William Pope, Newb. 256; The Thomas Swan, 6 Ben. 42.

The States bordering on a navigable river which flows between them possess the right of granting and controlling the privilege of ferrying from their respective shores, with such restrictions as to competition as may be deemed necessary to secure the proper accommodations for travel and trade, and with such regulations as will secure a speedy and comfortable passage across the river, and protect the rights and property of their citizens. Newport *v.* Taylor, 16 B. Mon. 699; State *v.* Hudson, 23 N. J. 206; s. c. 24 N. J. 718; Marshall *v.* Grimes, 41 Miss. 27; Mills *v.* St. Clair, 8 How. 569; s. c. 2 Gilman, 197; Conway *v.* Taylor, 1 Black, 603; s. c. 16 B. Mon. 699; Fanning *v.* Gregoire, 16 How. 524; Corporation *v.* Overton, 3 Yerg. 387; Phillips *v.* Bloomington, 1 Greene (Iowa), 498.

The concurrent action of both States is not necessary in order to establish a ferry over a navigable river flowing between them, for the ferry is in respect of the landing and not of the water. Conway *v.* Taylor, 1 Black, 603; s. c. 16 B. Mon. 699.

A State may regulate the rates of ferriage, although the ferry is between two States or a State and a foreign nation. It has the power to regulate the exercise of the right of ferry by any person holding a dock or wharf in the State, although the passage may in part be over the waters of an adjoining State. The jurisdiction of the State extends to the center of the stream, and the franchise may be regulated and controled to that extent, upon conditions which may affect the whole transit. State *v.* Hudson, 23 N. J. 206; s. c. 24 N. J. 718; People *v.* Babcock, 11 Wend. 586; Newport *v.* Taylor, 16 B. Mon. 699.

A State law requiring a license fee from ferry-boats carrying passengers between the State and a foreign nation, is valid. Chilvers *v.* People, 11 Mich. 43.

A ferry-boat duly licensed under the laws of one State may transport goods or passengers across a navigable river flowing between two States into another State, but can not carry goods or passengers from the latter State in violation of its laws granting an exclusive ferry privilege to others. Newport *v.* Taylor, 16 B. Mon. 699; s. c. 1 Black, 603.

A steamboat enrolled and licensed under the laws of the United States, is not authorized to engage in transporting goods and passengers across a navigable river flowing between two States, in violation of the laws of a State granting the exclusive ferry privilege to others. Newport *v.* Taylor, 16 B. Mon. 699; s. c. 1 Black, 603.

The owner of a ferry franchise has no right to exclude or restrain those who prosecute the business of commerce in good faith, without the regularity or purposes of ferry trips, and seek in nowise to interfere with the enjoyment of his franchise. Conway *v.* Taylor, 1 Black, 603; s. c. 16 B. Mon. 699.

Subject to State Laws.

Persons moving upon or using a navigable river for the purposes of trade and commerce, out of their own State, have not thereby a privilege to commit murders or robberies, or thefts or trespasses upon the person or property of others upon the shores, and a statute punishing such offenses is valid. McFarland *v.* McKnight, 6 B. Mon. 500; Steerman *v.* State, 10 Mo. 503.

Vessels, together with their masters and crews, while within the jurisdiction of a State, are subject to the operation of its laws passed with a view to the restraint and punishment of offenses against the person or property of its citizens, for such laws are police laws. Baker *v.* Wise, 16 Grat. 139.

The enrolment and license of a vessel confer on it no immunity from the valid laws of a State. Baker *v.* Wise, 16 Grat. 139; Smith *v.* State, 18 How. 71.

Internal Commerce.

Commerce with foreign nations signifies commerce which in some sense is necessarily connected with those nations—transactions which either immediately or at some stage of their progress must be extra territorial. The phrase can never be applied to transactions wholly internal between citizens of the same community, or to a polity and law whose ends, purposes and operations are restricted to the territory, soil and jurisdiction of such community. Veazie *v.* Moor, 14 How. 568; S. C. 32 Me. 343.

There is a commerce strictly internal to each State, over which Congress has no control, though it may be carried on by means of the navigable rivers of the United States. The Bright Star, Wool. 266.

Commerce among the States means commerce among the people of the States, and this commerce is internal as relates to the Government of the United States and its citizens, as contradistinguished from foreign commerce. Steamboat Co. *v.* Livingston, 3 Cow. 713; S. C. 1 Hopk. 150.

Comprehensive as the word "among" is, it may very properly be restricted to that commerce which concerns more States than one. The phrase is not one which would probably have been selected to indicate the completely interior traffic of a State, because it is not an apt phrase for that purpose, and the enumeration of the particular classes of commerce to which the power was to be extended, would not have been made had the intention been to extend the power to every description. The enumeration presupposes something not enumerated, and that something is the exclusively internal commerce of a State. The genius and character of the whole Government seem to be that its action is to be applied to all the external concerns of the nation, and to those internal concerns which affect the State generally, but not to those which are completely within a particular State, which do not affect other States, and with which it is not necessary to interfere for the purpose of executing some of the general powers of the Government. The completely internal commerce of a State, then, may be considered as reserved to the State itself. Gibbons *v.* Ogden, 9 Wheat. 1; S. C. 17 Johns. 488; 4 Johns. Ch. 150; Charleston *v.* Rogers, 2 McC. 495; Stokes *v.* New York, 14 Wend. 87; Moor *v.* Veazie, 31 Me. 360; S. C. 32 Me. 343; Morgan *v.* King, 18 Barb. 277; Sinnot *v.* Davenport, 22 How. 227.

The navigation of a public navigable river is not included in internal commerce, but composes a part of the coasting trade, and is subject to the regulation and control of Congress. Steamboat Co. *v.* Livingston, 3 Cow. 713; S. C. 1 Hopk. 150.

Congress has no jurisdiction over the navigable waters of a State, except as regards intercourse with other States or with a foreign country. A State law regulating pilots is valid so far as commercial intercourse may be carried on between parts of the State by the citizens thereof. Barnaby *v.* State, 21 Ind. 450.

Congress has no power to provide for a license and inspection of a vessel employed in navigation between ports in the same State. U. S. *v.* The Seneca, 10 A. L. Reg. 281; The Thomas Swan, 6 Ben. 42.

Congress has no power to interfere with the internal trade and business of the separate States, except as a necessary and proper means for carrying into execution some power expressly granted or vested. U. S. *v.* Dewitt, 9 Wall. 41.

A statute prohibiting the sale of a certain article within the limit of the several States, is void. U. S. *v.* Dewitt, 9 Wall. 41.

No regulation can be made by Congress of commerce among the States, but such as shall embrace two or more States. Halderman *v.* Beckwith, 4 McLean, 286.

This power does not impair the right of the State governments to legislate upon all subjects of internal police within their territorial limits, which is not forbidden by the Constitution, even though such legislation may indirectly and remotely affect commerce, provided it do not interfere with the regulations of Congress upon the same subject. Such are inspection, quarantine and health laws; laws regulating the internal commerce of the State; laws establishing and regulating turnpike roads, ferries, canals and the like. Corfield *v.* Coryell, 4 Wash. C. C. 371; Bennett *v.* Boggs, Bald. 60; Jolly *v.* Draw Bridge Co. 6 McLean, 237.

A State law regulating navigation is operative on commerce that is wholly within a State. Halderman *v.* Beckwith, 4 McLean, 286; Fitch *v.* Livingston, 4 Sandf. 492.

The grant of the power to regulate commerce contains no cession, either express or implied, of territory or of public or private property. The *jus privatum* which a State has in the soil covered by its waters, is totally distinct from the *jus publicum* with which it is clothed. The former, such as fisheries of all descriptions, remains common to all the citizens of the State to which it belongs, to be used by them according to their necessities or according to the laws which regulate their use. A law of the State regulating the use of the fisheries and oyster beds within the territorial limits of the State, does not interfere with the power of Congress to regulate commerce. Corfield *v.* Coryell, 4 Wash. C. C. 371; Bennett *v.* Boggs, Bald. 60; Fuller *v.* Spear, 14 Me. 417; Lunt *v.* Hunter, 16 Me. 9; Smith *v.* Levinus, 8 N. Y. 472; Smith *v.* State, 18 How. 71; The Martha Anne, Ole, 18; McCready *v.* Comm. 27 Grat. 985; S. C. 94 U. S. 391; Dunham *v.* Lamphere, 69 Mass. 268.

A statute which merely regulates the common property of the citizens of the State by forbidding it to be taken at improper seasons, or with destructive instruments, is not a commercial regulation, for it does not inhibit the buying and selling of the property after it has been lawfully gathered and has become an article of trade, but it forbids the removal unless under the regulation which the law prescribes. Corfield *v.* Coryell, 4 Wash. C. C. 371; Bennett *v.* Boggs, Bald. 60.

The shores of navigable waters and the soils under them, were not granted by the Constitution to the United States, but were reserved to the States respectively. Pollard *v.* Hagan, 3 How. 212; Guy *v.* Hermance, 5 Cal. 73; Seabury *v.* Field, 1 McA. 1; Griffing *v.* Gibb, 1 McA. 212; City *v.* Menard, 23 Tex. 349.

The new States have the same rights, sovereignty and jurisdiction over the shores of navigable waters and the soil under them as the original States. Mumford *v.* Wardwell, 6 Wall. 423; Weber *v.* Harbor Commissioners, 18 Wall. 57; Pollard v. Hagan, 3 How. 212; Withers *v.* Buckley, 20 How. 84; S. C. 29 Miss. 21; Griffing *v.* Gibb, 1 McA. 212.

Indians.

The Indian tribes in this clause are as clearly contradistinguished by a name appropriate to themselves from foreign nations as from the several States composing the Union. They are designated by a distinct appellation, and as this appellation can be applied to neither of the others, neither can the appellation distinguishing either of the others be in fair construction applied to them. The objects to which the power of regulating commerce might be directed are divided into three distinct classes : foreign nations, the several States, and Indian tribes. When forming the article, the convention considered them as entirely distinct. Cherokee Nation *v.* State, 5 Pet. 1.

Commerce with the Indian tribes means commerce with the individuals composing those tribes. U. S. *v.* Holliday, 3 Wall. 407.

Commerce can not without a palpable perversion of the term, be held applicable to ordinary business transactions occurring between individuals. Hicks *v.* Euhartonah, 21 Ark. 106.

Congress has the power to regulate commerce, traffic, or intercourse with an Indian tribe or with a member of such tribe, although the traffic is within the limits of a State. The locality of the traffic has nothing to do with the power. The right to exercise it in reference to any Indian tribe or any person who is a member of such tribe, is absolute without reference to the locality of the traffic or the locality of the tribe or of the member of the tribe with whom it is carried on. U. S. *v.* Holliday, 3 Wall. 407 ; U. S. *v.* 43 Gallons, 93 U. S. 188; Worcester *v.* State, 6 Pet. 515.

Congress has the power to forbid the introduction of spirituous liquors into a place near an Indian reservation, although it is within the limits of a State. U. S. *v.* 43 Gallons, 93 U. S. 188.

This provision does not apply to individual sales, or, at all events, not to sales of county lands granted to individual Indians by a State, but is confined to lands held in common by the tribes. Murray *v.* Wooden, 17 Wend. 531.

The power of Congress is not limited to the regulation of commerce between the Indian tribes and white people, or any particular people or persons, but extends to commerce with such tribes or any member thereof, however carried on. Congress may regulate commerce between different tribes and between individual Indians. U. S. *v.* Shawmux, 2 Saw. 304.

As the power to regulate commerce with the Indian tribes is given to Congress in the same clause of the Constitution and in the same words as the power to regulate commerce with foreign nations, it may be exercised to the same extent in one case as in the other. U. S. *v.* Cisna, 1 McLean, 254.

The Indian tribes referred to are those tribes which are in a condition to determine for themselves with whom they will have commerce, or in a condition to have Congress determine it for them, and not those small tribes or remnants of tribes yet denominated tribes, which are under the control and guardianship of a State, and are without power to carry on commerce or trade except by permission and under regulation of State laws. Moor *v.* Veazie, 32 Me. 343; S. C. 31 Me. 360.

If the tribal organization is preserved intact, and recognized by the political department of the Government as existing, then the tribe is a people distinct from others, capable of making treaties, separated from the jurisdiction of the State in which it is located, and to be governed exclusively by the Federal Government. The Kansas Indians, 5 Wall. 737; U. S. *v.* 43 Gallons, 93 U. S. 188.

The courts follow the action of the executive and other political departments of the Government, and if Indians are recognized as a tribe by them, the courts will do the same. U. S. *v.* Holliday, 3 Wall. 407; The Kansas Indians, 5 Wall. 737.

The rights of a tribe as against State laws can only be changed by treaty stipulation or a voluntary abandonment of their tribal organization. The Kansas Indians, 5 Wall. 737.

The Indian tribes residing within the territorial limits of the United States are subject to its authority; and where the country occupied by them is not within the limits of one of the States, Congress may by law punish any offense committed there, no matter whether the offender be a white man or an Indian. U. S. *v.* Rogers, 4 How. 567; s. c. Hemp. 450; U. S. *v.* Cha-to-kah-na-he-sha, Hemp. 27.

Congress has the power to extend its laws within the limits of municipal legislation over the Indian tribes when the territory occupied by them is not within the limits of a State. Cherokee Tobacco, 11 Wall. 616; s. c. 1 Dill. 264.

When the Indian territory is within the limits of a State, the power of Congress is limited to the regulation of a commercial intercourse with such tribes of Indians as exist as a distinct community, governed by their own laws, and resting for their protection on the faith of treaties and laws of the Union. Beyond this the power of the Federal Government in any of its departments can not be extended. U. S. *v.* Bailey, 1 McLean, 234; State *v.* Foreman, 8 Yerg. 256; U. S. *v.* Cisna, 1 McLean, 254.

The power to prohibit any intercourse with the Indians, except under a license, is within the power to regulate commerce with them, if such regulation could not be effectual short of an intercourse thus restricted. U. S. *v.* Cisna, 1 McLean, 254.

Congress can not effectually regulate commerce with the Indian tribes without adopting such provisions as shall effectually preserve them from an indiscriminate commercial intercourse with our own citizens. Their inferiority in the business of commerce is such, while in an uncivilized state, that their interests would be sacrificed if left to an unrestricted intercourse. U. S. *v.* Cisna, 1 McLean, 254.

Congress has no power to enact laws invalidating contracts entered into between an Indian and a white man within the limits of a State, and not on any Indian reservation. Hicks *v.* Euhartonah, 21 Ark. 106; Taylor *v.* Drew, 21 Ark. 485.

When the power to punish is derived exclusively from the power to regulate commerce, it must cease as soon as the power to regulate commerce ceases. U. S. *v.* Cisna, 1 McLean, 254.

Congress has no power to pass a law to punish a crime committed by one white man against another in Indian territory within the limits of a State. U. S. *v.* Bailey, 1 McLean, 234; U. S. *v.* Ward, 1 Wool. 17; Painter *v.* Ives, 4 Neb. 122.

The Federal courts have no jurisdiction of a crime committed by an Indian against a white man within the limits of a State and outside of the reservation. U. S. *v.* Yellow Sun, 1 Dillon, 271; S. C. 1 Abb. C. C. 377; 3 A. L. T. 113.

Congress has no authority, either by the power to regulate commerce or the power to make treaties, or by both combined, to punish the commission of a crime on an Indian reservation within the limits of a State. State *v.* Foreman, 8 Yerg. 256.

The legislation of Congress upon the subject of crimes committed in the Indian country is in its nature exclusive, and a plea of acquittal in an Indian court under the Indian laws for an offense punishable under the laws of the United States is bad. U. S. *v.* Ragsdale, Hemp. 497.

The Federal Government has the exclusive regulation of intercourse with the Indians, and so long as this power shall be exercised it can not be obstructed by a State. It is one of the powers parted with by the States and vested in the Federal Government. Worcester *v.* State, 6 Pet. 515.

Notwithstanding the peculiar relation which the Indian nations hold to the Government of the United States, the States have the power of a sovereign over their persons and property, so far as it is necessary to preserve the peace and protect them from imposition and intrusion. The power of a State to make such regulations to preserve the peace of the community is absolute and has never been surrendered. A State law for the protection of the Indians from the intrusion of the white people, and to preserve the peace, is not contrary to the Constitution. New York *v.* Dibble, 21 How. 366; S. C. 16 N. Y. 203; 18 Barb. 412.

Neither the Constitution of a State nor any act of its legislature, however formal or solemn, whatever rights it may confer upon the Indians or withhold from them, can withdraw them from the influence of an act of Congress which that body has the constitutional right to pass concerning them. U. S. *v.* Holliday, 3 Wall. 407.

An Indian tribe within the limits of a State constitutes a distinct community, occupying its own territory in which the laws of the State can have no force, and which the citizens of the State have no right to enter, but with the assent of the tribe, or in conformity with treaties or with acts of Congress. Worcester v. State, 6 Pet. 515; Blair v. Pathkiller, 2 Yerg. 407.

A State law which prohibits a white person from residing within the territory of an Indian tribe, unless he obtains a permit from the governor and takes an oath to support the State Constitution, is void. Worcester v. State, 6 Pet. 515.

The lands of Indian tribes within the boundaries of a State are within its jurisdiction, unless there is an express treaty that such lands shall not be included within the limits or jurisdiction of a State. McCracken v. Todd, 1 Kans. 148.

When the political jurisdiction of the tribe has been extinguished, either by law or by abandonment, the State has jurisdiction over the land, although it is owned by Indians as tenants in common. Telford v. Barney, 1 Greene (Iowa), 575; Webster v. Reid, 11 How. 437; S. C. Morris, 467; Wright v. Marsh, 2 Greene (Iowa), 94; Barney v. Chittenden, 2 Greene (Iowa), 165.

Except by compact, or the voluntary legislative action of the State, lands within its limits can not be withdrawn from its ordinary action. Lowry v. Weaver, 4 McLean, 82.

No Indian tribe can by treaty stipulate away any part of the sovereignty of a State guaranteed to it by the Federal Government on its admission into the Union. U. S. v. Lariviere, 19 I. R. R. 158.

A State can not impose a tax on the goods of a trader who carries on trade within the limits of an Indian tribe located in the State. Foster v. Commissioners, 7 Minn. 140.

If the tribal organization is preserved, a State can not levy a tax upon the lands of the Indians within its limits, if they are exempt by treaty, whether they are held in severalty or not. Kansas Indians, 5 Wall. 737; New York Indians, 5 Wall. 761; S. C. 23 N. Y. 420; She-mid-go-me-sia v. State, 36 Ind. 310; State v. Ross, 7 Yerg. 74; Lowry v. Weaver, 4 McLean, 82.

A State has jurisdiction to punish an Indian for an offense against another Indian committed within the limits of the State, and not on an Indian reservation. Hunt v. State, 4 Kans. 60.

So far as the administration of justice to persons not belonging to the Indian nation or tribe is concerned, a reserve forms an integral part of the county within whose boundaries it is included, and the State may punish a white man for a crime committed against another white person on the reserve. Millar *v.* State, 2 Kans. 174; U. S. *v.* Ward, 1 Wool. 17.

A State government has the power to punish its own citizens for offenses committed within its limits whether within an Indian territory or not. An Indian territory within a State can not be considered as a foreign jurisdiction. The State may exercise such jurisdiction over the territory as is not incompatible with the constitutional regulations of the General Government. U. S. *v.* Cisna, 1 McLean, 254.

A State may pass laws to punish a crime committed by one Indian against another Indian on an Indian reservation within the limits of the State. State *v.* Tassels, 1 Dudley, 229; State *v.* Foreman, 8 Yerg. 256; U. S. *v.* Ward, 1 Wool. 17; State *v* Ta-cha-na-tah, 64 N. C. 614; Ex parte George Peters, 2 Johns. Cas. 344.

Indians do not submit themselves to all the laws of a State, because they seek its courts for the preservation of rights and redress of wrongs sometimes voluntarily and sometimes by direction of the Secretary of the Interior. The Kansas Indians, 5 Wall. 737.

An Indian is liable to be sued in a State court. Jones *v.* Eisler, 3 Kans. 134; Murch *v.* Tomeer, 21 Me. 535 ; Rubideaux *v.* Vallie, 12 Kans. 28.

An Indian may maintain an action in a State court to enforce his right to the enjoyment of all property, real or personal. Lobdell *v.* Hall, 3 Nev. 507.

An Indian tribe can not institute a suit at law, in the name of the tribe, to recover a reservation held by them in common. Strong *v.* Waterman, 11 Paige, 607.

Indians may file a bill in equity on behalf of themselves and the residue of the nation on the reservation, to restrain a trespass upon their land. Strong *v.* Waterman, 11 Paige, 607.

If a contingency shall occur which shall render the Indians who shall reside in a State incapable of self government, either by moral degradation or a reduction of their numbers, it would undoubtedly be in the power of a State government to extend to them the ægis of its laws. Under such circumstances the agency of the Federal Government must of necessity cease. Worcester *v.* State, 6 Pet. 515.

From the settlement of the country, the Indians have been uniformly treated as a State, a distinct political society separated from others, capable of managing their own affairs and governing themselves. The numerous treaties made with them by the United States recognize them as a people capable of maintaining the relations of peace and war, of being responsible in their political character for any violation of their engagements, or for any aggression committed on the citizens of the United States, by any individual of their community. Cherokee Nation *v.* Georgia, 5 Pet. 1.

The condition of the Indians in relation to the United States, is perhaps unlike that of any other two people in existence. In general, nations, not owing a common allegiance are foreign to each other. The term foreign nation is with strict propriety, applicable by each to the other. But the relation of the Indians to the United States, is marked by peculiar and cardinal distinctions which exist nowhere else. The Indian territory is admitted to compose a part of the United States. In all maps, geographical treatises, histories and laws, it is so considered. In all intercourse with foreign nations, in commercial regulations, in any attempt at intercourse between Indians and foreign nations, they are considered as within the jurisdictional limits of the United States. They are not a State of the Union, nor can they with strict accuracy be denominated foreign nations. They may more correctly be denominated dependent nations. They occupy a territory to which the United States asserts a title independent of their will, which must take effect in point of possession, when their right of possession ceases. Meanwhile, they are in a state of pupilage. Their relation to the United States, resembles that of a ward to his guardian. They look to the Government for protection, rely upon its kindness and its power, and appeal to it for relief to their wants. They and their country are considered by foreign nations as being so completely under the sovereignty and dominion of the United States, that any attempt to acquire their lands or to form a political connection with them, would be considered as an invasion of its teritory, and an act of hostility. Cherokee Nation *v.* Georgia, 5 Pet. 1.

The Indian nations have always been considered as distinct independent political communities, retaining their original natural rights as the undisputed possessors of the soil from time immemorial, with the single exception of that imposed by irresistible power, which excluded them from intercourse with any other European potentate than the first discoverer of the coast of the particular region claimed. The very term "nation" so generally applied to them, means "a people distinct from others." The Constitution admits their rank among those powers who are capable of making treaties. At no time has the sovereignty of the country been recognized as existing in the Indians, but they have been always admitted to possess many of the attributes of sovereignty. All the rights which belong to self-government have been recognized as vested in them. Their right of occupancy has never been questioned, but the fee in the soil has been considered in the government. This may be called the right to the ultimate domain, but the Indians have a present right of possession. As they have the right of self-government they in some sense form a State. In the management of their internal concerns they are dependent on no power.

They punish offenses under their own laws, and in doing so they are responsible to no earthly tribunal. They make war and form treaties of peace. The exercise of these and other powers gives to them a distinct character as a people, and constitutes them in some respects a state. Their engagements with the United States do not divest them of the right of self-government nor destroy their capacity to enter into treaties or compacts. Every state is more or less dependent on those which surround it, but unless this dependence shall extend so far as to merge the political existence of the protected people into that of their protectors, they may still constitute a state. They may exercise the powers not relinquished and bind themselves as a distinct and separate community. Worcester v. State, 6 Pet. 515.

Indians on a reservation within the limits of a State, are not citizens or members of the body politic, but are considered as dependent tribes and alien communities governed by their own usages and chiefs. Goodell v. Jackson, 20 Johns. 693; Jackson v. Wood, 7 Johns. 290; Strong v. Waterman, 11 Paige, 607; Holden v. Joy, 17 Wall. 211.

The laws and usages of a conquered nation are only abrogated or superseded by positive enactments. The mere acquisition of the territory, whether by peace or war, has no such effect. The usages and customs of an Indian tribe continue to be their law, although the tribe is on a reservation within the limits of a State. Wall v. Williamson, 8 Ala. 48; S. C. 11 Ala. 826; Goodell v. Jackson, 20 Johns. 693.

Indian tribes may have laws and usages for their own internal government, and adopt other persons as members of their tribes. U. S. v. Ragsdale, Hemp. 497.

The Indian nations residing within the limits of a State, have a right to regulate their own civil policy, and their laws and customs regulating property, contracts and the relations between husband and wife are respected when drawn into controversy in the courts of the State and of the United States. Jones v. Laney, 2 Tex. 342; Dole v. Irish, 2 Barb. 639; Goodell v. Jackson, 20 Johns. 693.

The private property of the Indians on a reservation within the limits of a State, are not within the jurisdiction of State laws respecting administration, and no letters of administration can be granted on the estate of an Indian. Dole v. Irish, 2 Barb. 639; U. S. v. Shanks, 15 Minn. 369.

If an Indian dies before the laws of the State are extended over the reservation, a State court may grant letters of administration on his estate when they are so extended, as the debts which he may have owed can not be enforced in any other mode. Brashear v. Williams, 10 Ala. 630.

* The liability of an innkeeper who keeps an inn on an Indian reservation within the limits of a State is to be determined according to the laws of the tribe. Holland *v.* Pack, Peck, 151.

In the absence of proof the presumption is that, in a savage tribe, there are no laws regulating the descent of property, and that being in a state of nature the property of the deceased belongs to the first occupant. Brashear *v.* Williams, 10 Ala. 630.

So long as the Indians adhere to their tribal customs, and their affairs are managed by agents of the Federal Government, they are not subject to State laws so far as marriage and inheritance are concerned. Boyer *v.* Dively, 58 Mo. 510; Morgan *v.* McGhee, 5 Humph. 13; Wall *v.* Williamson, 11 Ala. 826; s. c. 8 Ala. 48.

A marriage between Indians, which is valid according to the usages of the tribe, will be deemed valid everywhere, although the tribe at the time was on a reservation within the limits of a State. Wall *v.* Williamson, 8 Ala. 48; S. C. 11 Ala. 826; Boyer *v.* Dively, 58 Mo. 510; Morgan *v.* McGhee, 5 Humph. 13; Johnson *v.* Johnson, 30 Mo. 72.

If a marriage between Indians is dissolved according to the law of the tribe, the dissolution will be deemed valid everywhere, although the tribe at the time was on a reservation within the limits of a State. Wall *v.* Williamson, 8 Ala. 48; S. C. 11 Ala. 826.

A marriage between Indians in a State after the tribe has removed from it, must conform to the laws of the State in order to be valid. Roche *v.* Washington, 19 Ind. 53.

The condition of an Indian on a reserve in a State, in reference to his contracts, is not distinguishable from that of a foreigner sojourning in the State. Murch *v.* Tomeer, 21 Me. 535.

Indians are not foreign citizens or subjects. Karrahoo *v.* Adams, 1 Dillon, 344.

An Indian may be a resident alien in a State. Parent *v.* Walmsley, 20 Ind. 82.

If an Indian leaves his tribe or nation and takes up his abode among the white population, he is entitled to all the rights and privileges which belong to an emigrant from any other foreign people. Dred Scott *v.* Sanford, 19 How. 393.

The Cherokee territory is a domestic territory, and its laws and proceedings stand on the same footing as those of other territories. Mackey *v.* Coxe, 18 How. 100.

A white man may incorporate himself with an Indian tribe, be adopted by it and become a member of the tribe. After adoption he is subject to all the burdens, and entitled to all the immunities of native born citizens or subjects. U. S. *v.* Ragsdale, Hemp. 497.

Naturalization.

(*d*) The power of naturalization is vested exclusively in Congress. Chirac *v.* Chirac, 2 Wheat. 259; U. S. *v.* Villato, 2 Dall. 370; Dred Scott *v.* Sanford, 19 How. 393; Matthews *v.* Ray, 3 Cranch C. C. 699; contra, Collet *v.* Collet, 2 Dall. 294.

The object to be attained by the exercise of the power of naturalization is to make citizens of the respective States. Ex parte Frank Knowles, 5 Cal. 300.

If the language is examined closely and according to the rules of rigid construction always applicable to delegated powers, it will be found that the power to naturalize in fact is not given to Congress, but simply the power to establish a uniform rule. The States are not forbidden to naturalize, nor is there anything in the exercise of the power by them incongruous or incompatible with the power of Congress to establish a uniform rule. That the States, if they choose to exercise the power as an original one, must abide by the rule which Congress makes, there can not be the slightest difference of opinion. The power given to Congress was intended to provide a rule for the action of the States, and not a rule for the action of the Federal Government. Ex parte Frank Knowles, 5 Cal. 300.

The power granted to Congress to establish an uniform system of naturalization is, by the well understood meaning of the word, confined to persons born in a foreign country under a foreign government. Dred Scott *v.* Sandford, 19 How. 393; U. S. *v.* Rhodes, 1 Abb. C. C. 281.

Indians may be naturalized by the authority of Congress like the subjects of any other foreign government, and become citizens of a State and of the United States. Dred Scott *v.* Sandford, 19 How. 393.

Congress has the power to admit by law to the rights of American citizenship, entire classes or races who were born and continue to reside within the United States, or upon soil acquired by the general government. Races, tribes and communities, irrespective of color, have been admitted in mass and by a single act of national sovereignty in repeated instances. People *v.* Washington, 36 Cal. 658.

Congress has the power by statute to confer the rights of citizenship upon all native born persons, now that the disability of slavery has been removed. People *v.* Washington, 36 Cal. 658.

Congress having power to make a uniform rule has the right to make the exercise of it a judicial power, and fix upon the class of courts which may be invested with the jurisdiction. This it can do as a part of the rule, although it may not directly confer the jurisdiction. Ex parte Frank Knowles, 5 Cal. 300; Ex parte Beavins, 33 N. H. 89.

Congress has the power to impart validity to an act which it may authorize a State tribunal to perform, although it may assume the form of a judicial act. If a State court has inherent jurisdiction adequate to the performance of everything required to be done in the process of naturalization, Congress may empower it to naturalize aliens and give validity to the act when done. Morgan v. Dudley, 18 B. Mon. 693; Rump v. Comm. 30 Penn. 475.

If a State law gives jurisdiction to the courts enumerated in the act of Congress, they may entertain proceedings for naturalization. Ex parte Frank Knowles, 5 Cal. 300; Rump v. Comm. 30 Penn. 475.

The Constitution does not point out any State functionaries or any State action as necessary or requisite to carry this power into effect. No power is conferred on Congress to require the aid of the States in its execution, while full power is conferred on Congress for that purpose. The States can not, therefore, be compelled to enforce the enactments of a uniform system of naturalization. Ex parte Beavins, 33 N. H. 89.

No State can confer the jurisdiction to entertain proceedings for naturalization on any tribunal which does not come within the terms of the act of Congress. State v. Whittemore, 50 N. H. 245.

A State may prohibit its courts from entertaining proceedings for naturalization. Ex parte Alexander Stephens, 70 Mass. 559; Ex parte Beavins, 33 N. H. 89.

Previous to the adoption of the Constitution, every State had the right to confer on whomsoever it pleased the character of citizen, and endow him with all its right. This power was not surrendered by the adoption of the Constitution. Each State may still confer the rights and privileges of a citizen upon an alien or any one it thinks proper, or upon any class or description of persons. No State however can, by naturalizing an alien, invest him with the rights and privileges secured to a citizen of a State under the Federal Government, although so far as the State alone is concerned he would be entitled to the rights of a citizen, and clothed with all the rights and immunities which the Constitution and the laws of the State attach to that character. The rights which he would acquire would be restricted to the State which gave them. Dred Scott v. Sandford, 19 How. 393; Ex parte Carl Wehlitz, 16 Wis. 443; Vaux v. Nesbit, 1 McCord Ch. 352.

The rights of citizenship which a State may confer within its own limits must not be confounded with the rights of citizenship as a member of the Union. It does not by any means follow because a person has all the rights and privileges of a citizen of a State, that he must be a citizen of the United States. Dred Scott v. Sandford, 19 How. 393.

A State by conferring the right to vote on aliens, thereby gives them an equal voice with any other citizen in the Government of the United States. Ex parte Carl Wehlitz, 16 Wis. 443.

No State can make the subject of a foreign prince a citizen of the State in any other mode than that provided by the naturalization laws of Congress. Lans *v.* Randall, 3 Cent. L. J. 688.

No State can superadd to the naturalization laws of Congress any requisitions before an alien can be relieved from the incapacities of alienage, and acquire the privileges and immunities of citizens. Comm. *v.* Towles, 5 Leigh, 743.

Bankruptcy.

(*e*) The subject is divisible in its nature into bankrupt and insolvent laws, though the line of partition between them is not so distinctly marked as to enable any person to say with positive precision what belongs exclusively to one and not to the other class of laws. The difficulty of discriminating with any accuracy between insolvent and bankrupt laws would lead to the opinion that a bankrupt law may contain those regulations which are generally found in insolvent laws, and that an insolvent law may contain those which are common to a bankrupt law. Sturges *v.* Crowninshield, 4 Wheat. 122.

The word bankruptcy is employed in the Constitution in the plural and as part of an expression, "the subject of bankruptcies." The ideas attached to the word in this connection are numerous and complicated. They form a subject of extensive and complicated legislation. Of this subject Congress has general jurisdiction. In re Edward Klein, 1 How. 277, note; s. c. 2 N. Y. Leg. Obs. 185; In re Silverman, 4 B. R. 523; s. c. 1 Saw. 410; 2 Abb. C. C. 243.

Bankruptcy bears a meaning co-extensive with insolvency, and is equivalent to that word in the Constitution. Kunzler *v.* Kohaus, 5 Hill, 317; Sackett *v.* Andross, 5 Hill, 327; Morse *v.* Hovey, 1 Barb. Ch. 404; s. c. 1 Sandf. Ch. 187.

The grant is a grant of plenary power over the "subject of bankruptcies." The subject of bankruptcies includes the distribution of the property of the fraudulent or insolvent debtor among his creditors, and the discharge of the debtor from his contracts and legal liabilities, as well as all the intermediate and incidental matters tending to the accomplishment or promotion of these two principal ends. Congress is given full power over this subject, with the one qualification, that its laws thereon shall be uniform throughout the United States. In re Silverman, 4 B. R. 523; s. c. 1 Saw. 410; 2 Abb. C. C. 243; In re Reiman & Friedlander, 11 B. R. 21; s. c. 13 B. R. 128; 7 Ben. 455; 12 Blatch. 562.

The power of Congress extends to all cases where the law causes the property of a debtor to be distributed among his creditors. This is its least limit. Its greatest is a discharge of the debtor from his contracts. All intermediate legislation affecting substance and form, but tending to further the great end of the subject—distribution and discharge—is in the competency and discretion of Congress. In re Edward Klein, 1 How. 277, note; S. C. 2 N. Y. Leg. Obs. 185; In re Silverman, 4 B. R. 523; S. C. 1 Saw. 410; 2 Abb. C. C. 243.

To this power there is no limitation, and consequently it is competent for Congress to act on the whole subject of bankruptcy with a plenary discretion. In re Irwine, 1 Penn. L. J. 291.

The power conferred is without restriction, save in its uniformity. It is plenary, and in reference to its subject may be exercised with the same latitude as the like power has been and may be by the British Parliament. Kunzler v. Kohaus, 5 Hill, 317; In re Edward Klein, 1 How. 277, note; S. C. 2 N. Y. Leg. Obs. 185.

Congress in passing laws on the subject of bankruptcies is not restricted to laws with such scope only as the English bankrupt laws had when the Constitution was adopted. The power is general, unlimited and unrestricted over the subject. In re Silverman, 4 B. R. 523; S. C. 1 Saw. 410; 2 Abb. C. C. 243; In re Reiman & Friedlander, 11 B. R. 21; S. C. 13 B. R. 128; 7 Ben. 455; 12 Blatch. 562; Thompson v. Alger, 53 Mass. 428.

The framers of the Constitution did not intend to limit the power to any particular class of persons. Morse v. Hovey, 1 Sandf. Ch. 187; S. C. 1 Barb. Ch. 404; In re Edward Klein, 1 How. 277, note; S. C. 2 N. Y. Leg. Obs. 185; Kunzler v. Kohaus, 5 Hill, 317; In re California Pacific R. R. Co. 11 B. R. 193; In re Silverman, 4 B. R. 523; S. C. 1 Saw. 410; 2 Abb. C. C. 243.

It is not necessary that a bankrupt law shall provide for the debtor's discharge. In re California Pacific R. R. Co. 11 B. R. 193.

Congress may establish a system of voluntary as well as involuntary bankruptcy. Loud v. Pierce, 25 Me. 233; Lalor v. Wattles, 8 Ill. 225; Kunzler v. Kohaus, 5 Hill, 317; In re Edward Klein, 1 How. 277, note; S. C. 2 N. Y. Leg. Obs. 185; Morse v. Hovey, 1 Sandf. Ch. 187; S. C. 1 Barb. Ch. 404; Thompson v. Alger, 53 Mass. 428; State Bank v. Wilborn, 6 Ark. 35; Keene v. Mould, 16 Ohio, 12; Cutter v. Folsom, 17 N. H. 139; McCormick v. Pickering, 4 N. Y. 276; Rowan v. Holcomb, 16 Ohio, 463; Dresser v. Brooks, 3 Barb. 429; Hastings v. Fowler, 2 Ind. 216; Reed v. Vaughan, 15 Mo. 137; In re Irwine, 1 Penn. L. J. 291.

The directly granted power over bankruptcies carries the incidental authority to modify the obligation of contracts so far as the modification may result from a legitimate exercise of the delegated power. A discharge may therefore be granted releasing the debtor from contracts subsisting at the time when the law was passed. Kunzler v. Kohaus, 5 Hill, 317; Sackett v. Andross, 5 Hill, 327; In re Edward Klein, 1 How. 277, note; S. C. 2 N. Y. Leg. Obs. 185; Morse v. Hovey, 1 Sandf. Ch. 187; S. C. 1 Barb. Ch.

404; Loud *v.* Pierce, 25 Me. 233; Keene *v.* Mould, 16 Ohio, 12; McCormick *v.* Pickering, 4 N. Y. 276; In re Irwine, 1 Penn. L. J. 291.

Congress may pass a law which will have the effect to make void an assignment which is valid under the State laws. In re Henry Brenneman, Crabbe, 456.

The power to enact a bankrupt law implies the power to make it efficient. The end implies the means. Russell *v.* Cheatham, 16 Miss. 703.

Congress has the power not only to establish uniform laws on the subject of bankruptcies, but also to commit the execution of the system to such Federal courts as it may see fit, and to prescribe such modes of procedure and means of administering the system as it may deem best suited to carry the law into successful operation. Sherman *v.* Bingham, 5 B. R. 34; S. C. 7 B. R. 490; S. C. 3 C. L. N. 258; Goodall *v.* Tuttle, 7 B. R. 193; S. C. 3 Biss. 219; Mitchell *v.* Manuf. Co. 2 Story, 648.

Congress has the power to define what and how much of the debtor's property shall be exempt from the claims of his creditors. In re Reiman & Friedlander, 11 B. R. 21; S. C. 13 B. R. 128; 7 Ben. 455; 12 Blatch. 562.

To come within the constitutional provision a bankrupt law must be a uniform law throughout the United States. A law which prescribes one rule in one district and a different one in another can not be regarded as a uniform law. Kittredge *v.* Warren, 14 N. H. 509.

The law established by Congress on the subject of bankruptcies under the power conferred by the Constitution must, indeed, be uniform throughout the United States. But the extent to which this power shall be exercised rests in the discretion of Congress. Uniformity is required in the national legislation only, and the laws of the several States may be left in force so long and to such extent as Congress may see fit. Day *v.* Bardwell, 3 B. R. 455; S. C. 97 Mass. 246.

The system of bankruptcy is, in a relative sense, uniform throughout the United States, when the assignee takes in each State whatever would have been available to the recourse of execution creditors if the bankrupt law had never been passed. Though the States vary in the extent of their exemptions, yet what remains the bankrupt law distributes equally among the creditors. The bankrupt act does not in any way vary or change the rights of the parties. All contracts are made with reference to existing laws, and no creditor could recover more from his debtor than the unexempted part of his assets, and as the thing is attained by the bankrupt law, it is uniform. In re Beckerford, 4 B. R. 203; S. C. 1 Dillon, 45; 1 L. T. B. 241; In re Jordan, 8 B. R. 180; In re Appold, 1 B. R. 621; S. C. 1 L. T. B. 83; 6 Phila. 469; In re Ruth, 1 B. R. 154; S. C. 7 A. L. Reg. 157; In re Wylie,

5 L. T. B. 330; In re Daniel Deckert, 10 B. R. 1 ; S. C. 1 A. L. T. (N. S.) 336; 9 A. L. J. 390; 6 C. L. N. 310.

A bankrupt law, to be constitutional, must be uniform, and whatever rule it prescribes for one, it must for all. If it provides that certain kinds of property shall not be assets under the law in one place, it must make the same provision for every other place within which it is to have effect. The provision that in each State property specified in the laws thereof, whether actually exempted by virtue thereof or not, shall be exempted, is unconstitutional and void. In re Daniel Deckert, 10 B. R. 1; S. C. 1 A. L. T. (N. S.) 336: 9 A. L. J. 390; 6 C. L. N. 310; In re Kerr & Roach, 9 B. R. 566; In re Geo. W. Dillard, 9 B. R. 8; s. c. 6 L. T. B. 490; In re Geo. T. Duerson, 13 B. R. 183; In re Shipman, 14 B. R. 570; Bush v. Lester, 55 Geo. 579; contra, In re Kean et al. 8 B. R. 367; In re John W. Smith, 8 B. R. 401; s. c. 6 C. L. N. 33; In re Willis A. Jordan, 10 B. R. 427; In re John W. A. Smith, 14 B. R. 295.

The uniformity required is as to the general policy and operation of the law. The bankrupt act in some minor particulars must necessarily operate differently in the different States. Thus, the bankrupt law regards as valid the legal and equitable liens existing by law in the several States, and as the nature, force and effect of such liens are dependent upon the local laws, they will in some respects be different in the different States. In re Jordan, 8 B. R. 180.

State Insolvent Laws.

The power granted to Congress may be exercised or declined as the wisdom of that body shall decide. If, in the opinion of Congress, uniform laws concerning bankruptcies ought not to be established, it does not follow that partial laws may not exist, or that State legislation on the subject must cease. It is not the mere existence of the power, but its exercise, which is incompatible with the exercise of the same power by the States. It is not the right to establish these uniform laws, but their actual establishment which is inconsistent with the partial acts of the States. Sturges v. Crowninshield, 4 Wheat. 122; Blanchard v. Russell, 13 Mass. 1 ; Farmer's Bank v. Smith, 3 S. & R. 63; Betts v. Bagley, 29 Mass. 572 ; Adams v. Storey, 1 Paine, 79; Pugh v. Bussel, 2 Blackf. 294 ; Alexander v. Gibson, 1 N. & McC. 480; contra, Vanuxem v. Hazelhursts, 4 N. J. 192; Oldens v. Hallet, 5 N. J. 466 ; Golden v. Prince, 3 Wash. 313; Mason v. Nash, 1 Breese, 16 ; Ballantine v. Haight, 16 N. J. 196.

One prominent reason why the power was given to Congress, was to secure to the people of the United States as one people, a uniform law by which a debtor might be discharged from his previous engagements, and his future acquisitions exempted from his previous engagements. The rights of debtor and creditor equally entered into the minds of the framers of the Constitution. The great object was to deprive the States of the dangerous power to abolish debts. In re Edward Klein, 1 How. 277, note; s. c. 2 N. Y. Leg. Obs. 185.

The peculiar terms of the grant deserve notice. Congress is not authorized merely to pass laws the operation of which shall be uniform, but to establish uniform laws on the subject throughout the United States. This establishment of uniformity is perhaps incompatible with State legislation on that part of the subject to which the acts of Congress may extend. Sturges *v.* Crowninshield, 4 Wheat. 122.

The right of the States to pass a bankrupt law is not extinguished but merely suspended by the enactment of a general bankrupt law. The repeal of that law can not confer the power on the States, but it removes a disability to its exercise, which was created by the act of Congress. Sturges *v.* Crowninshield, 4 Wheat. 122.

The bankrupt act, as soon as it took effect *ipso facto*, suspended all action upon future cases arising under the insolvent laws of the State, where the insolvent laws act upon the same subject-matter and the same persons as the bankrupt act; and all proceedings upon such cases commenced under the State laws after that time are null and void. Commonwealth *v.* O'Hara, 1 B. R. 86; s. c. 7 A. L. Reg. 765; 6 Phila. 402; Perry *v.* Langley, 1 B. R. 559; s. c. 1 L. T. B. 34; 7 A. L. Reg. 429; Van Nostrand *v.* Carr, 2 B. R. 485; s. c. 30 Md. 128; Martin *v.* Berry, 2 B. R. 629; s. c. 37 Cal. 208; 2 L. T. B. 180; Corner *v.* Miller et al. 1 B. R. 403; Shears *v.* Solhinger, 10 Abb. Pr. (N. S.) 287; in re Reynolds, 9 B. R. 50; s. c. 8 R. I. 485; in re Lucius Eames, 2 Story, 322; Bishop *v.* Loewen, 2 Penn. L. J. 364; Griswold *v.* Pratt, 49 Mass. 16; Rowe *v.* Page, 13 B. R. 366; s. c. 54 N. H. 190.

The State insolvent laws are not entirely abrogated. They exist and operate with full vigor until the bankrupt law attaches upon the person and property of the debtor. In re John Zeigenfuss, 2 Ired. 463; Reed *v.* Taylor, 4 B. R. 710; s. c. 32 Iowa, 209.

Two statutes having the same general object, and acting upon the same persons and the same cases, by different modes and in different jurisdictions, must be in conflict with each other. Though the modes by which the remedy is administered may vary, yet, where the bankrupt act and the State insolvent law have substantially the same scope and object, and act upon the same persons and cases, the State insolvent law is suspended. The act of Congress is both a bankrupt act and an insolvent act. Martin *v.* Berry, 2 B. R. 629; s. c. 37 Cal. 208; 2 L. T. B. 180; Van Nostrand *v.* Carr, 2 B. R. 485; s. c. 30 Md. 128.

The jurisdiction of the bankrupt act does not depend upon the right of the debtor to ultimately obtain a discharge. If his case comes within the provisions of the bankrupt act, he can not obtain a discharge under the State insolvent law, even though his assets are not sufficient to pay thirty per centum on the claims that may be proved against his estate. Van Nostrand *v.* Carr, 2 B. R. 485; s. c. 30 Md. 128.

If a State court has acquired jurisdiction, under a State law, of a case in insolvency, and is engaged in settling the debts and distributing the assets of the insolvent before or at the date at which the act of Congress upon the same subject takes effect, the State court may, nevertheless, proceed with the case to its final conclusion, and its action in the matter will be as valid as if no law upon the subject had been passed by Congress. Martin *v.* Berry, 2 B. R. 629; s. c. 37 Cal. 208; 2 L. T. B. 180; Meekins, Kelly & Co. *v.* Creditors, 3 B. R. 511; s. c. 19 La. Ann. 497; In re Eli Horton, 5 Law Rep. 462; In re Bela Judd, 5 Law Rep. 328; West *v.* Creditors, 5 Rob. (La.) 261; s. c. 8 Rob. (La.) 123; Dwight *v.* Simon, 4 La. Ann. 490; Larrabee *v.* Talbot, 5 Gill, 426; Lavender *v.* Gosnell, 12 B R. 282; s. c. 43 Md. 153; Longis *v.* Creditors, 20 La. Ann. 15.

If the debtor was divested of his property under the State insolvent law at the time of the adoption of the bankrupt law, the jurisdiction of the State court is not affected thereby. Judd *v.* Ives, 45 Mass. 401.

All proceedings on a petition to compel an insolvent debtor to surrender his property, which are pending at the time when the proceedings in bankruptcy were commenced, should be stayed until an assignee is appointed. West *v.* Creditors, 4 Rob. (La.) 88; s. c. 8 Rob. (La.) 123.

The jurisdiction of the State court attaches from the moment when it makes the order staying the creditors from all interference with the property of the debtor. From that time the State court has the legal custody and control of his estate. Martin *v.* Berry, 2 B. R. 629; s. c. 37 Cal. 208; 2 L. T. B. 180; Meekins, Kelly & Co. *v.* Creditors, 3 B. R. 511; s. c. 19 La. Ann. 497.

A suit to compel a new surrender is a new suit, and not a continuation of the suit in insolvency previously pending. The suspension of the State insolvent law by the enactment of the bankrupt law before the surrender was ordered, divested the State court of its jurisdiction over cases previously instituted, and no further proceedings can be had therein. Fisk *v.* Montgomery, 21 La. Ann. 446.

The State laws relating to insolvent corporations were superseded. The State courts have jurisdiction as far as the forfeiture of the charter of a corporation for insolvency is concerned; but with the decree of forfeiture their jurisdiction ends. They can not go on and administer upon the property of a corporation as the property of an insolvent corporation, for the insolvent laws of a State touching corporations are no longer in force. Thornhill et al. *v.* Bank of Louisiana et al. 3 B. R. 435; s. c. 5 B. R. 367;

1 Woods, 1; 1 L. T. B. 156; 3 L. T. B. 38; In re Merchants' Ins. Co. 6 B. R. 43; S. C. 3 Biss. 162; 2 L. T. B. 243.

The treatment which a corporation may receive at the hands of the State court can not avail to sustain that court's control over the assets. If the fact of insolvency exists, and the corporation is within the provisions of the bankrupt law, the Federal courts sitting in bankruptcy have exclusive jurisdiction of the property, and the fact that a State law does not purport or attempt to relieve the debtor from his debts can not be urged as a reason why the State court should hold the assets and administer them after proper proceedings in bankruptcy have been instituted in the Federal courts. So far as a State law attempts to administer on the effects of an insolvent debtor, and distribute them among creditors, it is, to all intents and purposes, an insolvent law, although it may not authorize the discharge of the debtor from further liability. If the fact of insolvency does not exist, the State court may probably have the right to administer the assets as an incident to a proceeding for the dissolution of the corporation, but when insolvency intervenes so as to make the debtor a proper subject for the operation of the bankrupt law, the exclusive jurisdiction of the bankrupt court attaches, and the State court, and those acting under its mandates, must surrender the control of the assets, whatever may be the final decree in regard to the continuance of the corporation. In re Merchants' Ins. Co. 6 B. R. 43; S. C. 3 Biss. 162; 2 L. T. B. 243; Thornhill et al. *v.* Bank of Louisiana et al. 3 B. R, 435; S. C. 5 B. R. 367; 1 Woods, 1; 1 L. T. B. 156; 3 L. T. B. 38; in re Independent Ins. Co. 6 B. R. 169, 260; S. C. 1 Holmes, 103; 2 Lowell, 97; Platt *v.* Archer, 6 B. R. 465; S. C. 9 Blatch. 559; Shryock *v.* Bashore, 13 B. R. 481.

A proceeding in bankruptcy is not the exclusive method of winding up insolvent corporations. The bankrupt act does not *ipso facto* suspend State laws for the collection of debts. Chandler *v.* Siddle, 10 B. R. 236; S. C. 3 Dillon, 477.

A State law to abolish imprisonment on civil process in certain cases, which is limited to the single instance of involuntary confinement, and whose aim and purpose is simply to liberate the person, is not superseded. Steelman *v.* Mattix, 36 N. J. 344; Shears *v.* Solhinger, 10 Abb. Pr. (N. S.) 287; in re Reynolds, 9 B. R. 50; S. C. 8 R. I. 485; Jordan *v.* Hall, 9 R. I. 218; in re Rank, Crabbe, 493.

If the distribution of the property is merely incidental to the release of the person from imprisonment, and the debt is not discharged, the proceeding is not a proceeding in bankruptcy. Steelman *v.* Mattix, 36 N. J. 344.

The bankrupt act can not affect the determination of a debtor's right to be discharged by taking the poor debtor's oath, and of his liability to imprisonment by way of punishment for fraud, upon proceedings which were commenced before the act took effect. Stockwell *v.* Silloway, 100 Mass. 287.

In an action on a bond given on the arrest of the debtor, and conditioned that he will apply for the benefit of the State insolvent laws, a plea that he has since obtained a discharge under the bankrupt law is a valid plea, unless the debt is one that is not released by a discharge. Hubert *v.* Horter, 14 B. R. 430; s. c. 81 Penn. 39; Barber *v.* Rogers, 71 Penn. 362 ; Nesbit *v.* Greaves, 6 W. & S. 120.

A bond to apply for the benefit of the State insolvent laws, and if he fails to be discharged to surrender himself to the sheriff, is valid. The undertaking is in the alternative, either to obtain a discharge or to return to the condition from which he was released. If he can not apply for the benefit of the State insolvent laws because they are suspended, he must perform the other alternative of the condition. Steelman *v.* Mattix, 36 N. J. 344.

A State insolvent law which merely protects the person from imprisonment, without affecting contracts, is not superseded, although it also provides for the distribution of the debtor's property. Sullivan *v.* Hieskill, Crabbe, 525 ; s. c. 4 Penn. L. J. 171.

A State law providing for the arrest and punishment of fraudulent debtors is not suspended by the bankrupt law, Scully *v.* Kirkpatrick, 79 Penn. 324.

The bankrupt law does not supersede the State laws relating to the settlement of the insolvent estate of lunatics, spendthrifts or deceased persons. Hawkins *v.* Learned, 54 N. H. 333.

A State law which makes a transfer by an insolvent with intent to give a preference, operate as an assignment for the benefit of all creditors, is not an insolvent law and is not superseded by the bankrupt law. Ebersole *v.* Adams, 13 B. R. 141 ; s. c. 10 Bush. 83; Linthicum *v.* Fenley, 11 Bush. 131.

The bankrupt law does not supersede a State law regulating assignments for the benefit of creditors. Mayer *v.* Hellman, 13 B. R. 440; s. c. 91 U. S. 496 ; in re Hawkins et al. 2 B. R. 378 ; s. c. 34 Conn. 548; Beck *v.* Parker, 65 Penn. 262; Maltbie *v.* Hotchkiss, 5 B. R. 485; s. c. 38 Conn. 80; Von Hein *v.* Elkus, 15 B. R. 195; s. c. 15 N. Y. Supr. 516.

The law allowing assignments for the benefit of creditors is not a part of the insolvent laws, and is not superseded by the bankrupt law. Cook *v.* Rogers, 13 B. R. 97; s. c. 31 Mich. 391; 14 A. L. Reg. 633.

A State law which provides the mode of apportioning the losses of a savings bank among the depositors, is valid although it was passed while the bankrupt law was in force. Simpson *v.* Savings Bank, 15 B. R. 385; s. c. 56 N. H. 466.

A provision in a State law, which prohibits an insolvent corporation from transferring its property with the intention of giving a preference, is superseded. French *v.* O'Brien, 52 How. Pr. 394.

An act which provides for the arrest of a debtor who removes or disposes of his property with the intent to defraud his creditors, is not superseded. Gregg *v.* Hilsen, 34 Leg. Int. 20.

An assignment made as a part of the machinery of a State insolvent law, and deriving all its validity and efficacy from the statute is void. Shryock *v.* Bashore, 13 B. R. 481; S. C. 15 B. R. 283; 82 Penn. 159; Rowe *v.* Page, 13 B. R. 366; s. C. 54 N. H. 190.

Whether an assignment in proceedings under a State insolvent law is void, is a question that may be raised in a collateral action. Shryock *v.* Bashore, 13 B. R. 481; S. C. 15 B. R. 283; 82 Penn. 159.

The insolvent laws are no further suspended than they seek upon notorious grounds to seize and distribute the effects of the debtor among his creditors generally. A statute for the more effectual appropriation of a debtor's property to satisfy an individual debt is not suspended. Berthelon *v.* Betts, 4 Hill, 577.

The State insolvent laws were not suspended until June 1, 1867. Day *v.* Bardwell et al, 3 B. R. 455; S. C. 97 Mass. 246; Martin *v.* Berry, 2 B. R. 629; s. C. 37 Cal. 208; 2 L. T. B. 180; Chamberlain *v.* Perkins, 51 N. H. 336; Augsbury *v.* Crossman, 17 N. Y. Supr. 387.

The State laws are operative to some extent and for some purposes. They are clearly operative in all cases which are not within the provisions of the bankrupt law. Shepardson's Appeal, 36 Conn. 23; Clarke *v.* Ray, 1 H. & J. 318; in re Winternitz, 4 B. R. (quarto), 127; S. C. 18 Pitts. L. J. 61.

The bankrupt law applies only to cases where the debtor owes debts provable under the act exceeding the amount of three hundred dollars. When the debts do not exceed that amount, the case is not within the purview of the act. Before proceedings under the State law can be held to be erroneous, it must affirmatively appear that the debts are more than that amount. Until then there is no conflict of laws, and courts will not presume that the debts are more or less than that amount. Shepardson's Appeal, 36 Conn. 23.

The State insolvent laws are still in force so far as they affect debts that will not be released by a discharge under the bankrupt act, such as debts created by the fraud of the bankrupt. Where the bankrupt act expressly excepts a class of cases, it must have been the intention of Congress not to interfere, in such specified class, with the laws of the several States. A party imprisoned under a judgment founded npon a fraudulent debt, may take the benefit of the State insolvent laws for the purpose ot obtaining a release and discharge from that debt. In re Winternitz, 4 B. R. (quarto), 127; s. c. 18 Pitts. L. J. 61; Stepp v. Stahl, 2 W. N. 80.

The State insolvent laws are suspended even as between citizens of the same State. Cassard et al. v. Kroner, 4 B. R. 569.

An attachment law which permits a writ of attachment to issue for the causes which would be sufficient to authorize the institution of proceedings in involuntary bankruptcy, and authorizes the distribution of the property equally among all the creditors, is superseded. Tobin v. Trump, 3 Brews. 288; s. c. 7 Phila. 123.

There is a material distinction between discharging a debtor and distributing his assets among his creditors. The bankrupt act was demanded and passed mainly for the former. The latter is in its nature incidental to the former, which is the principal thing. There probably existed in every State, at the time of the passage of the bankrupt law, some statutory provisions for the distribution of the effects of insolvent debtors among their creditors, and it can hardly be supposed that Congress intended to repeal or suspend those State laws, except so far as was necessary for the accomplishment of the main object in view, and that necessity may well be limited to those cases over which the Federal courts actually assert their jurisdiction within the time limited for that purpose. An assignment under the State law is good unless attacked within six months. If all the parties concerned desire that the estate may be settled in the State courts, it can be done. Should a case arise in which there will be an actual conflict of jurisdiction, the State courts must yield to the Federal courts, and when the bankrupt court, within the time limited, asserts its jurisdiction, the proceedings in the State court are thereby superseded. Should the State courts attempt to grant a certificate of discharge to an insolvent debtor, no court would give any effect to it. Maltbie v. Hotchkiss, 5 B. R. 485; s. c. 38 Conn. 80; Reed v. Taylor, 4 B. R. 710; s. c. 32 Iowa, 209.

If the debtor has not committed an act of bankruptcy, and declines to go into voluntary bankruptcy, a creditor may proceed against him under the State insolvent law, where such proceedings are in harmony with the purpose of the bankrupt law, for the State insolvent law remains in full force in respect to all persons and matters over which the bankrupt law declines to take jurisdiction. Geery's Appeal, 43 Conn. 289.

Whether a State insolvent law is unconstitutional is a question that can not be raised by the defendant in an action by an insolvent trustee to recover a debt due to the estate. Shryock v. Bashore, 13 B. R. 48; s. c. 15 B. R. 283; 82 Penn. 159.

As a bankrupt law merely suspends State insolvent laws without repealing them, they revive and are in force on the repeal of the bankrupt law, and need not be re-enacted. Lavender v. Gosnell, 12 B. R. 282; s. c. 43 Md. 153.

The bankrupt law must prevail in cases where it conflicts with the ordinance of 1787. Stow v. Parks, 1 Chand. 60.

Currency.

(*f*) The term money is used in different places in the Constitution, as it is elsewhere, in somewhat different senses. Here, however, it means metallic money—gold, silver and copper, or the metals used for coin, and no more. The phrase "coining" can not, without violence, be applied to the issue of paper money. To coin money is to make, stamp and issue coins as money. Coins are pieces of metal of a particular weight and standard, and to which a particular value is given in account and payment. The clause which follows, "to regulate the value thereof," evidently means to authorize the regulation of the value of the coins thus issued or the money coined, and that is metallic money. Metropolitan Bank v. Van Dyck, 27 N. Y. 400; Hague v. Powers, 39 Barb. 427; Thayer v. Hedges, 22 Ind. 282; Maynard v. Newman, 1 Nev. 271.

The National Government is to "coin money," that is, to fix the national stamp upon the metals which are to be used as money, to determine the character of the national currency, and what shall be the measure or standard of value, and what the different kinds used for money, and into what denominations the money shall be divided, or of what it shall consist. Hague v. Powers, 39 Barb. 427; Griswold v. Hepburn, 2 Duval, 20.

The language of the Constitution, by its proper signification, is limited to the faculty in Congress of coining and of stamping the standard of value upon what the Government creates or shall adopt, and of punishing the offense of producing a false representation of what may have been so created or adopted. Fox v. State, 5 How. 410.

The Constitution clearly designed to take all questions of currency, whether paper or metal, from the several States; and it is in the discretion of Congress to make of its tokens, whether of one substance or another, tenders in such amounts and for such purposes as may be determined upon. Van Husan v. Kanouse, 13 Mich. 303.

The power to regulate the value of money is without any limitation or restriction whatever. On that subject Congress has as supreme and unlimited powers as any sovereignty in the world. George v. Concord, 45 N. H. 434; Maynard v. Newman, 1 Nev. 271; Shollenberger v. Brinton, 52 Penn. 9.

The grant of the power to coin money does not contain an implied prohibition against the enactment of laws making treasury notes a legal tender. Legal Tender Cases, 12 Wall. 457.

The power to regulate the value of coin does not make that coin of necessity a legal tender at the value so fixed. Van Husan *v.* Kanouse, 13 Mich. 303.

The power to coin money is one power, and the power to declare anything a legal tender is another and different power. Thayer v. Hedges, 22 Ind. 282.

The power to declare what shall or shall not be a legal tender, or in other words lawful money of a country, is a necessary incident of sovereignty, and has ever been exercised by the sovereign power in all civilized nations. The power to make tender laws is an implied power, and may be derived from many of the express powers conferred upon Congress. Metropolitan Bank *v.* Van Dyck, 27 N. Y. 400; George *v.* Concord, 45 N. H. 434; Van Husan *v.* Kanouse, 13 Mich. 303; Maynard *v.* Newman, 1 Nev. 271; Shollenberger *v.* Brinton, 52 Penn. 9.

A statute making treasury notes a legal tender in time of war, with the design of preserving the Government, is valid. Dooley *v.* Smith, 13 Wall. 604; Railroad Co. *v.* Johnson, 15 Wall. 195; Legal Tender Cases, 12 Wall. 457; Black *v.* Lusk, 69 Ill. 70; Hague *v.* Powers, 39 Barb. 427; Reynolds *v.* Bank, 18 Ind. 467; Lick *v.* Faulkner, 25 Cal. 404; Curiac *v.* Albadie, 25 Cal. 502; Kierski *v.* Matthews, 25 Cal. 591; Thayer *v.* Hedges, 23 Ind. 141; George *v.* Concord, 45 N. H, 434; Latham *v.* U. S. 1 Ct. Cl. 149; S. C. 2 Ct. Cl. 573; Hintrager *v.* Bates, 18 Iowa, 174; Shollenberger *v.* Brinton, 52 Penn. 9; Jones *v.* Harker, 37 Geo. 503; contra, Hepburn *v.* Griswold, 8 Wall. 603; S. C. 2 Duval, 20.

The power to make treasury notes a legal tender is not to be resorted to except upon extraordinary and pressing occasions, such as war or other public exigencies of great gravity and importance, and should be no longer exerted than all the circumstances of the case demand. It is for the legislative department of the Government to judge of the occasions when, and of the times how long, it shall be exercised and in force. Legal Tender Cases, 12 Wall. 457.

There is no well-founded distinction between the constitutional validity of an act of Congress declaring treasury notes a legal tender for the payment of debts contracted after its passage, and that of an act making them a legal tender for the discharge of all debts, as well those incurred before as those made after its enactment. Legal Tender Cases, 12 Wall. 457.

The obligation of a contract to pay money, is to pay that which the law shall recognize as money when the payment is to be made. Every contract for the payment of money is subject to the constitutional power of the

Government over the currency, and the obligation of the parties is assumed with reference to that power. Legal Tender Cases, 12 Wall. 457.

The jurisdiction of the several States on the subject of taxation for all State purposes, is supreme, and over it the Federal Government has no power or control. If the State law requires the taxes to be paid in coin, its mandate must be obeyed, although Congress may have made something else a legal tender for debts. State *v.* Wright, 28 Ill. 509; Whitaker *v.* Haley, 2 Oregon, 128.

The power of coining money and regulating its value, was delegated to Congress by the Constitution, for the very purpose of creating and preserving the uniformity and purity of such a standard of value, and on account of the impossibility, which was foreseen, of otherwise preventing the inequalities and the confusion necessarily incident to different views of policy which in different communities would be brought to bear on this subject. The power to coin money being thus given to Congress, founded on public necessity, it must carry with it the correlative power of protecting the creature and object of that power. Hence Congress may provide for the punishment of the offense of uttering or circulating counterfeit coin. U. S. *v.* Marigold, 9 How. 560; Campbell *v.* U. S. 10 Law Rep. 400; contra, U. S. *v.* ———, 12 Law Rep. 90.

Weights.

(*g*) The States have the right to regulate weights and measures until Congress shall act on the subject. Weaver *v.* Fegley, 29 Penn. 27.

Counterfeiting.

(*h*) The term counterfeiting applies to the act of making, in contradistinction to the act of circulating, counterfeit coin. Campbell *v.* U. S. 10 Law Rep. 400.

There is a manifest distinction between counterfeiting and uttering false coin. The former is an offense directly against the Government, by which individuals may be affected; the latter is a private wrong by which the Government may be remotely, if it will in any degree, be reached. The criminality of the latter consists in obtaining, for a false representative of the true coin, that for which the true coin alone is the equivalent. The latter is an offense against the State, and may be punished by the laws of the State. Fox *v.* State, 5 How. 410; U. S. *v.* Marigold, 10 How 560; Harlan *v.* People, 1 Doug 207; State *v.* Antonio, 2 Tread. 776; People *v.* White, 34 Cal. 183; Sizemore *v.* State, 3 Head, 26.

A State may impose a penalty upon the act of keeping moulds and tools adapted and designed for producing counterfeit coin, coupled with the intent of using them for that purpose. State *v.* Brown, 2 Oregon, 221.

A State may punish the offense of keeping counterfeit coin with the intent to pass the same. Sizemore *v.* State, 3 Head, 26.

Congress has exclusive authority to declare the penalty for the acts necessary for the counterfeiting, that is, the making or producing of the false representation on metal, of the designs found on coin, and the Federal courts exclusive jurisdiction over its enforcement. State *v.* Brown, 2 Oregon, 221.

A national bank note is not current coin nor a security of the United States, and a State law to punish the counterfeiting thereof, is valid. State *v.* Randall, 2 Aik. 89.

Post-offices and Post-roads.

(*i*) The word "establish" means not merely to designate, but to create, erect, build, prepare, fix permanently. "To establish post-offices and post-roads," means *ex vi termini* not only the designation and adoption of an existing house and road for a post-office and a post-road, but also more comprehensively the renting or building of a house, and the construction and reparation of a road, and the appropriation of money for any of those national purposes whenever any of them shall be deemed useful. Dickey *v.* Turnpike Co. 7 Dana, 119.

The power to establish post-roads is something more than the power to establish post-offices. The former is as supreme and plenary as the latter, and both together were intended to embrace everything necessary and proper for regulating and transporting the mails in such manner as Congress might deem best. Dickey *v.* Turnpike Co. 7 Dana, 119.

The power to establish post-roads is deemed to be exhausted in the designation of roads on which the mails are to be transported. U. S. *v.* Railroad Bridge Co. 6 McLean, 517.

This comprehensive and express power was given not for authorizing the mere designation and use of State roads as post-roads, but for enabling the Government to make, repair and keep open such roads in every State as may, under any circumstances, be necessary for the most effectual and satisfactory fulfillment of the great national trust of transporting the national mails safely, certainly, speedily and punctually without any necessary dependence on the policy or will or purse of any one of the States. Searight *v.* Stokes, 3 How. 151; Neil *v.* State, 3 How. 720; Dickey *v.* Turnpike Co. 7 Dana, 119.

Congress has the power to make contracts relating to the establishment of post-roads. Searight *v.* Stokes, 3 How. 151.

A mail contractor can not use a road in a State without paying the same tolls as other citizens. Dickey *v.* Turnpike Co. 7 Dana, 119.

Congress has the power to authorize any telegraph company to construct, maintain and operate lines of telegraph along any of the military o post-roads of the United States. Pensacola Tel. Co. *v.* W. U. Tel. Co. Woods, 643.

Patents and Copyrights.

(*j*) The word "secure" does not mean the protection of an acknowledged legal right. Wheaton *v.* Peters, 8 Pet. 591.

No State can in any form interfere with the right of private persons under the copyright laws of the United States. Little *v.* Gould, 2 Blatch. 165, 362.

The Constitution does not authorize the protection of a dramatic composition which is grossly indecent and calculated to corrupt the morals of the people. Martinetti *v.* Maguire, 1 Deady, 216; s. c. 1 Abb. C. C, 356.

In the exercise of this power, Congress is limited to authors and inventors only. This clause, therefore, never can admit of so extensive a construction as to prohibit the respective States from exercising the power of securing to persons introducing useful inventions, without being the authors or inventors, the exclusive benefit of such inventions for a limited time. Livingston *v.* Van Ingen, 9 Johns. 507.

The power is general to grant to inventors, and it rests in the sound discretion of Congress to say when and for what length of time, and under what circumstances, the patent for an invention shall be granted. There is no restriction which limits the power of Congress to cases where the invention has not been known or used by the public. All that is required is that the patentee shall be the inventor. An act which gives a patent for an invention which was in public use and enjoyed by the community at the time of its passage, is not for that reason unconstitutional. Blanchard *v.* Sprague, 2 Story, 164; s. c. 3 Sum. 535; Evans *v.* Jordan, 1 Brock. 248; s. c. 9 Cranch, 199; Jordan *v.* Dobson, 4 Fish. 232; s. c. 27 Leg. Int. 292.

The power thus granted is domestic in its character, and necessarily confined within the limits of the United States. Brown *v.* Duchesne, 19 How. 183

This constitutional power might have been fully exercised by Congress in making special grants of patents.' Congress might have spent much time by such a course, and may not be the most competent body to investigate the facts and do equal justice to inventors, but this would be a question of expediency and not of constitutional power.' Bloomer *v.* Stolley, 5 McLean, 158.

The machinery through which the right to a patent is ordinarily applied for and obtained, may be dispensed with, and the title may be conferred by a legislative grant, and this may be done in regard to the extension of an exclusive right the same as in originally granting it. No constitutional restriction appears to exist against the exercise of this power by Congress. Bloomer *v.* Stolley, 5 McLean, 158.

Congress has the power to confer a new and extended term upon the patentee, even after the expiration of the first. Jordan *v.* Dobson. 4 Fish. 232; S. C. 27 Leg. Int. 292; Blanchard *v.* Haynes, 6 West. L. J. 82; Blanchard's Factory *v.* Warner, 1 Blatch. 258; Evans *v.* Robinson, 1 Car. Law Rep. 209.

The power of Congress to secure the rights and privileges of assignees upon extending a patent is incidental to the general power conferred by the Constitution on Congress to promote the progress of the useful arts by securing to inventors for limited times the exclusive right to their discoveries. The assignees of the original patentee are frequently most instrumental in putting the invention into general use, and bringing it successfully before the public by the expenditure of their time and money. More than half, probably, of the useful patented inventions have been thus brought into general public use, the successful results operating directly or indirectly for the benefit and interest of the patentees. Although this would not authorize the renewal of a grant to assignees, as no such power exists in the Constitution, still in exercising the power in favor of the inventor, it would be going too far to say that Congress has no right to regard incidentally the interests of meritorious assignees. Blanchard's Factory *v.* Warner, 1 Blatch. 258.

It is not the province of the judiciary to inquire into the reasons which induced the passage of the law, with the view of testing its validity. If constitutional, it must be enforced without regard to the policy or justice which dictated it. No inquiry as to the expenses and labor need be made when a patent is extended by a special act of Congress. Bloomer *v.* Stolley, 5 McLean, 158.

It does not follow from this power that Congress may from time to time, as they think proper, authorize an inventor to recall rights which he has granted to others, or reinvest in him rights of property which he has before conveyed for a fair and valuable consideration. Bloomer *v.* McQuewen, 14 How. 539.

Though changes in the patent laws may be retrospective in their operation, that is not a sound objection to their validity. The power of Congress to legislate upon the subject of patents is plenary by the terms of the Constitution, and as there are no restraints on its exercise, there can be no limitation of their right to modify them at their pleasure, so that they do not take away the rights of property in existing patents. M'Clurg *v.* Kingsland, 1 How. 202.

The property in inventions exists by virtue of the laws of Congress, and no State has a right to interfere with its enjoyment, or to annex conditions to the grant. If the patentee complies with the laws of Congress on the subject, he has a right to go into the open market anywhere within the United States, and sell his property. An act of a State legislature that attempts to direct the manner in which patent rights shall be sold in the State, is void. Ex parte Robinson, 4 Fish. 186; Hollida v. Hunt, 70 Ill. 109; Helm v. First National Bank, 43 Ind. 167; Crittenden v. White, 9 C. L. N. 110.

If a corporation is the owner of a patent, and its transactions in another State are connected with the sale, use or manufacture of the invention described in the patent, it is not subject to the provisions of the State laws relating to foreign corporations. Grover & Baker S. M. Co. v. Butler, 53 Ind. 454; Walter A. Wood Mowing Machine Co. v. Caldwell, 54 Ind 270.

No State can require that the consideration of a note given for a patent shall be expressed on the face thereof, and make such note subject in the hands of third parties to all defenses which could have been made against the payee. Hollida v. Hunt, 70 Ill. 109; Cranson v. Smith, 5 Cent. L. J. 386; s. c. 16 A. L. J. 330; Woolen v. Banker, 4 A. L. Rec. 236.

A State law regulating the sale of an article manufactured in pursuance of a patented invention, because it is dangerous, is valid, for there is a manifest distinction between the right of property in the patent and the right to sell the property resulting from the invention or patent. Patterson v. Comm. 11 Bush. 311.

The end of the statute is to encourage useful inventions, and to hold forth the exclusive use of his invention for a limited period as an inducement to the inventor. The sole operation of the statute is to enable him to prevent others from using the products of his labor except with his consent. But his own right of using it is not enlarged or affected. There remains in him, as in every other citizen, the power to manage his property or give direction to his labor at his pleasure, subject only to the paramount claims of society which require that his enjoyment may be modified by the exigencies of the community to which he belongs, and regulated by laws which render it subservient to the general welfare if held subject to State control. An attempt by the legislature in good faith, to regulate the conduct of a portion of its citizens in a matter strictly pertaining to its internal economy, is a legitimate exercise of power, although the law may sometimes indirectly affect the enjoyment of rights flowing from the Federal Government. A patent for a medicine does not confer upon the patentee the right to prescribe it for the sick without complying with the State laws for licensing physicians. Jordan v. Dayton, 4 Ohio, 294.

The right of property in an invention or discovery does not imply the unlimited power of using it. Its use is subject to the laws and under the control of the several States. Livingston v. Van Ingen, 9 Johns. 507.

A patent for a plan for constructing and drawing lotteries does not authorize the patentee to establish a lottery in a State whose laws prohibit lotteries on the ground that they are pernicious and destructive to frugality and industry, and introductive of idleness and immorality, and against the common good and general welfare. Vannini v. Paine, 1 Harrington, 65.

Piracy.

(*k*) Congress need not define in terms the offense of piracy, but may leave it to be ascertained by judicial interpretation. U. S. v. Smith, 5 Wheat. 153; U. S. v. Furlong, 5 Wheat. 184.

To define piracies in the sense of the Constitution is merely to enumerate the crimes which shall constitute piracy, and this may be done either by a reference to crimes having a technical name and determinate extent, or by enumerating the acts in detail upon which the punishment is inflicted. U. S. v. Smith, 5 Wheat. 153.

Congress may provide for the punishment of a conspiracy to burn a vessel with intent to injure underwriters. U. S. v. Cole, 5 McLean, 513.

Congress has the power to punish an attempt to commit a mutiny and revolt on a vessel on the high seas. U. S. v. Crawford, 1 N. Y. Leg. Obs. 288.

War.

(*l*) Congress alone has the power to declare a national or foreign war. Perkins v. Rogers, 35 Ind. 124; Prize Cases, 2 Black. 635; The Tropic Wind, 24 Law Rep. 144.

The authority to suppress rebellion may be found in the power to declare war. Texas v. White, 7 Wall. 700; contra, Norris v. Doniphan, 4 Met. (Ky.) 385.

War declared by Congress is not the only war within the contemplation of the Constitution. The Tropic Wind, 24 Law Rep. 144.

Rebels are at the same time belligerents and traitors, and subject to the liabilities of both; while the United States sustains the double character of a belligerent and sovereign, and has the rights of both. These rights co-exist, and may be exercised at pleasure. Prize Cases, 2 Black. 635; The Amy Warwick, 2 Sprague, 123.

The power to declare war involves the power to prosecute it by all means and in any manner in which war may be legitimately prosecuted. It, therefore, includes the right to seize and confiscate all property of an enemy, and to dispose of it at the will of the captor. Miller v. U. S. 11 Wall. 268.

Congress has the power to confiscate the property of public enemies, whether the war is a civil or a foreign war. Miller v. U. S. 11 Wall. 268; Tyler v. Defrees, 11 Wall. 331; Prize Cases, 2 Black. 635; The Ned, 1 Blatch. Pr. 119.

The Constitution confers absolutely on the Government the powers of making war and of making treaties; consequently it possesses the power of acquiring territory either by conquest or by treaty. Am. Ins. Co. v. Canter, 1 Pet. 511; Fleming v. Page, 9 How. 603.

Under the power to "declare war," Congress has the power to make treasury notes a legal tender for public and private debts. Legal Tender Cases, 12 Wall. 457; Dooley v. Smith, 13 Wall. 604; Railroad Co. v. Johnson, 15 Wall. 195; Black v. Lusk, 69 Ill. 70; Hague v. Powers, 39 Barb. 427; Reynolds v. Bank, 18 Ind. 467; Lick v. Faulkner, 25 Cal. 404; Curiac v. Abadie, 25 Cal. 502; Kierski v. Mathews, 25 Cal. 591; Thayer v. Hedges, 23 Ind. 141; George v. Concord, 45 N. H. 434; Hintrager v. Bates, 18 Iowa, 174; Shollenberger v. Brinton, 52 Penn. 9; Jones v. Harker, 37 Geo. 503; contra, Hepburn v. Griswold, 8 Wall. 603; S. C. 2 Duval, 20.

The word "declare" has several senses. It may mean to proclaim or publish. It should, however, be interpreted in the sense in which the phrase is used among nations when applied to such a subject-matter. A power to declare war is a power to make and carry on war. It is not a mere power to make known an existing thing, but to give life and effect to the thing itself. Metropolitan Bank v. Van Dyck, 27 N. Y. 400.

The power to declare war presupposes the right to make war. The power to declare war necessarily involves the power to carry it on, and this implies the means. The right to the means carries all the means in the possession of the nation. Every able-bodied man is at the call of the Government, for as there is no limit to the necessity in making war, there can be no limit to the force to be used to meet it. Therefore, if the emergency requires it, the entire military force of the nation may be called into service. But the power to carry on war, and to call the requisite force into service, inherently carries with it the power to coerce or draft. A nation, without the power to draw forces into the field, would not in fact possess the power to carry on war. The power of war, without the essential means, is really no power; it is a solecism. Voluntary enlistment is founded in contract. A power to command differs essentially from a power to contract. The former flows from authority; the latter from assent. The power to command implies a duty to obey, but the essential element of contract is freedom to assent or dissent. It is clear, therefore, that the power to make war, without the power to command troops into the field, is impotent; in point of fact is no governmental power, because it lacks the authority to execute itself. Kneedler v. Lane, 45 Penn. 238; S. C. 3 Grant, 465.

An act of Congress emancipating the slaves of those who aid in a rebellion is valid. Bure *v.* Parker, 63 N. C. 131; Jacoway *v.* Denton, 25 Ark. 625.

The power is not limited to victories in the field and the dispersion of the insurgent forces. It carries with it inherently the power to guard against the immediate renewal of the conflict, and to remedy the evils which have arisen from its rise and progress. Stewart *v.* Kahn, 11 Wall. 493; White *v.* Hart; 13 Wall. 646; s. c. 39 Geo. 306.

When the United States subdues a rebellious State, it has the right to determine and fix the conditions of returning peace. Jacoway *v.* Denton, 25 Ark. 625; Shorter *v.* Cobb, 39 Geo. 285.

Congress may pass an act suspending the statute of limitations during the existence of a rebellion. Stewart *v.* Kahn, 11 Wall. 493.

The genius and character of our institutions are peaceful, and the power to declare war was not conferred upon Congress for the purpose of aggression or aggrandisement, but to enable the General Government to vindicate by arms, if it should become necessary, its own rights and the rights of its citizens. A war, therefore, declared by Congress can never be presumed to be waged for the purpose of conquest or the acquisition of territory, nor does the law declaring the war imply an authority to the president to enlarge the limits of the United States by subjugating the enemy's country. Fleming *v.* Page, 9 How. 603.

Congress alone has the power to confiscate the property of an enemy, and debts due to an enemy. Brown *v.* U. S. 8 Cranch, 110; Britton *v.* Butler, 9 Blatch. 456.

A declaration of war does not of itself enact a confiscation of the property of the enemy within the territory of the belligerent. Brown *v.* U. S. 8 Cranch, 110.

The power to make rules concerning captures on land and water extends to captures within the United States as well as to those that are exterritorial, and is an independent substantive power not included in that of declaring war. Brown *v.* U. S. 8 Cranch, 110.

Congress may impose such conditions upon commercial intercourse with an enemy in time of war as it sees fit, and make a payment for a license a part of the conditions. Hamilton *v.* Dillin, 21 Wall. 74.

Raise Armies.

(*m*) The power to "raise and support armies" must not be confounded with that given over the militia of the country. Unlike that it is unrestricted, unless it be considered as a restriction that appropriations of money to the use of raising and supporting armies are forbidden for a longer term than two years. In one sense this is a practical restriction. Without appropriations no army can be maintained, and the limited period for which appropriations can be made enables the people to pass judgment upon the maintenance, and even existence, of the army every two years, and in every new Congress. But in this clause no limitation is imposed other than this indirect one, either upon the magnitude of the force which Congress is empowered to raise, or upon the uses for which it may be employed, or upon the mode in which the army may be raised. Kneedler *v.* Lane, 45 Penn. 238; S. C. 3 Grant, 465.

Congress may raise a military force by compulsory draft as well as voluntary enlistment. Kneedler *v.* Lane, 45 Penn. 238; S. C. 3 Grant, 465; In re Griner, 23 Wis. 423.

Congress may enact that a person shall be deemed in the military service from the time of the draft. Kneedler *v.* Lane, 45 Penn. 238; S. C. 3 Grant. 465.

In authorizing a national conscription by the National Government, the Constitution so far forth ignores the State governments entirely. With the action of the General Government they have legitimately nothing to do. If they attempt to aid they are wholly volunteers. Booth *v.* Woodbury, 32 Conn. 118.

Congress has power to make and authorize such orders and regulations as may be necessary to prevent those who are liable by law to military service from evading that duty. Allen *v.* Colby, 45 N. H. 544.

The power to raise and support armies is an exclusive power in Congress. Ferguson *v.* Landram, 1 Bush. 548.

The militia of the States is also that of the General Government. It is the whole able-bodied population capable of bearing arms, whether organized or not. It is the material, and the only material contemplated by the Constitution, out of which the armies of the Federal Government are to be raised. Whether gathered by coercion or enlistment, they are equally taken out of those who form a part of the militia of the States. The rights of the States can not be affected by the mode of taking. It is clear that the States hold their power over the militia subordinate to the power of Congress to raise armies out of the population that constitutes it. Kneedler *v.* Lane, 45 Penn. 238; S. C. 3 Grant, 465.

Congress has the power to enlist minors into the naval service. U. S. *v.* Bainbridge, 1 Mason, 71; Comm. *v.* Murray, 4 Binn. 487.

Where an act of Congress to provide for a draft of men into the army also allows of the acceptance of volunteers, a State may pass a law giving a bounty to those who volunteer. State *v.* Demarest, 32 N. J. 528; Taylor

v. Thompson, 42 Geo. 9; Coffman v. Knightly, 24 Ind. 509; Board v. Bearse, 25 Ind. 110; Wilson v. Burkman, 13 Minn. 441; Winchester v. Corinna, 55 Me. 9; Speer v. Directors, 50 Penn. 150; Booth v. Woodbury, 32 Conn. 118; Comer v. Folsom, 13 Minn. 219; Ahl v. Gleim, 52 Penn. 432; State v. Jackson, 31 N. J. 189; contra, Ferguson v. Landram, 1 Bush. 548.

Military Regulations.

(*n*) Congress has the power to provide for the trial and punishment of military and naval offenses by court martial, in the manner practiced by civilized nations, and the power to do so is given without any connection between it and the judicial power   The two powers are entirely independent of each other.   Dynes v. Hoover, 20 How. 65; In re Robert D. Bogart, 2 Saw. 396.

Militia.

(*o*) When it is said that Congress shall have the power to call forth the militia for three purposes, it is clear that it is not a call by the States of their own militia.   Kneedler v. Lane, 45 Penn. 238; S. C. 3 Grant, 465.

The power to call the militia into service is limited by express terms. It reaches only three cases. The call may be made "to execute the laws of the Union, to suppress insurrections, and to repel invasions," and for no other uses. The militia can not be summoned for the invasion of a country without the limits of the United States. They can not be employed therefore to execute treaties of offensive alliance, nor in any case where military power is needed abroad to enforce rights necessarily sought in foreign lands.   Kneedler v. Lane, 45 Penn. 238; S. C. 3 Grant, 465, 523.

Congress may lawfully provide for cases of imminent danger of invasion, as well as for cases where an invasion has actually taken place, for the power to provide for repelling invasions includes the power to provide against the attempt and danger of invasion, as the necessary and proper means to effectuate the object.   One of the best means to repel invasion is to provide the requisite force for action before the invader himself has reached the soil.   Martin v. Mott, 12 Wheat. 19.

By virtue of this power Congress may make laws to enforce the call; may inflict penalties for disobedience, and erect courts for trial of offenders. Comm. v. Irish, 3 S. & R. 176, note.

Congress may by law fix the period at which the militia, called forth by the president, enter into the service of the United States, and change their character from State to national militia.   This is included in the more extensive powers of calling forth the militia, organizing, arming, disciplining and governing them.   Houston v. Moore, 5 Wheat. 1; S. C. 3 S. & R. 169.

The authority to call forth the militia to execute the laws of the Union, suppress insurrections and repel invasions implies no prohibition against employing the army and navy for such purposes; nor does it imply that the militia can not be used for suppressing a rebellion as well as a mere insurrection. Metropolitan Bank *v.* Van Dyck, 27 N.Y. 400; Kneedler *v.* Lane, 45 Penn. 238; S. C. 3 Grant, 465; Texas *v.* White, 7 Wall. 700.

Instead of the power to call forth the militia being in exclusion of any of the preceding grants of the power of war, or operating as an exception or proviso, it is a continuation of the enumeration of powers, and is an additional grant subsidiary to the former, as its place in the section, its terms, its design and the subject-matter all import. While the framers of the Constitution intended that the nation should possess the primary and essential means of self-preservation, in its fullest extent, by the power to declare war, raise armies and maintain navies, and provide for the common defense; they also foresaw, through the genius of the people, the nature of the Government as a representative democracy, and the force of other powers and limitations operating, that it would be unlikely that a large standing army would always be on foot,'and the nation thereby ready for every emergency : hence the power to call out the militia in the three cases was added. Addition is not exclusion. Kneedler *v.* Lane, 45 Penn. 238; S. C. 3 Grant, 465.

A State law providing for the punishment of a person who neglects to obey an order calling forth the militia is valid. Houston *v.* Moore, 5 Wheat. 1; S. C. 3 S. & R. 169.

Government of Militia.

(*p*) There is a distinction between these two powers. Calling the militia forth is one thing, governing them when they are in actual service is another. Houston *v.* Moore, 3 S. & R. 169; S. C. 5 Wheat. 1.

So long as the militia are acting under the military jurisdiction of the State to which they belong, the powers over them are concurrent in the General and State Governments. Congress has power to provide for organizing, arming and disciplining them; and this power being unlimited, except in the two particulars of officering and training them according to the discipline to be prescribed by Congress, it may be exercised to any extent that may be deemed necessary by Congress. But as State militia, the power of the State governments to legislate on the same subject having existed prior to the formation of the Constitution, and not having been prohibited by that instrument, it remains with the States, subordinate nevertheless to the paramount law of the General Government operating upon the same subject. Houston *v.* Moore, 5 Wheat. 1; S. C. 3 S. & R. 169.

The power of the several States to govern their own militia is not derived from the Constitution. They had it before the adoption of the Constitution, and possess it still, except where it has been restricted or yielded to the United States. Houston *v.* Moore, 3 S. & R. 169; S. C. 5 Wheat. 1.

After a detachment of the militia has been called forth, and has entered into the service of the United States, the authority of the General Government over such detachment is exclusive. Over the national militia the State governments never had or could have jurisdiction. None such is conferred by the Constitution, consequently none such can exist. Houston *v.* Moore, 5 Wheat. 1; S. C. 3 S. & R. 169.

When a State law is to operate on the militia before they are in actual service, it may not only not interfere with the law of Congress, but have a powerful effect in aid of it. Houston *v.* Moore, 3 S. & R. 169; S. C. 5 Wheat. 1.

"Organizing" obviously includes the power of determining who shall compose the body known as the militia. The general principle is that a militia shall consist of the able-bodied male citizens, but this description is too vague and indefinite to be laid down as a practical rule. It requires a provision of positive law to ascertain the exact age which shall be deemed neither too young nor too old to come within the description. The power is given to the General Government to fix the age precisely, and thereby to put an end to doubt and uncertainty. Opinions of Justices, 80 Mass. 614.

The President may exercise his command of the militia by the officers of the militia duly appointed. There is no provision of the Constitution authorizing any officer of the army of the United States to command the militia. Opinions of Justices, 80 Mass. 548.

District of Columbia.

(*q*) In legislating for the District of Columbia, Congress is bound by the prohibitions of the Constitution. U. S. *v.* More, 3 Cranch, 160, note.

These terms are not limited by the principle that representation is inseparable from taxation. Loughborough *v.* Blake, 5 Wheat. 317.

In legislating for the District of Columbia, Congress necessarily preserves the character of the legislature of the Union, for it is in that character alone that the Constitution confers on it the power of exclusive legislation. Cohens *v.* Virginia, 6 Wheat. 264.

Congress possesses the power to lay and collect direct taxes within the District of Columbia in proportion to the census directed to be taken by the Constitution. Loughborough *v.* Blake, 5 Wheat. 317.

Congress may confer upon the city of Washington authority to assess upon the adjacent proprietors of lots, the expense of repairing streets with a new and different pavement, or repairing an old one. Willard *v.* Presbury, 14 Wall. 676.

Congress possesses the power to construct an aqueduct for the use of the District of Columbia, which shall, if necessary, draw its supply of water from within the limits of a State, and use and occupy land for that purpose in the State, with its permission and consent. Reddall *v.* Bryan, 14 Md. 444.

Forts.

(*r*) It seems apparent that the members of the convention who formed the Constitution, contemplated that places for forts, magazines, arsenals, dockyards and other buildings connected therewith, would be required to be purchased from individuals in the several States where their selection and erection might be deemed necessary, and that it was still more important to give exclusive legislation over the places ceded for public convenience and safety; but still the consent of the State legislature was required before such purchases could be made of individuals and the places so used. May it not also have been intended that forts and permanent garrisons should not be thus erected without the consent of the State? This inference would be warranted by the supposition that the States would view with natural jealousy the collection of numerous armed forces stationed among them in permanent works, established without their consent and beyond their control. McConnell *v.* Wilcox, 2 Ill. 344.

The United States can acquire the right of exclusive legislation within the territorial limits of a State, only in the mode pointed out in the Constitution. The essence of the provision is, that the State shall freely cede the particular place to the United States for one of the specific and enumerated objects. The jurisdiction can not be acquired tortiously or by disseizin of the State; much less can it be acquired by mere occupancy with the implied or tacit consent of the State, when such occupancy is for the purpose of protection. People *v.* Godfrey, 17 Johns. 225; Clay *v.* State, 4 Kans. 49; U. S. *v.* Tierney, 1 Bond, 571.

Ratification by the State in addition to purchase from the owner, is necessary to vest full sovereignty over land in the United States. U. S. *v.* Cornell, 2 Mason, 60; Comm. *v.* Young, Brightley, 302; U. S. *v.* Tierney, 1 Bond, 571.

An act of a State legislature will not vest the jurisdiction in the United States, unless there is some act on the part of the latter to show an acceptance of the grant. People *v.* Lent, 2 Wheel. Cr. Cas. 548.

Congress may relinquish jurisdiction over territory acquired from a State, for such jurisdiction is not an original and inherent power, but a secondary and acquired power. Renner *v.* Bennett, 21 Ohio St. 431.

When land has been purchased by the United States for military or other purposes, it can not be sold without the special authority of Congress. In such cases the purchase is made for a specific object, and being purchased with the consent of the State under the Constitution, there is a cession of jurisdiction as well as of property. To transfer property so acquired, and relinquish the jurisdiction, the authority of Congress is indispensable. U. S. *v.* Railroad Bridge Co. 6 McLean, 517.

Congress may own and use property within the limits of a State, without acquiring jurisdiction over the territory. Renner *v.* Bennett, 21 Ohio St. 431.

If the United States merely acquires land in a State from the owner, it holds the land in subordination to all the municipal regulations of the State. Comm. *v.* Young, Brightly, 302.

The power of exclusive legislation does not extend to land rented by the Government for a temporary purpose. U. S. *v.* Tierney, 1 Bond. 571.

Where jurisdiction over territory has been acquired for a temporary purpose, the consent of the State is not necessary to revest the jurisdiction when it is abandoned by the Government. Renner *v.* Bennett, 21 Ohio St. 431.

Congress may relinquish jurisdiction over territory acquired from a State without abandoning the use of the property. Renner *v.* Bennett, 21 Ohio St. 431.

A person who resides on land which has been ceded to the United States, is not liable to taxation in the State on account of such residence. Webster *v.* Seymour, 8 Vt. 135.

No offenses committed within the limits of territory purchased with the consent of the State, can be punished in the State courts. Comm. *v.* Clary, 8 Mass. 72; U. S. *v.* Ames, 1 W. & M. 76.

When a purchase of land for any of the enumerated purposes is made by the national government, and the State has given its consent to the purchase, the land so purchased by the very terms of the Constitution *ipso facto*, falls within the exclusive legislation of Congress, and the State jurisdiction is completely ousted. U. S. *v.* Cornell, 2 Mason, 60; s. c. 2 Mason, 91.

The Government has exclusive jurisdiction over the ceded territory, although the act of cession provides that civil and criminal process issued under the authority of the State may be executed within the ceded lands. Mitchell *v.* Tibbetts, 34 Mass. 298; U. S. *v.* Cornell, 2 Mason, 60; s. c. 2 Mason, 91; U. S. *v.* Davis, 5 Mason, 356; U. S. *v.* Travers, 2 Wheel. Cr. Cas. 490; Comm. *v.* Clary, 8 Mass. 72.

A State retains jurisdiction over lands ceded to the United States until the latter legislates for it. People *v.* Lent, 2 Wheel. Cr. Cas. 548.

Congress has no exclusive jurisdiction over land in a State which is purchased by a corporation created by an act of Congress. In re John O. Conner, 37 Wis. 379; contra, Sinks *v.* Reese, 19 Ohio St. 306.

Necessary Laws.

(*s*) This clause is placed among the powers of Congress, not among the limitations on those powers. Its term purports to enlarge, not to diminish, the powers vested in the Government. It purports to be an additional power, not a restriction on those already granted. M'Culloch *v.* State, 4 Wheat. 316.

This limitation on the means which may be used is not extended to the powers which are conferred. Gibbons *v.* Ogden, 9 Wheat. 1; S. C. 17 Johns. 488; 4 Johns. Ch. 150.

If the clause does not enlarge it can not be construed to restrain the powers of Congress, or to impair the right of the legislature to exercise its best judgment in the selection of measures to carry into execution the constitutional powers of the Government. If no other motive for its insertion can be suggested, a sufficient one is found in the desire to remove all doubts respecting the right to legislate on that vast mass of incidental powers which must be involved in the Constitution. A sound construction of the Constitution must therefore allow to the national legislature that discretion with respect to the means by which the powers it confers are to be carried into execution, which will enable that body to perform the high duties assigned to it in the manner most beneficial to the people. Let the end be legitimate, let it be within the scope of the Constitution, and all means which are appropriate, which are plainly adapted to that end, which are not prohibited, but consist with the letter and spirit of the Constitution, are constitutional. M'Culloch *v.* State, 4 Wheat. 316; Comm. *v.* Morrison, 2 A. K. Marsh, 75; U. S. *v.* Marigold, 9 How. 560; Mitchell *v.* Steelman, 8 Cal. 363; U. S. *v.* Fisher, 2 Cranch, 358; Dickey *v.* Turnpike Co. 7 Dana, 119.

It is essential to just construction that many words which import something excessive, should be understood in a more mitigated sense; in that sense which common usage justifies. The word "necessary" is of this description. It has not a fixed character peculiar to itself. It admits of all degrees of comparison, and is often connected with other words which increase or diminish the impression the mind receives of the urgency it imports. A thing may be necessary, very necessary, absolutely or indispensably necessary. To no mind would the same idea be conveyed by these several phrases. In its construction the subject, the context, and the intention of the person using it are all to be taken into view. M'Culloch *v.* State, 4 Wheat. 316; Comm. *v.* Morrison, 2 A. K. Marsh. 75.

It was impossible to enumerate all cases of necessity, and, therefore, it was left to Congress to judge of them, and their judgment must govern unless it should be so exercised as to be manifestly and flagrantly in breach of the Constitution. If a law is evidently useful in carrying into effect one of the powers vested in Congress, the court will not be over critical in inquiring into the degree of necessity. Comm. *v.* Lewis, 6 Binn. 266.

Congress is not authorized to enact laws, even in furtherance of a legitimate end, merely because they are useful, or because they make the Government stronger. There must be some relation between the means and the end; some adaptedness or appropriateness of the laws to carry into execution the powers created by the Constitution. Legal Tender Cases, 12 Wall. 457.

The relationship between the means and the end need not be direct and immediate. Legal Tender Cases, 12 Wall. 457; contra, U. S. *v.* Bailey, 1 McLean, 234.

It is not for the judiciary to determine whether a law of Congress has a direct relation as a means to the execution of an enumerated power. If, in any sense or in any degree, the means employed are appropriate or conducive to the exercise of the power—if there is any possible relation of the means to the end—the judiciary is limited to the inquiry whether the use of such means is repugnant to any provision of the Constitution. Metropolitan Bank *v.* Van Dyck, 27 N. Y. 400.

The judicial department of the Government can not declare that because to the judicial mind Congress, in the execution of a specified power, seems to have employed means not having a direct but a circuitous, remote and indirect relation to the end of such power, its act is constitutionally invalid. Metropolitan Bank *v.* Van Dyck, 27 N. Y. 400.

In the exercise of its powers and functions the Government must be allowed a wide discretion in the means to be employed. Occasions may arise for the use of means to accomplish the recognized objects of the Constitution, different from what its founders could have anticipated, and perhaps contrary to their expectations, and in such event the question of constitutional power is to be decided by a fair construction of the Constitution itself, and by the appropriateness of the proposed means to the end tested rather by the facts of the day than by the judgment of the past or its history. Metropolitan Bank *v.* Van Dyck, 27 N. Y. 400.

It is not essential that the statute shall be indispensably necessary to give effect to a specified power. Where various systems might be adopted for that purpose, it might be said with respect to each, that it was not necessary because the end might be attained by other means. Congress must possess the choice of means, and must be empowered to use any means which are in fact conducive to the exercise of a power granted by the Constitution. U. S. *v.* Fisher, 2 Cranch, 358.

Construction for the purpose of conferring a power should be resorted to with great caution, and only for the strongest and most persuasive reasons. Ex parte Beavins, 33 N. H. 89.

No trace is to be found in the Constitution of an intention to create a dependence of the Federal Government on the governments of the States, for the execution of the great powers assigned to it. Its means are adequate to its ends, and on those means alone was it expected to rely for the accomplishment of its ends. M'Culloch *v.* State, 4 Wheat. 316.

Where the means for the exercise of a granted power or the performance of an enjoined duty are given, no other or different means can be implied, either on account of convenience or as being more effectual. Ex parte Beavins, 33 N. H. 89.

A statute giving priority to the Government over the general creditors in cases of insolvency, is valid. U. S. *v.* Fisher, 2 Cranch, 358.

Congress may fix the rate of interest which a national bank may take upon a loan of money, and determine the penalty to be imposed for taking a greater rate. Central Bank *v.* Pratt, 115 Mass. 439.

Congress may make or authorize contracts with individuals for services to the Government; grant aids by money or land in preparation for and in the performance of such services, make any stipulations and conditions not contrary to the Constitution, and in its discretion exempt the agencies employed in such services from any State taxation which will really prevent or impede the performance of them. Thomson *v.* Pacific Railroad, 9 Wall. 579.

The Government is to pay the debt of the Union, and consequently has a right to make remittances by bills or otherwise, and to take those precautions which will render the transaction safe. U. S. *v.* Fisher, 2 Cranch, 358.

Congress may use all known and appropriate means of effectually collecting and disbursing the revenue, unless such means are forbidden in some other part of the Constitution. The power is not exhausted by the receipt of the money by the collector. The purpose of the power to collect and disburse the revenue, is to raise money and use it in the payment of the debts of the Government, and whoever may have possession of the public money until it is actually disbursed, the power to use those known and appropriate means continues. Murray *v.* Hoboken Co. 18 How. 272.

If it is necessary to render treasury notes effectual for the purpose for which they are issued—that they should be made a legal tender in payment of all debts, Congress may in its discretion adopt such means to carry out a conceded and delegated power. Metropolitan Bank *v.* Van Dyck, 27 N. Y. 400.

Congress has the power to provide that in case of the death of a collector without leaving estate sufficient for the payment of all his debts, the United States shall be first paid. Comm. *v.* Lewis, 6 Binn. 266.

The power of creating a corporation, though appertaining to sovereignty, is not like the power of making war, or levying taxes, or regulating commerce, a great substantive and independent power which can not be implied as incidental to other powers or used as a means of executing them. It is never the end for which other powers are exercised, but a means by which other objects are accomplished. The power of creating a corporation is never used for its own sake, but for the purpose of effecting something else. It may, therefore, pass as incidental to those powers which are expressly given if it be a direct mode of executing them. M'Culloch *v.* State, 4 Wheat. 316; Magill *v.* Parsons, 4 Conn. 317; contra, Comm. *v.* Morrison, 2 A. K. Marsh. 75.

Congress has the power to make any provisions which tend to promote the efficiency of national banks in performing the functions by which they were designed to serve the Government and to protect them, not only against interfering State legislation, but also against suits or proceedings in State courts, by which that efficiency would be impaired. Chesapeake Bank *v.* First Nat'l Bank, 40 Md. 269.

Congress has the power to prescribe the penalty to be incurred by a national bank for taking usurious interest. Farmers' National Bank *v.* Dearing, 91 U. S. 29; contra, First Nat'l Bank *v.* Lamb, 50 N. Y. 95; s. c. 57 Barb. 429.

The power of legislating upon the subject of the validity of private contracts made within the States, has not been granted by the Constitution to the Federal Government, but has ever rested with the States. Each one of them according to its own notions of policy, and without regard to the views of the others, has the right to prohibit and declare invalid within its own borders those contracts which it deems opposed to public morals or the welfare of its citizens. Each State had this right before the formation of the Federal Government, and has never surrendered it. When the people of all the States united in framing that Government, they carefully defined its powers, reserving to each State not merely its separate organization, but its sovereignty over its domestic affairs, granting to the Federal Government only the express powers enumerated in its written charter, together with authority to pass all laws necessary and proper for the execution of those enumerated powers, and in this form was the Constitution ratified by the States. If, for the execution of any express power vested in the Federal Government, it should become necessary to sanction or prohibit a particular class of contracts in opposition to the laws of the State where made, such a measure would not derive its validity from any power of Congress to legislate upon the subject of domestic contracts, but solely from the relation of the measure to the express power in the execution of which it was employed, and the existence of such a relation is a judicial question. In such a case the legislation of the State could be made to yield to that of the Federal Government, only to the extent to which the former constituted an obstruction to the accomplishment of the legitimate constitutional end which Congress had in view. First Nat'l Bank *v.* Lamb, 57 Barb. 429; S. C. 50 N. Y. 95.

Congress has the power to create, define and punish crimes and offenses whenever they deem it necessary by law to do so for effectuating the objects of the Government. U. S. *v.* Worrall, 2 Dall. 384; U. S. *v.* Marigold, 9 How. 560.

The power to prescribe an oath of office is an incidental power. Metropolitan Bank *v.* Van Dyck, 27 N. Y. 400.

The power of punishment appertains to sovereignty, and may be exercised whenever the sovereign has a right to act as incidental to his constitutional powers. It is a means for carrying into execution all sovereign powers, and may be used although not indispensably necessary. It is a right incidental to the power and conducive to its beneficial exercise. M'Culloch *v.* State, 4 Wheat. 316.

If the Constitution guarantees a right, the National Government is clothed with the appropriate authority and functions to enforce it. The fundamental principle is, that where the end is required the means are given; and where a duty is enjoined, the ability to perform it is contemplated to exist on the part of the functionaries to whom it is intrusted. Prigg *v.* Comm. 16 Pet. 539; U. S. *v.* Cruikshank, 1 Woods, 308; S. C. 91 U. S. 542.

The power of Congress to pass laws to enforce rights conferred by the Constitution, is not limited to the express powers of legislation enumerated in the Constitution. The powers which are necessary and proper as means to carry into effect rights expressly given and duties expressly enjoined, are always implied. The end being given, the means to accomplish it are given also by a just and necessary implication. Prigg *v.* Comm. 16 Pet. 539; Henry *v.* Lowell, 16 Barb. 268.

The method of enforcement, or the legislation appropriate to that end, will depend upon the character of the right conferred. It may be by the establishment of regulations for attaining the object of the right, the imposition of penalties for its violation, or the institution of judicial procedure for its vindication when assailed, or when ignored by the State courts; or it may be by all of them together. One method of enforcement may be applicable to one fundamental right, and not applicable to another. U. S. v. Cruikshank, 1 Woods, 308; s. c. 91 U. S. 542.

The Government which has a right to do an act, and has imposed on it the duty of performing that act, must, according to the dictates of reason, be allowed to select the means. M'Culloch v. State, 4 Wheat. 316.

Those who contend that the Government may not select any appropriate means, that one particular mode of effecting the object is excepted, take upon themselves the burden of establishing that exception. M'Culloch v. State, 4 Wheat. 316.

The Government has the right to employ freely every means not prohibited, necessary for its preservation, and for the fulfillment of its acknowledged duties. Legal Tender Cases, 12 Wall. 457.

Congress has the power to make laws for carrying into execution all the judgments which the judicial department has the power to pronounce. Wayman v. Southard, 10 Wheat. 1; Bank v. Halstead, 10 Wheat. 51.

Congress has the power to regulate the proceedings on executions, and direct the mode and manner, and out of what property of the debtor satisfaction may be obtained. Bank v. Halstead, 10 Wheat. 51.

The Constitution does not profess to enumerate the means by which the powers it confers may be executed. The powers given to the Government imply the ordinary means of execution. M'Culloch v. State, 4 Wheat. 316.

Congress may delegate to the courts the power of altering the modes of proceedings in suits. Wayman v. Southard, 10 Wheat. 1; Bank v. Halstead, 10 Wheat. 51.

If a measure is appropriate to the execution of a power, its necessity is to be determined by Congress alone. Where a law is not prohibited, but is really calculated to effect any of the objects intrusted to the Government, for the courts to undertake to inquire into the degree of its necessity would be to pass the line which circumscribes the judicial department, and to tread on legislative ground. M'Culloch v. State, 4 Wheat. 316; Metropolitan Bank v. Van Dyck, 27 N. Y. 400.

When a Territory becomes a State, it rests with Congress to declare to what tribunal the record of the Territorial court shall be transferred, and how its judgments shall be carried into execution, or reviewed on appeal or writ of error. Hunt v. Palao, 4 How. 589.

Congress may prescribe a limitation for actions to recover damages for acts done under the authority of the president. Milligan v. Hovey, 3 Biss. 13.

SECTION IX.

1. The migration or importation of such persons as any of the States now existing shall think proper to admit, shall not be prohibited by the Congress prior to the year one thousand eight hundred and eight, but a tax or duty may be imposed on such importation, not exceeding ten dollars for each person.

This clause does not in its words or meaning apply to State governments. Butler *v.* Hopper, 1 Wash. C. C. 499.

The power to prohibit the admission of "all such persons," includes necessarily the power to admit them on such conditions as Congress may think proper to impose, and therefore, as a condition, Congress has the unlimited power of taxing them. The whole power over the subject belongs exclusively to Congress, and connects itself indissolubly with the power to regulate commerce with foreign nations. It therefore follows that passengers can never be subject to State laws until they become a portion of the population of the State, temporarily or permanently. Passenger Cases, 7 How. 283; s. c. 45 Mass. 282.

2. The privilege of the writ of *habeas corpus* shall not be suspended, unless when, in cases of rebellion or invasion, the public safety may require it.

The president can not suspend the writ of *habeas corpus*. That is an act of legislative power which can only be performed by Congress. Griffin *v.* Wilcox, 21 Ind. 370; in re Nicholas Kemp, 16 Wis. 359; ex parte John Merryman, Taney, 246; contra, ex parte Field, 5 Blatch. 63.

Congress, in the cases mentioned, is the judge of whether the public safety does or does not require the suspension of the writ, and its judgment is conclusive. Ex parte John Merryman, Taney, 246; McCall *v.* McDowell, 1 Deady, 233; s. c. 1 Abb. C. C. 212.

The commander of a military district can not suspend the writ of *habeas corpus*. Johnson *v.* Duncan, 3 Mart. 531; ex parte Field, 5 Blatch. 63.

Congress has no power to suspend the issuing of a writ of *habeas corpus* by a State court. Griffin *v.* Wilcox, 21 Ind. 370; Kneedler *v.* Lane, 45 Penn. 238; s. c. 3 Grant, 465.

A stipulation in a treaty prohibiting the issuing of a writ of *habeas corpus* would be void, for the treaty making power is not competent to suspend the writ in time of peace. Ex parte Thomas Kaine, 10 N. Y. Leg. Obs. 257.

The language is, "the privilege of the writ shall not be suspended;" that is, the right to the writ, the privilege of having it issued and the case heard and determined shall not be suspended. It has no reference to the reasonable delay that may be occasioned in the disposition of such cases by a writ of review. Macready *v.* Wilcox, 33 Conn. 321.

A statute authorizing the president during a certain period to suspend the writ of *habeas corpus* whenever in his judgment the public safety requires it, is valid; for Congress does thereby exercise the discretion vested in it to determine that the emergency requires a suspension. In re Richard Oliver, 17 Wis. 681; McCall *v.* McDowell, 1 Deady, 233; S. C. 1 Abb. C. C. 212.

The suspension of the privilege of the writ is an express permission and direction from Congress to the executive to arrest and imprison all persons for the time being, whom he has reason to believe or suspect of intention or conduct in relation to the rebellion or invasion, which is or may be dangerous to the common weal. McCall *v.* McDowell, 1 Deady, 233; S. C. 1 Abb. C. C. 212.

The suspension of the privilege of the writ of *habeas corpus* being the virtual authorization of arrests without the ordinary legal cause or warrant, it follows that such arrests, pending the suspension and when made in obedience to the order or authority of the officer to whom that power is committed, are practically legal, and the persons making them are not liable to an action of damages therefor. McCall *v.* McDowell, 1 Deady, 233; S. C. 1 Abb. C. C. 212.

Congress may provide that an officer shall not be liable for an arrest made during the suspension of the privilege of the writ of *habeas corpus.* McCall *v.* McDowell, 1 Deady, 233; S. C. 1 Abb. C. C. 212.

The privilege of the writ of *habeas corpus* is the privilege of having judicial inquiry made into the cause of imprisonment, and a discharge if the detention be found to be unlawful, and a suspension thereof precludes all further proceedings on a writ already issued. Ex parte Fagan, 2 Sprague, 91; ex parte Dunn, 25 How. Pr. 467.

There is a plain distinction between the suspension of the writ in the sense of the Constitution and the right of a military commander to refuse obedience when justified by the exigencies of war, or the *ipso facto* suspension which takes place wherever martial law actually exists. But this kind of suspension which comes with war and exists without proclamation or other act, is limited by the necessities of war. It applies only to cases where the demands upon the officer's time and services are such that he can not, consistently with his superior military duty, yield obedience to the mandates of the civil authorities, and to cases arising within districts which are properly subjected to martial law. In cases of the latter description it is probable that the civil magistrates would be bound to take judicial notice of martial law; but as to the former, it would seem that the military officer should, if practicable, make return of the facts showing his excuse. In re Nicholas Kemp, 16 Wis. 359.

3. **No bill of attainder, or *ex post facto* law, shall be passed.**

This provision relates to criminal laws only. Comm. *v.* Lewis, 6 Binn. 266.

A statute making treasury notes a legal tender is not an *ex post facto* law. Metropolitan Bank *v.* Van Dyck, 27 N. Y. 400.

This provision applies not merely to criminal laws and cases, but to cases for the recovery of penalties and forfeitures. U. S. *v.* Hughes, 21 I. R. R. 84.

A statute which attempts to validate a punishment which would otherwise be illegal, is an *ex post facto* law. In re William Murphy, 1 Wool. 141.

Exclusion from any of the professions, or any of the ordinary avocations of life, for past conduct, is a punishment for such conduct. All enactments of this kind partake of the nature of bills of pains and penalties, and are subject to the constitutional inhibition against the passage of bills of attainder, under which general designation they are included. Ex parte Garland, 4 Wall. 333.

If a party who has once incurred a forfeiture seeks to avail himself of a defense granted by a subsequent law, he must take it subject to such terms and conditions as the legislature at the time when it passed the beneficial law, or at any future time, may please to prescribe. In such case the subsequent law can not be denominated *ex post facto*, because it does not, in any respect, change the condition of the party from what it was when the act was performed. U. S. *v.* Hall, 2 Wash. C. C. 366.

A statute excluding a person from the practice of a profession unless he will take an oath that he has not committed a certain act prior to the passage thereof, is an *ex post facto* law. Ex parte Garland, 4 Wall. 333; ex parte William Law, 35 Geo. 285; ex parte John Baxter, 14 A. L. Reg. 159.

A statute which imposes forfeiture of citizenship for a continuance of desertion by refusing to return after an assurance of pardon, is not an *ex post facto* law. Gotcheus *v.* Matheson, 58 Barb. 152; S. C. 40 How. Pr. 97.

If a statute, imposing a forfeiture of citizenship for a continuance of desertion after a proclamation, contemplates a trial by court martial to enforce the penalty, it is not a bill of attainder. Gotcheus *v.* Matheson, 58 Barb. 152; S. C. 40 How. Pr. 97.

A statute which in effect makes the non-payment of taxes for a certain period sufficient evidence of participation in rebellion, and forfeits the land absolutely therefor, is a bill of attainder. Martin *v.* Snowden, 18 Gratt. 100.

A statute providing for a forfeiture of the distillery premises for a violation of an internal revenue law, is not a bill of attainder. U. S. *v.* Distillery, 2 Abb. C. C. 192.

A treaty for the extradition of criminals is not an *ex post facto* law, although it provides for crimes committed before its adoption. Ex parte Angelo De Giacomo, 12 Blatch. 391.

4. No capitation or other direct tax shall be laid, unless in proportion to the census or enumeration hereinbefore directed to be taken.

The census referred to is a census exhibiting the numbers of the respective States. The omission to extend it to the District of Columbia or the territories, would not render it defective. The application of the power of direct taxation is not limited to the population contained in this census. The language of the clause does not imply this restriction. It is that no capitation or other direct tax shall be laid "unless in proportion to the census." This proportion may be applied to the District of Columbia or the territories. If an enumeration be taken of the population in the District of Columbia and the territories on the same principles on which the enumeration of the respective States is made, then the information is acquired by which a direct tax may be imposed on the District of Columbia and the territories. If the tax be laid in this proportion, it is within the very words of the restriction. Loughborough *v.* Blake, 5 Wheat. 317.

It was obviously the intention of the framers of the Constitution that Congress should possess full power over every species of taxable property except exports. The term taxes is generical, and was made use of to vest in Congress plenary authority in all cases of taxation. The general division of taxes is into direct and indirect. Although the latter term is not to be found in the Constitution, yet the former necessarily implies it. Indirect stands opposed to direct. There may, perhaps, be an indirect tax on a particular article that can not be comprehended within the description of duties, or imposts, or excises. In such case it will be comprised under the general denomination of taxes; for the term taxes is the genus, and includes: 1st. Direct taxes. 2d. Duties, imposts and excises. 3d. All other classes of an indirect kind, and not within any of the classifications enumerated under the preceding heads. Taxes of the last class may be laid by the rule of uniformity or not, as Congress shall think proper and reasonable. Hylton *v.* U. S. 3 Dall. 171.

CAPITATION TAX.

A general power is given to Congress to lay and collect taxes of every kind or nature, without any restraint, except on exports. But two rules are prescribed for their government, namely, uniformity and apportionment. Three kinds of taxes, to wit, duties, imposts and excises by the first rule, and capitation or other direct taxes by the second rule. Hylton *v.* U. S. 3 Dall. 171.

This clause gives a rule when the territories shall be taxed without imposing the necessity of taxing them. Loughborough *v.* Blake, 5 Wheat. 317.

The power to tax without apportionment extends to all other subjects. Taxes on other objects are included under the head of taxes not direct duties, imposts and excises, and must be laid and collected by the rule of uniformity. Veazie Bank *v.* Fenno, 8 Wall. 533.

The rule of apportionment is radically wrong, and can not be supported by any solid reasoning. It ought not, therefore, to be extended by construction. Apportionment is an operation on States, and involves valuations and assessments which are arbitrary, and should not be resorted to but in case of necessity. Uniformity is a visitant operation on individuals, without the intervention of assessments or any regard to States, and is at once easy, certain and efficacious. Hylton *v.* U. S. 3 Dall. 171.

The Constitution declares that a capitation tax is a direct tax, and both in theory and practice a tax on land is deemed to be a direct tax. In this way the terms, direct taxes and capitation and other direct taxes, are satisfied. Whether direct taxes, in the sense of the Constitution, comprehend any other tax than a capitation tax and a tax on land, is a questionable point. Hylton *v.* U. S. 3 Dall. 171.

The words "direct taxes," as used in the Constitution, comprehend only capitation taxes and taxes on lands, and perhaps taxes on personal property, by general valuation and assessment of the various descriptions possessed within the several States. Veazie Bank *v.* Fenno, 8 Wall. 533.

A tax on carriages kept for his own use by the owner is not a direct tax. Hylton *v.* U. S. 3 Dall. 171.

A tax upon the business of an insurance company is not a direct tax. Pacific Ins. Co. *v.* Soule, 7 Wall. 433.

A tax on bank circulation is not a direct tax. Veazie Bank *v.* Fenno, 8 Wall. 533.

A tax on income is not a capitation or other direct tax. Smedberry *v.* Bentley, 21 I. R. R. 38; Clark *v.* Sickel, 14 I. R. R. 6.

A succession tax is not a direct tax, but is an excise tax or duty. Scholey *v.* Rew, 23 Wall. 331.

5. No tax or duty shall be laid on articles exported from any State. No preference shall be given by any regulation of commerce or revenue to the ports of one State over those of another; nor shall vessels bound to or from one State be obliged to enter, clear or pay duties in another.

The prohibition is upon Congress, and is, by the fair import of the words and the connection in which they stand, subsidiary to a very important purpose, to wit, to restrain Congress from fostering or oppressing one port or the commerce of one State, to the end of destroying equality and uniformity as to levies of contributions from foreign commerce. It does not affect the States in the regulation of their domestic affairs. State *v.* Charleston, 10 Rich. 240; Munn *v.* Illinois, 94 Ill. 113.

This clause does not apply to a State tax upon an article brought into the State from another State. State *v.* Charleston, 10 Rich. 240.

This provision does not apply to the imposition of taxes on foreign vessels. It is within the discretion of Congress to totally prohibit the import or export trade in foreign vessels to or from our ports, or to grant them the privilege of bringing in or carrying out cargoes on such conditions and under such restrictions as may be most beneficial to the United States. Aguirre *v.* Marwell, 3 Blatch. 140.

A charge for a stamp on a package of tobacco intended for export, which is devised as a means to prevent fraud, and bears no proportion whatever to the value or size of the package on which it is affixed, is not a tax on exports. Pace *v.* Burgess, 92 U. S. 372.

The history of the provision as well as its language looks to a prohibition against granting privileges or immunities to vessels entering or clearing from the ports of one State over those of another. These privileges and immunities, whatever they may be in the judgment of Congress, must be common and equal in all the ports of the several States. This much is undoubtedly embraced in the prohibition, and it may certainly also embrace any other description of legislation looking to a direct privilege or preference of the ports of any particular State over those of another. State *v.* Wheeling Bridge Co. 18 How. 421.

It is a mistake to assume that Congress is forbidden to give a preference to a port in one State over a port in another State. Such preference is given in every instance where it makes a port in one State a port of entry and refuses to make another port in another State a port of entry. No greater preference in one sense can be more directly given than in this way, and yet the power of Congress to give such preference has never been questioned, nor can it be without asserting that the moment Congress makes a port in one State it is bound at the same time to make all other ports in all other States ports of entry. State *v.* Wheeling Bridge Co. 18 How. 421.

There are many acts of Congress passed in the exercise of the power to regulate commerce providing for a special advantage to the port or ports of one State, and which very advantage may incidentally operate to the prejudice of the ports in a neighboring State. The improvement of rivers and harbors, the erection of light houses and other facilities of commerce may be referred to as examples. The exercise of an admitted power of Congress conferred by the Constitution is not to be prohibited, because it appears or can be shown that the law may incidentally extend beyond the limitation of the power. State *v.* Wheeling Bridge Co. 18 How. 421.

The clause in terms seems to import a prohibition against some positive legislation by Congress to this effect, and not against any incidental advantages that may possibly result from the legislation of Congress upon other subjects connected with commerce, and confessedly within its power. State *v.* Wheeling Bridge Co. 18 How. 421.

What is forbidden is not discrimination between individual ports within the same or different States, but discrimination between States. State *v.* Wheeling Bridge Co. 18 How. 421.

A State tax upon capital invested in ships is not a preference of the ports of one State over the ports of another State. State *v.* Charleston, 4 Rich. 286.

A State may levy a tax upon money, although it is continuously invested in cotton purchased for exportation. People *v.* Tax Commissioner, 17 N. Y. Supr. 255.

This provision is a limitation upon the power of Congress to regulate commerce for the purpose of producing entire commercial equality within the United States, and also a prohibition upon the State to destroy such equality by any legislation prescribing a condition upon which vessels bound from one State shall enter the ports of another State. Passenger Cases, 7 How. 283; S. C. 45 Mass. 282; Alexander *v.* Railroad Co. 3 Strobh. 594.

This provision was intended to prevent vessels bound to or from a port in any State being obliged to enter, clear or pay duties in any State other than that to or from which they should be proceeding. U. S. *v.* The William, 2 Am. L. J. 255.

A statute regulating commercial intercourse with insurrectionary States, and imposing duties thereon, is valid. Folsom *v.* U. S. 4 Ct. Cl. 366.

This clause contemplates a restriction upon the powers of Congress, and not a restriction upon the legislation of the States in the regulation of their internal police. Baker *v.* Wise, 16 Gratt. 139.

A State may require the inspection of vessels bound for certain ports, although no inspection is required from vessels bound for other ports, if such requirement is a part of a police law. Baker *v.* Wise, 16 Gratt. 139.

A State law imposing half pilotage fees on vessels refusing to receive a pilot is not a duty. Cooley *v.* Philadelphia, 12 How. 299.

6. No money shall be drawn from the treasury, but in consequence of appropriations made by law; and a regular statement and account of the receipts and expenditures of all public money shall be published from time to time.

7. No title of nobility shall be granted by the United States, and no person holding any office of profit or trust under them shall, without the consent of the Congress, accept of any present, emolument, office or title of any kind whatever, from any king, prince or foreign State.

SECTION X.

1. No State shall enter into any treaty, alliance or confederation; grant letters of marque and reprisal; coin money (*a*); emit bills of credit (*b*); make anything but gold and silver coin a tender (*c*) in payment of debts; pass any bill of attainder (*d*), *ex post facto* (*e*) law, or law impairing the obligation of contracts; (*f*) or grant any title of nobility.

Coining Money.

(*a*) A State can not incorporate any number of individuals and authorize them to coin money. Such an act would be as much a violation of the Constitution as if the money were coined by an officer of the State under its authority. Briscoe *v.* Bank, 11 Pet. 257; S. C. 7 J. J. Marsh. 349.

Bills of Credit.

(*b*) A bill of credit is a paper issued by the sovereign power containing a pledge of its faith, and designed to circulate as money. Briscoe *v.* Bank,

11 Pet. 257; S. C. 7 J. J. Marsh. 349; City Nat'l Bank *v.* Mahan, 21 La. Ann. 751; Craig *v.* State, 4 Pet. 410.

To constitute a bill of credit within the Constitution, it must be issued by a State on the faith of the State, and be designed to circulate as money. It must be paper which circulates on the credit of the State, and is so received and used in the ordinary business of life. The individual or committee who issue the bill must have power to bind the State. They must act as agents, and, of course, do not incur any personal responsibility, nor impart as individuals any credit to the paper. These are the leading characteristics of a bill of credit which a State can not emit. Briscoe *v.* Bank, 11 Pet. 257; S. C. 7 J. J. Marsh. 349; Billis *v.* State, 2 McCord, 12; Curran *v.* State, 15 How. 304; S. C. 12 Ark. 321.

A bill of credit is unconstitutional, although it is not made a legal tender. The prohibition is general. It extends to all bills of credit, not to bills of a particular description. The Constitution considers the emission of bills of credit, and the enactment of tender laws, as distinct operations independent of each other, which may be separately performed. Both are forbidden. To sustain the one because it is not, also the other; to say that bills of credit may be emitted if they be not made a tender in payment of debts, is in effect to expunge that distinct independent prohibition, and to read the clause as if it had been entirely omitted. This can not be done. Craig *v.* State, 4 Pet. 410; Byrne *v.* State, 8 Pet. 40; Billis *v.* State, 2 McCord, 12; McFarland *v.* State Bank, 4 Ark. 44.

The prohibition can not be evaded by the mere omission of the State to pledge its faith for the redemption of the paper; nor, on the other hand, does the guaranty of the State for an emission of paper as the representative of money, conclusively stamp such paper as the bills of credit forbidden by the Constitution. Owen *v.* Branch Bank, 3 Ala. 258; Billis *v.* State, 2 McCord, 12; Darrington *v.* Branch Bank, 13 How. 12.

If the intention to create a currency is apparent, from the whole scope of the act, the emission is a bill of credit. State *v.* Hoge, 4 Rich. (N. S.) 185; State *v.* Auditor, 4 Rich. (N. S.) 311.

Although the issuing of bills of credit is a question of intent, yet the intent which must stamp the character of an instrument is that of the legislature which enacted the law, not of the officers who were to execute it, or of the persons who received the instrument. The legislative intent can be deduced from the legislative acts alone. In construing statutes, courts may look to the history and condition of the country as circumstances from which to gather the intention. Payaud *v.* State, 13 Miss. 491.

A State may grant acts of incorporation for the attainment of those objects which are essential to the interests of society. This power is incident to sovereignty, and there is no limitation in the Constitution in its exercise by the States in respect to the incorporation of banks. Consequently the notes issued by a bank are not bills of credit within the meaning of the Constitution. Briscoe *v.* Bank, 11 Pet. 257; S. C. 7 J. J. Marsh, 349; Craighead *v.* Bank, 1 Meigs, 199; Lampton *v.* Bank, 2 Litt. 300; Billis *v.* State, 2 McCord, 12; Bank *v.* Spilman, 3 Dana, 150; State *v.* Calvin, R. M. Charlt. 151; Owen *v.* Branch Bank, 3 Ala. 258; McFarland *v.* State Bank, 4 Ark. 44.

A bill of credit emanates from the sovereignty of the State. It rests for its currency on the faith of the State pledged by a public law. Whatever agency is employed to issue it, the State promises to pay it or to receive it in payment of public dues. When a particular fund is designated, out of which it is to be paid, it depends upon the faith of the State whether such fund shall be so appropriated. The State can not be sued ordinarily on such bill nor its payment exacted against its will. There is no fund or property which the holder of the bill can reach by judicial process. Such an instrument is altogether different in form and substance from a note issued by a bank whose capital is effectually chargeable with the redemption of its notes. Darrington *v.* Branch Bank, 13 How. 12; Curran *v.* State, 15 How. 304; S. C. 12 Ark. 321; Central Bank *v.* Little, 11 Geo. 346.

When a State becomes a stockholder in a bank, it imparts none of its attributes of sovereignty to the institution, and this is equally the case whether it owns the whole or a part of the stock of the bank. Darrington *v.* Branch Bank, 13 How. 12; Central Bank *v.* Little, 11 Geo. 346; Briscoe *v.* Bank, 11 Pet. 257; S. C. 7 J. J. Marsh, 249; Billis *v.* State, 2 McCord, 12; Owen *v.* Branch Bank, 3 Ala. 258; McFarland *v.* State Bank, 4 Ark. 44; Woodruff *v.* Trapnall, 10 How. 190; S. C. 8 Ark. 236.

The mere fact that the directors of a bank whose stock is owned solely by the State are elected by the legislature, will not make its notes bills of credit. Darrington *v.* Branch Bank, 13 How. 12.

The bank notes are not bills of credit, although the bank is owned by the State, and its officers give bond to the State for the faithful discharge of their duties. Billis *v.* State, 2 McCord, 12; contra, Linn *v.* State Bank, 3 Ill. 87.

An act which is prohibited can not be done by a State, either directly or indirectly. A State can not, by any device that may be adopted, emit bills of credit. Briscoe *v.* Bank, 11 Pet. 257; S. C. 7 J. J. Marsh, 349; Bank *v.* Clark, 4 Mo. 59; Griffith *v.* Bank, 4 Mo. 255.

A State can act only through its agents. It would therefore be absurd to say that an act was not done by a State which was done by its authorized agents. Briscoe *v.* Bank, 11 Pet. 257; S. C. 7 J. J. Marsh, 349.

The word "emit" is never employed in describing those contracts by which a State binds itself to pay money at a future day for services actually received, or for money borrowed for present use; nor are instruments executed for such purposes in common language denominated "bills of credit." Craig *v.* State, 4 Pet. 410; Payaud *v.* State, 13 Miss. 491.

A loan certificate issued on the faith of the State, and made receivable for taxes and debts due to the State, and for the salaries of State officers, is a bill of credit. Craig *v.* State, 4 Pet. 410; Byrne *v.* State, 8 Pet. 40.

A certificate of indebtedness which, by law, is receivable in payment of taxes, is not a bill of credit. State *v.* Cardozo, 5 Rich. (N. S.) 297.

A treasury note issued by a State to an individual as evidence of a loan, and not intended as a circulating medium, is not a bill of credit. Green *v.* Sizer, 40 Miss. 530.

An auditor's warrant, issued according to law for the payment of a demand against the State, is not a bill of credit. Payaud *v.* State, 13 Miss. 491.

States and municipal corporations may borrow money and give proper securities therefor, and such securities are not bills of credit. McCoy *v.* Washington Co. 3 Wall. Jr. 381; S. C. 3 Phila. 290.

The State may authorize a municipal corporation to issue certificates of indebtedness, and make them receivable in payment of public taxes. Mayor *v.* State, 15 Md. 376.

A State may authorize a municipal corporation to issue bills of credit. Smith *v.* New Orleans, 23 La. Ann. 5.

A municipal corporation may issue treasury notes, make them receivable for all debts due to it, and pledge its real estate for their redemption. Smith *v.* New Orleans, 23 La..Ann. 5.

A State government organized by a force in rebellion against the United States, can not issue bills of credit. McCracken *v.* Poole, 19 La Ann. 359.

Confederate notes were not bills of credit, for they were not issued by virtue of the sovereignty of a State, nor rest on the faith of a State for their currency. Bailey *v.* Milner, 35 Geo. 330.

A bill of credit is not a good consideration for a contract. Craig *v.* State, 4 Pet. 410; Bank *v.* Clark, 4 Mo. 59; Linn *v.* State Bank, 5 Ill. 87.

Legal Tender.

(*c*) If one person owes to another a certain sum of money, this is a debt. It is the duty of the debtor to produce to the creditor that sum of money, and offer to pay it to him; this is a tender. If the debt so tendered is not received by the creditor, the debtor is thereby discharged from the duty of tendering it again, until it shall have been legally demanded by the creditor. A tender may therefore, in general terms, be defined to be an act on the part of the debtor which affords some exemption to him, and works a correspondent inconvenience to the creditor. The Constitution therefore prohibits the States from passing laws, the effect of which will be to induce the creditor to receive something else than gold and silver coin in payment of the debt due him, in order to avoid an inconvenience that would result on his failure to do so. Baily *v.* Gentry, 1 Mo. 164.

The clause is not enabling, nor does it oblige the States to pass tender laws. Van Husan *v.* Kanouse, 13 Mich. 303.

A State has no power over the currency further than the right to establish banks, to regulate or prohibit the circulation within the State of foreign notes, and determine in what the public dues shall be paid. Woodruff *v.* Trapnall, 10 How. 190; S. C. 8 Ark. 236.

A statute which provides for a stay of execution for a certain period, unless the creditor will accept property at two-thirds of its appraised value, is unconstitutional. Baily *v.* Gentry, 1 Mo. 164.

If the charter of a bank attempts to make the notes of the bank a legal tender, this provision will be unconstitutional, but will not in any degree affect the constitutionality of the bank. Briscoe *v.* Bank, 11 Pet. 257; S. C. 7 J. J. Marsh, 349.

A statute requiring county scrip to be received for taxes due to the county is unconstitutional. Gaines *v.* Rives, 8 Ark. 220.

A statute requiring a bank to receive its own notes in payment of the note of another bank presented for payment by it is void. Bank *v.* Bank of Cape Fear, 13 Ired. 75.

A statute which provides for a stay of execution for a certain period, unless the creditor will accept the paper of a State bank in payment, is unconstitutional. Townsend *v.* Townsend, Peck. 1; Briscoe *v.* Bank, 11 Pet. 257; S. C. 7 J. J. Marsh, 349.

A statute making bank notes a legal tender is unconstitutional. Lowry *v.* M'Ghee, 8 Yerg. 242; Briscoe *v.* Bank, 11 Pet. 257; S. C. 7 J. J. Marsh, 349.

A State law authorizing the tender of scrip of a corporation in payment for damages assessed in favor of an individual whose property is taken for its benefit, is void. State *v.* Beackmo, 8 Blackf. 246.

The Legislature may from time to time prescribe in what currency debts due to a public corporation shall be paid, and may then make the notes of a State bank a legal tender therefor. Bush *v.* Shipman, 5 Ill. 186.

Attainder.

(*d*) A bill of attainder is a legislative act which inflicts punishment without a judicial trial. If the punishment is less than death, the act is termed a bill of pains and penalties. Within the meaning of the Constitution, bills of attainder include bills of pains and penalties. Cummings *v.* State, 4 Wall. 277; s. c. 36 Mo. 263.

All men have certain inalienable rights, among these are life, liberty, and the pursuit of happiness. In the pursuit of happiness all avocations, all honors, all positions are alike open to every one; and in the protection of these rights all are equal before the law. Any deprivation or suspension of any of these rights for past conduct is punishment. Cummings *v.* State, 4 Wall. 277; s. c. 36 Mo. 263.

What can not be done directly, can not be done indirectly. The Constitution deals with substance, not shadows. Its inhibition is leveled at the thing, not the name. It intends that the rights of the citizen shall be secure against deprivation for past conduct by legislative enactment, under any form, however disguised. Cummings *v.* State, 4 Wall. 277; s. c. 36 Mo. 263.

A bill of attainder may inflict punishment absolutely, or may inflict it conditionally. Cummings *v.* State, 4 Wall. 277; s. c. 36 Mo. 263.

Whether a statute excluding persons from pursuing certain vocations is a bill of attainder, must depend wholly upon what was the direct scope, object, and real intention of the act. If it were simply a measure of political wisdom, for the purposes of good government, it is a matter within the sovereign power, and valid beyond the reach of judicial condemnation. To bring it within the definition of a bill of attainder, it is absolutely necessary that it should be such by the very scope, operation, and intention of it. Murphy & Glover Cases, 41 Mo. 339.

A State law which deprives a party of the privilege of pursuing a certain avocation, unless he will take an expurgatory oath that he has not been guilty of a certain offense prior thereto, is invalid. Murphy & Glover Cases, 41 Mo. 339; State *v.* Heighland, 41 Mo. 388; Cummings *v.* State, 4 Wall. 277; s. c. 36 Mo. 263; contra, State *v.* Garesche, 36 Mo. 256.

A statute which deprives a party of the privilege of enforcing a contract, on account of an act previously done, is a bill of attainder. McNealy *v.* Gregory, 13 Fla. 417.

A statute of indemnity for acts done by virtue of military authority in times of civil war, is not a bill of attainder. Drehman *v.* Stifle, 41 Mo. 184; s. c. 8 Wall. 595; Hess *v.* Johnson, 3 W. Va. 645; Smith *v.* Owen, 42 Mo. 508; State *v.* Gatzweiller, 49 Mo. 18; Clark *v.* Dick, 1 Dillon, 8.

The right of suffrage being the creature of organic law, may be modified or withdrawn by the sovereign authority which conferred it, without inflicting any punishment. A State may therefore require that a party shall take an expurgatory oath that he has not done a certain act before he can be allowed to vote. Anderson *v.* Baker, 23 Md. 531; Randolph *v.* Good, 3 W. Va. 551; Blair *v.* Ridgley, 41 Mo. 63; State *v.* Neal, 42 Mo. 119; contra, Green *v.* Shumway, 39 N. Y. 418.

A statute depriving a party of a right to a rehearing of an attachment suit, unless he will take an oath that he has not theretofore done certain acts, is a bill of attainder. Pierce *v.* Carskadon, 16 Wall. 234; Kyle *v.* Jenkins, 6 W. Va. 371; Ross *v.* Jenkins, 7 W. Va. 284; Lynch *v.* Hoffman, 7 W. Va. 553; Lynch *v.* Hoffman, 7 W. Va. 578.

Ex Post Facto Laws.

(*e*) The prohibition that "no State shall pass any *ex post facto* law," necessarily requires some explanation, for naked and without explanation it is unintelligible, and means nothing. Literally it is only that a law shall not be passed concerning, and after the fact or thing done or action committed. The prohibition in the letter is not to pass any law concerning and after the fact, but the plain and obvious meaning and intention of the prohibition is this, that the legislatures of the several States shall not pass laws after a fact done by a subject or citizen which shall have relation to such fact, and shall punish him for having done it. The prohibition considered in this light is an additional bulwark in favor of the personal security of the subject to protect his person from punishment by legislative acts having a retrospective operation. Calder *v.* Bull, 3 Dall. 386; S. C. 2 Root, 350.

The fact contemplated by the prohibition, and not to be affected by a subsequent law, is some fact to be done by a citizen or subject. Calder *v.* Bull, 3 Dall. 386; S. C. 2 Root, 350.

The words *ex post facto* do mean "by matter of after fact, by something after the fact." But there is a manifest distinction between the case where one fact relates to and affects another fact, as where an after fact, by operation of law, makes a former fact either lawful or unlawful, and the case where a law made after a fact done is to operate on and to affect such fact. In the first case both the acts are done by private persons. In the second case the first act is done by a private person, and the second is done by the legislature to affect the first act. Calder *v.* Bull, 3 Dall. 386; S. C. 2 Root, 350.

This provision was not inserted to secure the citizen in his private rights of either property or contracts. The prohibition not to make anything but gold and silver coin a tender in payment of debts, and not to pass any law impairing the obligation of contracts, were inserted to secure private rights, but the restriction not to pass any *ex post facto* law was to secure the person of the subject from injury or punishment in consequence of such law. Calder *v.* Bull, 3 Dall. 386; S. C. 2 Root, 350.

The true distinction is between *ex post facto* laws and retrospective laws. Every *ex post facto* law must necessarily be retrospective, but every retrospective law is not an *ex post facto* law. The former only are prohibited. Calder *v.* Bull, 3 Dall. 386; S. C. 2 Root, 350; Bridgeport *v.* Hubbell, 5 Conn. 237; Stoddart *v.* Smith, 5 Binn. 355; Locke *v.* Dane, 9 Mass. 360; Society *v.* Wheeler, 2 Gallis. 105; Fisher *v.* Cockerill, 5 Mon. 129; Dash *v.* Van Kleeck, 7 Johns. 477; Davis *v.* Ballard, 1 J. J. Marsh. 563; Suydam *v.* Receivers, 3 N. J. Eq. 114; Byrne *v.* Stewart, 3 Dessau. 466; White *v.* Wayne, T. U. P. Charlt. 94; Forsyth *v.* Marbury, R. M. Charlt. 324; Andrews *v.* Russell, 7 Blackf. 474; Blackman *v.* Gordon, 2 Rich. Eq. 43; S. C. 1 Rich. Eq. 61; Sutherland *v.* De Leon, 1 Tex. 250; State *v.* Squires, 26 Iowa, 340; Caperton *v.* Martin, 4 W. Va. 138; Baugher *v.* Nelson, 9 Gill, 299; Coles *v.* Madison, Breese, 115; Carpenter *v.* Comm. 17 How. 456; Albee *v.* May, 2 Paine, 74; State *v.* Kline, 23 Ark. 587; Aldridge *v.* Tuscumbia R. R. Co. 2 Stew. & Port. 199; Locke *v.* New Orleans, 4 Wall. 172; Weister *v.* Hade, 52 Penn. 474; Ex parte Perkins, 2 Cal. 424; Lord *v.* Chadwick, 42 Me. 429; Butler *v.* Toledo, 5 Ohio St. 225; Stokes *v.* Rodman, 5 R. I. 405; Powers *v.* Dougherty Co. 23 Geo. 65; New Orleans *v.* Cordeviolle, 13 La. Ann. 268; Municipality *v.* Wheeler, 10 La Ann. 745.

The words *ex post facto* must be taken in their technical, which is also their common and general acceptation, and are not to be understood in their literal sense. Calder *v.* Bull, 3 Dall. 386; S. C. 2 Root, 350.

The provision of the Constitution can not be evaded by the form in which the power of the State is exerted. Cummings *v.* State, 4 Wall. 277; S. C. 36 Mo. 263.

The laws which are *ex post facto* within the words and intent of the prohibition are: 1st. Every law that makes an action done before the passing of the law, and which was innocent when done, criminal; 2d. Every law that aggravates a crime, or makes it greater than it was when committed; 3d. Every law that changes the punishment, and inflicts a greater punishment than the law annexed to the crime when committed; 4th. Every law that alters the legal rules of evidence, and receives less or different testimony than the law required at the time of the commission of the offense, in order to convict the offender. All these, and similar laws, are manifestly unjust and oppressive. Calder *v.* Bull, 3 Dall. 386; S. C. 2 Root, 350; Walston *v.* Comm. 16 B. Mon. 15; State *v.* Bond, 4 Jones (N. C.) 9.

The words *ex post facto* relate to crimes, and not to criminal proceedings. A statute regulating criminal proceedings is valid. Perry *v*. Comm. 3 Gratt. 632; Manning *v*. State, 14 Tex. 402; Walston *v*. Comm. 16 B. Mon. 15; People *v*. Mortimer, 46 Cal. 114.

A statute allowing the State a certain number of peremptory challenges is not an *ex post facto* law. Walston *v*. Comm. 16 B. Mon. 15; State *v*. Ryan, 13 Minn. 370.

A statute reducing the number of peremptory challenges is not an *ex post facto* law. Perry *v*. Comm. 3 Gratt. 632; Reynolds *v*. State, 1 Geo. 222.

A statute erecting a new tribunal to try past offenses is not an *ex post facto* law. Comm. *v*. Phillips, 28 Mass. 28; State *v*. Sullivan, 14 Rich. 281.

A statute changing the mode of summoning juries is not an *ex post facto* law. Perry *v*. Comm. 3 Gratt. 632.

A statute allowing the counsel for the State to open and close the argument before the jury, instead of alternating with the counsel for the defense, is valid. People *v*. Mortimer, 46 Cal. 114.

A statute changing the place of trial from one county to another, in the same district, or even to a different district from that in which the offense was committed, or the indictment found, is not an *ex post facto* law, though passed subsequent to the commission of the offense, or the finding of the indictment. Gut *v*. State, 9 Wall. 35.

A statute which deprives the accused of the right to object to an incompetent grand juror is an *ex post facto* law. Martin *v*. State, 22 Tex. 214.

A statute which operates only on the forms of the proceeding, rendering a defective indictment valid, is not unconstitutional, for it only provides the means by which a criminal may be brought to answer for that which was a crime when committed. Comm. *v*. Bean, Thach. Crim. Cas. 85; State *v*. Sears, Phil. 146.

A statute allowing an amendment of an indictment to correct a misnomer of the accused, is not an *ex post facto* law, for it merely has reference to the mode of conducting the proceedings on the prosecution. State *v*. Manning, 14 Tex. 402.

Any change which is referable to prison discipline, or penal administration, as its primary object, may also take effect upon past as well as future offenses, such as changes in the manner or kind of employment of convicts sentenced to hard labor, the system of supervision, or the like. Changes of this sort may operate to increase or mitigate the severity of the punishment, but do not raise any question under this provision. Hartung *v*. People, 22 N. Y. 95.

To aggravate the punishment of a crime by a law posterior to its commission, is forbidden by the same reason that restrains the legislature from converting into a crime an act innocent when committed. Dickinson *v.* Dickinson, 3 Murph. 327.

A law which increases the punishment is *ex post facto*, although it does not change the manner of the punishment. Shepherd *v.* People, 25 N. Y. 406.

A statute which adds a new punishment, or increases an old one, for an offense committed before its adoption, is an *ex post facto* law. Ross *v.* Riley, 19 Mass. 165; State *v.* Salomons, Riley, 99; Hartung *v.* People, 22 N. Y. 95; Hartung *v.* People, 26 N. Y. 167; Wilson *v.* O. & M. R. R. Co. 64 Ill. 542.

A statute which imposes a different punishment from that which existed at the time of the commission of the offense, is not an *ex post facto* law, if the punishment is not increased. Strong *v.* State, 1 Blackf. 193; Comm. *v.* Gardner, 77 Mass. 438; contra, Hartung *v.* People, 22 N. Y. 95; Shepherd *v.* People, 25 N. Y. 406; State *v.* McDonald, 20 Minn. 136.

No law is considered *ex post facto* within the prohibition that mollifies the rigor of the criminal law, but only those that create or aggravate the crime, or increase the punishment, or change the rules of evidence for the purpose of conviction. Calder *v.* Bull, 3 Dall. 386; S. C. 2 Root, 350; State *v.* Arlin, 39 N. H. 179.

It is perfectly competent for the legislature to remit any separable portion of the prescribed punishment. For instance, if the punishment were fine and imprisonment, a law which dispenses with either the fine or the imprisonment may be applied to existing offenses. The term of imprisonment may be reduced, or the number of stripes diminished in cases punishable in that manner. Hartung *v.* People, 22 N. Y. 95.

A statute changing the punishment for larceny from whipping and imprisonment in a jail to confinement in the penitentiary, mitigates the punishment, and is not *ex post facto*. State *v.* Kent, 65 N. C. 311.

A statute which provides a mitigated alternative punishment at the discretion of the jury, is not *ex post facto*. Turner *v.* State, 40 Ala. 21.

The substitution of imprisonment for life in place of death, is in the eye of the law a mitigation of the punishment. Comm. *v.* Gardner, 77 Mass. 438; contra, Hartung *v.* People, 22 N. Y. 95.

A statute which reduces the punishment, may take away from the accused the privilege of having counsel assigned him, and of being furnished with process to compel the attendance of witnesses. State *v.* Arlin, 39 N. H. 179.

A statute imposing an additional punishment for an offense committed after the passing of the statute, to be inflicted by the court upon coming to the knowledge of certain facts, is not *ex post facto*, although those facts are the commission of an offense before the passing of the statute. Ross *v.* Riley, 19 Mass. 165; Rand *v.* Comm. 9 Gratt. 738; Plumbly *v.* Comm. 43 Mass. 413; Ex parte Gutierrez, 45 Cal. 430.

A statute authorizing the jury to assess the amount of the fine to be imposed or punishment to be inflicted, only provides a different mode of ascertaining the amount of the fine or the duration of the imprisonment by substituting the opinion of the jury for that of the judge, and is not an *ex post facto* law. Holt *v.* State, 2 Tex. 363; Dawson *v.* State, 6 Tex. 347.

A statute repealing an amnesty act is an *ex post facto* law, for it renders that criminal which was not so before its adoption. State *v.* Keith, 63 N. C. 140.

A statute extending the time for prosecuting misdemeanors can not revive a right of prosecution which was barred at the time of its passage. State *v.* Sneed, 25 Tex. Supp. 66.

A law prohibiting the making of certain contracts is valid. Churchman *v.* Martin, 54 Ind. 380.

A statute allowing a divorce for an act which was no ground for granting a divorce at the time when it was committed, is an *ex post facto* law. Dickinson *v.* Dickinson, 3 Murph. 327; contra, Carson *v.* Carson, 40 Miss. 349.

A statute allowing the court in granting a divorce to decree that the guilty party shall not contract marriage with any other person during the lifetime of the other party, is not an *ex post facto* law. It simply leaves the party under the disability of his marriage contract, and does not impose any new punishment or penalty. Elliott *v.* Elliott, 38 Md. 357.

A statute which alters the legal rules of evidence, and receives less or different testimony than the law required at the time of the commission of the offense to convict the offender, is an *ex post facto* law. In a judicial inquiry no allegation can be taken as a fact unless it be admitted or proved. Unproved, it is the same as if it did not exist. *De non apparentibus et de non existentibus eadem est ratio.* If a person therefore is charged with the commission of an act which can be proved only by testimony of a particular kind or grade, a law passed for the purpose of admitting less testimony with a view to make conviction more easy, is the same as a law which makes an innocent act criminal. State *v.* Bond, 4 Jones, N. C. 9; Hart *v.* State, 40 Ala. 32.

A statute which permits marriage to be established by indirect evidence, when prior thereto it could only be established by direct evidence, is an *ex post facto* law. State *v.* Johnson, 12 Minn. 476.

A State law imposing a tax upon transactions during a preceding year, is not an *ex post facto*, although it imposes a penalty for failing to render an account thereof. State *v.* Bell, Phillips, 76.

A statute suspending the right of a party who has engaged in a rebellion against the Federal Government, to continue or prosecute a suit during the continuance of the rebellion, is an *ex post facto* law. Davis *v* Pierce, 7 Minn. 13; Keough *v.* McNitt, 7 Minn. 30; McFarland *v.* Butler, 8 Minn. 116; Jackson *v.* Butler, 8 Minn. 117.

A statute which deprives a citizen of the right to vote, unless he will take an expurgatory oath that he did not do a certain act prior to the passage thereof is valid, for the State has full powers to pass laws restrictive and exclusive, for the preservation or promotion of the common interests, as political and social emergencies may from time to time require, though in certain cases disabilities may directly flow as a consequence. Anderson *v.* Baker, 23 Md. 531; Blair *v.* Ridgley, 41 Mo. 63; Randolph *v.* Good, 3 W. Va. 551; State *v.* Neal, 42 Mo. 119; contra, Green *v.* Shumway, 39 N. Y. 418.

A statute which deprives a person of the right to hold certain offices and trusts, and to pursue certain avocations, unless he will take an expurgatory oath that he did not do a certain act prior to the passage thereof, is an *ex post facto* law. Cummings *v.* State, 4 Wall. 277; S. C. 36 Mo. 263; Murphy & Glover Cases, 41 Mo. 339; State *v.* Heighland, 41 Mo. 388; contra, State *v.* Garesche, 36 Mo. 256.

A statute which prevents a party from holding office under the State government, unless he will take an expurgatory oath that he did not do a certain act prior to the passage thereof, is not an *ex post facto* law. State *v.* Woodson, 41 Mo. 227.

A statute depriving a party of the right to a rehearing of an attachment suit unless he will take an oath that he has not theretofore done certain acts, is an *ex post facto* law. Pierce *v.* Carskadon, 16 Wall. 234; Kyle *v.* Jenkins, 6 W. Va. 371; Ross *v.* Jenkins, 7 W. Va. 284; Lynch *v.* Hoffman, 7 W. Va. 553; S. C. 7 W. Va. 578.

A statute which prohibits manufacturers and others who have manufactured or bought liquor before its passage from selling it or keeping it for sale within the State, is not an *ex post facto* law, for it does not retroact except by the civil consequence of lessening the value of the property. The statute, to meet the well settled definition, must not only retroact, but must retroact by way of criminal punishment upon that which was not a crime before its passage. State *v.* Paul, 5 R. I. 185; State *v.* Keeran, 5 R. I. 497.

An act which prescribes conditions under which alone a thing may be used in future, can not be *ex post facto*. It attaches neither guilt nor punishment to a past act, but looks forward to future acts, and prohibits the future use of the thing. Evans *v.* Jordan, 1 Brock. 248; s. c. 9 Cranch, 199; Evans *v.* Weiss, 2 Wash. C. C. 342; Evans *v.* Robinson, 1 Car. L. Rep. 209.

A law regulating escheats, which does not refer to crimes, pains or penalties, is not within the meaning of this prohibition. White *v.* Wayne, T. U. P. Charlt. 94.

A law that repeals a prior law before the performance of the acts necessary to give a vested right under it, is not an *ex post facto* law. Vanhorne *v.* Dorrance, 2 Dall. 304.

A law which grants a new trial in a case where the time to appeal from the decree has expired, is not an *ex post facto* law. Calder *v.* Bull, 3 Dall. 386; s. c. 2 Root, 350.

Obligation of Contracts.

(*f*) There is a distinction between a law which impairs a contract and one which impairs its obligation. It is a law which impairs the obligation of contracts, and not the contracts themselves, which is interdicted. The term "obligation" was well considered and weighed by those who framed the Constitution, and was intended to convey a different meaning from what the prohibition would have imported without it. Ogden *v.* Saunders, 12 Wheat. 213.

A contract is defined to be an agreement to do or not to do some particular thing. Ogden *v.* Saunders, 12 Wheat. 213; Sturgess *v.* Crowninshield, 4 Wheat. 122; Woodruff *v.* State, 3 Ark. 285; Trustees *v.* Rider, 13 Conn. 87; Robinson *v.* Magee, 9 Cal. 81; Farnsworth *v.* Vance, 2 Cold. 108.

The obligation of a contract can not commence before the date of the contract. Blair *v.* Williams, 4 Litt. 34.

The obligation of the contract continues until the debt is paid or the act performed. Baily *v.* Gentry, 1 Mo. 164.

Any law which impairs the obligation of the contract, whether the contract remains in its original shape or has been merged in a judgment, is within the operation of this provision. Whatever shape the contract may assume, the obligation remains until it is actually discharged, or until the law will imply its discharge from circumstances. Forsyth *v.* Marbury, R. M. Charlt. 324.

The great principle intended to be established by the Constitution was the inviolability of the obligation of contracts as the obligation existed and was recognized by the laws in force at the time the contracts were made.

It furnished to the legislatures of the States a simple and obvious rule of justice, which, however theretofore violated, should by no means be thereafter violated, and whilst it leaves them at full liberty to legislate upon the subject of all future contracts, and assign to them either no obligation or such qualified obligation as in their opinion may consist with sound policy and the good of the people, it prohibits them from retrospecting upon existing obligations upon any pretext whatever. Ogden v. Saunders, 12 Wheat. 213.

The word "obligation," as found in this provision, is not used in its widest sense. It is the " obligation of contracts " that can not be impaired. The obligation of other things than contracts is not protected. Robinson v. Magee, 9 Cal. 81.

The obligation of a contract is that which requires the performance of the legal duties imposed by it. The duties imposed upon one of the contracting parties are correlative with the rights of the other. What one party is obliged to perform the other has a right to have performed. Blann v. State, 39 Ala. 353.

Right and obligation are considered by all ethical writers as correlative terms. Whatever a party by his contract gives another the right to require, he by that act lays himself under an obligation to yield or bestow. The obligation of every contract consists then of that right or power over his will or actions which a party by his contract confers. Ogden v. Saunders, 12 Wheat. 213; Lapsley v. Brashears, 4 Litt. 47.

An agreement does not always, nay, seldom if ever upon its face, specify the full extent of the terms and conditions of the contract. Many things are necessarily implied and to be governed by some rule not contained in the agreement, and this rule can be no other than the existing law where the contract is made or to be executed. Parties must be understood as making their contracts with reference to existing laws, and impliedly assenting that such contracts are to be construed, governed and controlled by such laws. Ogden v. Saunders, 12 Wheat. 213.

The obligation of a contract is the law which binds the parties to perform their agreement. The law which has this binding obligation must govern and control the contract in every shape in which it is intended to bear upon it, whether it affects its validity, construction or discharge. That law is the municipal law of the State, whether written or unwritten. This is emphatically the law of the contract made within the State, and must govern it throughout wherever its performance is sought to be enforced. It forms a part of the contract, and travels with it wherever the parties to it may be found. Ogden v. Saunders, 12 Wheat. 213; Sturges v. Crowninshield, 4 Wheat. 122; Bronson v. Kinzie, 1 How. 311; McCracken v. Hayward, 2 How. 608; Blair v. Williams, 4 Litt. 34; Lapsley v. Brashears, 4 Litt. 47.

The Constitution refers to and preserves the legal not the moral obligation of a contract. Obligations purely moral are to be enforced by the operation of internal and invisible agents, not by the agency of human laws. The restraints imposed on States by the Constitution, are intended for those objects which would, if not restrained, be the subject of State legislation. Ogden *v.* Saunders, 12 Wheat. 213; Blair *v.* Williams, 4 Litt. 34.

The obligation of a contract consists in its binding force on the party who makes it. This depends on the laws in existence when it is made. These are necessarily referred to in all contracts, and form a part of them as the measure of the obligation to perform them by the one party and the right acquired by the other. There can be no other standard by which to ascertain the extent of either, than that which the terms of the contract indicate according to their settled legal meaning. McCracken *v.* Hayward, 2 How. 608; Johnson *v.* Duncan, 3 Mart. 531; Robinson *v.* Magee, 9 Cal. 81; Western Saving Fund *v.* Philadelphia, 31 Penn. 175; Wood *v.* Wood, 14 Rich. 148.

The obligation of a contract consists in the power and efficacy of the law which applies to and enforces performance of the contract, or the payment of an equivalent for non-performance. The obligation does not inhere and subsist in the contract itself *proprio vigore*, but in the law applicable to the contract. Ogden *v.* Saunders, 12 Wheat. 213.

Whatever the parties are authorized to and do stipulate for at the time of making the contract, or whatever provisions of law are then in force regulating the contract, either as to its construction or legal effect, or materially advantageous to one party or disadvantageous to the other, as to all such the legislature has no power afterwards to interfere, to change or modify the rights and relations thereby established. Smith *v.* Cleveland, 17 Wis. 556.

The law creates the obligation of the contract, and whenever therefore the *lex loci* prescribes for the dissolution of the contract, in any prescribed mode, the parties are presumed to have acted subject to such contingency. Ogden *v.* Saunders, 12 Wheat. 213; Blanchard *v.* Russell, 13 Mass. 1.

The Constitution embraces alike those laws which affect the validity, construction, discharge and enforcement of a contract, for they enter into and form a part of it. Van Hoffman *v.* Quincy, 4 Wall. 535; Walker *v.* Whithead, 16 Wall. 314; S. C. 43 Geo. 537.

Laws.

No law passed before a contract was made can impair its obligation. As it is the law which gives to the contract its obligation, so long as the law which was in force at the time the contract was made continues the same, the obligation of the contract must remain the same, and of course can not be impaired. Blair *v.* Williams, 4 Litt. 34; Bronson *v.* Kinzie, 1 How. 311; Moore *v.* Fowler, Hemp. 536; Sparrow *v.* Railroad Co. 7 Ind. 369; Bruns *v.* Crawford, 34 Mo. 330; Barry *v.* Iseman, 14 Rich. 129; Roby *v.* Boswell, 23 Geo. 51; Powers *v.* Dougherty Co. 23 Geo.65; Davis *v.* Bronson, 6 Iowa, 410.

The Constitution does not prohibit all legislation in respect to contracts. It only forbids the impairing of their obligation. Thornton *v.* Hooper, 14 Cal. 9.

No act of the legislature can alter the nature and legal effect of an existing contract to the prejudice of either party, nor to give to such a contract a judicial construction which shall be binding on the parties or on the courts of law. King *v.* Dedham Bank, 15 Mass. 447.

Whether the law professes to apply to the contract itself, to fix a rule of evidence, a rule of interpretation, or to regulate the remedy, it is equally within the true meaning of the Constitution if it in effect impairs the obligation of existing contracts. Ogden *v.* Saunders, 12 Wheat. 213.

A State law may divest vested rights, and yet not violate the Constitution, unless it also impairs the obligation of a contract. Charles River Bridge *v.* Warren Bridge, 11 Pet. 420; S. C. 24 Mass. 344; 23 Mass. 376; Watson *v.* Mercer, 8 Pet. 88; Cochran *v.* Van Surlay, 20 Wend. 365; Towle *v.* Forney, 4 Duer, 164.

Retrospective laws, which do not impair the obligation of contracts or partake of the character of *ex post facto* laws, are not condemned or forbidden by any part of the Constitution. Charles River Bridge *v.* Warren Bridge, 11 Pet. 420; S. C. 24 Mass. 344; 23 Mass. 376; Satterlee *v.* Matthewson, 2 Pet. 380; Davis *v.* Ballard, 1 J. J. Marsh. 563; Brown *v.* Storm, 4 Vt. 37; Andrews *v.* Russell, 7 Blackf. 474; Holman *v.* Bank, 12 Ala. 369; Balt. & S. R. R. Co. *v.* Nesbit, 10 How. 395; Wilson *v.* Hardesty, 1 Md. Ch. 66; Albee *v* May, 2 Paine, 74; Bay *v.* Gage, 36 Barb. 447; Drehman *v.* Stifle, 41 Mo. 184.

A law may be repealed at any time at the will of the legislature, and then it ceases to form any part of those contracts which may afterwards be entered into. The repeal is no more void than a new law would be which operates upon contracts to affect their validity, construction or duration. Both are valid as they may affect contracts afterwards formed, but neither are so if they bear upon existing contracts; and in the former case, in which the repeal contains no enactment, the Constitution would forbid the application of the repealing law to past contracts, and to those only. Ogden *v.* Saunders, 12 Wheat. 213; Atwater *v.* Woodbridge, 6 Conn. 223; Osborne *v.* Humphrey, 7 Conn. 335; Landon *v.* Litchfield, 11 Conn. 251.

A declaratory, like any other act, may be unconstitutional, as it impairs the obligation of prior contracts. Dundas *v.* Bowler, 3 McLean, 397.

The body upon which the prohibition rests is the legislative department of the State. Trustees *v.* Rider, 13 Conn. 87.

The States have, since the adoption of the Constitution, the authority to prescribe and declare by their laws prospectively what shall be the obligation of all contracts made within them. Such a power seems to be almost indispensable to the very existence of the States, and is necessary to the safety and welfare of the people. The whole frame and theory of the Constitution seems to favor this construction. The States were in the full enjoyment and exercise of all the powers of legislation on the subject of contracts before the adoption of the Constitution. The people of the States, in that instrument, transfer to and vest in Congress no portion of this power, except in the single instance of the authority given to pass uniform laws on the subject of bankruptcies throughout the United States, to which may be added such as result by necessary implication in carrying the granted powers into effect. The whole of this power is left with the States, as the Constitution found it, with the single exception that in the exercise of their general authority they shall pass no law "impairing the obligation of contracts." Ogden *v.* Saunders, 12 Wheat. 213.

Legislative powers over contracts, lawfully existing when the contracts are formed, affect the nature and enter into the obligation of those contracts. But such powers can be exerted only in the particular cases in reference to which they have been reserved, and they are inoperative in all other cases. Until such a case arises, the obligation of such a contract can no more be impaired than if it were under no circumstances subject to legislative control. Curran *v.* State, 15 How. 304; S. C. 12 Ark. 321.

The substance of the provision is that no State shall interfere in any way with the rights which citizens acquire by contract. A State Constitution is but a higher grade of State law than that passed by the legislature. A State convention has no more power to impair the obligation of contracts than a legislature. A State Constitution equally with a statute is within the prohibition. Rutland. *v.* Copes, 15 Rich. 84; Homestead Cases, 23 Gratt. 266; Moore *v.* Ill. Central R. R. Co. 4 C. L. N. 123; Union Bank *v.* State, 9 Yerg. 490; Logwood *v.* Planters' Bank, Minor, 23; Gunn *v.* Barry, 15 Wall. 610; Hazen *v.* Union Bank, 1 Sneed, 115; Edwards *v.* Jagers, 19 Ind. 407; Ex parte Oliver Lee & Co.'s Bank, 21 N. Y. 9; McNealy *v.* Gregory, 13 Fla. 417; Marsh *v.* Burroughs, 1 Woods, 463; Hawkins *v.* Filkins, 24 Ark. 286; Jacoway *v.* Denton, 25 Ark. 625.

The injunction is to the sovereignty. The whole people in any capacity or for any purpose assembled, can not constitute more than the State. Such assemblage is but the sovereign power of the State, and, of necessity, can not be more or greater than the State, and, therefore, the prohibition is to the sovereignty. The prohibition goes to the power of the State, and not to the manner or character of her action. Jacoway *v.* Denton, 25 Ark. 625.

A rebellious State can not adopt a law impairing the obligation of contracts in its Constitution preparatory to the restoration of its relation to the Union. In re Sarah Kennedy, 2 Rich. (N. S.) 116; Calhoun *v.* Calhoun, 2 Rich. (N. S.) 283; Gunn *v.* Barry, 15 Wall. 610; White *v.* Hart, 13 Wall. 646; s. C. 39 Geo. 306.

Congress can not, by authorization or ratification, give the slightest effect to a State law or Constitution in conflict with the Constitution of the United States. Gunn *v.* Barry, 15 Wall. 610; In re Sarah Kennedy, 2 Rich. (N. S.) 116; Calhoun *v.* Calhoun, 2 Rich. (N. S.) 283; White *v.* Hart, 13 Wall. 646; s. C. 39 Geo. 306.

A change of Constitution can not release a State from contracts made under a Constitution which permits them to be made. The moral obligations never die. Dodge *v.* Woolsey, 18 How. 331; Mathing *v.* Golden, 5 Ohio St. 361.

The obligation of a contract can not be impaired unwarrantably by judicial decisions any more than by legislation. Township *v.* Talcott, 19 Wall. 666; Butz *v.* City, 8 Wall. 575.

If a contract when made is valid by the laws of the State as then administered in its courts of justice, its validity and obligation can not be impaired by any subsequent decisions of the courts altering the construction of the law. Ohio Trust Co. *v.* DeBolt, 16 How. 416; s. C. 1 Ohio St. 563; Lee Co. *v.* Rogers, 7 Wall. 181; City *v.* Lamson, 9 Wall. 477; Olcott *v.* Supervisors, 16 Wall. 678; Gelpcke *v.* Dubuque, 1 Wall. 175; Havemeyer *v.* Iowa County, 2 Wall. 294; Thomson *v.* Lee County, 3 Wall. 327; Mitchell *v.* Burlington, 4 Wall. 270; Chicago *v.* Sheldon, 9 Wall. 50; contra, McClure *v.* Owen, 26 Iowa, 243.

If there is a remedy for the enforcement of a contract at the time when it is made, it can not be taken away by subsequent judicial decision. Butz *v.* City, 8 Wall. 575.

A law may be void in part and good in part, or in other words it may be void so far as it has a retrospective application to past contracts, and valid as applied prospectively to future contracts. Ogden *v.* Saunders, 12 Wheat. 213; Berry *v.* Haines, 2 Car. L. Rep. 428; Comm. *v.* Kimball, 41 Mass. 359; Norris *v.* Boston, 45 Mass. 282; State *v.* Paul, 5 R. I. 185; Barry *v.* Iseman, 14 Rich. 129.

Contracts.

The term contract, comprises in its full and more liberal signification every description of agreements, obligations or legal ties whereby one party binds himself, or becomes bound, expressly or impliedly, to pay a sum of money, or perform or omit to do a certain act. Woodruff *v.* State, 3 Ark. 285.

Whether the contract relates to real or personal estate, is executed or executory, or rests in parol, or is under seal, the Constitution preserves it inviolate from the action of a State legislature so far as it creates rights or contains obligations binding on the parties in law or equity. Trustees *v.* Rider, 13 Conn. 87; Taylor *v.* Stearns, 18 Gratt. 244.

The provision has no regard to the magnitude or values of contracts. The obligation of no contract shall be impaired, whether it be for much or little. Gault's Appeal, 33 Penn. 94.

The subject of the prohibition is every contract relating to property or some object of value, and which confers rights that may be asserted in a court of justice. Trustees *v.* Rider, 13 Conn. 87; Regents *v.* Williams, 9 G. & J. 365.

The Constitution recognizes no distinction between express and implied contracts. Myrick *v.* Battle, 5 Fla. 345.

The contracts designed to be protected are contracts by which perfect rights, certain, definite, fixed private rights of property are vested. Butler *v.* Pennsylvania, 10 How. 402.

The provision of the Constitution never has been understood to embrace other contracts than those which respect property or some object of value, and confer rights which may be asserted in a court of justice. Dartmouth College *v.* Woodward, 4 Wheat. 518.

This provision applies only to those contracts which impose obligations under the general principles of law. It does not extend to those which are void under the State Constitution, nor to those entered into without authority from the party sought to be bound. People *v.* Roper, 35 N. Y. 629.

All questions of property are within the jurisdiction of the respective States, and the individual members thereof, in forming a government, are not to be considered as contractors with the government thereby ordained in the sense in which that term is employed in the Constitution. It is but fair to suppose that individuals who sacrifice or part with a portion of their natural rights for the common good of all, have just reason to believe that the rights reserved will be respected or maintained inviolate, but this agreement is a social compact, and not *stricti juris* a contract. Billings *v.* Hall, 7 Cal. 1; State *v.* Paul, 5 R. I. 185.

CONTRACTS.

The Constitution does not give validity to contracts which confer no rights, nor add to those which they do confer. It prohibits a State from impairing the obligation of a contract—that is, the rights and duties which arise from it. It does not declare that every contract contains an obligation, or that it shall always be enforced, but it does declare that whatever obligations are created or rights secured shall not be impaired by an act of the legislature. It is obvious, therefore, that in every case in which the prohibition is attempted to be applied, the first inquiry is whether the case be one in which the subject-matter is a contract relating to property, or some object of value, and which imposes an obligation capable, in legal contemplation, of being impaired. If it be such a contract, the remaining inquiry is whether the act of the legislature impairs that obligation. Trustees *v.* Rider, 13 Conn. 87; Regents *v.* Williams, 9 G. & J. 365.

There is a distinction between those rights which the law gives to, or obligations which it imposes upon, persons in certain relations merely in carrying out its own views of policy, and independently of any stipulations which the parties may have made, and those rights which the law itself, even in carrying out some matter of general policy, authorizes to be made the subject of express contract between the parties. In the former case, the rights being derived entirely from the law, and not from the contract, laws changing them are not within the prohibition. But, in the latter case, although the law authorized the rights to be acquired, yet it authorized them to be acquired only by a contract stipulating for them, and when they are so acquired the contract is within the protection of the Constitution. Robinson *v.* Howe, 13 Wis. 341.

A claim arising out of a tort and not from a contract is not within the prohibition of this clause. Dash *v.* Van Kleek, 7 Johns. 477; Amy *v.* Smith, 1 Litt. 326; Thayer *v.* Seavey, 11 Me. 284.

It was not necessary, nor would it have been safe, to enumerate particular subjects to which the principle they intended to establish should apply. The principle was the inviolability of contracts. This principle was to be protected in whatsoever form it might be assailed. To what purpose enumerate the particular modes of violation which should be forbidden when it was intended to forbid all. Sturges *v.* Crowninshield, 4 Wheat. 122.

A compact between two States is a contract within the meaning of the Constitution. In fact the terms contract and compact are synonymous. Green *v.* Biddle, 8 Wheat. 1; Canal Co. *v.* Railroad Co. 4 G. & J. 1; Allen *v.* McKeen, 1 Sum. 276; Cox *v.* State, 3 Blackf. 193; Spooner *v.* McConnell, 1 McLean, 337; Hogg *v.* Canal Co. 5 Ohio, 410; Achison *v.* Huddleson, 12 How. 293; S. C. 7 Gill, 179; Stokes *v.* Searight, 3 How. 151; Neil *v.* State, 3 How. 720; State *v.* Wheeling Bridge Co. 13 How. 518.

A State can not pass any law impairing the obligation of a compact made by it with the United States. Lowry *v.* Francis, 2 Yerg. 534.

If a grant of land by the United States to a State is on conditions, the acceptance of the grant by the State constitutes a contract. McGee *v.* Mathis, 4 Wall. 143.

The character of the parties to the contract does not prevent the application of the prohibition. The contracting parties, whoever they may be, stand in this respect upon the same ground. Trustees *v.* Rider, 13 Conn. 87; Regents *v.* Williams, 9 G. & J. 365.

Although the Constitution does not mention corporations by name, yet they are within it as a part of the general law, for they are entitled to all the benefits of general laws, like natural persons, unless excluded therefrom by the charter. The contracts of corporations, therefore, have the full guaranty of the Constitution. Bank *v.* Bank of Cape Fear, 13 Ired. 75.

The questions as to the nature, form, extent, construction and validity of contracts is left to be determined by the judicial department of the Government. Trustees *v.* Rider, 13 Conn. 87.

Contracts with States.

There is no distinction between a contract by a State and a contract by an individual. The words are general, and are applicable to contracts of every description. Fletcher *v.* Peck, 6 Cranch, 87; Derby Turnpike Co. *v.* Parks, 10 Conn. 522; Green *v.* Biddle, 8 Wheat. 1; Terrett *v.* Taylor, 9 Cranch, 43; Pawlett *v.* Clark, 9 Cranch, 292; State *v.* Wilson, 7 Cranch, 164; S. C. 2 N. J. 300; Woodruff *v.* State, 3 Ark. 285; Trustees *v.* Rider, 13 Conn. 87; Astrom *v.* Hammond, 3 McLean, 107; Woodruff *v.* Trapnall, 10 How. 190; S. C. 8 Ark. 236; Stanmire *v.* Taylor, 3 Jones (N. C.) 207.

Impairing.

To impair means to alter, so as to make the contract more beneficial to one party and less so to the other, than by its terms it purports to be. Baily *v.* Gentry, 1 Mo. 164.

The impairing of contracts must mean their partial rescindment by legislative authority. Grimball *v.* Ross, T. U. P. Charlt. 175.

Any measure which lessens the value of contracts, that gives them a diminished value, takes from them any of the essential properties of contracts, or which divests them of that priority of lien, obligation or recovery which they would otherwise possess, impairs the obligation. Grimball *v.* Ross, T. U. P. Charlt. 175.

One of the tests that a contract has been impaired is that its value has by legislation been diminished. Planters' Bank *v.* Sharp, 6 How. 301; s. c. 12 Miss. 28.

It is not every statute which affects the value of a contract that impairs its obligation. Curtis *v.* Whitney, 13 Wall. 68.

There is no difference in principle between a law that in terms impairs the obligation of a contract, and one that produces the same effect in the construction and practical execution of it. Canal Co. *v.* Railroad Co. 4 G. & J. 1.

To be in conflict with the Constitution it is not necessary that the act of the legislature should import an actual destruction of the obligation of contracts. It is sufficient that the act imports an impairment of the obligation. If by the legislative act the obligation of contracts is in any degree impaired, or what is the same thing, if the obligation is weakened or rendered less operative, the Constitution is violated, and the act is so far inoperative. Lapsley *v.* Brashears, 4 Litt. 47.

Obligation and right are correlative terms. Whenever there exists a right in one person there is a corresponding obligation upon some other person. In the same proportion as the legal obligation is diminished, suspended or entirely destroyed by relaxing, suspending or abolishing the legal remedy, so in the same proportion is the legal right either impaired or destroyed. Lapsley *v.* Brashears, 4 Litt. 47; McCracken *v.* Hayward, 2 How. 608.

A law which authorizes the discharge of a contract by a smaller sum or at a different time, or in a different manner than the parties have stipulated, impairs its obligation by substituting for the contract of the parties one which they never entered into, and to the performance of which they, of course, had never consented. The old contract is completely annulled, and a legislative contract imposed upon the parties in lieu of it. The degree of injury to the creditor may not be so great as where the contract is declared to be void, but the principle is the same. Golden *v.* Prince, 3 Wash. 313; 5 Hall L. J. 502; Edmondson *v.* Ferguson, 11 Mo. 344.

The language and meaning of the inhibition were designed to embrace proceedings attempting the interpolation of some new term or condition foreign to the original agreement, and therefore inconsistent with and violative thereof. West River Bridge Co. *v.* Dix, 6 How. 507; s. c. 16 Vt. 446; McCauley *v.* Brooks, 16 Cal. 11.

Whatever law releases one party from any article of a stipulation voluntarily and legally entered into by him with another, without the direct assent of the latter, impairs its obligation, because the rights of the creditor are thereby destroyed, and these are ever correspondent to and co-extensive with the duty of the debtor. Jones *v.* Crittenden, 1 Car. L. Rep. 385; Townsend *v.* Townsend, Peck, 1; Pool *v.* Young, 7 Mon. 587; Greenfield *v.* Dorris, 1 Sneed, 548.

The obligation of a contract may be impaired without being entirely destroyed. The last must include the first, but the first does not necessarily include the latter. A statute can no more destroy than it can impair the obligation of a contract. Robinson *v.* Magee, 9 Cal. 81.

This provision does not prohibit all legislation in regard to existing contracts. The effect of the law must be looked to in every instance, and if it diminish the binding force of the contract on the party who makes it, then it is obnoxious to the Constitution, otherwise not. Nevitt *v.* Bank, 14 Miss. 513.

A contract is not to be impaired at all. This is not a question of degree or manner or cause, but of encroaching in any respect on its obligation, dispensing with any part of its force. Planters' Bank *v.* Sharp, 6 How. 301; S. C. 12 Miss. 28; Walker *v.* Whithead, 16 Wall. 314; S. C. 43 Geo. 547.

The objection to a law on the ground of its impairing the obligation of a contract, can never depend upon the extent of the change which the law effects in it. Any deviation from its terms by postponing or accelerating the period of performance which it prescribes, imposing conditions not expressed in the contract, or dispensing with the performance of those which are, however minute or apparently immaterial in their effect upon the contract of the parties, impairs its obligation. Green *v.* Biddle, 8 Wheat. 1; Blanchard *v.* Russell, 13 Mass. 1; McCracken *v.* Hayward, 2 How. 608; Commercial Bank *v.* State, 12 Miss. 439; Winter *v.* Jones, 10 Geo. 190; People *v.* Bond, 10 Cal. 563.

All legislation which materially affects the laws for the enforcement of a contract existing at the time it is made, impairs the obligation of the contract. This is the effect, although no reference is made to such laws by the contract, as fully as if they were written out at the time and incorporated into it. Nevitt *v.* Bank, 14 Miss. 513.

The legislature can not by a subsequent act impair the obligation of a contract by requiring the performance of other conditions not required by the law of the contract itself. The rights as well as the intentions of the parties are fixed by the existing law; therefore to require the performance of other conditions to make the contract operative, is to impair its obligation. The power to impose conditions after the contract is once complete and perfect, is nothing but the power to impair its obligation. Robinson *v.* Magee, 9 Cal. 81.

The obligation of a contract may be impaired by compelling either party to do more than he has promised. An act which should enforce payment before the debt becomes due, would be unconstitutional. The rights of both parties established by the contract are, in the eye of justice, equally sacred. Jones *v.* Crittenden, 1 Car. L. Rep. 385 ; Townsend *v.* Townsend, Peck, 1.

The terms and conditions of executory contracts can not be altered or interfered with in any respect by the legislature. The time, place, person or thing to be done can not be changed by act of assembly. Townsend *v.* Townsend, Peck, 1.

Where the contract is executed, it is impaired by a law operating to divest any right or estate which has passed or become vested under the grant. Phila. W. & B. R. R. Co. *v.* Bowers, 4 Houst. 506.

It is not true that the parties have in view only the property in possession when the contract is formed, or that its obligation does not extend to future acquisitions. Industry, talents and integrity constitute a fund which is as confidently trusted as property itself. Future acquisitions are therefore liable for contracts, and to release them from this liability impairs their obligation. Sturges *v.* Crowninshield, 4 Wheat. 122.

Just in proportion as delay, uncertainty. inadequacy or onerous exactions characterize the remedy, just in that proportion is the obligation actually diminished or impaired. Wood *v.* Wood, 14 Rich. 148.

The civil laws of a State can only have operation co extensive with the territorial limits of the State, and the obligation which contracts derive from those laws must necessarily be circumscribed by the same limits. It is, therefore, utterly impossible that an obligation derived from the laws of one State can be impaired by the laws of any other State. Lapsley *v.* Brashears, 4 Litt. 47.

The courts do refer to the laws of the State where the contract was made in deciding upon its nature and construction, but in doing so they do not proceed upon the notion that the contract brings with it the legal obligation which it derived from the laws of the State where it was made. In referring to the laws of a foreign State, the courts acknowledge that all persons are everywhere under a moral obligation to perform their contracts, and go upon the idea that wherever that moral obligation grows out of a contract conforming to the laws of the State where it was made, there is through the medium of remedies prescribed by the laws of the State where redress is sought, a legal force given to that moral obligation. But there is no provision in the Constitution which requires each State in the Union to give the same legal obligation to contracts made in any State. The Constitution, in that respect, has prescribed no limits to the power of the State. Lapsley *v.* Brashears, 4 Litt. 47.

State Contracts.

It is unquestionably true that one legislature can not, by ordinary legislation, bind or control, in any manner, subsequent legislatures. But it is equally true that by special legislation a subsequent legislature may be bound. Antoni *v.* Wright, 22 Gratt. 833; State Bank *v.* Knoop, 16 How. 369; Ohio Trust Co. *v.* Debolt, 16 How. 416; s. c. 1 Ohio St. 563; State *v.* County Court, 19 Ark. 360; State *v.* Bank, 2 Houst. 99; Humphrey *v.* Pegues, 16 Wall. 244; Wilmington Railroad *v.* Reid, 13 Wall 264; Tomlinson *v.* Branch Bank, 15 Wall. 460; Jefferson Bank *v.* Skelly, 1 Black, 436; s. c. 9 Ohio St. 606; People *v.* Auditor, 7 Mich. 84; Matheny *v.* Golden, 5 Ohio St. 361; Ill. Cent. R. R. Co. *v.* County, 17 Ill. 291; State Bank *v.* People, 5 Ill. 303; Mechanics' Bank *v.* Debolt, 18 How. 380; s. c. 1 Ohio St. 591; Camden & Amboy R. R. Co. *v.* Commissioners, 18 N. J. 71; Daughdrill *v.* Life Ins. Co. 31 Ala. 91; State *v.* Commercial Bank, 7 Ohio, 125; State *v.* Auditor, 5 Ohio St. 444; Ross County Bank *v.* Lewis, 5 Ohio St. 447; Bank *v.* New Albany, 11 Ind. 139; State *v.* Berry, 17 N. J. 81; Gardner *v.* State, 21 N. J. 557; Bank *v.* Edwards, 5 Ired. 516; Bank *v.* Deming, 7 Ired. 55; Municipality *v.* State Bank, 5 La. Ann. 394; Dodge *v.* Woolsey, 18 How. 331; Mechanics' Bank *v.* Thomas, 18 How. 384; Johnson *v.* Comm. 7 Dana, 338; contra, Mott *v.* Penn. R. R Co. 30 Penn. 9; Norwalk Co. *v.* Husted, 3 Ohio St. 586; Toledo Bank *v.* Bond, 1 Ohio St. 622; Exchange Bank *v.* Hines, 3 Ohio St. 1; Milan & R. Plank Road Co. *v.* Husted, 3 Ohio St. 578; Sandusky Bank *v.* Wilson, 7 Ohio St. 48.

A State legislature can not abandon the police power, or give a vested right to its exercise by a corporation or individual. Dingman *v.* People, 51 Ill. 277.

A State may contract with an individual by an act of the legislature. Canal Co. *v.* Railroad Co. 4 G. & J. 1; Winter *v.* Jones, 10 Geo. 190; Trustees *v.* Bailey, 10 Fla. 112.

Every contract with a State presupposes that some consideration is given, or is supposed to be given, by the party—that the community is to receive from it some public benefit which it could not obtain without his aid. Ohio Trust Co. *v.* Debolt, 16 How. 416; s. c. 1 Ohio St. 563.

It is not every declaration of the present will of the sovereign which constitutes a contract with the individual citizen. It does not necessarily follow that a law is intended as a contract from the use of language appropriate to a private agreement. The language must be construed with reference to those who use it, the subject to which they apply it, the context in which it is used, and the purpose for which it is employed. A general statute should not be construed to be a contract when it was obviously designed only as an expression of the legislative will, for the time being, in a matter of mere municipal regulation. When this is the object of the law, those who act on the faith of its provisions do so with notice that it is subject to revocation by the State whenever the public exigencies may demand. People *v.* Roper, 35 N. Y. 629.

Laws passed in the exercise of the ordinary legislative power of a State are not contracts within the purview of the Constitution, and laws which amend or repeal them do not fall beneath the constitutional inhibition. State *v.* Dews, R. M. Charlt. 397 ; Corning *v.* Greene, 23 Barb. 33.

The repeal of a statute before the party has taken all the steps necessary to give him a right under it, does not impair the obligation of a contract. Vanhorne *v.* Dorrance, 2 Dall. 304; Huntsman *v.* Randolph, 5 Hay, 263; Brinsfield *v.* Carter, 2 Geo. 143 ; Mobile R. R. Co. *v.* State, 29 Ala. 573; State *v.* Jones, 6 Wis. 334; State *v.* Gray, 4 Wis. 380; Wise *v.* Rogers, 24 Gratt. 169.

A statute which implies a contract executory, depending upon the further action of the legislature or its agents for its execution, and which is without any consideration in fact or law, may, before its execution and the existence of any consideration, be repealed, for such a contract does not create any rights or duties which can, in legal contemplation, be impaired. Trustees *v.* Rider, 13 Conn. 87.

General regulations for the descent and transmission of property in case of the death of the possessor, to his widow, heirs and next of kin, do not constitute a contract with them so as to bring those laws within the prohibition of the Constitution. In re Lawrence, 5 N. Y. Sur. 310.

A statute which contains a contract is not absolutely unchangeable, for it is a law as well as a contract, and it is of the very nature of law that those of its provisions which are merely legislative modes to give effect to the substantial purposes of the statute may need revision and alteration. The details may, as in other laws, be altered where the alteration does not affect the obligation of the contract. Thornton *v.* Hooper, 14 Cal. 9.

A statute by which a State waives the privilege of sovereignty, and permits itself to be sued, is not a contract, but an ordinary act of legislation. Consequently, the State may withdraw its consent to such waiver whenever it may suppose that justice to the public requires it, even though such withdrawal affects pending suits. Beers *v.* State, 20 How. 527; Bank of Washington *v.* State, 20 How. 530 ; Platenius *v.* State, 17 Ark. 518.

A statute granting an annuity in consideration of public services already rendered, is not a contract, and may be repealed. Pension laws are not contracts. Dale *v.* Governor, 3 Stew. 387.

A statute taking from the board of supervisors the power to make contracts for the publication of the delinquent tax list, and conferring it on another officer before the publication is commenced, does not impair the obligation of a contract previously made with the board, for the contractor must be deemed to have acted with reference to the fact that the matter was within the control of the legislature, and that the law might be changed before he would enter upon the performance of the work. Pott *v.* Supervisors, 25 Wis. 506.

A statute offering a bounty to those who do certain acts, is not a contract except as to those who earn the bounty while it is in force, and a repeal as to others is valid. Salt Co. *v.* East Saginaw, 13 Wall. 373; S. C. 19 Mich. 259.

A claim of personal exemption from taxation, from jury duty or military duty, is not in the nature of a right of property or a corporate franchise. A general law exempting those who have served in the militia for a certain period, from taxation, is valid. People *v.* Roper, 35 N. Y. 629.

It is immaterial whether the instrument by which the public faith is pledged, is in its terms a contract or in form a mere legislative enactment. In either event it is equally a contract within the meaning of the Constitution. Bridge Co. *v.* Hoboken Land Co. 13 N. J. Eq. 81; S. C. 1 Wall. 116.

A statute can not deprive a party of a bounty which has been already earned under a prior act. People *v.* Auditor, 9 Mich. 327.

If the laws in force at the time of the sale of land by the State, provide that the purchaser may revive his contract after a breach thereof, by paying the sum due, with interest, at any time before a second sale, this privilege can not be taken away by a subsequent act. Damman *v.* Commissioners, 4 Wis. 414.

Where a contract is made under authority of law, the right acquired arises not from the law itself, but from the contract to which it pertains as an incident, and the legislature can not divest the right thus acquired. State *v.* Barker, 4 Kans. 379, 435.

If a State authorizes a sale of stock held by it, it can not repeal the law after a sale has been made, and thus deprive a purchaser of the means of enforcing a contract. Baldwin *v.* Comm. 11 Bush, 417.

Where a statute enacts that a corporation shall be responsible and obligated in law to the laborers for work performed under contractors, rights acquired while it is in force can not be impaired by a subsequent statute. Streubel *v.* Mil. & M. R. R. Co. 12 Wis. 67.

A statute which provides that the coupons on a State bond shall be receivable in payment of all taxes, debts and dues to the State, is a contract with the holders, and can not be repealed so as to affect their rights. Antoni *v.* Wright, 23 Gratt. 833.

A person who has been an officer in the militia during the existence of a statute providing that such officers should be exempt from militia duty, may nevertheless be compelled to serve in the militia by a subsequent statute repealing the exemption. Comm. *v.* Bird, 12 Mass. 443.

It was not the purpose of this provision to impose on the courts the duty either of interposing between the legislature and the citizens in matters of pure governmental concern, of trammeling the States in the exercise of their general political powers, or of stamping municipal regulations for the time being with the seal of irrevocability. People *v.* Roper, 35 N. Y. 629.

Where a State gives a contract for printing the laws to one person for certain period, it can not subsequently make a contract with another for the same work. State *v.* Barker, 4 Kans. 379, 435.

A statute exempting the property of municipal corporations from forced sale on executions, is valid if no prior statute has authorized a levy thereon, for at common law no such levy could be made. Gilman *v.* Contra Costa, 8 Cal. 52.

If consolidated bonds, the payment of which is secured by a certain tax, are issued under a statute to compromise outstanding bonds, with a provision that they shall only be used to take up those bonds, no subsequent act can authorize the diversion of such bonds to any other use. McComb *v.* Board of Liquidation, 2 Woods, 48; s. c. 7 C. L. N. 251.

A statute providing a redemption fund to meet municipal indebtedness, may provide that a preference shall be given to the proposal that offers the largest amount of indebtedness for the least amount of money. Youngs *v.* Hall, 9 Nev. 212; contra, Bleakley *v.* Williams, 20 Pitts. L. J. 66.

A statute requiring the holders of county warrants bearing interest at the rate of ten per cent., to surrender them and accept in lieu thereof bonds bearing seven per cent. interest, is void. Brewer *v.* Otoe Co. 1 Neb. 373.

A statute providing that a warrant for a municipal indebtedness shall not be deemed to be valid unless it is presented to and passed by commissioners, is void, for the creditor can not be compelled to accept another and different mode of payment from that provided in his contract. Rose *v.* Estudillo, 39 Cal. 270.

A county government is a portion of the State government, and the county debt created by authority of law is a part of the public State debt; and in the same manner, as there is no remedy against the State, there may be none against the county. A statute may, therefore, change the mode and time of paying the county debt. Hunsaker *v.* Borden, 5 Cal. 288.

If an act passed to induce the creditors of a municipal corporation to surrender old bonds and take new ones, prohibits the issuing of bonds thereafter for any other purpose whatever, except in payment of the bonded debt of the corporation, this prohibition becomes a part of the contract, and is not subject to legislative repeal or amendment, so as to impair or diminish the security of the creditors. Smith *v.* Appleton, 19 Wis. 468.

If the contract in its inception was without a legal remedy for its violation or suspension, the legislature may repeal a statute subsequently passed whereby a remedy was provided. Young *v.* Oregon, 1 Oregon, 213.

The executory contracts of a State have no other than a moral sanction, and depend upon good faith for their performance. No money can be drawn without an appropriation, and no court can compel the legislative department to pass a law to make one. As there is no legal remedy to enforce a contract against a State, a statute forbidding the auditor to issue warrants does not impair the obligation of contracts. Swann *v.* Buck, 40 Miss. 268.

A State law providing for the discontinuance of work on a public building under a contract, is valid, for it leaves the contractor his remedy for damages for a breach of the contract. Lord *v.* Thomas, 64 N. Y. 107.

An act of the legislature authorizing a municipal corporation to subscribe to the stock of a railroad corporation is not a contract. List *v.* Wheeling, 7 W. Va. 501.

Where a fund is pledged for the payment of municipal bonds at the time of their issue, a subsequent statute can not authorize its diversion so as to impair the security of the bondholders. People *v.* Supervisors, 12 Cal. 300; People *v.* Woods, 7 Cal. 579; Western Saving Fund *v.* Philadelphia, 31 Penn. 185; People *v.* Bond, 10 Cal. 563; People *v.* Tillinghast, 10 Cal. 584; English *v.* Supervisors, 19 Cal. 172; Board *v.* Fowler, 19 Cal. 11; Trustees *v.* Bailey, 10 Fla. 112.

If an act authorizing a municipal corporation to issue bonds, provides for the levy and preservation of a tax to pay the same, this constitutes a contract with the bondholders which no subsequent ordinance can impair. Maenhut *v.* New Orleans, 2 Woods, 108; Ranger *v.* New Orleans, 2 Woods, 128.

If a corporation builds an improvement, under a statute which provides for the issue of bonds by the State, to be paid as fast as a fund accumulates for that purpose, an act providing for their redemption at less than par, and authorizing a loan of the fund if no bonds are tendered for redemption, is void. Goldsmith *v.* Brown, 5 Oregon, 418.

Where a statute pledging certain property to the payment of certain debts of a municipal corporation only authorizes a public sale, a subsequent act may provide a new mode for the disposition of those portions of the property which can not be advantageously disposed of at public sale in consequence of existing doubts as to the title thereto. Babcock *v*. Middleton, 20 Cal. 643.

If a municipal corporation obtains a loan by placing certain property in the hands of trustees as a security, and at the time promises not to change the selection or constitution of the trustees, it can not subsequently make any such change. Western Saving Fund *v*. Philadelphia, 31 Penn. 175; s. C. 31 Penn. 185.

If a statute authorizing a municipal corporation to condemn land for a park, provides that the bonds issued to pay for the same shall be a lien thereon, no subsequent act can authorize a sale of the land free from the lien, although the proceeds are to be turned into a sinking fund for the use of the bondholders. Brooklyn Park *v*. Armstrong, 45 N. Y. 234.

If the legislature pledges certain property to secure bonds at the time of their issue, it can not subsequently divest that lien, or postpone it to others. Trustees *v*. Beers, 2 Black, 448.

Executed Contracts.

A contract is a compact between two or more parties, and is either executory or executed. An executory contract is one in which a party binds himself to do or not to do a particular thing. A contract executed is one in which the object of the contract is performed, and this differs in nothing from a grant. A contract executed, as well as one which is executory, contains obligations binding on the parties. A grant, in its own nature, amounts to an extinguishment of the right of the grantor, and implies a contract not to re-assert that right. Since then, in fact, a grant is a contract executed, the obligation of which still continues, and since the Constitution uses the general term contract without distinguishing between those which are executory and those which are executed, it must be construed to comprehend the latter as well as the former. A law annulling conveyances between individuals, and declaring that the grantors shall stand seized of their former estates, would be as repugnant to the Constitution as a law discharging vendors of property from the obligation of executing their contracts by conveyances. Fletcher *v*. Peck, 6 Cranch, 87; Terrett *v*. Taylor, 9 Cranch, 43; Berrett *v*. Oliver, 7 G. & J. 191; Montgomery *v*. Kasson, 16 Cal. 189; Grogan *v*. San Francisco, 18 Cal. 590.

No consideration is necessary to render a grant irrevocable. Derby Turnpike Co. *v*. Parks, 10 Conn. 522.

If an act of the legislature of a State granting certain lands is obtained by fraud and corruption, and the grantee conveys the land to a *bona fide* purchaser for a valuable consideration, an act of the legislature divesting the rights of such purchaser will be unconstitutional and void. Fletcher *v.* Peck, 6 Cranch, 87.

The grant of a part of the land under water, affords no foundation for the inference of an intention in any manner to restrict or impair the right of the State to dispose of or improve the residue, and an improvement which affects the flow of the stream does not impair the obligation of the grant when the injury is remote and consequential. Lansing *v.* Smith, 8 Cow. 146; Hollister *v* Union Co. 9 Conn. 436.

The property of an alien, purchased by him under a special act of the legislature, can not be transferred to another without his consent by mere legislative power. Bonaparte *v.* Camden & Amboy R. R. Co. Bald. 205.

Where a religious corporation is under a disability to convey by its charter, a statute authorizing a sale, violates no contract. Burton's Appeal, 57 Penn. 213.

A grant made for the purpose of public instruction, religious or literary, is not subject to subsequent legislative control any more than if made for private use. Terrett *v.* Taylor, 9 Cranch, 43; Grammar School *v.* Burt, 11 Vt. 632.

The word irrevocable, in a grant, adds nothing to its force. Without that word the grant would be irrevocable. The exercise of the right of eminent domain is not a revocation of the grant. Ill. & Mich. Canal Co. *v.* Railroad Co. 14 Ill. 314.

A State may release its interest in an escheated estate to the occupant, although it has agreed to give one half thereof to an attorney who recovered it, for the release only passes the moiety belonging to the State. Mulligan *v.* Corbins, 7 Wall. 487.

If parties dedicate a square to public use, the legislature can not authorize its sale and use for a purpose foreign to the object of the grant. Warren *v.* Mayor, 22 Iowa, 351.

If a party, by the payment of the purchase money, has become entitled under a State law to a grant of a piece of land, the State can not by a subsequent act provide for a forfeiture of his right unless he obtains the grant within a certain period. Winter *v.* Jones, 10 Geo. 190; Fogg *v.* Williams, 2 Head, 474.

A statute which declares that land shall be forfeited unless improvements are made within a certain time, imposes a condition not contained in the grant, and is unconstitutional. Gaines *v.* Buford. 1 Dana, 481.

A statute giving the assent of the State to the purchase of lands by the United States is a grant of a right to purchase, which the State is not at liberty to qualify or impair by any subsequent act. U. S. *v.* Great Falls Manuf. Co. 21 Md. 119.

A grant of land to a railroad corporation upon certain conditions which are complied with is an executed contract, and the State can not subsequently revoke the grant. Davis *v.* Gray, 16 Wall. 203.

A grant made by the State of certain lands is an executed contract, and the State can not pass any law whereby the estate of those holding under the grant will be impaired or rendered null and void. Fletcher *v.* Peck, 6 Cranch, 87 ; People *v.* Platt, 17 Johns. 195 ; Gaines *v.* Buford, 1 Dana, 481 ; Crenshaw *v.* Slate River Co. 6 Rand. 245.

If a grant of lands includes both sides of an unnavigable river, the State can not by a subsequent law compel the owner to alter a dam already erected, so as to allow of the passage of fish up and down the stream. People *v.* Platt, 17 Johns. 195 ; State *v.* Glenn, 7 Jones (N. C.) 321 ; Cornelius *v.* Glen, 7 Jones (N. C.) 512.

If a mortgage made to a trustee provides a mode of perpetuating the trust, the legislature can not by a subsequent act provide a different mode. Fletcher *v.* R. & B. R. R. Co. 39 Vt. 535.

A statute allowing an occupant to recover compensation for improvements put by him on the land, does not impair the obligation of the grant from the State. Albee *v.* May, 2 Paine, 74; Armstrong *v.* Jackson, 1 Blackf. 374 ; Scott *v.* Mather, 14 Tex. 235 ; contra, Bristoe *v.* Evans, 2 Overt. 341 ; Nelson *v.* Allen, 1 Yerg. 360.

A law which restricts the rights of a claimant as against an occupant of land, in violation of a compact between two States, is unconstitutional. Green *v.* Biddle, 8 Wheat. 1 ; vide Bodley *v.* Gaither, 3 Mon. 57 ; Fowler *v.* Halbert, 4 Bibb, 52 ; Sanders *v.* Norton, 4 Mon. 464 ; M'Kinney *v.* Carroll, 12 Pet. 66; s. c. 5 Mon. 96 ; Fisher *v.* Cockerill, 5 Mon. 129.

A grant of a ferry franchise is a contract the obligation of which the legislature can not impair. McRoberts *v.* Washburne, 10 Minn. 23.

The grantee of a ferry right who pays no consideration for the grant, takes it subject to the power of the legislature to regulate the rates of ferriage. People *v.* Mayor, 32 Barb. 102 ; State *v.* Hudson, 23 N. J. 206 ; s. c. 24 N. J. 718.

If the grant of a license for a ferry is accompanied with a reservation of the power to a State court to establish a bridge alongside of the ferry, the legislature may make the grant directly to another without impairing the obligation of the grant to the licensee. Dyer *v.* Tuscaloosa Bridge Co. 2 Port 296.

The Constitution does not prevent the legislature of any State from enacting such laws as may have for their object the application to public use of the property of any member of the community. Jackson *v.* Winn, 4 Litt. 323; Beekman *v.* Railroad, 3 Paige, 45; Young *v.* McKenzie, 3 Geo. 31; Bloodgood *v.* Railroad Co. 18 Wend. 9.

Private property may be taken for public use, but such appropriations are constitutional and legal only when a fair and just equivalent is awarded to the owner of the property so taken. People *v.* Platt, 17 Johns. 195; Bonaparte *v.* Camden & Amboy R. R. Co. Bald. 205.

Subjecting the land of a grantee to the payment of his debts does not impair the rights derived to him under the grant, for in the very act the full effect of the transfer of interest to him is recognized and asserted. Because it is his is the direct and only reason for subjecting it to his debts. Livingston *v.* Moore, 7 Pet. 469.

A grant by a municipal corporation upon certain conditions requiring large expenditures, and the assumption of onerous obligations, and a compliance with those conditions, constitutes a contract. Brooklyn Central R. R. Co. *v.* Brooklyn City R. R. Co. 32 Barb. 358.

If a municipal corporation conveys land to an ecclesiastical corporation, to be used as a cemetery, with a covenant for quiet enjoyment, it may subsequently prohibit the use of the premises as a cemetery for the interment of the dead, for it has no power as a party to make a contract which shall control or embarrass its legislative powers and duties. Presbyterian Church *v.* New York, 5 Cow. 538.

A statute authorizing a municipal corporation to issue bonds, and thereby bind the citizens, does not impair any obligation contained in the grant of land to the individual citizens from the State. McCoy *v.* Washington Co. 3 Wall. Jr. 381; s. c. 3 Phila. 290.

A municipal corporation can make such contracts only as are allowed by the act of incorporation, and hence it can not abridge its legislative power or bind its legislative capacities. Gozzler *v.* Georgetown, 6 Wheat. 593; Presbyterian Church *v.* New York, 5 Cow. 538; Coates *v.* New York, 7 Cow. 585.

Every right from an absolute ownership in property down to a mere easement, is purchased and holden subject to the restriction that it shall be so exercised as not to injure others. Every purchaser is bound to know that his rights must yield to regular remedies for the suppression of nuisances. Hence a law may be passed to prohibit the use of a place as a cemetery, although there is a covenant in the grant that the place may be so used. Coates *v.* New York, 7 Cow. 585.

Registration Laws.

It is within the undoubted power of State legislatures to pass recording acts by which the elder grantee shall be postponed to a younger, if the prior deed is not recorded within a limited time, and the power is the same whether the deed is dated before or after the passage of the recording act. Though the effect of such a law is to render the prior deed fraudulent and void against a subsequent purchaser, it is not a law impairing the obligation of contracts. The time and manner of their operation, the exceptions to them, and the acts from which the time limited shall begin to run, will generally depend on the sound discretion of the legislature, according to the nature of the titles, the situation of the country, and the emergency which leads to their enactment. Jackson *v.* Lamphire, 3 Pet. 280; Varick *v.* Briggs, 6 Paige, 323; S. C. 22 Wend. 543; Tucker *v.* Harris, 13 Geo. 1; Boston *v.* Cummins, 16 Geo. 102; Stafford *v.* Lick, 7 Cal 479; Succession of John M. Nelson, 24 La. Ann. 25; Rochereau *v.* Delacroix, 26 La. Ann. 584.

A statute requiring the re-registration of deeds already in operation, and registered in conformity with the laws in force at its inception, does not impair the obligation of contracts. Miles *v.* King, 5 Rich. N. S. 146.

Confirmatory Statutes.

An act confirming deeds defectively acknowledged does not impair the obligation of contracts. So far as it has any legal operation, it goes to confirm and not to impair the contracts of the grantors. It gives the very effect to their acts and contracts which they intended to give, and which from mistake or accident has not been effected. Brinton *v.* Sievers, 12 Iowa, 389; Watson *v.* Mercer, 8 Pet. 88; Bell *v.* Perkins, Peck, 261; Barnet *v.* Barnet, 15 S. & R. 72; Tate *v.* Stooltzfoos, 16 S. & R. 35; Dulany *v.* Tilghman, 6 G. & J. 461; Maxey *v.* Wise, 25 Ind. 1; Raverty *v.* Fridge, 3 McLean, 230; Hughes *v.* Cannon, 2 Humph. 589; Barton *v.* Morris, 15 Ohio, 408; Bethune *v.* Dougherty, 30 Geo. 770; Dentzel *v.* Waldie, 30 Cal. 138; Journeay *v.* Gibson, 56 Penn. 57; Chesnut *v.* Shane, 15 Ohio, 599; contra, Pearce *v.* Patton, 7 B. Mon. 162.

A statute confirming a defective levy and sale under an execution, does not impair the obligation of a contract. Mather *v.* Chapman, 6 Conn. 54; Beach *v.* Walker, 6 Conn. 190; Booth *v.* Booth, 7 Conn. 350; Bell *v.* Roberts, 13 Vt. 582; Menges *v.* Wertman, 1 Penn. 218; Norton *v.* Pettibone, 7 Conn. 319; Selsby *v.* Redlon, 19 Wis. 17.

The legislatures of the States may pass a law confirming the doings of courts and other public bodies known to the law. Locke *v.* Dane, 9 Mass. 360; Walters *v.* Bacon, 8 Mass. 468; Patterson *v.* Philbrook, 9 Mass.

151; Goshen *v.* Stonington, 4 Conn. 310; Underwood *v.* Lilly, 10 S. & R. 97; Simmons *v.* Hanover, 40 Mass. 188; Kearney *v.* Taylor, 15 How. 494; Davis *v.* State Bank, 7 Ind. 316; Thornton *v.* McGrath, 1 Duvall, 349.

A statute confirming an illegal assignment of the limits of a jail, will defeat all liability upon a jail bond executed after the assignment, but before the passage of the law, when the alleged escape was simply an entrance into the limits so assigned. Locke *v.* Dane, 9 Mass. 360; Walter *v.* Bacon, 8 Mass. 468; Patterson *v.* Philbrook, 9 Mass. 151.

A statute which renders a judgment valid, which was entered upon a verdict rendered after the expiration of the term, is constitutional. Tilton *v.* Swift, 40 Iowa, 78.

A statute confirming a defective judgment does not impair the obligation of any contract. Underwood *v.* Lilly, 10 S. & R. 97.

A State may by a retroactive act cure any irregularity or want of authority in the levy of a tax, and thereby divest a right of action vested in an individual who has paid the tax under protest. Grim *v.* Weissenberg School District, 57 Penn. 433.

If the subscription of a municipal corporation to the stock of a private corporation is not made in pursuance of the power conferred upon it by statute, the legislature may confirm the act. McMillen *v.* Boyles, 6 Iowa, 304; Bass *v.* Mayor, 38 Geo. 875; Han. & St. Jo. R. R. Co. *v.* Marion, 36 Mo. 294.

The legislature may validate municipal bonds illegally issued. Kunkle *v.* Franklin, 13 Minn. 127; Comer *v.* Folsom, 13 Minn. 219.

If the act of a municipal corporation in subscribing to the stock of a private corporation is void, the legislature may confirm the act. City *v.* Railroad Co. 15 Conn. 475.

Marriage.

Marriage is more than a contract. It is a public institution. Hence, as between husband and wife there is no constitutional provision protecting the marriage itself or the property incident to it from legislative control by general law upon such terms as public policy may dictate. The sovereign power may by general enactment regulate and mold their relative rights and duties at pleasure. Noel *v.* Ewing, 9 Ind. 37; Kelly *v.* McCarthy, 3 Bradf. 7; Thurber *v.* Townsend, 22 N. Y. 517; White *v.* White, 5 Barb. 474.

This provision has never been understood to restrict the general right of the State legislature to legislate on the subject of divorces. Those acts enable some tribunal not to impair a marriage contract, but to liberate one of the parties because it has been broken by the other. Carson *v*. Carson, 40 Miss. 349; Cronise *v*. Cronise, 54 Penn. 255; Dartmouth College *v* Woodward, 4 Wheat. 518; Maguire *v*. Maguire, 7 Dana, 181; Adams *v*. Palmer, 51 Me. 480; Starr *v*. Pease, 8 Conn. 541; Tolen *v*. Tolen, 2 Blackf. 407; Clark *v*. Clark, 10 N. H. 380; Townsend *v*. Griffin, 4 Harring. 440; Cabell *v*. Cabell, 1 Metc. (Ky.) 319; Berthelemy *v*. Johnson, 3 B. Mon. 90; contra, State *v*. Fry, 4 Mo. 120; Bryson *v*. Campbell, 12 Mo. 498; Ponder *v*. Graham, 4 Fla. 23.

A statute which takes away the marital rights of the husband does not impair any contract. White *v*. White, 5 Barb. 474; Thurber *v*. Townsend, 22 N. Y. 517; contra, Holmes *v*. Holmes, 4 Barb. 295.

A statute exempting the property of the husband, from liability for the debts of the wife contracted prior to marriage is valid. Fultz *v*. Fox, 9 B. Mon. 499.

A statute allowing a *feme covert* to hold all property subsequently acquired for her own use, free from the control of her husband, is valid. Kelly *v*. McCarthy, 3 Bradf. 7; Starr *v*. Hamilton, 1 Deady, 268.

A statute enlarging or abridging the wife's right of dower is valid. Noel *v*. Ewing, 9 Ind. 37; Barbour *v*. Barbour, 46 Me. 9; Moore. *v*. Mayor, 8 N. Y. 110; Lucas *v*. Sawyer, 17 Iowa, 517; Magee *v*. Young, 40 Miss. 164.

A statute authorizing the surrogate to sell property so as to pass to the purchaser a title free from the widow's dower is valid. In re Lawrence, 5 N. Y. Sur. 310.

The disability of a *feme covert* to convey property granted to her for her sole and separate use flows from the nature of the use vested in her as implied in equity, and is wholly founded in the law of her relation, and not in the form of the terms of the grant, and may be removed by law without impairing the obligation of the grant contained in the deed. Jones' Appeal, 57 Penn 369.

Public Officers.

A public officer is the mere creature of law created by the sovereign power of the State for public purposes, as the agent of the body politic to give effect to its sovereignty and carry into effect its will. His office is a mere civil institution, established for public political purposes, and may be regulated or changed by society. The mere creature of law, he holds not by contract, and his duties change with the law. Hence the salary may be diminished or abolished during the term of his office. State *v*. Dews, R. M. Charlt. 397; People *v*. Auditor, 2 Ill. 537; Barker *v*. Pittsburgh, 4 Penn. 49; Conner *v*. New York, 2 Sandf. 355; Benford *v*. Gibson, 15 Ala.

521; Butler *v.* Pennsylvania, 10 How. 402; State *v.* Smedes, 26 Miss. 47; Coffin *v.* State, 7 Ind. 157; Hall *v.* State, 39 Wis. 79; Hyde *v.* State, 52 Miss. 665; Gilbert *v.* Commissioners, 8 Blackf. 81 ; Turpen *v.* Commissioners, 7 Ind. 172; Comm. *v.* Bacon, 6 S. & R. 322; Haynes *v.* State, 3 Humph. 480; People *v.* Burrows, 27 Barb. 89; Farwell *v.* Rockland, 62 Me. 296; Denver *v.* Hobart, 10 Nev. 28; Phillips *v.* Mayor, 1 Hilt. 483; Iowa City *v.* Foster, 10 Iowa, 189; Gilbert *v.* Commissioners, 8 Blackf. 81; People *v.* Devlin, 33 N. Y. 269; Swann *v.* Buck, 40 Miss. 268 ; People *v.* Lippincott, 67 Ill. 333; Walker *v.* Dunham, 17 Ind. 483 ; Walker *v.* Peele, 18 Ind. 264; Territory *v.* Pyle, 1 Oregon, 149 ; Bryan *v.* Cattell, 15 Iowa, 538.

The legislature may attach additional duties to a public office without increasing the compensation of the officer. Turpen *v.* Commissioners, 7 Ind 172.

An officer of a public corporation is a public officer. Iowa City *v.* Foster, 10 Iowa, 189; Augusta *v.* Sweeny, 44 Geo. 463 ; Comm *v.* Bacon, 6 S. & R. 322.

Licenses.

A statute permitting a party to establish a lottery merely grants an immunity which may be withdrawn if no contract made with others is thereby impaired. Gregory *v.* Shelby College, 2 Metc. (Ky.) 589; Bass *v.* Mayor, Meigs, 421 ; State *v.* Phalen, 3 Harring. 441 ; Phalen *v.* Comm. 1 Rob. (Va.) 713 ; S. C. 8 How. 163; Freleigh *v.* State, 8 Mo. 606 ; State *v.* Sterling, 8 Mo. 697.

If a contract has been made by a party holding an authority to establish a lottery, the legislature can not impair the contract. Gregory *v.* Shelby College, 2 Metc. (Ky.) 589; State *v.* Phalen, 3 Harring. 441 ; State *v.* Hawthorn, 9 Mo. 389.

If no bonus is given for a right to establish a lottery, the legislature may subsequently levy a tax on the franchise. Wendover *v.* Lexington, 15 B. Mon. 258.

A license to sell liquor is not a contract between the State and the person licensed, but is merely a temporary permit to do what otherwise would be an offense against the general law. It is issued as a part of the police system of the State, and is subject to modification or revocation. Calder *v.* Kurby, 71 Mass. 597; Metropolitan Board *v.* Barrie, 34 N. Y. 657; Fell *v.* State, 42 Md. 71 ; State *v.* Holmes, 38 N. H. 225.

Although the effect of a license to practice law or medicine, or to sell goods at public auction, gives to the members of the professions something of an exclusive character, and incidentally confers valuable privileges, yet the design of the license is to protect the community from the consequences of a want of professional qualifications, and to benefit the public by enabling the professions to acquire professional merits. Consequently the license may be modified in any manner which the public welfare may demand. A tax upon such as are licensed is not unconstitutional. State *v.* Gazlay, 5 Ohio, 14; Simmons *v.* State, 12 Mo. 268; New Orleans *v.* Turpin, 13 La. Ann. 56; State *v.* Waples, 12 La. Ann. 343; State *v.* Fellowes, 12 La. Ann. 344.

Where a foreign corporation is required to obtain a certificate before it can transact business in the State, such certificate does not constitute a contract so as to prohibit subsequent taxation by the laws of the State. Home Ins. Co. *v.* Augusta, 93 U. S. 116.

A statute requiring the oath of loyalty from an attorney does not impair the obligation of any contract. State *v.* Garesche, 36 Mo. 256.

Taxes.

If the State, for a valuable consideration, stipulates that certain lands shall be exempt from taxation, it can not pass any law to impair the obligation of such a contract. State *v.* Wilson, 7 Cranch, 164; S. C. 2 N. J. 300.

If a State in issuing scrip for land provides that the land shall be exempt from taxation for a certain period, it can not repeal the exemption as to lands paid for by scrip issued before the repeal. McGee *v.* Mathis, 4 Wall. 143.

If a statute which provides that all lands purchased from the United States shall be exempt from taxation for a certain period from the time of the purchase, the land can not be taxed until the expiration of that time. It is different from a statute merely exempting property from present taxation. In the one case there is a specific contract; in the other there is no contract and no obligation to extend the obligation beyond the present time. Thompson *v.* Holton, 6 McLean, 386.

If the privilege of exemption of taxation is annexed to the land itself, it will pass to a purchaser. State *v.* Wilson, 7 Cranch, 164; S. C. 2 N. J. 300.

A statute releasing a railroad corporation from a tax lawfully imposed upon it by a municipal corporation, impairs the obligation of the contract, and is void. City *v.* Ill. Central R. R. Co, 39 Iowa, 36.

A statute imposing a tax on a loan may authorize the borrower to deduct the amount of the tax from the interest, for taxation does not impair the obligation of contracts within the meaning of the inhibition. Maltby *v.* Reading & Col. R. R. Co. 52 Penn. 140.

A statute imposing a tax on a mortgage is valid, for it affirms the contract, and taxes the subject for maintaining it. Cook *v*. Smith, 30 N. J. 387.

A bond received as a security for the purchase money of property, or for the payment of a loan of money, may be taxed to any extent required by the State government, for all property is taken subject to the taxes that may be laid by the government which protects it. Weston *v*. Charleston, Harp. 340; s. c. 2 Pet. 449.

A tax upon annual rents reserved in leases does not impair the obligation of any contract. Loring *v*. State, 16 Ohio, 590; Livingston *v*. Hollenbeck, 4 Barb. 9.

A tax upon a new subject, or an increased tax on an old one, does not impair the obligation of a contract, although such taxation may affect particular contracts, as it may increase the debt of one person and lessen the security of another, or may impose additional burdens on one class and release the burdens of another. North Mo. Railroad *v*. Maguire, 20 Wall. 46; s. c. 49 Mo. 490.

A State may tax bonds issued by itself for borrowed money. Champaign Bank *v*. Smith, 7 Ohio St. 42.

A State tax upon bonds of a corporation held by non-residents is void, for no law of the State inconsistent with the terms of a contract made with or payable to parties out of the State, can have any effect upon the contract while in the hands of such parties or non-residents. State Tax on Foreign Held Bonds, 15 Wall. 300; contra, Maltby *v*. Reading & Col. R. R. Co. 52 Penn. 140; Susquehanna Canal Co. *v*. Comm. 72 Penn. 72; Del. R. R. Co. *v*. Comm. 66 Penn. 64; Pittsburgh F. W. & C. R R. Co. *v*. Comm. 66 Penn. 73; s. c. 3 Brews. 355.

The rights of a purchaser at a tax sale are derived from the contract which the law authorized to be made at the time of the sale, and if that was for an absolute deed, when the time for redemption expires, a statute which subsequently extends the time of redemption is void. Robinson *v*. Howe, 13 Wis. 341; Dikeman *v*. Dikeman, 11 Paige, 484; contra, Gault's Appeal, 33 Penn. 94.

A statute allowing a purchaser of land at a tax sale to recover the money paid to the collector above the taxes and costs does not, upon giving him an indemnifying bond, violate any contract against the consent of any person whose consent is necessary. Smith *v*. Merchand, 7 S. & R. 260.

A statute requiring that the holder of a certificate of tax sale shall give notice to the occupant of the land of his intention to apply for a deed a certain time before doing so, is valid. Curtis *v*. Whitney, 13 Wall. 68.

If the legislature does not attempt to lessen or impair the effect of a tax deed as evidence of matters contained in it, or graft upon the contract some new conditions, it may regulate the mere form or verbiage of the conveyance by an act passed after the sale. Lain *v.* Shepardson, 18 Wis. 59.

If a tax deed by the law existing at the time of its execution is conclusive evidence of the regularity of the sale, a subsequent act making it only *prima facie* evidence is void. Smith *v.* Cleveland, 17 Wis. 556.

Where a State issues bonds for its debts, and provides that the coupons shall be receivable for taxes, this provision can not be repealed by a subsequent act. Antoni *v.* Wright, 22 Gratt. 833.

Bank Notes.

If the charter of a bank whose stock is owned by the State, contains a provision that the notes of the bank shall be received in payment of all debts due to the State, a repeal of this provision can not affect the notes in circulation at the time of the repeal. Woodruff *v.* Trapnall, 10 How. 190; s. c. 8 Ark. 236; Paup *v.* Drew, 19 How. 218; s. c. 9 Ark. 205; Trigg *v.* Drew, 10 How. 224.

Where a statute at the time of the issue of the bills of a bank founded on the funds of the State, provides that such bills as are payable in gold or silver coin shall be receivable in payment of taxes, a law providing that depreciated bills shall not be received is valid. Graniteville Manuf. Co. *v.* Roper, 15 Rich. 138.

If a State, in establishing a bank as a State institution, provides that its notes shall be receivable for taxes due the State, this provision is a contract between the State and every noteholder, the obligation of which can not be impaired. Furman *v.* Nichol, 8 Wall. 44.

Such a guaranty is not a personal one. It attaches to the note the same as if it were written on the back of it, and goes with the note into the hands of every holder. Furman *v* Nichol, 8 Wall 44.

A statute appropriating the assets of a bank whose capital was furnished by the State to pay its debts, operates as an assignment, and can not be repealed by a subsequent act. Barings *v.* Dabney, 19 Wall. 1.

If a bank is created, and its capital furnished by the State, a statute appropriating its assets to pay a debt of the State guaranteed by the bank, to the prejudice of the creditors of the bank, is void. Barings *v.* Dabney, 19 Wall. 1.

If the notes of a bank are made payable at a particular place, a statute which requires it to receive them in payment of notes of other banks presented for payment by it, is void because it impairs the obligation of the notes. Bank *v.* Bank of Cape Fear, 13 Ired. 75.

A statute creating an agent for a bank without its knowledge or consent, and authorizing that agent to receive at his discretion, against the consent of the bank, whatever currency he may choose to receive in payment of debts due to the principal, and making such payment a satisfaction of the debt, is void. Bank *v.* McVeigh, 20 Gratt. 457.

A law which throws the burden of proof on the plaintiff, to show that bank bills which are the cause of action have never been used in aid of the rebellion, if the defendant will swear that he has reason to believe that they were so used, imposes upon the plaintiff an impossibility, and is tantamount to destroying the contract on the simple oath of the defendant as to his belief, and is void. Marsh *v.* Burroughs, 1 Woods, 463.

A statute which permits bank notes to be tendered for a debt due to the bank, but assigned before the passage of the statute, is unconstitutional. As between the original parties to a note, a law of set-off, though enacted subsequently to the execution of the note, may apply to it, for in this view it relates to the remedy. But when the note is in the hands of a *bona fide* assignee, an offset as between the original parties to the note can not be applied to it without essentially impairing the legal effect of the contract of assignment. Dundas *v.* Bowler, 3 McLean, 397.

Validating Contracts.

A law which gives validity to a void contract, does not impair the obligation of that contract. To create a contract, and to impair or destroy one, do not mean the same thing. Satterlee *v.* Matthewson, 2 Pet. 380; Hess *v.* Werts, 4 S. & R. 356; Bleakney *v.* Farmers' Bank, 17 S. & R. 64; Bridgeport *v.* Railroad Co. 15 Conn. 475; Central Bank *v.* Empire Stone Dressing Co. 26 Barb. 23.

A statute repealing a law which prohibited suits against Indians is valid, and does not impair the obligation of contracts. Stokes *v.* Redman, 5 R. I. 405.

A statute which makes previous payments of usurious interest valid, and allows the party to retain them, does not impair the obligation of the contract. Sparks *v.* Clapper, 30 Ind. 204.

A statute permitting the enforcement of usurious contracts is valid, although it applies to prior contracts. Woodruff *v.* Scruggs, 27 Ark. 26; Town *v.* Peace, 25 Gratt. 1; Curtis *v.* Leavitt, 15 N. Y. 9; Welch *v.* Wadsworth, 30 Conn. 149; Wood *v.* Kennedy, 19 Ind. 68; Andrews *v.*

Russell, 7 Blackf. 474; Wilson *v.* Hardesty, 1 Md. Ch. 66; Baugher *v.* Nelson, 9 Gill, 299; Savings Bank *v.* Bates, 8 Conn. 505; Grimes *v.* Doe, 8 Blackf. 371; Savings Bank *v.* Allen, 28 Conn. 97; contra, Morton *v.* Rutherford, 18 Wis. 298.

An act altering the statute of frauds, and giving validity to a contract which was previously void, does not violate the Constitution. Baker *v.* Herndon, 17 Geo. 568.

The repeal of a statute prohibiting stock-jobbing may give validity to prior contracts. Washburn *v.* Franklin, 35 Barb. 599.

A statute requiring a municipal corporation to pay for the services of an officer, rendered under a prior act which required that the services should be paid for by other persons, does not impair the obligation of a contract. Southworth *v.* City, 24 La. Ann. 312.

A State may make the breach of a pre-existing contract criminal, although it was before only the subject of a suit for damages. Blann *v.* State, 39 Ala. 353.

A State Constitution which provides that persons bound to service by contract or indenture without collusion or fraud, shall be held to the specific performance of their contracts or indentures, although the same were void when such State Constitution was adopted, is not in conflict with the Constitution of the United States. Phoebe *v.* Jay, Breese, 207.

Municipal Ordinances.

There is a distinction between a municipal ordinance for the public safety or good, and an ordinance for the pecuniary benefit of the corporation itself. An ordinance requiring a license fee after the granting of a right to run street cars in a city, is void. Mayor *v.* Second Av. R. R. Co. 34 Barb. 41.

A municipal corporation can not revoke a donation actually made, or impose new terms or duties upon the donee. Louisville *v.* University, 15 B. Mon. 642.

The repeal of an ordinance of a municipal corporation requiring a bond from an auctioneer, can not destroy or affect any right which was acquired by any person under the ordinance. McMechen *v.* Mayor, 2 H. & J. 41.

When a municipal corporation engages in things not public in their nature, it acts as a private individual—no longer legislates, but contracts—and is as much bound by its engagements as a natural person. Western Saving Fund *v.* Philadelphia, 31 Penn. 185; Western Saving Fund *v.* Philadelphia, 31 Penn. 175.

If a municipal corporation sells lots purporting to be bounded on a public street, the use of such space as a street passes as appurtenant to the grant, and the corporation can not afterward alter or defeat the dedication. Breed *v.* Cunningham, 2 Cal. 361.

Commercial Paper.

A statute which provides that if the last day of grace falls on a holiday, the negotiable note or bill shall be payable on the preceding day, is valid. Days of grace make no part of the original contract. Barlow *v.* Gregory, 31 Conn. 261.

A statute which provides that an indorser shall be bound without demand, notice or protest, impairs the obligation of the contract. Farmers' Bank *v.* Gunnell, 26 Gratt. 131.

A statute changing the mode of giving notice of protest to indorsers is valid, and applies to notes made prior to its passage. Levering *v.* Washington, 3 Minn. 323.

Special Instances.

The repeal of a law which is contrary to the Constitution of the State and void, does not impair the obligation of any contract. Vanhorne *v.* Dorrance, 2 Dall. 304; Walker *v.* Tipton, 3 Dana, 3.

If a statute is void, its repeal does not impair the obligation of contracts. Barings *v.* Dabney, 19 Wall. 1.

A vote of the people authorizing a municipal corporation to subscribe for stock in a railroad corporation does not form a contract. Until the subscription is actually made, the contract is unexecuted. List *v.* Wheeling, 7 W. Va. 501.

If a railroad commissioner merely has the power to approve or disapprove of the abandonment of a station, his consent upon condition that the corporation build a depot at another place, does not constitute a contract that binds the State. State *v.* New Haven & N. R. R. Co. 43 Conn. 351.

An act of the legislature is passed only when it has gone through all the forms made necessary by the State Constitution to give it force and validity as a binding rule of conduct for the citizen. Its passage dates from the time it ceases to be a mere proposition or bill and passes into a law. It can not impair a contract made while it is pending before the executive, any more than it can destroy a legal obligation existing before it was moved in by the legislature. Wartman *v.* Philadelphia, 33 Penn. 202.

If a professor accepts an office in a university controlled by the State, subject to law, his employment may be terminated at the discretion of the legislature. Head *v.* University, 19 Wall. 526; s. c. 47 Mo. 220.

A judgment for damages in a proceeding to appropriate private property to public uses, is not a contract, and the State may pass an act to set it aside. Until the property is actually taken and the compensation is made or provided, the power of the State over the matter is not ended. Garrison *v.* Mayor, 21 Wall. 196; In re Broadway, 61 Barb. 483; s. c. 49 N. Y. 150.

A State law discharging a testamentary trustee upon his own request, and appointing a new trustee, is valid, for no matter of contract is involved therein. Williamson *v.* Suydam, 6 Wall. 723.

A State law imposing a tax on bonds and stocks of foreign corporations owned by citizens of the State, is valid. Worthington *v.* Sebastian, 25 Ohio St. 1; Great Barrington *v.* Berkshire, 33 Mass. 572; McKeen *v.* Northampton, 49 Penn. 519.

A law providing for the distribution of the assets of persons dying insolvent, is valid as to the estate of a person dying after its passage, in the case of a judgment which was not a lien upon the estate, for a general creditor has no right to any particular part of the estate of the debtor. Deichman's Appeal, 2 Whart. 395.

A statute which declares all debts incurred by the State in aid of a rebellion against the Federal Government void, is valid. Leak *v.* Commissioners, 64 N. C. 132.

A statute providing for the sale of lands held by joint tenants or tenants in common, is valid, although it may have the effect to destroy a prior lease made by one of the tenants. Richardson *v.* Monson, 23 Conn. 94.

If a license to erect a dam in a navigable river is defeasible by the terms thereof, it may be modified or revoked. Monongahela Nav. Co. *v.* Coons, 6 W. & S. 101; Sus. Canal Co. *v.* Wright, 9 W. & S 9; Rundle *v.* Del. & R. Canal Co. 14 How. 80; s. c. 1 Wall. Jr. 275; Pratt *v.* Brown, 3 Wis. 603; vide Glover *v.* Powell, 10 N. J. Eq. 211; Crenshaw *v.* State River Co. 6 Rand. 245.

A State legislature may authorize an administrator to apply to a court for a sale of the real estate of an intestate to pay his debts. Florentine *v.* Barton, 2 Wall. 210.

Where a deed of trust authorizes the trustee, upon a default in paying certain notes, to sell the property, the sale can not be suspended for a fixed term. Taylor *v.* Stearns, 18 Gratt. 244.

A statute which releases the sheriff and his sureties from their liability on his official bond, is void. State *v.* Gatzweiller, 49 Mo. 18.

A statute changing a joint bond into a several bond, and permitting a suit against the representatives of a deceased surety, is void. Fielden *v.* Lahens, 6 Blatch. 524.

A statute which releases a tenant from his liability to pay rent under a covenant in the l ase where he has been compelled to pay it to the military authorities of the United States, is void. Clark *v.* Ticknor, 49 Mo. 144.

A statute authorizing a party to surrender the property for which the contract was made in full discharge of his indebtedness, is void. Abercrombie *v.* Baxter, 44 Geo. 36.

If a mortgage stipulates for priority for a subsequent loan to be made by the State, the State may authorize another to make the loan for a longer term, and without any provision for a sinking fund, without impairing the obligation of the contract, but not at a higher rate of interest. Campbell *v.* T. & N. O. R. R. Co. 2 Woods, 263.

A statute which provides that all contracts, without regard to the terms of payment made by the parties, shall be payable in instalments, is void. Jacobs *v.* Smallwood, 63 N. C. 112; Aycock *v.* Martin, 37 Geo. 124.

A statute authorizing the sale of property free from incumbrances before the maturity of a mortgage, is void if it expedites the payment of the loan. Randolph *v.* Middleton, 26 N. J. Eq. 543.

A statute allowing the plaintiff to recover damages in addition to the usual interest, enlarges the contract, and is void. Steen *v.* Finley, 25 Miss. 535.

A statute allowing interest on a debt which did not bear interest before that time, is void. Goggans *v.* Turnipseed, 1 Rich. N. S. 80.

An attempt to deprive a creditor of interest on an overdue debt, is an attempt to impair the implied obligation of the contract, and unconstitutional. Bleakley *v.* Williams, 20 Pitts. L. J. 66.

Interest, though an incident to the debt, is impliedly a part of the contract, and the contracting parties are to be presumed to have had reference to the law as it existed at the time the contract was made, and as a consequence no statute altering the rate of interest, can be made to affect contracts entered into before its passage. Myrick *v.* Battle, 5 Fla. 345; Lee *v.* Davis, 1 A. K. Marsh. 397; Bryan *v.* Moore, 1 Minor, 377; Hubbard *v.* Callahan, 42 Conn. 524.

A statute requiring an officer of the State to pay a higher rate of interest on moneys detained by him, than was allowed at the time the obligation arose, is void. Woodruff *v.* State, 3 Ark. 285.

A State law depriving a lessee of an action for forcible entry and detainer against the lessor is valid, if the action does not permit an inquiry into the title, although the lease stipulates for quiet possession. Drehman *v.* Stifle, 8 Wall. 595; S. C. 41 Mo. 184.

A State law which requires the plaintiff to prove the consideration where the defendant files a plea under oath, alleging that the obligation in whole or in part has been used for an illegal purpose, is void. Edwards *v.* Dixon, 53 Geo. 334.

A statute requiring a party to establish the genuineness of his certificate, in order to be entitled to a survey and a patent under it, is valid. League *v.* De Young, 11 How. 185.

The sureties upon the bond of a public officer can not be made liable for his failure to discharge the duties of another additional office imposed upon him by an act passed after the execution of the bond. Reynolds *v.* Hall, 2 Ill. 35.

A statute prohibiting a hazardous or pernicious business is valid, although it affects prior contracts. People *v.* Hawley, 3 Mich. 330.

If the legislature passes a law which declares that all contracts entered into after its passage shall be subject to the power of future legislatures, to make such changes in the obligations created by them as they may see fit, it is void. Goenen *v.* Schroeder, 8 Minn. 387.

If a scholarship, which is a contract for tuition in consideration of a prepaid subscription, does not name the place where the tuition is to be given, the locality of the college may be changed. Houston *v.* Jefferson College, 63 Penn. 428.

The legislature may remove the seat of justice from one place to any other place in the county, although the commissioners appointed to select the place have made a contract for the purchase of lands for the site, or received donations from those interested in the location. The designation of a place in which the courts of a county shall be held, the mode of making the selection, and of appointing the persons to act on behalf of the public in procuring or disposing of land for these purposes, or erecting the requisite buildings, are matters of political arrangement and expediency, and necessarily the subjects of legislative discretion. Alley *v.* Denson, 8 Tex. 297; Adams *v.* Logan, 11 Ill. 336; Harris *v.* Shaw, 13 Ill. 456; State *v.* Jones, 1 Ired. 414; Elwell *v.* Tucker, 1 Blackf. 285; Hamrick *v.* House, 17 Geo. 56; Newton *v.* Commissioners, 26 Ohio St. 618; Armstrong *v.* Commissioners, 4 Blackf. 208; Moses *v.* Kearney, 31 Ark. 261; contra, State *v.* Perry Co. 5 Ohio St. 497.

A statute requiring a party who has a contract with the State to submit his claim to a board of examiners for approval, is void. McCauley *v.* Brooks, 16 Cal. 11.

A statute mitigating the severity of the penalty in bonds, and allowing the party injured to recover as much as he deserves in equity and good conscience to receive, is valid, although it operates upon penalties and forfeitures previously incurred. Potter *v.* Sturdevant, 4 Me. 154.

The legislature can not make the opinion of the attorney general that a contract is illegal, conclusive upon the contractor. Young *v.* Beardsley, 11 Paige, 93.

A statute declaring contracts made during the war, the consideration whereof was slaves, void, impairs the obligation of contracts, and is void. Roach *v.* Gunter, 44 Ala. 209; McElvain *v.* Mudd, 44 Ala. 48; Fitzpatrick *v.* Hearne, 44 Ala. 171; Curry *v.* Davis, 44 Ala. 281; Osborn *v.* Nicholson, 13 Wall. 654; Boyce *v.* Tabb, 18 Wall. 546.

A provision in a State Constitution that prohibits the enforcement of contracts for slaves is void. Jacoway *v.* Denton, 25 Ark. 625; Calhoun *v.* Calhoun, 2 Rich. N. S. 283; McNealy *v.* Gregory, 13 Fla. 417; French *v.* Tomlin, 19 A. L. Reg. 641; White *v.* Hart, 13 Wall. 646; S. C. 39 Geo. 306; contra, Shorter *v.* Cobb, 39 Geo. 285; Armstrong *v.* Lecompte, 21 La. Ann. 528; Dranguet *v.* Rost, 21 La. Ann. 538.

A statute declaring contracts, the consideration whereof was confederate currency, void, impairs the obligation of the contract, and is null. Roach *v.* Gunter, 44 Ala. 209; Delmas *v.* Ins. Co. 14 Wall. 661; Forscheimer *v.* Holly, 14 Fla. 239; Marsh *v.* Burroughs, 1 Woods, 463; Hatch *v.* Burroughs, 1 Woods, 439.

A provision in a State Constitution declaring that all contracts, the consideration of which was confederate money, notes or bonds, are void, is invalid. Delmas *v.* Ins. Co. 14 Wall. 661.

A statute which declares that a certain consideration shall be deemed to be void, impairs the obligation of contracts based thereon. McNealy *v.* Gregory, 13 Fla. 417.

A statute which enacts that a party holding a contract which was intended to be paid in confederate money, or other paper currency, shall only recover the value of the confederate money or other paper at the time of the making of the contract, with interest, is void, for it allows a party by parol to set up another and different contract from that which the writing imports. Leach *v.* Smith, 25 Ark. 246; Woodruff *v.* Tilly, 25 Ark. 309.

If a contract is made payable in confederate notes, a statute which permits the jury to render a verdict according to the value of the consideration, and not according to the value of the currency, is void, for it substitutes the judgment of the jury upon the value of the contract for the value stipulated by the parties. Wilmington & Weldon R. R. Co. *v.* King, 91 U. S. 3.

A State law requiring the plaintiff to prove the consideration, when the defendant files a plea alleging that the obligation, in whole or in part, has been used for an illegal purpose, is void, when applied to a suit by the holder of a bank bill against a stockholder under a charter granted prior to the act. Branch *v*. Baker, 53 Geo. 502.

A statute allowing a guardian to sell his real estate and invest the proceeds in other securities for the protection of the infants, is valid, although a prior statute made their claim a lien on the land. Lobrano *v*. Nelligan, 9 Wall. 295.

A statute repealing a law imposing a personal liability upon the stockholders for the debts of the corporation, can not affect debts contracted before its passage. Conant *v*. Van Shaick, 24 Barb. 87 ; Hawthorne *v*. Calif, 2 Wall. 10; contra, Coffin *v*. Rich, 45 Me. 507.

A statute may relieve stockholders who subsequently subscribe from personal liability for the debts of the corporation, although the debts were contracted under a law which made stockholders personally liable. Ochiltree *v*. Railroad Company, 21 Wall. 249.

State Insolvent Laws.

An insolvent law which releases the debtor from a debt contracted prior to its enactment, impairs the obligation of the contract, and is unconstitutional. Sturges *v*. Crowninshield, 4 Wheat. 122 ; Oldens *v*. Hallet, 5 N. J. 466 ; Boardman *v*. De Forrest, 5 Conn. 1 ; Farmers' Bank *v*. Smith, 6 Wheat. 131 ; s. c. 3 S. & R. 63 ; Roosevelt *v*. Cebra, 17 Johns. 108 ; Post *v*. Riley, 18 Johns. 54 ; Golden *v*. Prince, 3 Wash. 313 ; 5 Hall L. J. 502 ; In re Wendell, 19 Johns. 153; contra, Adams *v*. Storey, 1 Paine, 79; Barber *v*. Minturn, 1 Day, 136.

If the law of the State at the time the contract was made in effect provided that the obligation of the contract should not be absolute, but qualified by the condition that the party should be discharged upon his becoming insolvent and complying with the requisitions of the insolvent law, the qualification attached to the contract by law the moment the contract was made, became inseparable from it, and traveled with it through all the stages of its existence, until the condition was consummated by the final certificate of discharge. Ogden *v*. Saunders, 12 Wheat. 213.

A discharge under a State insolvent law is valid where the contract was made between citizens of the State under whose law the discharge was obtained after the enactment of the law. Ogden *v*. Saunders, 12 Wheat. 213; Mather *v*. Bush, 16 Johns. 233 ; Blanchard *v*. Russell, 13 Mass. 1 ; Baker *v*. Wheaton, 5 Mass. 509 ; Smith *v*. Parsons, 1 Ohio, 236; Walsh *v*. Farrand, 13 Mass. 19; Pugh *v*. Bussel, 2 Blackf. 366 ; Wilson *v*. Matthews, 32 Ala. 332; Alexander *v*. Gibson, 1 N. & McC. 480; Jacques *v*. Marchand,

6 Cow. 497; contra, Vanuxem *v.* Hazlehursts, 4 N. J. 192; Smith *v.* Mead, 3 Conn. 253; Hammett *v.* Anderson, 3 Conn. 304; Herring *v.* Selding, 2 Ark. 12; Medbury *v.* Hopkins, 3 Conn. 472; Hinkley *v.* Marian, 3 Mason, 88; Ballantine *v.* Haight, 16 N. J. 196.

The proof of the debt, and the receiving of a dividend under proceedings in insolvency under an act which is void as against antecedent creditors, will not give validity to a discharge otherwise void. An act of the legislature which it has no constitutional right or power to pass, is a nullity, and all proceedings under it are void. The acts of individual citizens can give no force or effect to them. Kimberly *v.* Ely, 23 Mass. 440; Hammett *v.* Anderson, 3 Conn. 304; contra, Van Hook *v.* Whitlock, 26 Wend. 43; S. C. 7 Paige, 376.

A discharge not valid under the Constitution in the Federal courts, is equally invalid in the State courts. Ogden *v.* Saunders, 12 Wheat. 213; Frey *v.* Kirk, 4 G. & J. 509; Shaw *v.* Robbins, 12 Wheat. 369 n.; Cook Moffat, 5 How. 295; Poe *v.* Duck, 5 Md. 1; Spear *v.* Peabody, 10 La. Ann. 146; Fisher *v.* Wheeler, 5 La. Ann. 271; Beers *v.* Rhea, 5 Tex. 349; contra, Atwater *v.* Townsend, 4 Conn. 47; Smith *v.* Healy, 4 Conn. 49.

The power of the State over the contracts of its citizens is not limited by the power to make them parties to the proceedings in insolvency, for the insolvent law qualifies the contract from its inception. Stoddard *v.* Harrington, 100 Mass. 87.

If a foreign debtor removes to the State where the creditor resides, and there obtains a discharge, it will be valid against the creditor, for he is bound by the laws of his own State. Beal *v.* Burchstead, 64 Mass. 523.

If the indorsee and the maker of a note reside in the State at the time when the discharge is granted, the discharge will bar the debt, although the payee was a citizen of another State. Wheelock *v.* Leonard, 20 Penn. 440.

If both parties are citizens of the State, a discharge will be a bar to the debt, although the contract was made and was to be performed in another State. Marsh *v.* Putnam, 69 Mass. 551; contra, Smith *v.* Mead, 3 Conn. 253.

If a citizen of the State under whose laws the discharge was granted had previously obtained a judgment in his own State, and then recovered judgment in an action in another State upon the first judgment, the discharge will release the debtor from both judgments. Brest *v.* Smith, 5 Biss. 62.

The discharge will bar the debt of a citizen of the same State, although it has been merged in a judgment rendered in the courts of another State. Although a judgment for some purposes is considered as a merger of the former, and as constituting a new cause of action, yet when the essential rights of parties are influenced by the nature of the original contract, the courts will look into the judgment for the purpose of ascertaining what the nature of such original cause of action was. Betts *v.* Bagley, 29 Mass. 572.

If a contract was made between parties who at the time were not citizens of the State, but who became citizens of the State before the filing of the petition for a discharge, the discharge will be a bar to the debt. Hall *v.* Winchell, 38 Vt. 581; contra, Witt *v.* Follett, 2 Wend. 457.

If the contract was made in the State, and was to be performed in the State, and both parties resided there at the time the discharge was obtained, the discharge will bar an action upon the contract in the courts of another State. Both parties owe allegiance to the same laws, and by them their relations to each other are governed. Hempstead *v.* Reed, 6 Conn. 480; Pitkin *v.* Thompson, 30 Mass. 64; Williams *v.* Guignard, 2 How. (Miss.) 722; Stone *v.* Tibbetts, 26 Me. 110; Hall *v.* Boardman, 14 N. H. 38; Wheelock *v.* Leonard, 20 Penn. 440; Urton *v.* Hunter, 2 W. Va. 83.

If the creditor is a permanent resident in the State, both at the time when the debt is created and when the discharge is granted, the discharge will be a bar to his debt, although he is an alien. Vohn Glahn *v.* Varrence, 1 Dillon, 515.

An assignment in insolvency, as against citizens of the State, will pass property situate in another State. Hoag *v.* Hunt, 21 N. H. 106.

A citizen of the State where the proceedings in insolvency are pending can not levy an attachment upon property in another State. Wilson *v.* Matthews, 32 Ala. 332; Smith *v.* Brown, 43 N. H. 44; Einer *v.* Beste, 32 Mo. 240.

A State insolvent law can not dissolve an attachment made by a citizen of the State upon the property of the debtor in another State. Upton *v.* Hubbard, 28 Conn. 274.

A creditor who has obtained a judgment may show that the agreement which was the foundation of the judgment was made antecedent to the passing of the statute, for the purpose of taking it out of the operation of the discharge. Wyman *v.* Mitchell, 1 Cow. 316.

When the States pass beyond their own limits and the rights of their own citizens, and act upon the rights of citizens of other States, there arises a conflict of sovereign power, and a collision with the judicial powers granted to the United States, which renders the exercise of such power incompatible with the rights of other States, and with the Constitution. Baldwin *v.* Hale, 1 Wall. 223; S. C. 1 Cliff. 511.

Insolvent laws of one State can not discharge the contracts of citizens of other States, because they have no extra-territorial operation, and consequently the tribunal sitting under them, unless in cases where a citizen of such other State voluntarily becomes a party to the proceeding, has no jurisdiction in the case. Baldwin *v.* Hale, 1 Wall. 223; S. C. 1 Cliff. 511; Newmarket Bank *v.* Butler, 45 N. H 236; Gilman *v.* Lockwood, 4 Wall. 409; Babcock *v.* Weston, 1 Gallis. 168; Campbell *v.* Claudius, 1 Pet. C. C. 484; Ballantine *v.* Haight, 16 N. J. 196; Beers *v.* Rhea, 5 Tex. 349; Choteau *v.* Richardson, 94 Mass. 368; Collins *v.* Rodolph, 3 Greene (Iowa), 299; Atwater *v.* Townsend, 4 Conn. 47; Shelton *v.* Wade, 14 Tex. 52; Fisher *v.* Wheeler, 5 La. Ann. 271; Byrd *v.* Badger, 1 McA. 263; Kendall *v.* Badger, 1 McA. 523; Ogden *v.* Saunders, 12 Wheat. 213; Tabor *v.* Harwood, 5 Harring. 42; Vanuxem *v.* Hazlehursts, 4 N. J. 192; Whitney *v.* Whiting, 35 N. H. 457; Dinsmore *v.* Bradley. 71 Mass. 487; Ferrira *v.* Keevit, 18 Mo. 186; McMillan *v.* M'Neill, 4 Wheat. 209; Frey *v.* Kirk, 4 G. & J. 509; Clark *v.* Hatch, 56 Mass. 455; Donnelly *v.* Corbett, 7 N. Y. 500; Pugh *v.* Bussell, 2 Blackf. 366; Proctor *v.* Moore, 1 Mass. 139; Smith *v.* Smith, 2 Johns. 235; Van Raugh *v.* Van Arsdaln, 3 Caines, 154; Tebbetts *v.* Pickering, 59 Mass. 83; Potter *v.* Kerr, 1 Md. Ch. 275; Emory *v.* Greenough, 3 Dall. 369; Watson *v.* Bourne, 10 Mass. 337; Fiske *v.* Foster, 51 Mass 597; Palmer *v.* Goodwin, 32 Me. 335; Bancher *v.* Fisk, 33 Me. 316; Hinkley *v.* Marean, 3 Mason, 88; Bradford *v.* Farrand, 13 Mass. 18; Boyle *v.* Zacharie, 6 Pet. 348; Woodbridge *v.* Wright, 3 Conn. 525; Woodhull *v.* Wagner, 1 Bald. 296; Springer *v.* Foster, 2 Story, 383; Cook *v.* Moffat, 5 How. 295; Norton *v.* Cook, 9 Conn. 314; Boyle *v.* Turner, 6 Pet. 635; contra, Hale *v.* Ross, 2 Penn. 590; Blanchard *v.* Russell, 13 Mass. 1; Adams *v.* Storey, 1 Paine, 79; Hicks *v.* Brown, 12 Johns. 142; Wray *v.* Reily, 1 Cranch C. C. 513.

The terms "citizen of another State," "resident of another State," and "foreign creditors," are used in different decisions quite indiscriminately. The idea designed to be expressed is not that State insolvent laws can not operate *infra*-territorially upon all the people or inhabitants. or permanent residents of a State, as well as upon native or naturalized citizens, but that such laws can have no extra-territorial effect so as to operate upon the rights of non-residents of the State. Vohn Glahn *v.* Varrence, 1 Dillon, 515; Pratt *v.* Chase, 44 N. Y. 597; s. c. 19 Abb. Pr. 150.

If the creditors are residents of another State, the discharge will not release the debt. Whether they are citizens of the United States or foreigners is of no importance, if they are not citizens of the State under whose laws the discharge is obtained, nor subject to its territorial jurisdiction. Pratt *v.* Chase, 44 N. Y. 597; s. c. 19 Abb. Pr. 150.

A temporary residence does not change its character with the lapse of time. Whether it is longer or shorter it is temporary still. It possesses no elements of a superior state which time will mature. Although the foreign creditor was temporarily residing in the State at the time when the contract was made, the discharge will not bar the debt if he does not reside there when the petition for a discharge is filed. Easterly *v.* Goodwin, 35 Conn. 279.

The question whether a contract made after the passing of a State insolvent law is released by a discharge, depends upon the citizenship of the creditor, and not upon the place where the contract was made, or was to be performed. Baldwin *v.* Hale, 1 Wall. 223; S. C. 1 Cliff. 511; Hawley *v.* Hunt, 27 Iowa, 303.

The claim of a citizen of another State will not be barred by a discharge under the insolvent laws of the State, although the debt was made payable in the State. Baldwin *v.* Hale, 1 Wall. 223; S. C. 1 Cliff. 511; Baldwin *v.* Bank, 1 Wall. 234; S. C. 1 Cliff. 519; Demerritt *v.* Exchange Bank, 20 Law Rep. 606; Newmarket Bank *v.* Butler, 45 N. H. 236; Donnelly *v.* Corbett, 7 N. Y. 500; Riston *v.* Content, 4 Wash. C. C. 476; Anderson *v.* Wheeler, 25 Conn. 603; Felch *v.* Bugbee, 48 Me. 9; Chase *v.* Flagg, 48 Me. 182; Norton *v.* Cook, 9 Conn. 314; Kelly *v.* Drury, 91 Mass. 27; King *v.* Stevenson, 2 Cliff. 1; contra, Burrall *v.* Rice, 71 Mass. 539; Capron *v.* Johnson, 71 Mass. 339, n.; Scribner *v.* Fisher, 68 Mass. 43; Whitney *v.* Whiting, 35 N. H. 457; Bank *v.* Squires, 8 La. Ann. 318; Soule *v.* Chase, 39 N. Y. 342; S. C. 1 Robt. 222; Blanchard *v.* Russell, 13 Mass. 1; Parkinson *v.* Scoville, 19 Wend. 150; Brown *v.* Collins, 41 N. H. 405; Smith *v.* Brown, 47 N. H. 44; Brighton Bank *v.* Merick, 11 Mich. 405.

State insolvent laws are void as against a citizen of another State, without reference to the place where the contract is made. Poe *v.* Duck, 5 Md. 1; Baldwin *v.* Hale, 1 Wall. 223; S. C. 1 Cliff. 511; contra, Sherrill *v.* Hopkins, 1 Cow. 103; Raymond *v.* Merchant, 3 Cow. 147.

A debt contracted in another State with a citizen of that State, without any specific agreement as to the place where it shall be paid, will not be released by a discharge under the laws of the State where the debtor resides. Woodbridge *v.* Allen, 53 Mass. 470; Savoye *v.* Marsh, 51 Mass. 594.

A discharge under a State insolvent law will not release the debtor from a promissory note made in the State and given to a citizen of that State, but indorsed before maturity to a citizen of another State, by whom it was held at the time of the application for the benefit of the insolvent law. Braynard *v.* Marshall, 25 Mass. 194; Towne *v.* Smith, 1 W. & M. 115; Savoye *v.* Marsh, 51 Mass. 594; Anderson *v.* Wheeler, 25 Conn. 603; Smith *v.* Gardiner, 4 Bosw. 54; Ballard *v.* Webster, 9 Abb. Pr. 404; Houghton *v.* Maynard, 71 Mass. 552; Bancher *v.* Fisk, 33 Me. 316; Fessenden *v.* Willey, 84 Mass. 67; Eaton *v.* Sweetser, 84 Mass. 70, note; Felch *v.* Bugbie, 48 Me. 9; Chase *v.* Flagg, 48 Me. 182; contra, Bank *v.* Squires, 8 La. Ann. 318.

If the note was made between citizens of the State, and was held by a citizen of the State at the time of the application for a discharge, the discharge will bar any claim of a citizen of another State who subsequently takes it after it is overdue. Hall *v.* Boardman, 14 N. H. 38.

If a factor at the time of making the sale states that he is acting for a principal who lives out of the State, a discharge will not bar the debt, although the name of the principal was not disclosed. Isley *v.* Merriam, 61 Mass. 242.

If the contract was not to be performed in the State, a discharge under its laws will not release the debtor from the demand of a citizen of another State. McKim *v.* Willis, 83 Mass. 512.

If a promissory note, payable to the order of a citizen of the State, is indorsed after maturity, but before the filing of a petition for a discharge to a citizen of another State, it will be deemed to constitute a contract with him, and will not be released by a discharge. Fessenden *v.* Willey, 84 Mass. 67.

A subsequent indorsement of a promissory note, if made in pursuance of authority to that effect given at the time of the sale, confers the same rights upon the holder as if it had been previously made. Fessenden *v.* Willey, 84 Mass. 67.

If a foreign creditor places his claim in the hands of an attorney residing in the State, for collection, who takes a note therefor payable to himself as attorney, the discharge will not bar the debt, for the courts will regard the rights of the beneficial owner. Crow *v.* Coons, 27 Mo. 512.

The discharge will not avail, although it is pleaded in the courts of the State under whose laws it was given. Frey *v.* Kirk, 4 G. & J. 509; Hicks *v.* Hotchkiss, 7 Johns. Ch. 297; Savoye *v.* Marsh, 51 Mass. 594; Spear *v.* Peabody, 10 La. Ann. 146; contra, Penniman *v.* Meigs, 9 Johns. 325; Bank *v.* Squires, 8 La. Ann. 318; Scott *v.* Bogart, 14 La. Ann. 261.

The fact that the original indebtedness has been converted into a judgment in no way changes the legal rights and liabilities of the parties. A contract upon which a transitory action arises is not rendered local by a judgment rendered upon it. The character of the debt as due from citizens of one State to those of another, is not affected by the judgment, but the court will look behind the judgment to the original contract. Whitney *v.* Whiting, 35 N. H. 457.

The discharge will not affect a citizen of another State, although the debt, at the time the discharge was obtained, was merged in a judgment rendered in a court of the State under whose laws it was so obtained. A foreign creditor, by suing for a debt in a State court, does not adopt its insolvent laws, or thereby waive his constitutional immunity. Watson *v.*

Bourne, 10 Mass. 337; M'Carty v. Gibson, 5 Gratt. 307; Owen v. Bowie, 2 Met. 457; Wyman v. Mitchell, 1 Cow. 316; Donnelly v. Corbett, 7 N. Y. 500; Easterly v. Goodwin, 35 Conn. 279; Poe v. Duck, 5 Md. 1; Whitney v. Whiting, 35 N. H. 457; Choteau v. Richardson, 94 Mass. 368; Worthington v. Jerome, 5 Blatch. 279; Hawley v. Hunt, 27 Iowa, 303; Soule v. Chase, 39 N. Y. 342; S. C. 1 Robt. 222; contra, Davidson v. Smith, 1 Biss. 346.

If both parties were citizens of the State when the contract was made, the discharge will release the debtor from the contract, although the creditor had removed to another State before it was granted. Brigham v. Henderson, 55 Mass. 430; Converse v. Bradley, 55 Mass. 434; Stevens v. Norris, 30 N. H. 466; Stoddard v. Harrington, 100 Mass. 87.

If the plaintiff was a resident of the State at the time when the judgment was entered, a discharge will release the debt, although he removed from the State before the commencement of the proceedings in insolvency. Brown v. Bridge, 106 Mass. 563.

The provisions of a State law in regard to conveyances by a debtor in contemplation of insolvency do not apply to transfers made to citizens of another State. Larrabee v. Talbott, 5 Gill, 426; Potter v. Kerr, 1 Md. Ch. 275; Mead v. Dayton, 28 Conn. 33.

The pendency of proceedings in insolvency will not prevent a foreign creditor from attaching any property of the debtor that may be found in any other State. Beer v. Hooper, 32 Miss. 246; Dunlap v. Rogers, 47 N. H. 281; Crapo v. Kelly, 45 N. Y. 86; S. C. 16 Wall. 610.

If the property is within the State at the time of the execution of the assignment, the title of the assignee will prevail over that of any subsequent attachment by a non-resident creditor. Crapo v. Kelly, 16 Wall. 610; S. C. 45 N. Y. 86; Perry Manuf. Co. v. Brown, 2 W. & M. 449; contra, Owen v. Bowie, 2 Md. 457; White v. Winn, 8 Gill, 499; Poe v. Duck, 5 Md. 1; Glenn v. Glass Co. 7 Md. 287.

If a vessel which is upon the high seas at the time when the assignment is made, enters the port of another State, she can not be there attached by a citizen of that State, for at the time of the assignment she was legally and constructively within the territory of the State where the debtor resided, and subject to its laws. Crapo v. Kelly, 16 Wall. 610; S. C. 45 N. Y. 86.

A State insolvent law is valid against a foreign creditor, so far as it releases the person of the debtor from imprisonment. Choteau v. Richardson, 94 Mass. 368; Donnelly v. Corbett, 7 N. Y. 500; Carey v. Conrad, 2 Miles, 92.

A citizen of another State who voluntarily makes himself a party to the proceedings, and receives a dividend, abandons his extra-territorial immunity, and his claim is barred by the discharge. Clay *v.* Smith, 3 Pet. 411; Gardner *v.* Lee's Bank, 11 Barb. 558; Journeay *v.* Gardner, 65 Mass. 355; contra, Woodbridge *v.* Wright, 3 Conn. 523; Agnew *v.* Platt, 32 Mass. 417.

By proof of the debt in the proceedings a creditor makes himself a party thereto, and a discharge will be a bar to the demand, although no dividends have been received thereon. Blackman *v.* Green, 24 Vt. 17.

If an agent, without any authority from his principal, proves the debt in the proceedings, this will not render the discharge valid as against the principal. Blackman *v.* Green, 24 Vt. 17.

If a foreign creditor unites in recommending a trustee in insolvency, he thereby becomes a party to the proceedings. Jones *v.* Horsey, 4 Md. 306.

An attorney who holds a claim for collection has the power to unite in the recommendation of a trustee, and thereby make his client a party to the proceedings. Jones *v.* Horsey, 4 Md. 306.

A mere appearance in the proceedings to oppose the granting of a discharge will not render the discharge a bar to the debt of a citizen of another State. Norton *v.* Cook, 9 Conn. 314; M'Carty *v.* Gibson, 5 Gratt. 307; Collins *v.* Rodolph, 3 Greene (Iowa), 299.

Knowledge is one thing, and assent is another, and it by no means follows that because a party acts with reference to a knowledge of a particular act, that he thereby assents or acquiesces in that act. The mere knowledge of the legal effect of the insolvent laws, will not afford grounds for an inference of an assent to be bound by those laws. Glenn *v.* Glass Co. 7 Md. 287.

The act of waiving a constitutional privilege must be unequivocal. Donnelly *v.* Corbett, 7 N. Y. 500.

That part of a State insolvent law which discharges a person from imprisonment, may be valid, although the part which attempts to discharge the debt is void. Glenn *v.* Humphreys, 4 Wash. 424.

If the State court had no jurisdiction of the case, a participation in the proceedings will not make the discharge valid. Agnew *v.* Platt, 32 Mass. 417.

Corporations.

The charter of a private corporation is a contract, the obligation of which can not be impaired without violating the Constitution. Dartmouth

College *v.* Woodward, 4 Wheat. 518; Norris *v.* Abingdon Academy, 7 G. & J. 7; Canal Co. *v.* Railroad Co. 4 G. & J. 1; Regents *v.* Williams, 9 G. & J. 365; Enfield Bridge Co. *v.* Railroad Co. 17 Conn. 40; Michigan Bank *v.* Hastings, 1 Doug. 225; Young *v.* Harrison, 6 Geo. 130; Bank *v.* Bank of Cape Fear, 13 Ired. 75; Montpelier Academy *v.* George, 14 La. 395; Binghamton Bridge *v.* Chenango Bridge, 3 Wall. 51; S. C. 27 N. Y. 87; Phila. W. & B. R. R. Co. *v.* Bowers, 4 Houst. 506; Union Bank *v.* State, 9 Yerg. 490; Allen *v.* Buchanan, 9 Phila. 283; S. C. 20 Pitts. L. J. 128.

A general law for the organization of corporations is as special to each corporation as if no other institution were incorporated by it. State Bank *v.* Knoop, 16 How. 369.

A charter is a contract, both executed and executory. Phila. W. & B. R. R. Co. *v.* Bowers, 4 Houst. 506.

The objects for which a corporation is created are universally such as the government wishes to promote. They are deemed beneficial to the country, and this benefit constitutes the consideration, and in most cases the sole consideration, of the grant. Dartmouth College *v.* Woodward, 4 Wheat. 518.

The benefit which the community may derive from the objects for which the corporation was created constitutes the consideration for the charter, and no other is required to support it. Home of the Friendless *v.* Rouse, 8 Wall. 430; Regents *v.* Williams, 9 G. & J. 365.

A grant of franchises is not in point of principle distinguishable from a grant of any other property. Dartmouth College *v.* Woodward, 4 Wheat. 518; Derby Turnpike Co. *v.* Parks, 10 Conn. 522; Canal Co. *v.* Railroad Co. 4 G. & J. 1; Enfield Bridge Co. *v.* Connecticut River Co. 7 Conn. 28; Washington Bridge Co. *v.* State, 18 Conn. 53; Benson *v.* New York, 10 Barb. 223.

Whether the consideration is large or small is immaterial, as the motives or considerations which induced a sovereign State to make a contract can not be inquired into as affecting the validity of the act. Of the sufficiency of the consideration, the legislature is the exclusive judge. State Bank *v.* Knoop, 16 How. 369.

A charter is a stipulation on the part of the State, that the corporation shall be and continue a corporation for an indefinite time, or for the term limited in the charter, unless sooner forfeited for some cause recognized by existing laws as a cause of forfeiture; that its constitution, organization and mode of action, as prescribed by its charter, shall not be annulled or changed by the legislature; that members shall not be added or removed; that modes of election, expulsion or suspension of members shall not be altered, and that whatever belongs to its organic constitution and action as a body corporate, shall continue and be determined by the terms of the charter. In addition to which, the powers specially granted to it are not to be withdrawn or diminished. Comm. *v.* Farmers' Bank, 38 Mass. 542; Thorpe *v.* B. & R. R. R. Co. 27 Vt. 140.

The implied powers conferred by a charter, are held by a tenure as sacred as those which are expressly given. People *v.* Manhattan Co. 9 Wend. 351; Commercial Bank *v.* State, 12 Miss. 439.

The incidental or implied powers are, at most, only such powers as are essentially necessary to enable the corporation to fulfill its destiny—to do those things which it may do by express permission. It may be presumed that such powers were intended to be conferred; they are implied from those which are granted. Payne *v.* Baldwin, 11 Miss. 661; Commercial Bank *v.* State, 12 Miss. 439.

Every valuable privilege given by the charter, and which conduced to an acceptance of it and an organization under it, is a contract which can not be changed by the legislature, where the power to do so is not reserved in the charter. State Bank *v.* Knoop, 16 How. 369.

A statute conferring upon a corporation the right to collect additional tolls is a grant, and not a license. Derby Turnpike Co. *v.* Parks, 10 Conn. 522.

In examining a question of corporate rights and immunities, and the extent of the legislative power, the question is, whether the legislature can exercise the power consistently with the provisions of the charter and the rights of the corporation in any form. If the power exists, the mode of exercising it may be such as the legislature may direct. Comm. *v.* Farmers' Bank, 38 Mass. 542.

It is not a principle that a grant may be infringed upon if the variation be not great. As every variation violates, small injuries are as much prohibited as larger ones, and the least right is as anxiously protected as the greatest. Enfield Bridge Co. *v.* Connecticut River Co. 7 Conn. 28.

If the State is the sole stockholder in a corporation, the charter can not be deemed to be such a contract between the State and the corporation as is protected by the Constitution. Curran *v.* State, 15 How. 304; S. C. 12 Ark. 321.

Corporations are either public or private. Public corporations are generally esteemed such as exist for public political purposes only, such as towns, cities, parishes and counties, and in many respects they are so, although they involve some private interests; but strictly speaking, public corporations are such only as are founded by the government for public purposes, where the whole interests belong also to the government. The whole interests and franchises must be the exclusive property and domain of the government itself. Dartmouth College *v.* Woodward, 4 Wheat. 518; Allen *v.* McKeen, 1 Sumn. 276; Regents *v.* Williams, 9 G. & J. 365; University *v.* Maultsby, 8 Ired. Eq. 257.

If the foundation of a corporation is private, though under the charter of the government, the corporation is private, however extensive the uses may be to which it is devoted, either by the bounty of the founder or the nature and objects of the institution. Dartmouth College *v.* Woodward, 4 Wheat. 518; Trustees *v.* Bradbury, 11 Me. 118; Allen *v.* McKeen, 1 Sum. 276; Regents *v.* Williams, 9 G. & J. 365; State *v.* Heyward, 3 Rich. 389; Brown *v.* Hummel, 6 Penn. 86; Plymouth *v.* Jackson, 15 Penn. 44; Yarmouth *v.* Yarmouth, 34 Me. 411; Trustees *v.* State, 14 How. 268; S. C. 2 Ind. 293; Louisville *v.* University, 15 B. Mon. 642.

It by no means follows that, because the action of a corporation may be beneficial to the public, it is a public corporation. This may be said of all corporations whose objects are the administration of charities. But these are not public, though incorporated by the legislature, unless their funds belong to the government. Where the property of a corporation is private, it gives the same character to the institution, and to this there is no exception. State Bank *v.* Knoop, 16 How. 369.

A corporation may be private, and yet the charter may contain provisions of a purely public character, introduced solely for the public good, and as a general police regulation of the State. Regents *v.* Williams, 9 G. & J. 365.

The mere fact that the funds have been generally derived from the bounty of the government will not make the corporation public, for the government may as well bestow its bounty upon a private corporation as upon a public corporation. Louisville *v.* University, 15 B. Mon. 642; Allen *v.* McKeen, 1 Sum. 276; Regents *v.* Williams, 9 G. & J. 365; Sheriff *v.* Lowndes, 16 Md. 357; State *v.* Heyward, 3 Rich. 389; Yarmouth *v.* Yarmouth, 34 Me. 411; Richardson *v.* Brown, 6 Me. 355; Montpelier Academy *v.* George, 14 La. 395.

A corporation created for the purpose of investing school funds for a town and applying the income for the benefit of the schools in the town, is a private corporation. Trustees *v.* Bradbury, 11 Me. 118.

A banking corporation, the stock of which is owned by private individuals, is a private corporation. State Bank *v.* Knoop, 16 How. 369; Miner's Bank *v.* U. S. 1 Iowa, 553; Hazen *v.* Union Bank, 1 Sneed, 115.

Construction.

The object and end of all government is to promote the happiness and prosperity of the community by which it is established, and it can never be assumed that the government intended to diminish its power of accomplishing the end for which it was created. Whenever any power of the State is said to be surrendered or diminished, whether it be the taxing power or any other power affecting the public interest, this principle applies. Hence the rule for construing charters is, that any ambiguity in their terms must operate against the corporation and in favor of the public, and the corporation can claim nothing that is not clearly given to it by the act. The exercise of a corporate franchise, being restrictive of individual rights, can not be extended beyond the letter and spirit of the act of incorporation. No rights are taken from the public or given to the corporation beyond those which the words of the charter, by their natural and proper construction, purport to convey. Charles River Bridge *v.* Warren Bridge, 11 Pet. 420; S. C. 24 Mass. 344; 23 Mass. 376; Providence Bank *v.* Billings, 4 Pet. 514; Enfield Bridge Co. *v.* Connecticut River Co. 7 Conn. 28; Hartford Bridge Co. *v.* East Hartford, 16 Conn. 149; Turnpike Co. *v.* Railroad Co. 10 G. & J. 392; Tuckahoe Canal Co. *v.* Railroad, 11 Leigh, 42; Hartford Bridge Co. *v.* Union Ferry Co. 29 Conn. 210; Mills *v.* St. Clair, 6 How. 569; S. C. 2 Gilman, 197; Planters' Bank *v.* Sharp, 6 How. 301; S. C. 12 Miss. 28; Ohio Trust Co. *v.* Debolt, 18 How. 416; S. C. 1 Ohio St. 563; Collins *v.* Sherman, 31 Miss. 679; McLeod *v.* Burroughs, 9 Geo. 213; Richmond R. R. Co. *v.* Louisa R. R. Co. 13 How. 71.

A corporation is an artificial being, invisible, intangible, and existing only in contemplation of law. Being the mere creature of law, it possesses only those properties which the charter of its creation confers upon it, either expressly or as incidental to its very existence. This being does not share in the civil government of the country unless that be the purpose for which it was created. Dartmouth College *v.* Woodward, 4 Wheat. 518; Regents *v.* Williams, 9 G. & J. 365.

All contracts are to be construed to accomplish the intention of the parties, and in determining their different provisions, a liberal and fair construction will be given to the words either singly or in connection with the subject-matter. It is not the duty of a court, by legal subtlety, to overthrow a contract, but rather to uphold it and give it effect, and no strained or artificial rule of construction is to be applied to any part of it. If there is no ambiguity, and the meaning of the parties can be clearly ascertained, effect is to be given to the instrument used, whether it is a legislative grant or not. Binghamton Bridge *v.* Chenango Bridge, 3 Wall. 51; S. C. 27 N. Y. 87.

All rights which are asserted against the State must be clearly defined, and not raised by inference or presumption, and if the charter is silent about a power it does not exist. Binghamton Bridge *v.* Chenango Bridge, 3 Wall. 51; s. c. 27 N. Y. 87.

Where the instrument is susceptible of two meanings, the one restricting and the other extending the powers of the corporation, that construction is to be adopted which works the least harm to the State. Binghamton Bridge *v.* Chenango Bridge, 3 Wall. 51; s. c. 27 N. Y. 87.

If there is no ambiguity in the charter, and the powers conferred are plainly marked and their limits can be readily ascertained, then it is the duty of the court to sustain and uphold it, and to carry out the true meaning and intention of the parties to it. Binghamton Bridge *v.* Chenango Bridge, 3 Wall. 51; s. c. 27 N. Y. 87.

If on a fair reading of the instrument, reasonable doubts arise as to the proper interpretation to be given to it, those doubts are to be solved in favor of the State. Binghamton Bridge *v.* Chenango Bridge, 3 Wall. 51; s. c. 27 N. Y. 87.

When a right under a charter is claimed by construction merely, and the legislature has passed an act inconsistent with the right so claimed, a construction should not be given which will produce a conflict between the two acts, unless it is imperiously demanded by the general scope and evident design of all the provisions in the charter which bear upon the subject. Maysville Turnpike Co. *v.* How, 14 B. Mon. 426.

To establish a contract on the part of the legislature to relinquish any of its sovereign powers, plain and unequivocal words must be used. State *v.* Matthews, 3 Jones (N. C.) 451.

Instances.

If the charter allows the corporation a reasonable time to comply with the conditions whereby it may obtain an interest in land, the legislature can not shorten that time or impose any liability upon it, if it chooses to avail itself of all the time allowed by the charter. Nichols *v.* Som. & Ken. R. R. Co. 43 Me. 356.

The grant of an annual appropriation in a charter, in consideration of subscriptions by private individuals, is a contract and can not be repealed. Visitors *v.* State, 15 Md. 330.

The charter of an eleemosynary corporation can not be amended with the consent of the curators or directors. State *v.* Adams, 44 Mo. 570.

A statute giving a right of action to those who have been injured by the erection of a close bridge over a navigable creek, when such bridge was authorized by the charter, is void. Bailey *v.* Railroad Co. 4 Harring. 389.

Any act which impairs the charter by enlarging the power of the State over the body corporate, or by abridging the franchises, or by altering the charter in any material point, is void. Commercial Bank *v.* State, 14 Miss. 599.

A statute passed after the granting of a charter, and annexing a cause of forfeiture unknown to the charter, is unconstitutional. People *v.* Plankroad Co. 9 Mich. 285; State *v.* Tombecbee Bank, 2 Stew. 30; Washington Bridge Co. *v.* State, 18 Conn. 53; Aurora Turnpike Co. *v.* Holthouse, 7 Ind. 59.

A statute having the effect to abridge or restrict any power or privilege vested by the charter, which is material to the beneficial exercise of the franchise granted, and which must be supposed to have entered into the consideration which induced the corporators to accept the charter and to assume the duties imposed by it, is void. Phil. W. & B. R. R. Co. *v.* Bowers, 4 Houst. 506.

An officer of a corporation who, by the terms of the charter, holds his office during good behavior, with a fixed salary and certain fees annexed thereto, can not be deprived of that office by a statute purporting to amend the charter, although it is accepted by the corporation. Allen *v.* McKeen, 1 Sum. 276.

The legislature may, in a charter, impose duties and obligations upon a corporation, and inflict penalties and forfeitures as a punishment for its disobedience, which may be enforced against it in the form of criminal proceedings, and as the punishment of an offense against the law. Such penal provisions are not mere matters of contract. In legislative proceedings a forfeiture is always to be regarded as a punishment inflicted for the violation of some duty enjoined upon the party by law, and may be remitted after it has been incurred, although it was to be for the benefit of a municipal corporation. State *v.* Railroad Co. 3 How. 534; s. c. 12 G. & J. 399.

If the charter of a medical college confers upon the corporation the power to appoint a board of examiners to examine applicants and grant licenses upon the payment of ten dollars, and prohibits the practice of medicine without such license, this is merely a police regulation, and may be repealed. Regents *v.* Williams, 9 G. & J. 365; vide State *v.* Heyward, 3 Rich. 389.

A statute setting aside an inquisition of damages for land to be taken under a charter, and granting an inquisition *de novo* before a tender of the value assessed by the inquisition, does not impair the obligation of the charter when such tender is necessary to entitle the corporation to the land. Balt. & S. R. R. Co. *v.* Nesbit, 10 How. 395.

If the remedy provided in the charter for assessing damages for taking land, is unsuitable or insufficient, the legislature has the power to change it, both as to time and mode. Gowan *v.* Penobscot R. R. Co. 44 Me. 140.

A statute transferring the property of an insolvent corporation to a new corporation, in consideration of shares of the latter's stock, which are authorized to be sold for debts due by the insolvent corporation, is valid. Mudge *v.* Commissioners, 10 Rob. (La.) 460.

A State can not require a canal corporation to keep in repair the public bridges connecting the highways intersected by the canal. City *v.* Erie Canal Co. 59 Penn. 174.

A breach of the contract on the part of the State, furnishes no excuse to a corporation for disregarding the part which is a burden, while at the same time insisting upon the observance of the part which is beneficial. Turnpike Co. *v.* State, 3 Wall. 210.

A statute making the stockholders personally liable for the debts of the corporation, has no tendency to impair or in any way affect or modify any power, privilege or immunity pertaining to the franchise of the corporation, and is therefore within the just limits of legislative power. Gray *v.* Coffin, 63 Mass. 192; Coffin *v.* Rich, 45 Me. 507; Stanley *v.* Stanley, 26 Me. 191.

Banks.

A general statute making the suspension of specie payment by a bank a cause of forfeiture, when such cause is not stated in the charter, is void. State *v.* Tombecbee Bank, 2 Stew. 30.

A statute prohibiting a bank from transferring notes by indorsement, is valid, unless the power to do so is expressly granted in the charter, for the indorsement of a note is a new contract, the power to make which is derived from the law, and the statute simply takes this from the bank. Payne *v.* Baldwin, 11 Miss. 661; McIntyre *v.* Ingraham, 35 Miss. 25.

A statute authorizing the debtors of a bank to pay their debts in the notes and certificates of the bank is constitutional. Bank of Md. *v.* Ruff, 7 G. & J. 448.

If a State creates a bank of which it is the sole stockholder, and provides the capital therefor, whenever a credit is given to the bank on the faith of this assurance, a contract at once arises between the State and the creditor not to withdraw the capital to his injury, and the State can not withdraw the fund or any part of it without impairing its obligation. Curran *v.* State, 15 How. 304; S. C. 12 Ark. 321.

The general power to issue notes and bills, without any express grant as to small notes, is not a surrender of the right of the State to prescribe by law the lowest denomination for which notes or bills shall be allowed to circulate, but is subordinate to that right. No such surrender can be implied or presumed, for it is not only the right but the duty of the State to secure to its citizens, as far as it is able, a safe and sound currency, and to prevent the circulation of small notes when they become depreciated and are a public evil. The community have as deep an interest in preserving this right undiminished as they have the taxing power, and like the taxing power, it will not be construed to be relinquished unless the intention to do so is clearly expressed. Ohio Trust Co. *v.* Debolt, 16 How. 416; s. c. 1 Ohio St. 563; State *v.* Matthews, 3 Jones (N. C.) 451.

Bridges.

An undertaking to transport certain persons free of toll, in consideration of the removal of the county seat, will not prevent the State from authorizing the construction of a bridge which will divert the travel, for it thereby relieves the party from the burden of his contract. Shorter *v.* Smith, 9 Geo. 517.

A charter includes the laws defining its stipulations at the time of the grant. If the general laws at the time of the granting of a charter for a bridge, prohibit the erection of another bridge within a certain distance of one already existing, a subsequent statute allowing the erection of a bridge within that distance is void. Micou *v.* Tallassee Bridge Co. 47 Ala. 652.

The construction of a railroad bridge is not a violation of the exclusive right to construct a bridge for carriages in common use. McLeod *v.* Sav. A. & G. R. R. Co. 25 Geo. 445; Mohawk Bridge Co. *v.* Railroad Co. 6 Paige, 554; Bridge Co. *v.* Hoboken Land Co. 2 Beasely, 81; s. c. 1 Wall. 116; McRee *v.* Railroad Co. 2 Jones (N. C.) 186; Thompson *v.* Railroad Co. 3 Sandf. 625; contra, Enfield Bridge Co. *v.* Railroad Co. 17 Conn. 40.

A new road, canal or bridge materially diverting travel or business from an old one, established under a prior charter, is not unconstitutional unless the franchise is defined or made exclusive. Charles River Bridge *v.* Warren Bridge, 11 Pet. 420; s. c. 24 Mass. 344; 23 Mass. 376; Fort Plain Bridge Co. *v.* Smith, 30 N. Y. 44; Turnpike Co. *v.* State, 3 Wall. 260; Fall *v.* Suter, 21 Cal. 237; Indian Canon Road *v.* Robinson, 13 Cal. 519; Bush *v.* Peru Bridge Co. 3 Ind. 21; In re Hamilton Avenue, 14 Barb. 405; Ill. & Mich. Canal Co. *v.* Railroad Co. 14 Ill. 314; Salem Turnpike Co. *v.* Lyme, 18 Conn. 451; Oswego Bridge Co. *v.* Fish, 1 Barb. Ch. 547; Thompson *v.* Railroad Co. 3 Sandf. Ch. 625; Harrison *v.* Young, 9 Geo. 359; Shorter *v.* Smith, 9 Geo. 517; Fitch *v.* Railroad Co. 30 Conn. 38; Mohawk Bridge Co. *v.* Railroad Co. 6 Paige, 554; Collins *v.* Sherman, 31 Miss. 679; Curtis *v.* Morehouse, 12 La. Ann. 649; West End Co. *v.* Atlanta Co. 4 Geo. 151.

Turnpikes.

A statute authorizing commissioners to examine the condition of turnpike roads, and throw open the gates if they are out of repair, is void, for it impairs the right of the corporation to collect toll at its gates. Powell *v.* Sammons, 31 Ala. 552.

A charter authorizing the construction of a railroad does not impair the obligation imposed by a prior charter to a turnpike company, authorizing the construction of a turnpike between the same *termini*. Turnpike Co. *v.* Railroad Co. 10 G. & J. 392.

A statute appointing inspectors of turnpikes with power to direct proper repairs to be made, and to take down the toll gates for a refusal to make such repairs, does not impair the obligation imposed by the charters. State *v.* Bosworth, 13 Vt. 402.

If the charter of a turnpike company prescribes the form of the sign or board with the rates of tolls, it will prevail over a general statute subsequently passed. Nichols *v.* Bertram, 20 Mass. 342.

Railroads.

Where the charter provides that the directors may regulate the business of a railroad corporation, a statute requiring that the first train arriving at a crossing shall wait until the train upon the other road shall arrive, is void. State *v.* Noyes, 47 Me. 189.

If the State, in conferring a right or franchise lying solely in grant, stipulates, for a valuable consideration, that the grantee shall have and enjoy it undisturbed and unmolested by any act or permission on the part of the State, the grant has the same effect as if it were the grant of an exclusive right in terms. It is equivalent to a covenant for quiet enjoyment against the acts of the State and those claiming under it. If the charter of a railroad corporation contains a provision that no other road shall be built within a certain distance, the corporation can not be disturbed in the enjoyment of the franchise by any subsequent charter. The stipulations may be both an executory covenant and an executed contract. So far as it confers a present right it is executed; so far as it amounts to a stipulation that the covenantor will not disturb the enjoyment of the right granted, it may be deemed executory. Boston & L. R. R. Co. *v.* Salem & L. R. R. Co. 68 Mass. 1.

A law changing the tariff of freights which a railroad corporation is allowed by its charter to charge, is void. Hamilton *v.* Keith, 5 Bush, 458.

A State can not regulate the tolls of a corporation whose charter authorizes it to take such tolls as it may deem reasonable. Att. Gen. *v.* Railroad Companies, 35 Wis. 425.

Where the charter confers upon a railroad corporation the power to fix its tariff of charges, a statute regulating the rates is void. Sloan *v.* Mo. Pacific R. R. Co. 2 Cent. L. J. 781 ; Phila. W. & B. R. R. Co. *v.* Bowers, 4 Houst. 506 ; contra, Moore *v.* Ill. Cent. R. R. Co. 4 C. L. N. 123.

A State legislature has the power to regulate the rates to be charged by a railroad corporation for the transportation of freight or passengers. Chicago B. & Q. R. R. Co. *v.* Iowa, 94 U. S. 155 ; Winona & St. Peter R. R. Co. 94 U. S. 180.

Taxes.

A State may by contract based on consideration exempt the property of an individual or corporation from taxation either for a specified period or permanently, and it does not thereby relinquish its sovereign power. The taxing power may select its objects of taxation, and this is generally regulated by the amount necessary to answer the purposes of the State. The exemption of property from taxation is a question of policy and not of power. The act of making the contract, so far from parting with any portion of the sovereignty, is an exercise of it. State Bank *v.* Knoop, 16 How. 369; Ohio Trust Co. *v.* Debolt, 16 How. 416; S. C. 1 Ohio St. 563; State *v.* Georgia R. & B. Co. 54 Geo. 423; State *v.* County Court, 19 Ark. 360; Antoni *v.* Wright, 23 Gratt. 833; State *v.* Bank, 2 Houst. 99; Humphrey *v.* Pegues, 16 Wall. 244 ; Home of the Friendless *v.* Rouse, 8 Wall. 430; Wilmington Railroad Co. *v.* Reid, 13 Wall. 264; Tomlinson *v.* Branch Bank, 15 Wall. 460; People *v.* Auditor, 7 Mich. 84; Ill. Cent. R. R. Co. *v.* County, 17 Ill. 291 ; State Bank *v.* People, 5 Ill. 303; Camden & Amboy R. R. Co. *v.* Commissioners, 18 N. J. 71 ; Oliver *v.* Memphis & L. R. R. Co. 30 Ark. 128; Daughdrell *v.* Life Ins. Co. 31 Ala. 91 ; Bank *v.* New Albany, 11 Ind. 139 ; State *v.* Berry, 17 N. J. 81; Gardner *v.* State, 21 N. J. 557; Bank *v.* Edwards, 5 Ired. 516; Bank *v.* Deming, 7 Ired. 55; Municipality *v.* State Bank, 5 La. Ann. 394; Johnson *v.* Comm. 7 Dana, 338; contra, Mott *v.* Penn. R. R. Co. 30 Penn. 9; Norwalk Co. *v.* Husted, 3 Ohio St. 586; Toledo Bank *v.* Bond, 1 Ohio St. 622; Exchange Bank *v.* Hines, 3 Ohio St. 1; Milan & R. Plank Road Co. *v.* Husted, 3 Ohio St. 578; Sandusky Bank *v.* Wilbor, 7 Ohio, 481.

The taxing power is of vital importance and essential to the existence of government. The relinquishment of such a power is never to be assumed. The whole community is interested in retaining it undiminished, and has a right to insist that its abandonment ought not to be presumed in a case in which the deliberate purpose of the State to abandon it does not appear. Providence Bank *v.* Billings, 4 Pet. 514; Judson *v.* State, Minor, 150; Brewster *v.* Hough, 10 N. H. 138 ; Del. Railroad Tax, 18 Wall. 206 ; City *v.* Boatman's Ins. & Trust Co. 47 Mo. 150 ; State *v.* Dulle, 48 Mo. 282; Easton Bank *v.* Comm. 10 Penn. 442 ; Gordon *v.* Baltimore, 5 Gill, 231 ; Phila. & W. R. R. Co. *v.* State, 10 How. 376; Bank of Penn. *v.* Comm. 19 Penn. 144; State *v.* Minton, 23 N. J. 529.

The imposition of a tax upon a corporation does not impair the obligation of its charter, unless there is an express clause therein exempting the corporation from taxation. Providence Bank *v.* Billings, 4 Pet. 514; Portland Bank *v.* Apthorpe, 12 Mass. 252 ; Judson *v.* State, Minor, 150; North Mo. Railroad *v.* Maguire, 20 Wall. 46 ; S. C. 49 Mo. 490; Erie Railway Company *v.* Pennsylvania, 21 Wall. 492.

The mere reservation in a charter of a sum to be paid annually into the treasury does not contain an implied contract that no further tax shall be imposed. State *v.* Petway, 2 Jones Eq. 396 ; Minot *v.* P. W. & B. R. R. Co. 2 Abb. C. C. 323; Erie R. R. Co. *v.* Comm. 3 Brews. 368; Del. Railroad Tax, 18 Wall. 206 ; S. C. 7 Phila. 555 ; Louisville C. & L. R. R. Co. *v.* Comm. 10 Bush, 43 ; Evansville, H. & N. R. R. Co. *v.* Comm. 9 Bush, 438 ; State *v.* Parker, 32 N. J. 426.

A provision in the charter of an eleemosynary corporation, or of a university for learning, that its property shall be exempt from taxation, is a contract whose obligation can not be impaired. Home of the Friendless *v.* Rouse, 8 Wall. 430; Washington University *v.* Rouse, 8 Wall. 439; S. C. 42 Mo. 308.

If the charter stipulates that the corporation shall pay certain taxes annually in lieu of all taxes to which it would otherwise be subject, the amount of taxes can not be subsequently increased. State *v.* Auditor, 5 Ohio St. 444; Ross County Bank *v.* Lewis, 5 Ohio St. 447 ; Le Roy *v.* East. S. C. Railway, 18 Mich. 233; Farmers' Bank *v.* Comm. 6 Bush, 126; State Bank *v.* Knoop, 16 How. 369; Mechanics' Bank *v.* Debolt, 18 How. 380; S. C. 1 Ohio St. 591 ; State *v.* Commissioners, 37 N. J. 240; Franklin Bank *v.* State, 1 Black, 474; State *v.* Commercial Bank, 7 Ohio, 125; Wright *v.* Sill, 2 Black, 544; Jefferson Bank *v.* Skelly, 1 Black, 436; S. C. 9 Ohio St. 606; Matheny *v.* Golden, 5 Ohio St. 361 ; Dodge *v.* Woolsey, 18 How. 331 ; Mechanics' Bank *v.* Thomas, 18 How. 384 ; contra, Norwalk Co. *v.* Husted, 3 Ohio St. 586 ; Toledo Bank *v.* Bond, 1 Ohio St. 622; Exchange Bank *v.* Hines, 3 Ohio St. 1 ; Milan & R. Plank Road Co. *v.* Husted, 3 Ohio St. 578 ; Sandusky Bank *v.* Wilbor, 7 Ohio, 481.

If the charter stipulates that the property of the corporation shall be exempt from taxation, no tax can be levied or assessed thereon. Hardy *v.* Waltham, 24 Mass. 108.

If the charter exempts property used for the actual and necessary purposes of the corporation, a tax may be levied upon land leased to others, and not used for the purposes of the corporation. State *v.* Love, 37 N. J. 60.

If the charter exempts property used for the actual and necessary purposes of the corporation, no tax can be levied upon property used in the business of the corporation, although it may be used also by others. State *v.* Betts, 24 N. J. 555.

If a round sum or an annual charge is paid, or contracted to be paid, as the consideration for the grant of a franchise, the contract is a limitation upon the taxing power to impose any further tax on the franchise. The price is paid for the use of the privilege while it lasts, and any tax upon it would substantially be an addition to the price. Gordon *v.* Appeal Tax Court, 3 How. 133; S. C. 5 Gill, 231; Att. Gen. *v.* Bank of Charlotte, 4 Jones Eq. 287; vide Minot *v.* P. W. & B. R. R. Co. 2 Abb. C. C. 323; S. C. 18 Wall. 206; 7 Phila. 555; Mayor *v.* Balt. & O. R. R. Co. 6 Gill, 288.

It is not necessary that a bonus shall be paid in order to render the contract for exemption binding. The obligation is as strong on the State for the privileges granted and accepted as if a bonus were paid. State Bank *v.* Knoop, 16 How. 369.

A provision fixing the mode in which the taxes shall be assessed does not preclude the legislature from adopting another mode. Bailey *v.* Maguire, 22 Wall. 215; State *v.* Han. & St. Jo. R. R. Co. 60 Mo. 143.

Where the charter exempts the property and franchise of the corporation from taxation for a certain period, and after that time provides that the State may tax the capital stock not exceeding a certain amount, the State, after the expiration of the time, can not tax the property and the franchise, for the limitation to a particular mode includes a negative of every other mode. Raleigh & G. R. R. Co. *v.* Reid, 64 N. C. 155; S. C. 13 Wall. 269.

Where the charter provides that a tax to be levied on the happening of some future contingency, shall be in lieu of all other taxes, no tax can be levied prior to that time. McGavisk *v.* State, 34 N. J. 509.

A grant of all the rights, powers and privileges conferred by the charter of another corporation, includes an exemption from taxation conferred by an amendment of its charter then in force. Humphrey *v.* Pegues, 16 Wall. 244.

A statute merely exempting property from taxation, without any consideration, does not savor of a contract, and may be repealed. Hospital *v.* Philadelphia, 24 Penn. 229; Sandusky Bank *v.* Wilbor, 7 Ohio St. 481; St. Louis I. M. & S. R. Co. *v.* Loftin, 30 Ark. 693; People *v.* Commissioners, 47 N. Y 501; S. C. 53 Barb. 70; State *v.* County Treasurer, 4 Rich. N. S. 520; Holly Springs S. & I. Co. *v.* Marshall, 52 Miss. 281.

If property is given to an ecclesiastical society, for certain purposes, during the existence of a statute enacting that property so given shall be exempt from taxation, it can not be taxed as long as it is applied to those purposes, for the statute was a contract with the donors under which the property was given, and no subsequent legislature can divest the right thus vested in the society. Atwater *v.* Woodbridge, 6 Conn. 223; Osborne

v. Humphrey, 7 Conn. 335; Landon v. Litchfield, 11 Conn. 251 ; Seymour v. Hartford, 21 Conn. 481; Parker v. Redfield, 10 Conn. 490; Herrick v. Randolph, 13 Vt. 525 ; contra, Brainerd v. Colchester, 31 Conn. 407; Lord v. Litchfield, 36 Conn. 116.

The mere existence of a statute exempting lands sequestered to public, pious and charitable uses, from taxation at the time of the making of a grant by the State to a municipal corporation of land for the maintenance of the ministry, does not make it a condition of the grant, so as to exempt the land from subsequent taxation. Herrick v. Randolph, 13 Vt. 525.

A statute which provides that lands granted to public, pious or charitable uses, shall be forever exempt from taxation, has no effect upon prior grants, except while it remains in force, and may be repealed. Herrick v. Randolph, 13 Vt. 525.

If a statute exempts lands granted to a public or charitable use from taxation, a subsequent statute may render such land liable to taxation where it is conveyed without the reservation of an annual rent. New Haven v. Sheffield, 30 Conn. 160; Brainerd v. Colchester, 31 Conn. 407; Lord v. Litchfield, 36 Conn. 116.

If the exemption is spontaneous, and no service or duty or other remunerative condition is imposed on the corporation, it is a mere privilege, and may be withdrawn at any time. Rector v. Philadelphia, 24 How. 300; s. c. 24 Penn. 229; Brainerd v. Colchester, 31 Conn. 407 ; Lord v. Litchfield, 36 Conn. 116; Tucker v. Ferguson, 22 Wall. 527.

An exemption of the capital of a corporation from taxation extends to additional capital permitted under subsequent acts. State v. N. & W. R. R. Co. 30 Conn. 290.

The State can not authorize a municipal corporation to impose a tax which the State itself has no right to levy. O'Donnell v. Bailey, 24 Miss. 386; Camden & Amboy R. R. Co. v. Hillegas, 18 N. J. 11; Camden & Amboy R. R. Co. v. Commissioners, 18 N. J. 71.

A provision in a charter that a certain rate of taxes shall be paid in lieu of all taxes to the State does not exempt the corporation from liability for municipal taxes. Lexington v. Aull, 30 Mo. 480; Paris v. Farmers' Bank, 30 Mo. 575.

A provision exempting a corporation from taxation applies not merely to the State, but to every public corporation created by it. City of Richmond v. R. & D. R. R. Co. 21 Gratt. 604; Mayor v. Balt. & Ohio R. R. Co. 6 Gill, 288 ; Bank of Cape Fear v. Edwards, 5 Ired. 516; State Bank v. Charleston, 3 Rich. 342.

An exemption from taxation by the State does not exempt the corporation from taxation for county purposes. Pacific R. R. Co. v. Cass, 53 Mo. 17.

An exemption from State and county taxes does not relieve the corporation from taxes imposed upon its property by a city for municipal purposes. City v. Han. & St. Jo. R. R. Co. 39 Mo. 476.

If the charter merely exempts the corporation from State and county taxes, the corporation will be liable to a school tax. Livingston v. Han. & St. Jo. R. R. Co. 60 Mo. 516.

So long as a corporation uses its property for the purposes for which it was organized, it is entitled to the right of exemption from taxation under its charter. Washington University v. Rouse, 8 Wall. 439; s. c. 42 Mo. 308.

An exemption of the property of a corporation includes all which is obviously appropriate and convenient to carry into effect the franchise granted. State v. Hancock, 35 N. J. 537; s. c. 33 N. J. 315; State v. Woodruff, 36 N. J. 94.

The exemption is limited to such acquisitions as are incident to the existence of the corporation, to its objects and its uses, and are expedient and necessary for the full enjoyment of its franchises. State v. Newark, 26 N. J. 519; s. c. 25 N. J. 315; State v. Georgia R. R. & B. Co. 54 Geo. 423; State v. Mansfield, 23 N. J. 510; State v. Haight, 25 N. J. 40; Vermont C. R. R. Co. v. Burlington, 28 Vt. 193; State v. Flavell, 24 N. J. 370; State v. Powers, 24 N. J. 400; State v. Blundell, 24 N. J. 402; State v. Collector, 26 N. J. 519; State v. Collector, 38 N. J. 270; Cook v. State, 33 N. J. 474.

If a charter contains an exemption, the corporation may yield a part of the exemption and accept other terms in lieu thereof, without surrendering the whole. State v. Commissioners, 37 N. J. 240.

A provision exempting the property of a corporation from taxation, exempts the real and personal estate required for the successful prosecution of its business. Wilmington Railroad Co. v. Reed, 13 Wall. 264.

A contract not to tax a railroad company or its property, is broken by the levy of a tax upon its gross receipts for the transportation of freight and passengers. Pacific Railroad v. Maguire, 20 Wall. 36; s. c. 51 Mo. 142.

If the charter is renewed without a renewal of the exemption from taxation, the power to tax is revived. State v. Bank, 2 Houst. 99.

A contract exempting the franchise from taxation, will not exempt the stockholders from taxation on account of their stock. A franchise is recognized as property. The capital attached to the franchise is another property, owned in its parts by persons corporate or natural, for which they are liable to be taxed, as they are for all other property. Gordon *v.* Appeal Tax Court, 3 How. 133; S. C. 5 Gill, 231.

The bonds of a corporation are liable to taxation, although the corporation is exempt. State *v.* Branin, 23 N. J. 484.

If the corporation is exempt from taxation, the State can not tax the shares of the stockholders. State *v.* Branin, 23 N. J. 484; State *v.* Powers, 24 N. J. 400; State *v.* Bentley, 23 N. J. 532.

If the charter exempts the stock from liability to taxation, the State can not levy a tax upon the property held by the corporation. Ordinary *v.* Central R. R. Co. 40 Geo. 646; New Haven *v.* City Bank, 31 Conn. 106; Tax Cases, 12 G. & J. 117.

The exemption of the capital stock of a bank from any greater impost than that which is specified in its charter, does not exonerate the dividends of the stockholders from such taxes as the legislature from time to time may think proper to impose. State *v.* Petway, 2 Jones Eq. 396.

A provision that a bank shall be exempt from further taxation, exempts the stockholders from taxation on account of the stock which they own in the bank. Gordon *v.* Appeal Tax Court, 3 How. 133; S. C. 5 Gill, 231.

If the charter makes a distinction between capital stock and property, a tax may be laid on the property although the capital stock is exempt. St. Louis I. M. & S. R. R. Co. 30 Ark. 693.

If the charter merely exempts the capital, the property of the corporation is liable to taxation. Municipality *v.* Commercial Bank, 5 Rob. (La.) 151.

A provision exempting the property of a corporation from taxation, exempts its franchise. Wilmington Railroad Co. *v.* Reid, 13 Wall. 264.

If a statute allowing a corporation to unite with others, creates a new corporation, the exemption from taxation contained therein may be repealed, if the State Constitution then in force made all charters repealable, although the old charter could not have been repealed. State *v.* Northern Central R. R. Co. 44 Md. 131.

An exemption from taxation exempts the corporation from assessments for damages and expenses in opening streets, where they are assessed without regard to benefits. State *v.* Newark, 27 N. J. 185.

If the charter exempts the corporation from all taxes and assessments whatever, the corporation is not liable for assessments for grading streets. St. Paul & Pac. R. R. Co. *v.* St. Paul, 21 Minn. 526.

A provision exempting the corporation from taxation, applies to its property as well as its franchises. Camden & Amboy R. R. Co. *v.* Commissioners, 18 N. J. 71.

A mere provision in the charter of a passenger railway company, for the payment of a certain license fee for each car, does not prevent the legislature from imposing a higher license fee. Union Passenger Railway Co. *v.* Philadelphia, 34 Leg. Int. 330.

An exemption in a charter from all taxation is an exemption from a privilege tax. Grand Gulf & P. B. R. Co. *v.* Buck, 53 Miss. 246.

If the land is exempt, the buildings erected on it are also exempt. Osborne *v.* Humphrey, 7 Conn. 335.

Where the exemption is from taxes and assessments, the words must be taken to refer to the ordinary public taxes and assessments, and do not exempt the corporation from an assessment of benefits for opening a street. State Home Society *v.* Mayor, 35 N. J. 157; City *v.* Society, 24 N. J. 385; Mayor *v.* Proprietors, 7 Md. 517; Sheehan *v.* Good Samaritan Hospital, 50 Mo. 155.

The payment of taxes for twenty years will not prevent the owner from claiming the exemption. Landon *v.* Litchfield, 11 Conn. 251.

When two corporations are consolidated into one, an exemption from taxation contained in the charter of one of such corporations, will not, by such consolidation, be extended to the property of the other whose charter contained no such exemption. Phil. W. & B. R. R. Co. *v.* State, 10 How. 376; Tomlinson *v.* Branch, 15 Wall. 460; Del. Railroad Tax, 18 Wall. 206; Evansville H. & N. R. R. Co. *v.* Comm. 9 Bush, 438.

If the charter exempts the shares of the capital stock from taxation, an act imposing a tax on the franchise or property of the corporation is invalid. Han. & St. Jo. R. R. Co. *v.* Chacklett, 30 Mo. 550; State *v.* Han. & St. Jo. R. R. Co. 37 Mo. 265; Mayor *v.* Balt. & O. R. R. Co. 6 Gill, 288; Nichols *v.* N. H. & N. Co. 42 Conn. 103.

If the stock is exempt from taxation, no tax can be levied on a branch road which the corporation was authorized to construct by an amendment of its charter. A. & G. R. R. Co. *v.* Allen, 15 Fla. 637.

If a bank, in consideration of the payment annually of a certain sum upon its capital stock, purchase from the State the privilege of employing it in banking operations, a law which imposes in addition thereto an annual tax on the same capital thus employed, does impair the obligation of the contract. Union Bank *v.* State, 9 Yerg. 490.

If a statute grants land to a corporation to hold forever, with power to lease and to collect a sum in addition to the rent equal to the tax imposed by the State, and provides that the land shall forever be exempt from taxation, this privilege will not pass to a purchaser whose purchase is made under a subsequent statute authorizing a sale, and virtually repealing the first statute. Armstrong *v.* Treasurer, 16 Pet. 281; s. c. 10 Ohio, 235.

If the lessee of land which is exempt from taxation, covenants to pay such taxes as may be imposed thereon, he can not allege the unconstitutionality of an act imposing a tax. Hart *v.* Cornwall, 14 Conn. 228.

If the land is exempt from taxation, it will be exempt in the hands of a lessee. Hardy *v.* Waltham, 24 Mass. 108; Osborne *v.* Humphrey, 7 Conn. 335; Landon *v.* Litchfield, 11 Conn. 251; Matheny *v.* Golden, 5 Ohio St. 361; Kumler *v.* Traber, 5 Ohio St. 442.

If the lessee of a railroad agrees to pay all taxes assessed upon the property of the corporation, a tax on him in respect of his profits and earnings by the transportation of passengers and property, does not infringe a provision in the charter, exempting the corporation from taxation. State *v.* Del. L. & W. R. R. Co. 30 N. J. 473; s. c. 31 N. J. 531.

If, by terms of the lease, the buildings are not considered as a part of the lands, and an interest in them is created entirely distinct from an interest in the lands, the buildings may be taxed although the land is exempt. Parker *v.* Redfield, 10 Conn. 490.

If the charter of a library corporation authorizes it to build and rent a library building, and exempts its property from taxation, the parts which are leased as stores are exempt. State *v.* Leester, 29 N. J. 541.

If the State makes the immunity from taxation transferable, it can not tax the property in the hands of a purchaser. St. Paul & Pac. R. R. Co. *v.* Parcher, 14 Minn. 297; State *v.* Winona & St. Paul R. R. Co. 21 Minn. 315; A. & G. R. R. Co. *v.* Allen, 15 Fla. 637.

If the charter merely exempts the corporation and its property from taxation, the exemption does not pass to a party who purchases the property at a sale under a mortgage or execution. Morgan *v.* Louisiana, 93 U. S. 217; Trask *v.* Maguire, 18 Wall. 391.

Eminent Domain.

A grant is always understood to be made subject to those reserved rights in the State, which are indispensable to State sovereignty. These reserved rights of sovereignty, which are denominated the right of eminent domain, always exist as a condition or implied reservation in all grants. Hence, the legislature may take the benefit of the grant of a corporate franchise from the grantee for public use. Armington *v.* Barnet, 15 Vt. 745; Enfield Bridge Co. *v.* Railroad, 17 Conn. 40; Piscataqua Bridge Co.

v. N. H. Bridge Co. 7 N. H. 35; Boston Water Power Co. *v.* Railroad, 40 Mass. 360; Barber *v.* Andover, 8 N. H. 398; James River Co. *v.* Thompson, 3 Gratt. 270; West River Bridge Co. *v.* Dix, 6 How. 507; s. c. 16 Vt. 446; Richmond R. R. Co. *v.* Louisa R. R. Co. 13 How. 71; Newcastle R. R. Co. *v.* Peru & Ind. R. R. Co. 3 Ind. 464; Shorter *v.* Smith, 9 Geo. 517; Boston & L. R. R. Co. *v* Salem & L. R. R Co. 68 Mass. 1; Northern Railroad *v.* Concord Railroad, 27 N. H. 183; Central Bridge *v.* Lowell, 70 Mass. 474; Red River Bridge Co. *v.* Clarksville, 1 Sneed, 176; Crosby *v.* Hanover, 36 N. H. 404.

The tenure by which a corporation holds its property, forms no part of that which is of the essence of its charter. There is, therefore, nothing in the charter which can be so construed as to prevent the taking of the property for public uses. Ala. & Fla. R. R. Co. *v.* Kenney, 39 Ala. 307; Bellona Company's Case, 3 Bland, 442; Backus *v.* Lebanon, 11 N. H. 19; Turnpike Co. *v.* Railroad Co. 10 G. & J. 392; Boston Water Power Co. *v.* Railroad, 40 Mass. 360; Tuckahoe Canal Co. *v.* Railroad, 11 Leigh, 42; Crosby *v.* Hanover, 36 N. H. 404; In re Kerr, 42 Barb. 119; White River Turnpike Co. *v.* Railroad Co. 21 Vt. 590.

The reservation of a right to resume the charter at the end of a certain period, upon certain terms, does not prevent the legislature from exercising the authority of eminent domain, by taking a part of the property of the corporation. Backus *v.* Lebanon, 11 N. H. 19; Barber *v.* Andover, 8 N. H. 398.

The legislature may authorize the laying out of a common public highway over a road made by a turnpike corporation, although the charter is still in good force, provided compensation is made to the corporation for the property thus taken for public use. Barber *v.* Andover, 8 N. H. 398; Pierce *v.* Somersworth, 10 N. H. 369; Armington *v.* Barnet, 15 Vt. 745.

A statute which impairs a right under a charter, is unconstitutional unless it provides a legal indemnity. Enfield Bridge Co. *v.* Connecticut River Co. 7 Conn. 28.

Police Power.

As to their general liability to legislative control, corporations and natural persons stand upon the same ground. The great object of an incorporation is to bestow the character and properties of individuality on a collected and changing body of men. Any privileges which may exempt it from the burdens common to individuals, do not flow necessarily from the charter, but must be expressed in it or they do not exist. Thorpe *v.* B. & P. R. R. Co. 27 Vt. 140; Peters *v.* Railroad Co. 23 Mo. 107; Bank *v.* Hamilton, 21 Ill. 53.

The legislature has the same right of general control over corporations as it has over natural persons. By general laws it may require them to conform to such regulations of a police character as it may deem proper for the security of the rights of the citizens generally, and most conducive to quiet and good order, and the security of property. Nelson *v.* V. & C. R. Co. 26 Vt. 717; Thorpe *v.* B. & P. R. R. Co. 27 Vt. 140; Benson *v.* New York, 10 Barb. 223; Galena & C. R. R. Co. *v.* Loomis, 13 Ill. 548; Ohio & M. R. R. Co. *v.* McClelland, 25 Ill. 140; N. W. Fertilizing Co. *v.* Hyde Park, 70 Ill. 634; Gorman *v.* Pacific Railroad, 26 Mo. 441; New Alb. & S. R. R. Co. *v.* Tilton, 12 Ind. 3; B. C. & M. Railroad *v.* State, 32 N. H. 215; State *v.* Matthews, 3 Jones (N. C.) 451.

There is a distinction between those powers which are secured to corporations by contract and those which are mere endowments of existence. The former are their property, of which they can not be deprived without just compensation; the latter are elements of existence imparted to them by the law of their being, and are held by them like the natural rights of natural persons, subject to be controlled and modified by the legislature the same as it may control and modify the natural endowments of natural persons. Bank *v.* Hamilton, 21 Ill. 53.

Unless there is an express provision or a reasonable intendment that a right or faculty shall not be touched by subsequent legislation, it is held in the same subordination to governmental control as the rights and faculties of natural persons. Bank *v.* Hamilton, 21 Ill. 53.

A corporation which claims an exemption from the general police power must show either a relinquishment of the right in the charter, or that its exercise is inconsistent with and destructive of the particular rights, privileges or franchises therein enumerated. State *v.* Southern Pacific R. R. Co. 24 Tex. 80.

Powers, the exercise of which can only be justified as a police regulation, are such only as are so clearly necessary to the safety, comfort, or well being of society, or so imperatively required by the public necessity, as to lead to the rational and satisfactory conclusion that the framers of the Constitution could not, as men of ordinary prudence and foresight, have intended to prohibit their exercise in the particular case, notwithstanding the language of the prohibition would otherwise include it. People *v.* Plank Road Co. 9 Mich. 285.

The police power of the State comprehends all those general laws of internal regulation which are necessary to secure the peace, good order, health and comfort of society. Phila. W. & B. R. R. Co. *v.* Bowers, 4 Houst. 506.

Under the color of police laws the legislature can not destroy or impair the franchise, or any right or power essential to its beneficial exercise.

Sloan *v.* Mo. Pacific R. R. Co. 2 Cent. L. J. 781; Phila. W. & B. R. R. Co. *v.* Bowers, 4 Houst. 506.

The legislature has no power to establish laws to promote the mere convenience of the public, or of individuals, in contravention of the provisions of the charter of a private corporation. State *v.* Noyes, 47 Me. 189.

The legislature may at all times regulate the exercise of the corporate franchise by general laws passed in good faith for the legitimate ends contemplated by the police power of the State, but it can not, under color of such laws, destroy or impair the franchise itself, nor any of those rights and powers which are essential to its beneficial exercise. Phila. W. & B. R. R. Co. *v.* Bowers, 4 Houst. 506; T. W. & W. R. R. Co. *v.* City, 67 Ill. 37.

It is the province of the legislature to determine when the exigency exists calling for the exercise of the police power, and the province of the courts to decide what are the proper subjects of its exercise. Lake View *v.* Rose Hill Cem. Co. 70 Ill. 191.

Any act essentially paralyzing the franchise, or destroying the profits arising therefrom, is void, but beyond that the entire power of the legislative control resides in the legislature, unless such power is expressly limited in the grant to the corporation. Thorpe *v.* B. & C. R. R. Co. 27 Vt. 140.

So far as railroads are concerned, this police power which resides primarily and ultimately in the legislature, is twofold. 1st. The police of the roads which, in the absence of legislative control, the corporations themselves exercise over their operatives, and, to some extent, over all who do business with them, or come upon their grounds. There is no end of illustrations upon this subject. It may be extended to the supervision of the track, tending switches, running upon the time of other trains, running a road with a single track, using improper rails, not using proper precautions by way of safety beams in case of the breaking of axle-trees, the number of brakemen upon a train, with reference to the number of cars, employing intemperate or incompetent engineers and servants, running beyond a given rate of speed, and a thousand similar things. 2d. There is also the general police power of the State, by which persons and property are subjected to all kinds of restraints and burdens in order to secure the general comfort, health and prosperity of the State. The legislature may prohibit railroads from carrying freight which is regarded as detrimental to the public health, or morals, or the public safety generally, or they may probably be made liable as insurers of the lives and limbs of passengers, as they virtually are of freight. Thorpe *v.* B. & C. R. R. Co. 27 Vt. 140; Nelson *v.* V. & C. R. Co. 26 Vt. 717.

The right to regulate railroad crossings flows naturally from the police power of the State. P. & C. R. R. Co. *v.* S. W. P. R. R. Co. 77 Penn. 173.

A statute requiring a railroad corporation to keep a flagman at an ordinary crossing, where there is no unusual danger, is void. T. W. & W. R. R. Co. v. City, 67 Ill. 37.

The legislature may require a railroad corporation to ring a bell or sound a whistle at public crossings. Galena R. R. Co. v. Appleby, 28 Ill. 283.

The legislature may require a bell or whistle to be attached to each locomotive engine, and to be rung or whistled before crossing any other road. Galena & C. R. R. Co. v. Loomis, 13 Ill. 548.

A law regulating the speed of trains in a city is valid, although the charter authorizes the corporation to fix and regulate the speed of trains on its road. C. B. & Q. R. R. Co. v. Haggerty, 67 Ill. 113.

A statute requiring railroad corporations to construct fences and cattle guards along the line of their route is valid, as a mere police regulation for the safety of passengers and the security of animals. Blair v. Mil. & P. R. R. Co. 20 Wis. 254; Penn. R. R. Co. v. Riblet, 66 Penn. 164; Nichols v. Som. & Ken. R. R. Co. 43 Me. 356; New Alb. & S. R. R. Co. v. Tilton, 12 Ind. 3; Jones v. G. & C. R. R. Co. 16 Iowa, 6; Wenona & St. Peter R. R. Co. v. Waldron, 11 Minn. 515; Suydam v. Moore, 8 Barb. 358; Thorpe v. B. & C R. R. Co. 27 Vt. 140; Indianapolis R. R. Co. v. Kercheval, 16 Ind. 84; Ohio & M. R. R. Co. v. McClelland, 25 Ill. 140; Nelson v. V. & C. R. R. Co. 26 Vt. 717; Waldron v. Railroad Co. 8 Barb. 390; K. P. R. R. Co. v. Mower, 16 Kans 573; Gorman v. Pacific R. R. Co. 26 Mo. 441; Madison & Ind. R. R. Co. v. Whiteneck, 8 Ind. 217.

A statute passed after the granting of the charter may render railroad corporations liable for injuries caused by fire communicated from their engines. Lyman v. B. & W. R. R. Co. 58 Mass. 288; Rodemacher v. Mil. & St. P. R. R. Co. 41 Iowa, 297.

A statute imposing a penalty upon a corporation for taking unlawful toll or freight does not impair any right under the charter, for its only object is to compel the corporation to fulfill the contract. It neither violates, nor suffers a violation of the charter. Camden & Amboy R. R. Co. v. Briggs, 22 N. J. 623; Norris v. Androscoggin R. R. Co. 39 Me. 273.

A statute making railroad corporations criminally liable for the negligence and misconduct of their employees is valid. B. C. & M. Railroad v. State, 32 N. H. 215.

The legislature may authorize the appointment of commissioners to determine the duties and obligations of railroad companies who are authorized to connect their roads. Portland R. R. Co. v. Railway Co. 46 Me. 69.

A State law which prohibits a railroad corporation from constructing or maintaining a track on any highway, so near any depot of another railroad as to endanger the safe and convenient access thereto for ordinary purposes, is valid as a police regulation. P. S. & P. R. R. Co. *v.* B. & M. R. R. Co. 65 Me. 122.

A State may pass an act for the purpose of preventing an unjust discrimination in railway freights, whether as between individuals or communities, and enforce its observance by appropriate penalties. C. & A. R. R. Co. *v.* People, 67 Ill. 11.

A statute requiring a railroad corporation to build a depot for freight and passengers at a certain place on its road is valid. Railroad Commissioners *v.* P. & O. C. R. R. Co. 63 Me. 269.

Where the charter merely gives an implied right to take some toll, the legislature may regulate the rate of tolls for the transportation of freight and passengers. Winona & St. P. R. R. Co. *v.* Blake, 94 U. S. 180; s. c. 19 Minn. 418; C. B. & Q. R. R. Co. *v.* Iowa, 94 U. S. 155.

The imposition of a penalty upon banks for a refusal to pay their bank bills is not unconstitutional, unless there is some clause in the charter prohibiting such a law. Brown *v.* Penobscot Bank, 8 Mass. 445.

The power to regulate fares is not affected by the fact that the corporation has pledged its income for the security of its debts, and leased the road to a tenant who relies upon the earnings for the means of paying the rent. C. B. & Q. R. R. Co. *v.* Iowa, 94 U. S. 155.

If the charter provides that the corporation may obtain judgment on motion, after notice for twenty days, against a stockholder who fails to pay his assessments, the legislature may, at its discretion, modify and control this summary remedy. Ex parte Northeast R. R. Co. 1 Ala. Sel. Cas. 608; s. c. 37 Ala. 679.

A statute giving the legal representatives a right of action for an injury where the party injured would have had a right of action if death had not ensued, does not impair the obligation of a prior charter, for no corporation has a vested right to do wrong, or take human life intentionally or negligently. Southwestern R. R. Co. *v.* Paulk, 24 Geo. 356; Board *v.* Scearce, 2 Duvall, 576.

Although the charter authorizes the corporation to convert dead animals and animal matter into a fertilizer, yet a subsequent statute may prohibit the transportation thereof through a certain town. N. W. Fertilizing Co. *v.* Hyde Park, 70 Ill. 634.

Although the charter of a corporation contains a clause prohibiting the sale of spirituous liquors within a certain distance of the corporation, yet the State may subsequently license the sale of liquors within that distance. Dingman *v.* People, 51 Ill. 277.

If the charter permits the corporation to buy and hold a certain quantity of land, and use it for cemetery purposes, a subsequent statute prohibiting it from using a portion of the land for that purpose is void. Lake View *v.* Rose Hill Cem. Co. 70 Ill. 191.

A statute prohibiting the sale of malt liquors does not impair the obligation of a charter of a corporation created for the purpose of manufacturing malt liquors. Comm. *v.* Intoxicating Liquors, 115 Mass. 153.

A statute prohibiting lotteries is valid, and applies to a corporation whose charter gives it the right to establish lotteries for a certain period. Moore *v.* State, 48 Miss. 147.

The State may provide that a bank shall redeem several bills presented together as a single obligation. Reaper's Bank *v.* Willard, 24 Ill. 433.

The legislature may require that a certain proportion of the officers shall reside within the State. State *v.* Southern Pacific R. R. Co. 24 Tex. 80.

The legislature may require that the corporation shall make an annual report of the condition of its affairs. State *v.* Southern Pacific R. R. Co. 24 Tex. 80.

The State may make a failure to comply with a police regulation a ground for a forfeiture of the charter. State *v.* Southern Pacific R. R. Co. 24 Tex. 80.

The State may change the mode of assessing the property of a corporation. Bank *v.* Hamilton, 21 Ill. 53.

A statute rendering a corporation personally liable for the wages of laborers employed by contractors under it is valid. Peters *v.* Railroad Co. 23 Mo. 107; Branin *v.* Conn. & P. R. R. Co. 31 Vt. 214; Grannahan *v.* Railroad Co. 30 Mo. 546.

Although the charter provides that the insurance company can only be sued on a policy in the county where it is located, yet the legislature may render the corporation liable to such a suit in another county, if it does not affect injuriously any corporate right or subject the corporation to any additional loss or liability. Sanders *v.* Hillsborough Ins. Co. 44 N. H. 238; Howard *v.* Insurance Co. 13 B. Mon. 282.

Although the charter prescribes the mode in which process may be served on the corporation, yet a subsequent statute may prescribe a different mode. C. & F. R. R. Co. *v.* Hecht, 29 Ark. 661.

The State legislature has the power to subject the property and franchise of a corporation to the payment of its debts, and the exercise of such power does not impair the obligation of any contract between the State and the corporation. Louisville Turnpike Co. *v.* Lounsbury, 2 Met. (Ky.) 165.

A statute providing for the appointment of a receiver and the issuing of an injunction to restrain the exercise of the franchise when the corporation is insolvent or violates the provisions of its charter, is constitutional. Bank of Columbia *v.* Att. Gen. 3 Wend. 588; Suydam *v.* Receivers, 3 N. J. Eq. 114; Savings Institution *v.* Makin, 23 Me. 360; Aurora Turnpike Co. *v.* Holthouse, 7 Ind. 59.

A statute reviving a corporation whose charter has been forfeited, and legalizing contracts made by it after the forfeiture, is valid, for it merely removes an impediment or disability to the enforcement of contracts fairly entered into by debtors with it. Bleakney *v.* Farmers' Bank, 17 S. & R. 64; vide Officer *v.* Young, 5 Yerg. 320.

A statute which provides that, upon the institution of proceedings to have a charter declared forfeited, an injunction may issue to prevent the collection of all demands due to the corporation, until there is a final judgment of forfeiture or not, is valid, for the legislature may suspend the right of a corporation to sue until the charge of violating its charter is determined. Commercial Bank *v.* State, 12 Miss. 439; Comm. *v.* Farmers' Bank, 38 Mass. 542.

A general law passed after the granting of a charter, but before its expiration, and providing that all corporations should continue in existence for a certain period after the expiration of their charters, for the purpose of suing and being sued, does not violate the obligation of contracts, but provides a way of enforcing them both in favor of and against the corporation. A debtor to the corporation can not object, for the bringing of a suit would be an acceptance of a prolongation of the charter. The corporation can not object to a statute the object of which is to give a right of action upon contracts upon which it was legally and morally bound. The corporation can not object, for the debts are an equitable lien upon the stock, and the legislature has a right to provide the means of enforcing this moral obligation. Foster *v.* Essex Bank, 16 Mass. 245.

A debtor to a corporation can not object to a statute reviving the corporation, passed after the expiration of its charter. A legislature which limits itself to correcting mistakes and providing remedies for the furtherance of justice can not be charged with exceeding its authority. Lincoln Bank *v.* Richardson, 1 Me. 79.

A statute which provides that the debts due to a corporation shall not be released or extinguished by a judgment of forfeiture, but that a receiver may be appointed with authority to sue for and collect such debts, is constitutional. Nevitt *v.* Bank, 14 Miss. 513; Hall *v.* Carey, 5 Geo. 239; Carey *v.* Giles, 9 Geo. 253; Scearcy *v.* Stubbs, 12 Geo. 437.

Amendment.

A charter may be altered or modified with the consent of the corporation. Trustees *v.* Winston, 5 Stew. & Port. 17; Ehrenzeller *v.* Canal Co. 1 Rawle, 181; Commissioner *v.* Jarvis, 1 Mon. 5; Monongahela Nav. Co. *v.* Coon, 6 Penn. 379; S. C. 6 W. & S. 101; People *v.* Marshall, 1 Gilman, 672.

The assent of the corporation relates back to the date of the law. Ehrenzeller *v.* Canal Co. 1 Rawle, 181.

If there is no acceptance of a subsequent act, the rights under the charter remain unimpaired. Pingry *v.* Washburn, 1 Aik. 264; Allen *v.* McKeen, 1 Sum. 276; Comm. *v.* Cullen, 13 Penn. 133.

Where an act provides for an amendment in several particulars, and does not expressly authorize that some may be accepted and some rejected by the corporation, it must be accepted as it is offered or not at all. Marietta & Cin. R. R. Co. *v.* Elliott, 10 Ohio St. 57.

An inference of the assent of a corporation to an alteration of its charter can not be drawn from the mere non-user or misuser of its franchises. Regents *v.* Williams, 9 G. & J. 365.

If the funds of a charitable corporation accumulate to an amount which not only enables it to carry out and perfect the specific charity which gave rise to its creation, but to leave a surplus, it may apply for an amendment of the charter, so as to be enabled to apply this surplus to other charities. Att. Gen. *v.* Clergy Society, 10 Rich. Eq. 604; s. c. 8 Rich. Eq. 190.

The power of the legislature, with the consent of the corporation, to alter, repeal or provide for a surrender of the charter can be controlled by contracts made with the corporation only to the extent that the contracts and legal remedies must be left intact. Houston *v.* Jefferson College, 63 Penn. 428.

A corporation, by the very terms and nature of its political existence, is subject to dissolution by a surrender of its corporate franchises, or by a forfeiture of them for willful misuser or non-user. Every creditor must be presumed to understand the nature and incidents of such a body politic, and to contract with reference to them. The mere existence of a private contract of the corporation does not prevent a surrender of its charter, or force upon it a perpetuity of existence. Mumma *v.* Potomac Co. 8 Pet. 281.

The dissolution of a corporation by a surrender of its charter does not impair the obligation of its contracts, for the creditors may enforce their claims against any property belonging to the corporation which has not passed into the hands of *bona fide* purchasers, but is still held in trust for the corporation, or the stockholders thereof, at the time of its dissolution. Mumma *v.* Potomac Co. 8 Pet. 281.

If the incorporators have failed to comply with the requirements of law, so as to be legally incorporated, the legislature may pass an act curing the defects and giving to the corporation a right to sue upon contracts already made in its name. Syracuse Bank *v.* Davis, 16 Barb. 188.

Reserved Power to Alter.

If the power is reserved in the charter, the legislature may repeal, alter or modify the charter. Allen *v.* McKeen, 1 Sum. 276; Crease *v.* Babcock, 40 Mass. 334; McLaren *v.* Pennington, 1 Paige, 102; Monongahela Nav. Co. *v.* Coon, 6 Penn. 379; S. C. 6 W. & S. 101; Ferguson *v.* Miners' & Manuf. Bank, 3 Sneed, 609; Stephen *v.* Smith, 29 Vt. 160; Del. R. R. Co. *v.* Thorp, 5 Harring. 454; Perrin *v.* Oliver, 1 Minn. 202; Stephens *v.* Powell, 1 Oregon, 283.

If the legislature has the right to make grants, it of necessity must prescribe the terms upon which they shall be made. If it may limit the duration, it may also impose other restrictions. It may determine how much or how little, how large or how small, a franchise it will grant. It may grant absolutely, or on condition; so it may grant during pleasure, or until a certain event happens. If a grant is accepted on the terms prescribed, it becomes a compact, and the grantee can have no reason to complain of the execution of his own contract. Crease *v.* Babcock, 40 Mass. 334; Iron City Bank *v.* Pittsburgh, 37 Penn. 340.

The reservation of a right to repeal the charter is not a condition repugnant to the grant; it is only a limitation of the grant. Even in a commonlaw conveyance a power of revocation reserved to the grantor is valid. McLaren *v.* Pennington, 1 Paige, 102; Crease *v.* Babcock, 40 Mass. 334.

If a general statute provides that all charters thereafter granted shall be subject to alteration, suspension or repeal at the discretion of the legislature, a charter subsequently granted is subject to the power. Miller *v.* State, 15 Wall. 478; Sherman *v.* Smith, 1 Black, 587; Fort Plain Bridge Co. *v.* Smith, 30 N. Y. 44; Suydam *v.* Moore, 8 Barb. 358; White *v.* Railroad Co. 14 Barb. 559; Griffin *v.* Kentucky Ins. Co. 3 Bush, 592; State *v.* Person, 32 N. J. 134; Hyatt *v.* McMahon, 25 Barb. 457; Iron City Bank *v.* Pittsburgh, 37 Penh. 340; Central R. & B. Co. *v.* State, 54 Geo. 501; State *v.* Commissioners, 37 N. J. 228.

Whenever the power to repeal, alter or amend an act of incorporation has been reserved in the State Constitution, or in general laws on the subject, or in the special act of incorporation, its exercise does not impair the contract of which it forms a constituent part. Comm. *v.* Fayette County

R. R. Co. 55 Penn. 452; Pennsylvania College Cases, 13 Wall. 190; Miller *v.* State, 15 Wall. 478.

If the power to amend, alter or repeal is not reserved in the Constitution, it is a question in every case whether the legislature intended that the right to change or repeal should inhere in the charter, or whether the charter was perfect and not within the power of the legislature to impair its obligation. State *v.* Yard, 10 C. L. N. 90.

The reservation of the right to repeal or amend should not be extended beyond the terms in which it is expressed, and all the force which properly belongs to it is given when reservation is extended as far as the language justifies, and it should be extended no farther. State *v.* Yard, 10 C. L. N. 90.

A public statute which provides the manner in which a charter may be amended, is not a contract. State *v.* New Haven & N. R. R. Co. 43 Conn. 351.

The charter of a corporation may be made liable to repeal by an amendment accepted by the corporation, which reserves the power, notwithstanding the charter was before irrepealable. Monongahela Nav. Co. *v.* Coon, 6 Penn. 379; s. c. 6 W. & S. 101; Mobile R. R. Co. *v.* State, 29 Ala. 573.

If the right to repeal is reserved by one State Constitution, it can not be affected by the subsequent adoption of another Constitution. State *v.* Northern Central R. R. Co. 44 Md. 131.

A power to alter is not ordinarily to be intended as a power to repeal or a power to destroy. Hartford Bridge Co. *v.* East Hartford, 16 Conn. 149.

If the power to repeal depends on the abuse or misuse of the privileges conferred by the charter, it is not necessary that such abuse or misuse should be judicially ascertained. Crease *v.* Babcock, 40 Mass. 334; Miners' Bank *v.* U. S. 1 Iowa, 553; Erie & N. E. R. R. Co. *v.* Casey, 26 Penn. 287; s. c. 1 Grant, 274; contra, Mayor *v.* Pitts. & C. R. R. Co. 1 Abb. C. C. 9; Flint & F. P. Co. *v.* Woodhull, 25 Mich. 99.

Where the power to alter is reserved, the legislature may modify the charter by a general statute. State *v.* Commissioners, 37 N. J. 228; Bangor R. R. Co. *v.* Smith, 47 Me. 34; State *v.* Commissioners, 38 N. J. 472.

The statute may be passed in accordance with the forms prescribed by the State constitution in force at the time when the alteration is made, although those forms are not the same as were prescribed when the charter was granted. The sovereign people having reserved the power to alter, may, from time to time, designate the agents or organs by which, and prescribe the manner in which, the power shall be exercised. In re Reciprocity Bank, 29 Barb. 369; s. c. 22 N. Y. 9; 17 How. Pr. 323.

The alteration may be made by a change in the State constitution. In re Oliver Lee & Co.'s Bank, 21 N. Y. 9.

An act of incorporation may be repealed by implication, for there is no difference in the legislative proceeding by which an act of incorporation is repealed, and that by which any other act is repealed. Union Railroad Co. v. East Tenn. R. R. Co. 14 Geo. 327.

A power to alter or modify a charter is not exhausted by one alteration, but is a continuous and perpetual power. Proprietors v. Haskell, 7 Me. 474; State v. Commissioners, 37 N. J. 228; People v. Hills, 46 Barb. 340.

Where the power is reserved to repeal, alter or amend a charter, the legislature may repeal the charter, but it can not compel the corporation to accept an amendment, and an amendment is not binding without acceptance. Yeaton v. Bank, 21 Gratt. 593; Sage v. Dillard, 15 B. Mon. 340.

An alteration is binding upon the corporation, whether it assents or not. Att. Gen. v. Railroad Companies, 35 Wis. 425; Mayor v. N. & W. R. R. Co. 109 Mass. 103; Hyatt v. Whipple, 37 Barb. 595; Hyatt v. Esmond, 37 Barb. 601.

If an amendment goes farther than matters of policy, and those duties that immediately affect the public, the corporation may decline to accept an amendment, although the power to alter is reserved in the charter. Troy & Rutland R. R. Co. v. Kerr, 17 Barb. 581.

No formal vote to accept an amendment of the charter is necessary. The acceptance may be implied from proof of any regular corporate act. Bangor R. R. Co. v. Smith, 47 Me. 34; City of Roxbury v. Railroad Co. 60 Mass. 424.

Where the power is reserved to alter, repeal or amend the charter, the legislature may, if the interest and rights of creditors demand it, take away the custody of the assets of the corporation from the directors, and intrust the custody to a State officer, pending an investigation into the company's solvency. Lothrop v. Stedman, 42 Conn. 583; S. C. 15 A. L. Reg. 346.

Where the power is reserved to alter or amend the charter of a street railway corporation the legislature may authorize another company to lay a similar track through the same street, or to use the track of the first corporation, making compensation for the use and wear of the track, but without compensation for the diminution of its profits or the value of its franchise. Metropolitan R. R. Co. v. Highland Railway, 118 Mass. 290.

If the power to repeal or alter is reserved in the charter, a statute authorizing a receiver to make assessments on premium notes of an insurance company, instead of the directors, is valid, although it applies to notes issued before its passage. Hyatt v. McMahon, 25 Barb. 457.

The reservation of the power to repeal, alter or modify a charter, does not authorize the legislature to pass an act compelling the corporation to construct a highway across its property at its own expense. Miller *v*. Railroad Co. 21 Barb. 513.

Where a corporation has been exempted from the obligation to maintain a suitable and sufficient fishway, in consideration of its indemnifying the riparian owners whose rights are injured by its dam, and has expended considerable sums of money in pursuance of this requirement, it is not competent for the legislature, under its power to alter or amend the charter, to pass a law requiring the corporation to maintain a fishway. Comm. *v*. Essex Co. 79 Mass. 239.

Where there is a provision that the alteration shall work no injustice to the corporators, it is for the courts, and not for the legislature to decide, whether the modification works injustice to them. Iron City Bank *v*. Pittsburgh, 37 Penn. 340.

Where the power to alter is reserved in the charter, the legislature may modify a provision which requires the consent of a majority of the pew holders to the levying of a pew tax. Bailey *v*. Trustees, 6 R. I. 491.

Where the power to alter or repeal is reserved, the legislature may impose a tax different from that stipulated for in the original charter. Iron City Bank *v*. Pittsburgh, 37 Penn. 340.

Where the power is reserved to alter the charter, the legislature may require a railroad corporation to raise or lower the highways which its road crosses, as the security of the public requires. City of Roxbury *v*. Railroad Co. 6 Cush. 424.

Where the power to alter is reserved, a highway may be laid across a railroad track, and the corporation may be required to make the necessary excavations and embankments. Albany R. R. Co. *v*. Brownell, 24 N. Y. 345; Fitchburg R. R. Co. *v*. Grand Junction R. R. Co. 86 Mass. 198.

Where the power is reserved to alter the charter, the legislature may impose a burden clearly connected with the grant, and necessary to protect the public from the injurious consequences resulting from the exercise of the power conferred by the charter. English *v*. New Haven Co. 32 Conn. 240.

Where the power is reserved to alter the charter, the legislature may compel the corporation to widen a bridge over an excavation made by it. English *v*. New Haven Co. 32 Conn. 240.

Where the power is reserved to alter the charter, the legislature may increase the number of directors which a municipal corporation which is a stockholder, is entitled to elect. People *v.* Hills, 46 Barb. 340; Miller *v.* State, 15 Wall. 478.

Where the right is reserved to alter the charter, a State may prohibit an insolvent corporation from giving preferences. Robinson *v.* Gardiner, 18 Gratt. 509.

Where the power is reserved to alter or amend the charter, a State may impose a tax on the stock, although there is a clause in the charter that such tax shall not be imposed for a certain period. Comm. *v.* Fayette County R. R. Co. 55 Penn. 452.

A provision that the charter shall not be altered except by an act of the legislature is a sufficient reservation of the power to alter. Houston *v.* Jefferson College, 63 Penn. 428; Comm. *v.* Bonsall, 3 Whart. 559; Pennsylvania College Cases, 13 Wall. 190.

A legislature can not appoint additional trustees for a corporation, although it has reserved the right to repeal, alter, or amend the charter. Sage *v.* Dillard, 15 B. Mon. 340.

Where the power is reserved to repeal, alter, or amend the charter, a corporation authorized to construct a dam across a river may be required to construct a suitable fishway at its own expense. Commissioners *v.* Holyoke W. P. Co. 104 Mass. 446; Holyoke *v.* Lyman, 15 Wall. 500.

Where the power is reserved to repeal, alter, or amend the charter, the legislature may require a railroad corporation to construct cattle guards. Bulkley *v.* N. Y. & N. H. R. R. Co. 27 Conn. 479.

Where the power is reserved to alter, amend, or repeal the charter, the legislature may require a railroad corporation to fence its road. Staats *v.* Hudson River R. R. Co. 3 Keyes, 196.

Where the power is reserved to alter, amend, or repeal a charter, the corporation may be required to pay the excess of the dividend over six per cent. per annum to a hospital, instead of one-third of the net profits. Mass. Gen. Hospital *v.* State Mutual Life Insurance Co. 70 Mass. 227.

The reserved power to repeal, alter, or amend the charter may be exercised to almost any extent to carry into effect the original purposes of the grant, or to secure the due administration of its affairs, so as to protect the rights of the stockholders and of creditors, and for the proper disposition of the assets. Miller *v.* State, 15 Wall. 478; Holyoke *v.* Lyman, 15 Wall. 500.

Where the power is reserved to repeal, alter, or amend the charter, the legislature may repeal a clause in the charter exempting the corporation from taxation. State *v.* Miller, 30 N. J. 368; s. c. 31 N. J. 521; State *v.* Mayor, 31 N. J. 575; Union Improvement Co. *v.* Comm. 69 Penn. 140;

Comm. *v.* Fayette County R. R. Co. 55 Penn. 452; City *v.* Metropolitan Bank, 27 La. Ann. 648; Iron City Bank *v.* Pittsburgh, 37 Penn. 340; C. R. & B. Co. *v.* State, 54 Geo. 401; A. & G. R. R. Co. *v.* State, 55 Geo. 312; Tomlinson *v.* Jessup, 15 Wall. 454; West. Wis. R. R. Co. *v.* Supervisors, 35 Wis. 257; S. C. 93 U. S 595; Hewitt *v.* N. Y. & O. M. R. R. Co. 12 Blatch. 452.

Where the power is reserved to repeal, alter, or amend the charter, a railroad corporation may be required to erect a station-house at a certain place on its road, and cause trains to stop there. Comm. *v.* Eastern R. R. Co. 103 Mass. 254.

Where the power is reserved to repeal, amend, or alter the charter, a State may require several railroads to unite in a station in a city. Mayor *v.* N. & W. R. R. Co. 109 Mass. 103.

Where the power is reserved to repeal, amend, or alter the charter, a State may diminish the right to a ferry franchise from two miles to a quarter of a mile. Perrin *v.* Oliver, 1 Minn. 202.

Where the power is reserved to repeal the charter, the State may regulate tolls or rates for transportation of persons or property. Hinckley *v.* C. N. & St. P. R. R. Co. 38 Wis. 194; State *v.* Stone, 37 Wis. 204; Pick *v.* C. & N. W. R. R. Co. 94 U. S. 164; S. C. 6 Biss. 177; Shields *v.* State, 26 Ohio St. 86; Att. Gen. *v.* Railroad Company, 35 Wis. 425; Anon. 6 C. L. N. 333; M. W. & M. Plank Road Co. *v.* Reynolds, 3 Wis. 287; Parker *v.* Metropolitan R. R. Co. 109 Mass. 506.

If the power to alter, limit, annul, or restrain any of the powers vested in the corporation by the charter, is to be used as shall be judged necessary to promote the best interests of the corporation, the legislature can not extinguish its corporate existence. The legislature is constituted sole judge of what is the best interest of the corporation, but still it can not do anything pointedly destructive of that interest. Allen *v.* McKeen, 1 Sum. 276.

If the power is merely to alter, limit, annul, or restrain the powers vested in the corporation by the charter, the legislature can not intermeddle with its property. Allen *v.* McKeen, 1 Sum. 276.

Where the power to repeal or alter is reserved in the State Constitution, the right is not affected by the grant of authority by the legislature to consolidate with a corporation of another State. The corporation is still subject to the Constitution, and there is no authority anywhere to remove it beyond the reach of such authority. Anon. 6 C. L. N. 333.

The legislature can not touch the vested rights, privileges, or franchises of a corporation, except so far as the power is reserved by the charter. Allen *v.* McKeen, 1 Sum. 276.

The reservation of the power to repeal, alter, or modify the charter does not authorize the legislature to take the property of the corporation for public use without compensation. Miller *v.* Railroad Co. 21 Barb. 513.

Under the reserved power to alter and repeal, the legislature has no right to change the fundamental character of the corporation, and convert it into a different legal being. Buffalo & N. Y. City R. R. Co. *v.* Dudley, 14 N. Y. 336.

Under the reserved power to amend, the legislature can not compel the corporation to change the entire character of its business. An amendment must not only be granted, but accepted. The corporators do not agree to use the charter after an amendment, no matter how injurious to their interests. Troy & Rutland R. R. Co. *v.* Kerr, 17 Barb. 581; White.*v.* Railroad Co. 14 Barb. 559.

Although the charter contains a reservation of the right to alter or amend it, yet no amendment or alteration can take away the property or rights which have become vested under a legitimate exercise of the powers granted by the charter. Comm. *v.* Essex Co. 79 Mass. 239.

Where there is a reservation of the right to alter or amend, the legislature may make the stockholder personally liable for the debts of the corporation subsequently contracted. Sherman *v.* Smith, 1 Black, 587; Bailey *v.* Hollister, 26 N. Y. 112; In re Empire City Bank, 18 N. Y. 199; In re Reciprocity Bank, 29 Barb. 369; s. c. 22 N. Y. 9; 17 How. Pr. 323; In re Oliver Lee & Co.'s Bank, 21 N. Y. 9; Anderson *v.* Comm. 18 Gratt. 295.

Where the power is reserved to repeal, amend or alter the charter, the legislature may make the stockholders liable for all the debts of the corporation until the whole amount of the capital shall have been paid in, and a certificate thereof duly recorded. Butler *v.* Walker, 8 C. L. N. 92.

The power to repeal or alter the charter becomes by operation of law a part of every contract or mortgage made by the corporation. The shareholders and bondholders take their stock or their securities subject to this paramount condition, of which they in law have notice. Anon. 6 C. L. N. 333.

If the right to repeal or amend is reserved in the charter, a creditor of the corporation can not object to the repeal, for that is a contingency which he assumed when he made the contract. Read *v.* Frankfort Bank, 23 Me. 318; West. Wis. R. R. Co. *v.* Supervisors, 93 U. S. 595; s. c. 35 Wis. 257.

The power to destroy a contract made with a corporation by repealing its charter, does not give the legislature the power to impair or alter or destroy the contract in any manner the legislature may think fit, without repealing the charter. Curran *v.* State, 15 How. 304; s. c. 12 Ark. 321.

The power to repeal the charter does not confer the power to destroy the executory contracts of the corporation, and withdraw its property from the just claims of its creditors. Curran *v.* State, 15 How. 304; S. C. 12 Ark. 321.

The power to make by-laws for the government of the corporation does not give the corporation the right to enact a by-law which will affect the right to a scholarship previously taken, by imposing terms and conditions not embraced in the contract itself. Illinois College *v.* Cooper, 25 Ill. 148.

Contracts made between individuals and the corporation do not vary or in any manner change or modify the relation between the State and the corporation in respect to the right of the State to alter, amend or modify. Pennsylvania College Cases, 13 Wall. 190; Pick *v.* C. & N. W. R. R. Co. 6 Biss. 177.

Where a note is made payable at the bank, the legislature can not make a law allowing it to be paid at a branch bank, although the power was reserved to repeal, amend or alter the charter. Bank *v.* McVeigh, 20 Gratt. 457.

The legislature can not alter contracts made under a charter with the corporation, although the power was reserved to repeal, alter or amend the charter. Bank *v.* McVeigh, 20 Gratt. 457.

Effect of Amendment on Stockholders.

By acquiring an interest in a corporation, a stockholder enters into an obligation with it in the nature of a special contract, the terms of which are limited by the specific provisions, rights and liabilities detailed in the act of incorporation. To make a valid change in this contract, the assent of both parties is indispensable. The corporation on one part can assent by a vote of the majority; the individual, on the other part, by his own personal act. Union Locks & Canals *v.* Towne, 1 N. H. 44; Hartford & New Haven R. R. Co *v.* Crosswell, 5 Hill, 383.

The charter constitutes the fundamental articles of the association. It defines the rights and powers of the corporation, determines its objects and fixes the individual contract of the members with the corporation. These fundamental articles can not be altered by a vote of the majority against the consent of the minority, unless there is an express or implied provision in the charter itself that they may do it. The legislature has no greater power over the corporators than over the corporation. The contract subsisting between the members of a corporate body and the corporation is equally within the protection of the Constitution. Hence the legislature can not authorize an amendment of the charter against the wishes of any corporator, unless that power is expressly reserved. New Orleans, J. & G. N. R. R. Co. *v.* Harris, 27 Miss. 517; Mobile R. R. Co. *v.* State, 29

Ala. 573; McCray *v.* Junction Railroad Co. 9 Ind. 358; Stevens *v.* R. & B. Railroad Co. 29 Vt. 545.

Alterations may be made in the charter without changing the contract so essentially as to absolve the subscriber. Such is the case in respect to mere formal amendments, or those which are clearly enough beneficial, or at least not prejudicial, to his interests. A modification of the grant may frequently be advisable, if not necessary, in order to facilitate the execution of the very object for which the corporation was originally established. Hartford & N. H. Railroad Co. *v.* Croswell, 5 Hill, 383; Irvin *v.* Turnpike Co. 2 Penn. 466; Gray *v.* Monongahela Nav. Co. 2 W. & S. 156; Clark *v.* Monongahela Nav. Co. 10 Watts, 364; Banet *v.* Alton & Sangamon Railroad Co. 13 Ill. 504; Penn. & Ohio Canal Co. *v.* Webb, 9 Ohio, 136; Troy & Rutland Railroad Co. *v.* Kerr, 17 Barb. 581; Woodfork *v.* Union Bank, 3 Cold. 488.

Each subscriber, when he enters an association, is presumed to consent to whatever probably will and is intended to make the undertaking a success, and the investment profitable. Sprague *v.* Ill. Railroad Co. 19 Ill. 174; Ill. Railroad Co. *v.* Zimmer, 20 Ill. 654.

Such amendments of the charter as may be considered useful to the public and beneficial to the corporation, and which will not divert its property to new and different purposes, may be made without absolving the subscribers from their engagements. Banet *v.* Alton & Sangamon Railroad Co. 13 Ill. 504; Clark *v.* Monongahela Nav. Co. 10 Watts, 364.

No general rule can be laid down by which to determine whether a change is material or not. Each case must depend on its own circumstances, and be disposed of with due regard to the inviolability belonging to all private contracts. Hartford & New Haven Railroad Co. *v.* Crosswell, 5 Hill, 383.

Any corporation has a right to accept any amendment to its charter which it believes promotive of the objects and interests of the company. Of this the corporation is necessarily the judge, and so long as those who represent and act for the corporation act with an honest purpose and a *bona fide* intent, their action must be sustained as obligatory upon the corporation, the same as in the exercise of any other discretionary power. Ill. Railroad Co. *v.* Zimmer, 20 Ill. 654.

There must be a palpable abuse of power by the majority or governing authority, to the prejudice of the minority or dissenting portion, before an amendment can be held illegal. Sprague *v.* Ill. Railroad Co. 19 Ill. 174.

Bad faith or fraud will vitiate an amendment of a charter. Sprague *v.* Ill. Railroad Co. 19 Ill. 174; Ill. Railroad Co. *v.* Zimmer, 20 Ill. 654.

A grant of additional privileges to a corporation is not an invasion of the contract between it and the stockholders. Gray *v.* Monongahela Nav. Co. 2 W. & S. 156; P. & O. Railroad Co. *v.* Elting, 17 Ill. 429.

An amendment increasing the number of directors, and allowing a vote for each share of stock, is immaterial. Everhart *v.* Phila. & W. C. Railroad Co. 28 Penn. 339.

An amendment authorizing the corporation to take subscriptions and receive payment therefor, upon terms different from those upon which the original subscriptions were taken, will not release a subscriber. Ill. Railroad Co. *v.* Zimmer, 20 Ill. 654.

An amendment permitting an organization of the corporation upon a less subscription than was originally required, does not release a subscriber. Ill. Railroad Co. *v.* Zimmer, 20 Ill. 654; P. & O. Railroad Co. *v.* Elting, 17 Ill. 429.

A statute allowing the issue of preferred stock, with the consent of the majority of the stockholders, will bind the minority. City *v.* Cov. & Cin. Bridge Co. 10 Bush, 69.

An amendment changing the notice of a call for an instalment from ninety days to twenty days does not release a subscriber. Ill. Railroad Co. *v.* Zimmer, 20 Ill. 654; Ill. Railroad Co. *v.* Beers, 27 Ill. 185.

An amendment authorizing a call upon the subscribers in a particular locality, and devoting the funds to the construction of the road in their vicinage, does not release them. Ill. Railroad Co. *v.* Zimmer, 20 Ill. 654.

An amendment authorizing the issue of preferred stock and bonds, for the purpose of accomplishing the objects of the corporation, does not release a subscriber. Everhart *v.* Phila. & W. C. Railroad Co. 28 Penn. 339.

An amendment authorizing a corporation to borrow money and mortgage its property to secure the loan does not release a subscriber. P. & O. Railroad Co. *v.* Elting, 17 Ill. 429; Joy *v.* Jackson & Mich. Plank Road, 11 Mich. 155.

An amendment authorizing a corporation to purchase stock in another corporation does not release a subscriber. Terre Haute & Alton Railroad Co. *v.* Earp, 21 Ill. 291.

An amendment authorizing a railroad corporation to construct ferries across a river does not release a subscriber. P. & O. Railroad Co. *v.* Elting, 17 Ill. 429.

An amendment authorizing a corporation to increase its capital stock does not release a subscriber. P. & O. Railroad Co. *v.* Elting, 17 Ill. 429.

An amendment authorizing a corporation to issue new stock does not release a subscriber. Pacific Railroad *v.* Hughes, 22 Mo. 291.

If the stock is forfeited to the corporation for non-payment of assessments before the alteration, the alteration constitutes no defense to an action on a note given for one of the instalments.* Mitchell *v.* Rome Railroad Co. 17 Geo. 574.

An amendment confirming an organization made before the requisite amount of stock had been subscribed, is valid, and binds a subscriber whose subscription had been previously taken. Rice *v.* Rock Island & Alton Railroad Co. 21 Ill. 93.

A change in the route of a railroad or turnpike, which is a change from one enterprise to another, is a material change. Kenosha, Rockford & Rock Island Railroad Co. *v.* Marsh, 17 Wis. 13; Middlesex Turnpike Corporation *v.* Locke, 8 Mass. 268; Middlesex Turnpike Corporation *v.* Swan, 10 Mass. 384.

A road intended to secure the advantages of a particular line of travel and transportation can not be so changed as to defeat that general object. The corporation must remain substantially the same, and be designed to accomplish the same general purposes and subserve the same general interests. Banet *v.* Alton & Sangamon Railroad Co. 13 Ill. 504.

An amendment authorizing a railroad corporation to extend the line of its road does not release a subscriber. Rice *v.* Rock Island & Alton Railroad Co. 21 Ill. 93; Del. Railroad Co. *v.* Tharp, 1 Houst. 149; P. & O. Railroad Co. *v.* Elting, 17 Ill. 429; Terre Haute & Alton Railroad Co. *v.* Earp, 21 Ill. 291.

An immaterial deviation from the route prescribed in the charter will not release a subscriber. Champion *v.* Memphis & Charleston Railroad Co. 35 Miss. 692.

An amendment authorizing a railroad corporation to build branch roads does not release a subscriber. Pacific Railroad *v.* Hughes, 22 Mo. 291; Greenville & Col. Railroad Co. *v.* Coleman, 5 Rich. 118; P. & O. Railroad Co. *v.* Elting, 17 Ill. 429; Peoria & Rock Island Railroad Co. *v.* Preston, 35 Iowa, 115.

Whether a deviation from the route prescribed in the charter will release a subscriber, is a question that must be determined according to the circumstances of each particular case. Champion *v.* Memphis & Charleston Railroad Co. 35 Miss. 692; Witter *v.* M. O. & R. R. Railroad Co. 20 Ark. 463.

Where the primary object of the charter was to develop the interests along the line of the road, a change of intermediate points may be material. Witter *v.* M. O. & R. R. Railroad Co. 20 Ark. 463.

A material deviation from the route prescribed in the charter, will release a subscriber. Witter *v.* M. O. & R. R. Railroad Co. 20 Ark. 463; Winter *v.* Muscogee Railroad Co. 11 Geo. 438.

It is involved in the nature of a subscription to the stock of a corporation for making a road from one place to another, that the *termini* are part of the contract, and an amendment excusing the corporation from one *terminus* releases the subscriber. Plank Road Co. *v.* Arndt, 31 Penn. 317; Winter *v.* Muscogee Railroad Co. 11 Geo. 438; Marietta & Cin. Railroad Co. *v.* Elliott, 10 Ohio St. 57; Thompson *v.* Guion, 5 Jones Eq. 113.

An amendment which makes a material and fundamental alteration in the route of a railroad releases a subscriber. Hester *v.* Memphis & Charleston Railroad Co. 32 Miss. 378.

If the *termini* of the road remain the same, a change from an intermediate point will not release a stockholder from his subscription. Banet *v.* Alton & Sangamon Railroad Co. 13 Ill. 504; Irvin *v.* Turnpike Co. 2 Penn. 466; P. & O. Railroad Co. *v.* Elting, 17 Ill. 429.

An immaterial change in a terminative point of a road does not release a stockholder. Irvin *v.* Turnpike Co. 2 Penn. 466; Penn. & Ohio Canal Co. *v.* Webb, 9 Ohio, 136; Del. Railroad Co. *v.* Tharp, 1 Houst. 149; Pacific Railroad *v.* Hughes, 22 Mo. 291.

The straightening of the line of a road, the location of a bridge at a different place on a stream, or a deviation in the route from an intermediate point, will not have the effect to destroy or impair the contract between the corporation and the subscribers. Banet *v.* Alton & Sangamon Railroad Co. 13 Ill. 504.

A stockholder has no reason to complain of any line of transit which starts from the same point of business, accommodates the same travel and transportation, and substantially subserves the same general interests. Penn. & Ohio Canal Co. *v.* Webb, 9 Ohio, 136.

If an amendment materially altering the terms of the charter is made without the consent of a stockholder, he is released from liability on his subscription. Union Locks & Canals *v.* Towne, 1 N. H. 44; Middlesex Turnpike Corporation *v.* Locke, 8 Mass. 268; Hartford & New Haven Railroad Co. *v.* Crosswell, 5 Hill, 383; Turnpike Co. *v.* Phillips, 2 Penn. 184; Pitts. & S. Railroad Co. *v.* Gazzam, 32 Penn. 340; Middlesex Turnpike Corporation *v.* Swan, 10 Mass. 384.

The original purpose or object of the corporation can not be entirely changed or abandoned, and a new one undertaken, without releasing the subscribers. Sprague *v.* Illinois Railroad Co. 19 Ill. 174; Woodfork *v.* Union Bank, 3 Cold. 488.

The rule must be general in its operation. What will discharge one stockholder from the payment of his subscription, must be held to have the same effect as to others. The matter of injury to one, or of benefit to the others, can not affect their respective liabilities. Banet *v.* Alton & Sangamon Railroad Co. 13 Ill. 504; Irvin *v.* Turnpike Co. 2 Penn. 466; Fry *v.* L. & B. S. Railroad Co. 2 Metc. (Ky.) 314; Sprague *v.* Illinois Railroad Co. 19 Ill. 174.

The material change may consist either in advancing objects essentially different, or the same objects in methods essentially different from those originally contemplated. Union Locks & Canals *v.* Towne, 1 N. H. 44.

An act transferring the franchise and subscriptions of one corporation to another releases the subscriber to the stock of the former. New Orleans J. & G. N. Railroad Co. 27 Miss. 517.

An act dividing a corporation into two or more corporations, and apportioning the subscriptions between them, does not bind a stockholder. Turnpike Company *v.* Phillips, 2 Penn. 184; Supervisors *v.* Miss. & W. Railroad Co. 21 Ill. 338.

Where the power to consolidate existed at the time of the subscription, a subsequent consolidation does not release the subscriber, for his contract must be presumed to have been made with reference to it. Sparrow *v.* Evansville & Crawfordsville Railroad Co. 7 Ind. 369; Bish *v.* Johnson, 21 Ind. 299.

An amendment authorizing a railroad corporation, to consolidate or make connections with any other railroad corporation on the line of its route will not release a subscriber. Sprague *v.* Illinois Railroad Co. 19 Ill. 174; Illinois Railroad Co. *v.* Zimmer, 20 Ill. 654.

A consolidation of two corporations into one releases a stockholder from his subscription. McCray *v.* Junction Railroad Co. 9 Ind. 358; Lanman *v.* Lebanon Valley Railroad Co. 30 Penn. 42.

A corporation can not consolidate with another corporation without the consent of all the stockholders. Mowrey *v.* Ind. & Cin. Railroad Co. 4 Biss. 78.

A change in the charter of a railroad corporation, authorizing it to own and run a line of steamboats, is material. Hartford & New Haven Railroad Co. *v.* Crosswell, 5 Hill, 383; Marietta & Cin. Railroad Co. *v.* Elliott, 10 Ohio St. 57.

If a corporation is formed to loan money on movable property, an amendment allowing it to receive deposits and do a general banking business can be accepted only by the unanimous consent of the stockholders. State *v.* Accommodation Bank, 26 La. Ann. 288.

A change of name is immaterial. Clark *v.* Monongahela Nav. Co. 10 Watts, 364.

The mere acceptance of a material amendment, which the corporation has never attempted and may never attempt to use, does not release a subscriber. Hawkins *v.* Miss. & Tenn. Railroad Co. 35 Miss. 688; Fry *v.* L. & B. S. R. R. Co. 2 Met. (Ky.) 314; R. & B. R. R. Co. *v.* Thrall, 35 Vt. 536; P. & O. R. R. Co. *v.* Elting, 17 Ill. 429; M. O. & R. R. Railroad Co. *v.* Gaster, 24 Ark. 96.

A change in the height of a dam from four feet to eight feet is immaterial. Clark *v.* Monongahela Nav. Co. 10 Watts, 364; Gray *v.* Monongahela Nav. Co. 2 W. & S. 156.

An act amending a charter so as to permit the directors to make assessments upon the stock, alters the terms of the contract between the members and the corporation, and is unconstitutional. Brown *v.* Fairmount Co. 30 Leg. Int. 124.

If the construction of the road within a certain time was an essential inducement to the making of the contract, an amendment extending the time for the completion of the road will release a subscriber. Henderson *v.* Railroad Co. 17 Tex. 560.

A material alteration of the charter, accepted by the stockholders in general meeting duly organized, is binding upon each individual member, unless he expressly dissents therefrom before any debts are contracted, or rights inure to third parties, in carrying out the new design or enterprise. Martin *v.* Pen. & Geo. R. R. Co. 8 Fla. 370; Railroad Co. *v.* Leach, 4 Jones, 340.

If the alteration is material the subscriber will be released, although he was one of the directors who signed a petition to the legislature asking for the alteration. Middlesex Turnpike Corporation *v.* Swan, 10 Mass. 384.

If the alteration is material, the subscriber will be released, although he accepted the position of director after the adoption of the amendment. Middlesex Turnpike Corporation *v.* Walker, 10 Mass. 390.

Where an amendment changes the par value of the shares, and the proper number is assigned to a stockholder to meet his original subscription, a payment in part is an assent to the alteration. K. & P. R. R. Co. *v.* Palmer, 34 Me. 366.

A stockholder who, after the adoption of the amendment, votes at the election of the officers of the corporation, is estopped to deny the validity of his subscription. Clark *v.* Monongahela Nav. Co. 10 Watts, 364.

A consent to the alteration can not be implied from the acceptance and discharge of the office of director after the change has been made. Middlesex Turnpike Corporation *v.* Walker, 10 Mass. 390; Middlesex Turnpike Corporation *v.* Swan, 10 Mass. 384; O. & L. R. R. Co. *v.* Veazie, 39 Me. 571.

A subscriber who votes at the organization of the corporation and election of directors, after the acceptance of an amendment changing the amount of subscriptions required before an organization, assents to the change. Bedford Railroad Co. *v.* Bowser, 48 Penn. 29.

An assent to amendments extending the objects or increasing the powers or enlarging the liabilities of the corporation, is not to be presumed, but must be expressly shown. Union Locks and Canals *v.* Towne, 1 N. H. 44.

Effect of Reserved Power.

The right to bind subscribers who do not assent to the change derives no additional support from the fact that a power had been reserved to amend the charter. The corporation is not obliged to accept the amendment. It may assent or not, as it chooses. This is just what it might have done if the power of amendment had not been reserved. The question whether an individual subscriber is bound or not by the corporate assent must be determined by the same principles in either case. Kenosha, Rockford & Rock Island Railroad Co. *v.* Marsh, 17 Wis. 13; Zabriskie *v.* Hackensack & N. Y. R. R. Co. 18 N. J. Eq. 178; Black *v.* Del. & Rar. Canal Co. 24 N. J. Eq. 455; S. C. 22 N. J. Eq. 130.

Where the power is reserved to alter the charter, the stockholder subscribes to the stock subject to the power, and he can not complain of the exercise of the power. The agreement must be read with the legislative condition. Schenectady & Saratoga Plank Road Co. *v.* Thatcher, 11 N. Y. 102; Northern Railroad Co. *v.* Miller, 10 Barb. 260; White *v.* Syr. & Utica Railroad Co. 14 Barb. 559; Buffalo & N. Y. City Railroad Co. *v.* Dudley, 14 N. Y. 336; Meadow Dam Co. *v.* Gray, 30 Me. 547; Pacific Railroad *v.* Renshaw, 18 Mo. 210; Durfee *v.* Railroad Co. 87 Mass. 230; Story *v.* Jersey City P. R. Co. 16 N. J. Eq. 13.

If the reserved power to alter the charter is exercised without fraud, the alteration is valid, whether it is beneficial or injurious to the subscriber, for it is a question of power. Buffalo & N. Y. City Railroad Co. *v.* Dudley, 14 N. Y. 336.

To work a discharge where the power is reserved to alter the charter, the charter must be repealed or the legislation must be such as virtually to subvert the corporation itself, or at least to destroy its identity. Buffalo & N. Y. City Railroad Co. *v.* Dudley, 14 N. Y. 336.

The legislature can not authorize the extension of a railroad where such extension would be a different enterprise, although the power is reserved to repeal, alter or amend the charter. Zabriskie *v.* Hackensack & N. Y. Railroad Co. 18 N. J. Eq. 178.

A consolidation of two corporations will release the subscriber, although the power to amend was reserved in the charter. Booe *v.* Junction Railroad Co. 10 Ind. 93.

The legislature can not authorize the lease of a railroad for nine hundred and ninety-nine years, although the power is reserved to repeal, alter or amend the charter. Black *v.* Del. & Rar. Canal Co. 24 N. J. Eq. 455; s. c. 22 N. J. Eq. 130.

Although the power is reserved to alter the charter, the legislature can not, in effect, create a new corporation of a new and distinct character. White *v.* Syr. & Utica Railroad Co. 14 Barb. 559; Troy & Rutland Railroad Co. *v.* Kerr, 17 Barb. 581; Booe *v.* Junction Railroad Co. 10 Ind. 93; Buffalo & N. Y. City Railroad Co. *v.* Dudley, 14 N. Y. 336; Durfee *v.* Railroad Co. 87 Mass. 230; Zabriskie *v.* Hackensack & N. Y. Railroad Co. 18 N. J. Eq. 178; Tyson *v.* Va. & T. R. R. Co. 4 A. L. T. 223.

Where the power is reserved to alter the charter, a railroad corporation may shorten the line of its road. Troy & Rutland Railroad Co. *v.* Kerr, 17 Barb. 581.

Where the power is reserved to alter the charter, an amendment increasing the capital stock will not release a subscriber. Buffalo & N. Y. City Railroad Co. *v.* Dudley, 14 N. Y. 336.

Where the power is reserved to alter the charter, the name of the corporation may be changed without releasing a subscriber. Buffalo & N. Y. City Railroad Co. *v.* Dudley, 14 N. Y. 336.

Where the power is reserved to alter the charter, the legislature may authorize the corporation to subscribe to the capital stock of a foreign corporation. White *v.* Syr. & Utica Railroad Co. 14 Barb. 559.

Where the power is reserved to alter the charter, the corporation may be authorized to reduce its capital stock. Troy & Rutland Railroad Co. *v.* Kerr, 17 Barb. 581; Joslyn *v.* Pacific Mail Steamship Co. 12 Abb. Pr. N. S. 329.

Where the power is reserved to alter the charter, an amendment authorizing the corporation to borrow money to a certain amount, and to pay interest to stockholders on stock payments beyond calls, does not release a stockholder. Northern Railroad Co. *v.* Miller, 10 Barb. 260.

Where the power is reserved to amend the charter, an amendment extending the time for the completion of the road will not release a subscriber. Poughkeepsie & S. P. Plank Road Co. *v.* Griffin, 24 N. Y. 150; s. c. 21 Barb. 454; Agricultural Branch Railroad Co. *v.* Winchester, 95 Mass. 29.

Where the power is reserved to alter the charter, an amendment authorizing an extension of the road of a railroad corporation, will not release a subscriber. Buffalo & N. Y. City Railroad Co. *v.* Dudley, 14 N. Y. 336; Pacific Railroad Co. *v.* Renshaw, 18 Mo. 210; Pacific Railroad Co. *v.* Hughes, 22 Mo. 291.

Where the power is reserved to alter the charter, an amendment which increases the liabilities of the stockholders will not release a subscriber. Meadow Dam Co. *v.* Gray, 30 Me. 547.

Where the power is reserved to alter the charter, an amendment authorizing a railroad corporation to accept bonds issued by the State, and mortgage the road to secure the loan, will not release a subscriber. Pacific Railroad Co. *v.* Renshaw, 18 Mo. 210; Pacific Railroad Co. *v.* Hughes, 22 Mo. 291.

Where the power is reserved to alter the charter, an amendment may be made, allowing calls for instalments of subscriptions at the rate of five per centum per month instead of twenty-five per centum each year. B. & M. R. R. Co. *v.* White, 5 Iowa, 409.

Where a subscription is made upon the condition that the amount of capital required by the charter shall be subscribed, an amendment reducing the amount necessary to an organization will not render the subscriber liable. O. & L. Railroad Co. *v.* Veazie, 39 Me. 571.

Where the power is reserved to alter the charter, the legislature may authorize a railroad corporation to take a lease of another railroad. Durfee *v.* Railroad Co. 87 Mass. 230.

Where the power is reserved to alter the charter, an amendment to the charter of a plank road company, authorizing the construction of branch roads, does not release the stockholder. Schenectady & Saratoga Plank Road Co. *v.* Thatcher, 11 N. Y. 102; Northern Railroad Co. *v.* Miller, 10 Barb. 260.

If the power is reserved to alter and amend the charter, an act allowing a mutual insurance company to separate the risks of the inhabitants of the country from those of the towns, so that each class shall only be liable to contribute for a loss in its district, is binding on the minority if accepted by the majority of the stockholders. Currie *v.* Mutual Assurance Society, 4 H. & M. 315.

Public Corporations.

The charter of a public corporation created for purposes of government, can not be considered as a contract. Marietta *v.* Fearing, 4 Ohio, 427; People *v.* Morris, 13 Wend. 325; Bradford *v.* Cary, 5 Me. 339; Governor *v.* Gridley, Walk. 328.

A power to alter and change public corporations, created for purposes purely public, and to adapt them to the purposes they were intended to accomplish, is implied in their very nature. Bristol *v.* New Chester, 3 N. H. 524; State *v.* Railroad Co. 3 How. 534; S. C. 12 G. & J. 399; Bush *v.* Shipman, 5 Ill. 186; City *v.* Russell, 9 Mo. 507; Aspinwall *v.* Commissioners, 22 How. 364; Bridgeport *v.* Hubbell, 5 Conn. 237; Trustees *v.* Aberdeen, 21 Miss. 645; People *v.* Morris, 13 Wend. 325; Mayor *v.* State, 15 Md. 376; North Yarmouth *v.* Skillings, 45 Me. 133; Mills *v.* Williams, 11 Ired. 558; Gatzweiller *v.* People, 14 Ill. 142; Paterson *v.* Society, 24 N. J. L. 385.

A grant of a franchise to a public corporation may, at any time, be resumed by the State. Trustees *v.* Tatman, 13 Ill. 27.

Transactions between the legislature and a municipal corporation, in relation to public interests, are in the nature of legislation rather than of compact, and are not violated by subsequent legislative changes. Hartford *v.* Hartford Bridge Co. 10 How. 511; S. C. 16 Conn. 149; Trustees *v.* Tatman, 13 Ill. 27; Layton *v.* New Orleans, 12 La. Ann. 515; Police Jury *v.* Shreveport, 5 La. Ann. 661; Reynolds *v.* Baldwin, 1 La. Ann. 162; vide Benson *v.* New York, 10 Barb. 223.

The corporation which is subject to legislative control is one that is the mere instrument or agent of the State, through which it exercises some of its political or administrative powers and functions, or manages for its own purposes the public property of the State, or conducts transactions in which alone the State is interested. Louisville *v.* University, 15 B. Mon. 642.

The charter of a municipal corporation may be altered so as to change the person on whom service of process against the corporation may be made, and this will not impair the obligation of any contract previously made by the corporation. Perkins *v.* Watertown, 5 C. L. N. 472; S. C. 5 Biss. 320.

A law which repeals an act passed upon the division of a township, requiring that each of the new towns thus created should bear its proportion of the expense of the paupers supported at the time of the division, is unconstitutional. Bowdoinham *v.* Richmond, 6 Me. 112.

The power to divide the property of a municipal corporation is necessarily incident to the power to divide the territory of such corporation, and thus form two corporations. Bristol *v.* New Chester, 3 N. H. 524; Richland *v.* Lawrence, 12 Ill. 1; North Yarmouth *v.* Skillings, 45 Me. 133.

A State legislature may extend the limits of a municipal corporation without the consent of the citizens who live on or own the land comprising the part to be annexed. Manly *v.* Raleigh, 4 Jones Eq. 370; Morford *v.* Unger, 8 Iowa, 82.

A statute giving a municipal corporation the right to purchase the property of a private corporation at the expiration of its charter, may be repealed or modified at pleasure. Crescent C. G. Co. *v.* New Orleans G. Co. 27 La. Ann. 138.

The legislature may unite and divide townships and their school funds as it may think best. Greenleaf *v.* Township, 22 Ill. 236.

A statute taking part of the territory of one municipal corporation and giving it to another does not impair the obligation of the contract made by the former with its creditors. Wade *v.* Richmond, 18 Gratt. 583.

A State may repeal or alter the charter of an eleemosynary corporation established for educational purposes, where it is the sole contributor of the fund which supports it, and creates a corporation for the purpose simply of carrying out its objects. Dart *v.* Houston, 22 Geo. 506; Trustees *v.* Winston, 5 Stew. & Port. 17; Bass *v.* Fontleroy, 11 Tex. 698; Mobile School Com. *v.* Putnam, 44 Ala. 406.

The legislature may release a party from a contract entered into with a public corporation in relation to public property. The corporation is simply the agent authorized to bind the people. In conferring this authority the legislature acted for the people. The legislature can also revoke or resume this authority at any time, or confer it upon others. The legislature may also, either by its direct action, or by authority conferred upon and exercised by any designated agents, modify or rescind the contract, with the assent of the other party. People *v.* Fishkill Plank Road Co. 27 Barb. 445.

The legislature can not require a municipal corporation to rescind a contract for the sale of land held by it for the purposes of education. Butler *v.* Chariton, 13 Mo. 112.

The legislature can not alter or revoke a municipal charter so as to destroy the lawful contracts of the corporation, or enact a law impairing the obligation of a contract made by a municipal corporation. Bleakley *v.* Williams, 20 Pitts. L. J. 66.

If a charter of a private corporation provides that a municipal corporation may purchase the property of the former after the expiration of a certain time, and issue bonds therefor, any subsequent act forbidding the issue of the bonds or imposing onerous conditions upon their issue, as that the question of their issue shall be submitted to a vote of the electors, or that the ordinance allowing the issue shall provide for their payment, is void. Sala *v.* New Orleans, 2 Woods, 188.

If a State law authorizes a municipal corporation to issue bonds and levy a tax to pay the indebtedness, no subsequent act can destroy the corporation, and thus impair the obligation of the contract. Milner *v.* Pensacola, 2 Woods, 632.

An amendment to a charter allowing municipal corporations to subscribe to the stock may be repealed before the subscriptions are completed. Cov. & L. R. R. Co. *v.* Kenton, 12 B. Mon. 144.

A State can not release a municipal corporation from its contracts. Davenport Co. *v.* Davenport, 13 Iowa, 229.

The legislature may provide that the filing of the affidavits of the consent of the tax-payers to a subscription by a municipal corporation for the stock of a private corporation shall be conclusive evidence of such consent. People *v.* Mitchell, 45 Barb. 208.

A statute to be accepted by a municipal corporation and a private corporation may constitute a contract. Central Bridge *v.* Lowell, 81 Mass. 106.

The legislature may authorize a county corporation to change the mode of paying its subscription to a private corporation, with the consent of the latter. L. & N. R. R. Co. *v.* Davidson, 1 Sneed, 637.

A State may prohibit a public corporation from subscribing to the stock of a private corporation, although the subscription has been sanctioned by a vote of the people of the county or city, for until the subscription is made the contract is unexecuted, and obligatory upon neither party. Aspinwall *v.* Commissioners, 22 How. 364.

A State during a civil war has the right to take measures to remove those who refuse to take an oath of allegiance from the management of corporations of a public nature. State *v.* Adams, 44 Mo. 570.

The legislature may confirm an election of municipal officers made by mistake prior to the act of incorporation. State *v.* Kline, 23 Ark. 587.

The power conferred upon a municipal corporation to grant licenses may be withdrawn. Morris *v.* People, 13 Wend. 325; Gatzweiller *v.* People, 14 Ill. 142.

A forfeiture in favor of a municipal corporation may be waived, even after it has been incurred. State *v.* Railroad Co. 3 How. 534; S. C. 12 G. & J. 399; Coles *v.* Madison, Breese, 115.

The power conferred upon a municipal corporation to raise a revenue by taxation is a political power, and its application when collected must necessarily be within the control of the legislature for political purposes. People *v.* Power, 25 Ill. 187.

If a municipal corporation by its charter, or in any other way, is made the trustee of an estate, its right and title as such is subject to be defeated whenever the State shall deem it necessary to abolish its existence as a municipal organization. Montpelier *v.* East Montpelier, 29 Vt. 12; Bass *v.* Fontleroy, 11 Tex. 698.

If the legislature gives the revenues accruing from a ferry to a municipal corporation, without any consideration inuring to the State or onerous condition imposed upon the corporation, it does not deprive itself, by express or implied contract, of the power of repealing or altering the law at will. It may take those revenues, or a portion of them, from the corporation, and appropriate them to other purposes. Police Jury *v.* Shreveport, 5 La. Ann. 661; Marks *v.* Donaldson, 24 La. Ann. 242.

Where an act of Congress granting lands to the inhabitants of a township for the use of schools has been accepted by the State, the State legislature can not divert the fund from the use, although it may abolish the township. State *v.* Springfield, 6 Ind. 83; Morton *v.* Granada Academy, 16 Miss. 773.

A charter exempting the capital stock of the corporation from all taxation except for State purposes, is binding on a municipal corporation, for it is a modification of the charter of the latter. State Bank *v.* Madison, 3 Ind. 43; Bank *v.* New Albany, 11 Ind. 139.

The legislature can not divest a municipal corporation of its private property without the consent of its inhabitants. Milwaukee *v.* Milwaukee, 12 Wis. 93; Grogan *v.* San Francisco, 18 Cal. 590.

If an act of the legislature grants bonds to a municipal corporation, a subsequent statute vesting a right to the bonds in others is void. Spaulding *v.* Andover, 54 N. H. 38.

If money is raised by a municipal corporation by taxation to aid in building a railroad, and it takes stock in its own name, a subsequent statute requiring that the railroad corporation shall issue stock to the taxpayers in proportion to the taxes paid by them, does not impair the obligation of contracts. Commissioners *v.* Lucas, 93 U. S. 108.

Where a municipal corporation has condemned land as a highway, and paid for the same, a State can not diminish the width of the highway, and give the land back to the former owner. People *v.* Commissioners, 53 Barb. 70; s. c. 47 N. Y. 501.

Remedies.

The remedy is not a part of the contract itself, nor does the obligation of a contract consist in any particular form of the remedy. It is only necessary that there should be an adequate subsisting remedy. It is therefore competent for the legislature to change the remedy. Every form of remedy is a mere question of policy over which the legislature has entire control, so that the power to enforce the duty be not weakened. If the remedy given be as good as that which was taken away, the obligation of the contract is not thereby impaired. McMillan *v.* Sprague, 4 How. (Miss.)

647; Lapsley *v*. Brashears, 4 Litt. 47; Davis *v*. Ballard, 1 J. J. Marsh. 563; Bronson *v*. Kinzie, 1 How. 311; Commercial Bank *v*. State, 12 Miss. 439; Savings Institution *v*. Makin, 23 Me. 360; Van Rensselaer *v*. Snyder, 13 N. Y. 299; In re Trustees of Public Schools, 31 N. Y. 574; Longfellow *v*. Patrick, 25 Me. 18; Pratt *v*. Jones, 25 Vt. 303; Morse *v*. Gould, 11 N. Y. 281.

If a statute impairs the obligation of contracts, it is immaterial whether it is done by acting on the remedy or directly on the contract itself. In either case it is prohibited by the Constitution. Bronson *v*. Kinzie, 1 How. 311; Green *v*. Biddle, 8 Wheat. 1; Smith *v*. Morse, 2 Cal. 524; Johnson *v*. Duncan, 3 Mart. 531; Coffman *v*. Bank, 40 Miss. 29.

The obligation of a contract, in the sense in which those words are used in the Constitution, is that duty of performing it which is recognized and enforced by the law, and if the law is so changed that the means of legally enforcing this duty are materially impaired, the obligation of the contract no longer remains the same. Curran *v*. State, 15 How. 304; S. C. 12 Ark. 321; Green *v*. Biddle, 8 Wheat. 1; Von Baumbach *v*. Bade, 9 Wis. 559.

The epithet "material" is vague, uncertain and calculated to confuse and mislead. Taylor *v*. Stearns, 18 Gratt. 244.

The precise point at which laws cease to operate upon the remedy and begin to infringe upon the obligation of the contract can never be governed by any general rules, but must, in every case where the question is made, be governed by the circumstances of that case. Grimes *v*. Bryne, 2 Minn. 89; Von Baumbach *v*. Bade, 9 Wis. 559; Von Hoffman *v*. Quincy, 4 Wall. 535; Ex parte Pollard, 40 Ala. 77.

The legislature may alter remedies, but they must not, as far as regards antecedent contracts, be rendered less efficacious or more dilatory than those ordained by the law in being when the contract was made. Townsend *v*. Townsend, Peck, 1.

Although a new remedy may be deemed less convenient than the old one, and may in some degree render the recovery of debts more tardy and difficult, yet it will not follow that the law is unconstitutional. Bronson *v*. Kinzie, 1 How. 311; Guild *v*. Rogers, 8 Barb. 502.

A change of the remedy, in order to impair the obligation of a contract, must reach the intention of the parties resulting from the stipulations in the contract. Something contracted about must be changed. Commercial Bank *v*. State, 12 Miss. 439.

So long as contracts are submitted without legislative interference to the ordinary and regular course of justice, and the existing remedies are preserved in substance, the obligation of the contracts is not impaired. Holmes *v*. Lansing, 3 Johns Cas 73; Morse *v*. Gould, 11 N. Y. 281.

A condition will not render an act consistent with the Constitution, which, without such a condition, would be in collision with that instrument. Lapsley *v.* Brashears, 4 Litt. 47; Townsend *v.* Townsend, Peck, 1.

Although a State may change the remedies that are used before judgment, yet when the right is judicially ascertained, it can not interfere with the process to enforce that right so as to make it materially less efficient than that in existence when the contract was made. Oliver *v.* McClure, 28 Ark. 555.

Courts are erected for the purpose of deciding contested rights when those rights are drawn in question before them, through the instrumentality of remedies prescribed by law; but courts exist independent of those remedies, and, in a legal sense, compose no part of them. To create, alter and abolish courts, and to change their sessions, is a subject which falls properly within the sphere of legislative discretion. Lapsley *v.* Brashears, 4 Litt. 47; Rathbone *v.* Bradford, 1 Ala. 312; Ex parte Pollard, 40 Ala. 77; Woods *v.* Buie, 5 How. (Miss.) 285; Morse *v.* Gould, 11 N. Y. 281; Johnson *v.* Duncan, 3 Mart. 531; Wood *v.* Wood, 14 Rich. 148; State *v.* Barringer, Phil. 554; Newkirk *v.* Chapron, 17 Ill. 344; Johnson *v.* Higgins, 3 Met. (Ky.) 566.

If the alteration of the remedy is merely the consequence of a general law whose primary and essential object was to promote the administration of justice, and not specially to alter the remedy, the merely incidental delay following from the enactment of such a law, would not render it unconstitutional. Jones *v* Crittenden, 1 Car. L. Rep. 385; Townsend *v.* Townsend, Peck, 1; Rathbone *v.* Bradford, 1 Ala. 312; Wood *v.* Wood, 14 Rich. 148.

A change of the terms for holding courts which is not an incidental and subordinate result from a general and permanent change in the system of judicature, or the course of legal proceedings, but operates on contracts only, is void. Wood *v.* Wood, 14 Rich. 148; Jacobs *v.* Smallwood, 63 N. C. 112; Johnson *v.* Winslow, 64 N. C. 27.

The change of the remedy may affect pending actions. Read *v.* Frankfort Bank, 23 Me. 318; Oriental Bank *v.* Freeze, 18 Me. 109; Woods *v.* Buie, 5 How. (Miss.) 285; Lockett *v.* Usry, 28 Geo. 345.

A State has a right to prescribe a remedy if there be none. Commercial Bank *v.* State, 12 Miss. 439; Simmons *v.* Hanover, 40 Mass. 188; Milne *v.* Huber, 3 McLean, 212; Brandon *v.* Gaines, 7 Humph. 130.

A statute repealing a prior act under which a party was exempt from suit on his contracts, and rendering him liable to suit thereon, is valid. Stokes *v.* Rodman, 5 R. I. 405.

A mere change in one of two remedies does not impair the obligation of a contract. Heyward *v.* Judd, 4 Minn. 483.

A State may provide a new remedy to enforce an existing contract. Wheat *v*. State, Minor, 199; Anon. 2 Stew. 228.

A State legislature may repeal a statute under which a contract is illegal, and authorize a suit thereon. Milne *v*. Huber, 3 McLean, 212; Hill *v*. Smith, Morris, 70; Johnson *v*. Bentley, 16 Ohio, 97; Lewis *v*. McElvain, 16 Ohio, 347.

A statute which merely gives a remedy at law where it could previously have been made available in equity only, or *vice versa*, may consistently with the Constitution, operate retrospectively so as to embrace contracts already made. Paschall *v*. Whitsell, 11 Ala. 472; Baugher *v*. Nelson, 9 Gill, 299; Bethune *v*. Dougherty, 30 Geo. 770.

Every stipulation for a particular remedy is, in its own nature, conditional upon the lawful continuance of the process. The State is no party to the contract. It is bound to afford adequate process for the enforcement of rights, but it does not tie its own hands as to the modes by which it will administer justice. Those, from necessity, belong to the supreme power to prescribe, and their continuance is not the subject of contract between private parties. It may, therefore, abolish a particular remedy, although the parties have stipulated for it in their contract. Conkey *v*. Hart, 14 N. Y. 22.

If the covenant in a mortgage applies to the remedy and regulates it, fixing its terms and its credit, and there is no law forbidding it at the time it is made, no subsequent statute can alter or change those terms. Pool *v*. Young, 7 Mon. 587; Bronson *v*. Kinzie, 1 How. 311.

In time of war, commotion or epidemics, circumstances may imperiously demand for a while even a total suspension of judicial proceedings. In any time obnoxious to the due administration of justice, it is the duty and within the power of the legislature to pass laws to avert or diminish the consequences of the general calamity, and a law called for by such circumstances, and fairly intended to meet the exigency of the day, can not be properly classed among those which impair the obligation of contracts. Johnson *v*. Duncan, 3 Mart. 531; Ex parte Pollard, 40 Ala. 77.

The obligation of a contract and the rights of a party under it, may, in effect, be destroyed by denying a remedy altogether, or may be seriously impaired by burdening the proceedings with new conditions and restrictions so as to make the remedy hardly worth pursuing. Penrose *v*. Reed, 2 Grant, 472; Western Saving Fund *v*. Philadelphia, 31 Penn. 175; Bronson *v*. Kinzie, 1 How. 311; McCracken *v*. Hayward, 2 How. 608; Riggs *v*. Martin, 5 Ark. 506; Commercial Bank *v*. Chambers, 16 Miss. 9; Mundy *v*. Monroe, 1 Mich. 68; Curran *v*. State, 15 How. 304; S. C. 12 Ark. 321; Oatman *v*. Bond, 15 Wis. 20.

The right and the remedy, in the theory of all practical and just government, must stand or fall together. To deny the right is necessarily to deny the remedy; and to admit the right but deny the remedy, is to impair the right and to render it either partially or wholly inoperative. It is more consistent to deny both the right and the consequent remedy, than to admit the right and then, in the face of this admission, deny its inseparable incident. As the Constitution intended to prohibit the legislature from defeating a certain end, it does not matter how or by what means or in what manner this end is sought to be defeated, the statute is equally unconstitutional. If the purpose is defeated, the manner in which it is done is unimportant, and can not change the substantial result. The only end and object of a contract is the doing or not doing the particular thing mentioned. The practical result is the only end aimed at by the parties, and the obligation of the contract is the vital binding element that secures this practical consummation. A civil right without a remedy never can exist in the practical theory of government. It is not the intent of government to establish mere abstract and inoperative principles. A dormant right that can not be enforced is no right at all. To say that the law will give a party a judgment and yet refuse him an execution to enforce it, is to give him the shadow and withhold the substance. Robinson *v.* Magee, 9 Cal. 84.

A law absolutely recalling the power which a creditor enjoys of compelling his debtor *in foro legis* to perform the obligation of his contract, is a law destroying the obligation of the contract *in foro legis*, since a right without a legal remedy ceases to be a legal right. It impairs the obligation by reducing an obligation both *in foro legis* and *in foro conscientiæ* to an obligation *in foro conscientiæ* only—a legal and moral right to a moral right only. A law destroying or impairing the remedy is as unconstitutional as one affecting the right in the same manner, for *in foro legis* the effect of both laws is the same. Johnson *v.* Duncan, 3 Mart. 531.

Nothing is more material to the obligation of a contract than the means of its enforcement. The ideas of validity and remedy are inseparable, and both are parts of the obligation which is guaranteed by the Constitution against impairment. Walker *v.* Whitehead, 16 Wall. 314; S. C. 43 Geo. 537; Von Hoffman *v.* Quincy, 4 Wall. 535.

The remedy is incident to the contract. Although a party may have no right under the contract to any particular remedy, yet he has a right at all times to some adequate and available remedy to enforce it. Coffman *v.* Bank, 40 Miss. 29.

A State is no more permitted to impair the efficacy of a contract by changing the remedy, than to attack its vitality in any other manner. Walker *v.* Whitehead, 16 Wall. 314; S. C. 43 Geo. 537.

A judgment creates a contract, but is only on the side of the defendant, who thus acknowledges or assumes upon himself a debt which may be made the ground of an action. But, on the side of the plaintiff the necessity of resorting to certain means of enforcing the judgment is not an obligation arising out of contract, but one imposed upon him by the laws of the country, and hence the remedy may be changed. Livingston *v.* Moore, 7 Pet. 469; Williams *v.* Waldo, 4 Ill. 264 ; Grosvenor *v.* Chesley, 48 Me. 369; Sprott *v.* Reid, 3 G. Greene, 489.

A law regulating judgments and executions can not be considered as a law which enters into the nature of contracts, or which the parties have in view when they contract. A statute which deprives a judgment creditor of his judgment lien which was acquired by the recovery of the judgment alone, does not impair the obligation of contracts. McCormick *v.* Alexander, 2 Ohio, 285; Bank *v.* Longworth, 1 McLean, 35; Curry *v.* Landers, 35 Ala. 280; Daily *v.* Burke, 28 Ala. 328; Livingston *v.* Moore, 7 Pet. 469.

A law affecting judgments not rendered on a contract is valid, for the obligation created by such judgments is an obligation imposed by law and not an obligation of a contract made between the parties. Sprott *v.* Reid, 3 G. Greene, 489.

A statute may provide that a case shall not be tried at the return term, but at a subsequent term, thus allowing a parlance term between the return of the writ and the trial term, for the legislature may fix the time and mode of trial. Woods *v.* Buie, 5 How. (Miss.) 285.

The power to limit or extend the time for answering, or within which any other step in an action shall be taken, is and must be conceded. The only limit or qualification to its exercise is that the legislature shall confine their action within the bounds of reason and justice, and that they shall not so prolong the time within which legal proceedings are to be had, as to render them futile and useless in the hands of the creditor, or seriously impair his rights or securities. Von Baumbach *v.* Bade, 9 Wis. 559.

A statute changing the time for holding the court does not impair the obligation of a contract, although the laws of the State require an indorsee to sue the maker of a promissory note, at the first term held after its nonpayment. Rathbone *v.* Bradford, 1 Ala. 312.

A statute providing for a delay in the time of trial is valid. Ex parte Pollard, 40 Ala. 77.

A statute permitting either party to give in evidence the consideration and the value thereof at any time, and the intention of the parties as to the particular currency in which payment was to be made, and the value of such currency at any time, and directing that the verdict and judgment shall be on principles of equity, is valid. Robeson *v.* Brown, 63 N. C. 554; King *v.* W. & W. R. R. Co. 66 N. C. 277; Slaughter *v.* Culpepper, 35 Geo. 25; Taylor *v.* Flint, 35 Geo. 124; Rutland *v.* Copes, 15 Rich. 84;

Kirtland v. Molton, 41 Ala. 548; Tarleton v. Southern Bank, 41 Ala. 722; Herbert v. Easton, 43 Ala. 547.

A statute which allows the parties to show by parol evidence what the understanding was in regard to the kind of currency in which the contract was solvable, is valid, for it facilitates the means of ascertaining what the contract was. Woodfin v. Slader, Phillips, 200.

A State law providing that either party to a contract made during a civil war may give in evidence the consideration and value thereof, and the intention of the parties as to the particular currency in which payment was to be made, and the value of such currency, and that judgment shall be on principles of equity, is valid. Slaughter v. Culpepper, 35 Geo. 25.

A statute allowing the parties to give in evidence the consideration of the contract, the amount and value of the property owned by the debtor at the time the contract was made, the destruction or loss thereof, and in what manner it was destroyed or lost, and giving the jury the power to reduce the amount of the debt according to the equities of the case, and render such verdict as appears just and equitable, is valid. Cutts v. Hardee, 38 Geo. 350.

A statute of a State which permits an inquiry to be made into the consideration of a sealed instrument, and which was in force at the time of the execution of the contract in another State, does not impair the obligation of the contract, for the *lex fori* controls. Williams v. Haines, 27 Iowa, 251.

A statute passed after the execution of a tax deed, which enacts that the deed shall not be presumptive evidence of the regularity of the sale, is valid. Hickox v. Tallman, 38 Barb. 608.

The legislature can not cut off or destroy the rights of a *bona fide* holder for value of commercial paper by changing the rules of pleading or the laws of evidence. Cornell v. Hichens, 11 Wis. 353.

A statute which makes a protest of a promissory note evidence of the facts therein stated is valid, for it only affects the mode of proceeding. The legislature may prescribe what shall and what shall not be evidence of a fact, whether it be in writing or oral, and it makes no difference whether it be in reference to contracts existing at the time or prospectively. Fales v. Wadsworth, 23 Me. 553.

A statute dispensing with the necessity of proving the names of the individual partners in a suit against a firm is valid. Ballard v. Ridgley, Morris, 27.

A statute dispensing with the necessity of proving the signature to a written instrument in an action against the maker, unless he files a denial of the same under oath, is valid. Ingraham v. Dooley, Morris, 28.

A statute making parties competent witnesses in their own behalf is valid. Ralston *v.* Lothain, 18 Ind. 303; Neass *v.* Mercer, 15 Barb. 318.

The legislature may change the rules of evidence so as to affect prior contracts. People *v.* Mitchell, 45 Barb. 208.

A statute providing that no judgment shall be entered against a municipal corporation, except upon proof that the amount sought to be recovered still remains unexpended in the treasury to the credit of the appropriation for the specific object or purpose under the claim sued for, is void. Wood *v.* New York, 6 Robt. 463.

Where the law at the time of the sale makes a tax deed *prima facie* evidence of title, a subsequent statute may provide that secondary evidence of the deed shall not be *prima facie* evidence of the regularity of the sale. Roby *v.* City, 64 Ill. 447.

An act which merely accelerates the remedy, or gives a more summary remedy in case of a default in the performance of a contract, is valid. The legislature is not bound to continue the same forms and the same system of courts and proceedings for the accommodation of debtors or creditors. Stoddard *v.* Smith, 5 Binn. 355; Grubbs *v.* Harris, 1 Bibb, 567; Vanzant *v.* Waddell, 2 Yerg. 260; Livingston *v.* Moore, 7 Pet. 469; Rathbone *v.* Bradford, 1 Ala. 312; Maynes *v.* Moore, 16 Ind. 116; Hopkins *v.* Jones, 22 Ind. 310; Webb *v.* Moore, 25 Ind. 4; Smith *v.* Bryan, 34 Ill. 264; Wheat *v.* State, Minor, 199; Citizens' Bank *v.* Degnoodt, 25 La. Ann. 628.

A statute authorizing an attachment may apply to causes of action existing before its passage. Coosa River Steamboat Co. *v.* Barclay, 30 Ala. 120.

A law taking away the remedy by attachment is valid. Leathers *v.* Shipbuilders' Bank, 40 Me. 386; Bigelow *v.* Pritchard, 38 Mass. 169; Danley *v.* State Bank, 15 Ark. 16; Allis *v.* State Bank, 15 Ark. 19; Krebs *v.* State Bank, 15 Ark. 19.

A statute allowing an attachment to be issued and laid in the hands of the stockholders, without previously exhausting the assets of the bank, is valid. Smith *v.* Bryan, 34 Ill. 264.

An attachment law does not impair the obligation of the contract between the garnishee and the debtor, but merely provides that the former shall pay the money to a creditor of the latter, and thereby be discharged therefrom. Philbrick *v.* Philbrick, 39 N. H. 468; Klaus *v.* City, 34 Wis. 628.

- A statute permitting amendments in proceedings by attachment, which applies to pending as well as prospective suits is constitutional, for a bondsman assumes his responsibility subject to various amendments of the writ and declaration in matters of form, and to such modifications of the mode of proceeding as the legislature may think proper to make. It relates to the remedy alone. Knight *v.* Dorr, 36 Mass. 48.

A retrospective law depriving a party of the right to enforce a contract if the taxes have not been regularly paid thereon since the making thereof, is void. Walker *v.* Whithead, 16 Wall. 314; s. c. 43 Geo. 537; Griffiths *v.* Shipp, 49 Geo. 231; Lathrop *v.* Brown, 1 Woods, 474; Kimbro *v.* Bank, 49 Geo. 419; Gardner *v.* Jeter, 49 Geo. 195; Mitchell *v.* Cothrans, 49 Geo. 125; Dougherty *v.* Fogle, 50 Geo. 464.

A statute prohibiting persons aiding the rebellion against the United States from prosecuting or defending actions during the continuance of the rebellion is void. Davis *v.* Pierse, 7 Minn. 13; McFarland *v.* Butler, 8 Minn. 116; Jackson *v.* Butler, 8 Minn. 117.

A statute requiring suitors to take a test oath of loyalty in order to maintain a suit is valid. Beirne *v.* Brown, 4 W. Va. 72.

A statute creating a lien upon the property of the debtor in favor of existing contracts is valid, for it merely affects the remedy. Bolton *v.* Johns, 5 Penn. 145; Brien *v.* Clay, 1 E. D. Smith, 649; Gordon *v.* Canal Co. 1 McA. 513; contra, Kinney *v.* Sherman, 28 Ill. 520.

A statute enabling parties who have dealt with a contractor to file a lien claim, and obtain payment from the owner of the property, is valid, for it only provides a new remedy for the collection of a debt which one owes, and the other has the money of the debtor to pay with. Sullivan *v.* Brewster, 1 E. D. Smith, 681; Miller *v.* Moore, 1 E. D. Smith, 739.

A mechanics' lien law is altogether a statutory remedy created by the legislature as a boon to a favored class of the community, for the special encouragement of labor in the erection of houses, and is subject to the control of the legislature either to alter, vary, or modify it, or repeal it altogether. Evans *v.* Montgomery, 4 W. & S. 218.

If the mechanics' lien law has given a lien upon the property on which the improvements were made, without reference to the interest of the builder therein, it may be so modified as to restrict the lien to the interest and estate of the builder. Evans *v.* Montgomery, 4 W. & S. 218.

A statute enacting that the suit must be brought in the name of the real party in interest merely affects the remedy, and is valid. Hancock *v.* Ritchie, 11 Ind. 48.

A statute allowing an assignee of a *chose in action* to bring suit in his own name is valid in its application to instruments executed before its passage. It does not alter the nature of the instruments in any shape, or in any manner vary or affect the terms of the contracts. Ford *v.* Hale, 1 Mon. 23; Harlan *v.* Sigler, Morris, 39.

A statute authorizing the assignee of a *chose in action* to sue in his own name, can not prevent the maker from availing of the equities existing between him and the assignor at the time of its passage. Harlan *v.* Sigler, Morris, 39.

If a statute prohibiting the transfer of *choses in action* also prohibits any action thereon after a transfer either in the name of the assignee or the assignor, it is unconstitutional. Planters' Bank *v.* Sharp, 6 How. 301 ; S. C. 12 Miss. 28; McIntyre *v.* Ingraham, 35 Miss. 25 ; Jemison *v.* Planters' Bank, 23 Ala. 168; Montgomery *v.* Galbraith, 19 Miss. 555 ; Grand Gulf R. R. Co. *v.* State, 18 Miss. 428; vide Hyde *v.* Planters' Bank, 8 Rob. (La.) 416.

Imprisonment of the debtor may be a punishment for not performing his contract, or may be allowed as a means of inducing him to perform it. Imprisonment is no part of the contract, and simply to release the prisoner does not impair its obligation. A State, therefore, has the right to abolish imprisonment for debt altogether, and such law may extend to present as well as future punishment. Gray *v.* Munroe, 1 McLean, 528 ; Mason *v.* Haile, 12 Wheat. 370 ; Sommers *v.* Johnson, 4 Vt. 278 ; Oriental Bank *v.* Freeze, 18 Me. 109; People *v.* Carpenter, 46 Barb. 619; Brown *v.* Dillahunty, 12 Miss. 713 ; Woodfin *v.* Hooper, 4 Humph. 13; Fisher *v.* Lacky, 6 Blackf. 373 ; Beers *v.* Haughton, 9 Pet. 329 ; Mercer's Case, 4 Harring. 248 ; Donnelly *v.* Corbett, 7 N. Y. 500 ; Newton *v.* Tibbatts, 7 Ark. 150 ; Bronson *v.* Newberry, 2 Doug. 38.

When the statute in force at the time the bond was given reserves the right to change the limits of the jail, such change does not impair the obligation of the bond. Reed *v.* Fullum, 19 Mass. 158.

A State legislature may pass a statute assigning new limits for a prison, and thus affect jail bonds previously given. Reed *v.* Fullum, 19 Mass. 158; Walter *v.* Bacon, 8 Mass. 468 ; Holmes *v.* Lansing, 3 Johns. Cas. 73.

A statute may provide for the discharge of a jail bond in a manner different from that named in the bond. Morse *v.* Rice, 21 Me. 53; Oriental Bank *v.* Freeze, 18 Me. 109.

Where a creditor, at the time of the contracting of the debt, had the right, on a return of *nulla bona*, to have the rents, tolls, profits, rights and credits of a corporation sequestered, the State can not enact that a writ of sequestration shall not issue unless the corporation is guilty of mismanagement, misapplication of its funds, or willful delay in discharging its liabilities. Penrose *v.* Erie Canal Co. 56 Penn. 46.

A statute requiring a creditor to exhaust his securities before bringing suit on his claim, is valid, for it merely regulates the order in which several remedies shall be pursued. Swift *v.* Fletcher, 6 Minn. 550.

A statute which does not divest the remedy, but merely changes the form of it, is constitutional. Thayer *v.* Seavey, 11 Me. 284.

A statute which requires a party to record an abstract of his judgment within a certain time, in order to preserve his lien, is valid, for it leaves it entirely at the discretion of the creditor, whether he will preserve it or not. Tarpley *v.* Hamer, 17 Miss. 310.

A statute allowing a municipal corporation to set off a claim for benefits against a claim for damages, is valid. Baldwin *v.* Newark, 38 N. J. 158.

A statute allowing the bills of a bank to be tendered in payment of any debt due to it, is valid. Exchange Bank *v.* Tiddy, 67 N. C. 169; Bank *v.* Hart, 67 N. C. 264.

Where a State creates a bank, and invests its funds therein, a statute directing that the assets shall be sold and deposited in the treasury, without providing for the creditors of the bank, is void, for it withdraws the assets from the operation of all legal process. State *v.* Bank, 1 Rich. N. S. 63.

A statute which enacts that the obligors in official bonds shall not have the benefit of stay laws or appraisement laws, is valid, for it gives force to the contract by increasing the means to be used in enforcing performance of it. Pierce *v.* Mill, 21 Ind. 27.

A statute changing the manner of commencing the action, serving notice and proceeding to judgment, is valid. McCreary *v.* State, 27 Ark. 425.

A debtor in default has no vested right to have his property sold in any particular way. Tuolumne Redemption Co. *v.* Sedgwick, 15 Cal. 515.

A statute allowing the holder of a coupon detached from the bond to sue thereon in his own name is valid. Augusta Bank *v.* Augusta, 49 Me. 507.

So far as laws relating to executions are merely remedial, they may be modified or changed at any time. The sheriff may be allowed to give a deed instead of a certificate. Coriell *v.* Ham, 4 G. Greene, 455.

A statute which provides that no action shall be brought upon a promise to pay a debt from which the debtor has been discharged in bankruptcy, unless the promise is in writing, is valid, although it applies to prior verbal promises. Kingsley *v.* Cousins, 47 Me. 91.

The legislature may prescribe a different rule for the service of process on a corporation from that existing at the time when the charter was granted, for such a rule relates to the remedy and not to the obligation of the contract. New Albany & Salem Railroad Co. *v.* McNamara, 11 Ind. 543.

An alteration of the remedy to enforce the forfeiture of a charter, is valid, although it applies to prior charters. Aurora Turnpike Co. *v.* Holthouse, 7 Ind. 59.

A statute may reduce the costs below the legal amount by the law in force when the right of action accrued, or deny them altogether. Potter *v.* Sturdivant, 4 Me. 154; Free *v.* Haworth, 19 Ind. 404; Rader *v.* S. R. District, 36 N. J. 273.

A statute authorizing a corporation to sue in its own name upon notes made payable to its cashier, is valid, for it is strictly remedial, and carries out the contract according to its original intendment. Crawford *v.* Bank, 7 How. 279.

A statute allowing a judge and commissioner to reduce the account of a depositor in a savings bank, when the assets are less than the deposits, affects the remedy, and is valid. Simpson *v.* Savings Bank, 56 N. H. 466.

When the legislature requires a contract to be entered into collateral to the original, and as a part of the remedy to enforce it, the rights which it gives arise only out of the statute provision, and not out of any agreement of the parties, and are therefore liable to be modified by statute. Morse *v.* Rice, 21 Me. 53; Oriental Bank *v* Freeze, 18 Me. 109.

A statute allowing an administrator *de bonis non* to sue in the name of the State, on the bond of his predecessor, is valid, although the right did not exist when the bond was made, for it merely regulates the manner of enforcing the bond, without enlarging or varying the liabilities of the obligors. Graham *v.* State, 7 Ind. 470.

A statute which requires that the maker and indorsers of a promissory note shall be sued in joint actions does not impair the obligation of the contract. McMillan *v.* Sprague, 4 How. (Miss.) 647.

A statute requiring appraisement before a sale under an execution, relates to the remedy, and is valid. Catlin *v.* Munger, 1 Tex. 598.

A statute may provide that a corporation may be sued in the county where a tort committed by it occurs, for a suit is a remedy, and venue is but an incident of suit. Davis *v.* Central R. R. Co. 17 Geo. 323.

The appointment of a receiver upon the dissolution of a corporation, with a provision that all demands shall be prosecuted against him alone, is merely a change of the remedy. Read *v.* Frankfort Bank, 23 Me. 318; Leathers *v.* Shipbuilders' bank, 40 Me. 386.

A statute which provides that on all executions in favor of banks or their assignees, the notes of the banks shall be received in payment and discharge of the judgment is valid when it does not affect the rights of the *bona fide* holders of notes, for it affects the remedy. Bank *v.* Domigan, 12 Ohio, 220.

A statute allowing parties to institute suits upon an official bond, instead of issuing a *scire facias* upon a judgment already rendered in favor of another, merely changes the remedy and is valid. White *v.* Wilkins, 24 Me. 299.

A statute permitting one plaintiff to recover in an action of ejectment, although another joint plaintiff may fail to establish his title, does not impair any contract. Hinckle *v.* Riffert, 6 Penn. 196.

A statute which requires that a new promise to pay a debt barred by the statute of limitations shall be in writing is valid if it applies only to promises made after its passage. Joy *v.* Thompson, 1 Doug. 373.

A statute permitting one firm to sue another at law, although some parties are members of both firms, affects the remedy merely, and is valid. Hepburn *v.* Curts, 7 Watts, 300.

The right to dower arises solely by operation of law, and not by force of any contract, express or implied between the parties. A statute providing that the estate on the application of creditors shall be sold free from the dower, and the claim transferred to the proceeds, is remedial and valid. Lawrence *v.* Miller, 1 Sandf. 516; S. C. 2 N. Y. 245.

A statute which requires a minor, in enforcing his lien, to proceed against the land of the tutor most recently alienated, is valid, although he could previously have proceeded against any portion of it, for every person who is obliged to resort to the court to enforce his rights must submit to the forms and delays which the law may from time to time prescribe. Patin *v.* Prejean, 7 La. 301.

A State law providing that no *scire facias* shall be issued to revive a dormant judgment, is valid, for it leaves the creditor to his common-law remedy by an action of debt. Parker *v.* Shannonhouse, Phillips, 209.

A statute which takes from a creditor the right to proceed against the stockholders, and vests it in a trustee, and directs that the assets of the corporation shall be first exhausted, is valid. Story *v.* Furman, 25 N. Y. 214.

A statute anthorizing receivers to sell property free from encumbrances, and transferring the lien to the proceeds, does not impair the obligation of any contract, but merely affects the remedy. Potts *v.* Water Power Co. 9 N. J. Eq. 592.

A statute which provides that the securities shall be forfeited, if the creditor sues upon the claim without first exhausting them, is void. Swift *v.* Fletcher, 6 Minn. 550.

The courts, upon a proper case, may substitute one surety for costs in the place of another. There is no contract on the part of the person intended to be benefited by taking the surety. The law takes the surety to protect him from loss, and he has no right to ask more at the hands of the court than that this shall be done. He acquires no right by a contract to hold any particular person liable, provided the court will substitute another who can equally protect him from loss. Craighead *v.* Bank, 1' Meigs, 199.

The right of a purchaser at a tax sale to a deed, can not be taken away by a repeal of a statute authorizing the execution of a deed. Bruce *v.* Schuyler, 4 Gilman, 221.

Any law passed after the execution of a contract, which denies, obstructs or impairs the right to sell the property of the debtor under an execution at a fair public sale to the highest bidder, by superadding a condition that there shall be no sale for any sum less than the value of the property levied on, to be ascertained by appraisement or any other mode of valuation than a public sale, affects the obligation of the contract, and is repugnant to the Constitution. Hunt *v.* Gregg, 8 Blackf. 105; Shaffer *v.* Bolander, 4 G. Greene, 201; Burton *v.* Emerson, 4 G. Greene, 393; McCracken *v.* Hayward, 2 How. 608; Gantly *v.* Ewing, 3 How. 707; Smoot *v.* Lafferty, 2 Gilman, 383; Rosier *v.* Hale, 10 Iowa, 470; U. S. *v.* Conway, Hemp. 313; Bronson *v.* Kinzie, 1 How. 34; Baily *v.* Gentry, 1 Mo. 164; Rawley *v.* Hooker, 21 Ind. 144; contra, Waldo *v.* Williams, 4 Ill. 264; Catlin *v.* Munger, 1 Tex. 598.

Where a State has authorized a municipal corporation to contract and to exercise the power of local taxation to the extent necessary to meet its engagements, the power thus given can not be withdrawn until the contract is satisfied. The State and the corporation are equally bound. Von Hoffman *v.* Quincy, 4 Wall. 535; Lansing *v.* County, 1 Dill. 522; S. C. 2 Abb. C. C. 53.

A statute which prohibits a municipal corporation from levying taxes to pay a judgment, is void if it deprives the creditor of every efficient means for collecting his debt. Soutter *v.* Madison, 15 Wis. 30.

A statute which deprives a creditor of his remedy upon a judgment against a municipal corporation forever, unless the legislature shall in its discretion, at some future time, by a new law, provide for its payment, is void. Hadfield *v.* New York, 6 Robt. 501.

A statute making one municipal corporation liable on a contract, instead of another is valid, if all the rights of enforcing the judgment are preserved. Rader *v.* S. R. District, 36 N. J. 273.

A statute giving the grantee of a rent charge the right of re-entry for non-payment of the rent, is valid, for it merely affects the remedy. Van Rensselaer *v.* Ball, 19 N. Y. 100.

A statute authorizing the grantee of a rent charge to sue at law in his own name, is valid, for it operates on the remedy. Independently of the statute he could sue in the name of the grantor. Van Rensselaer *v.* Hays, 19 N. Y. 68.

An act taking away the priority of a claim for rent in case of the levy of an execution upon the goods of a tenant, is valid. Stocking *v.* Hunt, 3 Denio, 274.

A statute giving an action of covenant against the assignee of a leasehold estate, pertains to the remedy and is valid. Taggart *v.* McGinn, 14 Penn. 155.

A statute abolishing distress for rent is valid, and may apply to leases in which such a power is reserved. Conkey *v.* Hart, 14 N. Y. 22; Van Rensselaer *v.* Snyder, 13 N. Y. 299; Guild *v.* Rogers, 8 Barb. 502.

A statute providing that a mortgagor shall not be liable for rent after the date of the sale under the mortgage, if he remains in possession and redeems within the time limited by law, is void so far as it applies to prior contracts. Greenfield *v.* Dorris, 1 Sneed, 548.

A law which releases the sureties on a jail bond after condition broken, and assignment of the bond by the sheriff to the creditor, is unconstitutional. Starr *v.* Robinson, 1 Chip. 257; Lewis *v.* Brackenridge, 1 Blackf. 220.

A State statute authorizing the sale of property free from a mortgage, and transferring the lien thereof to the proceeds, is valid. Potts *v.* New Jersey Arms and Ordnance Co. 17 N. J. Eq. 395.

A statute allowing the proceeds of property sold free from incumbrances, without the consent of the mortgagee, to be applied first to pay indefinite costs other than those of the sale, is void. Martin *v.* Somerville Co. 3 Wall. Jr. 206.

A statute permitting a receiver to sell property free from incumbrances, without the consent of the mortgagee, whether it brings sufficient to pay the incumbrance or not, impairs the obligation of the mortgage. Martin *v.* Somerville Co. 3 Wall. Jr. 206.

If a mortgage contains a power in case of default, to sell according to law, a statute prescribing a shorter time for advertising before sale than existed at the time of the execution of the mortgage, is not repugnant to the Constitution. The remedy, instead of being impaired, is rendered more speedy and advantageous. James *v.* Stull, 9 Barb. 482.

The judicial mortgage resulting from the inscription of a judgment is no part of the contract on which the judgment is based, and may be taken away by statute. New Orleans *v.* Holmes, 13 La. Ann. 502.

REMEDIES.   223

The right to institute an action of ejectment upon the forfeiture of a mortgage is a part of the contract, and a statute which prohibits the institution of such a suit until after a foreclosure and sale of the property, is void. Mundy *v.* Monroe, 1 Mich. 68.

A statute extending the time from twenty days to six months before a default can be taken for want of an answer, is valid. Von Baumbach *v.* Bade, 9 Wis. 559; Holloway *v.* Sherman, 12 Iowa, 282.

A statute requiring six months advertisement prior to a sale under a mortgage, instead of six weeks, is valid. Von Baumbach *v.* Bade, 9 Wis. 559; Starkweather *v.* Hawes, 10 Wis. 125.

A statute diminishing the period required for the publication of a notice of foreclosure, is valid. Webb *v.* Moore, 25 Ind. 4; Hopkins *v.* Jones, 22 Ind. 310.

When the mortgagee does not resort to the power to sell, contained in the mortgage, but applies to the court for the enforcement of his mortgage, he must take the remedy as he finds it, and can not object that it is less beneficial than that afforded at the time the mortgage was executed. Heyward *v.* Judd, 4 Minn. 483.

A law which provides that property shall not be sold under an execution or a decree of foreclosure, unless it brings two-thirds of its appraised value, imposes conditions which will frequently render a sale impossible, and impairs the obligation of contracts. Bronson *v.* Kinzie, 1 How. 311; Grantly *v.* Ewing, 3 How. 707; contra, Waldo *v.* Williams, 4 Ill. 264.

Where the mortgage contains a power to sell, the legislature can not interfere with its exercise so as to change the estate which the trustee is authorized to sell, and extend the time for redemption. Heyward *v.* Judd, 4 Minn. 483; Goenen *v.* Schroeder, 8 Minn. 387; Carroll *v.* Rossiter, 10 Minn. 174.

A law which gives the mortgagor a certain period in which to redeem the property after a sale under the mortgage, confers upon him an equitable estate to which he was not entitled under the contract, and unquestionably impairs its obligation. Bronson *v.* Kinzie, 1 How. 311; Grantly *v.* Ewing, 3 How. 707; contra, Stone *v.* Bassett, 4 Minn. 298; Heyward *v.* Judd, 4 Minn. 483; Freeborn *v.* Pettibone, 5 Minn 277; Waldo *v.* Williams, 4 Ill. 264.

A statute allowing a creditor to redeem at any time within two years after the sale under a mortgage made prior to the passing of the statute, is void. Howard *v.* Bugbee, 24 How. 461; S. C. 32 Ala. 713; Malony *v.* Fortune, 14 Iowa, 417; Seale *v.* Mitchell, 5 Cal. 401; Thorn *v.* San Francisco, 4 Cal. 127; contra, Iverson *v.* Shorter, 9 Ala. 713.

A statute giving the mortgagor the right to remain in possession during the time of redemption, upon paying the interest and the taxes, is valid. Heyward *v.* Judd, 4 Minn. 483; Berthold *v.* Holman, 12 Minn. 335; Berthold *v.* Fox, 13 Minn. 501.

A statute requiring that the interest shall be paid in advance in order to enable the mortgagor to remain in possession after a sale, is valid. Stone *v.* Bassett, 4 Minn. 298.

The right to redeem is no part of the contract of indebtedness. It is a privilege given by statute. As the provision is only a matter out of which rights may grow, it may be repealed at any time before a party avails himself of it. Tuolumne Redemption Co. *v.* Sedgwick, 15 Cal. 515; contra, Cargill *v.* Power, 1 Mich. 369.

Although the law at the time of the execution of the mortgage provided that the property should not be sold for less than two-thirds of the appraised value, unless the mortgagor elected to have it sold subject to the right to redeem, a statute may take away the right of appraisement and redemption. Holland *v.* Dickerson, 41 Iowa, 367.

The right to redeem property sold under an execution pertains solely to the remedy, and exists solely by statute, and the legislature may repeal the statute at any time before it has been availed of by the parties entitled. Tuolumne Redemption Co. *v.* Sedgwick, 15 Cal. 515.

A State law allowing a redemption at any time within a certain period after a sale under an execution, when there was no redemption at the time of the making of the contract, is void. Oliver *v.* McClure, 28 Ark. 555; Scobey *v.* Gibson, 17 Ind. 572; Inglehart *v.* Wolfin, 20 Ind. 32; contra, Moore *v.* Martin, 38 Cal. 428; Turner *v.* Watkins, 31 Ark. 429.

Appeal.

A statute granting a writ of error or an appeal to a party after the expiration of the time for suing out the writ or taking the appeal, does not impair the obligation of a contract. Converse *v.* Burrows, 2 Minn. 229; Davis *v.* Ballard, 1 J. J. Marsh. 563; Braddee *v.* Brownfield, 2 W. & S. 271.

A statute permitting one of several parties against whom a judgment has been rendered, to sue out a writ of error without joining his codefendants, does not impair the obligation of a contract. Wilder *v.* Lumpkin, 4 Geo. 208.

A statute allowing an appeal to be taken without giving security for costs does not impair the obligation of any contract. Todd *v.* Neal, 49 Ala. 266.

A statute taking away the right of appeal is not unconstitutional. Grover *v.* Coon, 1 N. Y. 536.

EXEMPTIONS.   225

New Trial.

A statute allowing a new trial or a proceeding in the nature of an appeal after litigation actually commenced, or even after judgment, does not impair the obligation of a contract, although there was no provision for a new trial or appeal previously.   Calder *v.* Bull, 3 Dall. 386; S. C. 2 Root, 350 : Balt. & S. R. R. Co. *v.* Nesbit, 10 How. 395; League *v.* De Young, 11 How. 185; Colby *v.* Dennis, 36 Me. 9; vide Young *v.* State Bank, 4 Ind. 301.

A statute declaring a judgment void and granting a new trial impairs the obligation of contracts, and is void.   Weaver *v.* Lapsley, 43 Ala. 224.

Exemptions.

Such property as is subject to execution at the time the debt is contracted must remain subject to execution until the debt is paid. A statute which creates an additional exemption is therefore void so far as it affects prior contracts. Lessley *v.* Phipps, 49 Miss. 790; Alexander *v.* Kilpatrick, 14 Fla. 450; Jones *v.* Brandon, 48 Geo. 593; Quackenbush *v.* Danks, 1 Denio, 128; S. C. 3 Denio, 594; 1 N. Y. 129; Matthewson *v.* Weller, 3 Denio, 52; Homestead Cases, 23 Gratt. 266; Russell *v.* Randolph, 26 Gratt. 705; Cockran *v.* Darcy, 5 Rich. N. S. 125 ; Ex parte Hewett, 5 Rich. N. S. 409; De la Howe *v.* Harper, 5 Rich. N. S. 470; contra, Pol *v.* Hardie, 65 N. C. 447; Allen *v.* Shield, 72 N. C. 504; Robert *v.* Coco, 25 La. Ann. 199; Stephenson *v.* Osborne, 41 Miss. 119; Wilson *v.* Sparks, 72 N. C. 208; Garrett *v.* Cheshire, 69 N. C. 396; Bronson *v.* Kenzie, 1 How. 311; Rockwell *v.* Hubbell, 2 Doug. 197; Velder *v.* Alkenbrack, 6 Barb. 327; Helfenstein *v.* Cave, 3 Iowa, 287 ; In re Sarah Kennedy, 2 Rich. N. S. 116; Howze *v.* Howze, 2 Rich. N. S. 229; Sneider *v.* Heidelberger, 45 Ala. 126; Doughty *v.* Sheriff, 27 La. Ann. 355.

The contracting of a debt does not in any legal sense create a lien upon the debtor's property. The right which a creditor by becoming such acquires, is to have the use and benefit of the laws for the collection of debts. If a subsequent act increases the exemption, the question always is whether the law which prevailed when the contract was made has been so far changed that there does not remain a substantial and reasonable mode of enforcing it in the ordinary and regular course of justice. If it has not, the act is valid   Stephenson *v.* Osborne, 41 Miss. 119; Morse *v.* Gould, 11 N. Y. 281 ; Grimes *v.* Bryne, 2 Minn. 89.

If a new Constitution deprives the courts of jurisdiction to sell exempted property, there is no remedy to enforce the contract. Hardeman *v.* Downer, 93 Geo. 425.

No exemption can be allowed as against a mortgagee claiming under a mortgage made prior to the law allowing the exemption. Shelor *v.* Mason, 2 Rich. N. S. 233.

15

An exemption law which divests the lien of a judgment, and leaves no means for the collection of the debt, is unconstitutional. Gunn *v.* Barry, 15 Wall. 610; Forsyth *v.* Marbury, R. M. Charlt. 324; Smith *v.* Morse, 2 Cal. 524; McKeithan *v.* Terry, 64 N. C. 25; contra, In re Sarah Kennedy, 2 Rich. N. S. 116; Hardeman *v.* Downer, 39 Geo. 425; Adams *v.* Smith, 2 Rich. N. S. 228.

No State law can divest the lien of a judgment so as to give the homestead to the debtor, even after he abandons it. Tillotson *v.* Millard, 7 Minn. 513.

The subjection of property to execution, which was not so at the time the contract was made, does not in the slightest degree impair the obligation of the contract. It only extends and enlarges the remedy. Contracts are not made with an eye to the laws that shall enforce them, or to what property shall or shall not be liable to execution, but with an expectation of each party's performing with good faith what he has stipulated to do. Reardon *v.* Searcy, 2 Bibb, 202.

A homestead law is valid, although it leaves the debtor no property liable to execution. Hill *v.* Kessler, 63 N. C. 437.

A State law exempting a homestead is valid if it is such as sound policy, humanity, and the well-being of the community dictate. Cusic *v.* Douglas, 3 Kans. 23; Root *v.* McGrew, 3 Kans. 215.

The legislature may exempt real estate as well as personal property. Hill *v.* Kessler, 63 N. C. 437.

What are necessaries is a question for the legislature, and not for the court. Hill *v.* Kessler, 63 N. C. 437.

If the object of the law is not so much to secure the well-being of the citizens as to enable them to hold large amounts of property, with a view of making it available to their own aggrandizement, the statute is void. Cusic *v.* Douglas, 3 Kans. 23.

A State can not enact that the property of a debtor shall not be taken to satisfy his debts, if it was liable to such seizure and appropriation when the debt was incurred. Penrose *v.* Erie Canal Co. 56 Penn. 46; State *v.* Bank, 1 Rich. N. S. 63.

A statute permitting the declaration of a homestead is constitutional so far as it affects debts created after the passage of the statute, though prior to the declaration of the homestead, for the creditors knew, or are presumed to have known, at the time they gave credit, what rights and privileges the debtor was allowed by law, and to what property they must look for a satisfaction of their debts. In re Henkel, 2 Saw. 305.

Stay Laws.

A statute which grants a stay of execution for a certain period is unconstitutional. Jones *v.* Crittenden, 1 Car. L. Rep. 385; Townsend *v.* Townsend, Peck, 1; Grayson *v.* Lilly, 7 Mon. 6; Bumgardner *v.* Circuit Court, 4 Mo. 50; Baily *v.* Gentry, 1 Mo. 164; Dormire *v.* Cogly, 8 Blackf. 177; Strong *v.* Daniel, 5 Ind. 348; Aycock *v.* Martin, 37 Geo. 124; Hudspeth *v.* Davis, 41 Ala. 389; Stevens *v.* Andrews, 31 Mo. 205; Brown *v.* Ward, 1 Mo. 209; Barnes *v.* Barnes, 8 Jones (N. C.) 366; Burt *v.* Williams, 24 Ark. 91; Ex parte Pollard, 40 Ala. 77; Jacobs *v.* Smallwood, 63 N. C. 112; State *v.* Carew, 13 Rich. 498; Coffman *v.* Bank, 40 Miss. 29; Sequestration Cases, 30 Tex. 688; Canfield *v.* Hunter, 30 Tex. 712; Culbreath *v.* Hunter, 30 Tex. 713; Levison *v.* Norris, 30 Tex. 713; Levison *v.* Krohne, 30 Tex. 714; Webster *v.* Rose, 6 Heisk. 93; Garlington *v.* Priest, 13 Fla. 559.

A law procrastinating the remedy, generally speaking, destroys part of the right. He pays less who pays later—*Minus solvit qui serius solvit.* Any indulgence, therefore, in point of time afforded by the legislature to a debtor is a correlative injury to the creditor in the same degree, though of a different nature, as a correspondent indulgence by a proportional reduction of the debt. Johnson *v.* Duncan, 3 Mart. 531.

A statute providing for payment of a judgment in instalments, and a stay of execution so long as the instalments are paid, is void. Jones *v.* McMahan, 30 Tex. 319; Earle *v.* Johnson, 31 Tex. 164.

An act giving a stay of execution can not affect a judgment rendered prior to its passage. Dormire *v.* Cogly, 8 Blackf. 177.

A statute allowing of a stay of execution for an indefinite time, upon the consent of two-thirds of the creditors, is void. Bunn *v.* Gorgas, 41 Penn. 441.

Where the contract stipulates that there shall be no stay of execution beyond a certain limit, the legislature can not declare that there shall be a stay beyond that limit. The debtor's waiver of legal rights becomes a part of the obligation of his contract, and the legislature can no more impair that obligation than it can annul the entire contract. Billmeyer *v.* Evans, 40 Penn. 324; Lewis *v.* Lewis, 47 Penn. 127; Griffith *v.* Thomas, 34 Leg. Int. 150.

A provision for a stay of execution, unless the plaintiff will take the property levied on at two-thirds of its appraised value, is unconstitutional. Baily *v.* Gentry, 1 Mo. 164.

The right to suspend the recovery of a debt for one period implies the right of suspending it for another. Jones *v.* Crittenden, 1 Car. L. Rep. 385.

A statute which subjects parties in chancery to a longer credit than the law allowed when the contract between the respective parties was made is unconstitutional. January *v.* January, 7 Mon. 542 ; Pool *v.* Young, 7 Mon. 587.

A law which grants a stay of execution for a certain period, upon the defendant's superseding the judgment with sureties, does impair the obligation of contracts made before its adoption. Blair *v.* Williams, 4 Litt. 34 ; Lapsley *v.* Brashears, 4 Litt. 47 ; contra, Farnsworth *v.* Vance, 2 Cold. 108.

A statute which directs a stay of execution for one year, unless the property levied upon shall bring two-thirds of its appraised value is constitutional. Chadwick *v.* Moore, 8 W. & S. 49; Thompson *v.* Buckley, 34 Leg. Int. 148.

A statute passed in the time of a civil war, which enacts that no civil process shall issue or be enforced against any person mustered into the service of the State or of the United States during the term for which he is engaged in such service, and thirty days thereafter, is valid, for the stay is neither indefinite nor unreasonable. Breitenbach *v.* Bush, 44 Penn. 313 ; Coxe *v.* Martin, 44 Penn. 322; State *v.* McGinty, 41 Miss. 435.

A statute which provides that all actions shall stand continued during all the time that the defendant is in the actual military service of the United States, is valid. McCormick *v.* Rusch, 15 Iowa, 127.

A statute suspending all suits against a volunteer in the service of the United States, until his regiment or company returns home, is valid. Edmondson *v.* Ferguson, 11 Mo. 344; Lindsey *v.* Burbridge, 11 Mo. 545.

A statute exempting all persons from civil process while they are in the military service of the United States, or of the State, is void, for the suspension is indefinite. Hasbrouck *v.* Shipman, 16 Wis. 296.

When the enlistment is for the war, the time is indefinite, and a statute providing a stay of civil process for that time is unreasonable and invalid. Clark *v.* Martin, 49 Penn. 299 ; S. C. 3 Grant, 393.

No State can pass a law suspending the right of any person engaged in a rebellion against the Federal Government from prosecuting or defending a suit during the continuance of the rebellion. Davis *v.* Pierse, 7 Minn. 13 ; Keough *v.* McNitt, 7 Minn. 30; Wilcox *v.* Davis, 7 Minn. 23 ; Vernon *v.* Henson, 24 Ark. 242.

A statute which suspends all legal proceedings to obtain or enforce a judgment for money for the period of seven months, is valid, for it operates on the courts alone. Johnson *v.* Higgins, 3 Met. (Ky.) 566 ; Barkley *v.* Glover, 4 Met. (Ky.) 44.

A statute may provide that an execution issued upon a judgment obtained by confession or a warrant of attorney, shall be stayed until the demand is due, for it applies solely to the remedy. Wood *v.* Child, 20 Ill. 209.

A law which merely suspends temporarily proceedings for the collection of debts, is constitutional. Grimball *v.* Ross, T. U. P. Charlt. 175.

The legislature may provide for a stay of execution, providing that the stay is not so great and unreasonable as to amount to a substantial impairing of the obligation of contracts. Huntzinger *v.* Brock, 3 Grant, 243.

The State may grant a stay of execution upon a judgment due to a municipal corporation. Governor *v.* Gridley, Walk. 328.

Limitations.

A statute of limitations enacted with due discretion, and allowing a reasonable time for the commencement of suits on existing demands, is a wholesome and useful regulation, and not within the prohibition of the Constitution. Sampson *v.* Sampson, 63 Me. 328; Samples *v.* Bank, 1 Woods, 525; Briscoe *v.* Anketell, 28 Miss. 361; Lockhart *v.* Yeiser, 2 Bush, 231; Holcombe *v.* Tracy, 2 Minn. 241; Stearns *v.* Gittings, 23 Ill. 387; Barker *v.* Jackson, 1 Paine, 559; Lewis *v.* Broadwell, 3 McLean, 568; Newland *v.* Marsh, 19 Ill. 376; Smith *v.* Packard, 12 Wis. 371; State *v.* Jones, 21 Md. 432; Call *v.* Hagger, 8 Mass. 423; Jackson *v.* Lamphire, 3 Pet. 280; De Cordova *v.* Galveston, 4 Tex. 470; Cummings *v.* Maxwell, 45 Me. 190; Society *v.* Wheeler, 2 Gallis. 105; Blackford *v.* Peltier, 1 Blackf. 36; Miller *v.* Comm. 5 W. & S. 488; State *v.* Bermudez, 12 La. 352; Smith *v.* Morrison, 39 Mass. 430; Rexford *v.* Knight, 11 N. Y. 308; Beal *v.* Nason, 14 Me. 344; Bell *v.* Roberts, 13 Vt. 582; Butler *v.* Palmer, 1 Hill, 324; Griffin *v.* McKenzie, 7 Geo. 163; McKenny *v.* Compton, 18 Geo. 170; Lewis *v.* Harbin, 5 B. Mon. 564; Pearce *v.* Patton, 7 B. Mon. 162; Maltby *v.* Cooper, Morris, 59; Stephens *v.* St. Louis Nat'l Bank, 43 Mo. 385; Stone *v.* Bennett, 13 Minn. 153.

If a reasonable time is not allowed after the passage of the act for parties to institute proceedings for the enforcement of existing demands, but the act is permitted to take effect at once, thereby depriving them of all remedy for the recovery of those demands, the act violates the Constitution by impairing the obligation of contracts. Proprietors *v.* Laboree, 2 Me. 275; Society *v.* Wheeler, 2 Gallis. 105; Amy *v.* Smith, 1 Litt. 326; Forsyth *v.* Marbury, R. M. Charlt. 324; Garrett *v* Beaumont, 24 Miss. 377; Johnson *v.* Bond, 1 Hemp. 533; Robinson *v.* Magee, 9 Cal. 81; Auld *v.* Butcher, 2 Kans. 135; Pereles *v.* Watertown, 6 Biss. 79; Berry *v.* Ransdall, 4 Met. (Ky.) 292; Osborn *v.* Jaines, 17 Wis. 573.

In order to render the time for bringing a suit unreasonable, the court must be able to say that no substantial opportunity is afforded to the party affected to assert his rights after the passage of the law; that the unmistakable purpose and effect of the law is to cut off the right of the party, and not merely to limit the time in which he may begin to enforce it. Rexford v. Knight, 11 N. Y. 308.

Whether the time allowed for creditors to commence their actions is a reasonable time or not, is a question within the exclusive province of the court and not of the legislature, to determine. Pereles v. Watertown, 6 Biss. 79; contra, Smith v. Morrison, 39 Mass. 430.

Thirty days is not a reasonable time to allow for the bringing of a suit. Berry v. Ransdall, 4 Met. (Ky.) 292.

An extension of the time for bringing an action does not impair the obligation of a contract. Wardlaw v. Buzzard, 15 Rich. 158; Smith v. Tucker, 17 N. J. 82; Cox v. Berry, 13 Geo. 306; Edwards v. McCaddon, 20 Iowa, 520; Swickard v. Bailey, 3 Kans. 507; Winston v. McCormick, 1 Ind. 56; Gilman v. Cutts, 23 N. H. 376; Pleasants v. Rohrer, 17 Wis 577.

A statute prescribing the time within which the authority to establish a lottery may be exercised is valid. Phalen v. Comm. 8 How. 163; S. C. 1 Rob. (Va.) 713.

A statute requiring a new promise to be in writing is valid, if ample time is allowed to enforce the demand before it is affected by the new rule of evidence. Briscoe v. Anketell, 28 Miss. 361.

Who Can Not Object.

If a law affecting the remedy impairs the obligation of a contract, the creditor alone can complain that his guaranteed privileges are taken from him at the expense of the Constitution which protects them. If he does not complain, the debtor can not set up the unconstitutionality of an act which does not affect him, and can only prejudice his adversary. Small v. Hodgen, 1 Litt. 16.

A purchaser at a sale under an execution can not object to the unconstitutionality of an act allowing a redemption of the property. Iverson v. Shorter, 9 Ala. 713.

A surety who has superseded a judgment under a stay law which was unconstitutional can not set up the invalidity of the statute to defeat his liability. Berry v. Haines, 2 Car. L. Rep. 428; M'Kinney v. Carroll, 12 Pet. 66; S. C. 5 Mass. 96; Magruder v. Marshall, 1 Blackf. 333; contra, Strong v. Daniel, 5 Ind. 348.

It is competent for a party to waive the privileges or benefits secured by the Constitution, and if he does so by availing himself of an act, he can not afterwards complain that it is unconstitutional, because he has no interest affected or constitutional right violated. His adversary alone has ground of complaint. Hansford *v.* Barbour, 3 A. K. Marsh. 515; Barnett *v.* Barbour, 1 Litt. 396; M'Kinney *v.* Carroll, 12 Pet. 66; s. c. 5 Mon. 96; Chitty *v.* Glenn, 3 Mon. 424; Willard *v.* Longstreet, 2 Doug. 172.

A sheriff who has acted under a statute can not set up its unconstitutionality. Willard *v.* Longstreet, 2 Doug. 172.

A debtor who has given a bond to stay execution can not, after the expiration of the stay, raise the objection that the law was unconstitutional. M'Kinney *v.* Carroll, 12 Pet. 66; s. c. 5 Mon. 96.

The sureties to an improvement bond have no right to complain that the law under which it was given is unconstitutional, for they are not affected by it. M'Kinney *v.* Carroll, 12 Pet. 66; s. c. 5 Mon. 96.

A person who is not a party to the contract can not question the validity of a law on the ground that it impairs the contract. Gilman *v.* Sheboygan, 2 Black, 510.

The party whose rights are invaded is the only one who can plead the nullity of a law impairing the obligation of contracts. The law is binding on third parties. New Orleans C. & N. Co. *v.* New Orleans, 12 La. Ann. 364; Gilman *v.* Sheboygan, 2 Black, 510.

A purchaser at a sale under an execution can not object to the sale on the ground that the act regulating the terms of the sale is unconstitutional, because it impairs the obligation of contracts. Rudd *v.* Schlatter, 1 Litt. 19.

2. No State shall, without the consent of the Congress, lay any imposts (*a*) or duties on imports or exports, except what may be absolutely necessary for executing its inspection laws; and the net produce of all duties and imposts, laid by any State on imports or exports, shall be for the use of the treasury of the United States, and all such laws shall be subject to the revision and control of the Congress. No State shall, without the consent of Congress, lay any duty of tonnage (*b*), •keep troops or ships of war in time of peace, enter into any agreement (*c*) or compact with another State, or with a foreign power, or engage in war, unless actually invaded, or in such imminent danger as will not admit of delay.

Duties.

(*a*) An impost or duty on imports is a custom or tax levied on articles brought into a country, and is most usually secured before the importer is allowed to exercise his rights of ownership over them, because evasions of the law can be prevented more certainly by executing it while the articles are in its custody. It would not, however, be less an impost or duty on the articles if it were levied on them after they were landed. The policy and consequent practice of levying or securing the duty before or on entering the port does not limit the power to that state of things, nor consequently the prohibition, unless the true meaning of the clause so confines it. Imports are things imported. They are the articles themselves which are brought into the country. A duty on imports, then, is not merely a duty on the act of importation, but is a duty on the thing imported. Brown *v.* State, 12 Wheat. 419; Bode *v.* State, 7 Gill, 326; Hinson *v.* Lott, 8 Wall. 128; S. C. 40 Ala. 123; vide State *v.* Sluby, 2 H. & J. 480.

There is no difference in principle between a power to prohibit the sale of an article and a power to prohibit its introduction into the country. The one would be a necessary consequence of the other. No goods would be imported if none could be sold. No object of any description can be accomplished by laying a duty on importation, which may not be accomplished with equal certainty by laying a duty on the thing imported. It is obvious that the same power which imposes a light duty can impose a very heavy one, one which amounts to a prohibition. Brown *v.* State, 12 Wheat. 419.

A duty on imports is not, taken in its literal sense, confined to a duty levied while the article is entering the country, but extends to a duty levied after it has entered the country. Brown *v.* State, 12 Wheat. 419.

When the importer has so acted upon the thing imported that it has become incorporated and mixed up with the mass of property in the country, it has, perhaps, lost its distinctive character as an import, and has become subject to the taxing power of the State; but while remaining the property of the importer in his warehouse in the original form or package in which it was imported, a tax upon it is a duty on imports. Brown *v.* State, 12 Wheat. 419; Wynne *v.* Wright, 4 Dev. & Bat. 19; License Cases, 5 How. 504; S. C. 13 N. H. 536; State *v.* Charleston, 10 Rich. 240; State *v.* Shapleigh, 27 Mo. 344; State *v.* North, 27 Mo. 464; Low *v.* Austin, 13 Wall. 29.

This rule seems to have been suggested from that familiar principle, that if one mingle his money with another's so that the proportion can not be distinguished in the mass, the other shall have the whole. In some States and respecting some articles, this rule might operate with justness and propriety, but by far the greater proportion of foreign commodities, and those from other States, are never mixed with the mass of property, so as to lose their identity. Raguet *v.* Wade, 4 Ohio, 107.

If an importer breaks up his packages and travels with them as an itinerant peddler, or applies them to his own private use, they become incorporated with the general mass of property, and are liable to taxation. Brown *v.* State, 12 Wheat. 419.

After imported goods have become incorporated and mixed up with the mass of property in the country, a tax may constitutionally be imposed upon them, although they are taxed by the name of goods imported, or not of the production of the State, for a State may exercise its discretion in selecting the objects of taxation amongst those which are subject to taxation. Wynne *v.* Wright, 4 Dev. & Bat. 19; Biddle *v.* Comm. 13 S. & R. 405; Cowles *v.* Brittain, 2 Hawks, 204; Cummings *v.* Savannah, R. M. Charlt. 26; People *v.* Coleman, 4 Cal. 46; Tracey *v.* State, 3 Mo. 3; contra, State *v.* North, 27 Mo. 464.

An import ceases in the constitutional sense to be an import, the moment the importer becomes a vender, and sells the article. In the hands of the retailer or distributor, it is an article of the internal trade and commerce of the State. State *v.* Peckham, 3 R. I. 289.

After the imported goods have become incorporated with the general mass of property in the State, the State in laying taxes may discriminate against them in favor of domestic productions, and impose a higher tax on the former. Davis *v.* Dashiel, Phillips, 114.

If a State singles out imports as a special object for any impost or duty, it is unlawful, whether the imported goods remain with the original consignee or pass through the hands of any number of purchasers. People *v.* Moring, 47 Barb. 642; S. C. 3 Abb. App. 539.

While goods retain their character as imports, a tax upon them in any shape by a State, is within the constitutional prohibition, although the tax is the same as on any other property in the State. Low *v.* Austin, 13 Wall. 29.

The term "import," is used in the fiscal sense in the Constitution, and in that acceptation is wholly inapplicable to the interchange of commodities among the States, but is restricted in its meaning to such commodities only as are imported from abroad, introduced into the country through its several ports of entry, and are subject to the the taxing power of the Federal Government. A State tax on articles brought from another State, is not a tax on imports. License Cases, 5 How. 504; S. C. 13 N. H. 536; State *v.* Pinckney, 10 Rich. 474; State *v.* Charleston, 10 Rich. 240; Hinson *v.* Lott, 8 Wall. 148; s. c. 40 Ala. 123; Woodruff *v.* Parham, 41 Ala. 334; s. c. 8 Wall. 123; State Tax on Railway Gross Receipts, 15 Wall. 284; Harrison *v.* Mayor, 11 Miss. 581; Board *v.* Pleasants, 23 La. Ann. 349.

The power of imposing or levying duties on imports is a branch of the taxing power. This prohibition is an exception from the acknowledged power of the States to levy taxes. Gibbons *v.* Ogden, 9 Wheat. 1 ; s. c. 17 Johns. 488.; 4 Johns. Ch. 150.

The term "imports," means not only the act of importation, but the articles imported. Wynne *v.* Wright, 4 Dev. & Bat. 19.

If Congress has not established a port of entry within a State, for the introduction of foreign imports, the State can not pass an act that would be repugnant to this provision of the Constitution. Beall *v.* State, 4 Blackf. 107.

The prohibition is general, and not confined to a particular mode. A tax on the sale of an article imported only for sale is a tax on the article itself. A tax on the occupation of an importer is a tax on importation. It must add to the price of the article, and be paid by the consumer or by the importer himself in like manner as a direct duty on the article itself. This the State has no right to do. State *v.* North, 27 Mo. 464; Brown *v.* State, 12 Wheat. 419; License Cases, 5 How. 504; s. c. 13 N. H. 536; vide Biddle *v.* Comm. 13 S. & R. 405.

Pilot fees or penalties are not embraced within the words imposts or duties on imports, exports or tonnage. This provision was intended to operate upon subjects actually existing, and well understood when the Constitution was formed. Imposts and duties on imports, exports and tonnage were then known to the commerce of a civilized world as distinct from fees and charges for pilotage, and from the penalties by which commercial States enforced their pilot laws, as they were from charges for wharfage or towage or any other local port charges for services rendered to vessels or cargoes. It can not be denied that a tonnage duty or an impost on imports or exports may be levied under the name of pilot dues or penalties, and it is the thing and not the name which is to be considered. Cooley *v.* Philadelphia, 12 How. 299.

A State may impose a tax upon its citizens in proportion to the amount they are respectively worth, and the importing merchant is liable to this assessment like any other citizen, and is chargeable according to the amount of his property, whether it consist of money engaged in trade or of imported goods which he proposes to sell, or any other property of which he is owner. License Cases, 5 How. 504; s. c. 13 N. H. 536; State *v.* Pinckney, 10 Rich. 474.

By payment of the duty the importer purchases the right to dispose of his merchandise as well as bring it into the country. Brown *v.* State, 12 Wheat. 419; Hinson *v.* Lott, 8 Wall. 148; s. c. 40 Ala. 123.

A tax on water craft in which goods are sold by retail is valid, although the goods are brought from another State by a citizen of that State. When such a citizen comes into the State and makes sales, there is no reason why he should be exempted from the operation of its laws. Harrison *v.* Mayor, 11 Miss. 581.

A State may impose a penalty upon those who sell articles which are not of the product of the United States without a license. Beall *v.* State, 4 Blackf. 107; Raguet *v.* Wade, 4 Ohio, 107; People *v.* Coleman, 4 Cal. 46.

A statute requiring a license of retail dealers of spirituous liquors is constitutional. The regulation and superintendence of the houses and places where spirituous liquors are sold is an important subject of internal police, and is within the jurisdiction of the State government. State *v.* Peckham, 3 R. I. 289; Perdue *v.* Ellis, 18 Geo. 586; State *v.* Wheeler, 25 Conn. 290; Comm. *v.* Kimball, 41 Mass. 359; Ingersoll *v.* Skinner, 1 Denio, 540; Jones *v.* People, 14 Ill. 196; Smith *v.* People, 1 Parker Cr. Cas. 583; Comm. *v.* Clapp, 71 Mass. 97; License Cases, 5 How. 504; s. c. 13 N. H. 536; City *v.* Ahrens, 4 Strobh. 241; State *v.* Moore, 14 N. H. 451; Keller *v.* State, 11 Md. 525; Santo *v.* State, 2 Iowa, 165; State *v.* Donehey, 8 Iowa, 396.

A tax on legacies when the legatee is neither a citizen of the United States nor domiciled in that State is valid. It has no concern with commerce or with imports or exports. The mere fact that the owner intends to convert his property into money and send it abroad, does not relieve it from taxation Mager *v.* Grima, 8 How. 490.

A tax on auction sales of imported goods is a duty on imports, and invalid. People *v.* Moring, 3 Abb. App. 539; s. c. 47 Barb. 642.

A tax or duty on a bill of lading, although differing in form from a duty on the article shipped, is in substance the same thing; for a bill of lading, or some written instrument of the same import is necessarily always associated with every shipment of articles of commerce from the ports of one country to those of another. A tax on a bill of lading for articles exported is therefore void, as a tax on exports. Almy *v.* People, 24 How. 169; Brumagim *v.* Tillinghast, 18 Cal. 265.

A State may tax capital, although it is continuously invested in cotton purchased for exportation. People *v.* Tax Commissioner, 17 N. Y. Supr. 255.

A State law requiring hawkers and peddlers to take out a license is not a duty on imports. Comm. *v.* Ober, 66 Mass. 493.

A provision in the charter of a railroad corporation that all tonnage carried on the railroad shall be subject to a certain toll or duty per mile, is not a duty on imports or exports. Penn. R. R. Co. *v.* Comm. 3 Grant, 128.

A State law imposing a transit duty on foreign corporations for all goods and persons carried or transported in the State, is not a tax on imports or exports. State *v.* Del. L. & W. R. R. Co. 30 N. J. 473; s. c. 31 N. J. 531.

A tax upon the gross receipts of an express company engaged in carrying articles between States is valid. Southern Express Co. v. Hood, 15 Rich. 66.

A stamp tax on foreign bills of exchange drawn in the State, is not an impost or tax on exports. Ex parte James P. Martin, 7 Nev. 140.

A tax upon the gross sales of a party who purchases articles in their original packages from the importer, is not a tax on imports. Waring v. Mayor, 8 Wall. 110; S. C. 4 Ala. 139.

A tax upon a broker's sales of imported merchandise, which has not become incorporated with the property of the State, is void. People v. Moring, 3 Abb. App. 539; S. C. 47 Barb. 642.

A State law requiring a license from non-resident traders to vend foreign merchandise, is not a tax on imports or exports. Sears v. Commissioners, 36 Ind. 267.

A State may impose a higher tax on articles bought from non-residents than on those bought from manufacturers who reside in the State. Davis v. Dashiel, Phillips, 114.

A tax on sales is a tax on the proceeds, and not a tax on the imports. State v. Pinckney, 18 Rich. 474.

The removal or destruction of infectious or unsound articles is an exercise of the power of inspection, and forms an express exception to the prohibition. Brown v. State, 12 Wheat. 419.

A State has a right to lay a tax upon imports, the object of which is to pay for services performed in inspecting the articles, if the law is passed in good faith, and is not resorted to as a means of indirectly raising revenue. Green v. State, R. M. Charlt. 368.

The power to pass inspection laws involves the power to enforce such laws by adequate provisions for the remuneration of the officers charged with the duty of inspection. Such fees are not imposts. Addison v. Saulnier, 19 Cal. 82.

Inspection laws may apply to imported articles as well as to those intended for exportation. Neilson v. Garza, 2 Woods, 287.

Whether the fee allowed by a State law is excessive or not is a question that can only be determined by Congress. Neilson v. Garza, 2 Woods, 287.

The object of this prohibition is to protect both the vessel and cargo from State taxation while *in transitu*, and this prohibition can not be evaded and the same result effected by calling it a tax on the passengers or the master. Passenger Cases, 7 How. 283; S. C. 45 Mass. 282; People v. Downer, 7 Cal. 169; contra, In re Crandall, 1 Nev. 294.

Tonnage.

(*b*) A duty of tonnage signifies a tax, custom or toll. Sheffield *v.* Parsons, 3 Stew. & Port. 302.

A duty of tonnage, in the most obvious sense of the term, imports a tax or duty proportioned to the tonnage or size of the vessel. Johnson *v.* Drummond, 20 Gratt. 419; Inman Steamship Co. *v.* Tinker, 94 U. S. 238.

It is not only a *pro rata* tax which is prohibited, but any duty on the ship, whether a fixed sum upon its whole tonnage, or a sum to be ascertained by comparing the amount of tonnage with the rate of duty. Steamship Co. *v.* Port Wardens, 6 Wall. 31.

A duty or tax, or burden, imposed under the authority of the State, which is by the law imposing it to be measured by the capacity of the vessel, and is in its essence a contribution claimed for the privilege of arriving and departing from a port of the United States, is within the prohibition. Tobin *v.* Vicksburg, 4 Cent. L. J. 280; Cannon *v.* New Orleans, 20 Wall. 577; S. C. 27 La. Ann. 16.

Taxes levied by a State upon ships and vessels as instruments of commerce are within the prohibition, and it makes no difference whether the ships or vessels taxed belong to the citizens of the State which levies the tax, or the citizens of another State. State Tonnage Tax Cases, 12 Wall. 204; S. C. 3 Grant, 128.

The privilege extends to all vessels entitled to the privileges of vessels employed in the coasting trade, whether employed in commercial intercourse between ports in different States or between different ports in the same State. State Tonnage Tax Cases, 12 Wall. 204; S. C. 3 Grant, 128.

A tonnage tax is a means prohibited to the States, and can not be employed as a means of enforcing some law which is within their constitutional authority. Johnson *v.* Drummond, 20 Gratt. 419.

The mere fact that a tax does not go into the public coffers does not prevent its being a duty of tonnage. What is done with the money can not affect the question. Alexander *v.* Railroad Co. 3 Strobh. 594; Sheffield *v.* Parsons, 3 Stew. & Port. 302.

It is immaterial what form of expression is used in describing the tax or the object or subject, if, upon looking at its real character and effect, it is found to come within the meaning of a duty of tonnage. Thus the tax, instead of being called a tax on the vessel, may be called a tax upon the master or cargo; it may purport to be a tax upon some privilege to be enjoyed by the vessel, as the privilege of coming into a certain port or of riding at a particular anchorage, or of being served as she may have occasion by the wardens of a port, or the privilege of engaging in a particular trade, as the trade in wood, or corn, or oysters; yet, if really and substantially it is a duty of tonnage, it is equally within the prohibition as if the tax had been called by its right name. Johnson *v.* Drummond, 20 Gratt. 419.

A State law imposing half pilotage fees on vessels refusing to receive a pilot is not a duty, impost or excise. Cooley *v.* Philadelphia, 12 How. 299.

A charge for services rendered, or conveniences provided, is in no sense a tax or duty. It is not a hindrance or impediment to free navigation. The prohibition is designed to guard against local hindrances to trade and carriage by vessels, not to relieve them from liability to claims for assistance rendered and facilities furnished for trade and commerce. It is a tax or duty that is prohibited, something imposed by virtue of sovereignty, not claimed in the right of proprietorship. K. N. P. Co. *v.* Keokuk, 10 C. L. N. 91; s. c. 5 Cent. L. J. 504.

A charge for wharfage is not a tax or duty. It is an assertion, not of sovereignty, but of a right of property. K. N. P. Co. *v.* Keokuk, 10 C. L. N. 91; s. c. 5 Cent. L. J. 504; Cannon *v.* New Orleans, 20 Wall. 577; s. c. 27 La. Ann. 16.

The character of the service is the same whether the wharf is built and offered for use by a State, a municipal corporation, or a private individual. K. N. P. Co. *v.* Keokuk, 10 C. L. N. 91; s. c. 5 Cent. L. J. 504; Cannon *v.* New Orleans, 20 Wall. 577; s. c. 27 La. Ann. 16.

The State may regulate the compensation for wharfage, so as to prevent extortion. Cannon *v.* New Orleans, 20 Wall. 577; s. c. 27 La. Ann. 16.

A statute regulating dues for wharfage is not a statute imposing tonnage duties. The owners of the shores of navigable waters may, at considerable expense, make them convenient and useful for the masters of vessels, and the right to compensation results from the use of those conveniences. Sterrett *v.* Houston, 14 Tex. 153; Municipality *v.* Pease, 2 La. Ann. 538; The Ann Ryan, 7 Ben. 20.

A tax which is by its terms due from all vessels arriving and stopping in a port, without regard to the place where they may stop, whether it be in the channel of the stream or out in the bay, or landed at a natural river bank, can not be treated as compensation for the use of a wharf. Cannon *v.* New Orleans, 20 Wall. 577; s. c. 27 La. Ann. 16.

When a city or other municipality is the owner of wharves or piers built by its own money, to assist vessels landing within its limits, in the pursuit of their business, it may exact and receive a reasonable compensation for the use thereof, the same as individuals. Cannon *v.* New Orleans, 20 Wall. 577; s. c. 27 La. Ann. 16; Worsley *v.* Municipality, 9 Rob. 324.

Neither a State nor a municipal corporation can be permitted to impose a tax on tonnage under cover of laws ostensibly passed to collect wharfage. K. N. P. Co. *v.* Keokuk, 10 C. L. N. 91.

The prohibition was intended to protect the freedom of commerce, and nothing more, and should be so construed as to carry out that intent. K. N. P. Co. *v.* Keokuk, 10 C. L. N. 91.

If a municipal corporation improves a wharf on part of the water front, it may impose a reasonable wharfage for the use thereof, although it is graduated according to the tonnage of the vessel. N. W. Union Packet Co. *v.* St. Louis. 4 Cent. L. J. 58; Keokuk *v.* Packet Co. 4 Cent. L. J. 276; S. C. 10 C. L. N. 91; 5 Cent. L. J. 504.

An ordinance regulating the charges for wharfage, may be enforced, unless the defendant pleads and proves that they are beyond the limits of just compensation. Keokuk *v.* Packet Co. 4 Cent. L. J. 276.

A statute authorizing the collection of wharfage from vessels landing articles other than the production of the State, at any public wharf, is unconstitutional. Wharf Case, 3 Bland, 361.

A statute allowing fees to a harbor master for assigning a vessel to a berth at a wharf, is not a tonnage duty, although the fees are ascertained by the burden or tonnage. State *v.* Charleston, 4 Rich. 286; Benedict *v.* Vanderbilt, 1 Robt. 194; Port Wardens *v.* The Martha J. Ward, 14 La. Ann 289; Master *v.* Prats, 10 Rob. 459.

A State law requiring every vessel to pay a certain fee to the port warden or harbor master, whether he renders any services or not. is a duty on tonnage. Steamship Co. *v.* Port Wardens, 6 Wall. 31; Sheffield *v.* Parsons, 3 Stew. & Port. 302; Hackley *v.* Geraghty, 34 N. J. 332; Alexander *v.* Railroad Co. 3 Strobh. 594; Inman Steamship Co. *v.* Tinker, 94 U. S. 238; contra, Port Wardens *v.* The Charles Morgan, 14 La. Ann. 595; Port Wardens *v.* The Martha J. Ward, 14 La. Ann. 289; City *v.* The Nautilus, 8 I. R. R. 91.

A toll or duty on all tonnage carried on a railroad, at a certain rate per mile, is not a duty of tonnage. Penn. Railroad Co. *v.* Comm. 3 Grant, 128.

A municipal ordinance which imposes a charge on a vessel, to be regulated according to the tonnage, for arriving at and departing from a port, and not merely for the use of the wharf. is void. Northwestern U. P. Co. *v.* St. Paul, 3 Dillon, 454; S. C. 7 C. L. N. 331.

A toll to be applied to pay for improvements made upon a navigable river, is not in the nature of a tonnage duty or any duty at all, upon the vessel, within the meaning of the Constitution, any more than a toll at a turnpike gate is a duty upon the carriage. It is a compensation exacted for a privilege conferred, and in proportion to it. It is no more a tonnage duty than laws regulating wharfage or port charges. Thames Bank *v.* Lovell, 18 Conn. 500.

A State can not lay a tonnage duty on vessels employed as lighters for other vessels engaged in foreign commerce, although they ply exclusively within the waters of the State. Lott *v.* Morgan, 41 Ala. 246.

A statute requiring vessels carrying oysters taken in the State, to take out a license and pay therefor a tax of a certain amount for every ton that the vessel may measure, imposes a duty of tonnage, and is void. Johnson *v.* Drummond, 20 Gratt. 419.

A State law requiring a vessel to pay a fee to a pilot for inspection, is valid. Baker *v.* Wise, 16 Gratt. 139.

A State can not impose a duty of tonnage for the purpose of raising a revenue in order to defray the expenses of its quarantine regulations. Peete *v.* Morgan, 19 Wall. 581.

A State may tax a vessel owned by a citizen of the State, and engaged wholly and entirely in plying on waters exclusively within the State, although it is registered and enrolled by the United States. Lott *v.* Mobile Trade Co. 42 Ala. 578; Lott *v.* Cox, 43 Ala. 697.

A tax upon a vessel according to her valuation as property, and as part of the taxable property of the place where she is owned and registered, is not a duty of tonnage. The North Cape, 6 Biss. 505; State Tonnage Tax Cases, 12 Wall. 204; S. C. 3 Grant, 128; Perry *v.* Torrance, 8 Ohio, 521; State *v.* Charleston, 4 Rich. 286; Battle *v.* Corporation, 9 Ala. 234.

A tax levied on a vessel wholly irrespective of its value as property, and solely and exclusively on the basis of its tonnage, is a duty of tonnage. State Tonnage Tax Cases, 12 Wall. 204; S. C. 3 Grant, 128.

Agreement.

(*c*) The words "agreement" and "compact" can not be construed as synonymous with one another, and still less can either of them be held to mean the same thing with the word "treaty" in the preceding clause, into which the States are positively and unconditionally forbidden to enter, and which even the consent of Congress can not authorize. The words "agreement" and "compact" evidently mean something more than the word "treaty," and were designed to make the prohibition more comprehensive. The word "agreement" does not necessarily import any direct and express stipulation, nor is it necessary that it should be in writing. If there is a verbal understanding to which both parties have assented, and upon which both are acting, it is an "agreement." The use of all these terms, "treaty," "agreement," "compact," show that it was the intention of the framers of the Constitution, to use the broadest and most comprehensive terms, and that they anxiously desired to cut off all connection or communication between a State and a foreign power. The word "agreement" should therefore receive its most extended signification, and be so applied as to prohibit every agreement, written or verbal, formal or informal, positive or implied by the mutual understanding of the parties. The prohibition applies not only to a continuing agreement, embracing classes of cases or a succession of cases, but to any agreement whatever. Holmes *v.* Jennison, 14 Pet. 540.

No State can enter into an agreement with a foreign power in regard to the surrender of fugitives from justice. Holmes *v.* Jennison, 14 Pet. 540.

Agreement between States.

This provision is obviously intended to guard the rights and interests of the other States, and to prevent any compact and agreement between any two States which may affect the interests of the others injuriously. The right and the duty to protect these interests is vested in the General Government. Florida *v.* Georgia, 17 How. 478.

This prohibition only applies to such an agreement or compact as is in its nature political, or more properly, perhaps, such as may in any wise conflict with the powers which the States, by the adoption of the Constitution, have delegated to the General Government. This appears from the context, and from the reason and spirit of the prohibition. Union Railroad Co. *v.* East. Tenn. Railroad Co. 14 Geo. 327.

Two States may, by separate acts, authorize a corporation to erect a bridge over a navigable river flowing between them. If the charters are granted to different corporations with power to unite, their agreement so to do would not be an agreement or compact between the States. Dover *v.* Portsmouth Bridge, 17 N. H. 200.

A question of boundary between States is, in its nature, a political question to be settled by compact made by the political departments of the government. Florida *v.* Georgia, 17 How. 478.

It is not necessary that the consent of Congress to an agreement between the States shall be given in the form of an express and formal statement of every proposition of the agreement and of its consent thereto. Virginia *v.* West Virginia, 11 Wall. 39.

The Constitution makes no provision respecting the mode or form in which the consent of Congress is to be signified, very properly leaving that matter to the wisdom of that body to be decided upon according to the ordinary rules of law and right reason. The only question in cases which involve that point is, has Congress, by some positive act in relation to such agreement, signified the consent of that body to its validity? Green *v.* Biddle, 8 Wheat. 1; Canal Co. *v.* Railroad Co. 4 G. & J. 1.

A compact between States is binding upon the legislatures of those States. Green *v.* Biddle, 8 Wheat. 1.

A compact between two States can not operate as a restriction upon the powers of Congress under the Constitution. State *v.* Wheeling Bridge Co. 18 How. 421; Wilson *v.* Mason, 1 Cranch, 45.

ARTICLE II.

SECTION I.

1. The executive power shall be vested in a President of the United States of America. He shall hold his office during the term of four years, and, together with the Vice-president, chosen for the same term, be elected as follows :

The theory of the Constitution is that the great powers of the government are divided into separate departments, and so far as these powers are derived from the Constitution, the departments may be regarded as independent of each other. The executive power is vested in the President, and, as far as his powers are derived from the Constitution, he is beyond the reach of any other department, except in the mode prescribed by the Constitution through the impeaching power. Kendall *v.* U. S. 12 Pet. 524; S. C. 5 Cranch C. C. 163.

The President is invested with certain important political powers, in the exercise of which he is to use his discretion, and is accountable only to his country in his political character, and to his own conscience. To aid him in the performance of these duties, he is authorized to appoint certain officers, who act by his authority and in conformity with his orders. In such cases their acts are his acts, and whatever opinion may be entertained of the manner in which executive discretion may be used, still there exists, and can exist, no power to control that discretion. The subjects are political. They respect the nation and not individual rights ; and being intrusted to the executive, the decision of the executive is conclusive. Marbury *v.* Madison, 1 Cranch, 137.

The President has no power to dispense with or forbid the execution of any law. Kendall *v.* U. S. 12 Pet. 524 ; S. C. 5 Cranch C. C. 163 ; U. S. *v.* Smith, Trial of Smith & Ogden, 80.

The President has no common-law prerogative to interdict commercial intercourse with any nation, or to revive any act whose operation has expired. The Orono, 1 Gallis. 137.

If the President assumes powers which should have the authority or sanction of Congress, a ratification cures the defect. Prize Cases, 2 Black, 635.

The President is exempt from the writ of *habeas corpus*, not because he is above the law, or because he can do no wrong, but because he can not be held responsible except through the medium of impeachment; and to allow the writ to go to him would involve the necessity of punishing him for a refusal to obey it, and such a power does not belong to the judiciary. In re Geo. B. Keeler, Hemp. 306.

There are certain political duties imposed upon many officers in the executive departments, the discharge of which is under the direction of the President. Kendall *v.* U. S. 12 Pet. 524; S. C. 5 Cranch C. C. 163.

Congress may impose upon any executive officer any duty it may think proper, which is not repugnant to any right which is secured and protected by the Constitution; and in such cases the duty and responsibility grow out of and are subject to the control of law. Kendall *v.* U. S. 12 Pet. 524; S. C. 5 Cranch C. C. 163; Marbury *v.* Madison, 1 Cranch, 137.

Congress may authorize the President to restrict or regulate the introduction of merchandise into a Territory, under such penalties as Congress may prescribe. The Louisa Simpson, 2 Saw. 57; U. S. *v.* The Francis Hatch, 13 A. L. Reg. 289.

'2. Each State shall appoint, in such manner as the legislature thereof may direct, a number of electors, equal to the whole number of senators and representatives to which the State may be entitled in the Congress; but no senator or representative, or person holding an office of trust or profit under the United States, shall be appointed an elector.

When the legislature of a State directs the manner of appointment of electors, that law has its authority solely from the Constitution. It is a law passed in pursuance of the Constitution. Ex parte Henry E. Hayne, 9 C. L. N. 106; S. C. 1 Hughes, 571.

If the electors are elected by the people, the disqualification can not be removed by resigning the office, unless the resignation takes place before the election. In re Geo. H. Corliss, 16 A. L. Reg. 15.

The disqualification of the person having the highest number of votes does not have the effect to elect the minority candidate. In re Geo. H. Corliss, 16 A. L. Reg. 15.

Where the votes for electors are required to be canvassed by a returning board, the Houses may take notice of the fact that the board had no returns before it at all, or that the board which pretended to act was not a legal board. Electoral Count.

A judgment on a *quo warranto* against the electors can not affect the validity of votes previously cast on the day appointed by Congress for that purpose. Electoral Count.

No State legislature can change the appointment of electors after they have been elected and given their votes. Electoral Count.

The appointment of electors and mode of appointment belong exclusively to the State. Congress has nothing to do with it, and no control over it, except that Congress is empowered to determine the time of choosing the electors and the day on which they shall give their votes. In all other respects, the jurisdiction and power of the State are controlling and exclusive until the functions of the electors have been performed. Electoral Count.

If a person appointed an elector, has no official connection with the Federal Government when he gives his vote, such vote is not liable to exception. A disqualification at the time of the election is not material, if such disqualification ceases before he acts as an elector. Electoral Count.

If a person who is disqualified under the laws of the State, is elected and casts his vote, the vote must be counted. Electoral Count.

[3. The electors shall meet in their respective States, and vote by ballot for two persons, of whom one at least shall not be an inhabitant of the same State with themselves. And they shall make a list of all the persons voted for, and of the number of votes for each; which list they shall sign and certify, and transmit sealed to the seat of the Government of the United States, directed to the president of the Senate. The president of the Senate shall, in the presence of the Senate and House of Representatives, open all the certificates, and the votes shall then be counted. The person having the greatest number of votes shall be the President, if such number be a majority of the whole number of electors appointed; and if there be more than one who have such majority, and have an equal number of votes, then the House of Representatives shall immediately choose, by ballot, one of them for President; and if no person have a majority, then, from the five highest on the list, the said House shall, in like manner, choose the President. But, in choosing the President, the votes shall be taken by States, the representation from each State having one vote ; a quorum for this purpose shall consist of a member or members from two-thirds of the States, and a majority of all the States shall be necessary to a choice. In every case, after the choice of the President, the person having the greatest number of votes of the electors, shall be the Vice-president. But if there should remain two or more who have equal votes, the Senate shall choose from them, by ballot, the Vice-president.]

4. The Congress may determine the time of choosing the electors, and the day on which they shall give their votes; which day shall be the same throughout the United States.

5. No person, except a natural born citizen, or a citizen of the United States at the time of the adoption of this Constitution, shall be eligible to the office of of President ; neither shall any person be eligible to that office, who shall not have attained to the age of thirty-five years, and been fourteen years a resident within the United States.

6. In case of the removal of the President from office, or of his death, resignation, or inability to discharge the powers and duties of the said office, the same shall devolve on the Vice-president, and the Congress may, by law, provide for the case of removal, death, resignation, or inability, both of the President and Vice-president, declaring what officer shall then act as President, and such officer shall act accordingly, until the disability be removed, or a President shall be elected.

7. The President shall, at stated times, receive for his services a compensation, which shall neither be increased nor diminished during the period for which he shall have been elected, and he shall not receive within that period any other emolument from the United States, or any of them.

8. Before he enter on the execution of his office, he shall take the following oath or affirmation :

9. " I do solemnly swear [or affirm] that I will faithfully execute the office of President of the United

States, and will, to the best of my ability, preserve, protect, and defend the Constitution of the United States."

The oath to preserve, protect and defend the Constitution simply obliges the President to obey the Constitution himself, and to use the power which that instrument confers upon him, and none else, to cause others to obey it. Griffin v. Wilcox, 21 Ind. 370.

SECTION II.

1. The president shall be commander in chief (*a*) of the army and navy of the United States, and of the militia of the several States, when called into the actual service of the United States; he may require the opinion, in writing, of the principal officer in each of the executive departments, upon any subject relating to the duties of their respective offices; and he shall have power to grant reprieves and pardons (*b*) for offenses against the United States, except in cases of impeachment.

Military Power.

(*a*) The President may establish rules and regulations for the government of the army. The power to establish implies necessarily the power to modify or repeal or create anew. U. S. v. Eliason, 16 Pet. 291; U. S. v. Webster, 2 Ware, 46.

An instruction by the executive to a naval officer can not legalize an act which without it would have been a plain trespass. Little v. Barreme, 2 Cranch, 170.

The President has the authority during a war, to employ secret agents to enter the enemy's lines and obtain information respecting the strength, resources, and movements of the enemy, and contracts to compensate such agents are so far binding upon the Government, as to render it lawful for the President to direct payment of the amount stipulated out of the contingent fund under his control. Totten v. U. S. 92 U. S. 105.

If war is made by invasion of a foreign nation, the President is not only authorized but bound to resist force by force. He does not initiate the war, but is bound to accept the challenge without waiting for any special legislative authority. The Prize Cases, 2 Black, 635.

The President is bound to meet a civil war in the shape in which it presents itself, without waiting for Congress to baptize it with a name. The Prize Cases, 2 Black, 635.

The President has the power *jure belli* to declare a blockade of a hostile port in a civil as well as in a foreign war. The Tropic Wind, 24 Law Rep. 144; The Prize Cases, 2 Black, 635.

Whether the President, in fulfilling his duties as commander in chief in suppressing an insurrection, has met with such armed hostile resistance, and a civil war of such alarming proportions as will compel him to accord to them the character of belligerents, is a question to be decided by him, and the courts must be governed by the decisions and acts of the political department of the government. The Prize Cases, 2 Black, 635.

The power of the President, as commander in chief, though not defined by the Constitution, is limited by the laws and usages of nations. Of these laws and usages there is no principle better settled than that martial law is restricted to those places which are the theatre of war, and to their immediate vicinity. In re Nicholas Kemp, 16 Wis. 359; Ex parte Milligan, 4 Wall. 2.

The right of the President to temporarily govern localities through his military officers is derived solely from the fact that he is the commander in chief of the army, and is to see the laws executed, and he can exercise it to just the extent that a commanding general in the army of the United States could, and no farther. Where the laws are, or may be, executed without the interference of the President with the military force, he has no right thus to interfere. Griffin *v.* Wilcox, 21 Ind. 370.

The Constitution does not invest the President with power to arrest or imprison, or to authorize another to arrest or imprison, any person not subject to military law at any time or under any exigency, without some order, writ or precept or process of some civil court of competent jurisdiction. He can not extend martial law beyond the sphere of military operations. Jones *v.* Seward, 40 Barb. 563.

The right of a military officer to govern by martial law arises upon the fact of existing or immediately impending force, at a given place and time, against legal authority which the civil authority is incompetent to overcome, and it is exercised precisely on the principle on which self-defense justifies the use of force by individuals. Griffin *v.* Wilcox, 21 Ind. 370.

Martial law is the law of force, applied to govern persons and places where the civil law is expelled, and its officers rendered unable to execute it by forcible resistance. The right thus temporarily and locally to exercise martial law in case of necessity, is the war power of the President, and is all the war power that he possesses by virtue of which he can assume to govern, independently of the civil law. Griffin *v.* Wilcox, 21 Ind. 370.

The President has a right to govern through his military officers when and where the civil power of the United States is suspended by force. Where force prevails, martial law may be exercised. Griffin *v.* Wilcox, 21 Ind. 370; Ex parte Milligan, 4 Wall. 2.

The true test in cases of civil war is whether the civil authorities are able, by the ordinary legal process, to preserve order, punish offenders, and compel obedience to the laws. If they are, then the military commander has no jurisdiction. If, on the other hand, through the disloyalty of the civil magistrates, or the insurrectionary spirit of the people, the laws can not be enforced and order maintained, then martial law takes the place of civil law wherever there is a sufficient military force to execute it. In re Nicholas Kemp, 16 Wis. 359.

The precise limits of the jurisdiction of a military commander, in cases arising near the scene of strife, must be determined according to the circumstances of each case. In re Nicholas Kemp, 16 Wis. 359.

Martial law can not arise from a threatened invasion. The necessity must be actual and present, the invasion real, such as effectually closes the courts and deposes the civil administration. Ex parte Milligan, 4 Wall. 2.

In all parts of the country, where the courts are open and the civil power is not expelled by force, the Constitution and the laws rule, and no citizen not connected with the army can be punished by the military power of the United States, nor is he amenable to military orders. Griffin *v.* Wilcox, 21 Ind. 370; Skeen *v.* Monkeimer, 21 Ind. 1; In re Nicholas Kemp, 16 Wis. 359; Ex parte Milligan, 4 Wall. 2; Johnson *v.* Jones, 44 Ill. 142.

As necessity creates martial law, so it limits its duration, for if this government is continued after the courts are reinstated, it is a gross usurpation of power. Ex parte Milligan, 4 Wall. 2.

After an insurrection has been suppressed, and a provisional government established, and a State Constitution adopted, a citizen can not be tried by a court martial for an alleged crime. Ex parte James Eagan, 5 Blatch. 319.

Martial law is allowed only in case of necessity, and this necessity must be shown affirmatively by the party assuming to exercise this extraordinary power over the life, liberty and property of a citizen. Ex parte James Eagan, 5 Blatch. 319.

The United States, it is true, may extend its boundaries by conquest or treaty, and may demand the cession of territory as the condition of peace, in order to indemnify its citizens for the injuries they have suffered, or to reimburse the Government for the expenses of the war. But this can be done only by the treaty making power or the legislative authority, and is not a part of the power conferred upon the President by the declaration of war. His duty and his power are purely military. As commander in chief he is authorized to direct the movements of the naval and military forces placed by law at his command, and to employ them in the manner he may deem most effectual to harass, conquer and subdue the enemy. He may invade the hostile country and subject it to the sovereignty and authority of the United States. But his conquests do not enlarge the boundaries of the Union, nor extend the operation of our institutions and laws beyond the limits before assigned to them by legislative authority. Fleming v. Page, 9 How. 603.

If the conquered territory is ceded by the treaty of peace, the acquisition is confirmed, and the ceded territory becomes a part of the nation to which it is annexed, either on the terms stipulated in the treaty of cession, or on such as its new master shall impose. On such transfer the relations of the inhabitants with each other do not undergo any change. Their relations with their former sovereign are dissolved, and new relations are created between them and the government which has acquired the territory. The same act which transfers their country transfers the allegiance of those who remain in it, and the law which may be denominated political is changed, although that which regulates the intercourse and general conduct of individuals remains in force until altered by the newly created power. Am. Ins. Co. v. Canter, 1 Pet. 511; Leitensdorfer v. Webb, 20 How. 176.

The usage of the world is, if a nation be not entirely subdued, to consider the holding of conquered territory as a mere military occupation until its fate shall be determined by a treaty of peace. Am. Ins. Co. v. Canter, 1 Pet. 511.

Although the former political relations of the inhabitants of a conquered territory are dissolved, their private relations to each other and their rights of property remain undisturbed, except so far as they are in their nature and character found to be in conflict with the Constitution and laws of the United States, or with any regulations which the conquering and occupying authority may ordain. Among the consequences which are necessarily incident to a change of sovereignty is the appointment or control of the agents by whom and the modes in which the government of the occupant shall be administered. The ordinances of such provisional government displace and supersede every previous institution of the vanquished or deposed political power which is incompatible with them during the time that the territory is held by the United States as occupying conqueror. Leitensdorfer v. Webb, 20 How. 176.

The civil government established in the exercise of provisional rights over a conquered territory which is subsequently ceded to the Government by the treaty of peace, does not cease as a matter of course or as a necessary consequence of the restoration of peace. The President may dissolve it by withdrawing the officers who administer it. Congress may put an end to it. The right inference from the inaction of both is that it is meant to be continued until it is legislatively changed. Cross *v.* Harrison, 16 How. 164.

The President, as commander in chief, may exercise the belligerent rights of a conqueror, and form a civil government for conquered territory, which will continue to be operative until the ratification and exchange of a treaty of peace. Cross *v.* Harrison, 16 How. 164.

The ratification of a treaty of peace has no effect upon a civil government established in the exercise of belligerent rights over a conquered territory, until official information of the ratification is received by it. Cross *v.* Harrison, 16 How. 164.

If the conquered territory is retained by the conqueror, the ordinances of the provisional government do not terminate with the close of the war, nor are the former institutions thereby revived and re-established. The ordinances and institutions of the provisional government can only be revoked or modified by the United States either by direct legislation on the part of Congress, or by that of a territorial government in the exercise of powers delegated by Congress. Leitensdorfer *v.* Webb, 20 How. 176.

When a State government is overthrown by a rebellion against the United States, the President, on obtaining possession of the territory, may appoint a military governor. Rutledge *v.* Fogg, 3 Cold. 554; Texas *v.* White, 7 Wall. 700.

Wherever the territory which has been dominated by an insurgent power is occupied by the national forces, it is the duty of the National Government to provide, as far as possible, so long as the war continues, for the security of persons and property, and for the administration of justice. The duty of the National Government in this respect is no other than that which devolves upon the government of a regular belligerent occupying, during war, the territory of another belligerent. It is a military duty to be performed by the President as commander in chief. The Grapeshot, 9 Wall. 129.

A military governor may appoint a judge with authority to hold a court in his military district. Pennywit *v.* Eaton, 15 Wall. 382; Mechanics' Bank *v.* Union Bank, 22 Wall. 276.

A provisional governor may create courts for the administration of justice. Such tribunals are not State, but Federal courts, deriving their existence and all their powers from the Federal Government. Scott *v.* Billgerry, 40 Miss. 119.

The President, as commander in chief, may establish a provisional court in territory taken by the national forces from an insurgent power, to continue during the war. The Grapeshot, 9 Wall. 129; Kimball *v.* Taylor, 2 Woods, 37; Powell *v.* Boon, 43 Ala. 469; Burke *v.* Tregre, 22 La. Ann. 629; Armistead *v.* State, 43 Ala. 340.

While the State authorities are subverted, the question whether any and what civil government shall be permitted is a matter in the discretion of the Federal Government. During the military occupation, the laws of the State can only operate so far as it chooses to allow, and can only be administered by such agents as it pleases to appoint. The President can cause all the laws of the State to be administered and executed, or he can cause the whole to be disregarded and set at naught. Scott *v.* Billgerry, 40 Miss. 119.

A provisional government established over an insurrectionary State may levy and collect taxes under the municipal laws of the State which are not superseded by the will of the conqueror. Rutledge *v.* Fogg, 3 Cold. 554.

Taxes levied for municipal purposes under a provisional government may be collected after the military occupation has been terminated by the re-establishment of the State government. Rutledge *v.* Fogg, 3 Cold. 554.

When the President provides for calling a convention to form a State government, he may exclude those who have participated in the rebellion and not been pardoned, from voting for delegates. Ex parte Wm. H. Hughes, Phillips, 57.

If a rebellion overthrows a State government, the President may adopt measures to enable the people to meet in convention to form a State government. Ex parte Wm. H. Hughes, Phillips, 57.

The power of the President to establish a military government must be exercised in subordination to the Constitution. Scott *v.* Billgerry, 40 Miss. 119.

When an insurrection is suppressed, Congress may provide for the transfer of cases pending in a provisional court, and of its judgments and decrees, to the proper Federal courts. The Grapeshot, 9 Wall. 129.

The powers of a provisional governor are not restricted to the particular subjects specified in the proclamation appointing him, for the proclamation is not necessarily his only authority. Whatever power is possessed by the President may be delegated by him to the governor, and in the absence of any evidence that any particular act of the governor is disapproved by the President, it must be presumed that it was authorized beforehand, or subsequently ratified and adopted. Scott *v.* Billgerry, 40 Miss. 119.

Pardons.

(*b*) The language used in the Constitution conferring the power to grant reprives and pardons must be construed with reference to its meaning at the time of its adoption. At that time, both Americans and Englishmen attached the same meaning to the word "pardon." Without such a power of clemency to be exercised by some department or functionary of the government, it would be most imperfect and deficient in its political morality, and in that attribute of deity whose judgments are always tempered with mercy. Ex parte William Wells, 18 How. 307.

The word "pardon" was not meant to be used exclusively with reference to an absolute pardon, exempting the criminal from the punishment which the law inflicts for a crime he has committed. In common parlance it is forgiveness, release, remission; forgiveness for an offense, whether it be one for which the person committing it is liable in law or otherwise; release from pecuniary obligation; or it is the remission of a penalty to which one may have subjected himself by the non-performance of an undertaking or contract; or when a statutory penalty in money has been incurred and it is remitted by a public functionary having power to remit it. In law it has different meanings, which were as well understood when the Constitution was made as any other word in the Constitution now is. Such a thing as a pardon, without a designation of its kind, is not known in the law. Time out of mind in the earliest books of the English law, every pardon has its particular denomination. They are general, special or particular, conditional or absolute, statutory, not necessary in some cases and in some grantable of course. Ex parte William Wells, 18 How. 307.

The President may grant a conditional pardon. The language of the Constitution is general, that is, common to the class of pardons, or extending the power to pardon to all kinds of pardon known in the law as such, whatever may be their denomination. A conditional pardon is one of them. In this view of the Constitution, by giving to its words their proper meaning, the power to pardon conditionally is not one of inference at all, but one conferred in terms. Ex parte William Wells, 18 How. 307.

The power is unlimited with the exception stated. It extends to every offense known to the law, and may be exercised at any time after its commission, either before legal proceedings are taken or during their pendency, or after conviction and judgment. Ex parte Garland, 4 Wall. 333.

The power of the President is not subject to legislative control. Congress can neither limit the effect of his pardon nor exclude from its exercise any class of offenders. The benign prerogative of mercy reposed in him can not be fettered by any legislative restrictions. Ex parte Garland, 4 Wall. 333.

A pardon reaches both the punishment prescribed for the offense and the guilt of the offender, and when the pardon is full it releases the punishment and blots out of existence the guilt, so that in the eye of the law the offender is as innocent as if he had never committed the offense. Congress can not exclude him from a previously acquired right, by the exaction of an expurgatory oath covering the offense. Ex parte Garland, 4 Wall. 333.

If a person under the terms of a pardon, became entitled to a restoration of abandoned property, Congress can not provide that the Supreme Court shall dismiss a cause for want of jurisdiction, when it ascertains that he was entitled to the property by the pardon. U. S. v. Klein, 13 Wall. 128.

The grant to the President of the power to pardon, must be held to carry with it, as an incident, the power to release penalties and forfeitures which accrue from the offenses. Osborn v. U. S. 91 U. S. 474.

To the executive alone is intrusted the power of pardon, and it is granted without limit. Pardon includes amnesty. It blots out the offense pardoned, and removes all its penal consequences. Congress can not change the effect of a pardon. U. S. v. Klein, 13 Wall. 128.

The power to grant reprieves is not only to be used to delay a judicial sentence, when the President shall think the merits of the case, or some cause connected with the offender, may require it, but extends also to cases *ex necessitate legis*, as where a female after conviction is found to be *enceinte*, or where a convict becomes insane, or is alleged to be so. Ex parte William Wells, 18 How. 307.

The power of pardon is conferred on the office of President, and prior to delivery one President may recall and cancel a pardon granted by his predecessor. In re Moses De Puy, 3 Ben. 307.

A pardon is a deed, to the validity of which delivery is essential, and delivery is not complete without acceptance. It may be rejected by the person to whom it is tendered. U. S. v. Wilson, 7 Pet. 150; In re Theophilus C. Callicott, 8 Blatch. 89.

Until a pardon is delivered, all that may have been done is mere matter of intended favor, and may be canceled to accord with a change of intention. In re Moses De Puy, 3 Ben. 307.

Although a pardon has been properly signed and sealed, and sent to the marshal, it may be recalled and canceled before it is delivered to the warden of the prison where the criminal is confined. In re Moses De Puy, 3 Ben. 307.

The President may grant a pardon after the expiration of the term of sentence. The power to pardon continues so long as any of the legal consequences of the offense remain. Stetler's Case, 1 Phil. 302.

2. He shall have power, by and with the advice and consent of the Senate, to make treaties, (*a*) provided two-thirds of the senators present concur; and he shall nominate, and by and with the advice and consent of the Senate, shall appoint ambassadors, other public ministers, and consuls, judges of the Supreme Court, and all other officers (*b*) of the United States, whose appointments are not herein otherwise provided for, and which shall be established by law. But the Congress may, by law, vest the appointment of such inferior officers as they think proper, in the President alone, in the courts of law, or in the heads of departments.

Treaties.

(*a*) The power to make treaties is given by the Constitution in general terms, without any description of the objects intended to be embraced by it, and consequently it was designed to include all those subjects which in the ordinary intercourse of nations had usually been made subjects of negotiation and treaty, and which are consistent with the nature of our institutions, and distribution of powers between the general and State Governments. Holmes *v.* Jennison, 14 Pet. 540; U. S. *v.* 43 Gallons, 93 U. S. 188.

The power to make treaties is given without restraining it to particular objects in as plenipotentiary a form as it is held by any other sovereign in any other community. This principle results from the form and necessities of the Government as elicited by a general view of the Federal compact. Before the compact, the States had the power of treaty making as potentially as any power on earth. It extended to every subject. By the compact they expressly granted it to the Federal Government in general terms, and prohibited it to themselves. The General Government must therefore hold it as fully as the States held it, with the exceptions that necessarily flow from a proper construction of the other powers granted and those prohibited by the Constitution. People *v.* Gerke, 5 Cal. 381.

The recognition and enforcement of the principles of public law being one of the ordinary subjects of treaties, were necessarily included in the power conferred on the General Government. As the rights and duties of nations towards one another, in relation to fugitives from justice, are a part of the law of nations, and have always been treated as such by the writers upon public law, it follows that the treaty making power must have authority to decide how far the right of a foreign nation, in this respect, will be recognized and enforced when it demands the surrender of any one charged with offenses against it. This power can not be exercised by the States. Holmes *v.* Jennison, 14 Pet. 540; People *v.* Curtis, 50 N. Y. 321.

A State can not regulate the surrender of fugitives from justice to foreign countries, although no action has been taken by the Federal Government. People *v.* Curtis, 50 N. Y. 321.

A State law relating to the surrender of fugitives from justice from foreign countries, is void. People *v.* Curtis, 50 N. Y. 321.

A treaty allowing a reasonable time to those, after the death of the owner, who would be entitled to real estate upon the death of the owner, if they were not aliens, to sell the estate and withdraw the proceeds without molestation, is valid. People *v.* Gerke, 5 Cal. 381.

A treaty may give aliens the right to purchase and hold land in the United States. Chirac *v.* Chirac, 2 Wheat. 259.

The political rights of the people of the several States as such are not subjects of treaty stipulations. Pierce *v.* State, 13 N. H. 336; s. c. 5 How. 504.

An Indian treaty providing for a cession of land may stipulate that the law prohibiting the sale of spirituous liquor in the ceded territory shall remain in force, although it lies within the limits of a State. U. S. *v.* Lariviere, 23 I. R. R. 305.

The right of eminent domain is inseparably attached to national empire and sovereignty, and accompanies the right of making peace, whether that right be vested in one or many. Jones *v.* Walker, 2 Paine, 688.

Citizens abroad must look to the President for protection of person and of property, and for the faithful execution of the laws existing and intended for their protection. For this purpose the whole executive power of the country is placed in his hands under the Constitution and the laws passed in pursuance thereof. Durand *v.* Hollins, 4 Blatch. 451.

As the executive head of the nation, the President is made the only legitimate organ of the General Government to open and carry on correspondence or negotiations with foreign nations in matters concerning the interests of the country or its citizens. Durand *v.* Hollins, 4 Blatch. 451.

The duty of interposing for the protection of the lives or property of citizens abroad, must of necessity rest in the discretion of the President. Where the public act or order rests in the discretion of the executive, neither he nor his authorized agent is personally responsible civilly for the consequences. Durand *v.* Hollins, 4 Blatch. 451.

Offices.

(*b*) Some ambiguity of expression has found its way into this clause. If the relative "which" refers to the word "appointments," that word is referred to in a sense rather different from that in which it had been used. It is used to signify the act of placing a man in office, and referred to as signifying the office itself. The relative may, however, be construed as referring to the word "offices," which must be understood although not expressed. The Constitution then declares that all offices of the United States, except in cases where the Constitution may otherwise provide, shall be established by law. U. S. *v.* Maurice, 2 Brock. 96.

An office is a public charge or employment, and he who performs the duties of the office is an officer. U. S. *v.* Maurice, 2 Brock. 96.

Although an office is an employment, it does not follow that every employment is an office. A man may certainly be employed under a contract, express or implied, to do an act or perform a service without becoming an officer. U. S. *v.* Maurice, 2 Brock. 96.

If a duty is a continuing one, which is defined by rules prescribed by the Government, and not by contract, which an individual is appointed by Government to perform, who enters on the duties appertaining to his station, without any contract defining them—if those duties continue, though the person be changed—it is very difficult to distinguish such a charge or employment from an office, or the person who performs the duties, from an officer. U. S. *v.* Maurice, 2 Brock. 96.

The mere direction that a thing shall be done, without prescribing the mode of doing it, can not fairly be construed into the establishment of an office, for the purpose of the object can be effected without one. U. S. *v.* Maurice, 2 Brock. 96.

All offices except in cases where the Constitution itself may otherwise provide, must be established by law. U. S. *v.* Maurice, 2 Brock. 96.

A State magistrate who commits offenders against the criminal laws of the United States renders a voluntary service, and in an enlarged sense is *pro hac vice* an officer, but not one within the meaning of this clause. He is an officer of the State, and not a Federal officer. Ex parte Gist, 26 Ala. 156.

Congress can not by law designate the person to fill an office under the Government. U. S. *v.* Ferreira, 13 How. 40.

The heads of departments can make an appointment to office only in those cases where they have been authorized so to do by some act of Congress. U. S. *v.* Maurice, 2 Brock. 96.

Some point of time must be taken when the power of the executive over an officer not removable at his will must cease. That point of time must be when the constitutional power of appointment has been exercised, and this power has been exercised when the last act required from the person possessing the power has been performed. This last act is the signature of the commission. Marbury *v*. Madison, 1 Cranch, 137.

Neither the transmission of the commission to the appointee, nor an acceptance thereof, is necessary to complete his right. Marbury *v*. Madison, 1 Cranch, 137.

A formal delivery of the commission to the appointee is not essential to the validity of the commission. Marbury *v*. Madison, 1 Cranch, 137.

The appointing power designated in the latter part of the section was no doubt intended to be exercised by the department of the Government to which the officer to be appointed most appropriately belonged. The appointment of clerks of court properly belongs to courts of law, and that a clerk is one of the inferior officers contemplated by this provision of the Constitution can not be questioned. Ex parte Hennen, 13 Pet. 230.

The President can not make a temporary appointment in a recess, if the Senate was in session when or since the vacancy occurred. Case of District Attorney, 16 A. L. Reg. 786.

Congress can not extend an existing term in an office in such manner as to prolong absolutely or conditionally the tenure of a present incumbent. This can not be done otherwise than by a renomination or new appointment by the President, and concurrence of the Senate as to the additional period. Case of District Attorney, 16 A. L. Reg. 786.

Congress may vest the appointment of a commissioner in the Circuit Court, although his power is of a judicial nature. Ex parte H. Robinson, 6 McLean, 355.

The President, in his discretion, may remove any officer whether civil or military, unless Congress shall have given some other duration to the office. Gratiot *v*. U. S. 1 Ct. Cl. 258.

A civil officer has a right to resign his office at pleasure, and it is not in the power of the President to compel him to remain in office. It is only necessary that the resignation should be received to take effect, and this does not depend on the acceptance or rejection of the resignation by the President. U. S. *v*. Wright, 1 McLean, 509.

It has become the settled and well understood construction of the Constitution that the power to remove officers appointed by the President and Senate is vested in the President alone. Ex parte Hennen, 13 Pet. 230; U. S. *v*. Avery, 1 Deady, 204.

All inferior officers appointed by authority of law, under the President, or the courts of law, or the heads of departments, hold their office at the discretion of the appointing power. Ex parte Hennen, 13 Pet. 230; U. S. v. Avery, 1 Deady, 204.

A removal from office may be either express—that is, by a notification by order of the President that an officer is removed—or implied by the appointment of another person to the same office. But in either case the removal is not completely effected till notice is actually received by the person removed. Bowerbank v. Morris, Wall. Sr. 118.

3. The President shall have power to fill up all vacancies that may happen during the recess of the Senate, by granting commissions which shall expire at the end of their next session.

This power is not confined to vacancies which may happen in offices created by law. U. S. v. Maurice, 2 Brock. 96.

SECTION III.

1. He shall, from time to time, give to the Congress information of the state of the Union, and recommend to their consideration such measures as he shall judge necessary and expedient; he may, on extraordinary occasions, convene both houses, or either of them, and, in case of disagreement between them, with respect to the time of adjournment, he may adjourn them to such time as he shall think proper; he shall receive ambassadors and other public ministers, he shall take care that the laws be faithfully executed; and shall commission all the officers of the United States.

The President is not authorized to execute the laws himself, or through agents or officers civil or military appointed by himself, but he is to take care that they be faithfully carried into execution, as they are expounded and adjudged by the co-ordinate branch of the Government to which that duty is assigned. Ex parte John Merryman, Taney, 246.

The President is to take care that the laws are faithfully executed, but only by such means as the Constitution and laws themselves have given him power to employ, that is, by causing proceedings to be instituted according to law against those who violate the law, and by employing whatever force may be necessary to overcome all resistance that is offered to their execution. But he is to execute the laws, not to make or change them. If their more perfect execution requires additional laws, the President is wholly incompetent to provide this. It can be done by legislation only. So the oath to preserve and defend the Constitution gives the President no additional powers. He can not adopt all imaginable means that he may deem expedient for this purpose, but he is to defend it only by the use of such powers as the instrument itself and the laws enacted under it confer upon him. In re Nicholas Kemp, 16 Wis. 359.

SECTION IV.

1. The President, Vice-president, and all civil officers of the United States, shall be removed from office on impeachment for, and conviction of, treason, bribery, or other high crimes and misdemeanors.

The power of impeachment extends to a person who is charged with the commission of a high crime while he was a civil officer and acting in his official character, although he ceased to be such officer before the finding of articles of impeachment. Impeachment of Wm. W. Belknap.

A Senator who has been expelled from his seat is not, after such expulsion, liable to impeachment for acts done while he was a Senator. Impeachment of Wm. Blount, Whart. St. Tr. 250.

ARTICLE III.

SECTION I.

1. The judicial power of the United States shall be vested in one Supreme Court, and in such inferior courts as the Congress may, from time to time, ordain and establish. The judges, both of the Supreme and inferior courts, shall hold their offices during good behavior; and shall, at stated times, receive for their services a compensation which shall not be diminished during their continuance in office.

Judicial Power.

By the term "judicial power" is meant that power with which the courts are to be clothed for the purpose of the trial and determining of causes. Ex parte Gist, 26 Ala. 156.

It is not sufficient to bring a matter under the judicial power that it involves the exercise of judgment upon law and facts. U. S. *v.* Ferreira, 13 How. 40; Murray *v.* Hoboken Co. 18 How. 272; Ex parte Gist, 26 Ala. 156.

The power to hear and pass upon the validity of a claim in an *ex parte* proceeding is not a judicial power. U. S. *v.* Ferreira, 13 How. 40; U. S. *v.* Todd, 13 How. 52; Humphreys *v.* U. S. 1 Dev. 204.

A provision requiring an assessor to impose a certain penalty, if he shall find a return false, does not confer judicial power, and is valid. Doll *v.* Evans, 15 I. R. R. 143.

Congress can not empower a commissioner to commit a person for an alleged contempt. Ex parte George Doll, 7 Phila. 595.

The auditing of the accounts of a receiver of public moneys may, in an enlarged sense, be a judicial act. So are all those administrative duties the performance of which involves an inquiry into the existence of facts and the application to them of rules of law. The adjustment of the balances due from accounting officers is not necessarily and without regard to the consent of Congress a judicial controversy. Murray *v.* Hoboken Co. 18 How. 272.

Congress can neither withdraw from judicial cognizance any matter which, from its nature, is the subject of a suit at the common law, or in equity, or in admiralty, nor bring under the judicial power a matter which, from its nature, is not the subject of judicial determination. At the same time, there are matters involving public rights which may be presented in such form that the judicial power is capable of acting upon them, and which are susceptible of judicial determination, but which Congress may or may not bring within the cognizance of the courts of the United States, as it may deem proper. Murray *v.* Hoboken Co. 18 How. 272.

Congress may consent to a second trial of a claim against the United States, although a judgment thereon has been rendered in favor of the Government. Nock *v.* U. S. 2 Ct. Cl. 451.

Neither the legislative nor the executive branches of the Government can assign to the judicial any duties but such as are properly judicial, and to be performed in a judicial manner. Hayburn's Case, 2 Dall. 409; U. S. *v.* Ferreira, 13 How. 40.

Whether a foreign country has become an independent State is a question for the treaty making power to determine, and can not be decided by the judicial tribunals. Kennett *v.* Chambers, 14 How. 38; Gelston *v.* Hoyt, 3 Wheat. 246; Rose *v.* Himely, 4 Cranch, 241.

Congress can not confer any part of the judicial power upon an executive officer. Beatty *v.* U. S. 1 Dev. 231.

The condition of peace or war, public or civil, in a legal sense, must be determined by the political department of the Government, not the judicial U. S. *v.* 129 Packages, 11 A. L. Reg. 419.

This clause does not apply to the abnormal condition of conquered territory in the occupancy of a conquering army, nor prohibit the establishment of military courts in an insurrectionary State. Mechanics' Bank *v.* Union Bank, 22 Wall. 276; The Grapeshot, 9 Wall. 179.

Limited Jurisdiction.

The judicial power of the United States is to be exercised by courts organized for the purpose and brought into existence by an effort of the legislative power of the Union. Of all the courts which the United States may under their general powers constitute, one only, the Supreme Court, possesses jurisdiction derived immediately from the Constitution, of which the legislative power can not deprive it. All other courts created by the General Government possess no jurisdiction but what is given them by the power that creates them, and can be vested with none but what the power ceded to the General Government will authorize it to confer. Sheldon *v.* Sill, 8 How. 441; M'Intire *v.* Wood, 7 Cranch, 504; Kendall *v.* U. S. 12 Pet. 524; s. c. 5 Cranch C. C. 163; Cary *v.* Curtis, 3 How. 236; Bank *v.* Northumberland, 4 Conn. 333; s. c. 4 Wash. 108; U. S. *v.* Railroad Bridge Co. 6 McLean, 517; Bank of U. S. *v.* Roberts, 4 Conn. 323; U. S. *v.* Bedford Bridge, 1 W. & M. 401; Shute *v.* Davis, Pet. C. C. 431; U. S. *v.* Ta-wan-ga-ca, Hemp. 304; Hubbard *v.* Northern R. R. Co.' 3 Blatch. 84; Ex parte Joseph De Cabrera, 1 Wash. 232; Mayor *v.* Cooper, 6 Wall. 247; Turner *v.* Bank, 4 Dall. 8; Smith *v.* Allyn, 1 Paine, 453; Moffat *v.* Soley, 2 Paine, 103; contra, Dundas *v.* Bowler, 3 McLean, 204; Brainard *v.* Williams, 4 McLean, 122.

The Constitution declares that the judicial power shall be vested in one Supreme Court created by the Constitution, and in such inferior courts as Congress shall, from time to time, ordain and establish. The Constitution defines the portions of the judicial power vested in the Supreme Court, and leaves the residue to be distributed among the inferior courts, which may be established by law, and to be vested or not vested in them, respectively, from time to time, according to the discretion of Congress. The powers, therefore, not bestowed upon the Federal courts by legislative provisions remain dormant until some law shall call them into action by designating the particular tribunal which shall be authorized to exercise them. Bank of U. S. *v.* Roberts, 4 Conn. 323; Bank of U. S. *v.* Northumberland Bank, 4 Conn. 333.

The Federal courts can not exercise a common-law jurisdiction in criminal cases. U. S. *v.* Hudson, 7 Cranch, 32; U. S. *v.* Coolidge, 1 Wheat. 415; S. C. 1 Gallis. 488; contra, U. S. *v.* Ravara, 2 Dall. 297; U. S. *v.* Worrall, 2 Dall. 384.

The Federal courts can not proceed by information in criminal cases, unless the power is granted by Congress. U. S. *v.* Joe, 4 C. L. N. 105.

Congress may transfer a suit from one inferior tribunal to another. Stuart *v.* Laird, 1 Cranch, 299.

Territorial Courts.

Territorial courts are legislative courts created in virtue of the general right of sovereignty which exists in the Government, or in virtue of that clause which enables Congress to make all needful rules and regulations respecting the territory belonging to the United States. The jurisdiction with which they are invested is not a part of that judicial power which is defined in this article, but is conferred by Congress in the execution of those general powers which that body possesses over the territories of the United States. Am. Ins. Co. *v.* Canter, 1 Pet. 511; Stacy *v.* Abbott, 1 A. L. T. 84.

Congress may either define directly by its own act the jurisdiction of the Territorial courts created by it, or delegate the authority requisite for that purpose to the Territorial government. Leitensdorfer *v.* Webb, 20 How. 176.

If Congress, on admitting a Territory into the Union as a State, fails to provide for cases pending in the Supreme Court, it may do so by a subsequent act.. Freeborn *v.* Smith, 2 Wall. 160.

State Courts.

Congress can not vest any portion of the judicial power of the United States, except in courts ordained and established by itself. Martin *v.* Hunter, 1 Wheat. 304; Ely *v.* Peck, 7 Conn. 239; Davison *v.* Champlin, 7 Conn. 244; U. S. *v.* Lathrop, 17 Johns. 4; Jackson *v.* Rose, 2 Va. Cas. 34; Houston *v.* Moore, 5 Wheat. 1; S. C. 3 S. & R. 169; Ex parte Frank Knowles, 5 Cal. 300; State *v.* McBride, Rice, 400.

Congress can not compel a State court to entertain jurisdiction in any case, for they are not inferior courts in the sense of the Constitution. They are not ordained by Congress. State courts are left to consult their own duty from their own State authority and organization. Stearns *v.* U. S. 2 Paine, 300; Ex parte Alexander Stephens, 70 Mass. 559; Miss. River Tel. Co. *v.* First Nat. Bank, 7 C. L. N. 158.

A court is a creature of the Constitution and laws under which it exists. To exercise any power not derived from such Constitution and laws would be a usurpation. It is not, therefore, lawful for a State court to exercise jurisdiction conferred upon it by an act of Congress. Ex parte Frank Knowles, 5 Cal 300.

Congress can not give jurisdiction to or require services of any officer of a State government as such. Ex parte Wm. Pool, 2 Va. Cas. 276; Prigg v. Comm. 16 Pet. 539.

The Constitution directs that all the regular and permanent duties which properly belong to a court in the ordinary and popular signification of that term shall be performed by the courts described therein. There is, therefore, nothing in the Constitution which prevents a ministerial officer or other person by law directed to do and perform any act which may be necessary to bring an accused party before a court possessing the judicial power of determining his guilt or innocence. Ex parte Wm. Pool, 2 Va. Cas. 276; Prigg v. Comm. 16 Pet. 539; Ex parte Gist, 26 Ala. 156; Ex parte Martin, 2 Paine, 348; Ableman v. Booth, 21 How. 506; S. C. 3 Wis. 1, 145, 157.

Congress may authorize any citizen of the United States to perform any act which the Constitution does not require to be performed in a different manner. Ex parte Wm. Pool, 2 Va. Cas. 276; Ex parte Gist, 26 Ala. 156.

State Laws.

The jurisdiction of the Federal courts is derived alone from the Constitution and laws of the United States, and can not be enlarged, diminished, or affected by State laws. U. S. v. Drennen, Hemp. 320; Livingston v. Jefferson, 1 Brock. 203.

A State legislature can not confer jurisdiction upon Federal courts, or prescribe the means or mode of its exercise. That subject belongs exclusively to the Federal Government, and must be regulated solely by the Constitution and the laws of Congress. Greely v. Townsend, 25 Cal. 604.

No State can take away the privilege conferred upon citizens of other States to sue in the Federal courts by providing a special remedy in its own courts. Mason v. Boom Company, 3 Wall. Jr. 252.

Removal from State Courts.

The power to remove suits from State courts to Federal courts is not to be found in express terms in any part of the Constitution. It is only given by implication, as a power necessary and proper to carry into effect some express power. The removal of a cause is an indirect mode by which the Federal courts acquire original jurisdiction. Railway Company *v.* Whitton, 13 Wall. 270; Martin *v.* Hunter, 1 Wheat. 304.

Congress may provide for the removal of cases over which the Federal courts may take jurisdiction, from the State courts into the Federal courts. Railway Company *v.* Whitton, 13 Wall. 270; Fisk *v.* Union Pacific R. R. Co. 6 Blatch. 362; Murray *v.* Patrie, 5 Blatch. 343; Mayor *v.* Cooper, 6 Wall. 247; Tod *v.* Fairfield, 15 Ohio St. 377; Clark *v.* Dick, 1 Dill. 8; McCormick *v.* Humphrey, 27 Ind. 144; Johnson *v.* Monell, 1 Wool. 390; Martin *v.* Hunter, 1 Wheat. 304; Hodgson *v.* Millward, 3 Grant, 412; Kulp *v.* Ricketts, 3 Grant, 420; contra, Johnson *v.* Gordon, 4 Cal. 368.

Where the judicial power of the United States can be applied only because the case involves a controversy between citizens of different States, it rests entirely with Congress to determine at what time the power may be invoked, and upon what conditions; whether originally in the Federal court, or after suit brought in the State court; and in the latter case at what stage of the proceedings, whether before issue or trial by removal to a Federal court, or after judgment on appeal or writ of error. Gaines *v.* Fuentes, 92 U. S. 10.

A case may be removed from a State court to a Federal court where it arises under the Constitution or laws of the United States, as well as where it arises between citizens of different States. Kulp *v.* Ricketts, 3 Grant, 420.

A statute requiring a foreign corporation to file an agreement not to remove cases against it into the Federal courts, as a condition to the permission to transact business in the State, is void. Morse *v.* Ins. Co. 20 Wall. 445; s. c. 30 Wis. 496; Railway Co. *v.* Pierce, 27 Ohio St. 155; contra, N. Y. Life Ins. Co. *v.* Best, 23 Ohio St. 105; Continental Ins. Co. *v.* Kasey, 13 A. L. J. 311.

If the license to transact business in the State is made dependent upon the condition that the corporation shall not remove any case from a State to a Federal court, the State may revoke the license if such removal is made. State *v.* Doyle, 40 Wis. 175; Doyle *v.* Continental Ins. Co. 15 A. L. J. 267; contra, Hartford Fire Ins. Co. *v.* Doyle, 6 Biss. 461.

Compensation.

Congress can not create or limit any other tenure of the judicial office, or refuse to pay the stipulated salary of the judges at stated times, or diminish it during their continuance in office. Martin *v.* Hunter, 1 Wheat. 304.

Although Congress may establish courts of appellate jurisdiction, yet such courts must consist of judges appointed in the manner the Constitution requires, and holding their offices by no other tenure than that of good behavior. Hayburn's Case, 2 Dall. 409; U. S. *v.* Ferreira, 13 How. 40.

The fees allowed to a justice of the peace, appointed in the District of Columbia, can not be diminished during his continuance in office. U. S. *v.* More, 3 Cranch, 160, note.

SECTION II.

1. The judicial power shall extend to all cases in law and equity, arising under this Constitution, the laws of the United States, and treaties made, or which shall be made, under their authority ; to all cases affecting ambassadors, other public ministers and consuls ; to all cases of admiralty and maritime jurisdiction ; to controversies to which the United States shall be a party ; to controversies between two or more States ; between a State and citizens of another State ; between citizens of different States ; between citizens of the same State claiming lands under grants of different States ; and between a State, or the citizens thereof, and foreign States, citizens or subjects.

Construction.

The words "shall extend" are used in an imperative sense. They import an absolute grant of judicial power. They can not have a relative signification applicable to powers already granted, for the people had not made any previous grant. The Constitution was for a new Government organized with new substantive powers, and not a mere supplementary charter to a Government already existing. Martin *v.* Hunter, 1 Wheat. 304.

The language of the article throughout is manifestly designed to be mandatory upon the legislature. Its obligatory force is so imperative that Congress could not, without a violation of its duty, have refused to carry it into operation. It is a duty also to vest the whole judicial power. The language, if imperative as to one part, is imperative as to all. Martin *v.* Hunter, 1 Wheat. 304.

There are two classes of cases enumerated in the Constitution, between which a distinction seems to be drawn. The first class includes cases arising under the Constitution, laws and treaties of the United States; cases affecting ambassadors, other public ministers and consuls; and cases of admiralty and maritime jurisdiction. In this class the expression is that the judicial power shall extend to all cases, but in the subsequent part of the clause, which embraces all other cases of national cognizance, the word "all" is dropped, seemingly *ex industria*. In respect to the first class, it may well have been the intention of the framers of the Constitution imperatively to extend the judicial power either in an original or appellate form, to all cases, and in the latter class to leave it to Congress to qualify the jurisdiction, original or appellate, in such manner as public policy might dictate. Martin *v.* Hunter, 1 Wheat. 304; The Moses Taylor, 4 Wall. 411.

The Constitution imposes no limitation upon the class of cases involving controversies between citizens of different States to which the judicial power of the United States may be extended, and Congress may therefore lawfully provide for bringing, at the option of either of the parties, all such controversies within the jurisdiction of the Federal judiciary. Gaines *v.* Fuentes, 92 U. S. 10.

Congress may give the Federal courts original jurisdiction in any case to which the appellate jurisdiction extends. Osborn *v.* Bank, 9 Wheat. 738.

The mere question whether a collector of the customs is indebted to the United States, may be one of judicial cognizance. It is competent for the United States to sue any of its debtors in a court of law. It is equally clear that the United States may consent to be sued, and may yield this consent upon such terms and under such restrictions as it may think just. Murray *v.* Hoboken Co. 18 How. 272.

The judicial power may extend to all the cases enumerated in the Constitution. As the mode is not limited, it may extend to all such cases in any form in which judicial power may be exercised. It may, therefore, extend to them in the shape of original or appellate jurisdiction, or both, for there is nothing in the nature of the cases which binds to the exercise of the one in preference to the other. Martin *v.* Hunter, 1 Wheat. 304.

Laws.

The legislative, executive and judicial powers of every well constructed government are co-extensive with each other; that is, are potentially co-extensive. The executive department may constitutionally execute every law which the legislature may constitutionally make, and the judicial power may receive from the legislature the power to construe every such law. Bank of U. S. *v.* Roberts, 4 Conn. 323; Osborn *v.* Bank, 9 Wheat. 738.

The power is given in general terms. No limitation is imposed. The broadest language is used. "All cases" so arising are embraced. None are excluded. How jurisdiction shall be acquired by the inferior courts, whether it shall be original or appellate, or original in part and appellate in part, and the manner of procedure in its exercise after it has been acquired, are not prescribed. The Constitution is silent on those subjects. They are remitted without check or limitation to the wisdom of the legislature. Mayor *v.* Cooper, 6 Wall. 247.

This clause enables the judicial department to receive jurisdiction to the full extent of the Constitution, laws and treaties of the United States when any question respecting them shall assume such a form that the judicial power is capable of acting on it. That power is capable of acting only when the subject is submitted to it by a party who asserts his rights in the form prescribed by law. It then becomes a case, and the Constitution declares that the judicial power shall extend to all cases arising under the Constitution, laws and treaties of the United States. Osborn *v.* Bank, 9 Wheat. 738.

The judicial power covers every legislative act of Congress, whether it be made within the limits of its delegated powers, or be an assumption of power beyond the grants in the Constitution. Ableman *v.* Booth, 21 How. 506; S. C. 3 Wis. 1; Mayor *v.* Cooper, 6 Wall 247.

When a question to which the judicial power of the Federal Government is extended by the Constitution forms an ingredient of the original cause, it is in the power of Congress to give the Federal courts jurisdiction of that cause, although other questions of fact or law may be involved in it. The other questions may be decided as incidental to that which gives the jurisdiction. Osborn *v.* Bank, 9 Wheat. 738; Mayor *v.* Cooper, 6 Wall. 247.

The right of the plaintiff to sue can not depend on the defense which the defendant may choose to set up. His right to sue is anterior to that defense, and must depend on the state of things when the action is brought. The questions which the case involves must therefore determine its character, whether those questions be made in the cause or not. Osborn *v.* Bank, 9 Wheat. 738.

Whether the case arises in the State or Federal tribunals, it is within the reach of this power. Mayor *v.* Cooper, 6 Wall. 247.

Cases may arise under the laws of the United States by implication, so that they come under the judicial power of the Federal Government. It is not unusual for a legislative act to involve consequences not expressed. An officer, for example, is ordered to arrest an individual. It is not necessary, nor is it usual, to say that he shall not be punished for obeying the order. His security is implied in the order itself. The judicial power is the instrument employed by the Government in administering the security. Hodgson v. Millward, 3 Grant, 412.

To bring a case within the judicial power of the United States it need not be of an unmixed character. If the principal right, the right of property in the subject in controversy, is given or created by an act of Congress made in pursuance of the Constitution, it is sufficient. Bank of U. S. v. Roberts, 4 Conn. 323.

The construction of an act of Congress, when a claim or a defense arises out of it, is within the province of the Federal judiciary. Hodgson v. Millward, 3 Grant, 412.

When a defendant seeks protection under a law of the United States, it is a case arising under that law. Hodgson v. Millward, 3 Grant, 412; Kulp v. Ricketts, 3 Grant, 420.

Congress has no constitutional power to settle the rights under treaties, except in cases purely political. The construction of them is the peculiar province of the judiciary when a case shall arise between individuals. Wilson v. Wall, 6 Wall. 83.

The article does not extend the judicial power to every violation of the Constitution which may possibly take place, but to "a case in law or in equity," in which a right under such law is asserted in a court of justice. If the question can not be brought into a court, then there is no case in law or equity, and no jurisdiction is given by the words of the article. Cohens v. Virginia, 6 Wheat. 264.

The General Government has full authority to appoint and commission all courts, magistrates, and officers to carry the laws of Congress into effect without necessary reliance on those of the States. Ex parte Alexander Stephens, 70 Mass. 559.

Congress may provide that a national bank may sue and be sued in the Federal courts. Magill v. Parsons, 4 Conn. 317; Bank of U. S. v Roberts, 4 Conn. 323; Bank of U. S. v. Northumberland Bank, 4 Conn. 333; S. C. 4 Wash. 108; Bank v. Osborn, 9 Wheat. 738.

Admiralty.

The Constitution not only confers admiralty jurisdiction, but the word "maritime" is superadded, seemingly *ex industria*, to remove every latent doubt. "Cases of maritime jurisdiction" must include all maritime contracts, torts, and injuries which are in the understanding of the common law, as well as of the admiralty, "*causæ civiles et maritimæ.*" In this view there is a peculiar propriety in the incorporation of the term maritime into the Constitution. The disputes and discussions respecting what the admiralty jurisdiction was could not but be well known to the framers of that instrument. One party sought to limit it by locality, another by the subject-matter. It was wise, therefore, to dissipate all question by giving cognizance of all "cases of maritime jurisdiction," or what is precisely equivalent, of all maritime cases. Upon any other construction the word "maritime" would be mere tautology; but in this sense it has a peculiar and appropriate force. De Lovio *v.* Boit, 2 Gallis. 398 ; The Huntress, 2 Ware, 89 ; Kynoch *v.* Ives, Newb. 205 ; Davis *v.* The Seneca, 6 Penn. L. J. 213 ; S. C. Gilp. 10 ; vide U. S. *v.* Bedford Bridge, 1 W. & M. 401.

The terms admiralty and maritime belong to the law of nations as well as to our own domestic and municipal law. This is peculiarly true of the former – admiralty. A court of admiralty is a court of the law of nations, and in one branch of its jurisdiction, that of prize, both the law and the jurisdiction are derived solely from the law of nations. The Huntress, 2 Ware, 89.

The maritime law is a part of the common law. Thompson *v.* The Catharina, 1 Pet. Ad. 104.

The etymology or received use of the words "admiralty" and "maritime jurisdiction," include jurisdiction of all things done upon and relating to the sea, or, in other words, all transactions and proceedings relative to commerce and navigation, and to damages or injuries upon the sea. De Lovio *v.* Boit, 2 Gallis. 398 ; Scott *v.* The Young America, Newb. 101.

The admiralty and maritime jurisdiction of the Federal courts covers not merely the cognizance of the case, but the jurisprudence and principles by which it is to be administered. It covers the whole maritime law applicable to the case in judgment, without the slightest dependence upon or connection with the local jurisprudence of the State on the same subject. The subject-matter of admiralty and maritime law is withdrawn from State legislation, and belongs exclusively to the national Government and its proper functionaries. The Chusan, 2 Story, 455.

Cases in admiralty are not identical with cases arising under the laws and Constitution of the United States. The Constitution clearly contemplates these as three distinct classes of cases. Am. Ins. Co. *v.* Canter, 1 Pet. 511.

The admiralty jurisdiction can not be made to depend upon the power of Congress to regulate commerce. They are entirely distinct things having no necessary connection with each other, and are conferred in the Constitution by separate and distinct grants. The Belfast, 7 Wall. 624 ; The Genesee Chief *v.* Fitzhugh, 12 How. 443 ; The Sarah Jane, 1 Lowell, 203.

A law defining the jurisdiction of certain courts of the United States is not a regulation of commerce. The jurisdiction to administer the laws relating to commerce is not a regulation within the meaning of the Constitution. The Genesee Chief *v.* Fitzhugh, 12 How. 443.

The power of regulating commerce with foreign nations and among the States, is granted by another article of the Constitution, to the legislative department. This covers the whole maritime commerce of the country. The grant to the judicial department, of the cognizance of all causes of maritime jurisdiction, makes the judicial co-extensive with the legislative power. The Huntress, 2 Ware, 89.

The grant of admiralty power to the Federal courts was not intended to be limited or to be interpreted by what were cases of admiralty jurisdiction in England when the Constitution was adopted. Waring *v.* Clarke, 5 How. 441; De Lovio *v.* Boit, 2 Gallis. 398; The Huntress, 2 Ware, 89; Kynoch *v.* Ives, Newb. 205; Steele *v.* Thacher, 1 Ware, 91; Davis *v.* The Seneca, 6 Penn. L. J. 213; s. c. Gilp. 10; The Gold Hunter, 1 Bl. & H. 300; The Volunteer, 1 Sum. 551; New Jersey Co. *v.* Merchants' Bank, 6 How. 344.

The admiralty has jurisdiction over maritime contracts, although the voyage contemplated begins and ends in the State, and is prosecuted only in waters within the State. The Belfast, 7 Wall. 624; The Elmira Shepherd, 8 Blatch. 341; Leonard *v.* The Volunteer, 15 I. R. R. 59; s. c. 1 C. L. N. 185; The Mary Washington, 1 Abb. C. C. 1; The Leonard, 3 Ben. 263; The Sarah Jane, 1 Lowell, 203; Carpenter *v.* The Emma Johnson, 1 Cliff. 633; s. c. 1 Sprague, 527; contra, Maguire *v.* Card, 21 How. 248; The Troy, 4 Blatch. 355; Allen *v.* Newberry, 21 How. 244; New Jersey Co. *v.* Merchants' Bank, 6 How. 344.

The admiralty jurisdiction extends to torts committed on navigable waters although they are committed within the body of a county. Roberts *v.* Skolfield, 8 A. L. Reg. 156.

In cases purely dependent on the locality of the act done, the admiralty jurisdiction is limited to the sea and to tide waters as far as the tide flows, and does not reach beyond high-water mark. U. S. *v.* Coombs, 12 Pet. 72.

The cession of all cases of admiralty and maritime jurisdiction is not a cession of the waters on which those cases may arise. This article is not intended for the cession of territory or of general jurisdiction. The general jurisdiction over the place subject to this grant of power adheres to the territory as a portion of the sovereignty of the States not yet given away. U. S. *v.* Bevans, 3 Wheat. 336; Smith *v.* State, 18 How. 71; Ware *v.* Hyer, 2 Paine, 131; s. c. 1 Bl. & H. 235.

The power to regulate the fisheries belonging to the several States, and to punish those who should transgress these regulations, was exclusively vested in the States respectively at the time when the Constitution was adopted, and was not surrendered to the United States by the mere grant of admiralty and maritime jurisdiction to the judicial branch of the Government. Corfield *v.* Coryell, 4 Wash. C. C. 371; Bennett *v.* Boggs, Bald. 60; Smith *v.* State, 18 How. 71.

The grant of admiralty and maritime jurisdiction is a grant of power to Congress to legislate upon the subject, but without such legislation the Federal courts have no jurisdiction. Jackson *v.* The Magnolia, 20 How. 296.

Congress may give the courts the whole or so much of the admiralty jurisdiction as it sees fit. It may extend their jurisdiction over all navigable waters, and all ships and vessels thereon, or over some navigable waters and vessels of a certain description only. Jackson *v.* The Magnolia, 20 How. 296; U. S. *v.* Bevans, 3 Wheat. 336.

Congress can not create admiralty jurisdiction, because that jurisdiction is expressly granted to the Federal Government by the Constitution. Carpenter *v.* The Emma Johnson, 1 Cliff. 633; S. C. 1 Sprague, 527.

Congress may limit, or even control, the exercise of admiralty jurisdiction, by modifying or repealing existing laws and enacting others in their place. Carpenter *v.* The Emma Johnson, 1 Cliff. 633; S. C. 1 Sprague, 527.

The Constitution does not direct that the court shall proceed according to the ancient and established forms, or shall adopt any other form or mode of practice. The grant defines the subject to which the jurisdiction may be extended by Congress, but the extent of the power, as well as the mode of proceedings in which that jurisdiction is to be exercised, like the power and practice in all other courts of the United States, is subject to the regulation of Congress, except where that power is limited by the terms of the Constitution, or by necessary implication from its language. In admiralty and maritime cases, there is no such limitation as to the mode of proceeding, and Congress may, therefore, in cases of that description, give either party a right of trial by jury, or modify the practice of the court in any other respect that it deems more conducive to the administration of justice. Genesee Chief *v.* Fitzhugh, 12 How. 443.

The authority of Congress under this clause does not extend to punish offenses committed above and beyond high-water mark. U. S. *v.* Coombs, 12 Pet. 72.

A State legislature has no power to create a maritime lien. The Belfast, 7 Wall. 624.

No State law can regulate the lien for materials and supplies furnished to a foreign vessel. The Chusan, 2 Story, 455.

A State statute conferring a lien for repairs made on domestic ships is constitutional. The Chusan, 2 Story, 455; The Belfast, 7 Wall. 624.

It is not competent for the States by any local legislation to enlarge, or limit or narrow, the admiralty and maritime jurisdiction of the Federal courts. In the exercise of this jurisdiction they are exclusively governed by the legislation of Congress, and in the absence thereof by the general principles of the maritime law. The States have no right to prescribe the rules by which the Federal courts shall act, nor the jurisprudence which they shall administer. If any other doctrine were established, it would amount to a complete surrender of the jurisdiction of the Federal courts to the fluctuating policy and legislation of the States. If the latter have a right to prescribe any rule, they have a right to prescribe all rules, to limit, control or bar suits in the national courts. Such a doctrine has never been supported. The Chusan, 2 Story, 455.

Foreign Nations.

An Indian tribe within the United States is not a foreign State, and can not maintain an action in the Federal courts. Cherokee Nation *v.* State, 5 Pet. 1.

How far Exclusive.

As there is no express negation of jurisdiction to the State courts in the specified cases, their jurisdiction is not taken away, except as to such of the cases as they did not before hold cognizance of, and such as, from the nature of the jurisdiction, they could not hold cognizance of, from the incompatibility between the powers granted to the courts of the United States and a reservation of any portion of the same powers to the State courts. U. S. *v.* Lathrop, 17 Johns. 4; Jackson *v.* Rose, 2 Va. Cas. 34; State *v.* Randall, 2 Aik. 89; Houston *v.* Moore, 5 Wheat. 1; S. C. 3 S. & R. 169; Teal *v.* Felton, 12 How. 284; Delafield *v.* State, 2 Hill, 159.

The judicial power of the United States is unavoidably in some cases exclusive of all State authority, and in all others may be made so at the election of Congress. Martin *v.* Hunter, 1 Wheat. 304; The Moses Taylor, 4 Wall. 411.

The State tribunals can now constitutionally exercise concurrent jurisdiction with the Federal courts only in those cases where previous to the Constitution they possessed jurisdiction independent of national authority. Martin *v.* Hunter, 1 Wheat. 304.

There are several classes of cases where the State courts have constantly exercised concurrent powers, although the Federal courts have jurisdiction. The following cases may be mentioned: 1. Where the United States sue. 2. Where a State sues a citizen of another State. 3. Where a State sues an alien. 4. Where a citizen of one State sues a citizen of another State. 5. Where a citizen sues an alien. 6. Where an alien sues a citizen. Delafield *v.* State, 2 Hill, 159.

The State courts may entertain jurisdiction of cases arising under the laws of the United States, with or without an express provision in the acts of Congress, not as a matter of constitutional obligation, but upon those principles of comity which authorize the courts of every civilized State to administer law and justice to suitors, although not citizens of the State. Bank of U. S. *v.* Roberts, 4 Conn. 323; Houston *v.* Moore, 5 Wheat. 1; s c. 3 S. & R. 169; Jackson *v.* Rose, 2 Va. Cas. 34; Claflin *v.* Houseman, 93 U. S. 130.

So far as the judicial power is to be invoked in the execution of a treaty, it is exclusive in the Federal courts. Ex parte Juan Leon, 1 Edm. Sel. Cas. 311.

The Federal courts have cognizance of all those cases which are embraced in the first three clauses, because they are cases arising under the limited legislation of a government of limited powers. Of all those classes of cases their jurisdiction is exclusive. In all the other enumerated classes their jurisdiction is concurrent with the State courts. State *v.* McBride, Rice, 400.

The admiralty and maritime jurisdiction is vested exclusively in the Federal courts. Martin *v.* Hunter, 1 Wheat. 304.

The State courts may entertain an action to recover a penalty for the breach of a Federal statute. To sustain such a suit is not administering the criminal law of the United States. An action for a penalty is a civil action both in form and in substance. It is founded upon that implied contract which every person enters into with the Government to observe its laws. Stearns *v.* U. S. 2 Paine, 300; Claflin *v.* Houseman, 93 U. S. 130; Buckwalter *v.* U. S. 11 S. & R. 193; contra, Haney *v.* Sharp, 1 Dana, 442; Ely *v.* Peck, 7 Conn. 239; Davison *v.* Champlin, 7 Conn. 244; U. S. *v.* Lathrop, 17 Johns. 4; Jackson *v.* Rose, 2 Va. Cas. 34.

No part of the criminal jurisdiction of the United States can consistently with the Constitution be delegated to State tribunals. Martin *v.* Hunter, 1 Wheat. 304; State *v.* McBride, Rice, 400; State *v.* Wells, 2 Hill (S. C.) 687; Comm. *v.* Feely, 1 Va. Cas. 321; Huber *v.* Reily, 53 Penn. 112.

The commission of a crime against a national bank, which is not made an offense by an act of Congress, does not constitute a question or case arising under the Constitution or laws of the United States, and the

State courts have jurisdiction to try the same. State *v.* Buchanan, 5 H. & J. 317.

A State court may punish the offense of counterfeiting national bank notes, under a State law, although the act is punishable under the statutes of the United States, unless they have vested exclusive jurisdiction over the crime in the Federal courts. State *v.* Randall, 2 Ark. 89; State *v.* Tutt, 2 Bailey, 44; White *v.* Comm. 4 Binn. 418.

A State court has jurisdiction to punish the forgery of a land warrant, where it has not been made a crime by a Federal statute. Comm. *v.* Schaffer, 4 Dall. App. xxvi.

A State magistrate may commit a prisoner in order that he may be delivered over for prosecution to the United States. Ex parte Smith, 5 Cow. 273; Ex parte Gist, 26 Ala. 156; Ex parte Wm. Pool, 2 Va. Cas. 276; Prigg *v.* Comm. 16 Pet. 539; Ex parte Martin, 2 Paine, 348.

2. In all cases affecting ambassadors, other public ministers and consuls, and those in which a State shall be party, the Supreme Court shall have original jurisdiction. In all the other cases before mentioned, the Supreme Court shall have appellate jurisdiction, both as to law and fact, with such exceptions, and under such regulations as the Congress shall make.

Construction.

The first clause declares the extent of the judicial power, and the second clause prescribes the form, whether original or appellate, in which the Supreme Court shall exercise its jurisdiction. The latter clause confers no new powers, but only specifies the manner in which the powers already granted shall be exercised, so far as the Supreme Court is concerned. The words, "in all other cases before mentioned," plainly show that the second clause refers only to those cases to which the judicial power has been extended by the first clause. The power can not be enlarged by a mere declaration prescribing the form, original and appellate, in which it shall be exercised. Delafield *v.* State, 2 Hill, 159; Pennsylvania *v.* Quicksilver Co. 10 Wall. 553.

Every part of the article must be taken into view, and that construction adopted which will consist with its words, and promote its general intention. The court may imply a negative from affirmative words where the implication promotes, not where it defeats, the intention. Cohens *v.* Virginia, 6 Wheat. 264.

Original Jurisdiction.

It is left to Congress to organize the Supreme Court, to define its powers consistently with the Constitution as to its original jurisdiction, and to distribute the residue of the judicial power between it and the inferior courts. Rhode Island v. Massachusetts, 12 Pet. 657; Chisholm v. Georgia, 2 Dall. 490.

Congress can not assign original jurisdiction to the Supreme Court in cases other than those specified in this article. Marbury v. Madison, 1 Cranch, 137; Ex parte Clement L. Vallandigham, 1 Wall. 243; Ex parte Yerger, 8 Wall. 85.

The original jurisdiction of the Supreme Court, in cases where a State is a party, refers to those cases in which, according to the grant of power made in the preceding clause, jurisdiction might be exercised in consequence of the character of the party, and an original suit might be instituted in any of the Federal courts, not to those cases in which an original suit might not be instituted in a Federal court. Of the last description is every case between a State and its citizens, and perhaps every case in which a State is enforcing its penal laws. In such cases the Supreme Court can not take original jurisdiction. Cohens v. Virginia, 6 Wheat. 264.

A case which belongs to the jurisdiction of the Supreme Court, on account of the interest which a State has in the controversy, must be a case in which a State is either nominally or substantially a party. It is not sufficient that a State may be consequentially affected. Fowler v. Lindsey, 3 Dall. 411.

To give the Supreme Court jurisdiction, a State must be a party on the record. The fact that the State is a member of a corporation which is a party, does not make it a party. Bank v. Planter's Bank, 9 Wheat. 904.

The fact that land has been granted by, and is claimed under a State, does not make the State a party to a controversy between private persons concerning that land. Fowler v. Lindsey, 3 Dall. 411.

The Supreme Court is made the chosen arbiter to judge and determine the disputes and controversies that may arise between the respective States, and not each State in its individual capacity. Chancely v. Bailey, 37 Geo. 532.

A State can not prosecute a suit in the Supreme Court on the ground of any remote or contingent interest in itself, but if it has a direct interest in the controversy, the jurisdiction will be sustained. State v. Wheeling Bridge Co. 13 How. 518.

A State may bring an original suit in the Supreme Court against a citizen of another State, but not against one of her own. Pennsylvania v. Quicksilver Co. 10 Wall. 553.

The Supreme Court has jurisdiction of questions of boundary between two States, although the decision involves the construction of compacts or agreements between the States, or affects the territorial limits of the political jurisdiction and sovereignty of the States. Virginia *v.* West Virginia, 11 Wall. 39; Rhode Island *v.* Massachusetts, 12 Pet. 657.

A question of boundary between States is within the original jurisdiction of the Supreme Court. Florida *v.* Georgia, 17 How. 478.

The Supreme Court has no jurisdiction over questions of a political and not judicial character. State *v.* Stanton, 6 Wall. 50; Cherokee Nation *v.* State, 5 Pet. 1.

Although Congress has the right to prescribe the process and mode of proceeding in cases where the Supreme Court has original jurisdiction as fully as in any other court, yet the omission to legislate on the subject does not deprive the court of the jurisdiction conferred. In the absence of any legislation by Congress, the court itself may prescribe the mode and form of proceedings so as to attain the ends for which jurisdiction was given. Florida *v.* Georgia, 17 How. 478.

The original jurisdiction of the Supreme Court is special and limited, and its action must be confined to the particular cases, controversies and parties over which the Constitution has authorized it to act. Any action without the limits prescribed is *coram non judice*, and its action a nullity. Rhode Island *v.* Massachusetts, 12 Pet. 657.

A motion to dismiss for want of jurisdiction may be made, even after a plea to the merits. Rhode Island *v.* Massachusetts, 12 Pet. 657.

Where a State is a party plaintiff or defendant, the governor represents the State, and the suit may be in form a suit by him as governor in behalf of the State where the State is plaintiff, and he must be summoned or notified as the officer representing the State where the State is defendant. Comm *v.* Dennison, 24 How. 66.

Where a question of boundary is in dispute between two States, the United States may intervene if it has any interest in the controversy, and produce proof. Florida *v.* Georgia, 17 How. 478.

An indictment against a private person for an assault upon an ambassador or public minister, is not a case affecting such ambassador or minister. U. S. *v.* Ortega, 11 Wheat. 467.

A State court is deprived of jurisdiction over an offense committed by a consul against the laws of the State. Comm. *v.* Kosloff, 5 S & R. 546; contra, State *v.* De La Foret, 2 N. & M. 217.

The Supreme Court has no original jurisdiction of a proceeding by a private individual who is an alien, to obtain redress for a wrong done him by another private individual who is a citizen. Ex parte Barry, 2 How. 65.

Although the Constitution vests in the Supreme Court original jurisdiction in suits affecting ambassadors, ministers and consuls, it does not preclude Congress from exercising the power of vesting a concurrent jurisdiction in such inferior courts as may by law be established. St. Luke's Hospital *v.* Barclay, 3 Blatch. 259; Graham *v.* Stucken, 4 Blatch. 50; U. S. *v.* Ravara, 2 Dall. 297; Gittings *v.* Crawford, Tan. 1.

A State may be authorized to sue in the inferior courts. State *v.* Atkins 35 Geo. 315; contra, State *v.* Trustees, 5 B. R. 466; s. c. 1 Hughes, 133.

Appellate Jurisdiction.

Appellate jurisdiction is given by the Constitution to the Supreme Court in all cases where it has not original jurisdiction, subject, however, to such exceptions and regulations as Congress may prescribe. It is therefore capable of embracing every case enumerated in the Constitution which is not exclusively to be decided by way of original jurisdiction. Martin *v.* Hunter, 1 Wheat. 304.

In every case to which judicial power extends and in which original jurisdiction is not expressly given to the Supreme Court, its judicial power must be exercised in the appellate and only in the appellate form. The original jurisdiction can not be enlarged, but its appellate jurisdiction may be exercised in every case cognizable under this article in the Federal courts in which original jurisdiction can not be exercised. Cohens *v.* Virginia, 6 Wheat. 264.

The appellate powers of the Supreme Court are limited and regulated by the acts of Congress, and must be exercised subject to the exceptions and regulations made by Congress. Ex parte Clement L. Vallandigham, 1 Wall. 243; Durousseau *v.* U. S. 6 Cranch, 307; Barry *v.* Mercein, 5 How. 103; U. S. *v.* Moore, 7 Cranch, 159; Ex parte McCardle, 7 Wall. 506; Murdock *v.* Memphis, 20 Wall. 590; Martin *v.* Hunter, 1 Wheat. 304.

The Supreme Court can not exercise appellate jurisdiction over the Court of Claims. Gordon *v.* U. S. 2 Wall. 561.

In prize cases the Supreme Court can exercise appellate jurisdiction only. A case can not be docketed unless there is an order, decree or judgment in some inferior court, for appellate jurisdiction necessarily implies some judicial determination, some judgment, decree or order of an inferior tribunal from which an appeal is taken. The Alivia, 7 Wall. 571.

The Supreme Court may be vested with the power to issue a writ of *habeas corpus* to release a person committed by an inferior court, for the writ is appellate in its nature. Ex parte Bollman, 4 Cranch, 73; Ex parte Burford, 3 Cranch, 448; U. S. *v.* Hamilton, 3 Dall. 17; Ex parte Kearney, 7 Wheat. 38.

The appellate power of the Supreme Court is not limited by the terms of this article to any particular courts. The words are " in all other cases before mentioned the Supreme Court shall have appellate jurisdiction." It is the case, then, and not the court, that gives jurisdiction. The Constitution not only contemplated, but meant to provide for cases within the scope of the judicial power of the United States which might yet depend before State tribunals. It was foreseen that in the exercise of their ordinary jurisdiction State courts would incidentally take cognizance of cases arising under the Constitution, the laws, and treaties of the United States. Yet to all these cases the judicial power, by the very terms of the Constitution, is to extend. The appellate power of the United States must, therefore, in such cases, extend to State tribunals; and if in such cases, there is no reason why it should not equally attach upon all others within the purview of the Constitution. Martin v. Hunter, 1 Wheat. 304; Piqua Bank v. Knoup, 6 Ohio St. 342; Dodge v. Woolsey, 18 How. 331; Cohens v. Virginia, 6 Wheat. 264; Ableman v. Booth, 21 How. 506; s. C. 3 Wis. 1; Ferris v. Coover, 11 Cal. 175; contra, Hunter v. Martin, 4 Munf. 1; Johnson v. Gordon, 4 Cal. 368.

The principle on which the appellate jurisdiction of the Supreme Court over the State courts is allowed is, that no government can be efficient or just without the means of self-protection. And hence, that those who act under it, or claim rights beneath the shield of its laws should, within its own territory, be able to appeal to its own tribunals for relief. Scott v. Jones, 5 How. 343.

The provisions of the Constitution do not imply that the States will be willfully disregardful of the obligations solemnly placed upon them by the people, but that there may be interferences from their legislation, either with the Constitution or between their enactments and those of Congress. This suggested the necessity, or rather made it obvious, that the National Union would be incomplete and altogether insufficient for the great ends contemplated, unless a constitutional arbiter was provided to give certainty and uniformity in all of the States to the interpretation of the Constitution and the legislation of Congress, with powers to declare judicially what acts of the legislatures of the States might be in conflict with either. Had this not been done, there would have been no mutuality of constitutional obligation between the States, either in respect to the Constitution or the laws of Congress, and each of them would have determined for itself the operation of both, either by legislation or judicial action; in either way exempting itself and its citizens from engagements which it had not made by itself, but in common with other States of the Union equally sovereign, by which they bound their sovereignties to each other, that neither of them should assume to settle a principle or interest for itself in a matter which was the common interest of all of them. Such is certainly the common-sense view of the people when any number of them enter into a contract for their mutual benefit in the same proportions of interest. In such a case neither should assume the right to bind his compeers by his judgment as to the stipulations of their contract. Dodge v. Woolsey, 18 How. 331; Ableman v. Booth, 21 How. 506; s. C 3 Wis. 1.

The exercise of appellate jurisdiction is far from being limited by the terms of the Constitution to the Supreme Court. There can be no doubt that Congress may create a succession of inferior tribunals, in each of which it may vest appellate as well as original jurisdiction. The judicial power is delegated by the Constitution in the most general terms, and may therefore be exercised by Congress under every variety of form of appellate or original jurisdiction. As there is nothing in the Constitution which restrains or limits this power, it must therefore in all other cases subsist in the utmost latitude of which in its own nature it is susceptible. Martin *v.* Hunter, 1 Wheat. 304; s. c. 4 Munf. 1.

None but the Supreme Court can entertain jurisdiction by way of appeal from the judgments of State courts in cases originally cognizable and commenced in those courts; and any act of Congress giving such jurisdiction to any inferior court of the United States would be unconstitutional and void. Wetherbee *v.* Johnson, 14 Mass. 412; Patrie *v.* Murray, 43 Barb. 323.

3. **The trial of all crimes, except in cases of impeachment, shall be by jury; and such trial shall be held in the State where the said crime shall have been committed; but when not committed within any State, the trial shall be at such place or places as the Congress may, by law, have directed.**

The provisions of this clause are applicable to proceedings in the Federal courts only. Murphy *v.* People, 2 Cow. 815.

A proceeding to annul the license of a pilot for neglect of duty is not a criminal proceeding. Low *v.* Commissioners, R. M. Charlt. 302.

A citizen in civil life, in no wise connected with the military service, can not be tried by a military commission in a place where the Federal authority is unopposed, and its courts open to hear criminal accusations and redress grievances. Ex parte Milligan, 4 Wall. 2.

A statute which provides that a party may be tried by the court on a charge of libel is void, although it gives him the right to appeal to another court where the charge must be tried by a jury. The accused is entitled not to be first convicted by a court, and then to be acquitted by a jury, but to be acquitted or convicted in the first instance by a jury. Ex parte Charles A. Dana, 7 Ben. 1.

The form of asking a prisoner how he will be tried is wholly unnecessary. This provision is imperative upon the courts, and prisoners can be lawfully tried in no other manner. As soon, therefore, as it judicially appears of record that the party has pleaded not guilty, there is an issue in a criminal case which the courts are bound to direct to be tried by a jury. U. S. *v.* Gilbert, 2 Sum. 19.

A statute to confiscate the property of persons engaged in rebellion, in any district in which it may be found, is void. Norris *v.* Doniphan, 4 Met. (Ky.) 385.

A crime committed against the laws of the United States out of the limits of a State is not local, but may be tried at such place as Congress shall designate by law. United States *v.* Dawson, 15 How. 467.

SECTION III.

1. Treason against the United States shall consist only in levying war against them, or in adhering to their enemies, giving them aid and comfort. No person shall be convicted of treason unless on the testimony of two witnesses to the same overt act, or on confession in open court.

It is consonant to the principles of the Constitution that the crime of treason shall not be extended by construction. Ex parte Bollman, 4 Cranch, 75.

However flagitious may be the crime of conspiring to subvert the Government by force, such conspiracy is not treason. To conspire to levy war, and actually to levy war, are distinct offenses. The first must be brought into open action by the assemblage of men for a purpose treasonable in itself, or the fact of levying war is not committed. Ex parte Bollman, 4 Cranch, 75; U. S. *v.* Mitchell, 2 Dall. 348.

There must be an actual assemblage of men for a treasonable purpose to constitute a levying of war. Ex parte Bollman, 4 Cranch, 75.

The assemblage of men for the purpose of carrying into operation the treasonable intent, which will amount to levying war, must be an assemblage in force. U. S. *v.* Burr, 2 Burr's Trial, 401; U. S. *v.* Hoxie, 1 Paine, 265.

To constitute a levying of war there must be an assemblage of persons in force to overthrow the Government or coerce its conduct. The words embrace not only those acts by which war is brought into existence, but also those acts by which war is prosecuted. They levy war who create or carry on war. U. S. *v.* Greathouse, 2 Abb. C. C. 364.

If a body of men is actually assembled for the purpose of effecting by force a treasonable purpose, all those who perform any part, however minute or however remote from the scene of action, and who are actually leagued in the general conspiracy, are to be considered as traitors. Ex parte Bollman, 4 Cranch, 75.

Those who perform a part in the prosecution of the war, may correctly be said to levy war and to commit treason under the Constitution. U. S. v. Burr, 2 Burr's Trial, 401.

When a body, large or small, of armed men, is mustered in military array for a treasonable purpose, every step which any of them takes in part execution of that purpose, is an overt act of levying war, though not a warlike blow may have been struck. The marching of such a corps with such a purpose, in the direction in which a blow might be struck, is levying war. U. S v. Greiner, 4 Phila. 396.

It is not necessary that there should be any military array or weapons. The crime may be committed by those not personally present at the immediate scene of violence, if they are leagued with the conspirators and perform any part, however minute. Druecker v. Salomon, 21 Wis. 621.

The occupation of a fortress by a body of men in military array, in order to detain it against the Government, is treason on the part of all concerned, either in the occupation or detention of the post. U. S. v. Greiner, 4 Phila. 396.

If a party joins and marches with rebels, the only force which excuses him on the ground of compulsion, is force upon the person and present fear of death, which force and fear must continue during all the time of military service with the rebels. U. S. v. Greiner, 4 Phila. 396; U. S. v. Hodges, 2 Wheel. Cr. Cas. 477.

The overt act and the intention constitute the treason, for without the intention the treason is not complete. U. S. v. Fries, 2 Whart. St. Tr. 458; vide U. S. v. Hodges, 2 Wheel. Cr. Cas. 477.

The mere enlistment of men for service does not amount to levying war. Ex parte Bollman, 4 Cranch, 75.

War levied against the United States by citizens of the Republic, under the pretended authority of a rebellious State, or of Confederate States, is treason against the United States. Shortridge v. Macon, Chase, 136.

The offense is complete, whether the force be directed to the entire overthrow of the Government throughout the country, or only in certain portions of the country, or to defeat the execution and compel the repeal of one of its public laws. U. S. v. Greathouse, 2 Abb. C. C. 364.

The resistance of the execution of a law of the United States, accompanied with any degree of force, if for a private purpose, is not treason. To constitute that offense, the object of the resistance must be of a public and general nature. U. S. *v.* Hanway, 2 Wall. Jr. 140; U. S. *v.* Hoxie, 1 Paine, 265; U. S. *v.* Fries, 2 Whart. St. Tr. 458.

An assemblage by force, to prevent the operation or compel the repeal of a single act, is treason by levying war against the United States. U. S. *v.* Fries, 2 Whart. St. Tr. 458; U. S. *v.* Mitchell, 2 Dall. 348; U. S. *v.* Hanway, 2 Wall. Jr. 140.

Where the object of the assemblage is to prevent the operation or compel the repeal of a law, force is necessary to complete the crime, but the quantum of force is immaterial. U. S. *v.* Fries, 2 Whart. St. Tr. 458.

The following elements therefore constitute this offense: 1st. A combination or conspiracy, by which different individuals are united in one common purpose. 2d. This purpose must be to prevent the execution of some public law of the United States. 3d. The actual use of force by such combination, to prevent the execution of such law. Druecker *v.* Salomon, 21 Wis. 621.

The delivery of prisoners to the enemy is high treason against the United States. U. S. *v.* Hodges, 2 Wheel. Cr. Cas. 477.

If a party being with an enemy's squadron, comes to the shore with the intention to peaceably procure provisions for the use of the enemy, but stops short before anything is effected, this does not constitute an overt act of treason by adhering to the enemy. U. S. *v.* Pryor, 3 Wash. C. C. 234.

The term "enemies" applies only to the subjects of a foreign power in a state of open hostility with the United States. It does not embrace rebels in insurrection with their own Government. U. S. *v.* Greathouse, 2 Abb. C. C. 364; U. S. *v.* Cheneweth, 4 West. L. Mo. 165.

The provision that no person shall be convicted of treason unless upon the testimony of two witnesses to the same overt act, or on confession in open court, applies only to the trial of indictments, and is inapplicable to proceedings before grand juries, or to preliminary investigations. U. S. *v.* Greiner, 4 Phila. 396.

2. **The Congress shall have power to declare the punishment of treason, but no attainder of treason shall work corruption of blood or forfeiture, except during the life of the person attainted.**

This provision does not apply to the confiscation of enemies' property, even though those enemies are rebels against the Government, and therefore guilty of treason. Confiscation Cases, 1 Woods, 221.

ARTICLE IV.

SECTION I.

1. Full faith and credit shall be given in each State to the public acts, records, and judicial proceedings of every other State. And the Congress may, by general laws, prescribe the manner in which such acts, records and proceedings shall be proved, and the effect thereof.

The provision had for its object to prevent any such weakening of the bonds of the Federal Union as might follow from the States disregarding what was due to courtesy and comity when their respective proceedings should come under consideration, and opening anew the controversies and questions which in the jurisdiction having properly and primarily the control of them had once been determined. Its object was, so far as judgments are concerned, to preclude their being disregarded in other States when a proper tribunal, with competent jurisdiction, had rendered them. People v. Dawell, 25 Mich. 247.

This section has three distinct objects : 1. To declare that full faith and credit shall be given in each State to the public acts, records and judicial proceedings of every other State. 2. The manner of authenticating such public acts, records and judicial proceedings; and 3. Their effect when so authenticated. Green v. Sarmiento, 3 Wash. C. C. 17 ; s. c. 1 Pet. C. C. 74; Bissell v. Briggs, 9 Mass. 462; Comm. v. Green, 17 Mass. 514.

By the first member of this clause, the framers of the Constitution intended a general declaration that the records of the courts of the several States should be treated with great respect by full faith and credit being given to them in every other State. But as this general declaration was not defined with accuracy, and was subject to be misunderstood, they proceeded further to declare that Congress might, by a general law, mark out the effect and define the general power thus given. Curtis v. Gibbs, 2 N. J. 399.

The latter part of this clause was intended to provide the means of giving to judgments the conclusiveness of judgments upon the merits when it is sought to carry them into judgments by suits in the tribunals of another State. The authenticity of a judgment and its effect depend upon the law made in pursuance of the Constitution ; the faith and credit due to it as the judicial proceeding of a State, is given by the Constitution independently of all legislation. M'Elmoyle v. Cohen, 13 Pet. 312.

This clause does not mean that all the effects and consequences of a litigation in one State shall follow it into another. The rule that "*lis pendens*" is notice to all the world is limited to all persons within the jurisdiction of the State where the suit was pending. Shelton *v.* Johnson, 4 Sneed, 672.

This clause was not designed to extend the jurisdiction of local courts, or to extend beyond its just limits, the operation of a local decree, but to provide a mode of authenticating evidence of the record of a judicial proceeding had in one State, so that the proper general result of it might be conveniently attained in every other State, against persons and things justly within the range of the proceeding. Bowen *v.* Johnson, 5 R. I. 112.

It is manifest that the Constitution contemplated a power in Congress to give a conclusive effect to judgments in the State courts, otherwise this clause would be utterly unimportant and illusory. The common law would make such judgments *prima facie* evidence in the courts of another State. Mills *v.* Duryee, 7 Cranch, 481; M'Elmoyle *v.* Cohen, 13 Pet. 312; Warren Manuf. Co. *v.* Etna Ins. Co. 2 Paine, 501; Green *v.* Sarmiento, 3 Wash. 17; S. C. 1 Pet. C. C. 74.

Congress may declare what shall be the effect of a judgment of a State court in another State. M'Elmoyle *v.* Cohen, 13 Pet. 312; Green *v.* Sarmiento, 3 Wash. 17; S. C. 1 Pet. C. C. 74.

This clause places judgments in another State on a different footing from what are commonly called foreign judgments, and gives them all the force and effects of judgments in every State. Oldens *v.* Hallet, 3 N. J. 466; Gibbons *v.* Livingston, 6 N. J. 236; Gibbons *v.* Ogden, 6 N. J. 285.

The terms "faith and credit" evidently point to the attributes and qualities which such records and judicial proceedings shall have as evidence. Brengle *v.* McClellan, 7 G. & J. 434; Joice *v.* Scales, 18 Geo. 725; Shelton *v.* Johnson, 4 Sneed, 672; M'Elmoyle *v.* Cohen, 13 Pet. 312; Carter *v.* Bennett, 6 Fla. 214; Wilson *v.* Robertson, 1 Tenn. 266.

The Constitution has effected no change in the nature of a judgment. It only provides that, as a matter of evidence, it shall be entitled to full credit. In marshaling the assets of an insolvent estate, a judgment recovered in another State only ranks as a simple contract, and is not put upon the footing of judgments rendered in the State. M'Elmoyle *v.* Cohen, 13 Pet. 312; Harness *v.* Green, 20 Mo. 316; Brengle *v.* McClellan, 7 G. & J. 434; Cameron *v.* Wurtz, 4 McCord, 278; vide Colt's Estate, 4 W. & S. 314.

This clause does not give validity to a void decree. Ogden *v.* Saunders, 12 Wheat. 213; Vanuxem *v.* Hazlehursts, 4 N. J. 192.

The collision of a decree with a prior decree of the same court, is not embraced by this provision. Mitchell *v.* Lenox, 14 Pet. 49.

The records and judicial proceedings to which full faith and credit are to be given, are only such as are duly rendered by a court of competent jurisdiction against those who appeared to defend, or were duly notified to appear. Aldrich *v.* Kenney, 4 Conn. 380; Bissell *v.* Briggs, 9 Mass. 462.

The Constitution does not confer upon Congress to give to a judgment obtained in one State all the legal properties, rights and attributes to which it is entitled by the law of the State where it was rendered. Brengle *v.* McClellan, 7 G. & J. 434.

The Constitution makes no distinction between courts of record and those which are not such; nor between courts of the highest and most general jurisdiction and those tribunals whose authority is of the most limited and inferior character. Taylor *v.* Barron, 30 N. H. 78.

A judgment rendered before a justice of the peace is within the provision of the Constitution, although his court is not a court of record. Silver Lake Bank *v.* Harding, 5 Ohio, 545; Pelton *v.* Platner, 13 Ohio, 209.

Congress has the power to declare the effect and provide the mode of authenticating the records and judicial proceedings of the courts of the respective territories and countries subject to the jurisdiction of the United States. Hughes *v.* Davis, 8 Md. 271; Duvall *v.* Fearson, 18 Md 502; contra, Seton *v.* Hanahan, R. M. Charlt. 374; Adams *v.* Day, 33 Conn. 419; Haggin *v.* Squires, 2 Bibb, 334.

This clause relates only to judgments in civil actions, and not to judgments on criminal prosecutions. It has no effect whatever on judgments upon criminal suits, and in this respect the relation of the States to each other is wholly unaffected by the Constitution. Comm. *v.* Green, 17 Mass. 514.

A State may provide that an action of debt may be maintained on a judgment rendered in the courts of another State, for a State may give to such judgment any effect it may think proper, so that it does not derogate from the effect secured by the Constitution and the acts of Congress. Bissel *v.* Briggs, 9 Mass. 462.

A State law which declares that no action shall be maintained on any judgment rendered without the State against any person who at the time of the commencement of the suit was a resident of the State in any case where the cause of action would have been barred by any act of limitations of the State, is void. Christmas *v.* Russell, 5 Wall. 290; Dodge *v.* Coffin, 15 Kans. 277.

Prescription is a thing of policy growing out of its experience, and the time after which suits or actions shall be barred has been from a remote antiquity fixed by every nation, in virtue of that sovereignty by which it exercises its legislation for all persons and property within its jurisdiction.

The States, in the exercise of this right, may limit the time for remedies upon the judgments of other States, fixing a less or larger time than that of the common law to raise a presumption of payment, or altogether bar suits upon such judgments, if they are not brought within the time stated in the statute. A plea of the statute of limitations is a plea to the remedy, and consequently the *lex fori* must prevail. M'Elmoyle *v.* Cohen, 13 Pet. 312; Bacon *v.* Howard, 20 How. 22.

The law of a State may fix different times for barring the remedy in a suit upon a judgment of another State, and upon a judgment of its own tribunals. M'Elmoyle *v.* Cohen, 13 Pet. 312; Bacon *v.* Howard, 20 How. 22; Robinson *v.* Peyton, 4 Tex. 276.

The probate of a will, being but a decree *in rem*, is confined in its operation to things within the State setting up the court which takes the probate. "Full faith and credit" is given to it abroad when the same faith and credit is given to it which it has at home, and that is, that it is to be conclusive evidence of the validity of the will as affording title to things within the jurisdictional limits of the court at the death of the testator, whether such title comes in contest within or without those limits, but *de jure* no evidence whatever of title to things not then within those limits. Bowen *v.* Johnson, 5 R. I. 112; Olney *v.* Angell, 5 R. I, 198.

A discharge from imprisonment for debt under the laws of one State will not prevent an arrest under the laws of another State. Joice *v.* Scales, 18 Geo. 725.

SECTION II.

1. The citizens of each State shall be entitled to all privileges and immunities of citizens in the several States.

These expressions are confined to those privileges and immunities which are in their nature fundamental, which belong of right to the citizens of all free governments, and which have at all times been enjoyed by the citizens of the several States which compose this Union from the time of their becoming free, independent and sovereign. What these fundamental privileges are, it would perhaps be more tedious than difficult to enumerate. They may, however, be all comprehended under the following general heads: to wit, protection by the government; the enjoyment of life and liberty, with the right to acquire and possess property of every kind, and to pursue and obtain happiness and safety, subject, nevertheless, to such restraints as the government may justly prescribe for the general good of the whole. The right of a citizen of one State to pass through or to reside in any other State for purposes of trade, agriculture, professional pursuits or otherwise; to claim the benefit of the writ of *habeas corpus;* to institute and maintain actions of any kind in the courts of the State; to take, hold and dispose of property, either real or personal; an exemption from higher taxes or impositions than are paid by the other citizens of the State; may be mentioned as some of the particular privileges and immunities of citizens which are clearly embraced by the general description of privileges deemed to be fundamental; to which may be added the elective franchise, as regulated and established by the laws and Constitution of the State in which it is to be exercised. These and many others which might be mentioned, are, strictly speaking, privileges and immunities. Corfield *v.* Coryell, 4 Wash. C. C. 371; Bennett *v.* Boggs, Bald. 60; Comm. *v.* Milton, 12 B. Mon. 212.

Privilege and immunity are synonymous, or nearly so. Privilege signifies a peculiar advantage, exemption, immunity; immunity signifies exemption, privilege. Campbell *v.* Morris, 3 H. & McH. 535.

This clause means that the citizens of all the States shall have the peculiar advantage of acquiring and holding real as well as personal property, and that such property shall be protected and secured by the laws of the State in the same manner as the property of the citizens of the State is protected. It means that such property shall not be liable to any taxes or burdens which the property of the citizens is not subject to. It secures and protects personal rights. Campbell *v.* Morris, 3 H. & McH. 535; Ward *v.* Morris, 4 H. & McH. 330.

A particular and limited operation is to be given to these words, and not a full and comprehensive one. They do not mean the right of election, the right of holding office, or the right of being elected. Campbell *v.* Morris, 3 H. & McH. 535; Murray *v.* McCarty, 2 Munf. 393; Allen *v.* Sarah, 2 Harring. 434; Smith *v.* Moody, 26 Ind. 299.

This clause does not exempt the citizen of another State from any condition which the laws of the State impose upon its own citizens, nor confer upon him any privilege which the law gives to particular persons for special purposes, or upon prescribed conditions. Comm. *v.* Milton, 12 B. Mon. 212.

This clause does not apply to a person who, being a citizen of a State, migrates to another State, for then he becomes subject to the laws of the State in which he lives, and he is no longer a citizen of the State from which he removed. The State in which he resides may then determine his *status* or condition, and deny him the privileges and immunities enjoyed by other citizens. Dred Scott *v.* Sandford, 19 How. 393; Bradwell *v.* State, 16 Wall. 130; contra, Abbott *v.* Bayley, 23 Mass. 89.

An individual who permanently resides and is domiciled in a State, and who is entitled to all the privileges and immunities of a citizen of that State, can not be regarded otherwise than as a citizen of that State. Comm. *v.* Towles, 5 Leigh, 743.

The citizens of other States are not to be deemed aliens. They are not to be accounted as foreigners, or as persons who may become enemies. They are to have the right to carry on business; to inherit and transmit property; to enter upon, reside in, and remove from the territory of each State at their pleasure, yielding obedience to, and receiving protection from, the laws. Such are some of the privileges and immunities conferred by this clause, and all that are granted by it are of the same character. State *v.* Medbury, 3 R. I. 138.

No privileges are secured by this clause, except those which belong to citizenship. Rights attached by the law to contracts by reason of the place where such contracts are made or executed, wholly irrespective of the citizenship of the parties to those contracts, can not be deemed " privileges of a citizen " within the meaning of the Constitution. Conner *v.* Elliott, 18 How. 591.

This clause relieves citizens from the disabilities of alienage in other States. It inhibits discriminating legislation against them by other States. It gives them the right of free ingress into other States, and egress from them. It insures to them in other States the same freedom possessed by the citizens of those States in the acquisition and enjoyment of property, and in the pursuit of happiness; and it secures to them in other States the equal protection of their laws. Paul *v.* Virginia, 8 Wall. 168.

So far as the mere rights of persons are concerned, this provision is confined to citizens of a State who are temporarily in another State without taking up their residence there. It gives them no political rights in the State as to voting or holding office, or in any other respect, for a citizen of one State has no right to participate in the government of another. But if he ranks as a citizen in the State to which he belongs, then whenever he goes into another State, the Constitution clothes him, as to the rights of persons, with all the privileges and immunities which belong to citizens of the State. Dred Scott *v.* Sandford, 19 How. 393.

This clause gives to the citizens of each State entire freedom of intercourse with every other State, and any law which attempts to deny them free ingress or egress is void. Lemmon *v.* People, 20 N. Y. 562; S. C. 2 Sandf. 681; 26 Barb. 270.

The right of transit through each State, with every species of property known to the Constitution, and recognized by that paramount law, is secured by that instrument to each person, and does not depend on the uncertain and changeable ground of every mere comity. Ex parte Archy, 9 Cal. 147; Willard *v.* People, 5 Ill. 461; Julia *v.* McKinney, 3 Mo. 270.

This clause secures and protects the right of a citizen of one State to pass into any other State for the purpose of engaging in lawful commerce, trade, or business, without molestation; to acquire personal property; to take and hold real estate; and to maintain actions in the courts of the State. Ward *v.* Maryland, 12 Wall. 418; S. C. 31 Md. 279.

The main object of this clause was to prevent each State from discriminating in favor of its own people, or against those of any other. It secures not only absolute equality of rights and privileges with every citizen of each State, but all such privileges and immunities in any State as are by the laws and Constitution thereof secured and extended to her own people of the same class and otherwise similarly situated. Davis *v.* Pierce, 7 Minn. 13.

When in the regulation of any subject of internal police, a regard to justice and the due and convenient enforcement of its laws require a State to adopt a different mode of proceeding, or a modification of the regulation in respect to persons residing out of the State, in order to fairly meet and provide for the circumstance of their non-residence, the competency of the State so to act is not taken away by this clause. Baker *v.* Wise, 16 Gratt. 139.

This clause was not intended to give the laws of any one State the slightest force in another State. It secures to the citizens of each State in every other State, not the laws, or peculiar privileges which they may be entitled to in their own State, but such protection and benefit of the laws of any and every other State as are common to the citizens thereof in virtue of their being citizens. They do not, by force of this clause, acquire any peculiar privileges in another State, except upon the condition on which they may be held or enjoyed by the citizens of such other State. Comm. *v.* Milton, 12 B. Mon. 212; Reynolds *v.* Geary, 26 Conn. 179; Paul *v.* Virginia, 8 Wall. 168; Lemmon *v.* People, 5 Sandf. 681; S. C. 20 N. Y. 562; 26 Barb. 270.

A marked distinction has always been made between the rights and powers of the citizens of a State and the rights and powers of all other persons resident within the limits of the State, whether they are citizens of other States or foreigners. State *v.* Medbury, 3 R. I. 138.

This clause is intended to secure the citizens of one State against discriminations made by another State in favor of its own citizens, and not to secure the citizens of any State against discriminations made by their own State in favor of the citizens of other States, nor to secure one class of citizens against discriminations made between them and another class of citizens of the same State. Comm. *v.* Griffin, 3 B. Mon. 208.

A citizen of the State whose laws are complained of, can not claim the protection afforded by this clause. Bradwell *v.* State, 16 Wall. 130.

The citizens of other States are not entitled to greater privileges than the State grants to its own citizens. Lemmon *v.* People, 26 Barb. 270; S. C. 5 Sandf. 681; 20 N. Y. 562.

Where the laws of the several States differ, a citizen of one State asserting rights in another must claim them according to the laws of that State, and not according to those which obtain in his own State. Lemmon *v.* People, 26 Barb. 270; s. c. 5 Sandf. 681; 20 N. Y. 562.

No State can pass a law to punish a sale of property in another State where the right exists by the laws of the locality to make such a sale. People *v.* Merrill, 2 Parker C. C. 590.

The Constitution makes the people of the United States subjects of one government *quoad* everything within the national power and jurisdiction, but leaves them subjects of separate and distinct governments. Abbott *v.* Bayley, 23 Mass. 89.

It is most probable that the clause was intended to compel the general Government to extend the same privileges to the citizens of every State, and not permit that Government to grant privileges or immunities to citizens of some of the States and withhold them from those of others, and was never designed to interfere with the local policy of the State governments as to their own citizens. Kincaid *v.* Francis, Cooke, 49.

The clause may also mean that the citizens of other States shall be on the same footing with citizens of the State, in the payment of the debts of a deceased debtor. Campbell *v.* Morris, 3 H. & McH. 535.

The word "citizen," excludes every description of persons who were not fully recognized as citizens in the several States at the time of the adoption of the Constitution, and foreigners who have become citizens of some one of the States since that time, without naturalization. Dred Scott *v.* Sandford, 19 How. 393; Davis *v.* Pierse, 7 Minn. 13.

The word "citizen," means citizens of the United States. It does not authorize every one whom either of the States may recognize as a citizen, or may elevate to State citizenship, to demand in every State all the privileges and immunities accorded to its citizens. Davis *v.* Pierse, 7 Minn. 13.

The right to vote does not necessarily render a party a citizen. Foreigners not naturalized may be allowed to vote, yet this clause would not apply to them. Dred Scott *v.* Sandford, 19 How. 393.

The citizens here spoken of, are those who are entitled to all the privileges and immunities of citizens. The meaning of the language is, that no privilege enjoyed by, or immunity allowed to the most favored class of citizens of the State, shall be withheld from a citizen of any other State. State *v.* Claiborne, Meigs, 331.

The word "citizen," imports the same as the word "freeman," and means every person who by birth or naturalization is, or may be qualified to exercise and enjoy under like circumstances, all the rights which any

native-born white inhabitant of the State, does or can enjoy. Douglass
v. Stephens, 1 Del. Ch. 465.

A person may be a citizen, that is a member of the community who form the sovereignty, although he exercises no share of the political power, and is incapacitated from holding particular offices. Women and minors who form a part of the political family, can not vote, and when a property qualification is required, to vote or hold a particular office, those who have not the necessary qualification can not vote or hold the office, yet they are citizens. Dred Scott v. Sandford, 19 How. 393.

A free man of color, born within the United States, is a citizen of the United States. Smith v. Moody, 26 Ind. 299; contra, Amy v. Smith, 1 Litt. 326; Pendleton v. State, 6 Ark. 509; Hickland v. State, 8 Blackf. 365; State v. Cooper, 5 Blackf. 258; Baptiste v. State, 5 Blackf. 283; Shaw v. Brown, 35 Miss. 246.

The privileges and immunities are annexed to the *status* of citizenship. They are personal, and can not be assigned or imparted to any other person, natural or artificial. Slaughter v. Comm. 13 Gratt. 767.

The term "citizens," applies only to natural persons, members of the body politic, owing allegiance to the State, not to artificial persons created by the legislature, and possessing only the attributes which the legislature has prescribed. Paul v. Virginia, 8 Wall. 168.

Corporations are not citizens of the State which creates them, and can not be brought within the guaranty so as to entitle the corporations of each State to all privileges and immunities of corporations in the several States. Slaughter v. Comm. 13 Gratt. 767; Paul v. Virginia, 8 Wall. 168; Bank v. Earle, 13 Pet. 519; Ducat v. Chicago, 48 Ill. 172; Comm. v. Milton, 12 B. Mon. 212; Tatem v. Wright, 23 N. J. 429; Fire Department v. Helfevistein, 16 Wis. 136; State v. Lathrop, 10 La. Ann. 398; Warren Manuf. Co. v. Ætna Ins. Co. 2 Paine, 501 ; People v. Imlay, 20 Barb. 68; Phœnix Ins. v. Comm. 5 Bush, 68 ; F. & M. Ins. Co. v. Hurrah, 47 Ind. 236.

A statute imposing a tax upon foreign corporations, to which domestic corporations are not subjected, is not inconsistent with this clause. Att. Gen. v. Bay State Mining Co. 99 Mass. 148; Ducat v. Chicago, 48 Ill. 172; Phœnix Ins. Co. v. Comm. 5 Bush, 68; Comm. v. Milton, 12 B. Mon. 212; People v. Thurber, 13 Ill. 554; Paul v. Virginia, 8 Wall. 168; Tatem v. Wright, 23 N. J. 429; Slaughter v. Comm. 13 Gratt. 767 ; Firemen's Association v. Lounsbury, 21 Ill. 511; State v. Lathrop, 10 La. Ann. 398 ; Fire Department v. Noble, 3 E. D. Smith, 440; Fire Department v. Wright, 3 E. D. Smith, 453.

A statute providing that foreign corporations doing business in the State, may be sued by service of process on an agent in the State, is valid. If such corporations exercise franchises in the State, they will be deemed to have assented to the mode provided for instituting suits. Warren Manuf. Co. *v.* Ætna Ins. Co. 2 Paine, 501.

A statute requiring foreign corporations doing business in the State, to obtain a certificate from the State comptroller, is valid. People *v.* Imlay, 20 Barb. 68.

Citizens of other States are entitled to all immunity from taxation as respects their property in the State, which is enjoyed by citizens of the State. An act imposing higher taxes upon non-residents than upon citizens, is void. Wiley *v.* Parmer, 14 Ala. 627; Oliver *v.* Washington Mills, 93 Mass. 268; Smith *v.* Moody, 26 Ind. 299.

The property of a non-resident within the State, may be taxed equally with that of a resident. Duer *v.* Small, 4 Blatch. 263; Battle *v.* Corporation, 9 Ala. 234.

A State law imposing a discriminating tax on non-resident traders, is void. Ward *v.* Maryland, 12 Wall. 418; s. c 31 Md. 279.

A tax upon those who sell goods brought into the State from any other State, and not owned by persons domiciled in the State, is valid. People *v.* Coleman, 4 Cal. 46.

A tax upon non-resident traders or transient merchants, is valid where the taxation is the same as that imposed upon resident traders. Mount Pleasant *v.* Clutch, 6 Iowa, 546.

A State law requiring non-residents to take out a license to vend foreign merchandise, is valid. Sears *v.* Commissioners, 36 Ind. 267.

A State tax upon the sale of articles manufactured in the State, is valid. Downham *v.* Alexandria, 10 Wall. 173.

A State law which requires a license from all peddlers, except those who sell articles manufactured by themselves within the limits of the State, is valid. Seymour *v.* State, 51 Ala. 52.

A statute requiring a residence within the State for a certain number of years, in order to obtain a license to sell spirituous liquors, is valid. Austin *v.* State, 10 Mo. 591.

A mere difference in the modes of ascertaining the value of the property of residents and non-residents for taxation, where both modes are fair, does not amount to a discrimination between them so as to render the act invalid. Redd *v.* St. Francis Co. 17 Ark. 416.

The Constitution does not prohibit a discrimination between local freight and that which is extra-territorial when it commences its transit.

Such a discrimination denies to no citizen of another State, any privilege or immunity which it does not deny to the citizens of the State. Shipper *v.* Penn. R. R. Co. 47 Penn. 338.

The object of the Constitution was to secure to the citizens of every State an equal administration of justice, as it regarded their essential rights either of property or person, by the courts of every State, and was not at all intended to interfere with the mode of prosecuting those rights. The States are still left at liberty to prescribe the mode of commencing and conducting suits in their own courts, and if they provide extraordinary remedies for their own citizens, in extraordinary cases, it will not from thence follow that citizens of other States can claim them likewise. Hence the privilege of suing out an attachment may be limited to the citizens of the State. Kincaid *v.* Francis, Cooke, 49; Campbell *v.* Morris, 3 H. & McH. 535.

The right to institute actions of any kind, in another State, is one of the privileges and immunities to which the citizens of each State are entitled. Morgan *v.* Neville, 74 Penn. 52; Davis *v.* Peirse, 7 Minn. 13; McFarland *v.* Butler, 8 Minn. 116; Jackson *v.* Butler, 8 Minn. 117.

A law providing for the attachment of the property of non-residents for debt, is valid. Campbell *v.* Morris, 3 H. & McH. 535.

A citizen of one State has the right to sue out an attachment in another State, although the defendant and garnishee are residents of his own State. Morgan *v.* Neville, 74 Penn. 52.

A statute prohibiting all persons aiding the rebellion against the United States, from prosecuting or defending actions during the continuance of the rebellion, is void. Davis *v.* Peirse, 7 Minn. 13; McFarland *v.* Butler, 8 Minn. 116; Jackson *v.* Butler, 8 Minn. 117.

If a State legislature provides that a citizen, when commencing a suit, need not give security for costs, but that a plaintiff who is a citizen of another State, shall, the provision is not inconsistent with the Constitution. Kincaid *v.* Francis, Cooke, 49; Haney *v.* Marshall, 9 Ind. 194; Baker *v.* Wise, 16 Gratt. 139.

A citizen of one State can not, by virtue of this clause, claim the right to sue in another State, and there impeach an assignment made in his own State, which is valid by its laws but void by the laws of the State where he sues. Burlock *v.* Taylor, 33 Mass. 335.

A citizen of one State may sue a foreigner in the courts of another State, whether he comes there to embark for a foreign country, or to reside there for purposes of business. Barrell *v.* Benjamin, 15 Mass. 354.

A corporation itself, and its faculties or privileges as such, and the right of individuals to be or compose a corporation, and to act in a corporate capacity, are all peculiar privileges, creations of the local law, and can not, by the mere force of that law, exist or be exercised beyond its territorial jurisdiction. It therefore can operate in the territory of another sovereign only by his permission, express or implied. Comm. v. Milton, 12 B. Mon. 212; Slaughter v. Comm. 13 Gratt. 767.

A citizen of one State becoming entitled to property in another State, acquires and must hold it according to the laws of that State; and if the laws of the State prohibit its exportation, he can not export it. Allen v. Sarah, 2 Harring. 434.

Under this provision the citizens of the several States are not permitted to participate in all the rights which belong exclusively to the citizens of any other particular State, merely on the ground that they are enjoyed by those citizens. Nor is the legislature in regulating the use of the common property of the citizens of the State bound to extend to the citizens of all the other States the same advantages as are secured to its own citizens. A several fishery, either as the right to it respects running fish or such as are stationary, such as oysters, clams, or the like, is as much the property of the individual to whom it belongs as dry land or land covered with water. Where those private rights do not exist to the exclusion of the common right, that of fishing belongs to all the citizens or subjects of the State. It is the property of all. They may be considered as tenants in common of this property, and they are so exclusively entitled to the use of it that it can not be enjoyed by others without the tacit consent or express permission of the sovereign who has the power to regulate its use. The grant of privileges and immunities to the citizens of other States, does not amount to a grant of a cotenancy in the common property of the State. Corfield v. Coryell, 4 Wash. C. C. 371; Bennett v. Boggs, Bald. 60; McCready v. State, 94 U. S. 391; s. c. 27 Gratt. 985; Dunham v. Lamphere, 69 Mass. 268; State v. Medbury, 3 R. I. 138.

A statute passed for the purpose of preventing the escape of slaves may require an inspection of the vessels of non-residents, although the vessels of residents are not inspected. Baker v. Wise, 16 Gratt. 139.

A statute which makes a discrimination between the employment of vessels, but not between the persons owning or navigating them, does not discriminate in favor of citizens of the State, and is valid. The Ann Ryan, 7 Ben. 20.

A State law requiring an executor or administrator to pay the debts due to citizens of the State before paying debts due to citizens of other States, is valid. Douglass v. Stephens, 1 Del. Ch. 465.

Congress can not give privileges to citizens of one State over those of another by any measure which it can constitutionally adopt. Chapman v. Miller, 2 Spears, 769.

FUGITIVES FROM JUSTICE.   295

A provision in a statute of limitations that it shall not run when the defendant is out of the State, as against a resident, but shall as against a non-resident, is valid. Chemung Canal Bank *v.* Lowery, 93 U. S 72.

Pilot laws discriminating between vessels owned by citizens of the State and those owned by citizens of another State, are unconstitutional. Chapman *v.* Miller, 2 Spears, 769.

Congress can not give to a State the power to do a thing which it can not do itself. Chapman *v.* Miller, 2 Spears, 769.

A State law requiring a diploma from a regularly chartered medical school in order to practice medicine or surgery, except from those who have practiced within the State for ten years next preceding the passage of the law, is valid, and does not discriminate between citizens of different States. Ex parte Spinney, 10 Nev. 323.

The widows of the citizens of other States are not by this clause entitled to the same rights as the widows of persons resident in the State. Conner *v.* Elliott, 18 How. 591.

2. A person charged in any State with treason, felony, or other crime, who shall flee from justice, and be found in another State, shall, on demand of the executive authority of the State from which he fled, be delivered up, to be removed to the State having jurisdiction of the crime.

This clause by its terms applies only to criminals fleeing from one State to another State, and does not, in express terms, apply to those fleeing from a territory to a State. Ex parte James Romaine, 23 Cal. 585.

This clause does not contain a grant of power. It confers no right. . It is the regulation of a previously existing right. It makes obligatory upon every member of the Union the performance of an act which previously was of doubtful obligation. The whole effect of the Constitution is to confer on each member a right to demand from every other member a fugitive, and to make obligatory the surrender which was before discretionary. In re William Fetter, 23 N. J. 311.

The right of one State to claim the surrender of fugitives from justice who have escaped into another State, can be carried into effect only through the medium of laws and the intervention of magistrates. Comm. *v.* Tracy, 46 Mass. 536.

The purpose of this provision was two-fold: first, to impose an absolute obligation on each State to surrender criminals fleeing from the justice of another State; and second, to define clearly the class of criminals to be surrendered. Ex parte Peter Voorhees, 32 N. J. 141.

The words "treason, felony or other crime," in their plain and obvious import, as well as in their legal and technical sense, embrace every act forbidden and made punishable by a law of the State. The word "crime" of itself includes every offense from the highest to the lowest in the grade of offenses, and includes what are called misdemeanors as well as treason and felony. Comm. *v.* Dennison, 24 How. 66; Morton *v.* Skinner, 48 Ind. 123;. People *v.* Brady, 56 N. Y. 182; Ex parte John L. Clark, 9 Wend. 212; Ex parte Benjamin T. Greenough, 31 Vt. 279.

The word "crime" is a *nomen generalissamum*, and has always been considered as embracing every species of indictable offense. Ex parte Peter Voorhees, 32 N. J. 141.

All persons who are guilty of minor offenses, such as assaults, libels and the entire train of similar misdemeanors are embraced in the words of the Constitution. Ex parte Peter Voorhees, 32 N. J. 141.

The word "crime" embraces an act which was not criminal at the time of the adoption of the Constitution, but was made so by a subsequent statute. Ex parte Wm. H. Hughes, Phillips, 57; Ex parte Peter Voorhees, 32 N. J. 141; People *v.* Brady, 56 N. Y. 182.

This clause includes every offense made punishable by the law of the State in which it was committed, and gives the right to the executive authority of the State to demand the fugitive from the executive authority of the State in which he is found. The right given to demand, implies that it is an absolute right, and it follows that there must be a correlative obligation to deliver, without any reference to the character of the crime charged or to the policy or laws of the State to which the fugitive had fled. Comm. *v.* Dennison, 24 How. 66; Ex parte Peter Voorhees, 32 N. J. 141.

A person who commits a crime within a State, and withdraws himself from such jurisdiction without waiting to abide the consequences of such act, must be regarded as a fugitive from the justice of the State whose laws he has infringed. Ex parte Peter Voorhees, 32 N. J. 141.

It is the right of the sovereignty whose laws have been violated to decide what offenders it will pursue, and the State upon which the demand is made can not rightfully call in question that decision. Ex parte Peter Voorhees, 32 N. J. 141.

It is not necessary to show that the person is guilty. It is not necessary, as under the comity of nations, to examine into the facts alleged against him constituting the crime. It is sufficient that he is charged with having committed a crime. Ex parte John L. Clark, 9 Wend. 212; People *v.* Brady, 56 N. Y. 182.

The executive authority of the State is not authorized by this article to make the demand unless the party is charged in the regular course of judicial proceedings. It is equally necessary that the executive authority of the State upon which the demand is made, when called on to render his aid, should be satisfied by competent proof that the party is so charged. Comm. *v.* Dennison, 24 How. 66.

The duty to surrender is not one resting in discretion. If the demand is made in due form, and the requisite documents exhibited showing that the fugitive is charged with crime, the duty to surrender becomes merely ministerial. Under such circumstances, to refuse to authorize the extradition, is a clear infraction of the rule prescribed by the Constitution. The Constitution has made the surrender of a fugitive from justice, which, by the law of nations depended on the concessions of comity, a rule of law of perfect obligation and entirely imperative in its character. Ex parte Peter Voorhees, 32 N. J. 141.

The executive of the State upon whom the demand is made for the surrender of the fugitive, is not authorized to look behind the indictment or affidavit in which the crime against the State is charged, and inquire whether, by the laws of his own State, the facts alleged would constitute a crime in his own State. To refuse to deliver up a fugitive from justice, on the legally authorized demand of the executive officer of the State from which he fled, on the pretext that by the laws of the State in which the fugitive is found, he is not guilty of any criminal offense, would be an open, palpable violation of the Constitution. Johnston *v.* Riley, 13 Geo. 97.

The Constitution does not assume to deal with the question before the proper executive demand has been made, nor undertake, in the absence of a demand, to define the duties nor limit the authority of the State within which the fugitive may be found. A State law providing for the arrest and detention of a fugitive until a demand can be made, is valid. Ex parte John White, 49 Cal. 433; Comm. *v.* Tracy, 46 Mass. 536; Ex parte Cubreth, 49 Cal. 435.

A State law requiring the officer making the arrest to take the party before the nearest judge for identification, is valid. Robinson *v.* Flanders, 29 Ind. 10.

A State law which makes it the duty of the executive to issue the warrant upon a proper requisition, is constitutional. Ex parte Joseph Smith, 3 McLean, 121.

A State law which is intended to aid in the enforcement of the act of Congress relating to the surrender of fugitives from justice, is valid. Comm. *v.* Hall, 75 Mass. 262.

Congress has the power to vest in any national officer the authority to cause the arrest in any State of a fugitive from the justice of another State, and to surrender such fugitive on the requisition of the executive of the latter State. Ex parte Peter Voorhees, 32 N. J. 141.

Every sovereign nation has the right to surrender fugitives within its territory. No State is bound to harbor criminals within its borders, but may, at its option, surrender them to the government against whose laws they have offended. Hence a fugitive from justice from either of the United States, may, under the provisions of the Constitution, be arrested and detained preparatory to his surrender before a requisition is actually made by the executive of the State where the crime is committed. It is an exercise of power essential to the full operation of the Constitution. In re Wm. Fetter, 23 N. J. 311; People v. Schenck, 2 Johns. 479; In re Thomas F. Goodhue, 1 Wheel. Crim. Cas. 427; vide People v. Wright, 2 Caines, 213; Ex parte Edwin Heyward, 1 Sandf. 701.

3. No person held to service or labor in one State, under the laws thereof, escaping into another, shall, in consequence of any law or regulation therein, be discharged from such service or labor, but shall be delivered up on claim of the party to whom such service or labor may be due.

Congress has the power to pass laws to carry this provision into effect. Prigg v. Comm. 16 Pet. 539; Henry v. Lowell, 16 Barb. 268; Miller v. McQuerry, 5 McLean, 469; Norris v. Newton, 5 McLean, 92; Ex parte Martin, 2 Paine, 348; Ableman v. Booth, 21 How. 506; S. C. 3 Wis. 1; Jones v. Van Zandt, 5 How. 215; S. C. 2 McLean, 596; Butler v. Hopper, 1 Wash. C. C. 499; Ex parte Simmons, 4 Wash. C. C. 396; Ex parte Simeon Bushnell, 9 Ohio St. 76; Sims' Case, 61 Mass. 285; Comm. v. Aves, 35 Mass. 193; Comm. v. Fitzgerald, 7 Law Rep. 379; Comm. v. Griffith, 19 Mass. 11; Wright v. Deacon, 5 S. & R. 62; Hill v. Low, 4 Wash. C. C. 327; Johnson v. Tompkins, Bald. 571; Kauffman v. Oliver, 10 Penn. 514; Jack v. Martin, 12 Wend. 311; S. C. 14 Wend. 509; Floyd v. Recorder, 11 Wend. 180; Glenn v. Hodges, 9 Johns. 67; Graves v. State, 1 Ind. 368; Thornton's Case, 11 Ill. 32; Eells v. People, 5 Ill. 498; Fanney v. Montgomery, Breese, 188; Ex parte Perkins, 2 Cal. 424; Donnell v. State, 3 Ind. 480; State v. Hoppess, 2 West. L. J. 289; Ex parte Richards, 3 West. L. J. 563; Gittner v. Gorham, 4 McLean, 402; Opinion of Justices, 41 N. H. 553; Ex parte Long, 9 N. Y. Leg. Obs. 73; U. S. v. Williamson, 4 A. L. Reg. 5; Ray v. Donnell, 4 McLean, 504.

SECTION III.

1. New States may be admitted by the Congress into this Union; but no new State shall be formed or erected within the jurisdiction of any other State; nor any State be formed by the junction of two or more

States, or parts of States, without the consent of the legislatures of the States concerned, as well as of the Congress.

The power to expand the territory of the United States by the admission of new States is plainly given ; and in the construction of this power by all the departments of the Government, it has been held to authorize the acquisition of territory not fit for admission at the time, but to be admitted as soon as its population and situation would entitle it to admission. It is acquired to become a State, and not to be held as a colony and governed by Congress with absolute authority. And as the propriety of admitting a new State is committed to the sound discretion of Congress, the power to acquire territory for that purpose to be held by the United States until it is in a suitable condition to become a State upon an equal footing with the other States, must rest upon the same discretion. It is a question for the political department of the Government, and not the judicial; and whatever the political department of the Government shall recognize as within the limits of the United States, the judicial department is also bound to recognize and to administer in it the laws of the United States so far as they apply. Dred Scott *v.* Sandford, 19 How. 393.

The new States stand on an equal footing with the other States, and have the same powers and privileges. Pollard *v.* Hagan, 3 How. 212; Withers *v.* Buckley, 20 How. 84; S. C. 29 Miss. 21; Woodman *v.* Kilbourn Manuf. Co. 1 Abb. C. C. 158.

If an express stipulation were inserted in an act admitting a State into the Union granting the municipal right of sovereignty and eminent domain to the United States, such stipulation would be void and inoperative, because the United States have no constitutional capacity to exercise municipal jurisdiction, sovereignty, or eminent domain within the limits of a State or elsewhere, except in the cases in which it is expressly granted. Pollard *v.* Hagan, 3 How. 212 ; Strader *v.* Graham, 10 How. 82; Depew *v.* Trustees, 5 Ind. 8.

When a condition annexed to a State Constitution is rescinded with the assent of the State Government and the Federal Government, given through the constituted authorities of each, the powers disclaimed may be resumed and immediately exercised by the State authorities. Duke *v.* Navigation Co. 10 Ala. 82.

If Congress, upon the presentation of a Constitution by a territory, consents to admit it as a State upon condition that certain alterations are made therein, and these alterations are accepted by the territorial legislature, such alterations become a part of the State Constitution. Brittle *v.* People, 2 Neb. 198.

2. **The Congress shall have power to dispose of, and make all needful rules and regulations respecting**

the territory or other property belonging to the United States; and nothing in this Constitution shall be so construed as to prejudice any claims of the United States, or of any particular State.

The term "territory," as here used, is merely descriptive of one kind of property, and is equivalent to the word lands. Congress has the same power over it as over any other property belonging to the United States. This power is vested in Congress without limitation. U. S. *v.* Gratiot, 14 Pet. 526.

The words "other property," by every known rule of interpretation, must mean property of a different description from territory or land. Dred Scott *v.* Sandford, 19 How. 393.

The Constitution confers on the Government the powers of making war and of making treaties; consequently it possesses the power of acquiring territory either by conquest or by treaty. Am. Ins. Co. *v.* Canter, 1 Pet. 511.

This clause authorizes the passage of all laws necessary to secure the rights of the United States to the public lands, and to provide for their sale and to protect them from taxation. Pollard *v.* Hagan, 3 How. 212.

This clause does not confer on Congress any power to grant the shores of navigable waters, or the soil under them within a State. Pollard *v.* Hagan, 3 How. 212.

There can be neither a reservation nor appropriation of the public domain for any purpose whatever, without the express authority of law. Neither the President nor the executive officers in the several departments of the Government possess an absolute and inherent power to do any act not authorized by the Constitution or the acts of Congress. To the Constitution and laws alone they must look for the source of their power and authority, because they can derive them from no other. McConnell *v.* Wilcox, 2 Ill. 344.

Nothing but an act of Congress can authorize the exercise of the power to grant public property. Seabury *v.* Field, 1 McA. 1; U. S. *v.* Fitzgerald, 15 Pet. 407.

Congress can make all needful rules and regulations for the disposition and protection of public lands within the limits of a State, but beyond this it can exercise no other acts of sovereignty which it may not exercise in common over the lands of individuals. U. S. *v.* Railroad Bridge Co. 6 McLean, 517.

Until the Government has substantially parted with the land, and thereby divested itself of the jurisdiction over it conferred by the Constitution, it may provide for the protection and disposition thereof in such manner as may be necessary and adapted to those purposes. Congress may, therefore, provide that all contracts and transfers relating to such land, made before a patent issues, shall be void. Rose *v.* Buckland, 17 Ill. 309; Dyke *v.* McVey, 16 Ill. 41.

Congress has the absolute right to prescribe the times, the conditions, and the mode of transferring the public domain or any part of it, and to designate the persons to whom the transfer shall be made. No State legislation can interfere with this right or embarrass its exercise. Gibson *v.* Choteau, 13 Wall. 92; Irvine *v.* Marshall, 20 How. 558.

Congress has the sole power to declare the dignity and effect of titles emanating from the United States. Bagnell *v.* Broderick, 13 Pet. 436.

The power to dispose of the territory vests in Congress the power not only to sell, but also to lease the lands. The disposal must be left to the discretion of Congress. U. S. *v.* Gratiot, 14 Pet. 526.

A military officer at the head of a provisional government has no power, without an act of Congress, to authorize a grant of the public lands. Seabury *v.* Field, 1 McA. 1.

Congress may prohibit and punish trespassers on public lands within the limits of a State. Jourdan *v.* Barrett, 4 How. 169.

Congress has authority to dispose of the public lands as homesteads, and to secure the title to such grantees and *bona fide* purchasers free from liability for debts contracted prior to the issuing of the patent therefor, whether such lands are within the boundaries of a State or not. Russell *v.* Lowth, 21 Minn. 167; Gile *v.* Hallock, 33 Wis. 523; Miller *v.* Little, 47 Cal. 348.

A title to land may be conveyed by treaty, and no patent is necessary. U. S. *v.* Brooks, 10 How. 442; Eu-che-lah *v.* Welsh, 3 Hawks, 155.

The President and Senate, in concluding a treaty, may lawfully covenant that a patent shall issue to convey lands which belong to the United States, without the consent of Congress. Holden *v.* Joy, 17 Wall. 211.

No State can pass any law depriving a patentee of the possession and enjoyment of the property by reason of any delay in the transfer of the title after the initiation of proceedings for its acquisition. Gibson *v.* Choteau, 13 Wall. 92.

A State may tax persons occupying the public lands of the United States. The power of taxation for police or municipal purposes, whether for the benefit of local districts, or for the support of the State organization, is co-extensive with the persons of all who enjoy the protection of the State government, whether citizens or foreigners, whether occupying lands owned by themselves, or a part of the national domain. People *v.* Naglie, 1 Cal. 231.

No State law, whether of limitations or otherwise, can defeat the title of the United States to public land within the limits of a State. Jourdan *v.* Barrett, 4 How. 169.

A State statute requiring all persons engaged in mining on the public lands to take out a license, is not a regulation of the public lands. People *v.* Naglie, 1 Cal. 231.

In the admission of new States into the Union, compacts are entered into with the Federal Government, that they will not tax the lands of the United States. This implies that the States have the power to tax such lands, if unrestrained by compact. U. S. *v.* Railroad Bridge Co. 6 McLean, 517.

If, at the time of the purchase, the jurisdiction over the land is not ceded, the State may tax them. In many instances the States have taxed the lands on which custom houses and other public buildings have been constructed, and such taxes have been paid by the Federal Government. U. S. *v.* Railroad Bridge Co. 6 McLean, 517.

The proprietorship of land in a State, can not enlarge the sovereignty of the Federal Government, or restrict the sovereignty of the State. This sovereignty extends to the State limits over the territory of the State, subject only to the proprietary right of the lands owned by the Federal Government, and the right to dispose of such lands and protect them under such regulations as it may deem proper. U. S. *v.* Railroad Bridge Co. 6 McLean, 517; Camp *v.* Smith, 2 Minn. 155; State *v.* Batchelder, 5 Minn. 223.

A State may tax land after it has been entered and paid for, although no patent has been entered therefor. Carroll *v.* Safford, 3 How. 441; Levi *v.* Thompson, 4 How. 17; Carroll *v.* Perry, 4 McLean, 25; Astrom *v.* Hammond, 3 McLean, 107; Witherspoon *v.* Duncan, 4 Wall. 210; S. C. 21 Ark. 240.

In the discharge of the ordinary functions of sovereignty, a State has a right to provide for intercourse between the citizens, commercial or otherwise, in every part of the State, by the establishment of easements, whether they may be common roads, turnpike, plank or railroads. The kind of easement must depend on the discretion of the legislature. This power extends as well over the lands owned by the United States, as to lands owned by individuals. The right of eminent domain appertains to a State sovereignty, and is to be exercised free from the restraints of the Constitution. The property of individuals is subject to this right, and no reason is perceived why the public lands should not also be subject to it. U. S. *v.* Railroad Bridge Co. 6 McLean, 517; Ill. Cent. R. R. Co. *v.* U. S. 20 Law Rep. 630.

No State formed out of the territory of the United States has a right to the public lands within its limits, or can exercise any power whatever over them. Turner *v.* Missionary Union, 5 McLean, 344; U. S. *v.* Gratiot, 14 Pet. 526.

Where lands are reserved or held by the general Government for specified and national purposes, a State can not construct an easement which will in any degree affect such purposes injuriously. U. S. *v.* Railroad Bridge Co. 6 McLean, 517.

When the acts of Congress make a patent necessary to complete the title to public land, no State law can make anything else evidence that the title has passed. Wilcox *v.* Jackson, 13 Pet. 498.

In legislating for the territories, Congress exercises the combined power of the general and of a State government. Am. Ins. Co. *v.* Canter, 1 Pet. 511.

The right to govern the territory of the United States, is the inevitable consequence of the right to acquire territory. Dred Scott *v.* Sandford, 19 How. 393; Am. Ins. Co. *v.* Canter, 1 Pet. 511; U. S. *v.* Gratiot, 14 Pet. 526.

Congress possesses the absolute power of governing and legislating for the territories, and may give a territorial court jurisdiction over a suit brought by or against a citizen of a territory. Sere *v.* Pitot, 6 Cranch, 332.

A territorial legislature can not exercise the right of eminent domain over lands belonging to the United States, so as to impair the title of the latter, or hamper the primary disposal of the soil, by a claim derived from such authority. Pratt *v.* Brown, 3 Wis. 603.

The power to govern the territories subject to the Constitution is in Congress. It may do it mediately or immediately, either by the creation of a territorial government with power to legislate for the territory, subject to such restraints and limitations as Congress may impose upon it, or by the passage of laws directly operating upon the territory, without the intervention of a subordinate government. Edwards *v.* Panama, 1 Oregon, 418.

A territorial government is the only mode by which the purchasers and occupants of lands beyond the limits of any State, can be protected in their rights of person and property. Hence the implied power of Congress to establish such a government. U. S. *v.* Railroad Bridge Co. 6 McLean, 517; U. S. *v.* Gratiot, 14 Pet. 526; State *v.* Navigation Co. 11 Mart. 309.

The power to acquire necessarily carries with it the power to preserve and apply to the purposes for which it was acquired. It is therefore the duty of Congress to establish a government over the people in a territory.

The form of the government to be established necessarily rests in the discretion of Congress. Some form of civil authority is absolutely necessary to organize and preserve civilized society and prepare it to become a State, and what is the best form must always depend on the condition of the territory at the time, and the choice of the mode must depend upon the exercise of a discretionary power by Congress, acting within the scope of its constitutional authority. Dred Scott *v.* Sandford, 19 How. 393.

The power of Congress over the person or property of a citizen, can never be a mere discretionary power. The powers of the Government and the rights and privileges of the citizen, are regulated and plainly defined by the Constitution itself. When a territory becomes a part of the United States, the Federal Government enters into possession in the character impressed upon it by those who created it. It enters upon it with its powers over the citizen strictly defined and limited by the Constitution, from which it derives its own existence, and by virtue of which alone it continues to exist and act as a government and sovereignty. It has no power of any kind beyond it, and it can not, when it enters a territory of the United States, put off its character and assume discretionary or despotic powers, which the Constitution has denied to it. It can not create for itself a new character separated from the citizens of the United States, and the duties it owes them under the provisions of the Constitution. The territory being a part of the United States, the Government and the citizen both enter it under the authority of the Constitution, with their respective rights defined and marked out, and the Government can exercise no power over his person or property beyond what that instrument confers. Dred Scott *v.* Sandford, 19 How. 393 ; Ex parte Perkins, 2 Cal. 424.

This provision applies only to the property which the States held in common at the time of the adoption of the Constitution, and has no reference whatever to any territory or other property which the Government may have acquired since that time. The language used in the clause, the arrangement and combination of the powers, and the somewhat unusual phraseology it uses when it speaks of the political power to be exercised in the government of the territory, all indicate this design and meaning. It does not speak of *any* territory or of *territories*, but uses language which, according to its legitimate meaning, points to a particular thing. The power is given only in relation to *the* territory of the United States, that is, to a territory then in existence, and then known or claimed as the territory of the United States. It begins its enumeration of powers by that of disposing, in other words making sale, of the lands, or raising money from them. It then gives the power which was necessarily associated with the disposition and sale of the lands, that is, the power of making needful rules and regulations respecting the territory. These words are not the words usually employed by statesmen in giving supreme power of legislation. Whether the particular clause is taken by itself or in connection with the other provisions of the Constitution, it can not, by any just rule of interpretation, be construed to apply to any territory which the Government has since obtained from foreign nations. Dred Scott *v.* Sandford, 19 How. 393.

The principle has been established that discovery gives title to the government by whose subjects or by whose authority it is made, against all other European governments, which title may be consummated by possession. The exclusion of all other Europeans necessarily gives to the nation making the discovery the sole right of acquiring the soil from the natives, and establishing settlements upon it. It is a right with which no Europeans can interfere. It is a right which all assert for themselves, and to the assertion of which by others all assent. In the establishment of these relations, the rights of the original inhabitants were in no instance entirely disregarded, but were necessarily, to a considerable extent, impaired. They were admitted to be the rightful occupants of the soil, with a legal as well as just claim to retain possession of it, and to use it according to their own discretion, but their rights to complete sovereignty as independent nations were necessarily diminished, and their power to dispose of the soil at their own will, to whomsoever they pleased, was denied by the original fundamental principle that discovery gives exclusive title to those who make it. While the different nations of Europe respected the rights of the natives as occupants, they asserted the ultimate dominion to be in themselves, and claimed and exercised, as a consequence of this ultimate dominion, a power to grant the soil while yet in possession of the natives. These grants have been understood by all to convey a title to the grantees subject only to the Indian right of occupancy. The United States have unequivocally acceded to the great and broad rule by which its civilized inhabitants now hold this country. They maintain that discovery gave an exclusive right to extinguish the Indian title of occupancy, either by purchase or by conquest, and gave also a right to such a degree of sovereignty as the circumstances of the people would allow them to exercise. The existence of this power must negative the existence of any right which may conflict with and control it. An absolute title to lands can not exist at the same time in different persons, or in different governments. An absolute title must be an exclusive title, or at least a title which excludes all others not compatible with it. The absolute title of the government, subject only to the Indian right of occupancy, is incompatible with an absolute and complete title in the Indians. It has never been contended that the Indian title amounted to nothing. The right of possession has never been questioned. The claim of the Government extends to the complete, ultimate title charged with this right of possession, and to the exclusive power of acquiring that right. Johnson *v.* McIntosh, 8 Wheat. 543; Fletcher *v.* Peck, 6 Cranch, 87; Mitchell *v.* United States, 9 Pet. 712; Clark *v.* Smith, 13 Pet. 195; Latimer *v.* Poteet, 14 Pet. 4; Jackson *v.* Porter, 1 Paine, 457; Blair *v.*

Pathkiller, 2 Yerg. 407; Vanhorne v. Dorrance, 2 Dall. 304; Choteau v. Molony, 16 How. 203; Godfrey v. Beardsley, 2 McLean, 412.

The right of possession has never been questioned. The claim of the Government extends to the complete ultimate title charged with this right of possession, and to the exclusive power of acquiring that right. Johnson v. McIntosh, 8 Wheat. 543: Ogden v. Lee, 6 Hill, 546; Strong v. Waterman, 11 Paige, 607; Blair v. Pathkiller, 2 Yerg. 407.

A mere reservation of the Indian right to a certain part, within described boundaries, leaves the right reserved as it stood before the cession. Godfrey v. Beardsley, 2 McLean, 412; Wheeler v. Me-shin-go-me-sia, 30 Ind. 402; Penobscot Indians v. Veazie, 58 Me. 402.

An individual who purchases land from the Indians acquires only their title. The land remains a part of their territory, and is held under them by a title depending on their laws. The purchaser incorporates himself with them, so far as respects the property, and holds the title under their protection, and subject to their laws. If they annul the grant, the courts of the United States can not interpose for the protection of the title. A purchase can not be distinguished from a grant made to a native Indian, authorizing him to hold a particular tract of land in severalty. As such a grant can not separate the Indian from his nation, nor give a title which the courts of the United States can distinguish from the title of his tribe, as the land may be still conquered from, or ceded by his tribe, there is no legal principle which will authorize the assertion, that different consequences are attached to a purchase by a stranger. Johnson v. McIntosh, 8 Wheat. 543; Jackson v. Porter, 1 Paine, 457; Vanhorne v. Dorrance, 2 Dall. 306.

The Indians may dispose of their land with the consent of the executive, where the executive is authorized to give such consent by the provisions of any treaty or act of Congress. Hale v. Wilder, 8 Kans. 545.

The consent of the executive department to a sale of land by Indians, where it was not authorized by a treaty or an act of Congress, will not make a sale valid. Hale v. Wilder, 8 Kans. 545.

The consent of the Government to a sale of lands by Indians may be given by treaty or by an act of Congress, but in no other way. Hale v. Wilder, 8 Kans. 545.

A party who purchases the title subject to the Indian right of occupancy, acquires nothing but the right to purchase whenever the Indians may choose to sell. Ogden v. Lee, 6 Hill, 546; Fellows v. Lee, 5 Den. 628; Wadsworth v. Buffalo H. Association, 15 Barb. 82.

The Indian inhabitants are considered merely as occupants to be protected while in peace in the possession of their lands, but incapable of transferring an absolute title to others. Johnson *v.* McIntosh, 8 Wheat. 543.

The Indian right to land is not merely of possession; that of alienation is concomitant, subject only to ratification and confirmation by the Government. Mitchel *v.* U. S. 9 Pet. 711 ; Wilson *v.* Wall, 6 Wall. 83.

The Indians have a right to enjoy their possessions, and to use and occupy their lands in any manner agreeable to them, and for all time to come. Wadsworth *v.* Buffalo H. Association, 15 Barb. 82.

The Indians are not tenants of the State, but hold under their own original title. They are rightful lords of the soil, and may cut and sell the timber thereon. Ogden *v.* Lee, 6 Hill, 546.

The timber, while standing, is a part of the realty, and can only be sold as the land could be. Consequently, the timber can not be sold until rightfully severed. U. S. *v.* Cook, 19 Wall. 591.

The right of use and occupancy by the Indians is unlimited. They may exercise it at their discretion. If the lands in a state of nature are not in a condition for profitable use, they may be made so. U. S. *v.* Cook, 19 Wall. 591.

If desired for the purposes of agriculture, the lands may be cleared of their timber to such an extent as may be reasonable under the circumstances. The timber taken off by the Indians in such clearing, may be sold by them. But, to justify any cutting of the timber, except for use on the premises as timber or its product, it must be done in good faith for the improvement of the land. The improvement must be the principal thing, and the cutting of the timber the incident only. Any cutting beyond this is waste, and unauthorized. U. S. *v.* Cook, 19 Wall. 591; U. S. *v.* Foster, 2 Biss. 377.

The presumption is against the authority of the Indians to cut and sell the timber, and every purchaser from them is charged with notice of this presumption. U. S. *v.* Cook, 19 Wall. 591.

The Indians have the same rights in the lands of their reservations as a tenant for life has in the lands of a remainder-man. What a tenant for life may do upon the lands of a remainder-man, the Indians may do upon their reservations, but no more. U. S. *v.* Cook, 19 Wall. 591.

When the timber is rightfully severed, it is no longer a part of the land, and there is no restriction upon its sale. The timber may then be sold by the Indians. U. S. *v.* Cook, 19 Wall. 591; U. S. *v.* Foster, 2 Biss. 377.

If the timber is severed for the purposes of sale alone, the cutting is wrongful, and the timber when cut, becomes the absolute property of the United States. U. S. *v.* Cook, 19 Wall. 591.

When part of an Indian reservation is taken for public uses, with the consent of the tribe, it is not necessary to obtain the consent of the owner of the right of pre-emption, and when he purchases the land from the Indians he takes it subject to the servitudes or easements upon it, although no compensation was made to him. Wadsworth *v.* Buffalo H. Association, 15 Barb. 82.

The nature of the Indian title is not such as to be absolutely repugnant to a seizin in fee on the part of the State in which the land is situated. Fletcher *v.* Peck, 6 Cranch, 87.

A State law respecting lands in the Indian country, to take effect when the Indian title is extinguished, is valid, and will be enforced when the State acquires the soil. George *v.* Gamble, 2 Overt. 170.

A reservation to an Indian under a treaty, gives a right which is paramount to a grant from a State made while the Indian occupancy continued. Cornet *v.* Winton, 2 Yerg. 143.

A patent by a State, of land owned by it in an Indian country, is not void, but passes a title subject to the Indian right of occupancy. Clark *v.* Smith, 13 Pet. 195.

SECTION IV.

1. The United States shall guarantee to every State in this Union a republican form of government, and shall protect each of them against invasion, and on application of the legislature, or of the executive, when the legislature can not be convened, against domestic violence.

The recognition of the legality of a State government is political in its nature, and is placed in the hands of the political department. It rests with Congress to decide what government is the established one in a State; for, as the United States guarantee to each State a republican form of government, Congress must necessarily decide what government is established in a State before it can determine whether it is republican or not. Its decision is binding on every other department of the Government, and can not be questioned in a judicial tribunal. Luther *v.* Borden, 7 How. 1; Texas *v.* White, 7 Wall. 700; Calhoun *v.* Calhoun, 2 Rich. N. S. 283.

When the senators and representatives of a State are admitted into the councils of the Union, the authority of the government under which they are appointed, as well as its republican character, is recognized by the proper constitutional authority. Luther *v.* Borden, 7 How. 1; Blair *v.* Ridgeley, 41 Mo. 63.

Under this clause, Congress has the power to re-establish the broken relations of a rebellious State with the Union. Texas *v.* White, 7 Wall. 700.

In establishing a new government in a rebellious State, Congress may require that the new State Constitution shall pass any measure which Congress has the power to enact and enforce. Shorter *v.* Cobb, 39 Geo. 285; Hardeman *v.* Downer, 39 Geo. 425.

Congress is the only department of the Government authorized to reorganize and reconstruct rebellious States, and to provide for the establishment of civil governments therein. Powell *v.* Boon, 43 Ala. 469.

In the exercise of the power conferred by this clause, as in the exercise of every other constitutional power, a discretion in the choice of means is necessarily allowed. Texas *v.* White, 7 Wall. 700.

Where a rebellious State frames a Constitution which is approved by Congress, it is estopped to deny its validity. The action of Congress can not be inquired into, for the judicial is bound to follow the action of the political department. White *v.* Hart, 13 Wall. 646; s. c. 39 Geo. 306.

The approval of the Constitution of a rebellious State by Congress does not make the Constitution an act of Congress. Homestead Cases, 23 Gratt. 266; In re Sarah Kennedy, 2 Rich. N. S. 116; White *v.* Hart, 13 Wall. 646; s. c. 39 Geo. 306; Marsh *v.* Burroughs, 1 Wood. 463.

No particular government is designated as republican, nor is the exact form to be guaranteed in any manner especially indicated. A government may be republican, although women are not made voters. Minor *v.* Happersett, 21 Wall. 162.

It rests with Congress to determine the means proper to protect a State against invasion or domestic violence. Luther *v.* Borden, 7 How. 1.

A State may use its military power to put down an armed insurrection too strong to be controlled by the civil authority. The power is essential to the existence of every government, essential to the preservation of order and free institutions, and is as necessary to the States of this Union as to any other government. The State itself must determine what degree of force the crisis demands. If the State government deems the armed opposition so formidable as to require the use of its military force and the declaration of martial law, its authority can not be questioned by the courts. The established government may resort to the rights and usages of war to maintain itself and to overcome opposition. Luther *v.* Borden, 4 How. 1.

ARTICLE V.

1. The Congress, whenever two-thirds of both Houses shall deem it necessary, shall propose amendments to this Constitution, or, on the application of the legislatures of two-thirds of the several States, shall call a convention for proposing amendments, which, in either case, shall be valid, to all intents and purposes, as part of this Constitution, when ratified by the legislatures of three-fourths of the several States, or by conventions in three-fourths thereof, as the one or the other mode of ratification may be proposed by the Congress; provided that no amendment which may be made prior to the year one thousand eight hundred and eight, shall in any manner affect the first and fourth clauses in the ninth section of the first article; and that no State, without its consent, shall be deprived of its equal suffrage in the Senate.

ARTICLE VI.

1. All debts contracted and engagements entered into, before the adoption of this Constitution, shall be as valid against the United States under this Constitution as under the confederation.

2. This Constitution, and the laws of the United States which shall be made in pursuance thereof, and all treaties made, or which shall be made, under the authority of the United States, shall be the supreme law of the land; and the judges in every State shall be bound thereby, anything in the constitution or laws of any State to the contrary notwithstanding.

Supremacy.

The departments of the Government are legislative, executive and judicial. They are co ordinate in degree to the extent of the powers delegated to each of them. Each in the exercise of its powers is independent of the other, but all rightfully done by either is binding upon the others.

The Constitution is supreme over all of them, because the people who have ratified it have made it so. Consequently, anything which may be done unauthorized by it is unlawful. But it is not only over the departments of the Government that the Constitution is supreme. It is so to the extent of its delegated powers over all who made themselves parties to it, States as well as persons, within those concessions of sovereign powers yielded by the people of the States, when they accepted the Constitution in their conventions. Nor does its supremacy end there. It is supreme over the people of the United States aggregately and in their separate sovereignties. Dodge *v.* Woolsey, 18 How. 331.

The "supreme law of the land" is intended to be supreme, as construed and applied by the proper tribunal; in other words, it is not to be supreme solely in its dead letter, but in its practical construction. Its supremacy is not to be alone admitted in name, but in fact. As the laws of the Federal Government are made the supreme law of the land, and as the judicial power of the same Government extends to all cases in law and equity arising under this law, it follows as a necessary logical result, that the determination of the highest tribunal created by this supreme law must be final and conclusive upon all. If the law be supreme, the highest tribunal created by that law must also be supreme. If the law is supreme over the constitutions and laws of the States, then it is a necessary result that the interpretation of this law by the highest tribunal created by the law itself must be equally supreme over the constitutions and laws of the State. Warner *v.* Uncle Sam, 9 Cal. 697.

Statutes.

In declaring what shall be the supreme law of the land, the Constitution itself is first mentioned, and not the laws of the United States generally, but those only which shall be made in pursuance of the Constitution have that rank. Marbury *v.* Madison, 1 Cranch, 137.

An act of Congress repugnant to the Constitution, is void, for the Constitution is the fundamental and paramount law. Marbury *v.* Madison, 1 Cranch, 137.

The words "which shall be made in pursuance thereof," show the precision and foresight which marks every clause in the instrument. The sovereignty to be created was to be limited in its powers of legislation, and if it passed a law not authorized by its enumerated powers, it was not to be regarded as the supreme law of the land, nor were the State judges bound to carry it into effect. Ableman *v.* Booth, 21 How. 506; S. C. 3 Wis. 1.

The nullity of any act inconsistent with the Constitution, is produced by the declaration that the Constitution is the supreme law. The appropriate application of that part of the clause which confers the same supremacy on laws and treaties, is to such acts of the State legislatures as do not transcend their powers, but though enacted in the execution of acknowledged State powers, interfere with or are contrary to the laws of Congress made in pursuance of the Constitution, or some treaty made under the authority of the United States. In every such case the act of Congress or treaty is supreme, and the law of the State, though enacted in the exercise of powers not controverted, must yield to it. Gibbons v. Ogden, 9 Wheat. 1; S. C. 17 Johns. 488; 4 Johns. Ch. 150; Brown v. State, 12 Wheat. 419; Sinnot v. Davenport, 22 How. 227.

The Federal Government, though limited in its powers, is supreme, and its laws, when made in pursuance of the Constitution, form the supreme law of the land, "anything in the Constitution or laws of any State to the contrary notwithstanding." M'Culloch v. State, 4 Wheat. 316.

The laws of the United States are not to be considered as the laws of a foreign government. They are laws operating upon and binding on the same people as the government and laws of the several States. The laws of one State may be considered as foreign in relation to the government and actions of another State, because in no sense binding without the jurisdiction of the State. It is not so, however, with respect to the laws of the United States. The Government of the United States and that of the States, ought rather to be considered as parts of the same system. Stearns v. U. S. 2 Paine, 300; Gilmer v. Lime Point, 18 Cal. 229.

Treaties.

A treaty is but a part of the law of the land, and what is forbidden by the Constitution can no more be done by a treaty than by an act of Congress. People v. Washington, 36 Cal. 658; U. S. v. Rhodes, 1 Abb. C. C. 28.

A treaty is supreme only when it is made in pursuance of that authority which has been conferred upon the treaty-making department, and in relation to those subjects the jurisdiction over which has been exclusively intrusted to Congress. When it transcends these limits, like an act of Congress which transcends the constitutional authority of that body, it can not supersede a State law which enforces or exercises any power of the State not granted away by the Constitution. People v. Naglee, 1 Cal. 231.

The validity of a treaty is of two kinds, viz., necessary and voluntary. Necessary validity is that which results from the treaty's having been made by persons authorized by and for purposes consistent with the Constitution. Voluntary validity is that validity which a treaty that has become voidable by reason of violations, afterwards continues to retain, by the silent volition and acquiescence of the nation. Jones v. Walker, 2 Paine, 688.

TREATIES.

The necessary validity of a treaty is of a judicial nature, and the voluntary validity of a treaty is of a political nature. The former is referable to the judiciary and the latter to those departments which are charged with the political interests of the Government. The power given the judiciary to decide on the validity of treaties, is by the nature of the subject limited to their necessary validity,—necessary because while performed by one party it rests not on the volition of the other, but on that perfect obligation which contracts authorize, and not improperly impose on both parties. Jones v. Walker, 2 Paine, 688.

Ordinarily treaties are not rules prescribed by sovereigns for the conduct of their subjects, but contracts by which they agree to regulate their own conduct. This provision of the Constitution has made them part of the municipal law, but it has not assigned to them any particular degree of authority in the municipal law, nor declared whether laws so enacted shall or shall not be paramount to laws otherwise enacted. Taylor v. Morton, 2 Curt. 454.

When the terms of a stipulation import a contract, a treaty addresses itself to the political, not the judicial department, and Congress must execute the contract before it can become a rule of court. In re Metzger, 1 Parker Cr. Cas. 108; s. c. 1 Edm. Sel. Cas. 399; U. S. v. Ferreira, 13 How. 40; Taylor v. Morton, 2 Curt. 454; Foster v. Neilson, 2 Pet. 253; Turner v. Missionary Union, 5 McLean, 344.

Where money is required to be appropriated to carry out a treaty, the concurrence of Congress is required to give effect to the treaty; for money can not be appropriated by the treaty-making power. Turner v. Missionary Union, 5 McLean, 344.

A treaty is regarded as equivalent to an act of Congress whenever it operates of itself without the aid of any legislative provision. Foster v. Neilson, 2 Pet. 253; U. S. v. Percheman, 7 Pet. 51; U. S. v. Arredondo, 6 Pet. 691; Gordon v. Kerr, 1 Wash. C. C. 322.

Congress has the power to repeal a law contained in a treaty when it relates to subjects which the Constitution has placed under the legislative power. An act of Congress will therefore prevail over a treaty. Ropes v. Clinch, 8 Blatch. 304; Webster v. Reid, 11 How. 437; s. c. Morris, 467; Taylor v. Morton, 2 Curt. 454; The Clinton Bridge, 1 Wool. 150; s. c. 10 Wall. 454.

Whether an act of Congress shall prevail over a treaty is a question solely of municipal law as distinguished from public law. The foreign sovereign, between whom and the United States a treaty has been made, has a right to expect and require its stipulations to be kept with scrupulous good faith, but through what internal arrangements this shall be done is exclusively for the consideration of the United States. Taylor v. Morton, 2 Curt. 454.

No right can be incident to one department which necessarily goes to the suspension of a right incident to another, or to control, suspend or defeat its operation. Where the department authorized to annul a voidable treaty deems it most conducive to the national interest that it shall continue to be obeyed and observed, no right is incident to the judiciary to declare it void in a single instance. Jones *v.* Walker, 2 Paine, 688; Taylor *v.* Morton, 2 Curt. 454.

Four things are apparent on a view of this article: 1st. It is retrospective. 2d. The constitution or laws of any of the States, so far as either of them shall be found contrary to a treaty, are by force of this article prostrated before the treaty. 3d. The treaty has superior power to the legislature of any State, because no legislature of any State has any kind of power over the Constitution which was its creator. 4th. It is the declared duty of the State judges to determine any constitution or laws of any State contrary to any treaty made under the authority of the United States null and void. National or Federal judges are bound by duty and oath to the same conduct. Ware *v.* Hilton, 3 Dall. 199; Society *v.* New Haven, 8 Wheat. 464.

A treaty concluded by the President and Senate binds the nation in the aggregate, and all its subordinate authorities, and its citizens as individuals, to the observance of the stipulations contained in it. Fellows *v.* Denniston, 23 N. Y. 420.

A treaty can not change the Constitution, or be held valid if it be in violation of that instrument. The Cherokee Tobacco, 11 Wall. 616; s. c. 1 Dillon, 264.

If the Supreme Court possesses the power to declare a treaty void, it will never exercise it but in a very clear case indeed. Ware *v.* Hylton, 3 Dall. 199.

A treaty is a compact formed between two nations or communities having the right of self-government. It is not essential that each party shall possess the same attributes of sovereignty to give force to the treaty. The only requisite is that each of the contracting parties shall possess the right of self-government, and the power to perform the stipulations of the treaty. It must be admitted that the Indians sustain a peculiar relation to the United States. They do not constitute a foreign State, and yet having the right of self-government they, in some sense, form a State. In the management of their internal concerns they are dependent on no power. They punish offenses under their own laws, and in doing so they are responsible to no earthly tribunal. So far as the Indians, as distinct communities, have formed a connection with the Federal Government by treaties, such connection is political and equally binding on both parties. Worcester *v.* State, 6 Pet. 515.

The Constitution, by declaring treaties already made, as well as those to be made, to be the supreme law of the land, has adopted and sanctioned the previous treaties with the Indian nations, and consequently admits their rank among those powers who are capable of making treaties. The word "treaty" is applied to Indians as well as to other nations in the same sense. Worcester *v.* State, 6 Pet. 515.

After an Indian treaty has been executed and ratified by the proper authorities of the Government, no court can declare it invalid because the tribe was not represented by its chiefs and head men in the negotiation and execution of it. Fellows *v.* Blacksmith, 19 How. 366.

Treaties with Indian tribes have the same effect and dignity as treaties with foreign and independent nations. They are treaties within the meaning of the Constitution, and as such are the supreme law of the land. Turner *v.* Missionary Union, 5 McLean, 344; Worcester *v.* State, 6 Pet. 515; Fellows *v.* Denniston, 23 N. Y. 420.

After a treaty has been executed and ratified by the proper authorities of the Government, the courts can not go behind it for the purpose of annulling its operation by inquiring whether the tribe with whom it was made was properly represented. Fellows *v.* Blacksmith, 19 How. 366.

Supreme over States.

The convention which framed the Constitution was elected by the State legislatures. But the instrument, when it came from their hands, was a mere proposal without obligation or pretension to it. It was reported to the then existing Congress of the United States, with a request that it might "be submitted to a convention of delegates chosen in each State by the people thereof, under the recommendation of its legislature, for their assent and ratification." This mode of proceeding was adopted, and by the convention, by Congress and by the State legislatures, the instrument was submitted to the people. They acted upon it in the only manner in which they can act safely, effectively and wisely on such a subject, by assembling in convention. It is true they assembled in their several States, but the measures they adopted did not, on that account, cease to be the measures of the people themselves, or become the measures of the State governments. From these conventions the Constitution derives its whole authority. The Government proceeds directly from the people, and is ordained and established in the name of the people. The assent of the States in their sovereign capacity, is implied in calling a convention and thus submitting that instrument to the people. But the people were at perfect liberty to accept or reject it, and their act was final. It required not the affirmance, and could not be negatived by the State governments. The Constitution when thus adopted was of complete obligation, and bound the State sovereignties. The Federal Government is emphatically a government of the people. In form and substance it emanates from them. Its powers are granted by them, and are to be exercised directly on them and for their benefit. M'Culloch v. State, 4 Wheat. 316; Comm. v. Morrison, 2 A. K. Marsh. 75; Martin v. Hunter, 1 Wheat. 304; s. c. 4 Munf. 1.

Although the powers of the Federal Government are limited, yet within those limits it is a perfect government, as any other, having all the faculties and properties belonging to a government, with a perfect right to use them freely in order to accomplish the objects of its institution. U. S. v. Maurice, 2 Brock. 96 ; Cohens v. Virginia, 6 Wheat. 264.

The General Government, though limited as to its objects, is supreme as to those objects. Cohens v. Virginia, 6 Wheat. 264.

The powers of sovereignty are divided between the Federal Government and the governments of the States. They are each sovereign with respect to the objects committed to it, and neither sovereign with respect to the objects committed to the other. M'Culloch v. State, 4 Wheat. 316.

Within its limits the Government is sovereign and independent, and any interference by the State governments tending to the interruption of the full legitimate exercise of the powers granted to it is in conflict with that clause of the Constitution which makes the Constitution and the laws of the United States passed in pursuance thereof, "the supreme law of the land." The result of this doctrine is that the exercise of any authority by a State government, trenching upon any of the powers granted to the General Government, is to the extent of the interference, an attempt to resume the grant in defiance of constitutional obligation. Bank of Commerce v. New York, 2 Black, 620; s. c. 23 N. Y. 192; 32 Barb. 509.

State Powers Superseded.

The powers of Government may be divided into four classes: 1. Those which belong exclusively to the States. 2. Those which belong exclusively to the United States. 3. Those which may be exercised concurrently and independently by both. 4. Those which may be exercised by the States, but only with the consent, express or implied, of Congress. Farmers' National Bank v. Dearing, 91 U. S. 29.

There are but three cases in which the several States have no power to legislate: 1. Where they are expressly prohibited. 2. Where exclusive power is expressly vested in the United States. 3. Where the power vested in the United States is in its nature exclusive. Farmers' Bank v. Smith, 6 Wheat. 131 ; s. c. 3 S. & R. 63 ; Adams v. Storey, 1 Paine, 79; Cox v. State, 3 Blackf. 193; Passenger Cases, 7 How. 283; s. c. 45 Mass. 282; Prigg v. Comm. 16 Pet. 539; Jack v. Martin, 12 Wend. 311; s. c. 14 Wend. 509; People v. Naglee, 1 Cal. 231.

The mere grant of a power to Congress does not imply a prohibition on the States to exercise the same power. Sturges *v*. Crowninshield, 4 Wheat. 122.

Where an authority is granted to the Federal Government, to which a similar authority in the States would be absolutely and totally contradictory and repugnant, there the authority of the Federal Government is necessarily exclusive, and the same power can not be constitutionally exercised by the States. Holmes *v*. Jennison, 14 Pet. 540.

No legislation by Congress is wanted to make more binding upon the States what they have bound themselves in absolute terms not to do. Dodge *v*. Woolsey, 18 How. 331.

It does not always follow that the States have relinquished their own powers because they have granted similar powers to the United States. They retain their powers unless they are expressly deprived of them, or they have vested such powers in Congress as are in their own nature incompatible with the exercise of the same powers by themselves. Houston *v*. Moore, 5 Wheat. 1; s. c. 3 S. & R. 169; Blanchard *v*. Russell, 13 Mass. 1; Farmers' Bank *v*. Smith, 6 Wheat. 131; s. c. 3 S. & R. 63; Weaver *v*. Fegley, 29 Penn. 27.

When the prohibition is express, all power of the State ceased immediately on the adoption of the Constitution. Houston *v*. Moore, 5 Wheat. 1; s. c. 3 S. & R. 169.

Where the authority of the States is taken away by implication, they may continue to act until the United States exercise their power, because until such exercise there can be no incompatibility. Houston *v*. Moore, 5 Wheat. 1; s. c. 3 S. & R. 169; Cooley *v*. Philadelphia, 12 How. 299; Freeman *v*. Robinson, 7 Ind. 321.

This concurrent power of legislation does not extend to every possible case in which its exercise by the States has not been expressly prohibited. The confusion resulting from such a practice would be endless. Whenever the terms in which a power is granted to Congress, or the nature of the power, require that it should be exercised exclusively by Congress, the subject is as completely taken from the State legislatures as if they had been expressly forbidden to act on it. Sturges *v*. Crowninshield, 4 Wheat. 122; Holmes *v*. Jennison, 14 Pet. 540.

All State authority on a subject over which Congress may assume exclusive power does not cease when Congress has exercised the power only partially. The power of the States exists over such cases as the laws of the Union may not reach. Houston *v*. Moore, 5 Wheat. 1; s. c. 3 S. & R. 169; Sturges *v*. Crowninshield, 4 Wheat. 122; Eells *v*. People, 4 Scam. 498; Fitch *v*. Livingston, 4 Sandf. 492; Moore *v*. People, 14 How. 13; s. c. 5 Ill. 298; Nelson *v*. People, 33 Ill. 390.

Where Congress has exercised a power over a particular subject given to it by the Constitution, it is not competent for State legislation to add to the provisions of Congress upon that subject, for the will of Congress upon the whole subject is as clearly established by what it has not declared as by what it has expressed. The State legislatures have no right, by way of complement to the legislation of Congress, to prescribe additional regulations, and what they may deem auxiliary provisions for the same purpose. Prigg v. Comm. 16 Pet. 539; Jack v. Martin, 12 Wend. 311; s. c. 14 Wend. 509; People v. Brooks, 4 Denio, 469; Graves v. State, 1 Smith (Ind.) 258; Thornton's Case, 11 Ill. 32; In re George Kirk, 1 Parker Cr. Cas. 67; Henry v. Lowell, 16 Barb. 268; Donnell v. State, 3 Ind. 480; Degant v. Michael, 2 Ind. 396.

A State may pass a law to aid in accomplishing the purpose intended by an act of Congress. Robinson v. Flanders, 29 Ind. 10.

While a State is acting within the legitimate scope of its power as to the end to be attained, it may use whatsoever means, being appropriate to that end, it may think fit, although they may be the same, or so nearly the same as scarcely to be distinguishable from those adopted by Congress, acting under a different power, subject only to this limitation that, in the event of collision, the law of the State must yield to the law of Congress. Gibbons v. Ogden, 9 Wheat. 1; s. c. 17 Johns. 488; 4 Johns. Ch. 150; Mayor v. Miln, 11 Pet. 102; s. c. 2 Paine, 429; Charleston v. Rogers, 2 McC. 495; Norris v. Boston, 45 Mass. 282.

In considering whether it is competent for a State to pass any particular law, the courts look rather to the ends to be attained than to the particular enactments by which they are to be reached. Norris v. Boston, 45 Mass. 287.

Some State constitutions were formed before, some since that of the United States. Their relation to each other is not in any degree dependent on this circumstance. Their respective powers must be precisely the same as if they had been formed at the same time. McCulloch v. State, 4 Wheat. 316.

The Constitution was made by and for the protection of the people of the United States. The restraints imposed by that instrument upon the legislative powers of the several States can affect them only after they become States of the Union under the provisions of the Constitution, and consent to be bound by it. League v. De Young, 11 How. 185; Herman v. Phalen, 14 How. 79.

Congress can not in any manner regrant or reconvey to the States a power of which they have been divested by the Constitution. Cooley v. Philadelphia, 12 How. 299; City v. Churchill, 43 Barb. 550; s. c. 31 N. Y. 161; Homestead Cases, 23 Gratt. 266.

The States, or rather the people forming them, though sovereign as to the powers not delegated to the United States by the Constitution, or prohibited by it to the States, are not independent of each other in respect to the powers ceded in the Constitution. Their union by the Constitution was made by each of them conceding portions of their equal sovereignties for all of them, and it acts upon the States conjunctively and separately, and in the same manner upon their citizens, aggregately in some things and in others individually, in many of their relations of business, and also upon their civil conduct, so far as their obedience to the laws of Congress is concerned. In such a union the States are bound by all of those principles of justice which bind individuals to their contracts. They are bound by their mutual acquiescence in the powers of the Constitution, that neither of them shall be the judge, or shall be allowed to be the final judge, of the powers of the Constitution, or of the interpretation of the laws of Congress. This is not so because their sovereignty is impaired, but the exercise of it is diminished in quantity, because they have in certain respects put restraints upon that exercise in virtue of voluntary engagements. Dodge *v.* Woolsey, 18 How. 331.

To determine whether there is a conflict with the powers of the General Government, the alleged power must be considered with reference to its consequences; for its effects, when carried out, are the only criterion by which a judgment can be formed. Lin Sing *v.* Washburn, 20 Cal. 534.

The States are not to be divested of their powers by inferences, unless the inferences are inevitable. Farmers' Bank *v.* Smith, 6 Wheat. 131; S. C. 3 S. & R. 63; Weaver *v.* Fegley, 29 Penn. 27.

If a State law and an act of Congress relate to the same thing, and are different in their character, there is no necessary conflict between them if the intention of both acts can be fully carried out and practically applied; but if the intention of both can not be fully carried out, then there is a necessary conflict, and one or the other must yield. Mitchell *v.* Steelman, 8 Cal. 363.

Every citizen of the United States is also a citizen of a State or territory. He may be said to owe allegiance to two sovereigns, and may be liable to punishment for an infraction of the laws of either. The same act may be an offense or transgression of the laws of either. That either or both may, if they see fit, punish the offender, can not be doubted. Yet it can not be truly averred that the offender has been twice punished for the same offense, but only that by one act he has committed two offenses, for each of which he is justly punishable. He can not plead the punishment by one in bar to a conviction by the other. Moore *v.* People, 14 How. 13; S. C. 5 Ill. 298; Fox *v.* State, 5 How. 410; People *v.* Sheriff, 1 Parker Cr. Cas. 659; State *v.* Moore, 6 Ind. 436; Territory *v.* Coleman, 1 Oregon, 191.

In order to render a State statute unconstitutional because of its collision with the powers granted to the General Government, there must be some conflict or repugnancy or incompatibility. It must, either in its actual exercise or in its nature, be of a character to control, defeat, limit or impair some power of the General Government, or interfere with its action so that if admitted, that power could no longer be efficacious and adequate to accomplish the object for which it was given. If it merely operates upon the same subject-matter, but not in such a manner as to show a plain incompatibility, a direct repugnancy or an extreme practical inconvenience, it is not unconstitutional, because there may be a possible or potential inconvenience. Pierce v. State, 13 N. H. 336; s. c. 5 How. 504; U. S. v. Bedford Bridge, 1 W. & M. 401; Sinnot v. Davenport, 22 How. 227.

If, in a specified case, the people have thought proper to bestow certain powers on Congress as the safest depositary of them, and Congress has legislated within the scope of them, the people have reason to complain that the same powers should be exercised at the same time by the State legislatures. To subject them to the operation of two laws upon the same subject, dictated by distinct wills, particularly in a case inflicting pains and penalties, is something very much like oppression if not worse. Houston v. Moore, 5 Wheat. 1; s. c. 3 S. & R. 169.

Police Powers.

A State has the same undeniable and unlimited jurisdiction over all persons and things within its territorial limits as any foreign nation, where that jurisdiction is not surrendered or restrained by the Constitution. By virtue of this, it not only is the right but the bounden and solemn duty of a State to advance the safety, happiness and prosperity of its people, and to provide for its general welfare by any and every act of legislation which it may deem to be conducive to these ends where the power over the particular subject or the manner of its exercise is not surrendered or restrained. All those powers which relate to merely municipal legislation, or what may perhaps more properly be called internal police, are not thus surrendered or restrained, and consequently, in relation to these, the authority of a State is complete, unqualified and exclusive. Mayor v. Miln, 11 Pet. 102; s. c. 2 Paine, 429; License Cases, 5 How. 504; s. c. 13 N. H. 536; Fitch v. Livingston, 4 Sandf. 492; Ex parte Perkins, 2 Cal. 424.

The powers necessary to the regulation of the police, morals, health, internal commerce and general prosperity of the community, are subject to State regulation, and the objects to be accomplished by them are to be reached and effected by any appropriate means which do not interfere with the exercise of any of the powers vested in the General Government. Nelson v. People, 33 Ill. 390; Eells v. People, 5 Ill. 498; Fitch v. Livingston, 4 Sandf. 492; Comm. *v.* Kimball, 41 Mass. 359; Prigg *v.* Comm. 16 Pet. 539; Ex parte Perkins, 2 Cal. 424; Willard *v.* People, 5 Ill. 461.

The States may pass poor laws and laws to prevent the introduction of paupers or persons likely to become paupers. Norris *v.* Boston, 45 Mass. 282; Mayor *v.* Miln, 11 Pet. 102; S. C. 2 Paine, 429.

Every law relates to internal police which concerns the welfare of the whole people of a State, or any individual in it, whether it relates to their rights or their duties; whether it respects them as men or as citizens of the State; whether in their public or private relations; whether it relates to the rights of persons or of property, of the whole people of a State or of any individual within it, and whose operation is within the territorial limits of the State, and upon the persons and things within its jurisdiction. Mayor *v.* Miln, 11 Pet. 102; S. C. 2 Paine, 429.

The police power of a State can not be exercised in regard to a subject-matter which has been confided exclusively to the discretion of Congress. Henderson *v.* Mayor, 92 U. S. R. 259.

The police power of a State is one of the different means used by sovereignty to accomplish that great object, the good of the State. Police powers and sovereign powers are the same. Passenger Cases, 7 How. 283; S. C. 45 Mass. 282.

State Taxes.

The power of taxation is indispensable to the existence of the State governments, and is a power which, in its own nature, is capable of residing in and being exercised by different authorities at the same time. Taxation is the simple operation of taking small portions from a perpetually accumulating mass susceptible of almost infinite division, and a power in one to take what is necessary for certain purposes, is not in its nature incompatible with a power in another to take what is necessary for other purposes. Gibbons *v.* Ogden, 9 Wheat. 1; S. C. 17 Johns. 488; 4 Johns. Ch. 150; Biddle *v.* Comm. 13 S. & R. 405; M'Culloch *v.* State, 4 Wheat. 316; Comm. *v.* Morrison, 2 A. K. Marsh. 75; Raguet *v.* Wade, 4 Ohio, 107; People *v.* Naglee, 1 Cal. 231.

Taxation is an incident of sovereignty, and is coextensive with that to which it is an incident. All subjects over which the sovereign power of a State extends, are objects of taxation, but those over which it does not extend are upon the soundest principles exempt from taxation. The sovereignty of a State extends to everything which exists by its own authority or is introduced by its permission, but it does not extend to those means which are employed by Congress to carry into execution powers conferred on that body by the people of the United States. M'Culloch *v.* State, 4 Wheat. 316; City *v.* Churchill, 33 N. Y. 161; S. C. 43 Barb. 550.

21

The taxing power of the States must have some limits. It can not reach and restrain the action of the National Government within its proper sphere. It can not reach the administration of justice in the Federal courts, or the collection of the taxes of the United States, or restrain the operation of any law which Congress may constitutionally pass. It can not interfere with any regulation of commerce. Brown *v.* State, 12 Wheat. 419; Comm. *v.* Morrison, 2 A. K. Marsh. 75; Howell *v.* State, 3 Gill, 14.

The exemption of Federal agencies from State taxation is dependent, not upon the nature of the agents, or upon the mode of their constitution, or upon the fact that they are agents, but upon the effect of the tax; that is, upon the question whether the tax does in truth deprive them of the power to serve the Government as they were intended to serve it, or does hinder the efficient exercise of their power. Railroad Co. *v.* Peniston, 18 Wall. 5.

The agencies of the Federal Government are only exempt from State legislation so far as that legislation may interfere with or impair their efficiency in performing the functions by which they are designed to serve that Government. National Bank *v.* Comm. 9 Wall. 353.

The power to tax involves the power to destroy. The power to destroy may defeat and render useless the power to create. The several States have no power by taxation or otherwise to retard, impede, burden or in any manner control the operations of the constitutional laws enacted by Congress to carry into execution the powers vested in the General Government. M'Culloch *v.* State, 4 Wheat. 316; Weston *v.* Charleston, 2 Pet. 449; S. C. Harp. 340.

There is a difference between a tax imposed by the Federal Government and a tax imposed by the State Governments. The people of all the States have created the Federal Government, and have conferred upon it the general power of taxation. The people of all the States and the States themselves are represented in Congress, and by their representatives exercise this power. When they tax the chartered institutions of the State, they tax their constituents, and these taxes must be uniform. But when a State taxes the operations of the Federal Government, it acts upon institutions not created by itself, but by people over whom it claims no control. It acts upon the measures of a Government created by others as well as itself, for the benefit of others in common with its own people. M'Culloch *v.* State, 4 Wheat. 316.

The taxing power of a State is one of its attributes of sovereignty. Where there has been no compact with the Federal Government, or cession of jurisdiction for the purposes specified in the Constitution, this power reaches all the property and business within the State, which are not properly denominated the means of the General Government. This power may be exercised at the discretion of the State. Nathan *v.* Louisiana, 8 How. 73; People *v.* Coleman, 4 Cal. 46.

The measure of the power of taxation residing in a State is the extent of sovereignty which the people of a single State possess, and can confer on its government. M'Culloch *v.* State, 4 Wheat. 316; Howell *v.* State, 3 Gill, 14.

A State tax which remotely affects the efficient exercise of a Federal power is not for that reason alone prohibited. Railroad Co. *v.* Peniston, 18 Wall. 5.

No constitutional implication prohibits a State tax upon the property of an agent of the Government, merely because it is the property of such agent. Railroad Co. *v.* Peniston, 18 Wall. 5.

The State power of taxation is restrained by the Constitution whenever its exercise conflicts with the perfect execution of the powers delegated to the United States. That occurs when taxation by a State acts upon the instruments, emoluments and persons which the United States may use and employ as necessary and proper means to execute its sovereign powers. An officer is a means to execute those powers, and his salary is the means by which his services are procured and retained. Hence, the salary is not liable to State taxation. Dobbins *v.* Commissioners, 16 Pet. 435; s. c. 7 Watts, 513.

A State may tax the salary of a clerk in the post office, who is appointed upon the recommendation of the deputy postmaster, and the approval of the postmaster general. Melcher *v.* Boston, 50 Mass. 73.

A party who obtains a license to trade from the Government, is not an officer, nor as such exempt from taxation by a State. State *v.* Bell, Phillips, 76.

The taxing power of the State can not be exerted against the public money in the treasury, the precious metals in the mint, or the lots, structures, ships, material of war or other property devoted to public purposes by the General Government. City *v.* Churchill, 33 N. Y. 161; s. c. 43 Barb. 550.

A State tax on stock issued by the Government for loans is a tax on the contract, a tax on the power to borrow money on the credit of the United States, and consequently is repugnant to the Constitution. Weston *v.* Charleston, 2 Pet. 449; s c. Harp. 340; Bank *v.* Commissioners, 2 Black, 620; s. c. 23 N. Y. 192; 32 Barb. 509; Opinion of Justices, 53 N. H. 634; contra, People *v.* Commissioners, 37 Barb. 635; s. c. 26 N. Y. 163.

Congress may forbid any taxation of the stock and bonds of the United

States, if in its judgment such restriction is necessary to carry out the power to borrow money. Whether it exercises that power wisely or not is not for the courts to inquire. People *v.* Commissioners, 37 Barb. 635; S.C. 26 N. Y. 163.

A State can not tax the income derived from interest paid on bonds of the United States. Bank *v.* Comm. 9 Bush, 46; Opinion of Justices, 53 N. H. 634.

A State can not tax the stock or bonds of the United States, although it taxes the stock or bonds the same as all other property in the State. Bank *v.* Commissioners, 2 Black, 620; S. C. 23 N. Y. 192; 32 Barb. 509; Newark City Bank *v.* Assessor, 30 N. J. 1.

A person who deals in bonds of the United States is not liable to taxation under State laws on the capital in business thus invested. Chicago *v.* Lunt, 52 Ill. 414.

A State can not tax the notes of the United States issued and intended to circulate as money, when they are made exempt from taxation by Congress. Bank *v.* Supervisors, 7 Wall. 26; Montgomery *v.* Elston, 32 Ind. 27; Horne *v.* Green, 52 Miss. 452.

Internal revenue stamps issued by the United States as a means of collecting a tax are not liable to taxation by a State. Palfrey *v.* Boston, 101 Mass. 329.

A State can not tax a certificate of indebtedness issued by the United States. Banks *v.* Mayor, 7 Wall. 16; S. C. 37 N. Y. 9; State *v.* Haight, 34 N. J. 128; contra, People *v.* Gardiner, 48 Barb. 608.

There is no distinction between certificates of indebtedness issued for borrowed money and certificates of indebtedness issued directly to creditors in payment of their demands. Banks *v.* Mayor, 7 Wall. 16; S. C. 37 N. Y. 9.

The money of the Federal Government employed within the limits of a State as tax or revenue, and devoted in that character to its appropriate purposes, is exempt from taxation by the State; but if it is diverted from those purposes, and associated with the money of others in gainful transactions, it loses its sanctity, ceases to be tax or revenue, and becomes money, and in that character may be taxed by the State in which it is so employed, like that with which it is associated. Comm. *v.* Morrison, 2 A. K. Marsh. 75.

A State can not tax the property which constitutes the capital of a corporation when the capital is invested in stock or bonds of the United States. Bank *v.* Commissioners, 2 Black, 620; S. C. 23 N. Y. 192; 32 Barb. 509; Whitney *v.* Madison, 23 Ind 331; International Assurance Society *v.* Commissioners, 28 Barb. 318; Mechanics' Bank *v.* Bridges, 30 N. J. 112; St. Louis B. & S. Association *v.* Lightner, 42 Mo. 421.

A State tax on a corporation upon a valuation equal to its capital is void when that capital is invested in stock or bonds of the United States. Bank Tax Case, 2 Wall. 200.

A State may tax the shares held by an individual in a bank, although its capital is invested in bonds of the United States. Wright *v* Stilz, 27 Ind. 338; People *v.* Commissioners, 35 N. Y. 423; S. C. 4 Wall. 244; St. Louis B. & S. Association *v.* Lightner, 47 Mo. 393; contra, Whitney *v.* Madison, 23 Ind. 331.

If a savings bank has no capital stock or stockholders, a State may levy a tax of a certain per cent. on its deposits, although the deposits are invested in the bonds of the United States, for the tax is a tax on the franchise. Society *v.* Coite, 6 Wall. 594; S. C. 32 Conn. 173; Provident Institution *v.* Massachusetts, 6 Wall. 611; S. C. 94 Mass. 312.

If a State tax on the capital stock of a corporation, in excess of the value of its real estate and machinery, is a tax on the franchise, it is valid, although a part of the capital is invested in bonds of the United States. Hamilton Company *v.* Massachusetts, 6 Wall. 632; S. C. 94 Mass. 298.

A State tax upon the franchise of a corporation to an amount not exceeding the surplus earned and in its possession is valid, although the surplus is invested in bonds of the United States. Monroe Savings Bank *v.* Rochester, 37 N. Y. 365.

A collateral inheritance tax imposed by a State applies to that part of the estate which consists of bonds of the United States, for the tax is on the estate and not on the bonds. Strode *v.* Comm. 52 Penn. 181.

If the statute creating a national bank permits a State to tax the shares held by an individual, the tax may be levied, although its capital is invested in bonds or stocks of the United States. Van Allen *v.* Assessors, 3 Wall. 573; S. C. 33 N. Y. 161; 43 Barb. 550; People *v.* Commissioners, 4 Wall. 244; S. C. 35 N. Y. 423; National Bank *v.* Comm. 9 Wall. 353; S. C. 4 Bush, 98; State *v.* Haight, 31 N. J. 399; First Nat'l Bank *v.* Douglas, 3 Dillon, 330; People *v.* Assessors, 44 Barb. 148; Wright *v.* Stilz, 27 Ind. 338; Hubbard *v.* Supervisors, 23 Iowa, 130; contra, State *v.* Hart, 31 N. J. 434.

A State has no right to tax the means employed by the Government for the execution of its powers. M'Culloch *v.* State, 4 Wheat. 316; Banks *v.* Mayor, 7 Wall. 16; S. C. 37 N. Y. 9.

A State can not tax a national bank. M'Culloch *v.* State, 4 Wheat.

316; Osborne *v.* Bank, 9 Wheat. 738; Pittsburgh *v.* Nat'l Bank, 55 Penn. 45; Collins *v.* Chicago, 4 Biss. 472; contra, Comm. *v.* Morrison, 2 A. K. Marsh. 73.

A State can not tax the notes of a national bank. M'Culloch *v.* State, 4 Wheat. 316; Horne *v.* Green, 52 Miss. 452; contra, Montgomery *v.* Elston, 32 Ind. 27.

A tax upon the operations of a national bank is a tax on the operation of an instrument employed by the Federal Government to carry its powers into execution, and is unconstitutional. M'Culloch *v.* State, 4 Wheat. 316; Pittsburgh *v.* Nat'l Bank, 55 Penn. 45; contra, Comm. *v.* Morrison, 2 A. K. Marsh. 75.

The State may tax the dividends declared to an individual holder of stock in a national bank. State *v.* Collector, 2 Bailey, 654.

To tax the faculties, trade or occupation of a national bank is to tax the bank itself. To destroy or preserve the one is to destroy or preserve the other. If the trade of the bank is essential to its character as a machine for the fiscal operations of the Government, that trade must be as exempt from State control as the actual conveyance of the public money. Osborn *v.* Bank, 9 Wheat. 738.

A State can not tax a national bank for the privilege of transacting business in the State. Nat'l Bank *v.* Mayor, 8 Heisk. 814.

A State may tax the shares of stock held by an individual in a national bank. State *v.* Haight, 31 N. J. 399; State *v.* Hart, 31 N. J. 434; Stetson *v.* Bangor, 56 Me. 274; Bulow *v.* Charleston, 1 N. & M. 527; People *v.* Bradley, 39 Ill. 130; City *v.* Churchill, 31 N. Y. 161; S. C. 43 Barb. 550.

The shares held by an individual in a national bank, are not subject to taxation by a State, except by the permission of Congress. People *v.* Assessors, 44 Barb. 148.

Congress may permit the States to tax the national banks. Van Allen *v.* Assessors, 3 Wall. 573; S. C. 33 N. Y. 161; 43 Barb. 550; State *v.* Haight, 31 N. J 399; Frazer *v.* Seibern, 16 Ohio St. 614; Mintzer *v.* Montgomery, 54 Penn. 139; Austin *v.* Boston, 96 Mass. 359.

A State may tax or prohibit a business which is taxed by Congress, for the power of taxation is concurrent. Pervear *v.* Commonwealth, 5 Wall. 475.

A State tax on every passenger who leaves the State, or passes through it, is void. Crandall *v.* State, 6 Wall. 35; S. C. 1 Nev. 294.

The property of a private corporation created by Congress for individual trade and profit, and not for public and national purposes, may be taxed by a State. Union Pacific R. R. Co. *v.* Lincoln County, 1 Dillon, 314; Railroad Co. *v.* Peniston, 18 Wall. 5; Huntington *v.* Central Pac. R. R. Co. 2 Saw. 503.

The real estate or other property of a corporation not organized under an act of Congress, is not, in the absence of express legislation to that effect, exempt from State taxation, because of the employment of the corporation in the services of the Government. Thomson *v.* Pacific Railroad, 9 Wall. 579.

Congress may leave the States free to tax the shares of national banks in the hands of the shareholder. Van Allen *v.* The Assessors, 3 Wall. 573; s. c. 33 N. Y. 161; 43 Barb. 550; City *v.* Churchill, 33 N. Y. 161; s. c 43 Barb. 550; People *v.* Barton, 44 Barb. 148; People *v.* Commissioners, 4 Wall. 244; s. c. 35 N. Y. 423.

The implied inhibition is the same, whether the corporation whose property is taxed was created by Congress or by a State legislature. Railroad Co. *v.* Peniston, 18 Wall. 5.

If the capital of a corporation is converted into Government securities for a few days, for the express purpose of defeating any imposition of taxes, such investment is colorable and fraudulent, and its capital remains taxable to the same extent and in the same manner as if such conversion had never taken place. Holly Springs S. & I. Co. *v.* Marshall Co. 52 Miss. 281.

A national bank is subject to State legislation, except where such legislation is in conflict with some act of Congress, or tends to impair or destroy the utility of the bank as an agent or instrumentality of the United States, or interferes with the purposes of its creation. Waite *v.* Dowley, 9 C. L. N. 263.

A State law requiring a national bank to pay the tax on the shares of its stockholders, is valid. National Bank *v.* Comm. 9 Wall. 353; s. c. 4 Bush, 98; contra, Markoe *v.* Hartranft, 15 A. L. Reg. 487.

A State law which requires the cashier of a national bank to transmit to the clerk of the town in which each shareholder resides. a list of such shareholders and the number of shares held by each, is valid. Waite *v.* Dowley, 9 C. L. N. 263.

Secession.

A State, in the ordinary sense of the Constitution, is a political community of free citizens, occupying a territory of defined boundaries, and organized under a government sanctioned and limited by a written constitution, and established by the consent of the governed. Texas *v.* White, 7 Wall. 700.

The union of the States never was a purely artificial and arbitrary relation. It began among the colonies, and grew out of common origin, mutual sympathies, kindred principles, similar interests and geographical relations. It was confirmed and strengthened by the necessities of war, and received definite form and character and sanction from the articles of confederation. By these the Union was solemnly declared to "be perpetual." When these articles were found to be inadequate to the exigencies of the country, the Constitution was ordained "to form a more perfect Union." It is difficult to convey the idea of indissoluble unity more clearly than by these words. Texas *v.* White, 7 Wall. 700; Chancely *v.* Bailey, 37 Geo. 532.

The preservation of the States, and the maintenance of their governments, are as much within the design and care of the Constitution as the preservation of the Union and the maintenance of the National Government. The Constitution, in all its provisions, looks to an indestructible Union composed of indestructible States. Texas *v.* White, 7 Wall. 700.

A constitution is framed for ages to come, and is designed to approach immortality as nearly as human institutions can approach it. Its course can not always be tranquil. It is exposed to storms and tempests, and its framers must be unwise statesmen if they have not provided it, as far as its nature will permit, with the means of self-preservation from the perils it may be destined to encounter. No government ought to be so defective in its organization as not to contain within itself the means to secure the execution of its own laws against other dangers than those which occur every day. Cohens *v.* Virginia, 6 Wheat. 264.

The United States form, for many and for most important purposes, a single nation. In war we are one people. In making peace we are one people. In all commercial regulations we are one and the same people. In many other respects the American people are one, and the government which is alone capable of controlling and managing their interests in all these respects, is the government of the Union. It is their government, and in that character they have no other. America has chosen to be, in many respects and to many purposes, a nation, and for all these purposes her government is complete; to all these objects it is competent. Cohens *v.* Virginia, 6 Wheat. 264.

The people have declared that in the exercise of all powers given for national objects, the General Government is supreme. It can, in effecting these objects, legitimately control all individuals or governments within the American territory. The Constitution and laws of a State, so far as they are repugnant to the Constitution and laws of the United States, are absolutely void. These States are constituent parts of the United States. They are members of one great empire—for some purposes sovereign, for some purposes subordinate. Cohens *v.* Virginia, 6 Wheat. 264.

The Constitution was designed to operate upon States in their corporate capacities. It is crowded with provisions which restrain or annul the sovereignty of the States in some of the highest branches of their prerogatives. The tenth section of the first article contains a long list of prohibitions and disabilities imposed upon States. When such essential portions of State sovereignty are taken away or prohibited to be exercised, it can not be correctly asserted that the Constitution does not act upon the States. Martin *v.* Hunter, 1 Wheat. 304; s. c. 4 Munf. 1.

The powers of sovereignty are divided between the Federal Government and the governments of the States. They are each sovereign with respect to the objects committed to it, and neither sovereign with respect to the objects committed to the other. McCulloch *v.* State, 4 Wheat. 316; Comm. *v.* Morrison, 2 A. K. Marsh. 75; U. S. *v.* Cruikshank, 92 U. S. 542; s. c. 1 Woods, 308.

The Sovereignty of a State does not reside in the persons who fill the different departments of its government, but in the people from whom the government emanated, and who may change it at their discretion. Sovereignty abides with the constituency, and not with the agent. Spooner *v.* McConnell, 3 McLean, 337.

Allegiance is the duty which the citizen or subject owes to the sovereign. Allegiance is due to both the Federal and the State governments, the two constituting, in a legal point of view, one government in each State, so long as they keep within their respective constitutional limits. State *v.* Hunt, 2 Hill (S. C.) 1; Hawkins *v.* Filkins, 24 Ark. 286; U. S. *v.* Cruikshank, 92 U. S. 542; s. c. 1 Woods, 308.

The people made the Constitution, and the people can unmake it. It is the creature of their will, and lives only by their will. But this supreme and irresistible power to make or unmake resides only in the whole body of the people, not in any subdivision of them. The attempt of any of the parts to exercise it is usurpation, and ought to be repelled by those to whom the people have delegated their power of repelling it. Cohens *v.* Virginia, 6 Wheat. 264.

When a State becomes one of the United States, she enters into an indissoluble relation. The act which consummates her admission into the Union is something more than a compact; it is the incorporation of a new member into the political body. It is final. The union is as complete as perpetual, and as indissoluble as the union between the original States. Texas *v.* White, 7 Wall. 700.

A citizen can not withdraw his allegiance without the consent of the Government, express or implied, and the addition of a number of others similarly circumstanced can not confer what none possess. A State can not release its citizens from that allegiance, since the State itself is but a fractional part of a magnificent whole, and in its collective capacity is only the aggregation of its individual citizens, all of whom are alike incapable of effecting their own release, whether taken individually or collectively. Hence a State can not secede from the Union. Hood *v.* Maxwell, 1 W. Va. 219.

The Constitution expressly negatives the legal right of a State to secede, for a sovereign State may irrevocably bind itself by a voluntary compact. Chancely *v.* Bailey, 37 Geo. 532; Central R. R. Co. *v.* Ward, 37 Geo. 515; Sequestration Cases, 30 Tex. 688; White *v.* Hart, 13 Wall. 646; s. c. 39 Geo. 306.

The passage of an ordinance of secession by a State convention does not suspend or destroy the existence of the State government, but it continues to exist *de jure*, and its acts are valid and binding as though no attempt were made to secede. Hawkins *v.* Filkins, 24 Ark. 286; White *v.* Cannon, 6 Wall. 443; State *v.* Sears, Phil. 146; Harlan *v.* State, 41 Miss. 566.

An ordinance of secession is absolutely null. It is utterly without operation in law. After the adoption of such ordinance, the obligations of the State as a member of the Union, and of every citizen of the State as a citizen of the United States, remain perfect and unimpaired. The State does not cease to be a State, nor her citizens to be citizens of the Union. Texas *v.* White, 7 Wall. 700; U. S. *v.* Cathcart, 1 Bond, 586; White *v.* Hart, 13 Wall. 646; s. c. 39 Geo. 306; U. S. *v.* Morrison, Chase, 521.

The constitutional duties and obligations of a State are not affected by its rebellion, but remain the same. Homestead Cases, 23 Gratt. 266; White *v.* Hart, 13 Wall. 646; s. c. 39 Geo. 306.

A rebellious State is bound by the Constitution, and all acts in violation of it are void. Sequestration Cases, 30 Tex. 688.

A government of a rebellious State is not a *de facto* government, for a State has no existence outside of and independent of the Constitution. Penn *v.* Tollison, 26 Ark. 545; Thompson *v.* Mankin, 26 Ark. 586; Thomas *v.* Taylor, 42 Miss. 651.

Acts in furtherance or support of rebellion against the United States, or intended to defeat the just rights of citizens, must in general be regarded as invalid and void. Texas *v.* White, 7 Wall. 700; Hatch *v.* Burroughs, 1 Woods, 439.

Acts necessary to peace and good order among citizens, which would be valid if emanating from a lawful government, must be regarded in general as valid when proceeding from an actual, though unlawful government. Texas *v.* White, 7 Wall. 700; Sequestration Cases, 30 Tex. 688; Chappell *v.* Williamson, 49 Ala. 153; Cook *v.* Oliver, 1 Woods, 437.

The Confederate Government had no authority to confiscate and order a sale of the property of citizens of the United States, on the ground that they were alien enemies. Central R. R. Co. *v.* Ward, 37 Geo. 515; Keppel *v.* Petersburg R. R. Co. Chase, 167; Perdicaris *v.* Charleston Gaslight Co. Chase, 435.

An act to sequester debts due to loyal citizens is void, and the payment to the Confederate Government does not release the debtors. Sequestration Cases, 30 Tex. 688; Vance *v.* Burtis, 39 Tex. 88; Knox *v.* Lee, 12 Wall. 457; Shortridge *v.* Macon, Chase, 136.

An obligation incurred by a public corporation in aid of a rebellion can not be enforced after the rebellion has been suppressed. Bibb *v.* Commissioners, 44 Ala. 119.

Notes of a municipal corporation issued for the purpose of aiding a rebellion against the United States, are void, and can not be enforced. Evans *v.* Richmond, Chase, 551.

A statute which attempts to force the circulation of the bonds and treasury notes of the Confederate States, for the purpose of aiding the prosecution of the war of rebellion, is void. Ray *v.* Thompson, 43 Ala. 434; Irvine *v.* Armstead, 46 Ala. 363; Martin *v.* Hewitt, 44 Ala. 418.

Treasury notes issued by a State for the purpose of raising means to prosecute a rebellion against the United States, are void. Thomas *v.* Taylor, 42 Miss. 651.

An act repealing a statute requiring the indorsement of the governor as a prerequisite to the valid transfer of bonds belonging to it, passed by the legislature when the State is in rebellion against the United States, is a nullity as to bonds issued without such indorsement, and for the purpose of aiding the rebellion. Texas *v.* White, 7 Wall. 700; Texas *v.* Hardenberg, 10 Wall. 68.

Whether the alienation of bonds belonging to a State by a rebellious government divests the title of the State, depends on other circumstances than the quality of the government. The validity of the alienation depends on the object and purpose of it; if that was just and laudable in itself, the alienation is valid. Huntington *v.* Texas, 16 Wall. 402.

A payment to the officers of an insurrectionary State government of a debt due by a corporation to a State, for the purpose of enabling them to prosecute the rebellion, is void. Miss. C. R. R. Co. *v.* State, 46 Miss. 157.

The Confederate Government could not, by any statute or order of one of its departments, divest any right or property of the United States. U. S. *v.* Kechler, 9 Wall. 83.

The Confederate States was an unlawful assemblage, without corporate power to take, hold or convey a valid title to property, real or personal. Sprott *v.* U. S. 8 Ct. Cl. 499; s. c. 20 Wall. 469.

An investment of the funds belonging to an estate in Confederate bonds, by an executor, is illegal, although it was made under a law of the rebellious State, and was approved by the probate court. Horn *v.* Lockhart, 17 Wall. 570; Head *v.* Starke, Chase, 312; Houston *v.* Deloach, 43 Ala. 364; Powell *v.* Boon, 43 Ala. 469; Hall *v.* Hall, 43 Ala. 488.

The State is not liable for services rendered by an officer to a rebellious government established over it. Buck *v.* Vasser, 47 Miss. 551.

A judge elected by a rebellious State can not claim compensation for his services from a lawful government subsequently organized. Chisholm *v.* Coleman, 43 Ala. 204.

When a rebellious State is conquered the officers of the State can no longer exercise the functions of their respective offices. Cooke *v* Cooke, Phillips, 583.

When a rebellious State government is overthrown, the civil authorities do not necessarily cease at once to exist, but continue in being charged with the duty of maintaining order until superseded by the Government. Woodson *v.* Fleck, Chase, 305.

The statutes of a rebellious State intended solely to promote the good order and well being of society will be enforced. Wallace *v.* State, 33 Tex. 445; Hill *v.* Boyland, 40 Miss. 618; Buchanan *v.* Smith, 43 Miss. 90.

The statutes of a rebellious State which have been adopted by a government lawfully reorganized, will be deemed valid. Reynolds *v.* Taylor, 43 Ala. 420.

A charter of incorporation granted by the government of a rebellious State is valid. U. S. *v.* Home Ins. Co. 8 Ct. Cl. 449; s. c 22 Wall. 99.

A treasury note issued by a rebellious State in aid of the rebellion is not binding on a lawful government subsequently organized. Thomas *v.* Taylor, 42 Miss. 651; Rand *v.* State, 65 N. Ç. 194; Leak *v.* Commissioners, 64 N. C. 132.

A sale by a tax collector under the Confederate Government passed a valid title to the property of a citizen of the Confederate States. Cassell *v.* Backrack, 42 Miss. 56.

A contract which contains a stipulation for payment in Confederate notes may be enforced after the restoration of peace to the extent of its just obligation. Thorington *v.* Smith, 8 Wall. 1; Herbert *v.* Easton, 43 Ala. 547; Jordan *v.* Cobb, 47 Ala. 132; Mathews *v.* Rucker, 41 Tex. 636; contra, Latham *v.* Clarke, 25 Ark. 574; Reavis *v.* Blackshear, 30 Tex. 753; Shepard *v.* Taylor, 35 Tex. 774; Prigeon *v.* Smith, 31 Tex. 171; Lobdell v. Fowler, 33 Tex. 346; Brown v. Read, 33 Tex. 629; McGar v. Nixon, 36 Tex. 289.

Confederate notes were a valid consideration for a contract between citizens of the Confederate States. Rodes v. Patillo, 5 Bush, 271; Martin v. Horton, 1 Bush, 629; Rivers v. Moss, 6 Bush, 600; Naff v. Crawford, 1 Heisk. 111; Miller v. Gould, 38 Geo. 465; Sherfy v. Argenbright, 1 Heisk. 128; Taylor v. Turley, 33 Md. 500; Rodgers v. Bass, 46 Tex. 505; Delmas v. Ins. Co. 14 Wall. 661; Forcheimer v. Holly, 14 Fla. 239; Green v. Sizer, 40 Miss. 530; contra, Bailey v. Milner, 1 Abb. C. C. 261; Goodman v. McGehee, 31 Tex. 252; Wright v. Overall, 2 Cold. 336; Thornburg v. Harris, 3 Cold. 157; Hale v. Sharp, 4 Cold. 275; Fain v. Headerick, 4 Cold. 327; Hale v. Huston, 44 Ala. 134; Lawson v. Miller, 44 Ala. 616; Robertson v. Shores, 7 Cold. 164; Fox v. Woods, 34 Tex. 220; Wilson v. Bozeman, 48 Ala. 71; Dittmar v. Myers, 39 Tex. 295.

An administrator, executor or other person suing in a fiduciary capacity may maintain an action on a contract payable in Confederate currency. Shearon v. Henderson, 38 Tex. 245; Thompson v. Bohannon, 38 Tex. 241; Hamilton v. Pleasants, 31 Tex. 638; contra, Smith v. Nelson, 34 Tex. 516.

A bond issued by a rebellious State convention does not constitute a good consideration for a contract. Hanauer v. Woodruff, 15 Wall. 439.

The judicial proceedings of the courts in a rebellious State, so far as they do not impair or tend to impair the supremacy of the national authority or the just rights of citizens under the Constitution, are valid. Riddle v. Hill, 51 Ala. 224; Powell v. Young, 51 Ala. 518; Berry v. Bellows, 30 Ark. 198; Cook v. Oliver, 1 Woods, 437; Tarver v. Tankersley, 51 Ala. 309; Randolph v. Baldwin, 41 Ala. 305; Pepin v. Lachenmeyer, 45 N. Y. 27; Ray v. Thompson, 43 Ala. 434; White v. Cannon, 5 Wall. 443; Parks v. Coffey, 52 Ala. 32; Martin v. Hewitt, 44 Ala. 418; Shaw v. Lindsay, 46 Ala. 290; Hughes v. Stinson, 21 La. Ann. 540; French v. Tumlin, 19 A. L. Reg. 641; contra, Penn v. Tollison, 26 Ark. 545; Thompson v. Mankin, 26 Ark. 586; Timms v. Grace, 26 Ark. 598; Martin v. Hewitt, 44 Ala. 418; Carroll v. Boyd, 27 Ark. 183; Cowser v. State, 27 Ark. 444; Vinsant v. Knox, 27 Ark. 266.

A bail bond given for the surrender of an accused person while the State was in rebellion may be enforced. Thompson v. State, 31 Tex. 166.

A court organized by the Confederate Government was a nullity, and could exercise no rightful jurisdiction. Hickman v. Jones, 9 Wall. 197.

A decree of a probate court approving of an investment by an executor in Confederate bonds, is a nullity. Horn v. Lockhart, 17 Wall. 570.

Crimes committed during the existence of a rebellion may be punished under the laws of the State after the restoration of peace. Harlan v. State, 41 Miss. 566.

Federal and State Governments Distinct.

The General Government and the States, although both exist within the same territorial limits, are separate and distinct sovereignties, acting separately and independently of each other within their respective spheres. Collector *v.* Day, 11 Wall. 113.

A State court or judge who is authorized by the laws of the State, has the right to issue a writ of *habeas corpus* in any case where a party is imprisoned within its territorial limits, provided it does not appear when the application is made that the person imprisoned is in custody under the authority of the United States. The court or judge has a right to inquire in this mode of proceeding for what cause and by what authority the prisoner is confined within the limits of the State sovereignty. It is the duty of the marshal or other person having the custody of the prisoner to make known to the judge or court, by a proper return, the authority by which he holds him in custody. This right to inquire by process of *habeas corpus*, and the duty of the officer to make a return, grow necessarily out of the complex character of our Government and the existence of two distinct and separate sovereignties within the same territorial space, each of them restricted in its powers, and each, within its sphere of action prescribed by the Constitution, independent of the other. Ableman *v.* Booth, 21 How. 506; s. c. 3 Wis. 1; Ex parte Simeon Bushnell, 8 Ohio St. 599.

After a return is made to a writ of *habeas corpus*, and the State judge or court are judicially apprised that the party is in custody under the authority of the United States, they can proceed no further. They then know that the prisoner is within the dominion and jurisdiction of another government, and that neither the writ of *habeas corpus*, nor any other process issued under State authority, can pass over the line of division between the two sovereignties. He is then within the dominion and exclusive jurisdiction of the United States. If he has committed an offense against their laws, their tribunals alone can punish him. If he is wrongfully imprisoned, their judicial tribunals can release him and afford him redress. Ableman *v.* Booth, 21 How. 506; s. c. 3 Wis. 1.

Although it is the duty of the marshal or other person holding a prisoner to make known, by a proper return, the authority under which he detains him, it is at the same time imperatively his duty to obey the process of the United States, to hold the prisoner in custody under it, and to refuse obedience to the mandate or process of any other government. Consequently it is his duty not to take the prisoner, nor suffer him to be taken, before a State judge or court upon a *habeas corpus* issued under State authority. No State judge or court, after they are judicially informed that the party is imprisoned under the authority of the United States, has any right to interfere with him, or to require him to be brought before them. No judicial process, whatever form it may assume, can have any lawful authority outside of the limits of the jurisdiction of the court' or judge by whom it is issued. Ableman *v.* Booth, 21 How. 506; s. C. 3 Wis. 1; Ex parte Le Bur, 49 Cal. 160; People *v.* Fiske, 45 Barb. 294; State *v.* Gulich, 29 N. J. 409; Ex parte Charles E. Hopson, 40 Barb. 34; Ex parte J. J. Hill, 5 Nev. 154; Ex parte John D. Berwick, 25 How. Pr. 149; contra, Lockington's Case, Brightly, 269; Olmstead's Case, Brightly, 9; Ex parte H. H. Robinson, 6 McLean, 355.

The power of the General Government and of the State, although both exist and are exercised within the same territorial limits, are yet separate and distinct sovereignties, acting separately and independently of each other within their respective spheres; and the sphere of action of the General Government is as far beyond the reach of the judicial process issued by a State judge or a State court, as if the line of division was traced by landmarks and monuments visible to the eye. Ableman *v.* Booth, 21 How. 506; s. C. 3 Wis. 1.

A person who is liable to arrest for the non-payment of taxes may be arrested after he has enlisted in the army. Webster *v.* Seymour, 8 Vt. 135.

A State court has no jurisdiction to issue an injunction restraining a register and receiver acting under the laws of the United States from selling public lands. Brewer *v.* Kidd, 23 Mich. 440.

A State court has no jurisdiction to inquire into the regularity of a draft made under the laws of the United States, and the legality of the detention of the drafted man. Ex parte Jacob Spangler, 11 Mich. 298.

No judicial officer of a State has jurisdiction to issue a writ of *habeas corpus*, or to continue proceedings under the writ when issued for the purpose of inquiring into the validity of the enlistment of a soldier into the military service of the United States, and to discharge him from such service, when, in his judgment the enlistment has not been made in conformity to the laws of the United States. Tarble's Case, 13 Wall. 397; Ex parte Jacob Spangler, 11 Mich. 298; State *v.* Gulich, 29 N. J. 409; Ex parte Husted, 1 Johns. Cas. 136; Ex parte Jeremiah Ferguson, 9 Johns. 239; Ex parte Emanuel Roberts, 2 Hall's L. J. 192; Ex parte Wm. J. Jordan, 11 A. L. Reg. 749; Ex parte Ferrand, 1 Abb. C. C. 140; Phelan's Case, 9 Abb. Pr. 286; contra, Ex parte Carlton, 7 Cow. 471; State *v.* Dimish, 12 N. H. 194; Comm. *v.* Fox, 7 Penn. 336; Dabb's Case, 12 Abb. Pr. 113; Ex parte Barrett, 42 Barb. 479.

The State courts have concurrent jurisdiction with the Federal courts in all cases of illegal confinement under color of the authority of the United States, when that confinement is not the consequence of a suit or prosecution pending in the Federal courts in which the allegation upon which the commitment is made, will be tried. Ex parte Wm. Pool, 2 Va. Cas. 276; contra, State *v.* Plime, T. U. P. Charlt. 142.

A discharge under a State insolvent law does not entitle the insolvent to a release from imprisonment under an execution issued upon a judgment for a debt due to the United States. U. S. *v.* Wilson, 8 Wheat. 253; Duncan *v.* Darst, 1 How. 301 ; Glenn *v.* Humphreys, 4 Wash. 424 ; Sadlier *v.* Fallon, 2 Curt. 190.

No State can annul the judgment of a Federal court or destroy the rights acquired under it. U. S. *v.* Peters, 5 Cranch, 115; U. S. *v.* Bright, Brightley, 19.

A State court has jurisdiction of a proceeding to foreclose a mortgage, although the Government has purchased the land to secure a debt due to itself. Elliott *v.* Van Voorst, 3 Wall. Jr. 299.

If property is seized under process issued out of a Federal court, it can not be taken from the possession of the marshal under any process issued from a State court. Freeman *v.* How. 24 How. 450.

A State court has no jurisdiction to issue a writ of mandamus against an officer of the Government employed in disposing of the public land. M'Clung *v.* Silliman, 6 Wheat. 598.

A State court has no jurisdiction to enjoin proceedings on a judgment in a Federal court. M'Kim *v.* Voorhies, 7 Cranch, 279.

A State legislature can not regulate the modes of proceeding in suits in Federal courts, or the conduct of their officers in the service of executions issuing out of those courts. Wayman *v.* Southard, 10 Wheat. 1; Bank *v.* Halstead, 10 Wheat. 51; Homer *v.* Brown, 16 How. 354; Beers *v.* Houghton, 9 Pet. 329.

The several courts of the United States are domestic courts, and their respective seals prove themselves in the State courts. Adams *v.* Way, 33 Conn. 419; Pepoon *v.* Jenkins, 2 Johns. Cas. 119; Williams *v.* Wilkes, 14 Penn. 228; Womack *v.* Dearman, 7 Port. 513.

Power of Courts.

The courts have the power to declare an act of the legislature unconstitutional and void. Dawson *v.* Shaver, 1 Blackf. 204; Grimball *v.* Ross, T. U. P. Charlt. 175; Houston *v.* Moore, 5 Wheat. 1; s. c. 3 S. & R. 169; Eakin *v.* Raub, 12 S. & R. 330; Green *v.* Biddle, 8 Wheat. 1; Dausin *v.* Champlin, 7 Conn. 244; Baily *v.* Gentry, 1 Mo. 164; Winter *v.* Jones, 10 Geo. 190; Ableman *v.* Booth, 21 How. 506; s. c. 3 Wis. 145, 157; Marbury *v.* Madison, 1 Cranch, 137.

The question whether a law be void for its repugnancy to the Constitution, is at all times a question of much delicacy, which ought seldom, if ever, to be decided in the affirmative in a doubtful case. The court, when impelled by duty to render such a judgment, would be unworthy of its station could it be unmindful of the solemn obligations which that station imposes. But it is not on slight implication and vague conjecture that the legislature is to be pronounced to have transcended its powers, and its acts to be considered as void. The opposition between the Constitution and the law should be such that the judge feels a clear and strong conviction of their incompatibility with each other. Fletcher *v.* Peck, 6 Cranch, 87 ; Grimball *v.* Ross, T. U. P. Charlt. 175; Houston *v.* Moore, 5 Wheat. 1 ; s. c. 3 S. & R. 169; Dartmouth College *v.* Woodward, 4 Wheat. 518 ; Trustees *v.* Bradbury, 11 Me. 118; Charles River Bridge *v.* Warren Bridge, 24 Mass. 344; s. c. 23 Mass. 376; 11 Pet. 420; Eakin *v.* Raub, 12 S. & R. 330; Lapsley *v.* Brashears, 4 Litt. 47 ; Jones *v.* Crittenden, 1 Car. L. Rep. 385 ; Strong *v.* State, 1 Blackf. 193 ; Regents *v.* Williams, 9 G. & J. 365 ; Baugher *v.* Nelson, 9 Gill, 299; Butler *v.* Pennsylvania, 10 How. 402 ; Hartford Bridge Co. *v.* Union Ferry Co. 29 Conn. 210; Metropolitan Bank *v.* Van Dyck, 27 N. Y. 400.

No law will be declared to be void, except in a clear case. Calder *v.* Bull, 3 Dall. 386 ; s. c. 2 Root, 350.

No court ought, unless the terms of an act render it unavoidable, to give a construction to it which will involve a violation of the Constitution. Parsons *v.* Ballard, 3 Pet. 433; Payne *v.* Baldwin, 11 Miss. 661 ; Bailey *v.* Railroad Co. 4 Harring. 389.

The presumption is in favor of every legislative act, and the whole burden of proof lies on him who denies its constitutionality. Brown *v.* State, 12 Wheat. 419; Hylton *v.* U. S. 3 Dall. 171 ; Planters' Bank *v.* Sharp, 6 How. 301 ; s. c. 12 Miss. 28; Metropolitan Bank *v.* Van Dyck, 27 N. Y. 400.

The respect that is due from one branch of the Government to another will always lead the judiciary to decline to express an opinion on the subject of the constitutionality of a law in a case not requiring such a decision. Crandall *v.* State, 10 Conn. 339 ; Ex parte Randolph, 2 Brock. 447.

It is incumbent on those who affirm the unconstitutionality of an act of Congress to show clearly that it is in violation of the provisions of the Constitution. It is not sufficient for them that they succeed in raising a doubt. Legal Tender Cases, 12 Wall. 457.

Where there is a reasonable doubt as to the unconstitutionality of an act of Congress, the law should be sustained. In re Robert D. Bogart, 2 Saw. 396.

An act of Congress can not be declared invalid, merely because the court may think its provisions harsh and unjust. Legal Tender Cases, 12 Wall. 457.

If Congress, or any State legislature, shall pass a law within the general scope of their constitutional power, the court can not pronounce it to be void, merely because it is, in their judgment, contrary to the principles of natural justice. The ideas of natural justice are regulated by no fixed standard. The ablest and the purest men have differed upon the subject. All that the court could properly say in such an event would be that the legislature, possessed of an equal right of opinion, had passed an act which, in the opinion of the court, was inconsistent with the abstract principles of natural justice. Calder *v.* Bull, 3 Dall. 386; S. C. 2 Root, 350.

The power to make a law is all that the courts can judge of. They have no right to judge of its expediency. The legislative body exercises its powers at its own discretion, and is responsible only to the people to whom it owes its existence. Houston *v.* Moore, 5 Wheat. 1; S. C. 3 S. & R. 169; Charles River Bridge *v.* Warren Bridge, 24 Mass. 344; S. C. 23 Mass. 376; 11 Pet. 420; Bennett *v.* Boggs, Bald. 60.

A statute is judicially held to be unconstitutional because it is not within the scope of legislative authority. It may either propose to accomplish some object prohibited by the Constitution, or to accomplish some lawful and even laudable object by means repugnant to the Constitution. Comm. *v.* Clapp, 71 Mass. 97.

The courts of one State have the right to decide upon the validity and constitutionality of an act of assembly of another State. Stoddart *v.* Smith, 5 Binn. 355.

A statute may be void in part and valid in part. If some of the provisions of a statute violate the Constitution, while others are consistent with it, the latter will be maintained if they can be separated from and stand without the unconstitutional and void parts of the law. Mobile R. R. Co. *v.* State, 29 Ala. 573; Kneedler *v.* Lane, 45 Penn. 238; S. C. 3 Grant, 465; Comm. *v.* Clapp, 71 Mass. 97.

If the parts held respectively constitutional and unconstitutional are so mutually connected with and dependent on each other as conditions, considerations and compensations for each other as to warrant a belief that the legislature intended them as a whole, and if all could not be carried into effect the legislature would not pass the residue independently, all the provisions which are thus dependent, conditional, or connected with the unconstitutional parts, must fall with them. State *v.* Perry Co. 5 Ohio St. 497.

When the principal part of a statute is void, the subordinate parts which are adjuncts of and dependent upon the main theory are also void. People *v.* Commissioner, 9 C. L. N. 270.

The constitutionality of a law can not be called in question on a summary motion. Brien *v.* Clay, 1 E. D. Smith, 649.

Although a charter may contain one unconstitutional feature, yet it can not be deemed entirely void at the instance of a person who may call it in question collaterally. Rar. & Del. R. R. Co. *v.* Del. & Rar. Canal Co. 18 N. J. Eq. 546.

After a statute has been repealed, the court will not pass upon its constitutionality simply to dispose of a question of costs. Burbanks *v.* Williams, Phillips, 37.

An unconstitutional law affords no justification to a State officer for an act injurious to an individual. Astrom *v.* Hammond, 3 McLean, 107.

A purchaser at a sale under an execution issued upon a judgment rendered under an unconstitutional law, obtains a good title. Webster *v.* Reid, Morris, 467 ; s. c. 11 How. 437.

Who may object.

The debtors of a bank incorporated under the laws of a State can not raise the objection that the charter of the bank is a violation of the Constitution. After having borrowed the paper of the institution, both public policy and common honesty require that the borrowers shall repay it. Snyder *v.* Bank of Ill. 1 Ill. 122.

If parties having conflicting claims to a ferry enter into an agreement to submit their rights to the legislature, they can not afterwards object to the constitutionality of the act determining their rights. Walker *v.* Tipton, 3 Dana, 3.

This obligation is imperative upon the State judges in their official, and not merely in their private capacities. From the very nature of their judicial duties they would be called upon to pronounce the law applicable to the case in judgment. They were not to decide merely according to the laws or Constitution of the State, but according to the Constitution, laws and treaties of the United States, the supreme law of the land. Martin *v.* Hunter, 1 Wheat. 304; s. c. 4 Munf. 1.

3. **The senators and representatives before mentioned, and the members of the several State legislatures, and all executive and judicial officers, both of the United States and of the several States, shall be bound by oath or affirmation, to support this Constitution : but no religious test shall ever be required as a qualification to any office or public trust under the United States.**

The acts of the members of the legislature are not made void for a failure to take the oath to support the Constitution. The provision is merely directory, and the omission to take the oath does not affect the validity of their legislation. Hill *v.* Boyland, 40 Miss. 618 ; contra, White *v.* McKee, 19 La. Ann. 111 ; Thomas *v.* Taylor, 42 Miss. 651.

ARTICLE VII.

1. The ratification of the conventions of nine States shall be sufficient for the establishment of this Constitution between the States so ratifying the same.

Done in Convention, by the unanimous consent of the States present, the seventeenth day of September, in the year of our Lord one thousand seven hundred and eighty-seven, and of the Independence of the United States of America the twelfth. In witness whereof, we have hereunto subscribed our names.

GEORGE WASHINGTON, *President*,
and deputy from Virginia.

New Hampshire.—John Langdon, Nicholas Gilman.
Massachusetts.—Nathaniel Gorham, Rufus King.
Connecticut.—William Samuel Johnson, Roger Sherman.
New York.—Alexander Hamilton.
New Jersey.—William Livingston, David Brearly, William Patterson, Jonathan Dayton.
Pennsylvania.—Benjamin Franklin, Thomas Mifflin, Robert Morris, George Clymer, Thomas Fitzsimons, Jared Ingersoll, James Wilson, Gouverneur Morris.
Delaware.—George Read, Gunning Bedford, jr., John Dickinson, Richard Bassett, Jacob Broom.
Maryland.—James McHenry, Daniel of St. Thomas Jenifer, Daniel Carroll.
Virginia.—John Blair, James Madison, jr.
North Carolina.—William Blount, Richard Dobbs Spaight, Hugh Williamson.
South Carolina.—John Rutledge, Charles Cotesworth Pinckney, Charles Pinckney, Pierce Butler.
Georgia.—William Few, Abraham Baldwin.

Attest: WILLIAM JACKSON, *Secretary.*

AMENDMENTS TO THE CONSTITUTION.

[The following Amendments were proposed at the first session of the first Congress of the United States, which was begun and held at the city of New York, on the 4th of March, 1789, and were adopted by the requisite number of States. 1 Stat. 21.]

Of two constructions, either of which is warranted by the words of an amendment, that is to be preferred which best harmonizes the amendment with the general tenor and spirit of the act so amended. Ex parte Cæsar Griffin, 25 Tex. Supp. 623; S. C. Chase, 364.

No limit can be imposed on the people when exercising their sovereign power in amending the Constitution. Ex parte Cæsar Griffin, 25 Tex. Supp. 623; S. C. Chase, 364.

The Constitution was ordained and established by the people of the United States for themselves, for their own government, and not for the government of the individual States. Each State established a Constitution for itself, and in that Constitution provided such limitations and restrictions on the powers of its particular government as its judgment dictated. The people of the United States framed such a government for the United States as they supposed best adapted to their situation, and best calculated to promote their interests. The powers they conferred on this government were to be exercised by itself, and the limitations on power, if expressed in general terms, are naturally and necessarily applicable to the government created by the instrument. They are limitations of powers granted in the instrument itself, not of distinct governments framed by different persons and for different purposes. Barron *v.* Mayor, 7 Pet. 243.

The amendments contain no expression indicating an intention to apply them to the State governments, and they can not be so applied. Barron *v.* Mayor, 7 Pet. 243.

All the amendments adopted by Congress at its first session, and afterwards sanctioned by the requisite number of States, were intended to apply to the General Government only, for the purpose of limiting and restricting its powers, but without any intention of limiting or controlling State legislation. Livingston *v.* Mayor, 8 Wend. 85; Murphy *v.* People, 2 Cow. 815; Jackson *v.* Wood, 2 Cow. 819; Livingston *v.* Moore, 7 Pet. 469; Barker *v.* People, 3 Cow. 686; Fox *v.* State, 5 How. 410; Comm. *v.* Hitchings, 71

Mass. 482; Comm. v. Pomeroy, 71 Mass. 486; James v. Comm. 12 S. & R. 220; Bryan v. State, 4 Iowa, 349; Lincoln v. Smith, 27 Vt. 328; Barron v Mayor, 7 Pet. 243; Withers v. Buckley, 20 How. 84; S. C. 29 Miss. 21; State v. Paul, 5 R. I. 185; State v. Shricker, 29 Mo. 265; North Mo. R. R. Co. v. Maguire, 49 Mo. 490; S. C. 20 Wall. 46; Hill v. State, 53 Geo. 472;. State v. Barnett, 3 Kans. 250; Pervear v. Commonwealth, 5 Wall. 475; Baker v. Wise, 16 Gratt. 139; State v. Millain, 3 Nev. 407; Twitchell v. Comm. 7 Wall. 321.

The prohibition in these amendments is not confined to the States, but the words are general, and extend to the whole territory over which the Constitution gives Congress the power to legislate, including those portions of it remaining under territorial government, as well as that covered by States. It is a total absence of power everywhere within the dominion of the United States, and places the citizens of a territory, so far as these rights are concerned, on the same footing with citizens of the States, and guards them as plainly and firmly against any inroads which the Government might attempt, under the plea of implied or incidental powers. Dred Scott v. Sandford, 19 How. 393.

Congress can confer no power on any local government established by its authority to violate the provisions of the Constitution. Dred Scott v. Sandford, 19 How. 393.

ARTICLE I.

1. Congress shall make no law respecting an establishment of religion, or prohibiting the free exercise thereof; or abridging the freedom of speech, or of the press; or the right of the people peaceably to assemble, and to petition the Government for a redress of grievances.

Congress has no power to punish individuals for disturbing assemblies of peaceable citizens. That is the prerogative of the several States. It belongs to the preservation of the public peace and the fundamental rights of the people. U. S. v. Cruikshank, 92 U. S. 542; S. C. 1 Woods, 308.

ARTICLE II.

1. A well regulated militia being necessary to the security of a free State, the right of the people to keep and bear arms shall not be infringed.

This provision is restrictive only of the powers of the Federal Government. State *v.* Newsom, 5 Ired. 250; Andrews *v.* State, 3 Heisk. 165; Fife *v.* State, 31 Ark. 455.

This amendment has no other effect than to restrict the powers of the National Government, leaving the people to look for their protection against any violation by their fellow-citizens of the rights it recognizes to the several States. U. S. *v.* Cruikshank, 92 U. S. 542; S. C. 1 Woods, 308.

The word "arms" refers to the arms of a militiaman or soldier, and is used in its military sense. English *v.* State, 35 Tex. 473.

The provision does not prevent the passage of a law to prevent the carrying of concealed weapons. State *v.* Buzzard, 4 Ark. 18; Nunn *v.* State, 1 Geo. 243; State *v.* Chandler, 5 La. Ann. 489; State *v.* Smith, 11 La. Ann. 633; State *v.* Jumell, 13 La. Ann. 399.

A statute prohibiting the bearing of arms openly is in conflict with the Constitution, and invalid. Nunn *v.* State, 1 Geo. 243.

A statute prohibiting the carrying of dirks, daggers, slung shots, swordcanes, brass-knuckles, and bowie knives, is valid. English *v.* State, 35 Tex. 473.

A higher punishment may be prescribed for an unlawful assault with one of the dangerous weapons which it is lawful to carry than with another. Cockrum *v.* State, 24 Tex. 394.

ARTICLE III.

1. No soldier shall, in time of peace, be quartered in any house without the consent of the owner, nor in time of war but in a manner to be prescribed by law.

ARTICLE IV.

1. The right of the people to be secure in their persons, houses, papers, and effects, against unreasonable searches and seizures, shall not be violated, and no warrants shall issue but upon probable cause, supported by oath or affirmation, and particularly describing the place to be searched, and the persons or things to be seized.

This amendment can not affect proceedings under the authority of the States. It was not adopted with the intent to restrict the powers of the

States, but to limit the power of the United States, and to prescribe fixed rules relative to searches and seizures under the authority of the National Government. Reed *v.* Rice, 2 J. J. Marsh. 44; Smith *v.* State, 1 How. 71; Weimer *v.* Bunbury, 30 Mich. 201.

This amendment only protects those who are parties to the Constitution. Comm. *v.* Griffith, 19 Mass. 11.

A statute allowing a supervisor of internal revenue to issue a summons for the production of books and papers is valid. Ex parte Meador, 1 Abb. C. C. 317; Ex parte Mark Strouse, 1 Saw. 605; Stanwood *v.* Green, 2 Abb. C. C. 184.

This provision applies to criminal cases only. Ex parte Meador, 1 Abb. C. C. 317.

This provision does not prohibit a search or seizure made in attempting to execute a military order issued under a law to prevent citizens from evading a draft. Allen *v.* Colby, 45 N. H. 544.

A statute which authorizes the production of books and papers on a proceeding for a forfeiture under the internal revenue laws is valid. U. S. *v.* Distillery, 8 C. L. N. 57.

A warrant of commitment which does not state some good cause certain, supported by oath, is illegal. Ex parte Burford, 3 Cranch, 448.

Provisions for searches and seizures to aid in the collection of revenue by duties, are not repugnant to this clause. In the Matter of John R. Platt et al. 7 Ben. 261; S. C. 19 I. R. R. 132.

This article has no reference to civil proceedings for the recovery of debts of which a search warrant is not made a part. The process issued from the treasury to enforce the payment of balances due from accounting officers is termed a warrant of distress. The name bestowed upon it can not affect its constitutional validity. In substance, it is an extent authorizing a levy for the satisfaction of a debt, and as no other authority is conferred to make searches or seizures than is ordinarily embraced in every execution issued upon a recognizance, or a stipulation in the admiralty, it is not invalid because it is issued without the support of an oath or affirmation. Murray *v.* Hoboken Co. 18 How. 272.

An order of the war department directing the arrest without warrant of persons liable to draft is void. Ex parte Field, 5 Blatch. 63.

An executive officer can justify his acts by showing a regular warrant from a magistrate having jurisdiction over the subject, without showing that it was founded on a complaint under oath. It will not do to require of executive officers before they shall be held to obey precepts directed to them, that they shall have evidence of the regularity of the proceedings of the tribunal which commands the duty. Such a principle would put a stop to the execution of legal process, as officers so situated would be necessarily obliged to judge for themselves, and would often judge wrong as to the lawfulness of the authority under which they are required to act. It is a general and known principle that executive officers obliged by law to serve legal writs and processes are protected in the rightful discharge of their duty, if those precepts are sufficient in point of form, and issue from a court or magistrate having jurisdiction of the subject-matter. Sanford *v.* Nichols, 13 Mass. 286.

In order to protect an executive officer, it is necessary that the precept under which the officer acts in arresting the body or seizing the goods, and especially in entering a dwelling house by force, shall be lawful on the face of it. Sanford *v.* Nichols, 13 Mass. 286.

In the case of smuggled goods it may be difficult to describe them with minuteness, and this is not required. It is not difficult to mention the kind of goods to be searched for, or at least to describe them as having been taken out of some certain vessel, so that the officer who shall undertake such a search, may not conceive himself at liberty to rifle the house and disturb the arrangements of the family occupying it. Sanford *v.* Nichols, 13 Mass. 286.

A direction to search for goods, wares and merchandise without any specification of their character, quality, number, weight or any other circumstance tending to distinguish them, is not such a particular description as the Constitution requires. Sanford *v.* Nichols, 13 Mass. 286.

A warrant directing a search in the houses of Thomas Sanford & Co. will not justify a search in the house of Thomas Sanford. Sanford *v.* Nichols, 13 Mass. 286.

ARTICLE V.

1. No person shall be held to answer for a capital or otherwise infamous crime, unless on a presentment or indictment (*a*) of a grand jury, except in cases arising in the land or naval forces, or in the militia when in actual service, in time of war or public danger; nor shall any person be subject, for the same offense, to be twice put in jeopardy (*b*) of life or limb; nor shall be compelled in any criminal case to be a witness (*c*) against himself; nor be deprived of life, liberty, or property, without due process (*d*) of law; nor shall private property be taken for public use (*e*) without just compensation.

This provision is intended solely as a limitation on the exercise of power by the Government of the United States, and is not applicable to the legislation of the States. Hollister *v.* Union Co. 9 Conn. 436; Barker *v.* People, 3 Cow. 686; Barron *v.* Mayor, 7 Pet. 243; Bonaparte *v.* Camden & Am. R. R. Co. Bald. 205; Livingston *v.* Mayor, 8 Wend. 85; Murphy *v.* People, 2 Cow. 815; Jackson *v.* Wood, 2 Cow. 819; Railroad Co. *v.* Davis, 2 Dev. & Bat. 451; Withers *v.* Buckley, 20 How. 84; s. c. 29 Miss. 21; Powers *v.* Dougherty Co. 23 Geo. 65; Boyd *v.* Ellis, 11 Iowa, 97; Concord Railroad *v.* Greely, 17 N. H. 47; State *v.* Jackson, 21 La. Ann. 574; Clark *v.* Dick, 1 Dillon, 8; Weimer *v.* Bunbury, 30 Mich. 201; Prescott *v.* State, 19 Ohio St. 184; State *v.* Schumpert, 1 Rich. N. S. 85.

Indictment.

(*a*) A party may be tried in a State court for an alleged crime, without a previous indictment by a grand jury. State *v.* Keyes, 8 Vt. 57.

The several States may dispense with any matter of form or substance which was deemed essential to the validity of an indictment at common law. Jane *v.* Comm. 3 Met. (Ky.) 18.

This clause relates to times of war as well as peace. In re Nicholas Kemp, 16 Wis. 359.

The words "infamous crime" have a fixed and settled meaning. In a legal sense, they are descriptive of an offense that subjects a person to infamous punishment or prevents his being a witness. The fact that an offense may be or must be punished by imprisonment in the penitentiary, does not necessarily make it in law infamous. U. S. *v.* Maxwell, 3 Dillon, 275; s. c. 21 I. R. R. 148; U. S. *v.* Sheppard, 1 Abb. C. C. 431; U. S. *v.* Waller, 1 Saw. 701; U. S. *v.* Block, 9 C. L. N. 234.

This provision does not say that all offenses must be prosecuted with the sanction of a grand jury, but only that certain classes of offenses must be. The fair implication is that other offenses than those falling within the classes specifically described may be prosecuted otherwise than through the intervention of a grand jury. And certainly, as respects offenses not capital and not infamous, there is no restriction upon Congress as to the mode of procedure; and as to such offenses, it is entirely competent for Congress to provide that they shall be prosecuted upon indictment or information, or in either mode. U. S. *v.* Maxwell, 3 Dillon, 275; s. c. 21 I. R. R. 148.

Misdemeanors can not, by any construction or interpretation, be brought within the term "infamous." At the time of the adoption of the amendment, attention was no doubt called to existing constitutional provisions, and had the requirement that all classes of crimes should be passed on by grand juries before trial been intended, suitable language for that purpose would have been employed. Indeed, by the use of the words "capital or otherwise infamous crimes," it may be readily inferred that a grand jury was to pass on such and such only. U. S. *v.* Ebert, 1 Cent. L. J. 205.

The clause in the fifth amendment "when in actual service in time of war or public danger," evidently only refers to the militia. It has no reference to the army or navy of the United States. Such is the reasonable grammatical construction. In re Robert D. Bogart, 2 Saw. 396.

Congress may confer jurisdiction upon the military and naval authorities to try military and naval offenses by courts martial, and this jurisdiction may be exercised both in peace and in war. In re Robert D. Bogart, 2 Saw. 396.

Congress may authorize a trial by court martial for military and naval offenses committed while the offender was in actual service, after his connection with the service has ceased. It is not merely a "case" that the court is to try, but a "case arising in the land or naval force." A case, in ordinary parlance, is that which falls, comes or happens—an event—also a state of facts involving a question for discussion. But the event—that which happens—the state of facts presenting the question for discussion—must have arisen—must have had an origin. Among the ordinary and most common definitions of the word "arise" are "to proceed, to issue, to spring;" and a case arising in the land or naval forces, upon a fair and reasonable construction of the whole article, is a case proceeding, issuing or springing from acts in violation of the naval laws and regulations committed while in the naval forces or services—a case originating in the naval force or service; or, in other words, offenses against the laws regulating the navy, committed while in the naval forces. In re Robert D. Bogart, 2 Saw. 396.

Jeopardy.

(*b*) The expression "jeopardy of limb" was used in reference to the nature of the offense, and not to designate the punishment for an offense, for no such punishment as loss of limb was inflicted by the laws of any of the States at the adoption of the Constitution. Punishment by deprivation of the limbs of the offender would be abhorrent to the feelings and opinions of the enlightened age in which the Constitution was adopted, and it had grown into disuse in England for a long period antecedently. The term "jeopardy of limb" refers to offenses which in former ages were punishable by dismemberment, and intends to comprise the crimes denominated in the law felonies. People *v.* Goodwin, 18 Johns. 187.

The rule means no more than this—that no man shall be twice tried for the same offense. The test by which to decide whether a person has been once tried can only be by a plea of *autrefois acquit* or a plea of *autrefois convict*. The power to discharge a jury in cases of supreme and absolute necessity does exist, and may be exercised without operating as an acquittal of the prisoner. It extends to felonies as well as to misdemeanors. In a legal sense a prisoner is not once put in jeopardy until the verdict of the jury is rendered for or against him. U. S. *v.* Perez, 9 Wheat. 579; U. S. *v.* Haskell, 4 Wash. 402; People *v.* Goodwin, 18 Johns. 187; State *v.* Moor, Walk. 134; Comm. *v.* Merrill, Thach. Cr. Cas. 1; Hoffman *v.* State, 20 Md. 425.

The court may, in its discretion, discharge the jury in a capital case, as well as in case of a misdemeanor. U. S. *v.* Haskell, 4 Wash. 402.

Where the jury, from the length of time they have been considering a cause, and their inability to agree, may be fairly presumed as never likely to agree, unless compelled so to do from the pressing calls of famine or bodily exhaustion, they may be discharged, and such discharge will not operate as an acquittal. People *v.* Goodwin, 18 Johns. 187; U. S. *v.* Perez, 9 Wheat. 579.

If the jury do not agree on the last day of the term, they may be discharged. State *v.* Moor, Walk. 134.

If one of the jurors is attacked with a sudden illness, the jury may be discharged. Comm. *v.* Merrill, Thach. Cr. Cas. 1.

If the jury is impaneled and sworn by inadvertence, in a case of misdemeanor, before the prisoner has been arraigned, or in any manner answered to the indictment, the proceeding is a nullity, and may be disregarded, and a jury impaneled in the regular order. U. S. *v.* Riley, 5 Blatch. 204.

Where a jury is impaneled and sworn, but subsequently discharged without the consent of the accused, on account of the absence of witnesses for the State, this does not prevent a subsequent trial. Hoffman *v.* State, 20 Md. 425.

If the court, after the jury is impaneled and sworn in a case of misdemeanor, finds that a juror is so biased either against the prisoner or the Government that he is unfit to sit in the cause, it may discharge the jury and continue the cause. U. S. *v.* Norris, 1 Curt. 23.

The illness of the district attorney or the absence of witnesses when such illness did not occur, and the absence of the witnesses was not first made known until after the swearing of the jury, is not a ground for discharging the jury. U. S. *v.* Watson, 3 Ben. 1.

The court may discharge the jury on account of the insanity of one of the jurymen. U. S. *v.* Haskell, 4 Wash. 402.

If the district attorney enters a *nolle prosequi* after the jury is impaneled and sworn, in an action for feloniously taking letters from the mail, the accused can not be again indicted for the same offense. U. S. *v.* Shoemaker, 2 McLean, 114.

This provision is designed to shield the prisoner against oppression and injustice, and puts it out of the power of the court to subject him to the danger of another trial, except at his election and request. He, however, has the right to waive the protection, and may do so by applying for a new trial. U. S. *v.* Williams, 1 Cliff. 5; U. S. *v.* Harding, 1 Wall. Jr. 127; U. S. *v.* Keen, 1 McLean, 429; U. S. *v.* Conner, 3 McLean, 573; U. S. *v.* Macomb, 5 McLean, 286; contra, U. S. *v.* Gilbert, 2 Sum. 19.

The principle asserted by this provision, applies to all cases where a second punishment is attempted to be inflicted for the same offense by a judicial sentence. Ex parte Lange, 18 Wall. 163.

When a punishment has been in part executed, the court can not vacate the judgment entirely, and without reference to what has been done, impose another punishment on the prisoner on the same verdict. Ex parte Lange, 18 Wall. 163.

Where the indictment, on demurrer, is held bad, the prisoner may be remanded for further proceedings. U. S. *v.* Townmaker, Hemp. 299.

Witness.

(*c*) The words "criminal case," mean a case in which punishment for crime is sought to be visited upon the person of the offender in the ordinary course of criminal prosecution, in contradistinction to a proceeding *in rem* to effect a forfeiture of the thing to which the offense primarily attaches. U. S. *v.* Parker, 21 I. R. R. 251; U. S. *v.* Distillery, 8 C. L. N. 57.

Where a charge of misconduct is made against an officer, whether amounting to an indictable offense or only to his discredit as such officer, which might furnish grounds for his removal or impeachment, he is not bound to be a witness against himself. U. S. *v.* Collins, 1 Woods, 499.

This provision applies to criminal cases only. Ex parte Meador, 1 Abb. C. C. 317.

A statute permitting an assessor of internal revenue to summon a party before him to produce his books and submit to an examination for the purpose of ascertaining the tax due from him, is valid, for it is a civil proceeding. Ex parte Mark Strouse, 1 Saw. 605; Ex parte John T. Phillips, 10 I. R. R. 107.

Due Process.

(*d*) The Constitution contains no description of those processes which it was intended to allow or forbid. It does not even declare what principles are to be applied to ascertain whether it be due process. It is manifest that it was not left to the legislative power to enact any process which might be devised. The article is a restraint on the legislative as well as on the executive and judicial powers of the Government, and can not be so construed as to leave Congress free to make any process "due process of law" by its mere will. Murray *v.* Hoboken Co. 18 How. 272; Newcomb *v.* Smith, 1 Chand. 71; U. S. *v.* Taylor, 3 McLean, 539.

"Due process of law" does not necessarily import a jury trial as essential in every case to deprive a person of his life, liberty or property. Ex parte Meador, 1 Abb. C. C. 317.

The words "due process" of law were undoubtedly intended to convey the same meaning as the words "by the law of the land" in Magna Charta. Murray *v.* Hoboken Co. 18 How. 272.

This amendment does nothing more than declare a great common-law principle applicable to all governmeats, both State and Federal, which has existed from the time of *Magna Charta.* Young *v.* McKenzie, 3 Geo. 31; Parkham *v.* Justices, 9 Geo. 341; Ervine's Appeal, 16 Penn. 256.

Due process of law ordinarily implies and includes a complainant, a defendant, and a judge, regular allegations, an opportunity to answer, and a trial according to some settled course of judicial proceeding. Huber *v.* Reily, 53 Penn. 112.

In general, "due process of law" means a legal proceeding under the direction of a court. Congress may regulate the proceedings if the substantial rights of the party are protected by forms prescribed by law. Newcomb *v.* Smith, 1 Chand. 71.

A law abolishing imprisonment for debt does not disturb vested rights, for remedies are always subject to such modifications as the legislature in the constitutional exercise of its power shall think proper to adopt. Gray *v.* Munroe, 1 McLean, 528.

It is of no consequence whether the property is real or personal estate, because the Constitution protects a man in the enjoyment and dominion of his personal as potentially as of his real estate. Ervine's Appeal, 16 Penn. 256.

No person can be deprived of his liberty on the ground that he has neglected to assert his rights. Allen *v.* Sarah, 2 Harring. 434.

If a party purchases a machine from a patentee without any limitation as to the time for which it is to be used, it becomes his property. Its only value consists in its use. A special act of Congress passed afterwards, depriving him of the right to use it, can not be regarded as due process of law, and if a special act extending a patent had that effect, it would be so far unconstitutional. Bloomer *v.* McQuewen, 14 How. 539.

Provisions for searches and seizures to aid in the collection of the revenue by duties, are not repugnant to this clause. In the matter of John R. Platt, 7 Ben. 261; S. C. 19 I. R. R. 132.

Congress has no power to organize a board of revision to nullify titles confirmed many years before by the authorized agents of the Government. Reichart *v.* Felps, 6 Wall. 160.

A statute which perfects a voidable entry and gives a patent therefor, is valid, although it divests a grant made after the entry but before its passage. Williams *v.* Norris, 12 Wheat. 117.

A board of election officers constituted under State laws is not a judicial tribunal, and has no power to adjudge the guilt or innocence of an alleged violator of the laws of the United States. A trial before such officers is not due process of law. Huber *v.* Reily, 53 Penn. 112.

Congress has no power to provide for the absolute forfeiture of land, as a penalty for the non-payment of taxes, without any process. Martin *v.* Snowden, 18 Gratt. 100.

This section prohibits the passage of a law by Congress, authorizing the arrest of a citizen without just cause, because such arrest deprives him of his liberty. Griffin *v.* Wilcox, 21 Ind. 370.

A statute repealing a prior grant of land is void. U. S. *v.* Minn. & N. W. R. R. Co. 1 Minn. 127; S. C. 1 Black, 358.

The law of the land authorizes the employment of auditors, and an inquisition without notice, and a warrant of distress, to enforce the payment of balances due from receivers of the revenue. Although "due process of law" generally implies and includes *actor, reus, judex*, regular allegations, opportunity to answer, and a trial according to some settled course of judicial proceedings, yet this is not universally true. Murray *v.* Hoboken Co. 18 How. 272.

Whenever the Government seeks the property of the citizen, in the exercise of the right of taxation, the processes for seizure and assessment are in the most plenary sense within the discretion of the legislature. Pullan *v.* Kinsinger, 2 Abb. C. C. 94.

Congress can not annul the judgment of a court already rendered, or the rights determined thereby. When they have passed into judgment they become absolute. State *v.* Wheeling Bridge Co. 18 How. 421.

After the entry of a decree requiring the removal of an obstruction to navigation, Congress may pass an act legalizing the obstruction, and the decree can not then be enforced. Congress may interfere with that part of the decree which remains executory. State *v.* Wheeling Bridge Co. 18 How. 421.

A statute authorizing the filing of a bill of review, to set aside a decree rendered in favor of a fictitious person, does not divest any vested right, and is not an exercise of judicial powers. Sampeyreac *v.* U. S. 7 Pet. 222.

A rebel may lawfully be slain in battle and thus be deprived of life, or he may be lawfully captured in battle and thus deprived of liberty, because these being acts of war are authorized by those other provisions of the Constitution which authorize the prosecution of the war. Norris *v.* Doniphan, 4 Metc. (Ky.) 385.

A statute which makes an order of the President a sufficient defense for an act previously done, is void. Johnson *v.* Jones, 44 Ill. 142.

A statute which attempts to deprive a person of his right to recover a rent which had previously been paid to a provost marshal, is unconstitutional. Clark *v.* Mitchell, 64 Mo. 564.

Public Use.

(*e*) The right to appropriate private property to private use, has been deemed to be precluded by the provision authorizing it to be taken for public use only upon just compensation. Newcomb *v.* Smith, 1 Chand. 71.

This clause was established for the protection of personal safety and private property. It addresses itself to the common sense of the people, and ought not to be filed away by legal subtleties. It has its foundations in natural justice, and without its pervading efficacy other rights would be useless. If the legislature possessed an irresponsible power over every man's private estate, whether acquired by will, deed or inheritance, all inducement to acquisition, industry and economy would be removed. The principal object of government is the administration of justice and the promotion of morals. But if property is subject to the caprice of an annual assemblage of legislators acting tumultuously and without rule or precedent, and without hearing the party, stability in property will cease and justice be at an end. If the Government is interdicted from taking private property, even for public use, without just compensation, how can the legislature take it from one man and dispose of it as they think fit ? The great principle is that a man's property is his own, and that he shall enjoy it according to his pleasure, until it is proved in due process of law that it is not his, but belongs to another. Ervine's Appeal, 16 Penn. 256.

The power of the Government respecting public improvements, is a sovereign power. It rests in the wisdom of Congress to determine when and in what manner the public necessities require its exercise, and with the reasonableness of the exercise of that discretion the courts will not interfere. Swan *v.* Williams, 2 Mich. 427; Avery *v.* Fox, 1 Abb. C. C. 246.

The constitutionality of the right is not measured by the precise amount or degree of the public benefit to be conferred. Wherever there is even an apparent public interest to sustain a statute, the legislative power, or such subordinate person or body as it may designate, is the proper judge of its necessity. The question in all such cases is, not whether the law is indispensable, but whether it may be useful and convenient. Newcomb *v.* Smith, 1 Chand. 71.

The Constitution does not recognize military necessity, nor any other necessity whatever, as an authority for "taking private property for public use," in peace or in war, without just compensation. Norris *v.* Duniphan, 4 Metc. (Ky.) 385; Corbin *v.* Marsh, 2 Duvall, 193.

Extraordinary and unforseen occasions arise in cases of extreme necessity in time of war, or of immediate and impending public danger, in which private property may be impressed into the public service, or may be seized and appropriated to the public use, or may even be destroyed, without the consent of the owner. U. S. *v.* Russell, 13 Wall. 623.

The right of the Government to destroy or appropriate private property, without compensation, in cases of emergency, is not confined to enemy's country, but may be exercised wherever military operations are carried on upon which the emergency arises. Taylor *v.* Railroad Co. 6 Cold. 646.

The public danger must be immediate, imminent and impending, and the emergency in the public service must be extreme and imperative, and such as will not admit of delay or a resort to any other source of supply, and the circumstances must be such as imperatively require the exercise of that extreme power in respect to the particular property so impressed, appropriated or destroyed. U. S. *v.* Russell, 13 Wall. 623.

The necessity which justifies the taking by a military officer need not be an overpowering necessity, which admits of no alternative; but if the interests of the Government may probably be promoted thereby, it his right and duty to take and appropriate it. Taylor *v.* Railroad Co. 6 Cold. 646.

While active military operations are being carried on, the military commander is the judge of the necessity for taking private property, and he can not be held responsible in a civil tribunal for mere errors of judgment. Taylor *v.* Railroad Co. 6 Cold. 646.

If a military commander, in a time of war, acts in good faith for the accomplishment of the purposes of the war, his acts, whether of destruction or appropriation, are valid. Taylor *v.* Railroad Co. 6 Cold. 646.

If movable property is taken in good faith by a military commander for the public use, with the intent to appropriate it absolutely and permanently to such use, the title vests in the Government, and will not revert to the original owner upon the subsequent discovery that it is not necessary actually to consume the property in such use. Taylor *v.* Railroad Co. 6 Cold. 646; Williams *v.* Wickerman, 44 Mo. 484.

The rightful taking of private property for use or destruction when the public exigency demands it, by a military officer, is an exercise of the right of eminent domain, and compensation must be made by the Government to the owner. Grant *v.* U. S. 1 Ct. Cl. 41; s. c. 2 Ct. Cl. 551; Wiggins *v.* U. S. 3 Ct. Cl. 412.

The courts can not interfere and declare such acts void, unless in cases of palpable and wanton abuse of power, or when the evidence of a departure from the rule of public use is manifest on the face of the act. Newcomb *v.* Smith, 1 Chand. 71.

The Constitution only provides for the general principle. The means of ascertaining the just compensation are left to be decided by the public authority which shall give the power to take private property for public use. Ches. & O. Canal Co. *v.* Key, 3 Cranch C. C. 599.

As the Constitution does not provide any mode in which the amount of compensation shall be ascertained, it is fairly to be presumed that the framers of that instrument intended to leave that subject to be regulated in such manner as Congress, in its discretion, might deem best calculated to carry into effect the constitutional provision, according to its spirit and intent. Swan *v.* Williams, 2 Mich. 427.

The Constitution does not require that the value shall be paid, but that just compensation shall be given. Just compensation means a compensation which will be just in regard to the public as well as in regard to the individual. Ches. & O. Canal Co. *v.* Key, 3 Cranch C. C. 599.

A statute which allows the jury to consider the benefits from a public improvement in estimating the damages, is valid. Ches. & O. Canal Co. *v.* Key, 3 Cranch C. C. 599.

If the law taking private property for public use provides a special tribunal for ascertaining the compensation, the owner can not resort to any other. Meade *v.* U. S. 2 Ct. Cl. 224.

The framers of this clause did not intend that every subordinate officer, or petty agent of the United States, might undertake to decide for himself when the exigency has occurred, or the necessity exists, for the seizure and appropriation of the property of the citizen, and every attempt on the part of any public officer to do so, unless justified by some pressing emergency or overruling necessity, is a simple trespass, for which he is amenable to the law, but for which, being beyond the scope of his powers, the United States is in nowise responsible. Pitcher *v.* U. S. 1 N. & H. 7.

This provision has always been understood as referring only to a direct appropriation, and not to consequential injuries resulting from the exercise of lawful power. Legal Tender Cases, 12 Wall. 457; contra, Hepburn *v.* Griswold, 8 Wall. 603 ; s. c. 2 Duvall, 20.

A statute which makes treasury notes a legal tender in payment of debts is valid, for it makes the notes as valuable as gold coin for all commercial purposes. The difference between the value of gold coin and the value of such notes can not be regarded, because it is not recognized by law. Metropolitan Bank *v.* Van Dyck, 27 N. Y. 400.

A proceeding by complaint to assess damages for taking land for public use, where the right of trial by jury is preserved, is due process of law. Newcomb *v.* Smith, 1 Chand. 71.

Whether the statute does or does not require that notice shall be given to the owner of the property of the proceedings to assess the damages, will not affect its constitutionality. Swan *v.* Williams, 2 Mich. 427.

The title of the owner is not divested until indemnity is afforded him. Corbin *v.* Marsh, 2 Duvall, 193.

A statute diminishing tolls which have been mortgaged to secure bonds, is void, because it takes private property for public use without due compensation. U. S. *v.* Louisville Canal Co. 1 Cent. L. J. 101.

This provision is not applicable to taxation. Michigan Central R. R. Co. *v.* Slack, 22 I. R. R. 337.

The power to confiscate the property of public enemies is not affected by the restrictions imposed by this amendment. Miller *v.* U. S. 11 Wall. 268.

A statute authorizing the taking of private property for use as mill sites and mill dams, is valid. Newcomb *v.* Smith, 1 Chand. 71.

The grant of the power to a corporation to condemn land for the purpose of constructing a canal or railroad is valid. If the object designed by the legislature in the granting of the charter is the public interest, to be secured by the exercise of powers delegated for that purpose, then, although private interest may be incidentally promoted, the corporation is essentially the trustee of the Government for the promotion of the objects desired—a mere agent to which authority is delegated to work out the public interest through the means provided by the Government for that purpose, and broadly distinguishable from one created for the attainment of no public end, and from which no benefit accrues to the community, except such as results incidentally and not necessarily from its operations. In the creation of this class of corporations, public duties and public interests are involved, and the discharge of those duties and the attainment of those interests are the primary objects to be worked out through the powers delegated to them. To secure these, the right of eminent domain may be exercised by the condemnation of lands to their use. Governments more frequently effect these objects through the aid of corporations than by their immediate agents, and experience proves that this is the most wise and economical method. The grant to the corporation is in no essential particular different from the employment of commissioners or agents. Swan *v.* Williams, 2 Mich. 427; Balto. & Ohio R. R. Co. *v.* Van Ness, 4 Cranch C. C. 593; Ches. & O. Canal Co. *v.* Key, 3 Cranch C. C. 599.

A statute providing for the condemnation of land for a private way, is valid. Ex parte Robert Barnard, 4 Cranch C. C. 294.

In the exercise of the power to establish post offices and post roads, Congress can not take private property without the consent of the owner, or a just compensation for the property. Dickey *v.* Turnpike Co. 7 Dana, 119.

Congress in improving the navigable waters of the United States can not divert the water from a natural channel without providing compensation for the riparian owner who is injured thereby. Avery *v.* Fox, 1 Abb. C. C. 246.

The power to appropriate land or other property within the States for its own use belongs to the Federal Government, for it is essential to its independent existence and perpetuity. Kohl *v.* United States, 91 U. S. 367.

No State can condemn property for the use of the United States. The power of the Federal Government is complete in itself. It can neither be enlarged nor diminished by a State, nor can any State prescribe the manner in which it must be exercised. The consent of a State can never be a condition precedent to its exercise. Kohl *v.* United States, 91 U. S. 367; Trombley *v.* Humphrey, 23 Mich. 471; Darlington *v.* U. S. 33 Leg. Int. 409; contra, Gilmer *v.* Lime Point, 18 Cal. 229; Burt *v.* Merchants' Ins. Co. 106 Mass. 356.

ARTICLE VI.

1. In all criminal prosecutions, the accused shall enjoy the right to a speedy and public trial, by an impartial jury of the State and district wherein the crime shall have been committed, which district shall have been previously ascertained by law, and to be informed of the nature and cause of the accusation; to be confronted with the witnesses against him; to have compulsory process for obtaining witnesses in his favor; and to have the assistance of counsel for his defense.

This amendment does not apply to the acts of the legislatures of the several States. Twitchell *v.* Comm. 7 Wall. 321 ; Ex parte Newell Smith, 10 Wend. 449; Murphy *v.* People, 2 Cow. 815; Jackson *v.* Wood, 2 Cow. 819; Campbell *v.* State, 11 Geo. 353; Guillote *v.* New Orleans, 12 La. Ann. 432.

This provision applies only to the case of offenses committed within the limits of a State. U. S. *v.* Dawson, 15 How. 467.

The trial for a criminal offense must be in a district ascertained by law previous to the commission of the offense. An indictment found in a district created after the commission of the offense is void. U. S. *v.* Maxon, 5 Blatch. 360.

The framers of the Constitution meant to limit the right of trial by jury in the sixth amendment to those persons who are subject to indictment or presentment in the fifth. Ex parte Milligan, 4 Wall. 2.

All other persons except those who are connected with the army or the navy, citizens of States where the courts are open, if charged with crimes, are guaranteed the privilege of trial by jury, and can not be tried by a military commission. Ex parte Milligan, 4 Wall. 2.

A party can not be tried under the laws of one State for an act done in another State. People *v.* Merrill, 2 Parker Cr. Cas. 590.

A proceeding to annul the license of a pilot for neglect of duty is not a criminal proceeding. Low *v.* Commissioners, R. M. Charlt. 302.

The power to confiscate the property of public enemies is not affected by the restrictions imposed by this amendment. Miller *v.* U. S. 11 Wall. 268.

An indictment must set forth the offense with clearness and all necessary certainty, to apprise the accused of the crime with which he stands charged. U. S. *v.* Cruikshank, 1 Woods, 308; s. C. 92 U. S. 542.

If the defendant, for the purpose of obtaining a trial, admits that the absent witnesses will testify to the facts set forth in the affidavit produced on behalf of the United States, he thereby waives his right to be confronted with the witnesses. U. S. *v.* Sacramento, 2 Mont. 239.

ARTICLE VII.

1. In suits at common law, where the value in controversy shall exceed twenty dollars, the right of trial by jury shall be preserved ; and no fact tried by a jury shall be otherwise re-examined in any court of the United States, than according to the rules of the common law.

This provision does not apply to the legislation of the several States. Justices *v.* Murray, 9 Wall. 274; Foster *v.* Jackson, 57 Geo. 206; Edwards *v.* Elliott, 21 Wall. 532; Livingston *v.* Moore, 7 Pet. 469; Walker *v.* Sauvinet, 92 U. S. 90; Livingston *v.* Mayor, 8 Wend. 85; Colt *v.* Eves, 12 Conn. 243; Dawson *v.* Shaver, 1 Blackf. 204; Boring *v.* Williams, 17 Ala. 510; Lee *v.* Tillotson, 24 Wend. 337; Railroad Co. *v.* Heath, 9 Ind. 558; State *v.* Keyes, 8 Vt. 57; Huntington *v.* Bishop, 5 Vt. 186.

The State legislature, in regulating the rights of property, can not radically change the mode of proceeding prescribed for the Federal courts, or direct those courts in a trial at common law, to appoint commissioners for the decision of questions which a court of common law must submit to a jury. Bank *v.* Dudley, 2 Pet. 492; Green *v.* Biddle, 8 Wheat. 1.

The phrase "common law" found in this clause, is used in contradistinction to equity, and admiralty, and maritime jurisprudence. It is well known that in civil causes in courts of equity and admiralty juries do not intervene, and that courts of equity use the trial by jury only in extraordinary cases, to inform the conscience of the court. When, therefore, the amendment requires that the right of trial by jury shall be preserved in suits at common law, the natural conclusion is that this distinction was present to the minds of the framers of the amendment. By common law they meant not merely suits which the common law recognized among its old and settled proceedings, but suits in which legal rights were to be ascertained and determined, in contradistinction to those where equitable rights alone were recognized and equitable remedies administered, or where, as in the admiralty, a mixture of public law and of maritime law and equity was often found in the same suit. Probably there were few, if any States, in which some new legal remedies, differing from the old common-law forms, were not in use, but in which, however, the trial by jury intervened, and the general regulations in other respects were according to the course of the common law. In a just sense, the amendment may well be construed to embrace all suits which are not of equity and admiralty jurisdiction, whatever may be the peculiar form which they may assume, to settle legal rights. Parsons *v.* Bedford, 3 Pet. 433; Ins. Co. *v.* Comstock, 16 Wall. 258.

The only modes known to the common law to re-examine facts tried by a jury are the granting of a new trial by the court where the issue was tried, or to which the record was properly returnable, or the award of a *venire facias de novo* by the appellate court for some error of law which intervened in the proceedings. Parsons *v.* Bedford, 3 Pet. 433; U. S. *v.* Wonson, 1 Gallis. 5; Wetherbee *v.* Johnson, 14 Mass. 412; Patrie *v.* Murray, 43 Barb. 323.

This restriction is general, and applies to all the departments of the Government alike, especially to the legislative and judicial branches, so that neither Congress nor the courts can, by law or rules of practice, deny to a citizen the right thereby secured. Congress has no power, or by delegation of power to another body of its own creation, to deny this right to a citizen of a territory. Kleinschmidt *v.* Dunphy, 1 Mont. 118.

"Trial by jury" had, at the time of the adoption of the Constitution, a fixed legal signification, and from time immemorial has meant a trial by a tribunal of twelve men, acting only upon a unanimous determination. Unanimity of twelve jurors alone constitutes a legal verdict, and no statute can dispense with either attribute or essential of a verdict. Kleinschmidt *v.* Dunphy, 1 Mont. 118.

This provision does not apply to preliminary inquiries which do not involve a trial of the merits of the controversy. Ex parte Martin, 2 Paine, 348.

A trial by referees without the consent of the parties is not sanctioned by the Constitution. U. S. *v.* Rathbone, 2 Paine, 578.

This provision does not apply to the imposition of a fine for a failure to comply with inspection laws. Green *v.* Savannah, R. M. Charlt. 368.

A proceeding for a judgment on a forfeited recognizance, under special statutory provisions, is not a suit at common law. People *v.* Quigg, 59 N. Y. 83.

Any attempt to set up wager of law is utterly inconsistent with the right of trial by jury, so that the wager of law is now abolished. Childress *v.* Emory, 8 Wheat. 642.

A statute may provide that when a judgment is affirmed, a summary judgment may be entered against the surety on the appeal bond without a trial by jury. Hiriart *v.* Ballou, 9 Pet. 156.

A nonsuit can not be ordered in any case without the consent and acquiescence of the plaintiff. Elmore *v.* Grymes, 1 Pet. 469; D'Wolf *v.* Rabaud, 1 Pet. 476.

The right of trial by jury may be denied in a proceeding which is not a proceeding at common law, but a proceeding under statutory provisions and forms specially provided. Miller *v.* McQuerry, 5 McLean, 469; Ex parte Martin, 2 Paine, 348; Ableman *v.* Booth, 21 How. 506; s. c. 3 Wis. 1, 145, 157.

In a proceeding to assess damages, which is neither a suit at common law nor the trial of a right in a court of common-law jurisdiction, the damages may be assessed without the intervention of a jury. Bonaparte *v.* Camden & Am. R. R. Co. Bald. 205.

A statute which authorizes a judgment by default, unless the party on notice produces his books and papers, is valid. U. S. *v.* Distillery, 8 C. L. N. 57.

A statute appointing commissioners to determine titles and making their award final, unless a suit is brought within a certain period, does not take away the right of trial by jury. Barker *v.* Jackson, 1 Paine, 559.

This provision does not apply to a proceeding to annul the license of a pilot for neglect of duty. Low *v.* Commissioners, R. M. Charlt. 302.

When there is a default in a proceeding under the confiscation laws, in a seizure on land, there is no fact to be ascertained, and no jury trial is necessary. Miller *v.* U. S. 11 Wall. 268.

This provision does not embrace the established exclusive jurisdiction of courts of equity, nor that which they have exercised as concurrent with courts of law, but is limited to rights and remedies peculiarly legal in their nature, and such as it is proper to assert in courts of law and by the appropriate modes and proceedings of courts of law. Shields *v.* Thomas, 18 How. 253; Kleinschmidt *v.* Dunphy, 1 Mont. 118; Ely *v.* M. & B. Manuf. Co. 4 Fish. 64; Motts *v.* Bennett, 2 Fish. 642.

The power to issue an injunction in chancery, in its legitimate use, does not impair, supersede or prevent a trial by jury, where it has ever existed. Woodworth *v.* Rogers, 3 W. & M. 135.

A court of equity can not be authorized to award damages or compensation for the breach of a contract for the sale and delivery of personal property. Scott *v.* Billgerry, 40 Miss. 119.

This is not an inhibition upon the mode of trial of suits which are not exclusively suits at common law. It refers to suits at common law alone, and does not embrace suits in admiralty. It does not, therefore, prohibit suits in admiralty, although the courts of common law have a concurrent jurisdiction. Waring *v.* Clarke, 5 How. 441; U. S. *v.* Bright, Bright. 19; The Huntress, 2 Ware, 89; vide Bains *v.* The James Catherine, Bald. 544.

An information *in rem* to enforce a penalty for a violation of the laws of the United States, which occurs on navigable waters, in a case of admiralty jurisdiction, is not a suit at common law but an admiralty proceeding, where the trial is never by jury. U. S. *v.* La Vengeance, 3 Dall. 297; The Margaret, 9 Wheat. 421; U. S. *v.* Irma, 12 I. R. R. 42; U. S. *v.* The Betsey, 4 Cranch, 443; Whelan *v.* U. S. 7 Cranch, 112; U. S. *v.* The Queen, 4 Ben. 237; Clark *v.* U. S. 2 Wash. 519.

If the seizure is made on land, the claimant in an information *in rem*, is entitled to a trial by jury. U. S. *v.* Fourteen Packages, Gilp. 235.

A proceeding *in rem*, under the internal revenue laws, is a suit at common law within the meaning of this article, and the party is entitled to a jury trial. U. S. *v.* Distillery, 8 C. L. N. 57.

In a proceeding *in rem*, to enforce a forfeiture for a violation of the internal revenue laws, the claimant is entitled to a jury trial. U. S. *v.* 130 Bbls. 1 Bond, 587.

This provision applies to tribunals established under a provisional government. Scott v. Billgerry, 40 Miss. 119.

A territorial statute prohibiting a trial by jury in actions at law, where the amount involved exceeds twenty dollars, is void. Webster v. Reid, 11 How. 437; s. C. Morris, 467; Whallon v. Bancroft, 4 Minn. 109.

A territorial statute allowing a verdict to be rendered upon the agreement of three-fourths of the jurors is void. Kleinschmidt v. Dunphy, 1 Mont. 118.

This provision does not prevent a territorial legislature from extending the right of jury trial to cases at law involving less than twenty dollars. Whallon v. Bancroft, 4 Minn. 109.

Had the terms been that "the trial by jury shall be preserved," it might have been contended that they were imperative and could not be dispensed with. But the words are that "the right of trial by jury shall be preserved," which place it on the foot of a *lex pro se introducta*, and the benefit of it may therefore be relinquished. Bank v. Okely, 4 Wheat. 235; U. S. v. Rathbone, 2 Paine, 578; Parsons v. Armor, 3 Pet. 415.

Whenever a party is concluded by his own act, and held to have waived any right or privilege, such act should not be left doubtful, but should be plain and explicit. Every reasonable presumption should be made against the waiver, especially when it relates to a right or privilege deemed so valuable as to be secured by the Constitution. U. S. v. Rathbone, 2 Paine, 578.

The second clause is a substantial and independent clause, and applies to cases of Federal cognizance coming into the Federal courts from the State courts. Justices v. Murray, 9 Wall. 274.

ARTICLE VIII.

1. Excessive bail shall not be required, nor excessive fines imposed, nor cruel and unusual punishments inflicted.

This amendment was intended only for Congress and the Federal courts, and does not extend to the State governments, which are left at liberty to regulate their own criminal codes as they may deem proper, without reference to the laws or Constitution of the United States. James v. Comm. 12 S. & R. 220; Barker v. People, 3 Cow. 686.

The Supreme Court can not, on a writ of *habeas corpus*, revise the sentence of an inferior court in a criminal case, on the ground that the fine imposed was excessive. Ex parte Tobias Watkins, 7 Pet. 568.

ARTICLE IX.

1. The enumeration in the Constitution of certain rights, shall not be construed to deny or disparage others retained by the people.

ARTICLE X.

1. The powers not delegated to the United States by the Constitution, nor prohibited by it to the States, are reserved to the States respectively, or to the people.

This amendment omits the word "expressly," contained in the articles of confederation, thus leaving the question whether the particular power which may become the subject of contest has been delegated to the one government or prohibited to the other, to depend on a fair construction of the whole instrument. The men who drew and adopted this amendment had experienced the embarrassments resulting from the insertion of this word in the articles of confederation, and probably omitted it to avoid those embarrassments. McCulloch *v.* State, 4 Wheat. 316; George *v.* Concord, 45 N. H. 434.

Under the Constitution all possible powers must be found in the Federal Government or the States, or else they remain among those reserved rights which the people have retained, as not essential to be vested in any government. That which is forbidden to the States is not necessarily in the Federal Government, because it may be among the reserved powers. But if that which is essential to government is prohibited to one, it must, of necessity, be found in the other, and a prohibition in such a case on the one side is equivalent to a grant on the other. Van Husan *v.* Kanouse, 13 Mich. 303.

The Government can claim no powers which are not granted to it by the Constitution, and the powers actually granted must be such as are expressly given, or given by necessary implication. Martin *v.* Hunter, 1 Wheat. 304; S. C. 4 Munf. 1.

The principle that the Government is a government of limited powers, is misapplied when an attempt is made to use it to restrict the right to exercise a power expressly given. It is of value when the inquiry is whether a power has been conferred, but of no avail to strip a power given, in general terms, of any of its attributes. The powers of the Federal Government are limited in number, not in their nature. A power vested in Congress is as ample as it would be if possessed by any other legislature. It is not enlarged or diminished by the character of its possessor. Kneedler *v.* Lane, 45 Penn. 238; S. C. 3 Grant, 465.

The United States is a government, and consequently a body politic and corporate, capable of attaining the objects for which it was created by the means which are necessary for their attainment. It requires no argument to prove that one of the means by which some of these objects are to be accomplished is contract. The Government, therefore, is capable of contracting, and its contracts may be made in the name of the United States. The capacity of the United States to contract is coextensive with the powers and duties of government. Every contract which subserves to the performance of a duty may be rightfully made. U. S. *v.* Maurice, 2 Brock. 96.

The Federal Government, under the Constitution, has no power to impose on a State officer, as such, any duty whatever, and compel him to perform it; for if it possessed this power it might overload the officer with duties which would fill up all his time, and disable him from performing his obligations to the State, and might impose on him duties of a character incompatible with the rank and dignity to which he was elevated by the State. Comm. *v.* Dennison, 24 How. 66.

Prohibitions on the States are not to be enlarged by construction. Anderson *v.* Baker, 23 Md. 531.

When the American people created a national legislature, with certain enumerated powers, it was neither necessary nor proper to define the powers retained by the States. These powers proceed not from the people of America, but from the people of the several States, and remain, after the adoption of the Constitution, what they were before, except so far as they may be abridged by that instrument. Sturges *v.* Crowninshield, 4 Wheat. 122.

The Constitution was not intended to furnish the corrective for every abuse of power which may be committed by State governments. The interest, wisdom and justice of the representative body, and its relations with its constituents, furnish the only security against unwise legislation, where there is no contract. Providence Bank *v.* Billings, 4 Pet. 514.

The power to direct and regulate the mode of selling by citizens of the State, and within its own territories, is one of the acknowledged powers of the State governments. It is in virtue of this power that all laws respecting hawkers, peddlers, auctioneers and others are made. Comm. *v.* Kimball, 41 Mass. 359.

There is nothing in the Constitution which forbids the legislature of a State to exercise judicial functions. Satterlee *v.* Matthewson, 2 Pet. 380.

The establishing courts of justice, the appointment of judges, and the making regulations for the administration of justice within each State according to its laws, on all subjects not intrusted to the Federal Government, are the peculiar and exclusive province and duty of the State legislatures. Calder *v.* Bull, 3 Dall. 386; S. C. 2 Root, 350; Lapsley *v.* Brashears, 4 Litt. 47.

There is no constitutional objection to the exercise of the power to make a binding contract by a State. It necessarily exists in the sovereignty. A denial of this is a denial of State sovereignty. It takes from the State a power essential to the discharge of its functions as sovereign. If it does not possess the attribute, it could not communicate it to others. There is no power possessed by it more essential than this. Through the instrumentality of contracts, the machinery of government is carried on. Money is borrowed and obligations given for payment. Contracts are made with individuals, who give bonds to the State. State Bank *v.* Knoop, 16 How. 369; Ohio Trust Co. *v.* Debolt, 16 How. 416; S. C. 1 Ohio St. 563; Boston & L. R. R. Co. *v.* Salem & L. R. R. Co. 68 Mass. 1.

The power to regulate suffrage in a State, and to determine who shall or shall not be a voter, belongs exclusively to the State itself. The right of suffrage at a State election is a State right, a franchise conferrable only by the State, which Congress can neither give nor take away. Huber *v.* Reily, 53 Penn. 112.

Every State has the right to determine the *status* or domestic and social condition of the persons domiciled within its territory, except in so far as the powers of the States in this respect are restrained or duties and obligations imposed upon them by the Constitution. Strader *v.* Graham, 10 How. 82.

The several State legislatures retain all the powers of legislation delegated to them by the State constitutions which are not expressly taken away by the Constitution of the United States. Calder *v.* Bull, 3 Dall. 386; S. C. 2 Root, 350; Comm. *v.* Kimball, 41 Mass. 359; People *v.* Naglee, 1 Cal. 231.

The Constitution makes no provision for protecting the citizens of the respective States in their religious liberties. This is left to the State constitutions and laws. There is no inhibition, in this respect, imposed by the Constitution on the States. Permoli *v.* Municipality, 3 How. 589.

The several States, for all purposes except those of a national character embraced in the Constitution, are foreign to and independent of each other. Buckner *v.* Finley, 2 Pet. 586; Bank *v.* Daniel, 12 Pet. 33; Augusta *v.* Earle, 13 Pet. 520; Dodge *v.* Woolsey, 18 How. 350.

SUITS AGAINST STATES. 365

[The following amendment was proposed at the second session of the third Congress. 1 Stat. 22.]

ARTICLE XI.

1. The judicial power of the United States shall not be construed to extend to any suit in law or equity, commenced or prosecuted against one of the United States by citizens of another State, or by citizens or subjects of any foreign State.

There is nothing in the Constitution to deprive a State court of the jurisdiction over suits against a State which it possessed before the Constitution was adopted. Garr *v.* Bright, 1 Barb. Ch. 157.

This amendment applied to past as well as future cases. Hollingsworth *v.* Virginia, 3 Dall. 378.

The mere suggestion of title in a State to property in the possession of an individual, does not arrest the proceedings or prevent the court from looking into the suggestion and examining the validity of the title. U. S. *v.* Peters, 5 Cranch, 115.

This amendment is, of necessity, limited to those suits in which a State is a party on the record. Osborn *v.* Bank, 9 Wheat. 738; U. S. *v.* Peters, 5 Cranch, 115; Davis *v.* Gray, 16 Wall. 203; U. S. *v.* Bright, Bright. 19; Olmstead's Case, Bright. 9; Swasey *v.* N. C. R. R. Co. 1 Hughes, 1; S. C. 71 N. C. 571.

By a suit commenced by an individual against a State, is meant process sued out by that individual against the State, for the purpose of establishing some claim against it by the judgment of a court, and the prosecution of that suit is its continuance. Cohens *v.* Virginia, 6 Wheat. 264.

A suit is the prosecution of some demand in a court of justice. To commence a suit is to demand something by the institution of process in a court of justice, and to prosecute the suit is, according to the common acceptation of language, to continue that demand. Cohens *v.* Virginia, 6 Wheat. 264.

The amendment was intended for those cases, and for those only, in which some demand against a State is made by an individual in the Federal courts. Cohens *v.* Virginia, 6 Wheat. 264.

A writ of error prosecuted by a citizen against his own State, is not within the prohibition. Cohens *v.* Virginia, 6 Wheat. 264.

Where a State obtains a judgment against an individual, and the court rendering such judgment overrules a defense set up under the Constitution or laws of the United States, the transfer of the record into the Supreme Court for the sole purpose of inquiring whether the judgment violates the Constitution or laws of the United States, can not be denominated a suit commenced or prosecuted against the State whose judgment is so far re-examined. Nothing is demanded from the State. No claim against it of any description is asserted or prosecuted. Cohens *v.* Virginia, 6 Wheat. 264.

The Federal courts may entertain a suit against a corporation although a State is one of the corporators. Bank *v.* Planters' Bank, 9 Wheat. 904; Louisville R. R. Co. *v.* Letson, 2 How. 497.

The Federal courts may entertain a suit against a corporation although a State is the sole proprietor of the stock. Bank *v.* Wister, 2 Pet. 318.

Where the chief magistrate of a State is sued not by his name but by his style of office, and the claim made upon him is entirely in his official character, the State itself may be considered as a party on the record. Governor *v.* Madrazo, 1 Pet. 110.

An independent foreign sovereign can not be sued, and does not appear in court. But a friend of the court comes in, and by suggestion gives it to understand that his interests are involved in the controversy. The interests of the sovereign in such a case, and in every other where he chooses to assert them under the name of the real party to the cause, are as well defended as if he were a party to the record. Osborn *v.* Bank, 9 Wheat. 738.

The right of a State to assert as plaintiff any interest it may have in a subject which forms the matter of controversy between individuals in a Federal court is not affected by this amendment, nor can it be so construed as to oust the court of jurisdiction should such claim be suggested. The amendment simply provides that no suit shall be commenced or prosecuted against a State. The State can not be made a defendant to any suit brought by an individual. U. S. *v.* Peters, 5 Cranch, 115; Osborn *v.* Bank, 9 Wheat. 738.

A mere suggestion of title in a State to property in the possession of an individual, will not arrest proceedings in a Federal court between individuals, and prevent its looking into the suggestion and examining the validity of the title. U. S. *v.* Peters, 5 Cranch, 115; Osborn *v.* Bank, 9 Wheat. 738.

If the Federal court decides that the State has no title or claim to property in a suit between individuals, the State has no constitutional right to resist the legal process which may be directed in the cause. U. S. *v.* Peters, 5 Cranch, 115.

A Federal court has no power to compel the officers of a State to execute its laws. To do so, would be to substitute the court for the executive officers of the State, to supplant their views of duty and the obligations imposed upon them by their official oaths by the discretion of the court and its official oath. In other words, it would be an undertaking on the part of the court to administer the State Government. This the court has no power to do. Macauley *v.* Kellogg, 2 Woods, 13; S. C. 1 Cent. L. J. 164.

[The three following sections were proposed as amendments at the first session of the eighth Congress. 1 Stat. 22.]

ARTICLE XII.

1. The electors shall meet in their respective States, and vote by ballot for President and Vice-President, one of whom, at least, shall not be an inhabitant of the same State with themselves; they shall name in their ballots the person voted for as President, and in distinct ballots the person voted for as Vice-President; and they shall make distinct lists of all persons voted for as President, and of all persons voted for as Vice-President, and of the number of votes for each, which lists they shall sign and certify, and transmit sealed to the seat of the Government of the United States, directed to the president of the Senate; the president of the Senate shall, in the presence of the Senate and House of Representatives, open all the certificates, and the votes shall then be counted; the person having the greatest number of votes for President, shall be the President, if such number be a majority of the whole number of electors appointed; and if no person have such majority, then from the persons having the highest numbers, not exceeding three, on the list of those voted for as President, the House of Representatives shall choose immediately, by ballot, the President. But in choosing the President, the votes shall be taken by States, the representation from each State having one vote; a quorum for this purpose shall consist of a member or members from two-thirds of the States, and a majority of all the States shall be necessary to a choice. And if the House of Representatives shall not choose a President, whenever the right of choice

shall devolve upon them, before the fourth day of March next following, then the Vice-President shall act as President, as in the case of the death or other constitutional disability of the President.

Fraud and misconduct on the part of the State authorities, constituted for the very purpose of declaring the final will of the State, is not a subject over which the two Houses of Congress have jurisdiction to institute an examination. Electoral Count.

The utmost that the two Houses of Congress can do, is to ascertain whether the State has made the appointment according to the form prescribed by its laws. Electoral Count.

If the State is in the enjoyment of its proper relations to the Federal Government, the two Houses can not inquire whether the tumults and disorders existing therein at the time of the election, or the presence of troops sent there by the President for the purpose of preserving the peace, had such an influence as to render the election void. Electoral Count.

Congress can not institute a scrutiny into the appointment of electors by a State. While the two Houses of Congress are authorized to canvass the electoral vote, no authority is given them to canvass the election of the electors themselves on the suggestion of fraud, or for any other cause. Electoral Count.

The two Houses of Congress may inquire whether the certificate of the executive is genuine, whether it is plainly false, and whether it contains a clear mistake of fact. Electoral Count.

The powers of the president of the Senate are merely ministerial. He is not invested with any authority for making any investigation outside of the joint meeting of the two Houses. He can not send for persons or papers. He is utterly without the means or power to do more than to inspect the documents sent to him, and he can not inspect them until he opens them in the presence of the two Houses. Electoral Count.

2. The person having the greatest number of votes as Vice-President, shall be the Vice-President, if such number be a majority of the whole number of electors appointed ; and if no person have a majority, then from the two highest numbers on the list, the Senate shall choose the Vice-President ; a quorum for the purpose shall consist of two-thirds of the whole number

of Senators, and a majority of the whole number shall be necessary to a choice.

3. But no person constitutionally ineligible to the office of President, shall be eligible to that of Vice-President of the United States.

[The following amendment was proposed at the second session of the thirty-eighth Congress. 13 Stat. 774.]

ARTICLE XIII.

SEC. 1. Neither slavery nor involuntary servitude, except as a punishment for crime, whereof the party shall have been duly convicted, shall exist within the United States, or any place subject to their jurisdiction.

SEC. 2. Congress shall have power to enforce this article by appropriate legislation.

Contracts relating to slaves, if valid when made, are not impaired by this amendment. Osborne *v.* Nicholson, 13 Wall. 654; S. C. 1 Dill. 219; Boyce *v.* Tabb, 18 Wall. 546; Hall *v.* Keese, 31 Tex. 504; Roundtree *v.* Baker, 52 Ill. 241; McElvain *v.* Mudd, 44 Ala. 48; Calhoun *v.* Calhoun, 2 Rich. N. S. 283; White *v.* Hart, 13 Wall. 646; S. C. 39 Geo. 306; contra, Wainwright *v.* Bridges, 19 La. Ann. 234; Austin *v.* Sandel, 19 La. Ann. 309; Halley *v.* Hoeffner, 19 La. Ann. 518; Lytle *v.* Whicher, 21 La. Ann. 182; Gautden *v.* Stoddard, 41 Geo. 329; Cherry *v.* Jones, 41 Geo. 579; Rodrigues *v.* Bienvenu, 22 La. Ann. 300; Succession of Woodward, 22 La. Ann. 305.

The object of this provision was not only to effect the emancipation of all persons then held in slavery, but also to forever thereafter deprive both Congress and the respective States of any and all power to reduce either the persons so emancipated, or any others within the jurisdiction of the United States, to the condition of slavery or involuntary servitude, except as a punishment for crime whereof the party shall have been duly convicted. To secure personal freedom to all within the purview of its provisions was the first great and leading object of the amendment. People *v.* Washington, 38 Cal. 658.

Personal security and the right to acquire and enjoy private property, are powerful auxiliaries to the maintenance of personal liberty. The continued enjoyment of personal liberty can not well be assured without the enjoyment of personal security. The right to acquire and enjoy private property is necessary to give that independence and freedom from want essential to the full enjoyment of personal liberty. Whatever, therefore, tends to maintain and assure to a person personal security, and to protect him in the acquisition and enjoyment of private property, aids in the maintenance of personal liberty. People *v.* Washington, 38 Cal. 658; Smith *v.* Moody, 26 Ind. 299.

The establishment of different rules as to the competency of evidence applicable to different classes of persons, may tend to the advantage of one class and to the oppression and encroachment upon the personal liberty of another. A law providing that the same rule of evidence shall apply to both classes, placing the class likely to be reduced to servitude upon an equal footing with the other, in respect to the right to testify as to the encroachment upon their personal liberty, strongly conduces to the enforcement of this amendment. People *v.* Washington, 38 Cal. 658; U. S. *v.* Rhodes, 1 Abb. C. C. 28.

Legislation which practically tends to facilitate the securing to all, through the aid of the judicial and executive departments of the government, the full enjoyment of personal freedom, is appropriate. People *v.* Washington, 38 Cal. 658.

A law which only permits the same class of persons to testify against a black man as are allowed to testify against a white man, in a matter where personal liberty is concerned, tends to enforce this amendment. People *v.* Washington, 38 Cal. 658; contra, Bowlin *v.* Comm. 2 Bush, 5.

Colored children may be excluded from the schools for white children, where separate schools are provided for them. Ward *v.* Flood, 48 Cal. 36; Cory *v.* Carter, 48 Ind. 327.

The utmost legal effect of this clause is to declare the colored as free as the white race in the United States. It certainly gave the colored race nothing more than freedom. It did not elevate them to social or political equality with the white race. It neither gave, nor aimed to give them, in defiance of State laws, all the rights of the white race, but left them equally free in all the States, and equally subject to State jurisdiction and State laws. Bowlin *v.* Comm. 2 Bush, 5.

"Power to enforce this article by appropriate legislation," imports nothing more than to uphold the emancipating section and prevent a violation of the contemplated liberty of the enfranchised race. It does not mean that Congress shall have power to legislate over their civil rights and remedies in the States, any more than over those of all other citizens. Bowlin *v.* Comm. 2 Bush, 5.

This is not merely a prohibition against the passage or enforcement of any law inflicting or establishing slavery or involuntary servitude, but is a positive declaration that slavery shall not exist. It prohibits the thing. In the enforcement of this article, therefore, Congress has to deal with the subject-matter. U. S. v. Cruikshank, 1 Woods, 308 ; s. c. 92 U. S. 542.

That a personal servitude was meant is proved by the use of the word "involuntary," which can only apply to human beings. The exception of servitude as a punishment for crime gives an idea of the class of servitudes that is meant. The word servitude is of larger meaning than slavery, as the latter is popularly understood, and the obvious purpose was to forbid all shades and conditions of African slavery. Slaughter House Cases, 16 Wall. 36.

This clause does not authorize Congress to pass laws for the punishment of ordinary crimes and offenses against persons of the colored race, or any other race. That belongs to the State government alone. All ordinary murders, robberies, assaults, thefts and offenses whatsoever, are cognizable only in the State courts, unless the State should deny to the class of persons referred to the equal protection of the laws. U. S. v. Cruikshank, 1 Woods, 308 ; s. c. 92 U. S. 542.

[By a joint resolution adopted at the first session of the thirty-ninth Congress (two thirds of both houses concurring), the following article was proposed to the legislatures of the several States as an amendment to the Constitution of the United States, to become a part of the Constitution when ratified by the legislatures of three-fourths of the States. 15 Stat. 706.]

ARTICLE XIV.

SEC. 1. All persons born or naturalized in the United States, and subject to the jurisdiction thereof, are citizens of the United States, and of the State wherein they reside. No State shall make or enforce any law which shall abridge the privileges or immunities of citizens of the United States ; nor shall any State deprive any person of life, liberty, or property, without due process of law, nor deny to any person within its jurisdiction, the equal protection of the laws.

SEC. 2. Representatives shall be apportioned among the several States according to their respective numbers, counting the whole number of persons in each State, excluding Indians not taxed. But when the right to vote at any election for the choice of electors for President and Vice-President of the United States, representatives in Congress, the executive and judicial officers of a State, or the members of the legislature thereof, is denied to any of the male inhabitants of such State, being twenty-one years of age, and citizens of the United States, or in any way abridged, except for participation in rebellion or other crime, the basis of representation therein shall be reduced in the proportion which the number of such male citizens shall bear to the whole number of male citizens twenty-one years of age in such State.

Sec. 3. No person shall be a senator or representative in Congress, or elector of President and Vice-President, or hold any office, civil or military, under the United States, or under any State, who, having previously taken an oath as a member of Congress, or as an officer of the United States, or as a member of any State legislature, or as an executive or judicial officer of any State, to support the Constitution of the United States, shall have engaged in insurrection or rebellion against the same, or given aid or comfort to the enemies thereof; but Congress may, by a vote of two-thirds of each house, remove such disability.

Sec. 4. The validity of the public debt of the United States authorized by law, including debts incurred for payment of pensions and bounties for services in suppressing insurrection or rebellion, shall not be questioned. But neither the United States, nor any State, shall assume or pay any debt or obligation incurred in aid of insurrection or rebellion against the United States, or any claim for the loss or emancipation of any slave; but all such debts, obligations, and claims, shall be held illegal and void.

Sec. 5. The Congress shall have power to enforce, by appropriate legislation, the provisions of this article.

Citizenship.

This clause declares that persons may be citizens of the United States without regard to their citizenship of a particular State, and overturns the Dred Scott decision, by making all persons born within the United States, and subject to its jurisdiction, citizens of the United States. The phrase "subject to its jurisdiction," was intended to exclude from its operation children of ministers, consuls and citizens or subjects of foreign States born within the United States. Slaughter House Cases, 16 Wall. 36.

No white person born within the limits of the United States, and subject to its jurisdiction, or born without those limits, and subsequently naturalized under its laws, owes the status of citizenship to this amendment. Van Valkenburg v. Brown, 43 Cal. 43.

Slaves who escaped to Canada before the adoption of the amendment, where they now reside, are not citizens of the United States. Hedgman v. Board, 26 Mich. 51.

The child of slaves who escaped to Canada, where he was born, is not a citizen of the United States. Hedgman v. Board, 26 Mich. 51.

This clause evidently refers to natural persons. The birth referred to is a natural one, and not artificial nor procuced in some legislative body. People v. C. & A. R. R. Co. 6 C. L. N. 280.

An Indian whose tribe has ceased to maintain its tribal integrity, and who is taxed by the State, is subject to the jurisdiction of the United States, and a citizen thereof. U. S. v. Elm, 23 I. R. R. 419.

Immunities.

The words "citizen" and "person" are synonymous terms, and by the term person is meant a natural person, a citizen of the United States, and of the State in which he may reside. People v. C. & A. R. R. Co. 6 C. L. N. 280.

A corporation is not a citizen of the United States, as that term is used in the amendment. Ins. Co. v. New Orleans, 1 Woods, 85.

A corporation is not a person within the meaning of this amendment. Ins. Co. v. New Orleans, 1 Woods, 85.

Women may be citizens of the United States. Minor v. Happersett, 21 Wall. 162.

The amendment did not add to the privileges or immunities of a citizen as they existed at the time it was adopted. Minor v. Happersett, 21 Wall. 162.

It is only the privileges and immunities of citizens of the United States which are placed by this clause under the protection of the Federal Constitution, and the privileges and immunities of citizens of a State, whatever they may be, are not intended to have any additional protection by this paragraph of the amendment. Slaughter House Cases, 16 Wall. 36.

The distinction between citizenship of the United States and citizenship of a State, is clearly recognized and established. Not only may a man be a citizen of the United States without being a citizen of a State, but an important element is necessary to convert the former into the latter. He must reside within the State to make him a citizen of it, but it is only necessary that he should be born or naturalized in the United States to be a citizen of the Union. Slaughter House Cases, 16 Wall. 36; U. S. v. Cruikshank, 1 Woods, 308; s. c. 92 U. S. 542.

The privileges and immunities are the same as those secured to the citizens of each State by section two of article four. Slaughter House Cases, 16 Wall. 36.

This clause includes only such privileges or immunities as are derived from or recognized by the Constitution. State v. McCann, 21 Ohio St. 198.

When political rights and privileges are secured in the Constitution only by a declaration that the State or the United States shall not violate or abridge them, it is at once understood that they are not created or conferred by the Constitution, but that the Constitution only guarantees that they shall not be impaired by the State or the United States, as the case may be. The fulfillment of this duty by the United States, is the only duty with which that Government is charged. The affirmative enforcement of the rights and privileges themselves, unless something more is expressed, does not devolve on it, but belongs to the State government as a part of its residuary sovereignty. U. S. v. Cruikshank, 1 Woods, 308; s. c. 92 U. S. 542; contra, U. S. v. Hall, 13 I. R. R. 181; s. c. 3 C. L. N. 260.

There can be no constitutional legislation of Congress for directly enforcing the privileges and immunities of citizens of the United States by original proceedings in the Federal courts, where the State has passed no law adverse to them. U. S. v. Cruikshank, 1 Woods, 308; s. c. 92 U. S. 542.

Each State has the right to regulate the immunities and privileges of its own citizens, provided that in so doing it does not abridge the privileges and immunities of citizens of the United States. Slaughter House Cases, 16 Wall. 36.

A State law which prohibits persons from practicing medicine or surgery unless they have received a diploma from some regularly chartered medical school, excepting those who have practiced in the State for ten years next preceding the passage of the law, is valid. Ex parte Spinney, 10 Nev. 323.

A statute regulating slaughter houses is a part of the police power of the State, and does not deprive a party of his property without due process of law, or deny him the equal protection of the laws. Slaughter House Cases, 16 Wall. 36; contra, Slaughter House Case, 1 Woods, 21.

A trial by jury in suits at common law pending in the State courts, is not a privilege or immunity of national citizenship, which the States are forbidden to abridge. Walker v. Sauvinet, 92 U. S. 90.

The right to sell intoxicating liquors is not one of the rights growing out of citizenship of the United States, and is not protected by this provision. Bartemeyer v. Iowa, 18 Wall. 129.

The right to admission to practice law in the State courts, is not one of the privileges or immunities which is protected by this clause. Bradwell v. State, 16 Wall. 130.

A statute prohibiting the intermarriage of the white and colored races is valid, for the right of intermarriage among the races is not one of the privileges or immunities protected by the amendment. Lonas v. State, 3 Heisk. 287; State v. Gibson, 36 Ind. 389; Ex parte Wm. B. Hobbs, 1 Woods, 537; contra, Burns v. State, 48 Ala. 195.

The right of voting, or the privilege of voting, is a right or privilege arising under the Constitution of a State, and not of the United States. If the right belongs to any particular person, it is because such person is entitled to it as a citizen of the State where he offers to exercise it, and not because of citizenship of the United States. U. S. v. Anthony, 11 Blatch. 200; U. S. v. Cruikshank, 1 Woods, 308; s. c. 92 U. S. 542.

A female can not claim the right to vote under the provisions of this amendment, for it is not a privilege or immunity that is protected thereby. Van Valkenburg v. Brown, 43 Cal. 43; Minor v. Happersett, 21 Wall. 162; U. S. v. Anthony, 11 Blatch. 200; Spencer v. Board, 1 McArthur, 169.

An arrest made by an officer of the State militia, in pursuance of military power granted to him by the governor against persons in insurrection, does not abridge the privileges or immunities of citizens. In re Bergen, 2 Hughes, 512.

Congress can not protect a citizen in the right to use a public conveyance for local travel. Cully v. Balt. & O. R. R. Co. 1 Hughes, 536.

Due Process.

Due process of law is process due according to the law of the land. This process in the States is regulated by the law of the State. A party is not deprived of his property without due process of law, although the case is tried without a jury. Walker v. Sauvinet, 92 U. S. 90.

The words "due process of law" mean law in its regular course of administration according to the prescribed forms and in accordance with the general rules for the protection of individual rights, and do not prohibit the States from prosecuting for felonies by information instead of by indictment, if they choose to abolish the grand jury system. Rowan *v.* State, 30 Wis. 129.

This provision adds nothing to the rights of one citizen as against another. It simply furnishes an additional guaranty against any encroachment by the States upon the fundamental rights which belong to every citizen as a member of society. Sovereignty for the purpose of protecting the rights of life and personal liberty when assailed by others, rests in the States alone. U. S. *v.* Cruikshank, 92 U. S. 542; S. C. 1 Woods, 308.

The Federal Government has no power to punish individuals for conspiring to deprive a person of life or liberty, without due process of law. U. S. *v.* Cruikshank, 92 U. S. 542.

A State law regulating a pursuit or profession, or regulating the use of property, does not in any manner abridge the liberty of citizens. Munn *v.* People, 69 Ill. 80; S. C. 94 U. S. 113; Ex parte Spinney, 10 Nev. 323.

The entry of a judgment on a forfeited recognizance does not take the property of the cognizor without due process of law. People *v.* Quigg, 59 N. Y. 83.

A State law which prohibits common carriers from discriminating against passengers on account of race or color, does not deprive them of property without due process of law. Decuir *v.* Benson, 27 La. Ann. 1.

A levy by a collector in pursuance of a State law, to collect a tax, is due process of law. McMillen *v.* Anderson, 27 La. Ann. 18.

A State law allowing overseers of the poor to commit an alleged vagrant to the workhouse on an *ex parte* hearing, is void, for it deprives him of his liberty without due process of law. An *ex parte* decision is not such process. Portland *v.* Bangor, 65 Me. 120.

A statute authorizing a commissioner to ascertain whether lewd and debauched women are among the passengers, and to prevent them from landing, is valid. Ex parte Ah Fook, 49 Cal. 402.

A statute regulating the use, or even the price of the use of private property, does not necessarily deprive an owner of his property without due process of law. Under some circumstances it may, but not under all. Munn *v.* Illinois, 94 U. S. 113; S. C. 69 Ill. 80.

When private property is affected with a public interest, it ceases to be *juris privati* only. Property becomes clothed with a public interest when used in a manner to make it of public consequence and affect the community at large. When one, therefore, devotes his property to a use in which the public has an interest, he in effect grants to the public an interest in that use, and must submit to be controlled by the public for the common good to the extent of the interest he has thus created. Munn *v.* Illinois, 94 U. S. 113; S. C. 69 Ill. 80.

A State statute regulating the charges for the storage of grain by warehouses is valid. Munn v. Illinois, 94 U. S. 113; s. c. 69 Ill. 80.

If no state of facts could exist that would justify a statute regulating the use of private property, then the act would be void; but if it could, the presumption is that it did. The legislature is the exclusive judge of the propriety of interference within the scope of legislative power. Munn v. Illinois, 94 U. S. 113; s. c. 69 Ill. 80.

What is a reasonable compensation for the use of property is a legislative and not a judicial question, when the legislature has acted on the subject. Munn v. Illinois, 94 U. S. 113; s. c. 69 Ill. 80.

The assessment of a tax is necessarily summary, and need not be by a judicial proceeding. It is valid, although the party had no opportunity to be present when he was assessed. McMillen v. Anderson, 6 A. L. J. 335.

An arrest made by an officer of the State militia in pursuance of authority granted to him by the governor against persons in insurrection, does not deprive any person of liberty without due process of law, for in times of insurrection the sword is due process of law. In re Bergen, 2 Hughes, 512.

Equal Protection.

This provision does not add anything to the rights which one citizen has under the Constitution against another. The equality of the rights of citizens is a principle of republicanism. Every republican government is in duty bound to protect all its citizens in the enjoyment of this principle, if within its power. That duty was originally assumed by the States, and still remains there. The only obligation resting upon the United States is to see that the States do not deny the right. This the amendment guarantees, but no more. The power of the National Government is limited to the enforcement of this guaranty. U. S. v. Cruikshank, 1 Woods, 308; s. c. 92 U. S. 542.

Any outrages, atrocities, or conspiracies, whether against the colored race or white race, which do not flow from the war of races, but spring from the ordinary felonious or criminal intent which prompts to such unlawful acts, are not within the jurisdiction of the United States, but within the sole jurisdiction of the States, unless the States, by their laws, deny to any particular race equality of rights. U. S. v. Cruikshank, 1 Woods, 308; s. c. 92 U. S. 542.

The war of race, whether it assumes the dimensions of civil strife or domestic violence, whether carried on in a guerilla or predatory form, or by private combinations, or even by private outrage or intimidation, is subject to the jurisdiction of the Government of the United States, and when any atrocity is committed which may be assigned to this cause, it may be punished by the laws and in the courts of the United States. U. S. *v.* Cruikshank, 1 Woods, 308; s. c. 92 U. S. 542.

If the wrong is of that character which permits of its being done only by certain classes of persons, or by one sex, and not by the other, the Constitution does not require that the remedy shall be broader than the evil, or be made to act upon persons other than those whose conduct produces the mischief, or stand in the way of the legislature's directing the remedy by special designation against the class or sex to which the wrong or evil is exclusively due. Ex parte Nellie Smith, 38 Cal. 702.

A statute which authorizes a recovery of double the value of the live stock destroyed by railroad trains at points where the roads are not fenced, and where the right to fence exists, is valid, and does not deprive the corporation of the equal protection of the laws. Tredway *v.* S. C. & St. P. R. Co. 43 Iowa, 527.

A statute prohibiting females from being in places where liquors are sold, after a certain hour at night, is valid. Ex parte Nellie Smith, 38 Cal. 702.

A State law prohibiting Chinese from testifying in any action wherein a white person is a party, does not, in criminal cases, deprive them of the equal protection of the laws. People *v.* Brady, 40 Cal. 198.

All persons, whether native or foreign, high or low, are, while within the jurisdiction of the United States, entitled to the equal protection of the laws. Equality of protection implies not only equal accessibility to the courts for the prevention or redress of wrongs, and the enforcement of rights, but equal exemption, with others of the same class, from all charges and burdens of every kind. Ex parte Ah Fong, 3 Saw. 144.

A statute regulating the charges for storage in warehouses, in certain places, does not deprive the owners of the equal protection of the laws. Munn *v.* Illinois, 94 U. S. 113.

A State, while providing a system of education, can not exclude colored children from its benefits merely because of their African descent, for this would deny them the equal protection of the laws. Ward *v.* Flood, 48 Cal. 36; contra, Marshall *v.* Donovan, 10 Bush, 681.

Unless separate schools are in fact maintained for colored children, all children, whether white or colored, have an equal right to become pupils at any common school organized under the laws of the State. Ward *v.* Flood, 48 Cal. 36.

A statute providing for the education of colored children in schools separate from those provided for the education of white children, is valid. Ward *v.* Flood, 48 Cal. 36; Cory *v.* Carter, 48 Ind. 327; State *v.* McCann, 21 Ohio St. 198.

A State law which inflicts a more severe punishment for adultery or fornication, where the parties are of different races, than where they are of the same race, is valid. Ford *v.* State, 53 Ala. 150; Ellis *v.* State, 42 Ala. 525.

Disability.

The intention of the people was to create a disability to be made operative by the legislation of Congress, in its ordinary course. Legislation by Congress is necessary to give effect to the prohibition by providing for the removal. The exercise by an officer of his functions until removed, in pursuance of such legislation, is not unlawful. Ex parte Cæsar Griffin, 25 Tex. Supp. 623 ; s. c. Chase, 364 ; Powell *v.* Boon, 43 Ala. 469.

A person engaged in the rebellion, who held office under the Confederate Government, or voluntarily aided the rebellion by personal services or contribution other than charitable, of anything that was useful or necessary in the confederate service, is disqualified. Worthy *v.* Barrett, 63 N. C. 199.

A sheriff who took an oath to support the Constitution is within this prohibition. Worthy *v.* Barrett, 63 N. C. 199.

A county attorney who took the oath to support the Constitution is within the prohibition. In re William L. Tate, 63 N. C. 308.

Did not this amendment bar any other punishment? Ex parte Jefferson Davis, Chase, 1.

Confederate Debt.

No contract to be paid in confederate notes can be enforced, for that would be a payment of the confederate debt. Smith *v.* Nelson,. 34 Tex. 516.

[The following amendment was proposed at the third session of the fortieth Congress. 16 Stat.]

ARTICLE XV.

SEC. 1. The right of citizens of the United States to vote, shall not be denied or abridged by the United States or by any State on account of race, color, or previous condition of servitude.

SEC. 2. The Congress shall have power to enforce this article by appropriate legislation.

This amendment does not establish the right of any citizen to vote. It merely declares that race, color, or previous condition of servitude shall not exclude him. U. S. *v.* Cruikshank, 1 Woods, 308; s. c. 92 U. S. 542.

The object and effect of this amendment was to place the colored man in the matter of suffrage on the same basis with the white. It does not give him the right to vote independent of the restrictions and qualifications, such as age and residence, imposed by the State laws upon the white man. Anthony v. Halderman, 7 Kans. 50.

No person can claim the right to vote under this provision, unless he is a citizen of the United States. Hedgman v. State, 26 Mich. 51.

This amendment deprives the provisions of the State constitutions and laws restricting the exercise of suffrage to white persons of all legal force and efficacy. Wood v. Fitzgerald, 3 Oregon, 568; Anthony v. Halderman, 7 Kans. 50.

The amendment does not confer an authority to impose a penalty for every wrongful refusal to receive the vote of a qualified elector at State elections. It is only where the wrongful refusal at such an election is because of race, color or previous condition of servitude, that Congress can interfere and provide for its punishment. U. S. v. Reese, 92 U. S. 214.

This amendment does not confer the right of suffrage upon any one. It prevents the States from giving preference to one citizen of the United States over another, on account of race, color or previous condition of of servitude. It has invested the citizens of the United States with a new constitutional right which is within the protective power of Congress. U. S. v. Reese, 92 U. S. 214; U. S. v. Cruikshank, 1 Woods, 308; s. c. 92 U. S. 542.

The limitation which is prescribed by the amendment must not be overlooked. It is not the right to vote which is guaranteed to all citizens. Congress can not interfere with the regulation of that right by the States, except to prevent by appropriate legislation, any distinction as to race, color or previous condition. U. S. v. Cruikshank, 1 Woods, 308; s. c. 92 U. S. 542; U. S. v. Petersburg Judges, 14 A. L. Reg. 105, 238.

This clause confers a positive right which did not exist before. The language is peculiar. It is composed of two negatives. The right shall not be denied. That is, the right shall be enjoyed; the right, namely, the right to be exempt from the disability of race, color or previous condition of servitude, as respects the right to vote. U. S. v. Cruikshank, 1 Woods, 308; s. c. 92 U. S. 542.

The right conferred and guaranteed is not an absolute, but a relative one. This clause does not confer the right to vote. That is the prerogative of the State laws. It only confers a right not to be excluded from voting by reason of race, color or previous condition of servitude, and this is all the right that Congress can enforce. U. S. v. Cruikshank, 1 Woods, 308; s. c. 92 U. S. 542.

*A State may exclude a citizen from voting on the ground of sex. Van Valkenburg *v.* Brown, 43 Cal. 43.

The proclamation of the Secretary of State acting in behalf of the President is *prima facie* evidence of the legal ratification of the amendment. Wood *v.* Fitzgerald, 3 Oregon, 568.

When State laws impose duties upon persons, whether officers or not, the performance or non-performance of which affects rights under the Federal Government, Congress may make the non-performance of those duties an offense against the United States, and punish it accordingly. U. S. *v.* Given, 17 I. R. R. 289.

APPENDIX.

APPENDIX.

THE DECLARATION OF INDEPENDENCE.

A Declaration by the Representatives of the United States of America in Congress assembled:

When, in the course of human events, it becomes necessary for one people to dissolve the political bands which have connected them with another, and to assume, among the powers of the earth, the separate and equal station to which the laws of nature and of nature's God entitle them, a decent respect to the opinions of mankind requires that they should declare the causes which impel them to the separation.

We hold these truths to be self-evident: that all men are created equal; that they are endowed, by their Creator, with certain unalienable rights; that among these are life, liberty, and the pursuit of happiness. That to secure these rights, governments are instituted among men, deriving their just powers from the consent of the governed; that whenever any form of government becomes destructive of these ends, it is the right of the people to alter or to abolish it, and to institute a new government, laying its foundation on such principles, and organizing its powers in such form as to them shall seem most likely to effect their safety and happiness. Prudence, indeed, will dictate, that governments long established should not be changed for light and transient causes; and, accordingly, all experience hath shown, that mankind are more disposed to suffer while evils are sufferable, than to right themselves by abolishing the forms to which they are accustomed. But when a long train of abuses and usurpations, pursuing invariably the same object, evinces a design to reduce them under absolute despotism, it is their right, it is their duty to throw off such government, and to provide new guards for their future security. Such has been the patient sufferance of these colonies; and such is now the necessity which constrains them to alter their former systems of government. The history of the present king of Great Britain is a history of repeated injuries and usurpations, all having in direct object the establishment of an absolute tyranny over these States. To prove this, let facts be submitted to a candid world.

He has refused his assent to laws the most wholesome and necessary for the public good.

He has forbidden his governors to pass laws of immediate and pressing importance, unless suspended in their operation till his assent should be obtained; and when so suspended, he has utterly neglected to attend to them.

He has refused to pass other laws for the accommodation of large districts of people, unless those people would relinquish the right of representation in the legislature—a right inestimable to them, and formidable to tyrants only.

He has called together legislative bodies at places unusual, uncomfortable, and distant from the depository of their public records, for the sole purpose of fatiguing them into compliance with his measures.

He has dissolved representative houses repeatedly, for opposing, with manly firmness, his invasions on the rights of the people.

He has refused, for a long time after such dissolutions, to cause others to be elected; whereby the legislative powers, incapable of annihilation, have returned to the people at large, for their exercise, the State remaining, in the mean time, exposed to all the dangers of invasion from without, and convulsions within.

He has endeavored to prevent the population of these States; for that purpose obstructing the laws for naturalization of foreigners; refusing to pass others to encourage their migration hither, and raising the conditions of new appropriations of lands.

He has obstructed the administration of justice, by refusing his assent to laws for establishing judiciary powers.

He has made judges dependent on his will alone, for the

tenure of their offices, and the amount and payment of their salaries.

He has erected a multitude of new offices, and sent hither swarms of officers, to harass our people, and eat out their substance.

He has kept among us, in times of peace, standing armies, without the consent of our legislatures.

He has affected to render the military independent of, and superior to, the civil power.

He has combined with others to subject us to a jurisdiction foreign to our constitution, and unacknowledged by our laws; giving his assent to their acts of pretended legislation:

For quartering large bodies of armed troops among us:

For protecting them, by a mock trial, from punishment for any murders which they should commit on the inhabitants of these States:

For cutting off our trade with all parts of the world:

For imposing taxes on us without our consent:

For depriving us, in many cases, of the benefits of trial by jury:

For transporting us beyond the seas to be tried for pretended offenses:

For abolishing the free system of English laws in a neighboring province, establishing therein an arbitrary government, and enlarging its boundaries, so as to render it at once an example and fit instrument for introducing the same absolute rule into these colonies:

For taking away our charters, abolishing our most valuable laws, and altering, fundamentally, the powers of our governments:

For suspending our own legislatures, and declaring themselves invested with power to legislate for us in all cases whatsoever.

He has abdicated government here, by declaring us out of his protection, and waging war against us.

He has plundered our seas, ravaged our coasts, burnt our towns, and destroyed the lives of our people.

He is at this time transporting large armies of foreign mercenaries to complete the works of death, desolation, and tyranny, already begun with circumstances of cruelty and perfidy, scarcely paralleled in the most barbarous ages, and totally unworthy the head of a civilized nation.

He has constrained our fellow-citizens, taken captive on the high seas, to bear arms against their country, to become the executioners of their friends and brethren, or to fall themselves by their hands.

He has excited domestic insurrection among us, and has endeavored to bring on the inhabitants of our frontiers the merciless Indian savages, whose known rule of warfare is an undistinguished destruction of all ages, sexes, and conditions.

In every stage of these oppressions we have petitioned for redress in the most humble terms: our repeated petitions have been answered only by repeated injury. A prince, whose character is thus marked by every act which may define a tyrant, is unfit to be the ruler of a free people.

Nor have we been wanting in attention to our British brethren. We have warned them, from time to time, of attempts by their legislature to extend an unwarrantable jurisdiction over us. We have reminded them of the circumstances of our emigration and settlement here. We have appealed to their native justice and magnanimity, and we have conjured them by the ties of our common kindred to disavow these usurpations, which would inevitably interrupt our connections and correspondence. They too have been deaf to the voice of justice and of consanguinity. We must, therefore, acquiesce in the necessity which denounces our separation, and hold them, as we hold the rest of mankind—enemies in war, in peace, friends.

We, therefore, the representatives of the UNITED STATES OF AMERICA, in general congress assembled, appealing to the Supreme Judge of the world for the rectitude of our intentions, do, in the name and by the authority of the good people of these colonies, solemnly publish and declare, That these United Colonies are, and of right ought to be, FREE and INDEPENDENT STATES; that they are absolved from all allegiance to the British crown, and that all political connection between them and the state of Great Britain is, and ought to be, totally dissolved; and that, as FREE and INDEPENDENT STATES, they have full power to levy war, conclude peace, contract alliances, establish commerce, and to do all other acts and things which INDEPENDENT STATES may of right do. And for the support of this Declaration, with a firm reliance on the protection of DIVINE PROVIDENCE, we mutually pledge to each other our lives, our fortunes, and our sacred honor.

JOHN HANCOCK.

New Hampshire.—Josiah Bartlett, William Whipple, Matthew Thornton.

Massachusetts Bay.—Samuel Adams, John Adams, Robert Treat Paine, Elbridge Gerry.

Rhode Island.—Stephen Hopkins, William Ellery.

Connecticut.—Roger Sherman, Samuel Huntington, William Williams, Oliver Wolcott.

New York.—William Floyd, Philip Livingston, Francis Lewis, Lewis Morris.

New Jersey.—Richard Stockton, John Witherspoon, Francis Hopkinson, John Hart, Abraham Clark.

Pennsylvania.—Robert Morris, Benjamin Rush, Benjamin Franklin, John Morton, George Clymer, James Smith, George Taylor, James Wilson, George Ross.

Delaware.—Cæsar Rodney, George Read, Thos. M'Kean.

Maryland.—Samuel Chase, William Paca, Thomas Stone, Charles Carroll of Carrollton.

Virginia.—George Wythe, Richard Henry Lee, Thomas Jefferson, Benjamin Harrison, Thomas Nelson, Jr., Francis Lightfoot Lee, Carter Braxton.

North Carolina.—William Hooper, Joseph Hewes, John Penn.

South Carolina.—Edward Rutledge, Thomas Hayward, Jr., Thomas Lynch, Jr., Arthur Middleton.

Georgia.—Button Gwinnett, Lyman Hall, George Walton.

Resolved, That copies of the Declaration be sent to the several assemblies, conventions, and committees or councils of safety, and to the several commanding officers of the continental troops; that it be proclaimed in each of the United States and at the head of the army.

THE ARTICLES OF CONFEDERATION.

To all to whom these presents shall come, we, the undersigned delegates of the States, affixed to our names, send greeting: whereas, the delegates of the United States of America in Congress assembled did, on the 15th day of November, in the year of our Lord 1777, and in the second year of the Independence of America, agree to certain articles of confederation and perpetual union between the States of New Hampshire, Massachusetts Bay, Rhode Island and Providence Plantations, Connecticut, New York, New Jersey, Pennsylvania, Delaware, Maryland, Virginia, North Carolina, South Carolina, and Georgia, in the words following, viz.:

ARTICLES OF CONFEDERATION AND PERPETUAL UNION, BETWEEN THE STATES OF NEW HAMPSHIRE, MASSACHUSETTS BAY, RHODE ISLAND AND PROVIDENCE PLANTATIONS, CONNECTICUT, NEW YORK, NEW JERSEY, PENNSYLVANIA, DELAWARE, MARYLAND, VIRGINIA, NORTH CAROLINA, SOUTH CAROLINA, AND GEORGIA.

ARTICLE 1. The style of this confederacy shall be "THE UNITED STATES OF AMERICA."

ART. 2. Each State retains its sovereignty, freedom, and independence, and every power, jurisdiction, and right, which is not by this confederation expressly delegated to the United States in Congress assembled.

ART. 3. The said States hereby severally enter into a firm league of friendship with each other, for their common defense, the security of their liberties, and their mutual and general welfare, binding themselves to assist each other against all force offered to, or attacks made upon them, or any of them, on account of religion, sovereignty, trade, or any other pretense whatever.

ART. 4. The better to secure and perpetuate mutual friendship and intercourse among the people of the different States in this union, the free inhabitants of each of these States (paupers, vagabonds, and fugitives from justice excepted), shall be entitled to all privileges and immunities of free citizens in the several States, and the people of each State shall have free ingress and regress to and from any other State, and shall enjoy therein all the privileges of trade and commerce, subject to the same duties, impositions, and restrictions, as the inhabitants thereof respectively:·*Provided* that such restrictions shall· not extend so far as to prevent the removal of property imported into any State, to any other State, of which the owner is an inhabitant: *Provided, also,* that no imposition, duties, or restriction, shall be laid by any State on the property of the United States, or either of them.

2 If any person guilty of, or charged with treason, felony, or other high misdemeanor in any State, shall flee from justice, and be found in any of the United States, he shall, upon demand of the governor or executive power of the State from which he fled, be delivered up and removed to the State having jurisdiction of his offense.

3 Full faith and credit shall be given in each of these States, to the records, acts, and judicial proceedings of the courts and magistrates of every other State.

1 Art. 5. For the more convenient management of the general interests of the United States, delegates shall be annually appointed in such manner as the legislature of each State shall direct, to meet in Congress on the first Monday in November, in every year, with a power reserved to each State to recall its delegates, or any of them, at any time within the year, and to send others in their stead, for the remainder of the year.

2 No State shall be represented in Congress by less than two, nor by more than seven members; and no person shall be capable of being a delegate for more than three years, in any term of six years; nor shall any person, being a delegate, be capable of holding any office under the United States, for which he, or any other for his benefit, receives any salary, fees, or emolument of any kind.

3 Each State shall maintain its own delegates in any meeting of the States, and while they act as members of the committee of these States.

In determining questions in the United States in Congress assembled, each State shall have one vote.

Freedom of speech and debate in Congress shall not be impeached or questioned in any court or place out of Congress, and the members of Congress shall be protected in their persons from arrests and imprisonments during the time of their going to and from, and attendance on Congress, except for treason, felony, or breach of the peace.

ART. 6. No State, without the consent of the United States in Congress assembled, shall send any embassy to, or receive any embassy from, or enter into any conference, agreement, alliance, or treaty, with any king, prince, or State; nor shall any person holding any office of profit or trust under the United States, or any of them, accept of any present, emolument, office, or title of any kind whatever, from any king, prince, or foreign State: nor shall the United States in Congress assembled, or any of them, grant any title of nobility.

No two or more States shall enter into any treaty, confederation, or alliance whatever, between them, without the consent of the United States in Congress assembled, specifying accurately the purposes for which the same is to be entered into, and how long it shall continue.

No State shall lay any imposts or duties which may interfere with any stipulations in treaties entered into by the United States in Congress assembled, with any king, prince, or State, in pursuance of any treaties already proposed by Congress to the courts of France and Spain.

No vessels of war shall be kept up in time of peace by any State, except such number only as shall be deemed necessary by the United States in Congress assembled, for the defense of such State or its trade; nor shall any body of forces be kept up, by any State, in time of peace, except such number only as, in the judgment of the United States in Congress assembled, shall be deemed requisite to garrison the forts necessary for the defense of such State; but every State shall always keep up a well regulated and disciplined militia, sufficiently armed and accoutered, and shall provide and have constantly ready for use, in public stores, a due number of field-pieces and tents, and a proper quantity of arms, ammunition, and camp equipage.

No State shall engage in any war without the consent of the United States in Congress assembled, unless such State be actually invaded by enemies, or shall have received certain advice of a resolution being formed by some nation of Indians to invade such State, and the danger is so imminent as not to admit of a delay till the United States in Congress assembled can be consulted; nor shall any State grant commissions to any ships or vessels of war, nor letters of marque or reprisal, except it be after a declaration of war by the United States in Congress assembled, and then only against the kingdom or State, and the subjects thereof, against which war has been so declared, and under such regulations as shall be established by the United States in Congress assembled, unless such State be infested by pirates, in which case vessels of war may be fitted out for that occasion, and kept so long as the danger shall continue, or until the United States in Congress assembled shall determine otherwise.

ART. 7. When land forces are raised by any State for the common defense, all officers of or under the rank of colonel shall be appointed by the legislature of each State respectively by whom such forces shall be raised, or in such manner as such State shall direct, and all vacancies shall be filled up by the State which first made the appointment.

ART. 8. All charges of war, and all other expenses that shall be incurred for the common defense or general welfare, and allowed by the United States in Congress assembled, shall be defrayed out of a common treasury, which shall be supplied by the several States, in proportion to the value of all land within each State, granted to or surveyed for any person, as such land and the buildings and improvements thereon shall be estimated, according to such mode as the United States in Congress assembled shall, from time to time, direct and appoint. The taxes for paying that proportion shall be laid and levied by the authority and direction of the legislatures of the several States within the time agreed upon by the United States in Congress assembled.

ART. 9. The United States in Congress assembled, shall

have the sole and exclusive right and power of determining on peace and war, except in the cases mentioned in the sixth article; of sending and receiving ambassadors; entering into treaties and alliances: *Provided* that no treaty of commerce shall be made whereby the legislative power of the respective States shall be restrained from imposing such imposts and duties on foreigners as their own people are subjected to, or from prohibiting the exportation or importation of any species of goods or commodities whatsoever; of establishing rules for deciding in all cases what captures on land or water shall be legal, and in what manner prizes taken by land or naval forces in the service of the United States shall be divided or appropriated; of granting letters of marque and reprisal in times of peace; appointing courts for the trial of piracies and felonies committed on the high seas; and establishing courts for receiving and determining finally appeals in all cases of captures: *Provided* that no member of Congress shall be appointed a judge of any of the said courts.

The United States in Congress assembled, shall also be the last resort on appeal in all disputes and differences now subsisting, or that hereafter may arise between two or more States concerning boundary, jurisdiction, or any other cause whatever; which authority shall always be exercised in the manner following: Whenever the legislative or executive authority or lawful agent of any State in controversy with another, shall present a petition to Congress, stating the matter in question, and praying for a hearing, notice thereof shall be given by order of Congress to the legislative or executive authority of the other State in controversy, and a day assigned for the appearance of the parties by their lawful agents, who shall then be directed to appoint, by joint consent, commissioners or judges to constitute a court for hearing and determining the matter in question; but if they can not agree, Congress shall name three persons out of each of the United States, and from the list of such persons each party shall alternately strike out one, the petitioners beginning, until the number shall be reduced to thirteen; and from that number not less than seven nor more than nine names, as Congress shall direct, shall, in the presence of Congress, be drawn out by lot; and the persons whose names shall be so drawn, or any five of them, shall be commissioners or judges to hear and finally determine the controversy, so always as a major part of the judges, who shall hear the cause, shall agree in the determination: and if either party shall neglect to attend at the day appointed, without showing reasons which Congress shall judge sufficient, or being present shall refuse to strike, the Congress shall proceed to nominate three persons out of each State, and the secretary of Congress shall strike in behalf of such party absent or refusing; and the judgment and sentence of the court, to be appointed in the manner before prescribed, shall be final and conclusive: and if any of the parties shall refuse to submit to the authority of such court, or to appear to defend their claim or cause, the court shall nevertheless proceed to pronounce sentence or judgment, which shall in like manner be final and decisive; the judgment or sentence and other proceedings being in either case transmitted to Congress, and lodged among the acts of Congress, for the security of the parties concerned: *Provided*, that every commissioner, before he sits in judgment, shall take an oath, to be administered by one of the judges of the Supreme or Superior Court of the State, where the cause shall be tried, "well and truly to hear and determine the matter in question, according to the best of his judgment, without favor, affection, or hope of reward:" *Provided, also,* that no State shall be deprived of territory for the benefit of the United States.

3 All controversies concerning the private right of soil claimed under different grants of two or more States, whose jurisdictions, as they may respect such lands, and the States which passed such grants are adjusted, the said grants or either of them being at the same time claimed to have originated antecedent to such settlement of jurisdiction, shall, on the petition, of either party to the Congress of the United States, be finally determined, as near as may be, in the same manner as is before prescribed for deciding disputes respecting territorial jurisdiction between different States.

4 The United States in Congress assembled, shall also have the sole and exclusive right and power of regulating the alloy and value of coin struck by their own authority, or by that of the respective States; fixing the standard of weights

and measures throughout the United States; regulating the trade and managing all affairs with the Indians, not members of any of the States; provided that the legislative right of any State, within its own limits, be not infringed or violated; establishing or regulating post offices from one State to another, throughout all the United States, and exacting such postage on the papers passing through the same, as may be requisite to defray the expenses of the said office; appointing all officers of the land forces in the service of the United States, excepting regimental officers; appointing all the officers of the naval forces, and commissioning all officers whatever in the service of the United States; making rules for the government and regulations of the said land and naval forces, and directing their operations.

The United States in Congress assembled, shall have authority to appoint a committee, to sit in the recess of Congress, to be denominated, "*A Committee of the States*," and to consist of one delegate from each State; and to appoint such other committees and civil officers as may be necessary for managing the general affairs of the United States under their direction; to appoint one of their number to preside: *Provided* that no person be allowed to serve in the office of president more than one year in any term of three years; to ascertain the necessary sums of money to be raised for the service of the United States, and to appropriate and apply the same for defraying the public expenses; to borrow money or emit bills on the credit of the United States, transmitting every half year to the respective States, an account of the sums of money so borrowed or emitted; to build and equip a navy; to agree upon the number of land forces, and to make requisitions from each State for its quota, in proportion to the number of white inhabitants in such State, which requisition shall be binding; and thereupon the legislature of each State shall appoint the regimental officers, raise the men, and clothe, arm, and equip them, in a soldier-like manner, at the expense of the United States; and the officers and men so clothed, armed, and equipped, shall march to the place appointed, and within the time agreed on by the United States in Congress assembled; but if the United States in Congress assembled, shall, on consideration of circumstances, judge proper that any State should not raise men, or should raise a smaller number than its quota, and that any other State should raise a greater number of men than the quota thereof, such extra number shall be raised, officered, clothed, armed, and equipped in the same manner as the quota of such State, unless the legislature of such State shall judge that such extra number can not be safely spared out of the same, in which case they shall raise, officer, clothe, arm, and equip as many of such extra number as they judge can be safely spared, and the officers and men so clothed, armed, and equipped, shall march to the place appointed, and within the time agreed on by the United States in Congress assembled.

6 The United States in Congress assembled shall never engage in a war, nor grant letters of marque and reprisal in time of peace, nor enter into any treaties or alliances, nor coin money, nor regulate the value thereof, nor ascertain the sums and expenses necessary for the defense and welfare of the United States, or any of them, nor emit bills, nor borrow money on the credit of the United States, nor appropriate money, nor agree upon the number of vessels of war to be built or purchased, or the number of land or sea forces to be raised, nor appoint a commander in chief of the army or navy, unless nine States assent to the same; nor shall a question on any other point, except for adjourning from day to day, be determined, unless by the votes of a majority of the United States in Congress assembled.

7 The Congress of the United States shall have power to adjourn to any time within the year, and to any place within the United States, so that no period of adjournment be for a longer duration than the space of six months, and shall publish the journal of their proceedings monthly, except such parts thereof relating to treaties, alliances, or military operations, as in their judgment require secrecy; and the yeas and nays of the delegates of each State, on any question, shall be entered on the journal, when it is desired by any delegate; and the delegates of a State, or any of them, at his or their request, shall be furnished with a transcript of the said journal, except such parts as are above excepted, to lay before the legislatures of the several States.

Art. 10. The committee of the States, or any nine of them,

shall be authorized to execute, in the recess of Congress, such of the powers of Congress as the United States in Congress assembled, by the consent of nine States, shall, from time to time, think expedient to vest them with; provided that no power be delegated to the said committee, for the exercise of which, by the articles of confederation, the voice of nine States, in the Congress of the United States assembled, is requisite.

Art. 11. Canada acceding to this confederation, and joining in the measures of the United States, shall be admitted into, and entitled to all the advantages of this union; but no other colony shall be admitted into the same, unless such admission be agreed to by nine States.

Art. 12. All bills of credit emitted, moneys borrowed, and debts contracted by or under the authority of Congress, before the assembling of the United States, in pursuance of the present confederation, shall be deemed and considered as a charge against the United States, for payment and satisfaction whereof the said United States and the public faith are hereby solemnly pledged.

Art. 13. Every State shall abide by the determination of the United States in Congress assembled, on all questions which by this confederation are submitted to them. And the articles of this confederation shall be inviolably observed by every State, and the union shall be perpetual; nor shall any alteration at any time hereafter be made in any of them, unless such alteration be agreed to, in a Congress of the United States, and be afterward confirmed by the legislatures of every State.

And whereas, it hath pleased the great Governor of the world to incline the hearts of the legislatures we respectively represent in Congress to approve of, and to authorize us to ratify the said articles of confederation and perpetual union, Know ye, that we, the undersigned delegates, by virtue of the power and authority to us given for that purpose, do by these presents, in the name and in behalf of our respective constituents, fully and entirely ratify and confirm each and every of the said articles of confederation and perpetual union, and all and singular the matters and things therein contained. And we do further solemnly plight and engage the faith of our respective constituents, that they shall abide by the determination of the United States in

Congress assembled, on all questions which by the said confederation are submitted to them; and that the articles thereof shall be inviolably observed by the States we respectively represent, and that the union shall be perpetual. In witness whereof, we have hereunto set our hands, in Congress.

Done at Philadelphia, in the State of Pennsylvania, the ninth day of July, in the year of our Lord one thousand seven hundred and seventy-eight, and in the third year of the Independence of America.

On the part and behalf of the State of New Hampshire.—Josiah Bartlett, John Wentworth, Jr. (August 8, 1778).

On the part and behalf of the State of Massachusetts Bay.—John Hancock, Samuel Adams, Elbridge Gerry, Francis Dana, James Lovell, Samuel Holten.

On the part and behalf of the State of Rhode Island and Providence Plantations.—William Ellery, Henry Marchant, John Collins.

On the part and behalf of the State of Connecticut.—Roger Sherman, Samuel Huntington, Oliver Wolcott, Titus Hosmer, Andrew Adams.

On the part and behalf of the State of New York.—James Duane, Francis Lewis, William Duer, Gouv. Morris.

On the part and behalf of the State of New Jersey.—John Witherspoon, Nath. Scudder (November 26, 1778).

On the part and behalf of the State of Pennsylvania.—Robert Morris, Daniel Roberdeau, Jona. Bayard Smith, William Clingan, Joseph Reed (July 22, 1778).

On the part and behalf of the State of Delaware.—Thomas McKean (February 12, 1779), John Dickinson (May 5, 1779), Nicholas Van Dyke.

On the part and behalf of the State of Maryland.—John Hanson (March 1, 1781), Daniel Carroll (March 1, 1781).

On the part and behalf of the State of Virginia.—Richard Henry Lee, John Banister, Thomas Adams, Jno. Harvie, Francis Lightfoot Lee.

On the part and behalf of the State of North Carolina.—John Penn (July 21, 1778), Corns. Harnett, John Williams.

On the part and behalf of the State of South Carolina.—Henry Laurens, William Henry Drayton, Jno. Matthews, Richard Hutson, Thos. Heyward, Jr.

On the part and behalf of the State of Georgia.—Jno. Walton (July 24, 1778), Edwd. Telfair, Edward Langworthy.

INDEX.

26

INDEX.

ACCOUNT,
>of public money, 108.
>to be published, 108.

ADJOURN,
>when either house of Congress may, 12.
>President may, when Congress can not agree, 258.

ADMIRALTY,
>jurisdiction in, 265.
>extent of, 268.
>distinct from power to regulate commerce, 269.
>not limited to jurisdiction in England, 270.
>when voyage begins and ends in the State, 270.
>cases of tort, 270.
>jurisdiction not a cession of the soil, 270.
>not include power to regulate fisheries, 271.
>a grant to Congress alone, 271.
>Congress may limit jurisdiction in, 271.
>Congress may grant jury trial, 271.
>a State can not create a maritime lien, 271.
>a State can not regulate jurisdiction in, 272.

ALIENS,
>not eligible to the office of president, 245.
>naturalization of, 67.

AMBASSADORS,
>appointment of, 254.
>President to receive, 258.
>judicial power extends to, 265.
>jurisdiction of Supreme Court over, 274.
>jurisdiction of inferior courts over, 276.

AMENDMENTS,
    how made to the Constitution, 310.
    to bills, 13.

APPELLATE JURISDICTION. *See* JUDICIAL POWER.

APPOINTMENT,
    of officers in the militia, 17.
    of electors, 243.
    of senators during vacancy of legislatures, 9.
    of officers, 254.
    Congress can not make, 256.
    when heads of department may make, 254, 256.
    when complete, 256.
    during recess, 258.
    when vacancy occurs during session of Senate, 257.

APPROPRIATION,
    for army limited to two years, 16.
    no money drawn from treasury except by, 108.

ARMS,
    Congress can not infringe right to keep, 342.

ARMY,
    Congress may raise, 16.
    power to raise unrestricted, 88.
    may be raised by draft, 89.
    States can not raise, 89.
    States may give bounties, 89.
    Congress may make rules to govern, 16.
    President commander-in-chief of, 246.
    punishment of persons in, 345.

ARREST,
    members of Congress exempt from, 12.

ATTAINDER,
    Congress can not pass, 103.
    State can not pass, 108.
    definition of, 103, 113.
    what are bills of, 113.
    bills of can not be passed indirectly, 113.

BAIL,
    excessive not to be required, 361.

BANKRUPTCY,
Congress may establish uniform laws, 16.
definition of, 69.
not limited to provisions of English laws, 70.
not limited to particular persons, 70.
voluntary bankruptcy, 70.
impairing obligation of contracts, 70.
selection of courts, 71.
uniform laws required, 71.
exemptions law, 71.
State insolvent laws superseded, 72.
State court retains pending cases, 74.
State laws relating to corporations, 74.
State laws relating to release from imprisonment, 75.
assignments for benefit of creditors, 76.
repeal revives State law, 79.

BILLS,
to raise revenue must originate in the House, 13.
to be signed by President, 13.
when become law, 14.
order resolution or vote to be same as, 15.

BILLS OF CREDIT,
State can not emit, 108.
what are, 108.
bank bills are not, 110.

CENSUS,
to be taken every ten years, 8.
capitation and direct taxes laid in proportion to, 104.

CITIZENS,
alone eligible to office of president, 245.
how long must be to be senator, 9.
judicial power extends to controversies between between, 265.
entitled to privilege and immunities in other States, 286.
to what privileges entitled, 286.
who are, 290, 371.
taxation in other States, 292.

CITIZENS—*continued*.
>right to sue, 293.
>right to catch oysters, 294.
>widows of, 295.
>no State to abridge immunities of, 371.

COIN,
>Congress may coin money, 16.
>no State can coin money, 108.
>no State can make anything but coin a legal tender, 108.

COMMERCE,
>Congress may regulate, 16.
>extent of power, 26.
>rivers, 34.
>how far power of Congress exclusive, 36.
>State legislation, 37.
>pilots, 41.
>State taxation, 42.
>transportation of persons, 49.
>bridges, 50.
>dams, 54.
>ferries, 54.
>persons engaged in subject to State laws, 56.
>internal, 56.
>with the Indians, 58.
>duty of tonnage prohibited, 231, 237.
>no preference to port of one State over another allowed, 106.

COMPENSATION,
>of senators, 12.
>of President, 245.
>of judges, 259.
>for private property taken for public use, 345.

CONFISCATION,
>Congress may provide for, whether war is civil or foreign, 87.

CONGRESS,
>legislative power vested in, 7.
>consist of a Senate and House of Representatives, 7.
>manner of electing members of, 10.
>when to assemble, 10.

CONGRESS—*continued.*

    judge of the qualification of members, 10.
    each house to determine the rules of its proceedings, 10.
    each house may punish for contempt, 10.
    to keep journal of its proceedings, 12.
    adjournment of, 12, 258.
    powers of, 15.
    to lay taxes, 15, 21.
    to borrow money, 16, 25.
    to regulate commerce, 16, 26.
    to establish rule of naturalization, 16, 67.
    to establish bankrupt laws, 16.
    to coin money, 16, 79.
    to punish counterfeiting, 16, 81.
    to establish post offices and post roads, 16, 82.
    to grant copyrights, 16, 85.
    to grant patents, 16, 85.
    to create inferior tribunals, 16.
    to punish piracies and other felonies, 16, 86.
    to declare war, 16, 86.
    to raise armies, 16, 88.
    regulate military forces, 16, 90.
    to call forth the militia, 16, 90.
    to govern the militia, 16, 91.
    to legislate for the District of Columbia, 17, 92.
    to govern places purchased with consent of legislature, 17, 93.
    to make all necessary laws, 17, 95.
    may prohibit the importation of persons, 191.
    may suspend the writ of *habeas corpus*, 191.
    can not pass bill of attainder, 103.
    can not pass *ex post facto* law, 103.
    may consent to officers receiving presents from foreign States, 108.
    may allow State to lay duties on imports, 231.
    may allow to lay duty of tonnage, 231.
    may allow State to keep troops, 231.
    may allow State to enter into contract with another State, or with a foreign power, 231.

CONGRESS—*continued.*
    may determine time of choosing electors, 245.
    may provide for vacancy in the office of president, 245.
    may provide for appointment of inferior officers, 254.
    receive information from president, 258.
    may regulate appellate jurisdiction of the Supreme Court, 274.
    may provide for trial of crimes not committed within a State, 279.
    may provide for the proof of records in other States, 283.
    admit new States, 298.
    dispose of territory, 299.
    propose amendments to Constitution, 310.

CONTRACTS,
    Congress may impair obligation of, 20.
    State can not impair obligation of, 108.
    definition of, 120.
    what laws do affect, 122.
    what are within protection, 126.
    with States, 128.
    impairing, 128.
    what statutes are contracts, 132.
    executed, 137.
    registration laws, 141.
    confirmatory statute, 141.
    marriage, 142.
    public officers, 143.
    license, 144.
    taxes, 145.
    bank notes, 147.
    laws giving validity to, 148.
    municipal ordinances, 149.
    acts not contracts, 150.
    statutes which do impair contracts, 151.
    sale of property free from incumbrances, 152.
    interest, 152.
    State insolvent laws, 155.
    charters, 162.
    acts which impair charters, 167.

CONTRACTS—*continued.*
    charters of banks, 169.
    charters of bridge companies, 170.
    charters of turnpike companies, 171.
    charters of railroad companies, 171.
    taxation of corporations, 172.
    eminent domain against corporations, 179.
    police power over corporations, 180.
    amendment of charters, 187.
    effect of reserved power to alter charters, 188.
    effect of amendments on stockholders, 195.
    rights of stockholders where power is reserved to alter, 202.
    public corporations, 204.
    remedies, 208.
    appeal, 224.
    new trial, 225.
    exemptions, 225.
    stay laws, 227.
    statute of limitations, 229.
    who may object, 230.

COPYRIGHT,
    power to grant to author, 16.
    State can not interfere with, 83.

CORPORATIONS,
    obligations of charter can not be impaired, 162.
    construction of charter, 166.
    statutes affecting charter void, 167.
    bank charters, 169.
    bridge companies, 170.
    turnpike companies, 171.
    railroad companies, 171.
    taxation of, 172.
    taking property of for public uses, 179.
    police power, 180.
    amendment of charter, 187.
    effect of reserved power to alter, 188.
    effect of amendment on stockholders, 195.

410 INDEX.

CORPORATIONS—*continued*.
 effect on stockholders of reserved power to alter charters, 202.
 public corporations, 204.

COUNSEL,
 accused has right to assistance of, 356.

COUNTERFEITING,
 Congress may provide for punishment of, 16.
 what acts State may punish, 81.

COURTS. *See* JUDICIAL POWER.

CRIMES,
 when indictment necessary, 345, 346.
 trial by jury, 279.
 where tried, 279.
 accused not compellable to testify, 345.
 rights of accused, 356.
 cruel punishments prohibited, 361.
 may be punished by involuntary servitude, 369.
 surrender of fugitives from justice, 395.

DEBT,
 validity of public not to be questioned, 372.
 confederate, not to be assumed, 372.
 of United States Congress to pay, 15.
 State can not make anything exceptg oldand silver a tender in payment of, 108.

DISTRICT OF COLUMBIA,
 exclusive jurisdiction over, 17.
 what acts for valid, 92.

DUTIES. *See* TAXES.

ELECTIONS,
 of representatives, 7.
 of senators, 9.
 in case of vacancy in representation, 8.
 of president and vice-president, 243.
 how votes by electors taken, 367.
 Congress may regulate, of senators and representatives, 10.
 each house judge of its own, 10.
 no abridgment of right to vote on account of race or color, 379.

ELECTORS,
>   appointment of, 243.
>   who disqualified to be, 243.
>   mode of voting, 367.
>   transmission of vote of, 367.

EMINENT DOMAIN,
>   does not impair obligation of contracts, 179.
>   over franchise and property of corporations, 179.
>   no exercise of without compensation, 345.
>   State can not exercise for United States, 356.

EXCISE. *See* TAXES.

EXPORTS,
>   no tax on, 106.
>   State can not tax, 231.

EX POST FACTO LAWS,
>   Congress can not pass, 103.
>   State can not pass, 108.
>   what are, 114.
>   regulating criminal proceedings, 116.

FELONY,
>   Congress may punish when committed on the high seas, 16.
>   members of Congress arrested for, 12.
>   fugitives from justice delivered up, 295.

FINES,
>   excessive not to be imposed, 361.

FORTS,
>   Congress to exercise exclusive legislation over, 17.
>   extent of jurisdiction over, 93.

FUGITIVES FROM JUSTICE,
>   to be surrendered, 295.
>   what crimes surrendered for, 296.
>   demand for surrender of, 297.
>   State laws, 297.

GRAND JURY,
>   when indictment by necessary, 345.

HABEAS CORPUS,
when writ of, suspended, 101.
State court can not issue for person held under Federal authority, 334.

HEADS OF DEPARTMENTS,
President may require to give opinion in writing, 246.
appointment of inferior officers may be vested in, 254.

HOUSE OF REPRESENTATIVES,
Congress consists of Senate and, 7.
when members of, chosen, 7.
qualifications of electors, 7.
who may be representatives, 7.
how representatives apportioned, 7.
how vacancies in filled, 8.
choose speaker and other officers, 9.
has sole power of impeachment, 9.
Congress may regulate elections of representatives, 10.
when to meet, 10.
judge of the election of its own members, 10.
what constitutes a quorum, 10.
may compel the attendance of absent members, 10.
may adopt rules of proceeding, 10.
power to punish members, 10.
    expel members, 10.
    punish contempt, 10.
to keep a journal, 12.
when yeas and nays entered on, 12.
power to adjourn, 12.
compensation of, 12.
members privileged from arrest, 12.
    not liable for debate, 12.
    not eligible to certain offices, 13.
sole right to originate bills for revenue, 13.
when may elect President, 367.
when to be convened by President, 258.
when to be adjourned by President, 258.

IMMUNITIES. *See* CITIZENS.

IMPEACHMENT,
>   House of Representatives has sole power of, 9.
>   Senate has sole power to try, 9.
>   who presides on trial of, 9.
>   what vote necessary for conviction, 9.
>   judgment in cases of, 10.
>   party liable to indictment after, 10.
>   not subject of pardon, 246.
>   for what crimes officers may be removed, 259.
>   no trial by jury, 279.

IMPOSTS. *See* TAXES.

INDIANS,
>   Congress may regulate commerce with, 15.
>   what commerce with subject to regulation by Congress, 58.
>   commerce with when in State, 60.
>   Congress may punish offenses by, 60.
>   jurisdiction of crimes committed by, 61.
>   when State laws void, 62.
>   rights of, 64.
>   when citizens, 371.

INDICTMENT,
>   when necessary, 345.

INSOLVENT LAWS,
>   State may pass, 72.
>   suspended by bankrupt law, 73.
>   can not impair obligation of contract, 155.
>   may affect subsequent contracts, 155.
>   can not affect citizens of other States, 157.

INSPECTION LAWS,
>   State may pass, 231.

INSURRECTION,
>   Congress may suppress, 16.
>   Congress to protect State against, 308.

JEOPARDY,
>   no person twice put in for same offense, 345.
>   when second trial allowed, 347.

JOURNAL,
>   each house to keep, 12.

JOURNAL—*continued.*
    when yeas and nays entered on, 12.
    when objections of President to be entered on, 13.

JUDGES,
    President may nominate, 254.
    hold office during good behavior, 259.
    compensation not be diminished, 259.
    bound by Constitution, 310.

JUDGMENTS. *See* RECORDS.

JUDICIAL POWER,
    in what courts to be vested, 259.
    limited jurisdiction of Federal courts, 261.
    territorial courts, 262.
    can not be vested in State courts, 262.
    not affected by State laws, 263.
    removal from State courts, 263.
    to what causes extends, 265.
    cases under acts of Congress, 266.
    cases in admiralty, 268.
    over foreign nations, 272.
    how far jurisdiction of Federal courts exclusive, 272.
    jurisdiction of Supreme Court, 274.

JURY,
    trial of crimes by, 279.
    indictment by grand, 345.
    from what district taken in case of crimes, 356.
    trial by, preserved at common law, 357.

MARQUE AND REPRISAL,
    Congress may grant letters of, 16.
    State can not grant, 108.

MARRIAGE,
    not a contract, 142.
    rights arising from not protected, 142.

MARTIAL LAW,
    when allowed, 247.

MILITIA,
    Congress may call forth, 16.
        provide for organizing, 16.

MILITIA—*continued.*
    State may appoint officers of, 17.
    President commander in chief of, 246.
    necessity of, 342.
    when offenses in tried without indictment, 345.

MONEY,
    Congress has power to borrow, 16.
                        coin, 16.
    appropriation of, limited to two years, 16.
    not drawn from treasury without appropriation, 108.
    State can not coin, 108.

NATIONAL BANK,
    Congress may create, 98.
    State may punish crimes against, 273.
                        counterfeiting notes of, 274.
        can not tax, 325.

NATURALIZATION,
    Congress may regulate, 16.
    who are subjects of, 67.
    State laws, 68.

NAVY,
    Congress may provide, 16.
                        make rules for government of, 16.
    trial of persons in, 345.
    President commander in chief of, 246.

NOBILITY,
    Congress can not grant title of, 108.
    State can not grant title of, 108.

OATH,
    in case of impeachment, 9.
    of President, 245.
    to support Constitution, 339.
    no warrant to issue without, 343.

OBLIGATION OF CONTRACTS. *See* CONTRACTS.

OFFICERS,
    when President may appoint, 254.
    when others may appoint, 254.

OFFICERS—*continued.*
    when appointment complete, 256.
    removal of, 257.
    resignation, 257.
    appointment during recess, 258.
    removal by impeachment, 259.

PARDONS,
    President may grant, 246.
    different kinds of, 252.,
    to what extends, 252.
    not subject to legislative control, 252.
    effect of, 253.
    recalled before delivery, 253.

PATENTS,
    Congress may regulate, 16.
        grant for thing in public use, 83.
          extended term, 84.
    State can not regulate, 85.

PIRACIES,
    Congress may punish, 16.

POLICE POWER,
    over corporations, 180.
    of State, 320.

PORTS,
    no preference to, in one State over that of another, 106.

POST OFFICES,
    Congress may establish, 16.
    extent of power, 82.

PRESENT,
    officers not allowed to accept from king, prince or foreign State, 108.

PRESIDENT,
    chief justice presides on impeachment of, 9.
    all bills to be presented to, 13.
    orders, resolutions and votes to be presented to, 15.
    executive power vested in, 242.
    electors of, appointed by State, 243.
    Congress to determine the time of choosing electors, 245.

PRESIDENT—*continued.*
> who is eligible, 245.
> who may act in case of removal, death, resignation or inability, 245.
> compensation of, 245.
> oath, 245.
> to be commander in chief, 246.
> require written opinion from heads of departments, 246.
> may grant pardons, 246.
> military power, 246.
> when may govern by martial law, 247.
> power over conquered territory, 249.
> power over rebellious State, 250.
> may make treaties, 254.
> may appoint officers, 254.
> fill vacancies during recess of Senate, 258.
> may recommend measures, 258.
> may convene Congress, 258.
> when may adjourn Congress, 258.
> to receive public ministers, 258.
> remove from office on impeachment, 259.
> mode of casting votes for, 367.
> mode of counting votes for, 367.
> mode of electing when electors fail to elect, 367.

PRESS,
> Congress can not make any law abringing the freedom of, 342.

PRIVATE PROPERTY. *See* EMINENT DOMAIN.

PRIVILEGES AND IMMUNITIES. *See* CITIZENS.

QUORUM,
> what constitutes, 10.
> what constitutes in choosing President, 367.
> what constitutes for the election of Vice-President, 368.

REBELLION,
> Congress may suppress, 86.
> confiscation of property of rebels, 87.

REBELLION—*continued.*
    President may appoint Governor for rebellious State, 250.
    Congress may reorganize rebellious States, 309.
    a State can not secede, 328.
    legal effect of secession, 230.

RECORDS,
    full faith and credit given to in other States, 283.
    effect merely as evidence, 284.
    a foreign judgment ranks merely as simple contract, 284.
    what State laws valid, 285.

RELIGION,
    Congress can make no law respecting establishment of, 342.
    no religious test required as qualification to office, 339.

REMEDY. *See* CONTRACTS.

REPRESENTATIVES. *See* HOUSE OF REPRESENTATIVES.

REPRIEVES. *See* PARDON.

REPRISAL. *See* MARQUE AND REPRISAL.

REPUBLICAN GOVERNMENT,
    Congress must guarantee to every State, 308.

RESOLUTION,
    when to be approved by the President, 15.

RIGHTS,
    to religious freedom, 339, 342.
    to freedom of speech, 342.
    to assemble peaceably, 342.
    to petition for redress of grievances, 342.
    to bear arms, 342.
    soldiers not to be quartered on citizen without consent, 343.
    against unreasonable searches and seizures, 343.
    to warrant under oath, 343.
    to indictment by grand jury, 345.
    not to be twice put in jeopardy, 345.
    not compellable to be witness against himself, 345.
    not to be deprived of life, liberty or property without due process of law, 345, 371.
    property not to be taken for public use without compensation, 345.
    of criminal to speedy and public trial, 356.
    to trial in district where crime was committed, 279, 356.

RIGHTS—*continued*.
>   to be informed of the nature and cause of the accusation, 356.
>   to be confronted with witnesses, 356.
>   to compulsory process to obtain witnesses, 356.
>   to assistance of counsel, 356.
>   to trial by jury at common law, 357.
>   to moderate bail, 361.
>   to moderate fine, 361.
>   to moderate punishment, 361.
>   to freedom, 369.
>   to privileges and immunities, 286, 371.
>   to equal protection of the laws, 371.
>   to vote, 379.
>   to trial by jury in criminal eases, 279.

SEARCHES,
>   people protected against unreasonable, 343.

SECESSION. *See* REBELLION.

SEIZURES,
>   people protected against unreasonable, 343.

SENATE,
>   Congress consists of, and House of Representatives, 7.
>   number of senators, 9.
>   how senators chosen, 9.
>   division of senators into classes, 9.
>   mode of filling vacancies, 9.
>   qualification of senator, 9.
>   who is president of senate, 9.
>   choosing officers of, 9.
>   when president *pro tempore* chosen, 9.
>   sole power to try impeachment, 9.
>   time, place and manner of choosing senators, 10.
>   when to assemble, 10.
>   judge the election of its own members, 10.
>   what constitutes a quorum, 10.
>   power to expel a member, 10.
>   power to punish contempt, 10.

SENATE—*continued.*
    to keep a journal, 12.
    when yeas and nays entered on journal, 12.
    when journal published, 12.
    can not adjourn without consent of representatives, 12.
    compensation of senators, 12.
    privileged from arrest, 12.
    senators not liable for speech or debate, 12.
    senator can not be appointed to office created during his term, 13.
    officer can not be senator, 13.
    can not originate bill for revenue, 13.
    bills to be presented to President, 13.
    resolutions to be presented to President, 15.
    no State to be deprived of its suffrage in, 310.
    votes of electors to be transmitted to president of, 367.
    who can not be senator, 72.
    senators to take oath to support the Constitution, 329.

SLAVERY,
    abolished, 369.
    slaves included in representation, 7.
    importation of slaves prohibited, 101.
    return of fugitive slaves, 298.

SOLDIER,
    not to be quartered on citizen in time of peace, 343.

SPEECH,
    when senators and representatives not to be questioned for, 12.
    Congress can not abridge freedom of, 342.

STATE,
    elect representatives, 7.
    representative must be inhabitant of, 7.
    apportionment of representatives among, 7.
    each State entitled to one representative, 8.
    mode of filling vacancies in representation of, 8.
    choosing senators from, 9.
    senator must be inhabitant of, 9.
    mode of filling vacancies among senators, 9.

STATE—*continued.*
    exports from, not liable to tax, 106.
    no preference to be given to ports of, 106.
    can not make a treaty, 108.
    can not grant letters of marque and reprisal, 108.
    can not coin money, 108.
    can not emit bills of credit, 108.
    can not make anything but gold and silver a legal tender, 108.
    can not pass bill of attainder, 108.
    can not make *ex post facto* law, 108.
    can not impair the obligation of contracts, 108.
    can not grant title of nobility, 108.
    can not lay duty on imports or exports, 231.
    can not lay duty of tonnage, 231.
    can not keep troops or ships of war, 231.
    can not enter into compact with other State or foreign power, 231.
    can not engage in war, 231.
    shall appoint electors, 243.
    to what controversies judicial power extends, 265.
    original jurisdiction of Supreme Court, 274.
    full faith given to acts of, 283.
    privileges and immunities of citizens of, 286.
    surrender of fugitives from justice, 295.
    admission of new, 298.
    republican government guaranteed to, 308.
    not deprived of suffrage in Senate, 310.
    bound by Constitution, 315.
    when powers of, superseded, 316.
    police powers preserved, 320.
    when taxation by, restricted, 321.
    can not secede, 328.
    can not interfere with operation of Federal Government, 334.
    officers must take oath to support the Constitution, 329.
    powers reserved to, 302.
    can not be sued in a Federal court, 365.

SUPREME COURT. *See* JUDICIAL POWER.

TAXES,

Congress may lay, 15.
how bills for raising must originate, 13.
how direct taxes to be apportioned, 7.
in the District of Columbia, 92.
on importation of persons, 101.
mode of levying capitation or direct tax, 104.
on exports prohibited, 106.
State can not tax commerce, 42.
State can not tax imports or exports, 231.
State can not lay any duty of tonnage, 231.
State power concurrent with Federal Government, 321.
State can not tax agencies of Federal Government, 322.
power of State over territory, 301.
State may contract not to levy, 145.
when on corporation by State valid, 172.

TENDER,

State can not make anything but gold and silver, 108.
Congress may make notes legal tender, 25, 87.

TERRITORY,

Congress to legislate for, 17.
Congress may acquire, 299.
Congress may make regulations for, 299.
power of State over, 301.
power of Congress in legislating for, 303.
establishment of courts in, 303.
establishment of government for, 303.

TEST,

no religious, required as qualification to office, 339.

TONNAGE,

no State can lay duty of, 231.
what is, 237.
charge for wharfage, 238.
fees to harbor master, 239.
taxation of vessels, 240.

TREASON,

senator or representative may be arrested for, 12.
removal from office on conviction of, 259.

TREASON—*continued.*
>definition of, 280.
>Congress may declare punishment of, 282.
>not to work corruption of blood, 282.
>surrender of fugitive charged with, 295.

TREATY,
>President may make, 254.
>judicial power extends to cases arising under, 265.
>the supreme law, 310.
>no State can enter into, 108.

VACANCIES,
>in House of Representatives, how filled, 8.
>in Senate, how filled, 9.
>President may fill that happen in recess of Senate, 258.

VETO POWER. *See* PRESIDENT.

VICE-PRESIDENT,
>President of Senate, 9.
>when may vote, 9.
>when Senate may choose a president *pro tempore*, 9.
>chosen for four years, 242.
>mode of electing, 367.
>electing when electors fail to elect, 368.
>who is ineligible, 369.
>when to act as President, 245.
>removed by impeachment, 259.

VOTE,
>each senator has one, 9.
>when Vice-President may, 9.
>when taken by yeas and nays, 14.
>of electors, 367.
>of House of Representatives in electing President, 367.
>diminution of representatives, when right is denied, 371.
>right not to be abridged on account of race, color or previous condition, 379.

WAR,
    Congress may declare, 16.
        suppress rebellion, 86.
    powers incidental to, 87.

WARRANTS,
    must be under oath, 343.

WEIGHTS,
    Congress may regulate, 16.

WITNESS,
    no person compellable to be against himself, 345.
    right to be confronted by, 356.
        compulsory process to obtain, 356.
    how many necessary to convict of treason, 280.

YEAS AND NAYS,
    when entered on journal, 12.
    on passage of bill over veto, 14.

www.ingramcontent.com/pod-product-compliance
Lightning Source LLC
Chambersburg PA
CBHW031954300426
44117CB00008B/757